E. P. SANDERS

JESUS AND JUDAISM

SCM PRESS LTD

British Library Cataloguing in Publication Data

Sanders, E. P.
Jesus and Judaism.
1. Jesus Christ
I. Title
232   BT202

ISBN 0–334–02091–3

First published 1985
by SCM Press Ltd
26–30 Tottenham Road, London N1 4BZ
Fourth impression 1994

Phototypeset by Input Typesetting Ltd
Printed and bound in Great Britain by
Biddles Ltd, Guildford and King's Lynn

For Laura

CONTENTS

PART THREE   CONFLICT AND DEATH

PREFACE

This book was begun during 1975–76 with the support of a Senior Research Scholarship from the Killam Program of the Canada Council. For various reasons completion was delayed. I was finally able to rewrite it entirely during 1982, thanks to the support of a Leave Fellowship and a Research Grant from the Social Sciences and Humanities Research Council of Canada. During this period I was also Visiting Fellow Commoner at Trinity College, Cambridge. I am grateful to the officers of the Killam Program for their great patience and understanding and to the officers of the SSHRC for giving me a final chance to complete the work. To the Master and Fellows of Trinity College, Cambridge, I owe an enormous debt for the privilege of being one of their company for even a short time. The generosity and hospitality of the College, both the Fellows and the Staff, never ceased to evoke surprise and appreciation.

One of the Fellows of the College, and my sponsor while there, was the Right Reverend Dr John A. T. Robinson. His recent death has deprived many of us of a dear friend and the Church of a far-sighted spokesman. My dearest memories of 1982 are the evenings spent in his rooms, discussing my work and his. A memorial on his work as New Testament scholar and theologian would be out of place here. Appreciations and tributes have been and will be offered by many more qualified than I. Here I can say only that my life and work were greatly enhanced by him.

The final typing of the book has been done with the aid of a grant from McMaster University. Its completion marks a time of transition in my long and happy tenure there, and I wish to say a more general word of thanks to the administrative officers, both past and present, who have served during the last seventeen years. I think that no university can have been more fortunate in its choice of so many administrators over so many years. I am especially indebted to Alvin A. Lee, now the President of the University, who has been my administrative superior in one office or another since 1971. He has throughout actively and forcefully supported both my own research and that of my colleagues in the area of Judaism and

Christianity in the Graeco-Roman World. We would all have accomplished less without him.

Chapter 6 is an appreciably revised and somewhat expanded form of an article which appeared as 'Jesus and the Sinners' in *JSNT* 19, 1983, pp. 5–36. Parts of the article are reproduced here with the kind permission of Dr Bruce Chilton. I am grateful to those who responded to the article; their comments have aided me in revising it.

I have discussed the book, in whole and in parts, with numerous people, usually to my great benefit – and sometimes, I fear, to their consternation. Several institutions have provided the opportunity to lecture on the subject of the book. I am grateful to them all. I must single out for special thanks two of my colleagues, Albert Baumgarten and Ben F. Meyer, who have been regularly available to exchange ideas and thrash out problems.

Phyllis DeRosa Koetting performed her customary magic with the typescript, the bibliography and the indexes. The requirement to read the proof and paginate the index, however, came at a very awkward time, and I am grateful to Jean Cunningham of SCM Press for assistance above and beyond the call of duty, and to Margaret Davies of the University of Bristol for unselfishly giving assistance at very short notice.

The years during which the work was in progress or on the shelf have been challenging and often trying ones, both professionally and personally. Numerous friends and colleagues, including the ones just named, have helped see me through. The unflagging support and friendship of four other men have also been vital on both levels. They are my teachers, David Daube, W. D. Davies, W. R. Farmer and Louis Martyn. I owe them more than I can say, and I can only hope that I can do for someone else what they have so unfailingly done for me. But the most important person during this – and any other – period, whose cheerful acceptance, steady affection and buoyant good spirits have always been an inspiration, is my daughter. The book is dedicated to her with love and gratitude.

ABBREVIATIONS

AGAJU	Arbeiten zur Geschichte des antiken Judentums und des Urchristentums, Leiden
AJ	Josephus, *Antiquitates Judaicae*
ANRW	*Aufstieg und Niedergang der römischen Welt*, ed. H. Temporini and W. Haase, Berlin and New York
Ap.	Josephus, *Contra Apionem*
ATANT	Abhandlungen zur Theologie des Alten und Neuen Testaments, Zürich
BETL	Bibleotheca Ephemeridum Theologicarum Lovaniensium, Louvain
Bibl	*Biblica*, Rome
BJ	Josephus, *De Bello Judaico*
BZNW	Beiheft zur *Zeitschrift für die neutestamentliche Wissenschaft*, Giessen, Berlin
CBQ	*Catholic Biblical Quarterly*, Washington, D. C.
CBQMS	*Catholic Biblical Quarterly* Monograph Series, Washington, D. C.
ET	English translation
ETL	*Ephemerides Theologicae Lovanienses*, Louvain
ExpT	*Expository Times*, Edinburgh
HNT	Handbuch zum Neuen Testament, Tübingen
HTR	*Harvard Theological Review*, Cambridge, Mass.
HUCA	*Hebrew Union College Annual*, Cincinnati
IEJ	*Israel Exploration Journal*, Jerusalem
Interpr	*Interpretation*, Richmond, Va.
JBL	*Journal of Biblical Literature*, Philadelphia, Missoula, Mont., et al.
JBLMS	*Journal of Biblical Literature* Monograph Series
JE	*Jewish Encyclopaedia*, 12 vols., New York 1901–06
JJS	*Journal of Jewish Studies*, London
JSJ	*Journal for the Study of Judaism*, Leiden
JSNT	*Journal for the Study of the New Testament*, Sheffield
JSOT	*Journal for the Study of the Old Testament*, Sheffield

JSOTSuppl	Supplements to *Journal of Old Testament Studies*, Sheffield
JSS	*Journal of Semitic Studies*, Manchester
JTS	*Journal of Theological Studies*, Oxford
LCL	Loeb Classical Library, London and New York
Legat.	Philo, *Legatio ad Gaium*
NovT	*Novum Testamentum*, Leiden
NovTSuppl	Supplements to *Novum Testamentum*, Leiden
n.s.	new series
NTS	*New Testament Studies*, Cambridge
PGM	*Papyri Graecae Magicae*, ed. K. Preisendanz, 3 vols., Dresden 1928–42
RQ	*Revue de Qumran*, Paris
SANT	Studien zum Alten und Neuen Testament, Munich
SBLDS	Society of Biblical Literature Dissertation Series, Philadelphia, Missoula, Mont., et al.
SBT	Studies in Biblical Theology, London and Naperville, Ill.
Sib.Or.	Sibylline Oracles
SJT	*Scottish Journal of Theology*
SNTSMS	Society for New Testament Studies Monograph Series, Cambridge
SNTU	Studien zum Neuen Testament und seiner Umwelt, Freistadt
SUNT	Studien zur Umwelt des Neuen Testaments, Göttingen
TDNT	*Theological Dictionary of the New Testament*, ed. G. Kittel and G. Friedrich, ET ed. G. Bromiley, Grand Rapids 1964–76
TLZ	*Theologische Literaturzeitung*, Leipzig
TU	Texte und Untersuchungen zur Geschichte der altchristlichen Literatur, Leipzig, Berlin
WMANT	Wissenschaftliche Monographien zum Alten und Neuen Testament, Neukirchen
WUNT	Wissenschaftliche Untersuchungen zum Neuen Testament, Tübingen
ZAW	*Zeitschrift für die alttestamentliche Wissenschaft*, Giessen, Berlin
ZNW	*Zeitschrift für die neutestamentliche Wissenschaft und die Kunde des Urchristentums*, Giessen, Berlin
ZTK	*Zeitschrift für Theologie und Kirche*, Tübingen

INTRODUCTION

The Problem

It is the purpose of the present work to take up two related questions with regard to Jesus: his intention and his relationship to his contemporaries in Judaism.[1] These questions immediately involve us in two others: the reason for his death (did his intention involve an opposition to Judaism which led to death?) and the motivating force behind the rise of Christianity (did the split between the Christian movement and Judaism originate in opposition during Jesus' lifetime?).[2] These are questions on which there are numerous viewpoints, and gathered about which are enormous bodies of scholarly literature, so that it is with some trepidation that one advances another essay in an attempt to answer them.

There are some general aspects of the study of these and related problems in contemporary research which call for special note. First, to one who early imbibed the theological position that research into problems concerning the historical Jesus was and should be dead (since faith should not seek security in historical data), the persuasiveness and vitality of much that is being written today is impressive. There are numerous fresh attempts to give a general account of Jesus' teaching and activity, and several focus on just the problems which were mentioned in the first paragraph. One thinks, for example, of Paul Winter's work on the trial of Jesus[3] and the extensive debate triggered by his hypothesis,[4] of such detailed studies as Martin Hengel's *Nachfolge und Charisma*,[5] of Joachim Jeremias's volume on the *Proclamation of Jesus*,[6] of the essay by Eduard Schweizer in his *Jesus*,[7] of C. H. Dodd's brilliantly written *The Founder of Christianity*,[8] of the works of Vermes[9] and Bowker,[10] which are especially addressed to the question of Jesus and Judaism, of Meyer's *The Aims of Jesus*,[11] and of Harvey's recent *Jesus and the Constraints of History*.[12] What is characteristic of many of these works is that, despite the recognition of how difficult it is to be certain of the historical reliability of any individual pericope, the authors seem confident of the ability to present a reasonably accurate sketch of what Jesus taught and how he behaved.[13] One finds, for example, in the works of Jeremias, Dodd, Vermes and Meyer, new, or at least freshly stated, overall descriptions of Jesus which are coherent, which are based on material in the Gospels, and which intend to answer historical questions on historical grounds. The dominant view today seems to be that we can know pretty well what Jesus was out to accomplish, that we can know a lot about what he said, and that those two things make sense within the world of first-century Judaism.[14]

A second aspect of the current situation is that such questions about Jesus as those contemplated here are being asked without special reference to the debate on the relationship between knowledge about the historical Jesus and Christian faith.[15] It was that theological problem which actually lay behind Ernst Käsemann's decision to reopen the question of the historical Jesus,[16] and his defence of his position was thoroughly theological.[17] Only incidentally did he make historical assertions about Jesus;[18] the real interest on the part of Käsemann and those who debated with him was whether or not one *ought* to make such statements. Thus Käsemann was ready to give a quick description of the relationship between Jesus and Judaism,[19] but this comes in the context of a very long essay on the proper theological position about the historical Jesus, and there is neither here nor elsewhere any very thorough attempt to ground the accuracy of the point of conflict. It is quite otherwise in the books referred to in the second paragraph. In these and other works it is either assumed or argued (usually assumed) that it is worthwhile to know and to state clearly whatever can be known about Jesus, and great effort is expended in establishing what can be known. The present work is written very much in the latter vein. To speak personally for a moment, I am interested in the debate about the significance of the historical Jesus for theology in the way one is interested in something that he once found fascinating. The present work is written without that question in mind, however, and those who wish an essay on that topic may put this book down and proceed farther along the shelf.

The last general comment about the present state of research is this: it seems that real progress has recently been made on the two questions with which we are concerned. This is not the result of a rapid increase in knowledge, but rather of a shift of attitude.[20] It used to be almost a taboo question in many circles to ask what Jesus was up to. That must have seemed a Roman Catholic question, for the very question might seem to imply that he had in mind a programme which included the continuation of the church.[21] Recent scholars seem less fearful on this point. Secondly, the question of Jesus' relation to Judaism has all too often been locked in later religious controversy and apologetics: either Jesus has been depicted as standing completely superior to the contemporary Judaism[22] (which is viewed as a decline from the prophetic period),[23] or he has been claimed by Jewish scholars as one of their own, with the development of Christianity being described as a Pauline innovation.[24] It has proved difficult to do justice to the question posed by Joseph Klausner: how was it that Jesus lived totally within Judaism, and yet was the origin of a movement that separated from Judaism, since *ex nihilo nihil fit*, nothing comes from nothing, or, more idiomatically, where there is smoke there is fire.[25] Nevertheless, many fairly recent studies have attempted to do justice even to this problem, without lapsing either into polemics or apologetics.[26]

In saying that progress has been made, I do not mean to imply that the works listed above are necessarily complementary or lead to the same conclusions. The progress consists, rather, in the way in which serious and important historical questions have been put about Jesus and the way in which the material of the Gospels and, to some extent, of Jewish literature, has been put to good use, despite some uncertainties about final answers to questions of authenticity and reliability. The method which is being followed more and more, and the one which it seems necessary to follow in writing about Jesus, is to construct hypotheses which, on the one hand, do rest on material generally considered reliable without, on the other hand, being totally dependent on the authenticity of any given pericope.[27] Hypothetical reconstructions which are based on (but which may not be strictly exegetical treatments of) material considered reliable are subject to criticism on one of two grounds. One may criticize the selection of material or the suppositions which are made in putting it together. I wish now to lay out as clearly as possible the way in which the material will be handled and the suppositions which lie behind the reconstruction which follows.

Method of Proceeding

The securest evidence

No one will dispute the principle that, given the conglomeration of evidence about Jesus and the early church which one finds in the Gospels, one should begin with what is relatively secure and work out to more uncertain points. But finding agreement about the ground rules by which what is relatively secure can be identified is very difficult. One of the reasons for this is, I believe, that most studies of Jesus focus on Jesus as a teacher or preacher – at any rate, primarily a messenger – and thus move immediately to try to establish the centre of his message.[1] One may start with what comes first in the Gospels (repentance in view of the coming of the kingdom), with what strikes one as most characteristic (such as the call of sinners), with the sayings material which seems to have been least subject to alteration (often held to be the parables), or with the sayings which could not conceivably have been created in the early church ('Jesus said to him, "Why do you call me good?" ', Mark 10.18); but in any case one starts with a core of sayings material and proceeds to a depiction of Jesus' message and, sometimes, his intention and the cause of the conflict with Judaism.

There are two considerations which make us look elsewhere for the most secure and the best evidence if we wish to understand Jesus. The first is simply that scholars have not and, in my judgment, will not agree on the authenticity of the sayings material, either in whole or in part. There are a few sayings on which there is wide consensus, but hardly enough to allow a full depiction of Jesus. We return to the question of criteria for establishing authenticity in the next subsection, and we shall take up some of the principal sayings in ch. 4.

Secondly, when the study of Jesus is equated with the study of his sayings, there is the unspoken assumption that what he really was, was a teacher. He is then either a clear, straightforward teacher whose parables make his message about God and the kingdom plain, or, as in some recent studies, a difficult, riddling teacher, whose meaning is not and was not altogether clear, or even one who intended to be ambiguous.[2] Whatever sort of teacher he is held to have been, it is difficult to move from 'Jesus the teacher' to 'Jesus, a Jew who was crucified, who was the leader of a group which survived his death, which in turn was persecuted, and which formed a messianic sect which was finally successful'. It is difficult to make his teaching offensive enough to lead to execution or sectarian enough to lead to the formation of a group which eventually separated from the main body of Judaism. This is not to say that scholars have not tried to find links between Jesus' teaching, his death, and the rise of the Christian movement; but only that the links are difficult to establish. Further, the most common ones (e.g., he directly opposed Moses and this aroused opposition) are, at best, dubious. These matters, again, will be explored more fully later, especially in the section on 'the state of the question', and I have to be content here only to say that the various proposed connections between

'Jesus the teacher' and the conclusion and aftermath of his career are not fully satisfactory.

We see, then, that the enormous labour which for generations has been expended on the investigation of the teaching material in the Gospels has not yielded a convincing historical depiction of Jesus – one which sets him firmly in Jewish history, which explains his execution, and which explains why his followers formed a persecuted messianic sect. What is needed is more secure evidence, evidence on which everyone can agree and which at least points towards an explanation of these historical puzzles. Such evidence, if it is produced, could then be supplemented in various ways; but the first goal of this study is to seek and establish that evidence. I think that it exists. There are *facts* about Jesus, his career, and its consequences which are very firm and which do point towards solutions of historical questions; and the present study is based primarily on facts about Jesus and only secondarily on a study of some of the sayings material.

Fuchs some years ago proposed placing first Jesus' behaviour and using that as a framework for the sayings.[3] The concrete behaviour which he had in mind was Jesus' association with sinners, which correlates with the sayings which call sinners and promise them the kingdom. In common with many modern interpreters, I shall later argue that such behaviour and sayings were characteristic of Jesus and become important for understanding him and his relationship to his contemporaries. To understand the importance of Jesus' calling sinners to be with him, however, we must understand rather a lot about who the sinners were and about what Jesus meant by the kingdom, which in turn requires the very understanding of Jesus and Judaism which we are trying to illuminate. The discussion which proceeds from Jesus' association with sinners, to understanding his intention in calling them, to making inferences about his relationship to Judaism (made up of the sinners and the righteous alike) is a fruitful one; but it turns out not to be a good starting-point. Not only does Jesus' association with sinners depend on other important points which must first be clarified before its significance can be seen, but also (as I shall argue in ch. 6) the most common understanding of it is incorrect. It is a fact which must be explained and correlated with Jesus' message;[4] but the meaning is sufficiently in doubt that it does not provide the best point of entry for our study.

Recently two scholars have pointed to the existence of facts about Jesus, and they use them in different ways to derive a full picture of him. Morton Smith has pointed out that ' . . . the external framework of Jesus' life – the what, when, and where – is reasonably certain'.[5] He notes another important fact: 'Whatever else Jesus may or may not have done, he unquestionably started the process that became Christianity.'[6] Anthony Harvey similarly comments that 'the evidence for at least the main facts of the life and death of Jesus is as abundant, circumstantial and consistent as is the case with any other figure of ancient history.'[7] Harvey mentions as beyond reasonable doubt the following facts:

> that Jesus was known in both Galilee and Jerusalem; that he was a teacher; that he carried out cures of various illnesses, particularly demon-possession, and that these were widely regarded as miraculous; that he was involved in controversy with fellow Jews over questions of the law of Moses: and that he was crucified in the governorship of Pontius Pilate.[8]

These two scholars come to different views about Jesus, though agreeing on the whole about these facts. Smith argues that the first and surest fact about Jesus is that he was a miracle worker, and he is confident that in Jesus' own ministry it was healing which attracted the crowds to whom he preached.[9] The crowds began to think of him as the Messiah. The expectations thus aroused, if they affected enough people, might lead the authorities to fear him (p. 16; cf. 43f.). Thus Smith can trace a reasonable line of development from 'miracle worker' to 'messianic pretender' to the crucifixion. He also argues that the title 'son of God' arose because of Jesus' miracles (pp. 80–83; 101–3; cf. 14). Finally, he points out that a lot of teachers and some prophets were known in Israel, but that there was no tendency to make them miracle workers. It is comprehensible, however, that one first known for the latter activity became known for the others: 'the rest of the tradition about Jesus can be understood if we begin with the miracles, but the miracles cannot be understood if we begin with a purely didactic tradition' (p. 16; cf. 129).

The teaching attributed to Jesus does not figure prominently in Smith's treatment, although he does drop the tantalizing hint that Jesus' being a 'magician' correlates with the statement that he preached the gospel to the poor (p. 24). It appears that Smith, were he to treat the teaching material in more detail, would consider some to have come from Jesus and to have been widely known because of his fame as a magician, some to have been attributed to him on the principle that famous names attract famous sayings.

The guild of New Testament scholars has not paid Smith's latest work the attention which it deserves, despite the fact that in it Smith offers to us another deposit of material from his unrivalled treasury of learning. The title 'magician' may be a hindrance, as may Smith's habit of tweaking the noses of the pious. We should not, however, allow ourselves to be so easily deflected from considering the work for what it is: a serious effort to explain historically some of the principal puzzles about Jesus, specifically why he attracted attention, why he was executed, and why he was subsequently deified. I earlier indicated that regarding Jesus as essentially a teacher does not answer these and related questions. The point will, I think, be clearly seen if one compares two recent books on Jesus as teacher, those by Scott and Breech,[10] with the work of Smith. Both of these are based on the assumption that the bedrock material about Jesus consists of a small core of sayings and parables. In these works, Jesus appears as an enigmatic symbol-maker (Scott) or parable-weaver (Breech), offering things which, though mysterious then, are seen, when finally puzzled out twenty centuries later, to be striking in manner but not especially in matter. The Jesus of those works, I think, could not have been an important historical figure. I think that it is fair to say that he is not regarded as such in these two works. Breech is explicit: ' . . . there is absolutely no basis for assuming that Jesus shared the cosmological, mythological, or religious ideas of his contemporaries',[11] and on this reading there would have been no reason for them to have paid attention to him one way or the other. Scott similarly argues that, for Jesus, 'kingdom' was a symbol to the exclusion of concept.[12] He does not explicitly say that Jesus did not speak the same language as his contemporaries, but it seems to follow. A Jesus who was only a teacher, but as teacher did not even communicate striking ideas to his audience, surely was a person of little consequence.

These books are, to be sure, extreme and one-sided, and others who have seen Jesus as primarily a teacher have depicted his teaching as relevant to his contemporaries and have even tried to find in his teaching such offensive matter that he was executed.[13] The success of these efforts will be considered later. But when one shifts from extreme books about Jesus as teacher to Smith's extreme and one-sided account of him as magician, one whiffs not only fresh air, but also the earnest sweat which comes from the effort to explain history.

I have said that Smith's book is one-sided, and it will be helpful to give an instance. In commenting on the Lord's prayer, he recognizes that ' "thy kingdom come" [Matt. 6.10] has no clear magical parallel', since it derives 'from Jewish eschatological thought' (p. 132). Yet he considers that the frequent repetition of the names of gods in the Greek Magical Papyri may illuminate the preceding line, 'hallowed be thy name' (Matt. 6.9). It would be better to look to Jewish hopes for restoration if we wish parallels to the line about sanctifying the name. In a much earlier work, in fact, Smith cited a line from the Kaddish as parallel to the line in Matthew: 'Let thy great name be magnified and hallowed.'[14] The new evidence now adduced from the *PGM* might lead us to examine in a wider context the phrases about magnifying, glorifying and sanctifying the name of God; but it is surely one-sided – as Smith doubtless would grant – to cite only the *PGM*.

This leads us to the consideration which counts against simply adopting Smith's procedure and beginning the investigation of facts about Jesus with miracles. We should bear in mind the general context of Jesus' life and work and start with a fact about Jesus which corresponds best to that context. The reasoning is this: Jesus lived in a mixed culture, and *elements* of his life and work may be illuminated by drawing on information from here and there in the ancient world. I intend here to include the magical papyri. But we know the principal context of Jesus' work: Jewish eschatology. As I shall argue later, the line from John the Baptist to Paul and the other early apostles is the line of Jewish eschatology, and it would be misleading to move the centre of our investigation off that line.

I take it that Smith has struck a blow for redressing the balance in the study of Jesus; that is, for moving us away from the almost exclusive concentration on him as a teacher. Further, building on the undoubted fact that Jesus was known as a miracle worker, he has brought forward evidence for showing that, in this activity, Jesus followed some of the standard practices of magicians. Third, he has made a substantial contribution to methodology. We should study the facts about Jesus and try to understand their significance in his context. I depart from Smith because I think that there are other facts which fit Jesus unmistakably into a context other than that of magic.

Harvey also constructs his book by setting known activities of Jesus into their context, which in turn sets definite limits to their significance. Thus the title, *Jesus and the Constraints of History*. His procedure may be exemplified by quoting him on the question of Jesus as teacher.

> ... we shall find that those bare biographical statements, which are established with a high degree of historical certainty but which seem at first to convey little information that is of interest to the theologian, take on considerable significance. The statement, for example, that Jesus was a teacher, when set in the context of the constraints which bore upon any teacher of his time and culture and of the relatively small number of options which was open to anyone who wished to give a new lead in religious understanding while remaining intelligible to the majority of his hearers – such a statement is capable of yielding a surprising amount of information about the kind of person Jesus must have been and the kind of achievement

at which he aimed; and this information is of great relevance to the ultimate question of Christology: who and what was Jesus?[15]

I shall confess to the reader that, when I read those words, I thought that Harvey had succeeded in publishing first a book on which I had been engaged, off and on, for almost ten years. That turned out not to be the case, and I now recall the moment in order to indicate how appropriate to the problem of how to describe Jesus his procedure is. It will turn out that we do not employ precisely the same list of facts,[16] that we assess the range of possible meanings within Judaism quite differently, and that – as is always the case – we disagree about individual pericopes. Further, as the quoted paragraph makes clear, Harvey is concerned to press his discussion towards the problem of christology, and he spends considerable effort on the question how a modern can make sense of ancient thinking.[17] I prescind from both topics.

The phrase 'must have been', which occurs in the quotation from Harvey, and similar phrases, are extremely common in his book. This indicates the degree to which he is obliged to write what we may call 'aprioristic' history: if Jesus did X, it must have meant Y. The present work is by no means without that sort of argument, although I do not use it as heavily as does Harvey. Such arguments are not necessarily bad ones. Their value depends on several factors, of which we may name the two most important: how sure we are of the possible range of meanings of any given action or saying; how many lines of evidence converge towards the same meaning.

The method which one sees articulated by Smith and Harvey, and which I am attempting to clarify and to pursue systematically, is not in fact new. It has often been followed here and there, though with relatively little or no conscious reflection. We may exemplify the method and its problems by citing an instance (one which is returned to below) from Ernst Käsemann's essay which formally reopened the quest for the historical Jesus. He stated that the first, second and fourth antitheses of the Sermon on the Mount are authentic, and he drew the conclusion that Jesus thereby either cut himself off from Judaism 'or else he brings the Messianic Torah and is therefore the Messiah'.[18] The conclusion about the two possible meanings of the sayings about not being angry, not lusting, and not swearing is based on a prior assumption: normal Judaism could not tolerate such sayings. Here the prior assumption is based on a misunderstanding of Jewish law and the permissible bounds of individual disagreement. For the present I mention only one point: it is not against the law to be more strict and rigorous than the law requires.

I hope that both the method and its pitfalls are clear. In principle it is possible to argue from facts to meaning or significance. Further, this sort of argument is necessary if one is to answer significant questions about Jesus. What is hard is to develop such arguments successfully and convincingly: to avoid too much circularity, to start at the right point, to get the facts straight, and to assess correctly their possible significance in their original context.

There is, as is usual in dealing with historical questions, no opening which does not involve one in a circle of interpretation, that is, which does not depend on points which in turn require us to understand others. Historians always work in this kind of circle, moving from evidence to tentative conclusions, then back to the evidence with renewed insight, and so on. In discussing Smith's book, I have already mentioned a circle of interpretation which I have followed and which will be presented fully below: enough evidence points towards Jewish eschatology as the general framework of Jesus' ministry that we may examine the particulars in the light of that framework. One must be careful to enter the circle at the right point, that is, to choose the best starting place. This, in turn, is a point which is secure historically and whose meaning can be established with some degree of independence from the rest of the evidence. One must also, of course, avoid circular arguments, the basing of two points each on the other. These occur with surprising frequency, and we shall see an important one in discussing Matt. 12.28//Luke 11.20. They result not so much from deficiencies in knowledge of logic as from lack of attention to what is and is not bedrock in the tradition. Conclusions about Jesus are based on passages, especially sayings, whose authenticity and meaning depend on a context which is, in turn, provided by the conclusion. Thus the conclusion that Jesus thought that in his exorcisms the kingdom was shown to be or was made present depends on Matt. 12.28 and par. The verse is known to be both authentic and meaningful because it reflects Jesus' feeling of eschatological power. But Jesus' feeling of eschatological power is known to us only through conclusions and arguments based on Matt. 12.28 and one or two other sayings (see ch. 4).

The simplest way to avoid these and other problems of argumentation is to found the study on bedrock, and especially to begin at the right point. Once a beginning is made, a context is set which will influence the interpretation of subsequent evidence.

We start by determining the evidence which is most secure. There are several facts about Jesus' career *and its aftermath* which can be known beyond doubt.[19] Any interpretation of Jesus should be able to account for these. The almost indisputable facts, listed more or less in chronological order, are these:

1. Jesus was baptized by John the Baptist.
2. Jesus was a Galilean who preached and healed.
3. Jesus called disciples and spoke of there being twelve.
4. Jesus confined his activity to Israel.
5 Jesus engaged in a controversy about the temple.
6. Jesus was crucified outside Jerusalem by the Roman authorities.
7. After his death Jesus' followers continued as an identifiable movement.
8. At least some Jews persecuted at least parts of the new movement (Gal. 1.13, 22; Phil. 3.6), and it appears that this persecution endured at least to a time near the end of Paul's career (II Cor. 11.24; Gal. 5.11; 6.12; cf. Matt. 23.34; 10.17).

In the course of the present work I have tried several starting points, working them out either mentally or on paper, in an effort to find the one which is most satisfactory. The aim is always to move from the evidence which is most secure and least ambiguous to more uncertain evidence. If we knew enough about any of the eight points it would serve as an adequate beginning point. If we knew, for example, whether or not there was a direct connection between the Roman execution of Jesus and the Jewish persecution of some of his followers, many of the puzzles about early Christianity and its relationship to Judaism would be solved. If we knew enough about the reported trials and the motives for the execution of Jesus, we would have a firm clue to start the unravelling of the interrelated themes which are under discussion here.[20] But on the one point our information is non-existent, on the other uncertain and unreliable. A sound answer to the question of the cause of Jesus' death requires us to solve a lot of other problems, and the fact of his execution cannot be the starting point for our study. Similarly, if we could definitely establish whether or not there was an intrinsic connection between the preaching of Jesus and the subsequent formation of his disciples into a group with its own distinctive identity, we could safely begin our study there. Yet this question remains one of the most debated points in the study of Christian origins. I have chosen to begin with the temple controversy, about which our information is a little better and which offers almost as good an entry for the study of Jesus' intention and his relationship to his contemporaries as would a truly eye-witness account of the trial.[21] The temple controversy can also be isolated to some degree from other questions. It thus gives a point of entry for the study of Jesus' career and historical setting, and it will also open the way to re-examine the question of 'Jesus and the Kingdom'.

A special word should be said about the use of facts after Jesus' death to shed light on his intention and his relationship to Judaism. In the Anglo-Saxon world it has often been argued, usually in response to liberal German Protestant discussions of Jesus, that something about Jesus could be inferred from, in fact was necessitated by, the faith which sprang up among his disciples. To quote from Robert Morgan's criticism of this response, the argument has been that 'the phenomenon of Christianity necessarily demands more than a liberal Protestant Jesus to explain it.'[22] In somewhat the same vein, John Knox wrote that 'if we could not trust any of the sayings or any of the deeds, we could still trust the impression of the sayer and the doer, which the Gospels convey.'[23] Knox's position is not the same as the English tradition from Rawlinson to Moule,[24] but for the immediate point they may be considered together. What has been at stake in the English discussion is, as Morgan's essays show, incarnational christology: while historical research itself can portray only an historical Jesus, and cannot be the basis for Christian faith, some historical descriptions of Jesus will be more congruent with the doctrine of the incarnation than others.[25] Knox's argument was directed to the church: the reader who is a Christian can *know* what Jesus really *was* by examining the early church, in which the impact of his life and work was embedded.

I do not wish to challenge or confirm the positions of (for example) Lightfoot and Knox.[26] I shall, however, sometimes attempt to infer causes from results. I shall attempt, among other things, to see what can be known about Jesus by studying what happened after his death. When pursuing this line of enquiry, I shall have in mind only the historical sequence already described, the one which terminates in the persecution of the early Christian movement by some within Judaism, not the one which results in the confession of John 20.28. The question is simply whether or not Jesus did or said anything which pushed his followers in the direction of forming a sect, a group within Judaism which could be identified and subjected to punishment. In advance I do not consider it likely that the link between Jesus and the consolidation and persecution of his followers lies in a common view of his *person*. Paul gives only one motive for persecution: the question of circumcision, and thus, by extrapolation, the question of the law.[27] I do not wish to try to settle this issue here, but only to point out that there is a difference between my effort to link causes and results and that which has been most common in Anglo-Saxon scholarship. In the subsection on 'a good hypothesis' I shall describe more fully my view of how to infer causes from result.

The sayings

Although the sayings material has just been assigned a relatively secondary role, especially considering the dominance which it has generally enjoyed, it remains important in this study. A full examination of the reliability and authenticity of the sayings material is beyond the bounds of the present work,[28] but I shall explain in brief form the general stance towards the sayings material which is taken here.

I belong to the school which holds that a saying attributed to Jesus can seldom be proved beyond doubt to be entirely authentic or entirely non-authentic, but that each saying must be tested by appropriate criteria and assigned (tentatively) to an author – either to Jesus or to an anonymous representative of some stratum in the early church.[29] This appears to be a neutral stance, placing the burden of proof equally on those who would assign a saying to Jesus and those who would assign it to the church. If one were writing a history of the synoptic sayings material, such a position probably would be neutral. When one writes about Jesus, however, this attitude has the effect of shifting the burden of proof to the shoulders of those who affirm the authenticity[30] of a saying or group of sayings. I find that I am not neutrally canvassing the material, assigning it as best I can to an appropriate place. I am looking for information about Jesus, and looking with a somewhat sceptical eye; I want to be *convinced* that a given saying is at least probably by Jesus before employing it.

The question of where the burden of proof falls, which has been so often discussed, is in fact very simple: it falls on the one who argues a case.[31] Were this a book about Matthew, I would need to show that the material which I use represents Matthew, not, for example, a pre-Matthaean redactor. Since the book is about Jesus, I must bear the burden of proof and show that the material which I use probably provides accurate knowledge about Jesus.

We should be able to obtain general agreement on this way of stating the question of the burden of proof. Important disagreements about the reliability of the Gospels will, however, remain. Different scholars have different overall views of the Gospel material, and these will markedly affect their judgments about the number of instances in which one may successfully argue that a passage is authentic. I stand, as I have indicated,

on the sceptical side, and I should here lay out briefly my judgments about
the nature of the material.

1. One of the principal arguments of the form critics – namely, that we
have the material as it was handed down by the church, and that it has
been adapted for use by the church – is to be maintained.[32] The most
vigorous attempt to provide an alternative to form criticism is that of Birger
Gerhardsson, who for years has argued for a fundamentally different
evaluation of the synoptic material. Gerhardsson has now been joined by
others,[33] and we should pause to consider the possibility of revising the
most common overall view of the material.

I shall not rehearse the history of Gerhardsson's original statement,[34]
the criticisms directed against it,[35] and his reponse.[36] This discussion will
be restricted to his latest statement, which I find often convincing, at least
with regard to how we view the origin and history of the material in the
Gospels, even though it does not decisively change my position with regard
to authenticity.[37]

Of principal importance are two points: outside the Gospels we do not
find a substantial body of traditions about Jesus; inside the Gospels we
have full *texts*, not just essential points.[38] When these two points are
combined, they effectively refute the basic form-critical position that much
of the material was created in 'typical situations' to serve diverse needs of
the church.[39] We have, rather, parenesis without Jesus-material, as in
James, and much Jesus-material which would serve parenesis (especially
in Matthew), but no evidence that the need for ethical exhortation led to
the creation of material about Jesus. Gerhardsson notes that in such
activities as exhortation and apologetic the church needed primarily *points*,
not necessarily the reading of full *texts*.[40] He seeks a special activity in the
life of the church which accounts for the preservation of texts which
contain sayings of Jesus, and he finds it by considering the dual transmission
of the Hebrew Scriptures. There was a free transmission, one which often
altered Scripture appreciably, and which is represented in the haggada of
the midrashim and in the targums. There were also activities in which
the precise text was maintained: worship, study, and the professional
preservation and transmission of the written text.[41] Since the material
about Jesus exists in full texts, he proposes that it – or at least some of it –
was kept and preserved in a way analogous to that of the Hebrew
Scripture.[42]

There are two clear instances in which we can be certain that, from the
very earliest time, the church preserved texts: the saying on divorce (I Cor.
7.10f.; Matt. 5.31f.; Matt. 19.9; Mark 10.11f.: Luke 16.18) and the words

of institution (I Cor. 11.23–26; Matt. 26.26–29 and parr.).[43] It is noteworthy that even here we do not find the concern for precise *wording* which Gerhardsson several times proposes as having characterized the preservation of the material about Jesus.[44] Not only does the wording vary from version to version, but there are also substantial variations. Did Jesus say of the cup, 'this is my blood' (Matthew and Mark) or 'this is the new covenant in my blood' (Paul and Luke)? Did he forbid women to leave their husbands (Paul and Mark), or did he mention only men (Matthew and Luke)?

Gerhardsson repeatedly says that the church changed the material: it deleted, added, altered and occasionally created Jesus-material.[45] But once that is granted, and is seen to be true even in the two texts which we know to have existed very early, it seems that the analogy with the text of the Hebrew Scriptures should be dropped. I am persuaded by Gerhardsson that the Gospel material was not created and transmitted in the ways proposed by the form critics – i.e., separately according to function in diverse activities of the early church, such as teaching and debate.[46] But we still do not have an analogy from the ancient world which will explain how it was handled. Gerhardsson effectively refutes form criticism's view of how the church's creativity was exercised (in typical activities which gave rise to certain forms), but we do not have a persuasive alternative, and the creativity itself is not to be denied. The most certain point is the one with which we began, and which Gerhardsson grants: the material was subject to all sorts of alteration, and we have it as it was transmitted by the church.

2. The form-critical tests which were used to establish the earlier form of tradition, which have often been used in attempts to establish authenticity, are unreliable. I have in mind principally Semitisms, brevity and details. Sayings in general do not tend to become either more or less 'Semitic', longer or shorter, or more or less detailed.[47]

3. We know very little of the practices and interests of the early church (apart from the Pauline mission) before the Gospels were written.[48] In a few instances there is indisputable evidence that a saying has been altered or perhaps created after the death of Jesus,[49] but we can give nothing like a catalogue of the kinds of changes that may have been introduced.

When these three points are taken together we must conclude that the material was subject to change and may have changed, but that we do not know just how it changed.[50] It is not the case that I am decisively convinced that Jesus did not say the bulk of the things attributed to him in the synoptic Gospels, but rather that I regard the material as having been subject to change in ways that cannot be precisely assessed. Thus the sayings material alone does not offer us enough firm ground to explore successfully the problems which we have set ourselves.

The weaknesses of form criticism should not lead us to the view that the alternative is to accept the general reliability of the tradition except when it can be disproved. The form critics were right in thinking that the material changed; they were wrong in thinking that they knew how it changed. Dibelius and Bultmann, for example, thought that the material tended to depart from its original, 'pure' form. The observations that 'pure' forms may be only scholarly reconstructions,[51] and that in any case we do not know that material tends to become increasingly mixed or 'impure',[52] mean that *we do not have the rather optimistic confidence of form criticism* that reconstructions of the original text can be achieved. When one tries to reconstruct the life and message of Jesus, this situation, as we have already said, shifts the burden of proof from the shoulders of those who doubt authenticity to the shoulders of those who affirm it. This is not to say that the burden cannot be borne in individual cases, but only to say that it must be borne.[53]

The principal test which scholars have recently used for assessing authenticity is the test of double 'dissimilarity', and to that test we now turn.[54]

The test is this: material which can be accounted for neither as traditional Jewish material nor as later church material can be safely attributed to Jesus. There are well-known difficulties in applying the test. We know first-century Judaism very imperfectly, and knowledge about the interests of the church between 70 and 100 CE (when the Gospels were completed) is slender indeed.[55] Nevertheless, the test can occasionally be successfully applied, and it is used below in the discussion of Matt. 8.21f.//Luke 9.59f. Yet a problem remains. The test rules out too much. We should assume that part of what Jesus said and did became constitutive of Christian preaching, so that the elimination of all Christian motifs would result in the elimination of material which also tells us something about Jesus. Similarly, we should be prepared to assume a broad ground of positive relationships between Jesus and his contemporaries in Judaism. Another way of stating this problem with the test of double dissimilarity is to observe that it provides too little material to allow a satisfactory reconstruction of the life and teaching of Jesus. The material which remains after the test is applied is biased towards uniqueness.

Secondly, the remaining material does not interpret itself or necessarily answer historical questions. It must still be placed in a meaningful context, and that context is not automatically provided by summarizing sayings which are atypical, as far as we know, of both Judaism and the Christian church.

We have earlier agreed that, in dealing with Jesus, one has to begin with relatively secure evidence. That is not to say, however, that a summary of the most nearly certain sayings of Jesus will provide a satisfactory depiction of his career. If our assumption is true that Jesus also said things which were in agreement with the contemporary Judaism or with the views of the later church, a summary of the sayings which pass the test of double dissimilarity would be inadequate for a meaningful presentation of his teaching.

The inadequacy remains even if the list of sayings which are held to be authentic is expanded by employing other criteria, such as attestation in more than one source or attestation in more than one form.[56] No matter what criteria for testing the sayings are used, scholars still need to move beyond the sayings themselves to a broader context than a summary of their contents if they are to address historical questions about Jesus.[57]

Since historical reconstruction requires that data be fitted into a context, the establishment of a secure context, or framework of interpretation, becomes crucial. There are basically three kinds of information which provide help in this endeavour: such facts about Jesus as those outlined above (p. 11, nos. 1–6); knowledge about the outcome of his life and teaching (cf. nos. 7 and 8); knowledge of first-century Judaism.

Different scholars have tried to correlate sayings and other information in various ways. I have already indicated that in the present work emphasis will be placed on unassailable facts about Jesus, their possible significance in his own time, and the outcome of his life and work. Once the context is established and integrated with sayings which are very probably authentic, it will be possible to draw in other material in the synoptics.

One of the points of emphasis, the one which justifies the title of the book, is on the third source of information, first-century Judaism. 'Everything which enlarges our knowledge of' Palestinian Judaism, which is Jesus' environment, 'indirectly extends our knowledge of the historical Jesus himself.'[58] Judaism will not, however, be the subject of an independent account. Rather, keeping to the outline sketched above of facts about Jesus' life and work, we shall attempt to draw special attention to the significance of Jesus' deeds and words in first-century Jewish Palestine. I have previously attempted an account of some features of Jewish thought in the period 200 BCE to 200 CE, and some elements of that account will be presupposed.[59] Thus I take it for granted that no body of Jewish leaders would have taken offence at the proclamation of God's willingness to forgive *repentant* sinners.[60] The forgiveness of repentant sinners is a major motif in virtually all the Jewish material which is still available from the period. Such general theological points will not be again demonstrated in detail. On the other hand, it will be necessary to explore more fully some aspects of Jewish practice and belief, especially about the temple cult. Here I shall be in quest not of a common-denominator 'pattern of religion' which underlay all sorts of Judaism over a prolonged period but of evidence about individual points which can be definitely dated before 70.

Our study will lead to a hypothesis, and a hypothesis is derived not only from the available information, but also from prior suppositions about what a hypothesis could and should look like. In order that these suppositions should be clear, a few words will be said about them.

A good hypothesis

In the first place, a good hypothesis with regard to Jesus' intention and his relationship to Judaism should meet Klausner's test: it should situate Jesus believably in Judaism and yet explain why the movement initiated by him eventually broke with Judaism. That a hypothesis should meet both these expectations will not be conceded on all sides, and a few comments should be made about each point.

Earlier generations of scholars sometimes made Jesus so unique (and Judaism so inferior) that the reader is now forced to wonder how it could be that Jesus grew up on Jewish soil. Thus Bousset, for example, while conceding some formal similarities between Jesus and his contemporaries (e.g., the use of parables), denied any similarity at all on essentials. 'In the one case we have mere exposition of the Scriptures, in the other a living piety. There the parables are designed to illustrate the distorted ideas of a dead learning. . . . Here the parable was handled by one whose whole soul was set . . . upon the real.'[61] Although many of Bousset's basic views about Judaism are still unhesitatingly repeated by New Testament scholars,[62] the crudity of his description of Judaism has pretty well disappeared, and with it the stark contrast between Jesus, who represents everything good, pure and enlightened, and Judaism, which represents everything distorted, hypocritical and misleading. There is still an appreciable drive on the part of New Testament scholars to depict Jesus as transcending the bounds of Judaism (which in this context is always considered a good thing to do), but the inclination to have Jesus so superior to his contemporaries that he is deprived of a living context in Judaism seems to have been overcome by better judgment and better historical understanding. There is today virtually unanimous consent to the first of Klausner's propositions: Jesus lived as a Jew.[63] The question which remains is how to determine what Jesus' relationship to his contemporaries was, and there is wider disagreement on how to answer that question, as we shall see in the next section. The precise delineation of Jesus' attitude towards and relations with his contemporaries is one of the major concerns of scholarship on Jesus and occupies a prominent place in the present work.

The second half of Klausner's position – that something in Jesus' own activity should have prepared in some way for the eventual split of Christianity from Judaism – is more controversial and may be argued against in a variety of ways. It has been held by many that this was not the case, but that only the resurrection experiences account for the existence of the Christian movement at all.[64] That the resurrection experiences of the disciples provided the motivating force behind the proclamation of Jesus as the Christ and as Lord, and much of its content, is not in dispute. The question is whether the resurrection is the sole explanation of the Christian movement, or whether there is also a more than accidental connection between Jesus' own work and the emergence of the Christian church. This is not a question which can be answered in advance. Klausner's argument that there must have been such a connection on the grounds that *ex nihilo nihil fit* is not necessarily convincing as a formal argument; for those who find no connection between the intention of Jesus and the emergence of Christianity do not argue that something developed out of nothing. They argue, rather, that the resurrection called the disciples back together and allowed them to see the ministry of Jesus in a new light, so that they could appeal to it even though nothing in what Jesus said or did had prepared them in advance to constitute a special group. There is nothing formally impossible about such a hypothesis, and certainly a connection should not be forced if there is not good evidence for one.

The fullest argument against attributing to Jesus an intention which had results is that of Henry J. Cadbury in *The Peril of Modernizing Jesus*.[65] He described the modern view as being that 'the person's aim is to be deduced from his recorded words and actions. These words and actions were motivated by his aim. They were chosen with a view to their effectiveness towards the end that was conceived' (pp. 120f.). In Jesus' day, however, 'to plot a career *de novo* would occur to almost nobody' (p. 123). He suggested 'an unreflective vagabondage' as having characterized Jesus (p. 125). Cadbury's argument was directed against both Schweitzer's consistent eschatology (pp. 127f.) and the view of Jesus as a social or political reformer (pp. 128–30). It is 'too easy', warned Cadbury, 'to arrive at a man's purpose by seeing what he accomplished' (p. 137). He explicitly noted the argument that where there is smoke there is fire, but urged that 'the ratio of smoke and fire varies enormously, and the smoke often is misleading as to the exact location of the fire' (p. 40). In place of the modern view that the 'fire' which produced the smoke must have been Jesus' own intention, Cadbury offered another:

> What I wish to propose is that Jesus probably had no definite, unified, conscious purpose, that an absence of such a program is *a priori* likely and that it suits well the historical evidence (p. 141).

Cadbury's warning against imposing modern categories and ways of thought on the ancient world is salutary, but in this case not convincing. Consciously intended programmes were not as alien to the ancient world as he suggests, nor need we look far to find instances. Two of the sectarian or semi-sectarian groups in the Judaism of Jesus' day had such programmes: the *ḥaberim* and the Essenes.[66] The former wanted to sanctify the entirety of life, to make common life as holy as the temple, filled with the presence of God.[67] *To this end* they agreed to handle, sell and eat food in virtually the same state of purity as that which the Bible prescribes for the priests who serve in the temple. The Essenes (as known from the Dead Sea Scrolls) sought a purified, 'true' Israel (although the term is not altogether accurate),[68] one composed of people dedicated to keeping 'the covenant of Moses' as it was interpreted by the sect's leaders. *To achieve this end* they went to extreme steps, such as requiring the communal pooling of possessions and limiting intercourse with strangers very strictly. After his crucifixion Jesus' followers constituted a sect or a semi-sectarian group within Judaism. There is every reason to attribute to them the same degree of intentionality which we can attribute to the *ḥaberim* and the Dead Sea community. Their programme, as it emerges for example in Paul's letters, was clear and straightforward, and it determined their activities. They intended to prepare Israel and, secondarily, the 'full number' of the Gentiles for the return of the Lord.[69] *To this end* they organized missions, divided responsibility (Gal. 2.6–10), and even held a conference to make sure that their various endeavours converged on the common goal (Gal. 2.1f.).

Thus the question is not whether or not ancients in general and ancient Jews in particular formulated aims and shaped their actions so as to accomplish them. They did so. The question is whether or not *Jesus'* intention can be inferred from the results. Can we, for example, draw a line from Jesus' intention to that of his followers after his death?

I have thus far urged that the historian should examine the question and probe for evidence. It is not a question which should be dismissed as inappropriate to the ancient world or as theologically inappropriate (it is often feared that too much history will damage faith). We should not, of course, coerce the evidence.

In our endeavour, however, we must give strict attention to one of Cadbury's admonitions. It is his comment about smoke and fire. They do not always precisely correspond. It is true that the early church came to believe that Jesus was a transcendent being, that God sent him to save the world, that he would soon return in glory, and that all who believed in him would be saved. Historians should attempt to account for the origin and development of these and other beliefs, but it would be foolhardy – or worse – to rush to the conclusion that the historical Jesus must have corresponded to such beliefs. It seems intrinsically likely that beliefs about Jesus' relation to God and his imminent return depend very heavily on the resurrection appearances. It was surely such an appearance that convinced Paul that Jesus had not died in vain (Gal. 2.21) and that he would return from heaven (I Thess. 4.16) – beliefs which Paul held without benefit of having known Jesus. In the realm of dogmatic belief we have a lot of smoke – a lot of firm beliefs – but we must be very cautious about describing the fire which produced it.

It is otherwise, however, when we ask about other matters, such as the disciples' existence as a sect and their living out of the conviction that the last days were upon them. We can explain Paul's conviction that the Lord would return from heaven and that the resurrection would not be of a physical body (I Cor. 15.44–50) by the resurrection appearance. It is more difficult to attribute to the same cause the general eschatological framework in which he lived and worked.

It is true that the eschatological framework within which the early Christian church stood need not have been given entirely by Jesus; something could have come from the general environment. It is my intention here only to point out that in some instances it is more reasonable to infer causes from results – fire from smoke – than it is in others.

Cadbury said that, on his reading, the evidence suits a purposeless Jesus better than it does a programme-orientated Jesus. Here we come to the crunch. I shall say in advance of the detailed argument that, on my reading, the evidence points towards Jesus' having had a definite programme.

The only way to avoid circularity in this area is the exercise of caution and the use of converging lines of argument. Cadbury's *a priori* assumption that ancients on the whole did not have conscious programmes might be seen as informing his reading of the evidence about Jesus. My contrary assumption might lead me to find intention where there is none. The reader will have to judge how good the evidence is. My own perception is that my prior assumption that Jesus may well have had an intention which resulted in corresponding consequences has led me to look for evidence, but not to create or force it. Further, I propose that a hypothesis which does offer a reasonable and well-grounded connection between Jesus and the Christian movement is better than one which offers no connection, but which appeals, finally, to accident and to the resurrection experiences to explain why Jesus' mission did not end with his death.[70] This also urges that one seek evidence. The reader, again, will have to judge its value.

A second aspect of a good hypothesis about Jesus' intention and his relationship with his contemporaries is that it should offer a connection between his activity and his death.[71] Again, this is not absolutely clear in advance. It could be the case, and the case has often been well argued, that Jesus was put to death more or less accidentally; he and his followers created a disturbance which the Roman authorities incorrectly took as indicating the possibility of insurrection, and Jesus did not die over a conflict with his contemporaries which was paramount in his own life and teaching.[72] This is also possible, but again it seems preferable to posit a connection between what he did and said and the reason for his execution.

To put these two points together and as baldly as possible: it is conceivable that Jesus taught one thing, that he was killed for something else, and that the disciples, after the resurrection, made of his life and death still something else, so that there is no causal thread between his life, his death and the Christian movement. This is possible, but it is not satisfying historically. Further, I think – and this is far more important than *a priori* suppositions – that the evidence shows that there was a causal connection: that there is substantial coherence between what Jesus had in mind, how he saw his relationship to his nation and his people's religion, the reason for his death, and the beginning of the Christian movement. It is the intention of the present work to explore that evidence. We should first, however, give some review of scholarly opinions on these points so that the issues will be sharply focused.

State of the question

The purposes of this review of the state of the question are very limited. I do not wish to summarize every opinion, but only to situate the present work in recent New Testament scholarship. For this reason the discussion will be limited to general works which give a more or less comprehensive view of Jesus and will not include special studies of particular points. Some of the latter will be taken up in subsequent chapters. Further, I do not intend to offer a point-by-point evaluation of the views summarized. The subsequent chapters will reveal where I agree or disagree with the several points and positions which are considered here. The purpose, rather, is to see what are some of the main lines of research and to achieve a view of how some major New Testament scholars see the questions of the intention of Jesus and his relationship to his contemporaries.[1]

It was Albert Schweitzer who most sharply posed the hypothesis that Jesus had some intention which went beyond the reformation of crass, materialistic and nationalistic ideas about the kingdom of God.[2] His well-known argument will not be repeated in any detail. It was, in brief, that Jesus expected the kingdom to come in a literal sense within a few months, that he saw himself as its messenger, that he structured his activity to anticipate its arrival, and that, when it did not arrive on schedule, he took upon himself the sufferings which he supposed the kingdom required in an attempt to force its appearance. Jesus stood firmly anchored in the Judaism of his time, being dominated by an 'eschatological dogma' which was thoroughly Jewish, and differing from his contemporaries not with regard to theology and ideas about God, but only because of his conception of his own role in the scheme of things.[3]

The reaction to Schweitzer was so intense that the force and validity of his positive points seem to have been missed (in distinction from his analysis of everybody else, which was widely appreciated). What is wrong with Schweitzer's reconstruction is immediately clear: he used the material in the Gospels too arbitrarily, his hypothesis does not arise naturally from the study of the texts but seems to be imposed upon them, and the dogma which he ascribes to Jesus may not in fact even be thoroughly grounded in the contemporary Jewish expectation. The expectation of sufferings before the Messiah comes, for example, which is absolutely crucial to Schweitzer's hypothesis,[4] may not precede the two wars with Rome, and numerous other elements of his eschatological scheme may be queried.[5] His work has the great merit, however, of attempting to find an inner connection between the intention of Jesus, his death, and the church's subsequent expectation of the parousia.[6] These are attempts which it would be profitable to pursue, even if Schweitzer's hypothesized inner connection is found unconvincing.

The merit of Schweitzer's attempt to ground Jesus in Judaism and to find a thread which ties together his intention, his death and the early church can in part be seen by contrast with more or less contemporary works which made no such attempt.[7] It is instructive in this regard to re-read Bousset's books on Jesus and Judaism.[8] If Schweitzer's particular hypothesis is unconvincing and finally incredible, Bousset's is unbelievable in quite a different way. He offers, by contrast, not a dogmatic hypothesis arbitrarily imposed on the Gospels, but a fairy tale. Many elements of the fairy tale have been repeated, and for that reason a brief examination is useful. The aspect of Bousset's work which gives it its 'fairy tale' quality has been mentioned in the preceding section: Jesus was so different from and superior to Judaism in every way that it is hardly believable that he was born and reared a Jew. One is immediately struck by Bousset's utter disdain for what he understood Judaism to be, a disdain which is all the more disconcerting when one realizes that Bousset's work on Judaism is still considered a standard text:[9]

> Everything turned upon the letter of the law and its exegesis. The merely legal and ceremonial side, with its mass of ordinances, occupied by far the largest space in it. Much that was good and useful for religion and morals was no doubt let fall by the way, but only by the way – it could not be enjoyed to the full. Trained acumen, a system of explaining separate passages of Scripture by the most artificial rules, idle, fantastic combinations, devices of greater or less ingenuity, punning interpretations and burlesque anecdotes – these were the characteristics of the rabbinic discourses (pp. 37f.).

Jesus was completely different:

> But with him the Scriptures and the law were never an end in themselves, but only a means to an end; his business was, not to expound the Scriptures, but to lead men to the living God. Whatever he could make use of for that purpose he took from the Scriptures; whatever was useless simply glanced aside from his largeness of soul and his devotion to the real (pp. 38f.)

> Here, then, lay the difference. The message he brought was a living reality, not a clinging to the skirts of a vanished world . . . (p. 29).

> His desire was to teach, not to ask riddles or to make ingenious puns and witticisms in order to arouse a superficial interest (p. 41).

In the one case we have mere exposition of the Scriptures, in the other a living piety. There the parables are designed to illustrate the distorted ideas of a dead learning, and therefore often – though by no means always – themselves become distorted and artificial. Here the parable was handled by one whose whole soul was set, clearly and simply and with nothing to impede its vision, upon the real (p. 44).

On the one hand was the artificiality of a hair-splitting and barren erudition, on the other the fresh directness of the layman and the son of the people; here was the product of long generations of misrepresentation and distortion, there was simplicity, plainness, and freedom; here a clinging to the petty and the insignificant, a burrowing in the dust, there a constant dwelling upon the essential and a great inward sense of reality; here the refinement of casuistry, formula- and phrase-mongering, there the straightforwardness, severity, and pitilessness of the preacher of repentance; here a language which was scarcely to be understood, there the inborn power of the mighty orator; here the letter of the law and there the living God. It was like the meeting of water and fire. This close corporation of the professionally learned could never forgive the simple outsider for making a greater effect than they, and for the fact that the people listened to him. Between these two there must have been mortal enmity from the outset. And on the other hand, Jesus' love of truth and feeling for reality, offended by such caricatures of true piety,[10] broke through all the limits of forbearance, self-restraint, and consideration, and allowed the passionate wrath of his soul to pour forth far and wide (pp. 67–69).

Since the point has been made elsewhere, I shall simply report here as a matter of fact that the person to whom the Rabbis' language was incomprehensible was Bousset,[11] and he understood Rabbinic religion as little as he did their language. It is clear simply from the tone of these passages that Bousset's contrast is dictated primarily by theology and has little to do with historical description.[12]

What that theology was has been described by Moore: many Christian scholars, having lost confidence in the creeds, sought the distinctiveness and superiority of Christianity in a contrast of Jesus with Judaism; and they thus found it necessary to paint Judaism as black as possible.[13] Thus the fairy tale quality of Bousset's description: Jesus is completely different and unique. The contrast is like fire and water. There could only have been implacable hatred from the outset.

On other levels, however, Bousset did not so entirely lose touch with the probabilities of historical reality. In addition to the basic antipathy between Jesus and Judaism which we have just cited, he described the conflict in other terms. Jesus, argued Bousset, agreed with his Pharisaic contemporaries with regard to the authority of the Torah in principle. Because of his intention not to expound Scripture, but to lead people to the living God, however, he could, '*if only half-consciously*', break the scriptural limits. Bousset continues, 'But just as he saw authority in the Scriptures, so he submitted with equal earnestness and humility to the laws of God as he read them in nature and in the life of man.'[14] As we shall see, this view of Jesus' attitude towards the law becomes important in later discussion.

A second concrete point of opposition besides Jesus' willingness to break the law (though only half-consciously) is the definition of the kingdom. For Judaism, the kingdom was always the kingdom *of Israel*. Jesus, by emphasizing *of God*, made a fundamental change, one which broke with Jewish nationalism (pp. 86–98). Again, however, the fundamental opposition was more implicit than explicit: 'With the idea of the kingdom of God the universalism of the Gospel is already present in embryo' (p. 94). 'And while with sure though gentle hand he released religion from its ancient forms, he nevertheless created *no new forms*, nothing material to place between God and His disciples' (p. 108).[15]

Despite the severity of these points of opposition – the implacable hatred between Jesus and the scribes and Pharisees because of their fundamental religious antipathy, Jesus' implicit abrogation of the law, and his embryonic universalizing of religion – Jesus' death did not, in Bousset's view, result from any or all of them. Bousset notes that the scribes and Pharisees are replaced in Jerusalem by the high priests and others as Jesus' opponents (p. 16), and he argues that the cause of Jesus' death was his messianic claim, which threatened the Jerusalem hierarchy rather than the scribes and Pharisees (p. 17). Thus the content of the disputes on matters of religious significance did not actually influence the outcome of Jesus' career. The thread which Schweitzer sought is not present. As historical explanation, Bousset's work fails at every point. It presents no believable point of opposition between Jesus and other Jewish teachers, the opposition which is described depends on a regrettable denigration and perversely misleading description of Judaism, and the opposition in any case had nothing to do with subsequent events. The occasion of Jesus' trial and death is stated baldly, without any attempt to explain why a messianic claim should have led to death.

I believe that the best way to explain Bultmann's book on Jesus[16] is to say that he was Bousset's student and he fully registered the impact of some of Schweitzer's points (in addition to the standard and correct observation that he worked primarily with existentialist categories). Bultmann and Dodd offered the major responses to Schweitzer's theory of 'thorough-going eschatology', Dodd proposing 'realized eschatology'[17] and Bultmann existential eschatology (the kingdom *is* wholly future, but it determines the present; its chief characteristic is that it demands decision; see pp. 51f.). Bultmann, however, unlike Dodd,[18] did not mention Schweitzer as someone whose views should be taken seriously.[19] Despite this, the counter to Schweitzer is explicit. Jesus was *not* an apocalypticist (p. 39), and Jesus' ethics are *not* interim ethics (pp. 127–29). The definition of the kingdom of God takes into account the future definition insisted on by Weiss[20] and Schweitzer, while taking away the concrete meaning.[21] The claim that the kingdom is coming is always present in the word,[22] confronts every individual through all generations in his own historicity,[23] and always demands a decision. This makes creative theological use of the work of Weiss and Schweitzer, and Bultmann's ability to deal in a creative way with the future prediction that the kingdom was coming is one of his chief contributions to the history of New Testament theology. This is intended as genuine but limited praise. For it is clear that Bultmann's interpretation deprives the proclamation of the kingdom of the only meaning it could have had in Jesus' own lifetime. Once it becomes timeless truth (even if always occurring in 'true history' in Bultmann's terms), it has been pulled out of its concrete historical setting.

Schweitzer's principal insight – that one should seek an inner connection between the teaching of Jesus and his death – is not discussed by Bultmann, but it is by implication denied, and denied in a way that bears a marked resemblance to Bousset's position. As in the case of Bousset's book, a great deal of Bultmann's book consists of specifying differences between the teaching of Jesus and the rest of Judaism, and like Bousset Bultmann finds no intrinsic connection between the contrast of Jesus' teaching with that of Judaism and the cause of Jesus' death. The movement initiated by Jesus, the entry to Jerusalem, and his death can be explained only if Jesus 'spoke as a Messianic prophet' (p. 124).[24] (Bultmann, unlike Bousset, hesitates to say that Jesus claimed the title 'Messiah'.[25]) Thus the detailed analysis of the teaching of Jesus and its contrast with Judaism do not explain the historical circumstances leading to his death and the rise of Christianity. Further, there is still no explanation of why speaking as a messianic prophet should result in death.

Some of the points at which Bultmann finds Jesus to differ from Judaism echo Bousset. Thus, in Bultmann's view, the law was not explicitly combated, for if Jesus had opposed the law the attitude of the early church could not be explained (pp. 62f.). Jesus differed only in how he interpreted the law (p. 64). It turns out, however, that against his own intention (and apparently without knowing it!) Jesus actually attacked the law: 'In such polemic [as Mark 7.9–13] Jesus apparently intends to attack merely a particular scribal interpretation of the Old Testament. Actually he opposes not only a whole group of Old Testament laws, but the Old Testament itself as formal legal authority' (p. 76). This is almost precisely Bousset's view. On the question of the nationalism or universalism of the kingdom, Bultmann's view is more nuanced than Bousset's. Bultmann does find that nationalistic exclusivism is broken by Jesus ('belonging to the Jewish race does not constitute a right to a share in the Kingdom', p. 45), but universalism is equally renounced.

> The Kingdom is an eschatological miracle, and those destined for it are not destined because of their humanity but because they are called of God. To begin with, the Jewish people are called, and the connection of the Kingdom with the Jewish people demonstrates most clearly how far from universalistic is the thought of the Kingdom, how utterly every human claim on God disappears; for the calling of the nation depends wholly on God's choosing. On the other hand, a nationalistic misinterpretation is avoided, since the call to repentance is directed to the chosen people, and this call rejects every claim of the individual based on the fact that he belongs to this people (pp. 46f.).

This is a great deal more sophisticated than Bousset, but it is still noteworthy that Bultmann holds the view that Jesus abrogated the law without intending to do so and that he overcame Jewish nationalism in principle.

It should be emphasized that, despite the structural similarity with Bousset's *Jesus*, Bultmann's actual contrast of the teaching of Jesus with that of Judaism has a completely different *tone*. The rest of Judaism is still presented as a religion which has failed, with which Jesus can properly be contrasted, but the scornful, disdainful phraseology has disappeared. Further, Bultmann presents Jesus as addressing the problems posed within Judaism (and as offering successful answers in contrast to the rest of Judaism),[26] which gives his work much more a feeling of reality than Bousset's. We may consider the discussion of God as distant and remote as an example. The *idea* that God is both remote and near, he writes, is basic to Judaism: God is God of the world and supramundane, but the world is dependent on God (pp. 137f.). It is a Jewish idea, and a good one, that the two ideas of God should be held in unity, but this was never achieved in Judaism apart from Jesus. 'The thought of the God of the future stands with one-sided emphasis and definite colouring so in the foreground that it is often not clear how this God can also be the Lord of the present' (p. 141). By the end of the page it has been concluded that God is not God of the present in Judaism and 'the whole idea of God is hence endangered'. In swift strokes Bultmann maps out how this future emphasis further leads to the calculation of merit for the future judgment. One's deeds are directed not by God in the present, but they become works which aim towards achieving future righteousness (p. 146). In the teaching of Jesus, on the other hand, 'the remote and the near God are one' (p. 151). The possibility of Judaism was not realized there, but only in Jesus. And so it goes for point after point.[27]

Perhaps it need hardly be said that Bultmann's description of Judaism and his contrast of Jesus with it do not rest on a fresh study of Judaism. He in fact seems to have known of 'late Judaism' only what he read in Bousset and Billerbeck, and his description of God as remote from man, no longer God of the present, is simply a sophisticated version of what can be read in numerous treatments of Judaism in Christian scholarship. It has been repeatedly shown that the view cannot actually be supported from the surviving literature.[28] Our immediate aim, however, is not to debate the accuracy of Bultmann's description of Judaism, but to see how he proceeded. The description of the contrast between Jesus and the rest of Judaism centres (as with Bousset) on teaching: on theological content. Jesus differs by being superior. The way in which the superiority is worked out is different, the philosophical categories are different, and the treatment has more of a realistic ring. Jesus is not totally removed from Judaism, he is seen rather as having brought to fulfilment what it could not. Despite these differences from Bousset, the fundamental agreement with Bousset is clear: it is Jesus' teaching which differs by being superior; the superiority, while constituting a contrast with Judaism, is not what led to Jesus' death.

When Günther Bornkamm's book on Jesus was published,[29] it created something of a sensation, since he made a few more statements about the history of Jesus than had Bultmann. As Morgan has pointed out, he had no more historical evidence than had Bultmann, nor a different way of establishing it. He was, rather, less hostile to incarnational theology and more inclined to see Jesus as the Word, rather than just the bearer of it.[30]

On the points under review, however, he remained very close to Bultmann, though introducing some modifications. He found, in the first place, a basic difference between Jesus and his contemporaries which has to do with the authority of Jesus and his making the kingdom of God immediately real to his hearers:

What is essential is the indissoluble connection between what has been said here [*scil.*, about Jesus' authority] and Jesus' message about the reality of God, his kingdom and his will. This alone lends to Jesus' history and person the character of unmediated presence, gives the force of an actual event to his preaching, and makes his words and deeds so incomparably compelling. To make the reality of God present: this is the essential mystery of Jesus. This making-present of the reality of God signifies the end of the world in which it takes place. This is why the scribes and Pharisees rebel, because they see Jesus' teaching as a revolutionary attack upon law and tradition. This is why the demons cry out, because they sense an inroad upon their sphere of power 'before the time' (Mt. viii.29). This is why his own people think him mad (Mk. iii.21). But this is also why the people marvel and the saved praise God (p. 62).

It seems readily apparent that this is more *post factum* theological evaluation than historical description. The implied contrast with Jesus' contemporaries is that for them God was not present.[31] That contrast is still based on no study of Judaism to see whether or not God was perceived to be present; one is rather reading here a theological assessment of the significance of Jesus for Christians. It is noteworthy that the contrast implied by Bornkamm is the same as that proposed by Bousset, although the language is both temperate and less blunt: Jesus is a living reality in contrast to the Jewish teachers immersed in dead erudition, for whom God was not present. We have seen the same contrast in other terms in Bultmann.

Discussing Matt. 10.5f. and 8.11f. (both of which he apparently takes to be genuine), Bornkamm comes to Bultmann's position on the question of Jesus and Jewish nationalism:

> ... Jesus has by no means substituted the idea of a kingdom of God embracing all men for the hope of the coming of the kingdom of God to Israel alone. But it is no less clear that through Jesus' words and attitude the illusion of the inalienable, as it were, legal rights of Israel and its fathers is attacked at the root and shaken to pieces (p. 78).

Bornkamm differs from his teacher, however, in his analysis of Jesus' attitude towards the law: 'Significant above all . . . is the open conflict with the law which causes the mounting antagonism of the Pharisees and scribes' (p. 97). He considers first the Sabbath law, but concludes that here Jesus opposed only 'that Sabbath casuistry developed in Judaism to the greatest degree of pedantry', but not the Torah itself (p. 97). The Torah is directly opposed on two points: the laws of cleanness (accepting the authenticity of Mark 7.14–23), although even here Bornkamm says that Jesus may not have seen this controversy as an attack on the law; and the law on divorce. On these two points Jesus reveals his unrivalled authority over the law. Jesus' intention, however, was not to 'abolish the scriptures and the law, and to replace them by his own message'. Rather, 'they are and remain the proclamation of God's will. For Jesus, however, the will of God is present in such immediate fashion that the letter of the law may be gauged by it' (pp. 99f.). Yet it soon turns out that Jesus did, apparently against his own intention, in fact abolish the law:

> He liberates the will of God from its petrifaction in tables of stone, and reaches for the heart of man which seeks seclusion and safety behind the stronghold of observance of the law. He detaches the law of God from the 'traditions of men' and sets it free, and makes man in a new sense a captive – man who deludes himself that his life is in order under the existing regime (p. 105).

To the degree that this is considered by Bornkamm to be a historical statement, and not further Christian theological reflection on the significance of Jesus, it seems to mean that Jesus countered the authority of the Mosaic law in principle.

Bornkamm follows the line taken by Bousset and Bultmann in not connecting the theological disagreements between Jesus and his contemporaries immediately with Jesus' death. He does offer, however, a somewhat fuller account of how Jesus' entry into Jerusalem and his conflict with the authorities there led to his death. 'The reason why Jesus sets out with his disciples on his journey to Jerusalem cannot be doubted. It was to deliver the message of the coming kingdom of God in Jerusalem also . . . ' (p. 154). The entry may or may not have been intended by Jesus as strictly messianic. But in any case Jesus claimed that the kingdom of God 'is dawning in his word, and that the final decision will turn upon himself' (p.158). The cleansing of the temple was not just a purification of polluting practice; rather, Jesus 'cleanses the sanctuary for the approaching kingdom of God' (pp. 158f.). The entry and the cleansing provoked the Jewish authorities in Jerusalem (p. 159), and it is probable that they turned him over to Pilate as a political suspect (p. 164).

We have now come to a formulation of the situation which is very common. The essential elements are these: Jesus opposed the law on one or two points, and therefore in principle, by appealing to the immediate will of God, even if he himself did not intend to oppose the law as such or fully see the implications of his own words and deeds; Jesus did not universalize the idea of the kingdom explicitly, although he implicitly abrogated Israel's national hopes; he differed theologically from his contemporaries and was their superior, but this had no immediate bearing on his death; he went to Jerusalem to force the issue there, to present there the claim that the kingdom was coming and to challenge the hierarchy to decide for his message or against it; he alarmed the hierarchy by his claims and was put to death at their behest.

Implicit in this is the view that Jesus did not intend anything else: he did not have in mind establishing a community to carry on after his death; he did not think he could force the coming of the kingdom of God; he had no intention of reforming Judaism. He was a messenger primarily, but in a way that made him more than a mere messenger, for the response to him and his message was crucial. In Bornkamm's words, 'the final decision will turn upon himself' (p. 158).

The main features of this position can be seen before Bornkamm, in Dibelius's book on Jesus.[32] In Galilee, Jesus' work constituted an eschatological and messianic movement (p. 61). He went to Jerusalem to demand a decision (p. 63), and the cleansing of the temple represents his effort to force a decision as to his cause (p. 127). Dibelius differs from the Bousset/Bultmann school, however, in arguing that Jesus did intend to leave a community behind, 'one devoted to the Messianic expectation, as a witness and pledge of a personal attachment to him' (p. 100). The primary evidence here is the Last Supper. This is not, however, a point on which Dibelius dwells. He still sees Jesus' basic intention to be to announce the kingdom of God. But the announcement is more than bare announcement: 'Jesus himself, in his own person, in his words and deeds, is the decisive sign of the Kingdom' (p. 101).

In one sense, in Dibelius's view, Jesus remained within the 'frame of the traditional religion': he addressed only his own people (p. 107). Despite this, he broke fundamentally with the law. Jesus demands, 'under certain circumstances, even the renunciation of duties'.

> Here one sees most clearly the difference from the legal religion: the whole Jewish system of commandments and prohibitions with its absolute jurisdiction comes in question, since God himself is entering into the world with absolute majesty, absolute justice and holiness (p. 114).

Dibelius cites the Sabbath commandment as an example of a law which 'must be broken if God requires it'. He sees the statement about leaving the dead to bury the dead (Matt. 8.22) as evidence that not even filial duty should restrain one who hears the call of the kingdom (p. 114). Dibelius puts the matter most clearly a few pages later:

> The center of Jesus' message, the announcement of the Kingdom of God,

could readily be combined with the Jewish hope. The radicalism of this announcement, however, the exclusive insistence that 'one thing is necessary,' devalued the claim of all other duties, including the ritual, the legal, and the nationalistic. And Jesus gave expression to this devaluation in his own life: he broke the Sabbath when he felt that God bade him act; he excused his disciples . . . from . . . fasting; and the burning national question whether one had really to pay the poll tax to the foreign power of occupation . . . he answered in the affirmative, but he viewed it as a secular concern and pointed his questioners to the essential duty, 'Give to God what belongs to him' (p. 124).

In this way he ran into conflict with the Jewish teachers, since they laid burdens on people and were 'silent about the essential things' (p. 125, citing Matt. 23.23 as reliably describing other Jewish teachers). Dibelius saw more clearly than the other scholars whom we have thus far considered how all this must have looked to Jesus' contemporaries: 'The devaluation of those duties through the principle that "one thing is necessary" must have appeared to them as threatening to undermine and ruin the whole system of piety' (p. 125). He does not, however, explain why this must have been the case.

There was another point of opposition: Jesus did not share the general hope for the restoration of the nation's splendour. Dibelius cites Matt. 25.25, Luke 14.18, Matt 11.16f., and Mark 12.1–9 as evidence that Jesus knew that Israel would waste its inheritance and reject the kingdom (pp. 125f.).

The most fundamental point of opposition, however, had to do with Jesus' assertion of his own authority against the Torah.

The law with its precepts could have become for men the occasion for recognizing the absolute will of God. But men have defrauded themselves of this opportunity by their expansion of the precepts into a legal system. As a result, Jesus was now obliged to announce what must obtain in the Kingdom of God, viz. the pure will of God. . . . He spoke as one who possessed authority and power, and not like their scribes (Matt. 7.29) – but in the eyes of the Jews that could be viewed only as heresy. For the voices of the prophets were now silent, and no one had the right to announce the will of God on his own account (p. 126).

Jesus's self-claim was, in fact, that he would be Messiah (p. 95); this was construed to mean that he was a pretender to the throne, and for this he was crucified (p. 102). Thus there is in Dibelius's view more coherence between what Jesus intended, what he taught, and the reason for his death than we found in the works of Bousset, Bultmann and Bornkamm: the central point is Jesus' self-claim, which puts him into opposition both to the law and to the temple hierarchy, and which leads to his death by being understood as being a claim to the throne.

Before we consider a selection of the most recent general treatments of Jesus, we should pay some attention to the essays of Käsemann and Fuchs. Although not full treatments of Jesus, these are significant contributions to the recent discussion. Chronologically both Käsemann's and Fuchs's principal essays on Jesus come after Dibelius and before Bornkamm; but Bornkamm, though differing in some ways from Bultmann, is truer to his views than either Käsemann or Fuchs. We should further note that it is to Bultmann's position that Käsemann and Fuchs are replying, not to the intervening work of Dibelius and others.[33]

Käsemann, in opening a new era in the discussion of Jesus, began his brief summary[34] with the assertion that Jesus claimed 'an authority which rivals and challenges that of Moses'. He continued: 'But anyone who claims an authority rivalling and challenging Moses has *ipso facto* set himself above Moses.' The basis for the assertion is the unquestioned authenticity of the first, second and fourth antitheses of the Sermon on the Mount. Käsemann immediately draws the conclusion: 'For the Jew who does what is done here has cut himself off from the community of Judaism – or else he brings the Messianic Torah and is therefore the Messiah' (p. 37). Here Käsemann sets out a proposition that will become more and more prevalent: that Jesus *intentionally* set himself above Moses, and that doing so constitutes an implicit messianic claim. Käsemann proceeds to cite Jesus' attitude towards the Sabbath and ceremonial purity as instances in which the Torah is 'shattered' (p. 38). Breaching the laws of ceremonial purity, which permits association with sinners, is especially significant; for by making the breach Jesus removed 'the distinction (which is fundamental to the whole of ancient thought) between the *temenos*, the realm of the sacred, and the secular' (p. 39). Jesus was thus apparently the first modern man. In Käsemann's view Jesus' attitude towards the law caused his death, shook the foundations of Judaism, and, most profoundly, 'cuts the ground from under the feet of the ancient world-view with its antithesis of sacred and profane and its demonology' (p. 41). Perhaps one might remark that this is rather a lot to base on the somewhat dubious authenticity of Mark 7.15.

The contrast between Jesus and contemporary teachers is the standard one which appears also in Bousset and Bultmann: Jesus demanded 'intelligent love' in opposition 'to the demand of the rabbinate for blind obedience' (p. 42).[35]

Jesus' intention was the proclamation that the day of the kingdom had dawned 'and of how God was come near to man in grace and demand' (p. 45). Jesus apparently had no other concrete plan; and, as we indicated, he died for opposing the authority of Moses, although Käsemann in his sketch does not indicate how his death came about historically.

Fuchs[36] agreed with Käsemann that the legal challenges to the Torah (Sabbath-breaking and the like) go back to Jesus' own situation, but he did not regard this as the central point of Jesus' intention or as the central point of opposition (pp. 25f.). For Fuchs, the central point is Jesus' own decision to suffer. I must confess that the argument is not altogether clear to me, but it is apparently that suffering is necessary if there is to be new life (resurrection). The decision to suffer Fuchs finds proved in two other *acts* of Jesus (arguing that Jesus' behaviour is the context for his teaching, rather than vice versa, p. 21): he drew sinners to himself[37] and he formed a community in the midst of a perverse world. It is not the case, however, that suffering is the accidental result of association with sinners and forming a community: rather, the goal is suffering.[38]

> God loses no one. Hence resurrection takes the place of death. Apart from resurrection the suffering of faith would be pointless (cf. also I Cor. 15). On the other hand resurrection would be no real goal, were it not preceded by suffering; for resurrection is both grace and faithfulness (cf. also Matt. 6.1–8). Therefore, when Jesus directs the sinner beyond death to the God of grace he knows he must suffer. Precisely because Jesus himself assumes the standpoint of God's grace, he assumes also for himself the standpoint of suffering. His threats and calls of woe, and also the severity of his demand, all stem from his stringent will to suffer. For in all this Jesus opposed his adversaries, even though he was fully aware of the violent death of the Baptist (p. 26).

As he trenchantly puts it a few sentences earlier: 'The secret turning-point of truth is really still death (cf. Mark 8.35).' The connections between points remain difficult, and it is perhaps not surprising that the one point which many have taken from Fuchs is the observation that Jesus' behaviour is more reliably accessible than his sayings and should serve to interpret them. The view that Jesus' will was to suffer, because beyond suffering lies grace, has not become a major point in interpreting Jesus, despite its force as a theological proposition.[39]

In the view of W. G. Kümmel,[40] Jesus' principal intention was to call Israel to repentance in view of the approaching end (p. 36). The calling of the twelve makes visible 'his claim to be calling the entire twelve-tribe nation to repentance', and they in no way represent a sect, nor did they possess a community consciousness (pp. 37f.). The idea of repentance itself is well known to Judaism, being 'one of the basic views of Judaism in Jesus' time'. But Jesus' call, by changing the emphasis, is fundamentally different from what is found in Judaism:

> ... Jesus ventures to proclaim that God takes pleasure, not in the righteous man who boasts before God of his being righteous, but in the sinner who is conscious of his lost condition (Luke 18.9–14). And therein Jesus fundamentally distinguishes himself from contemporary Judaism, which strongly emphasizes God's readiness to forgive and man's being directed to God's forgiveness, it is true, but always added; 'If this is granted to those who transgress his will, how much more to those who do his will' (Bab. Talmud, Makkoth 24b) (p. 43).

In addition to this basic difference of theological orientation, Kümmel cites as points of opposition Jesus' willingness to 'set aside the written law as well as the rules of the scribes' (p. 51) and his transcending the limitations of Jewish nationalism (p. 56). The principal examples of setting aside the law are the transgression of the Sabbath (Mark 2.23–28 and parr.; p. 51), the abolishing of the distinction between clean and unclean (Mark 7.15; p. 52), the abolishing of divorce (Mark 10.2–9; p. 52), and the antitheses of the Sermon on the Mount (pp. 52f.). Kümmel subsequently cites Luke 16.16//Matt. 11.12 as indicating that Jesus 'clearly affirms that with his coming the time of the law and the prophets is ended' (p. 66).

Kümmel somewhat curiously finds the transcending of nationalism in the coupling of the two love commandments: 'This coordination of them by Jesus unmistakably has the intention of naming all that man has to do in the sight of God', apparently neglecting Jesus' citation elsewhere of other commandments (Matt. 19.17f. and parr.).[41] Kummel continues:

> The response to the encounter with God in Jesus and to the promise of the kingdom of God can only be love for God which is actualized in love for one's neighbor. If love for one's neighbor grows out of the encounter with God's love and is inseparable from love of God, then such love for one's neighbor knows no limits: Jesus explicitly abolishes both cultic and national limitations on love (Mark 3.1ff. par.; Luke 10.29ff.) (pp. 55f.).

Here the parable of the Good Samaritan is taken as indicating the abolition of the national limitation on love, while the healing of a man on the Sabbath indicates the abolition of a cultic (!) limitation on love. This is somewhat confusing, not only because the Sabbath commandment is not cultic, but because it is not clear whether or not a distinctive point is being made.

The question of nationalism usually has to do with soteriology: what are the restrictions, if any, on who will be admitted to the kingdom. Kümmel here addresses the question of to whom one should show love, and there is an implied contrast with Judaism. But Kümmel cites no material to show that Jews traditionally understood that love should be shown only to members of their own race.

We have already seen that, in Kümmel's view, Jesus' abrogation of the law was based on his own self-claim: he brings the law and the prophets to an end (Kümmel, p. 66). Similarly, Jesus' death receives a christological interpretation: it has more to do with what Jesus thought of himself than with concrete opposition on the part of his Jewish and/or Roman contemporaries. After arguing that Jesus identified himself with the future 'man' (pp. 76–84), and further predicted his own sufferings as 'part of his divine commission' (p. 90), Kümmel explains his death as follows:

> Thus Jesus was so keenly conscious of being in the service of God as the one to bring in the dawning kingdom of God that he entered upon the way to death imposed upon him by God and therein completed his mission. In this being delivered up to sinful men which was imposed upon him, and from which Jesus did not shrink, the love of God which in Jesus seeks out the sinner and encounters rejection comes to consummation and fulfillment. Even though Jesus very probably did not give any more specific interpretation of his death, still in the willingly accepted reality of his death a divine action appears, which the Christians later had to make comprehensible. And even if Jesus did not speak directly about his being raised by God – in any case we have no certain early witness for this – still he undoubtedly regarded his death as the transition to the coming which he anticipated as 'the Man' from God, and thus confronted the Christians with the task of interpreting his person, his work, and his dying in the light of the experience of his resurrection, which at the time of the last supper still lay in the obscurity of the future. But this all says that the incorporation by earliest Christianity of Jesus' death and resurrection in the understanding of Jesus' person was sketched by Jesus in the interpretation of his death, and was not first inserted by the first community as something utterly strange and unexpected for the understanding of Jesus (pp. 94f.).

Despite his efforts to head off this objection, Kümmel's view seems most naturally to be understood as a retrojection of Christian theology back into the mind of Jesus. Here we have not really a historical explanation of the causes which led to Jesus' death, but a theological interpretation of the value of his death ('the love of God . . . comes to consummation . . . '; 'a divine action appears').[42]

Kümmel sees Jesus' activity and death as being basically shaped by his own self-conception, and in this sense he is closer to Schweitzer than most subsequent writers: what really matters is what was going on in Jesus' own mind; his own dogmatic view determines what he should do, even to the point of determining that he should die. Kümmel differs completely from Schweitzer, however, in arguing that the dogmatic intent behind Jesus' deeds corresponds precisely to Christian interpretation. On this point Schweitzer saw only a negative connection: Christian theology, faced with the delay of the parousia, had to Hellenize the expectation of an imminent eschaton into belief in immortality.[43] For Kümmel, on the other hand, the delay was anticipated by Jesus himself.

Eduard Schweizer,[44] while agreeing with Kümmel (and many others) on the points of theological contrast between Jesus and Judaism, is much less specific about what Jesus had in mind. He is, if anything, even more extreme than Bultmann and Bornkamm in viewing Jesus as one who had no intention beyond the proclamation of repentance, forgiveness and the presence of God. The twelve, writes Schweizer, were called to be with Jesus (p. 41, quoting Mark 3.14), and it is hard to be more specific than that. Just what they did is not known. One can say that they are neither a remnant nor a gathering of a religious élite. Jesus, rather, sought all Israel. In fact, he was prepared to go even beyond the bounds of Israel in his call (p. 42, citing Mark. 7.15, 29; Matt. 8.11f.). Thus Schweizer easily accepts the view that Jesus contradicted Jewish exclusivism. Besides this, however, Jesus' intention is defined only negatively. Schweizer makes it a main point that Jesus fitted no preconceived pattern, had no programme that met the desires of any group, and cannot be defined by one of the usual categories of Jewish expectation (pp. 42f.). All who hoped in him for the fulfilment of their own plans were disappointed (p. 43). Positively, he can say that Jesus' purpose was to give faith (p. 45), but it is a little difficult to know what the specific content of the faith was.

The negative points are clearer. Jesus set himself solidly against the essentials of Judaism. The principal point is the customary contrast between Jesus' personal authority and the law: 'It is clear . . . that Jesus spoke to tax collectors, who were excluded from the people of God . . . , summoning them to fellowship at his table and thus to fellowship with God; in other words, he offered forgiveness as though he stood in the place of God' (p. 14). He personally had the authority to offer the kingdom, and the Torah is abrogated by the antitheses (p. 14). Schweizer cites as further instances in which Jesus abrogated the law the saying on divorce, transgression of the Sabbath (which he considers to be beyond doubt), and ritual purity (p. 32). The best summary statement of Jesus' distinction from and opposition to his contemporaries is this:

> They [his contemporaries] would have understood and tolerated an ascetic who wrote off this world for the sake of the future kingdom of God. They would have understood and tolerated an apocalypticist. . . . They would have understood and tolerated a Pharisee who urgently summoned people to accept the kingdom of God here and now in obedience to the law, for the sake of participating in the future kingdom of God. They would have understood . . . a realist or sceptic who . . . [declared] himself an agnostic with respect to any future expectations. But they could not understand a man who claimed that the kingdom of God came upon men in what he himself said and did, but nevertheless with incomprehensible caution refused to perform decisive miracles; healed individuals, but refused to put an end to the misery of leprosy or blindness; spoke of destroying the old temple and building a new one, but did not even boycott the Jerusalem cult like the Qumran sect . . .; who above all spoke of the impotence of those who can only kill the body, but refused to drive the Romans from the country; who left all these matters to God knowing that God would one day honor the promises and commitments now made by Jesus (p. 26).

Thus the principal difficulty with Jesus was his complete non-conformity and his refusal to do anything decisive, but rather only to call for faith and leave the rest to God.

It was not, however, this puzzling non-conformity which led to Jesus' death, nor his opposition to the Torah, but his assuming the role of God by forgiving sinners:

> With an assurance that must have struck his hearers as unexampled, he equates God's merciful conduct with his own conduct towards the tax collectors. Who but Jesus could venture to describe such incredible and absolutely unexpected conduct on the part of the father towards his windbag of a son? Who but Jesus would have the authority to assume the role of God himself in his parable and proclaim a celebration on behalf of the sinner who has been restored to fellowship with God? Those who nailed him to the cross because they found blasphemy in his parables – which proclaimed such scandalous conduct on the part of God – understood his parables better than those who saw in them nothing but the obvious message, which should be self-evident to all, of the fatherhood and kindness of God, meant to replace superstitious belief in a God of wrath.
>
> But Jesus identifies himself so with the cause of God that he dies for the truth of his parables (pp. 28f.).

We see here the same lack of concern with reasonable historical explanation which often marks discussions of Jesus' death. He died, in short, for the gospel. But how did it happen? Who were those Jews who opposed the offer of grace to sinners? Where is there any indication that the parables were understood as blasphemy? Which Jews denied the fatherhood and mercy of God and held superstitious beliefs about his wrath? Where is the evidence that there is a connection between Jesus' parabolic teaching, the accusation of blasphemy, and the crucifixion? One marvels at the sentence which begins 'those who nailed him to the cross because they found blasphemy in his parables': were the Romans offended by the 'blasphemy' of the offer of grace to sinners? There is here an apparent loss of touch with historical reality.

There are, to be sure, unstated views about the connection of events which, when made explicit, show that Schweizer's view is quite coherent, even if historically dubious. The line of argument would go something like this: In his parables Jesus proclaimed the forgiveness of sinners. Since forgiveness is the prerogative of God, he both intended and was understood to mean that he set himself in God's place. This constitutes blasphemy. The Jewish trial is on the charge of blasphemy. The Roman trial was actually held at the instigation of the Jewish leaders, so that Jesus was *de facto*, if not *de jure*, executed for blasphemy. Thus Jesus' intention, his teaching and his death cohere. One may recall for the sake of contrast Bousset's view, shared by many scholars, that the opposition which led to Jesus' death was not necessarily connected to an opposition to Judaism which is reflected in his teaching.

To the degree that a trend has thus far become visible, it is this: there seems to have developed a greater willingness to see Jesus as consciously setting himself against the law and the other essentials of Judaism. The explanation of his doing so is not a matter on which there is a consensus. Everyone agrees that he did so in the name of the will of God, but there is no agreement on the question of whether or not he had anything in mind other than the bare assertion that in particular cases he could discern that the will of God required the direct disobedience of the law. In the next studies to be reviewed, we see more emphasis on a positive intention in the sense of a plan or programme lying behind Jesus' opposition to particulars of the law.

We may cite first Moule's brief treatment of the question in his *The Birth of the New Testament*.[45] After commenting on the Christian instinct to argue for continuity with Israel, he points out that there also emerged an awareness of difference and newness. He continues,

There was no desire (unless it was in a radical type of thought – possibly that of the martyr Stephen) to break away or to start a new religion. It was only that the character of Christian experience and the centre of gravity in Christian teaching were so different that, sooner or later, they had to be acknowledged. And the seeds of this revolutionary differentiation were sown by Jesus, even if his explicit teaching did not formulate it. His ministry was marked by an attitude to those religious authorities with whom he came into collision, and a manifestation of his own personal authority, which were entirely unacceptable to them. They evidently sought authority in tradition or written documents rather than in the personal encounter, the dialogue, between the living God and man. . . . In a word, those with whom Jesus collided were 'authoritarian', not 'prophetic'. Jesus himself, by contrast, reached out a hand – so far as he reached backwards at all and was not altogether forward-looking, new, and different – not to the authoritarian scribes' religion of the post-prophetic period but to the mighty prophets of Israel. . . . All this is only another way of saying that the ministry of Jesus pointed to such a new covenant as is described in Jer. xxxi – a relation between God and man not of propositional statement . . . , but of personal obedience. . . . And one more way of expressing this is to say that the community which Jesus formed round himself was the community of the new age: it was Israel, indeed, but it was the Israel of the latter days; and in committing their loyalty to Jesus, the Twelve and others with them were constituted in that sense a new community (pp. 52–54).

He continues by noting that the term 'new Israel' does not occur. Nevertheless, '*God's* Israel, *true* Israel, was so radically different from what counted as Israel in the contemporary world, that there is an undeniable sense in which it is "new" ' (p. 54).

In one respect, and in only one, Moule's position is somewhat reminiscent of Bousset's. Moule sees Jesus as different from his contemporaries: he is either new, or else he harks back to the Old Testament. The important point, however, is the introduction of the notion of the 'new Israel'. Moule sees Jesus as intending the beginning of a community which, while still being called 'Israel', is not constituted according to its acceptance of the Mosaic covenant. Moule claims much more than that Jesus countered the law on some particulars and thus in principle abrogated it. The substantial abrogation, rather, in Moule's view, was Jesus' intention.

This general position was worked out in more detail by Dodd in his last published work.[46] Dodd first puts Jesus' intention very tentatively. Discussing ethics, he states that Jesus' purpose was to bring about an 'awakening of conscience'. 'If we ask what overt result Jesus may have hoped for, the answer is not easy, because he issued no program of religious

or political reform, any more than he laid down precise regulations for
individual behaviour. He disclaimed any intention to reform the existing
system' (p. 86). Dodd works out a more definite statement of Jesus'
intention, however, beginning the argument with a discussion of John the
Baptist. John, according to Dodd, clearly meant that being an Israelite 'is
no passport to membership of the true people of God'. John looked for a
creative act of God to bring the 'new "Israel" out of the existing system'.
He immediately points out: 'it is unlikely that Jesus was less radical' (pp.
87f.).

Jesus' view was that Israel was doomed. The nation faced not only a
political crisis but a spiritual one. 'In terms of the existing situation, the
present Jewish establishment is doomed; the true people of God will
emerge from its ruins' (p. 89). Jesus' prediction of the destruction of the
temple indicates the situation as he saw it:

> The temple stands for a way of religion and a community embodying it.
> The manifest disintegration of the existing system is to be preliminary to
> the appearance of a new way of religion and a new community to embody
> it. And yet, it is the *same* temple, first destroyed, that is to be rebuilt. The
> new community is still Israel; there is continuity through the discontinuity.
> It is not a matter of replacement but of resurrection (p. 90).

Thus Dodd reaches his first proposition about the intention of Jesus: 'His
aim was to constitute a community worthy of the name of a people of God,
a divine commonwealth, through individual response to God coming in his
kingdom' (ibid.). The disciples are both recruiting agents and foundation
members (p. 91). Those who hear Jesus' call to repentance are members
'of the Israel-to-be' (p. 92). The conclusion, it is to be noted, is completely
non-eschatological.[47] The change does not take place at the eschaton, but
within normal history. In 'the company of the followers of Jesus . . . the
people of God was to die in order to live again' (p. 96).

Jesus' death was the direct result of this activity. As the founder of the
Israel-to-be, he at least functioned as Messiah. The charge on which he
was executed, of claiming to be 'king of the Jews', is simply the way in
which the Jewish leaders put the matter to the Romans. The actual charge
was that he claimed to be Messiah. As such he not only 'set himself to
constitute the new Israel under his own leadership' but he also 'nominated
its foundation members, and admitted them into the new "covenant", and
he laid down its new law. That was his mission' (p. 102).

Jesus went to Jerusalem to force a decisive response there with regard
to his mission (p. 139; cf. p. 144). The response, as we have already seen,

was a charge that led to his death. We should, however, give a fuller account of the conflict between Jesus and his contemporaries as Dodd depicts it. The conflict which resulted in his death was preceded by a period of growing opposition (p. 69). The terms in which Dodd puts the points of conflict are quite striking: he had 'a certain impatience with minutiae of religious etiquette' (e.g., tithing, p. 70); he 'sat loose to other current rules of discipline' (e.g., Sabbath observance, p. 71, to attack which was 'to blur the national image', p. 72). Accepting the authenticity of Mark 7.15, Dodd sees Jesus as abrogating the laws of clean and unclean (pp. 73f.). The point at issue was this: Jesus feared that current practice resulted in 'such an emphasis on the overt act that the inner disposition was forgotten' (p.73). Jesus' conviction was that 'with the coming of the kingdom of God a new era in relations between God and man had set in. Morality might now draw directly from fresh springs. The whole apparatus of traditional regulations lost its importance.' Somewhat curiously, in view of his firm view of Jesus' intention, Dodd then remarks that Jesus did not *intend* to wage a campaign against the law, but that it was his opponents who 'rightly divined that his teaching threatened the integrity of Judaism as a system in which religion and national solidarity were inseparable'. 'This was the secret of the fatal breach' (p. 77, agreeing with Klausner). But, continues Dodd, the fear from the Jewish side was deeper even than the threat posed to Jewish nationalism, although that was a hot issue in the current climate. The clinching charge was blasphemy.

> The charge of blasphemy expresses not so much a rational judgment as a passionate, almost instinctive, revulsion of feeling against what seems to be a violation of sanctities. There must have been something about the way in which Jesus spoke and acted which provoked this kind of revulsion in minds conditioned by background, training and habit. It was this, over and above reasoned objections to certain features of his teaching, that drove the Pharisees into an unnatural (and strictly temporary) alliance with the worldly hierarchy, whose motives for pursuing Jesus to death were quite other (pp. 78f.).

Thus Dodd bridges the gap which we first observed in Bousset's view: Jesus is depicted as opposing the scribes and Pharisees on points of law, but it is the Jerusalem hierarchy which hands him over for death for threatening the temple. The gap is bridged by the theory of an alliance. Jesus' conflict with the Jerusalem hierarchy is presented in usual, though sharply put, terms. Jesus said that the 'new temple should be for all nations'. They saw it otherwise, and further saw challenged here the authority of the *law of Moses* (not, it should be noted, just their own authority) (pp. 148f.). The doom of the present establishment is presented in the parable of the vineyard, which 'reads almost like a declaration of war' (p. 149). The priests got the point and launched a counter-attack. There were two charges: blasphemy, which was designed to discredit him among his compatriots, and the claim of kingship, which was designed to get the Romans to execute him (pp. 158f.). Thus Dodd again bridges an old difficulty, that of the relationship of the trials before the Jewish and the Roman authorities.

Dodd offers a thorough and complete hypothesis: he accounts for major aspects of Jesus' activity (the calling of the twelve); the conflict described is based on the sayings and controversies attributed to Jesus; the various conflicts and opponents (the Pharisees, the priests and the Romans) are accounted for; Jesus is seen as having a concrete mission; the mission is one which has a setting in the life of Judaism; the mission and the opposition it aroused led to Jesus' death. Dodd does not make much of the statements concerning Jesus' association with tax-collectors and sinners, and he continues his rejection of eschatological views on the part of Jesus. Precisely these two points become main themes in the work of Jeremias, who presents what is in many ways the most complete hypothesis since Schweitzer's with regard to the intention of Jesus, his relationship to Judaism, and the conflict that led to his death.[48]

With regard to the proclamation of the kingdom, Jesus' preaching, according to Jeremias, is distinctive in only two respects. One is that the kingdom is present in the ministry of Jesus (pp. 100–08, the other is that it is for the 'poor' or the 'sinners' (p. 108). Precisely who these are will be a major point of discussion later, and Jeremias's views will be considered more thoroughly then. We note here only that they are primarily identified as the *'amme ha-arets*, whom Jeremias understands to be non-Pharisees (p. 112). It is the second point of distinction in Jesus' message that is offensive. 'One example of the difference between Jesus and the Judaism of his time would be his message of God's love for sinners; this was so offensive to the majority of his contemporaries that it cannot be derived from the thinking current in his environment' (p. 2; cf. p. 109). More fully:

The good news was a slap in the face to all the religious feelings of the time. The supreme religious duty for contemporary Judaism was to keep away from sinners. Table-fellowship in Qumran was open only to the pure, to the full members. For the Pharisee, 'dealings with sinners put at risk the purity of the righteous and his membership within the realm of the holy and the divine'.[49] 'A Pharisee does not dwell with them (the *'amme ha-arets*) as

a guest, nor does he entertain one of them at home in his garments'[50]. . . .
Certainly, Judaism knew that God was merciful and could forgive. But his
help was for the righteous; judgment was the destiny of the sinner. Even
the sinner could be saved, but only when he had proved the earnestness of
his repentance by making good and altering his way of life. Then, and only
then, did the Pharisee see him as the object of the love of God. First he had
to become a righteous man.

For Jesus, the love of the Father was directed even towards the despised
and lost children. That he called them, and not the righteous (Mark 2.17),
was apparently the dissolution of all ethics. . . . Thus the stumbling block
arose from the good news – and not primarily from Jesus' call to repentance
(Matt. 11.6 par.) (pp. 118f.).

For all the errors which I believe there to be in Jeremias's description of
Judaism,[51] it must be granted that he has put his finger on a vital point. He
sees that Judaism believed thoroughly in the efficacy of repentance, so that
there is nothing distinctive about saying that God accepts repentant sinners: if
they are repentant they are not sinners. Jesus proclaimed God's love to
sinners *before* they repented. Jeremias regards this as both unique and
offensive. We shall have occasion later to examine the issue in detail.[52]

Jeremias makes Jesus' call more radical yet: the implication of Jesus'
wording is that *only* the 'poor' or the 'sinners' are called (p. 121).

Jeremias finds further points of opposition between Jesus and his Jewish
contemporaries besides the basic one just outlined. Jesus opposed the
priests for profiteering from the temple service, and this was the immediate
cause of his death (p. 145). He opposed the scribes for saying and not
doing (pp. 145f.). He opposed the Pharisees most strenuously of all: 'All
the charges against the Pharisees are connected with their claim to
represent the true Israel and the community of the time of salvation,
through strict fulfilment of the commandments and works of supererogation' (p. 146). In Jeremias's view, Jesus criticized the Pharisees especially
for not taking sin seriously. They trivialized it by casuistry and by the
idea of merit. By casuistry Jeremias means that the specification and
categorization of sins shows that it was not seen as rebellion against God.
Merit implies the idea of storing up good deeds to compensate for bad at
the judgment. If sins can be compensated for, they are not very serious
(pp. 147f.). Jeremias subsequently returns to Jesus' opposition to what he
believes to be the remnant theology of the Pharisees and the Essenes:
'Again and again in the first three Gospels it is said how offensive,
provocative and disturbing was Jesus' rejection of Pharisaic and Essene
special claims to be realizing the holy remnant' (p. 177).

While it is not the intention here to debate points, I must note that I disagree entirely with all of Jeremias's points in the last paragraph. I do not think that the Pharisees – or even the Essenes – claimed to be the remnant.[53] Jeremias misunderstands the force of the categorization of sin and simply ignores all the Rabbinic passages which deal with rejection of a commandment as implying rejection of the redemption from Egypt (in Jeremias's terms, as implying rebellion against God).[54] On the question of merit, he shares a widespread but erroneous view.[55] It is hard to believe that Jesus opposed the Pharisees for views which, as far as we know, they did not hold. Further, there is a marked incongruence in Jeremias's argument. He sees the Pharisees as being criticized for claiming to be the only true Israel, while maintaining that Jesus identified the 'poor' or the 'sinners' as the only true Israel. He then argues that this identification is evidence of the '*boundlessness* and unconditional character of *grace*' in Jesus' preaching (p. 177). It would seem that his own position would require him to argue that Jesus simply turned society on its head. One exclusivist remnant group, just because composed of previous rebels and outcasts, is not necessarily superior to another, just because composed of these who earnestly tried to obey the conditions of the covenant.

With regard to the law, Jeremias takes the more or less standard position that Jesus abolished individual points of the Mosaic code (divorce, the antitheses of Matt. 5.33–37 and 5.38–42; p. 207). Yet Matt. 5.17 shows that 'Jesus is not concerned with destroying the law but with filling it to its full eschatological measure'. Jesus did not oppose the cult, although he did predict its demise (pp. 207f.). The oral Torah was rejected entirely (Jeremias puts here the Sabbath disputes and purity; Jesus did not challenge the dietary laws; pp. 208–10).

> Thus it was Jesus himself who shook the foundations of the ancient people of God. His criticism of the *Torah*, coupled with his announcement of the end of the cult; his rejection of the *Halakah* and his claim to announce the final will of God, were the decisive occasion for the action of the leaders of the people against him, finally brought into action by the cleansing of the Temple. They took Jesus to be a false prophet. . . . This accusation brought him to the cross (p. 211).

As did Dodd, Jeremias finds Jesus' actions and sayings to be based on 'a particular programme' which he had in mind. The first evidence for this is the call of the twelve (p. 234). The number twelve represents not just the twelve tribes of the historical Israel; it means, rather, that Jesus intends to establish 'the eschatological people of God' which would ultimately include Gentiles (p. 235). Jesus' programme to establish the people of God is based on his view of salvation history:

> First, God's promise must be fulfilled and Israel must be offered salvation. First, the servant of God must pour out his blood for the many, before the hour of the Gentiles comes. It lies beyond the passion, and the help that Jesus grants to Gentiles in individual instances belongs in the series of anticipations of the complete fulfilment (p. 247).

Jesus' view of salvation history, then, also involves his own suffering.

> Everywhere we find the explanation of this suffering to be the representation of the many (Mark 10.45; 14.24) by Jesus. The only answer to the question how it could be possible that Jesus attributed such unlimited atoning power to his death must be that he died as the servant of God, whose suffering and death is described in Isa. 53. It is innocent (v. 9), voluntary (v. 10) suffering, patiently borne (v.7), willed by God (vv. 6, 10) and therefore atoning for others (vv. 4f.) (p. 299).

Thus Jeremias finds not only external factors which led to Jesus' death (his opposition to Judaism on crucial points), but also a dogmatic factor in Jesus' own mind. His death is a necessary part of *Heilsgeschichte*.

Before considering the views of two important Jewish scholars, we shall conclude this summary of Christian scholarship by presenting the conclusions of two works which have focused on three of the major questions under consideration – the intention of Jesus, his relationship with his contemporaries and the cause of his death.

Ben Meyer's description of *The Aims of Jesus* is the richest and best nuanced one that I know, and it will be necessary to return to his recent book in discussing points along the way and in the conclusion. Many of Meyer's suppositions and intentions are harmonious with those presented earlier in this work: a survey of the teaching of Jesus is not 'history in the proper sense'; 'history is reconstruction through hypothesis and verification' (p. 19). Jesus should be related to the history of Israel, especially of the post-Maccabean period, and also to early Christianity (p. 222).

Jesus' intention, as described by Meyer, was to prepare Israel for what God had prepared:

> What had he prepared for Israel and the nations? For Israel, climactic and definitive restoration; for the nations, participation in the salvation of Israel. . . . Present by operation but future in its fulness, the reign of God was being mediated by its proclaimer. . . . Jesus' message, summons,

promise was specially directed to an unexpected combination of groups and classes within Israel: the simple, the afflicted, and the outcasts (p. 171).

This description, like any other about Jesus, is not unique, but the argument is striking. Meyer begins with John the Baptist and proceeds to discuss Jesus' public teaching, his public actions, and his private teaching, arguing that all converge towards the same conclusion. Meyer pointedly puts emphasis on the traditions most often denied authenticity, those concerning Jesus in discourse with his disciples alone, but they are taken to explain Jesus' intention rather than to prove its main outlines, and they come into play after the main points have been established on other grounds: 'the esoteric traditions provide the fully differentiated context in which to set the whole of his career' (p. 221). What is learned from them is this:

> Synoptic data individually and in the mass thus bring us to two ascertainments: Jesus understood his immediate messianic task to be the division of Israel between faith and unfaith; and he understood his messianic destiny (formally, enthronement and rule) to be scheduled for fulfilment only as the outcome and reversal of repudiation, suffering, and death (p. 216).

In an important chapter Meyer sets the career of Jesus in the context of Israel and offers reflections on the relationship between Jesus' own view and what actually emerged. Jesus relates positively to a long Israelite and Jewish history in looking for restoration, although his view of restoration is not to be precisely identified with that of one of the prophets or any one of the parties and sects. In other respects, however, Jesus was in direct and bitter conflict with the Zealots (Mark 12.17 and parr.), he hit at the heart of Pharisaic Torah piety (tradition, the Sabbath, ritual observances), and in the view of the Sadducees he virtually broke with the covenant (the temple) (pp. 235–9). Collectively the conflicts led to his death, the last one being the one for which he paid with his life (pp. 235, 238).

Meyer's view of Jesus' career also gains confirmation from early Christian self-understanding.

> From the start this was an essentially ecclesial self-understanding. Its first categories – the community of the outpoured Spirit, the Zion of the last days, the remnant of Israel, the restored qāhāl of the desert – corresponded in substance and sometimes in striking detail to what we take to have been Jesus' goal (p. 239).

Further, a substantial part of the church's understanding of Jesus conformed to his understanding of his own role. It saw him as withstanding the test in the wilderness and being transformed, thus providing the representation of the 'new Israel' which the church saw itself as typifying. Jesus himself had thought Israel would be restored in connection with his suffering and vindication (pp. 240f.).

Although John Bowker does not offer a general account of the life and teaching of Jesus, his book on *Jesus and the Pharisees* should also be considered here, since it is addressed to two of our principal questions: Jesus' relationship to his contemporaries and the connection between that and his death. Bowker's view in part depends on his analysis of the use of the terms *pharisaioi* and *perushim* in Josephus, Mark and Rabbinic literature. His argument is basically this: that there was a general drive on the part of the *ḥakamic* movement to achieve purity, that the drive towards purity was taken to an extreme point by some, and that their extremism caused them finally to be separatists from the main movement. Thus he accounts for the alteration from Josephus's *pharisaioi* – a party actively involved in life in Jerusalem – to the *perushim* of such passages as Sotah 22b – ascetic extremists criticized by the Talmud. He finds the transition to be faithfully reflected in Mark. The *pharisaioi* there sometimes represent the position of the *ḥakamim* (the question about divorce, plucking grain on the Sabbath) (pp. 38f.), while at other times Mark's *pharisaoi* adopt extremist positions (Mark 2.16; 2.18; 3.1ff.; 7.1ff.; p. 38). Further, Mark accurately reflects the historical situation of Jesus, for already then the extremists (*perushim*) were separated from the *ḥakamim*. For this reason they do not appear at the trial, since they by their extremism have dissociated themselves from the governing authorities (p. 42). Bowker proposes, however, that the extremists may have 'alerted others in authority to the dangers implicit in Jesus' position' (ibid.).

Besides crossing swords with these extremists, Jesus offended the essentials of Judaism on the question of authority (p. 42). He

appeared to be claiming that . . . the relation of God to a human situation is possible even where no attempt at all is being made to accept and implement what God has commanded in Torah: sin can apparently be forgiven by a word (Mk. ii.1–12). Jesus did not necessarily deny the observance of Torah (note the preceding incident, Mk. i.40–4), but he certainly resisted the view that its observance is an indispensable and prior condition of the action of God; faith is, if anything, the prior condition (p. 43).

Even this opposition, however, would not have been a cause of crucifixion, 'particularly if Jesus had kept [his views] to himself' (p. 45).

There were many unorthodox teachers and sects around at the time, but scarcely any record survives of their having been crucified, and even then it may not have been for their teaching, or sectarian beliefs, alone. The difference, in Jesus' case, lies in the fact that he did *not* keep his claims or teachings to himself, and that they were, in fact, deeply threatening, not simply to the principles of the Hakamim, or to the authority of the Temple, but to the basic structure of Jewish life as a response to God's gift of Torah to his people. . . . He clearly believed that the relationship could obtain, even when the details of the covenant, as specified in Torah, were not being kept; . . . (p. 45).

Bowker proposes that the actual offence of Jesus was that he was a 'rebellious elder' (p. 46). The immediate charge had to do with a threat to the temple (p. 49), but Jesus proved himself a rebellious elder, not by saying 'I am', 'but in the fact that he said nothing. Silence was the offence, because it was a contempt of court which made him, in effect, a rebel against it' (p. 50). Bowker admits that this last proposal is hypothetical and lacks direct evidence (p. 51).

Bowker's history of the terms *pharisaioi* and *perushim* is itself not convincing. He offers no dating criteria for the Rabbinic passages, but it seems likely that the negative use (extremist) developed no earlier than the second century.[56] There is certainly no reason for retrojecting the negative sense of Sotah 22b (extremist ascetic) into the period before 70, when it seems undoubted that the term 'Pharisee' referred to a member of a major party within Judaism. In Rabbinic literature, all the uses of *perushim* which definitely refer to the period before 70 refer to the party known as the Pharisees, while all the references to the *perushim* which refer to a group of the second century or later refer to ascetics or extremists.[57] (I leave aside passages in Rabbinic literature which equate *perushim* and *qedoshim*, since in them the terms do not refer to any group at all, but define a characteristic of any good Jew: he should be separate from the things which God commanded one should be separate from: sin and defilement, not other people.[58])

Bowker's principal hypothesis with regard to Jesus' opposition to the Torah as the presupposition of the covenantal relationship, however, does not actually depend on his discussion of the *pharisaioi* and the *perushim*. Here we see one more instance in which a New Testament scholar is willing to see a basic opposition on the part of Jesus to what is essential to Judaism, and the terms in which Bowker states it are appropriate. The law and the cultus were considered by Judaism to be the response to the God who redeemed Israel and offered the covenantal promises, and keeping them became the condition for remaining in the covenant.[59] Rejecting them would be as revolutionary as Bowker suggests.

If there is increasing willingness on the part of Christian scholars to see Jesus as deliberately opposing the authority of the law (rather than unconsciously subverting it in principle), Jewish scholars have maintained with remarkable consistency that he did not consciously set himself against the Torah of Moses.[60] Klausner,[61] for example, argued that Jesus often stood on the side of the Pharisees. The Gospels now retain only a few evidences of this (e.g. Mark 12.28–34), but they were influenced by the subsequent struggle between Judaism and Christianity. Such agreements must in fact have been numerous (pp. 319f.). The criticisms of Matt. 23 Klausner regards as in part unjustified, while granting that in part they could refer to a few (p. 321). He regards the chapter as authentic and sees in it the beginning of opposition of Jesus: 'Jesus, however, by his generalizations and abuse, provoked the indignation of the Pharisees and their followers' (p. 322). Klausner grants that Pharisaism did have one defect which merited criticism: it gave almost equal significance to the commandments between human and God (often incorrectly called 'cultic' or 'ceremonial')[62] and those between human and human ('ethical') (pp. 215f.). It is noteworthy that Klausner, in accord with the general religious spirit of the times, regards this as a bad thing: what counts are ethics and interior religious disposition. Emphasis on forms and ceremonies is bad. The value judgment is the same as Bousset's, for example, although Klausner correctly states the balance: 'almost as much importance' in contrast to Bousset's view that 'ceremonial' laws virtually drove out the others.

At any rate, this fault on the part of Pharisaism became the real point of opposition from Jesus' side, just as his unfair criticisms triggered opposition from the Pharisees' side (p. 220). There were other points of disagreement: Jesus emphasized the near approach of the Messiah and the kingdom more than did the Pharisaic teachers; the method of teaching differed in emphasis, the Pharisees relying on interpreting the Torah and using parables only by the way, Jesus centring his teaching on parables and relying on Scripture only slightly; Jesus gave equal importance to his teaching and to miracles, while the Pharisees gave less emphasis to miracles than to teaching (p. 255). Jesus' choice of associates would prove offensive to the Pharisees, *since he himself was a Pharisee*, as would the fact that he and his disciples did not fast (p. 274). There is a hint towards abolishing the ceremonial laws, but it is so slight that even the disciples did not get it (as the later behaviour of Peter and James proves) (p. 275). In general,

Jesus remained 'steadfast to the old *Torah*: till his dying day he continued to observe the ceremonial laws like a true Pharisaic Jew' (p. 275). On all these points of conflict, then, there is no open breach between Jesus and the Pharisees (p. 276).

Jesus' principal offence in the Pharisees' view was healing the man with the withered hand (p. 278). This led the Pharisees to turn the people against Jesus (p. 279). He offended the scribes on the question of handwashing (p. 288). It is the statement with regard to clean and unclean food, however (accepting Mark 7.17–23 as authentic), by allowing what Moses expressly forbade, which completed the breach between Jesus and the Pharisees (p. 291). But even so, he was not *criminally* guilty in the eyes of the Pharisees. The challenge to the temple comes closer to being the cause of his death:

> The Pharisees, hitherto Jesus' main opponents, cease now to play a prominent part; their place is taken by the Sadducees and the priestly class whom Jesus had irritated by the 'cleansing of the Temple' and by his reply concerning the Law of Moses and the resurrection of the dead. The Pharisees objected to Jesus' behaviour – his disparagement of many ceremonial laws, his contempt of the words of the 'sages' and his consorting with publicans and ignorant folk and doubtful women. They considered his miracles sorcery and his messianic claims effrontery. Yet for all that, *he was one of themselves*: his convinced belief in the Day of Judgment and the resurrection of the dead, the messianic age and the kingdom of heaven, was a distinctively Pharisaic belief; he taught nothing which, by the rules of the Pharisees, rendered him criminally guilty (p. 335).

Thus Klausner's view may again be compared with Bousset's: Jesus offended the Pharisees, but that did not lead to his death. But in Klausner's view, it was not even the challenge to the temple and the hierarchy which really led to his death. The real reason for his execution was this: the hierarchy knew that Pilate would use any excuse to 'demonstrate the power of Rome' by inflicting punishment on the Jews. The Jerusalem leaders, though irritated and angered by Jesus' behaviour in the temple, were primarily removing a cause of offence to Rome – for Jesus and his followers were potentially offensive to Rome – in arranging for him to be executed (p. 348).

Although Jesus did not set aside the ceremonial law, he so devalued it that this became the point on which Paul broke with Judaism (Klausner regards Paul as the *fons et origo* of the break):[63]

Ex nihilo nihil fit: had not Jesus' teaching contained a kernel of opposition to Judaism, Paul could never *in the name of Jesus* have set aside the ceremonial laws, and broken through the barriers of national Judaism. There can be no doubt that in Jesus Paul found justifying support (p. 369).

Klausner does not explain how Paul, but not James and Peter, could have found support for the abrogation of the law in Jesus' words and deeds, but his position is similar to that of Bultmann and others, who have held that Jesus abrogated the law in principle and without intending to do so. Klausner goes one step further by tracing a line from Jesus' attitude to Paul. The opposition to Judaism in Jesus' teaching, primarily directed against the ceremonial law, had further implications. Since Judaism is not only a religion but a way of life (p. 371), Jesus' attitude implies a denial of Judaism itself. Although Jesus' attitude is only an extreme example of what can be found in the Jewish tradition, the exaggeration of Judaism becomes, in effect, non-Judaism (p. 376).

Klausner attempts to explain Jesus' behaviour by finding a setting in Judaism for him. In Galilee, explains Klausner, there were no Pharisees or Sadducees, but only Zealots on the one hand and the 'meek' on the other. The latter 'abandoned interest in temporal things to dream of a future life, a life based on the ethics of the prophets and the messianic idea'. Jesus was one of these (p. 173). His intention was simply to implant his messianic ideas in Israel and to hasten the end by calling for repentance and good works (p. 368). In agreement again with the temper of the times, Klausner writes that Jesus abolished the political aspects of messianism and made it 'purely mystical and ethical' (p. 202; cf. pp. 227f., 236). One may again compare Bousset's view that Jesus abolished all outward forms in favour of true interiority. Thus, in Klausner's view, the priests who saw Jesus as a potential threat were alarmed not by any real political movement, but only by their knowledge of Pilate's extreme reaction to any disturbance at all.

The general line followed by Geza Vermes,[64] while being better informed both by modern critical study of the New Testament and also by a real care in dating Jewish materials, is in important respects similar to Klausner's. Jesus was a Galilean charismatic, of a type known from Jewish literature (p. 42). As did they, he healed and taught, and he shared with them a lack of interest in legal and ritual affairs (p. 77). As a Galilean, he could have been 'guilty' in the eyes of the Jerusalemites of 'the charge of religious impropriety levelled at the Galileans in general' (p. 55). Under this head Vermes lists his consorting with publicans and whores, his disregard for the regulations concerning levitical purity and tithing, and even the conflict in the temple: 'He was more concerned to keep business dealings out of the precincts of the sanctuary than with the quality of sacrificial victims or the type of currency used for Temple donations' (pp. 55f.). These points would naturally lead to conflict with the Pharisees, 'not because they were obsessed with trivialities, but because for them the trivial was an essential part of the life of holiness, every small detail of which was meant to be invested with religious significance' (p. 56). There was inevitably conflict between the charismatics, such as Jesus, and the Pharisees. The points just mentioned ('refusal to conform in matters of behaviour and religious observance', p. 80) are less important than a more fundamental clash: 'the threat posed by the unrestrained authority of the charismatic to the upholders of the established religious order'. The conflict on this point can be seen not only with regard to Jesus but also in the stories concerning other charismatics, specifically Honi and Hanina (p. 80). Vermes puts the point of hostility this way: 'The charismatics' informal familiarity with God and confidence in the efficacy of their words was also deeply disliked by those whose authority derived from established channels' (p. 81).

Apart from the conflicts just mentioned, there are no points of opposition between Jesus and the Pharisees. The healing of the man with a withered hand on the Sabbath does not constitute a breach of Sabbath observance, since the healing was done without work, but only by a word (p. 25). Mark's presentation of Jesus as opposing Jewish dietary laws is his own interpretation. 'The one apparent doctrinal conflict between Jesus and Judaism is due to a deliberate twist given to a probably genuine saying of Jesus by the redactor of the Greek Mark' (p. 29). Jesus did have a serious dispute with the Sadducees on the question of the resurrection, but here as in other places he agrees with the Pharisees (p. 35). There is no evidence for 'an active and organized participation on the part of the Pharisees in the planning and achievement of Jesus' downfall' (p. 36). On the contrary, he was put to death by the political establishment (p. 36). Even though he was not a Zealot, he was executed as one, perhaps because he was from Galilee (p. 50). The fullest explanation of Jesus' death is this:

> Taking into consideration the spirit of first-century A.D. Palestine, with its eschatological, political and revolutionary ferment, it is quite conceivable that Jesus' denial of Messianic aspirations failed to be accepted by his friends as well as his foes. His Galilean partisans continud to hope, even after the crushing blow of his death on the cross, that sooner or later he would reveal himself and 'restore the kingdom of Israel'. Moreover, his Jerusalem prosecutors were bound to suspect that this Galilean, whose

popular impact was now spreading in Judea itself, was impelled by motives of subversion (p. 154).

Thus Vermes argues that Jesus did not set himself in opposition to the Torah in principle, nor even in any important particular, although his behaviour and attitudes may have been offensive to Pharisaism. In any case, he was executed not on account of this opposition, but because he was mistaken to be a political revolutionary.

The situation seems to be this: those who presumably know the most about Judaism, and about the law in particular – Jewish scholars – do not find any substantial points of disagreement between Jesus and his contemporaries, and certainly not any which would lead to death.[65] Christian scholars, on the other hand, seem to have become increasingly convinced that there was a fundamental opposition between Jesus and Judaism and that the opposition was *intentional* on Jesus' part. It is difficult to know precisely what has led to the greater willingness on the part of Christian scholars to hold this view. It does not seem to be based on fresh information about Judaism and the tolerable limits of dissent. It may stem, rather, from the motive which we mentioned earlier: a hypothesis is on *a priori* grounds superior if it draws a line of connection between Jesus' teaching and activity, his death, and the rise of Christianity. There are really just two possible lines of connection, and both have appeared in this survey. One is Jesus' self-consciousness. If he made a strong personal claim which was sufficient to lead to his execution, that fact would help account for several elements of his teaching, his death and the rise of Christianity. The difficulty here is finding a sufficiently strong personal claim to account for execution, especially as long as one stays within the confines of traditional terminological studies. The claim to be Messiah, if Jesus made it, would not seem to be an indictable offence (unless construed, as some have suggested, as a challenge to Rome). The claim to be the Son of man, or to know that he was coming, is not blasphemy. Stauffer, to be sure (followed by Schoeps), finds in Jesus' words a claim of divinity which might be construed as blasphemy, but the evidence cannot be considered persuasive.[66]

Thus most scholars who wish to find the thread to which we have referred have turned to Jesus' attitude towards the law. If he opposed the validity of the Mosaic code, his doing so would account for his meeting opposition during his public ministry, it might well account for an opposition to the death (although this is not the charge in the trial accounts), and it would account for a new sect which broke with Judaism. The trouble with this thread is that the apostles in Jerusalem apparently did not know that the Torah had been abrogated: that was the contribution of Paul and possibly other apostles to the Gentiles. In Paul's case, the issue was argued on the ground that faith in Christ, not keeping the Torah, is the basis of salvation and that Gentiles must be admitted on equal footing with Jews (Rom. 3.28–30; 4.24f.; 10.4–17; 11.20–23 and elsewhere). Paul does not seem to be able to refer to Jesus' attitude to the law for support (contrary to Klausner).

The fact that the early disciples did not know that Jesus had opposed the law has led some to suggest that he did so only implicitly, without knowing, or fully knowing, that he was doing so. It is hard to know what this amounts to as an historical explanation. It does not explain Christianity's subsequent break with Judaism. If neither Jesus nor the early apostles knew that he implicitly opposed the law, there would be no chain of transmission which would permit Jesus' words and deeds to influence Paul and the ultimate outcome. The implication would become clear only after the outcome had been achieved. The break would not be based on any *intention* on the part of Jesus, although, after the break had been made, support from Jesus' lifetime might be found for it. At any rate, implicit rejection seems to explain nothing; neither Paul's rejection nor the Jerusalem apostles' maintenance of the law.

Further, and more important, it is intrinsically unlikely that Jesus could have opposed the law in principle but without knowing what he was doing. If, for example, he did say that the dietary laws should not be observed, he could not have seen this as a dismissal of what is irrelevant to true religion. The explanation that Jesus did not know what he was doing, though repeated in the twentieth century, is essentially a nineteenth-century explanation, being determined by the view that Jesus' intention was to purge Judaism of crass materialism and externalities. The understanding was that Jesus *intended* to oppose only a few externalities, but that since these are part of the Mosaic code, which is one, he actually opposed the law itself. What must be recognized is that Jesus could not possibly have seen things in the way this proposal requires. It is unrealistic to regard Jesus as a modern man[67] or as someone who did not know the standard Jewish view that the law is unitary. And even if he (an untutored Galilean) could have been ignorant of this, the error would have been quickly pointed out by his adversaries. *For the principle on which the law rests is perfectly clear: God gave the Torah to Israel by the hand of Moses; obedience to the Torah is the condition for retaining the covenant promises; intentional and unrepenting disobedience implies rejection of the law, rejection of the covenant for which it is the condition, and rejection of the God who gave the law and the covenant.* This is an understanding which is so uniform in the literature which survives from the approximate period[68] that Jesus and his followers could not possibly have been ignorant of it. Thus we must reject the hypothesis that Jesus opposed the law but did not know that he was doing so. Either he opposed the law and intended something by it, or he did not oppose it. (It remains possible that he accepted it but still debated points within its framework, even to the point of using one scriptural passage against another. This device was well known to the Rabbis, for example.[69] We shall see below that most of the reputed disputes about the law are not outside the bounds of Jewish debate.)

We said earlier that many scholars are prepared to find a thread between Jesus' intention and his death and the subsequent rise of the church. There are difficulties with all the main proposals: (1) the thread is his self-assertion (the evidence is weak); (2) the thread is implicit abrogation of the law (no evident chain of transmission); (3) the thread is explicit abrogation of part of the law, which leads to rejection of all (those who know the law best see no crucial break).

This situation seems to make it easy to return to another large option: there was no link between the content of Jesus' teaching in Galilee and the cause of his death in Jerusalem: Jesus opposed the scribes and Pharisees during his teaching activity (whether basically or only marginally), but he was killed either because the Romans (perhaps on the advice of the Jerusalem leaders) took him to be a Zealot or because he offended and threatened the Jewish hierarchy by his challenge to the temple. We have thus far said that this theory, in its turn, suffers from an *a priori* difficulty: it would be preferable to find a thread from Jesus' intention to his death to the church. We may now observe that, in addition to this deficiency, there are even graver objections. It presupposes that Jesus' activity in the temple had no intrinsic connection with the teaching. This presupposition rests on the same misapprehension which we pointed out in connection with the theory that Jesus did not know that he opposed the law: that he did not know that interrupting the temple arrangements could be seen only as a direct affront not merely to the priests' authority, but to Moses, and thus to God, who commanded the daily performance of the sacrifices. The view that Jesus went about Galilee healing, calling for repentance, and rousing the ire of the Pharisees, and that he then went to Jerusalem and interfered with the temple, rousing the ire of the priests, but that there is no connection between the two, supposes that Jesus acted with a lack of coherence that is almost incredible. Could it be that Jesus encouraged his disciples to think that something was to come of his ministry, that he was inconveniently killed along the way for reasons unconnected with his teaching, but that the cause which seemed lost was rescued by the resurrection? What is wrong with this possibility is that it supposes that Jesus intended something different when he 'cleansed' the temple from what he intended to achieve by his teaching. Or, alternatively, it supposes that Jesus intended throughout to abolish external inessentials in the name of true religion, without intending directly to oppose the law of Moses. We have already seen the improbability of the second alternative. The first is equally unlikely, for it equally requires us to believe that Jesus did not really know what he was doing or what the significance of his actions was. How could it be that something as serious as interfering with the temple sacrifices could have been seen by him as something different from his teaching and as unconnected with his calling disciples? How could it be that his activity in Jerusalem alarmed a quite different set of opponents, and for different reasons, from those whom he met in Galilee? One would have to think that Jesus quite literally did not know what he was doing. He called disciples simply to be with him, he taught simply to promote repentance, he interfered with temple practice because of a dislike of business dealings in the temple area, he was executed as a rebel or rabble rouser; and the disciples, who expected nothing in particular to come of his ministry, were galvanized into unity and activity solely by the resurrection experiences: it is possible, but it is not likely.

That the problem we have posed is not susceptible of a rock-hard answer which absolutely excludes all others is shown not only by the difficulties which can be brought against any hypothesis, but also by the very large number of hypotheses. It is almost a foregone conclusion that a fresh attempt to unravel the problem – or rather set of problems – which we have posed will not come up with a totally new answer. There are no totally new answers (except for fictional constructions) to be offered. We shall, however, investigate the most pertinent points in an effort to come up with the *best* answer. One is looking for a hypothesis which explains more (not everything), which gives a good account (not the only one) of what happened, which fits Jesus realistically into his environment, and which has in view cause and effect. The strategy to be followed was described in preceding sections, and we turn now to the point of departure, the temple controversy.

PART ONE

THE RESTORATION OF ISRAEL

1

JESUS AND THE TEMPLE

Having named Jesus' activity in the temple as the surest starting point for our investigation, I must hasten to say that the question of Jesus and the temple brings with it the amount of uncertainty which is usual in the study of the Gospels. There is neither firm agreement about the unity and integrity of the basic passages concerning the 'cleansing of the temple' (Mark 11.15–19 and parr.),[1] nor is there absolute certainty of the authenticity of either or both of the sayings about the destruction of the temple (Mark 13.2 and parr.;[2] Matt. 26.61//Mark 14.58.[3]) Despite all this, it is overwhelmingly probable that Jesus did something in the temple and said something about its destruction.[4] The accusation that Jesus threatened the temple is reflected in three other passages: the crucifixion scene (Matt. 27.39f.//Mark 15.29f.); Stephen's speech (Acts 6.13f.); and, with post-Easter interpretation, in John 2.18–22. The conflict over the temple seems deeply implanted in the tradition, and that there was such a conflict would seem to be indisputable.[5]

The 'cleansing' of the temple (Mark 11.15–19 and parallels)

The older understanding of the event, and the one which still predominates, is that it was just what the title of the pericope in modern synopses says: the *cleansing* of the temple. This implies a prior profanation or contamination, and the profanation has been readily found in the conducting of trade in or around[6] the temple precincts. To many this is self-evidently a debasing of true religion, and Jesus was intending to purify the temple so that it should better fulfil its purpose. Thus, for example, Edersheim was of the view that 'the whole of this traffic – money-changing, selling of doves, and market for sheep and oxen – was in itself, and from its attendant circumstances, a terrible desecration'.[7] It is noteworthy that Abrahams, in disagreeing with Edersheim, nevertheless accepted his major premises: what is external is bad, and Jesus was right to attack it. Edersheim accepted the charge of corruption ('den of thieves', Mark 11.17) as being necessarily a part of any trading.[8] Abrahams countered with the observation that while some individual abuses might have occurred, a general charge would be unjustified.[9] Yet he himself also wrote that he approved of Jesus' attack on 'externalism'. 'When Jesus overturned the money-changers and ejected the sellers of doves from the Temple he did a service to Judaism.'[10] This is a strange position for one to adopt who argued that buying and selling were necessary for the continuation of the temple sacrifices.[11] It shows the pervasiveness of the view that Jesus opposed externals in the name of true religious interiority.[12]

This same view, though now expressed differently, is seen in more recent exegetical remarks. After rejecting (correctly, in my view) what he identifies as the two principal recent interpretations of the 'cleansing' – that it expresses the opposition of the early church to the temple cultus[13] and that it represents 'the present power of the raised [Christ] in the confession of the post-Easter community'[14] – Roloff gives his own interpretation: the action was 'a prophetic sign which intended to bring about the repentance and return of Israel in the last days'.[15] 'He charged Judaism with its own recognition of the holiness of the temple as the place of the presence of God and demonstrated that its practice stood in contradiction to that holiness.'[16] Jesus' action constituted a 'requirement of the absolute maintenance of the holiness of the existing temple'.[17] There was, it seems from this remark, an interior holiness which was being besmirched or obscured by the actual conduct of the temple's affairs.

Other recent scholars, without explicitly expressing the view that religion must be devoid of crass materialism, also understand Jesus' action as being a 'cleansing' of defiling trade. Thus Jeremias proposed that the 'cleansing' was directed against the priestly class because 'They misuse their calling . . . by carrying on business to make profit.'[18] Similarly Aulén remarked that 'To transform the court of the temple to a market place – and for their own profit – was a violation of the law concerning the holiness of the temple . . .'[19] We may also cite Trocmé's view: the action was 'in defence of the honour of God',[20] which the trade apparently called into question. Harvey speaks of 'the abuse of Jewish institutions'[21] which Jesus attacked and characterizes the action as a prophetic one which represents 'the divine judgment on a particular use which was being made of the temple'.[22] That 'use' was trading, and Harvey writes that Jesus had good grounds for thinking that trade should not have been taking place in the temple precincts.[23]

Such comments as these are doubtless intended to distinguish the temple ordained by God – which Jesus did not attack – from the Jewish 'abuse' of the divine institution – which Jesus did attack. The way in which the distinction is made, however, implies that it is just the trade itself – the changing of money, the purchase of sacrifices, and probably also the charge for their inspection – which is the focus of the action. The assumption seems to be that Jesus made, and wanted his contemporaries to accept, a distinction between this sort of 'practice' and the 'real purpose' of the temple. This seems to owe more to the nineteenth-century view that what is external is bad than to a first-century Jewish view.[24] Those who write about Jesus' desire to return the temple to its 'original', 'true' purpose, the 'pure' worship of God,[25] seem to forget that the principal function of any temple is to serve as a place for sacrifice, and that sacrifices *require* the supply of suitable animals. This had always been true of the temple in Jerusalem. In the time of Jesus, the temple had long been the only place in Israel at which sacrifices could be offered, and this means that suitable animals and birds must have been in supply at the temple site. There was not an 'original' time when worship at the temple had been 'pure' from the business which the requirement of unblemished sacrifices creates. Further, no one remembered a time when pilgrims, carrying various coinages, had not come. In the view of Jesus and his contemporaries, the requirement to sacrifice must always have involved the supply of sacrificial animals, their inspection, and the changing of money. Thus one may wonder what scholars have in mind who talk about Jesus' desire to stop this 'particular use' of the temple. Just what would be left of the service if the supposedly corrupting externalism of sacrifices, and the trade necessary to them, were purged? Here as often as we see a failure to think concretely and a preference for vague religious abstractions.

In order to solidify the present point, and to gain perspective on the possible range of meanings of Jesus' action in the temple, we should lay out more thoroughly the common view of the temple, the sacrifices, the changing of money, and the sale of birds. The common view was that the temple was where sacrifices to God were offered, and that these sacrifices were not only appropriate but necessary. Josephus, in commenting on the strategic importance of fortified places in the city, gives clear expression to this view:

> Whoever was master of these [fortified places] had the whole nation in his power, for sacrifices could not be made without (controlling) these places, and it was impossible for any of the Jews to forgo offering these, for they would rather give up their lives than the worship which they are accustomed to offer God (*AJ*. XV.248).

The importance of sacrifice emerges in another way in Josephus, in his account of the beginning of the revolt. One Eleazar persuaded the priests who were then serving 'to accept no gift or sacrifice from a foreigner'. Josephus continues:

> This action laid the foundation of the war with the Romans; for the sacrifices offered on behalf of that nation and the emperor were in consequence rejected. The chief priests and the notables earnestly besought them not to abandon the customary offering for their rulers, but the priests remained obdurate (*BJ* II.409.f).

Everyone agreed that sacrifices were integral to the function of the temple. They were essential to the religion of Judaism, and withholding sacrifices for the Romans was the final sign that a true revolt, rather than just another round of rock-throwing, was at hand. The notion that the temple should serve some function other than sacrifice would seem to be extremely remote from the thinking of a first-century Jew.

But could the sacrifices continue without the changing of money and the selling of birds? It is hard to see how.[26] The money changers were probably those who changed the money in the possession of pilgrims into the coinage acceptable by the temple in payment of the half-shekel tax levied on all Jews.[27] The word 'levied' itself requires interpretation, for payment of the tax was voluntary, being enforced only by moral suasion.[28] Yet we know that Jews from all parts of the Diaspora paid it out of loyalty to the Jerusalem temple.[29] The desire of the authorities to receive the money in a standard coinage which did not have on it the image of an emperor or king is reasonable, and no one ever seems to have protested this. The money changers naturally charged a fee for changing money,[30] but they can hardly have been expected to secure enough Tyrian coinage to meet the demands of worshippers and to supply their services for free. The buyers and sellers were similarly required for the maintenance of the temple service, and they provided a convenient service for pilgrims. If a Galilean, for example, wished or was required to present a dove as a sacrifice, it was more convenient to sell the dove in Galilee and buy one in Jerusalem which was certified as unblemished than to carry the dove from Galilee to the temple. A charge was made in Jerusalem for the service, but this was doubtless to be preferred to the alternative: bringing one's own dove from Galilee and running the risk of having it found blemished after the trip. The charge for inspection would be made in any case. The most important point to recognize here is that the requirement to present an *unblemished* dove as a sacrifice for certain impurities or transgressions was a requirement *given by God to Israel through Moses*.[31] The business arrangements around the temple were *necessary* if the commandments were to be obeyed. An attack on what is necessary is not an attack on 'present practice'.

If these were the circumstances, was there anything at all about the temple which could give rise to attacks on 'present practice' as distinct from the temple service itself? As it happens, we know of attacks which rest on a distinction between 'practice' and 'ideal' and which have in view the purity of the temple. Will these help us fit Jesus into the mould of a religious reformer, bent on cleansing the temple? It seems not. The attacks otherwise known rest on charges about which the Gospels are silent: the suitability of the priests for their office. Such charges appear already in the biblical period. Thus in Malachi 3 the 'messenger of the covenant' will 'purify the sons of Levi' until they present 'right offerings'. This may have been taken in an eschatological sense subsequently, but the thrust of the chapter itself is that the Levites were impure (3.3) and that all Israel was robbing God by withholding part of the tithes (3.6–10). They should mend their ways or face destruction.

Such accusations continue in the later period. In the days of the Hasmoneans, there were objections to their combining the offices of priest and king[32] and against their 'usurping' the high priesthood.[33] The author[s] of the Psalms of Solomon also objected to the contemporary priests because they served the temple in a state of immorality and impurity. They are accused of committing adultery, robbing the sanctuary, and offering sacrifice when impure because of having come into contact with menstrual blood (8.9–14). God duly punished them (the Hasmonean priests) by sending the Romans (8.15–19). The Dead Sea Sectarians accused the 'Wicked Priest' of committing abominable deeds and defiling the temple (1QpHab 12.8f.). He also 'robbed the Poor of their possessions' (ibid. 12.10; cf. 9.5), but this apparently refers to his actions as king, as is clear in 8.8–11 (cf. 11.4–7). Similar accusations are seen in the Covenant of Damascus:

Also they convey uncleanness to the sanctuary, inasmuch as they do not keep separate according to the Law, but lie with her that sees 'the blood of her flux'. And they marry each man the daughter of his brother and the daughter of his sister. . . . (CD 5.6–8; cf. 4.18).

The charge of impurity in part reflects such halakic disputes as the duration of a woman's impurity following her menstrual period,[34] and there were other halakic disputes. Thus the Dead Sea Sect would have followed a different calendar from that used in Jerusalem, with the result that all the sacrifices were, from their point of view, on the wrong day (see again 1QpHab II.7).[35] We should also suppose that the Pharisees quarrelled with the Sadducean practice because of halakic disagreements.[36]

Criticism of anyone who handles money or goods is easy and obvious – so much so that the priests of the second temple are still assumed to have been dishonest.[37] Many New Testament scholars quite readily suppose that such concerns lay behind Jesus' demonstration.

If Jesus were a religious reformer, however, bent on correcting 'abuse' and 'present practice', we should hear charges of immorality, dishonesty and corruption directed *against the priests*.[38] But such charges are absent from the Gospels (except for Mark 11.17), and that is not the thrust of the action in the temple. On the contrary, the attack was against the trade which is necessary for sacrifices no matter who are the priests and without mention of the *halakot* which they follow. Thus far, it appears that Jesus' demonstration was against what all would have seen as necessary to the sacrificial system, rather than against present practice.

If the saying in Mark 11.17 and parr. were Jesus' own comment on why he 'cleansed' the temple, however, we would have to accept that it was indeed trade and sacrifice which bothered him, possibly because dishonesty was involved.[39] In that verse the conflated quotation from Isa. 56.7 and Jer. 7.11 says that the temple should be a house of prayer (Mark has 'for all the Gentiles'), while 'you' have made it a den of robbers. The saying, however, is quite correctly rejected by most scholars as an addition.[40] Roloff regards v. 17 as an addition because of the introductory 'and he taught them and said'.[41] A. E. Harvey has recently proposed that the quotations in Mark 11.17 cannot represent a saying of Jesus. 'House of prayer for all the Gentiles' 'could hardly be extracted from the Hebrew version which Jesus would have used.' He adds that 'robbers' cave' is inappropriate, since 'robber' always means raider, never swindler.[42] That these and other scholars who reject v. 17 nevertheless think that Jesus opposed present practice, not the temple itself, shows how deeply embedded is the view that Jesus opposed corrupting externalism. They must take it that the mere fact of buying and selling, without any charge of thievery, was seen by Jesus as in contradiction to the purity of the temple.

If one overlooked the 'thievery' part of Mark 11.17 and focused on the 'house of prayer' part, one could argue that Jesus was against sacrifice itself. This view has occasionally been championed,[43] and it could be supported by citing the quotation of Hos. 6.6 in Matt. 9.13 and 12.7, 'I want mercy and not sacrifice.' As Davies points out in correctly dismissing this view, 'Matt. 5:23-24 and Acts 2:46 become inexplicable on such a view of Jesus.'[44] We have here the same problem which we shall meet in discussing Jesus' view of the law. If he actually explicitly opposed one of the main institutions of Judaism, he kept it secret from his disciples.

There is one last possibility for seeing Jesus as bent on purification and reform: he wanted the trade moved entirely outside the temple precincts. If any trade was conducted inside the temple precincts, it was conducted in the court of the Gentiles.[45] We shall immediately consider the question of whether or not it was precisely the Gentiles for whom Jesus was concerned, and we now limit our attention to the fact that the court of the Gentiles was within the temple precincts. Did Jesus differ from his contemporaries simply by wishing to extend the holy area to the outermost court? To my knowledge, no one has proposed this precise interpretation, although one might do so.[46] Such a view could have been suggested by the last sentence of Zech. 14.20f.:

> And on that day there shall be inscribed on the bells of the horses, 'Holy to the Lord'. And the pots in the house of the Lord shall be as the bowls before the altar; and every pot in Jerusalem and Judah shall be sacred to the Lord of hosts, so that all who sacrifice may come and take of them and boil the flesh of the sacrifice in them. And there shall no longer be a trader in the house of the Lord of hosts on that day.

In a context in which all the cooking utensils in Jerusalem are to be ritually pure, so that they can be used in preparing sacrificed meat, there will be no traders in the house; the entire area will be purified.

It is very unlikely that we have here the motive behind Jesus' action. One passage, Mark 7.1–5 and par., depicts Jesus' followers as not accepting an extension to lay people of the biblical purity laws which govern the priests. I doubt the authenticity of this dispute, but in any case there is certainly no evidence for attributing to Jesus a concern to extend the purity code in the way hoped by Zechariah.

This leads us to see once more that the notion behind the discussion of 'purity' in New Testament scholarship is a modern one. New Testament scholars who write about Jesus' concern for the purity of the temple seem to have in mind a familiar Protestant idea: 'pure' worship consists in the Word, and all external rites should be purged. In first-century Judaism, however, a concern to extend purity would almost certainly have involved extending the rites, such as washing, connected with it. I think that we should drop the discussion of Jesus' action as one concerned with purifying the worship of God.[47]

I shall shortly propose an alternative explanation, and one which seems to fit better into the probable outlook of Palestinian Jews of Jesus' day.[48] We should first of all note that other views have been advanced. Principally to be noted are Brandon's view that Jesus' action was part of a carefully planned attempt to take the leadership of the country by arms[49] and Davies' view that what was at stake was the status of Gentiles.[50] On the latter view the key is given by the fact that trade was conducted in the court of the Gentiles.[51] Since that was the area that was cleansed, Jesus must have been 'concerned with the right of, and the hopes of Judaism for, the Gentiles as with the Temple itself'.[52] Both of these views rest on reconstructions of Jesus' activity which are informed by numerous points of evidence, and it would be out of place to discuss them fully in this chapter. Brandon's view, in fact, will get no full airing at all, since I consider that it has been sufficiently refuted;[53] it cannot in any case be said to have influenced many.

Jesus' attitude towards the Gentiles, on the other hand, will be discussed in more detail in ch. 7. Meanwhile, it will have to suffice to say that Jesus does not seem to have made a definite gesture in favour of including Gentiles in the kingdom, although he may well have envisaged their inclusion at the eschaton. The evidence to be discussed below will show Jesus not to have been *directly* concerned with the Gentiles. In light of this, the place of the trade, and consequently of Jesus' action, should be seen as coincidental and not determinative for the meaning of the event.[54] Any public action must have been performed in a place in which activities related to the temple were carried out and to which Jesus had access. In order to derive the meaning of the event directly from the place where it was carried out (presumably the court of the Gentiles), or from the particular activity which was attacked (the trade necessary as a preliminary to sacrifice), we would have to think that Jesus selected the place and the activity from among several available. This, however, seems not to have been the case. Jesus might have gained access to the Priests' Court, and thus to a place more directly connected with the preparation of sacrifices, had he pretended to have a sin- or guilt-offering to present; but apart from the employment of such a ruse there would seem to be nothing other than the trade in the court of the Gentiles which he could have attacked.

The proposal that Jesus' action was in favour of the Gentiles, however, has the merit of understanding it as symbolic, a point to which we shall return.

There is one other frequently met scholarly assertion about the significance of Jesus' action at the temple which should be noted. It is generally thought that Jesus' action would have been primarily resented by the temple hierarchy, those who had a vested interest in the profit derived from the sale of bird-offerings and the exchange of money. Thus, for example, Trautmann argues that Jesus objected to the *Sadducean* priesthood for combining politics and economics with the temple and also opposed *their* theology of atonement by means of sacrifice and the cult[55] – as if other Jews did not believe in atonement through sacrifice. We have seen that a distinction has often been made between Jesus' attack on the law, which is believed to have been directed against the Pharisees and scribes, and his attack on the temple trade, directed against the priests and the Sadducees.[56] This distinction, which is often made sharply, is quite misleading. The law was generally revered, while the temple was the focus of religious hope and devotion throughout Judaism. I earlier pointed out that there is no indication that Jesus' action was directed only against some particular practice. Now we must note that it would not have been offensive to only one group. More than just the priests thought that the sacrifices were ordained by God and atoned for sins. We shall return to this point later in this chapter and also in ch. 10, when assessing Jesus' opponents and the points of opposition.

Thus far we have seen reason to doubt many of the prevalent views about the event in the temple area: that the action was that of a religious reformer, bent on 'purifying' current practice; that the locale, the court of the Gentiles, indicates that the action primarily had to do with opening the worship of the temple to non-Jews; that the action was, and was perceived to be, primarily against the temple officers and the Sadducean party.

There is another frequently met interpretation, however, which I regard as entirely correct. Jesus' action is to be regarded as a symbolic demonstration.[57] The question, of course, is what the action symbolized. We have already considered and rejected the principal proposal, that it symbolized the inclusion of Gentiles.

Let us first consider how the action must have looked to others. Jesus did not actually bring all buying and selling to a halt. As Hengel has pointed out, any real effort to stop the trade necessary to the temple service would have required an army, and there is no evidence of a substantial martial conflict.[58] It is reasonable to think that Jesus (and conceivably some of his followers, although none are mentioned) overturned some tables as a demonstrative action. It would appear that the action was not substantial enough even to interfere with the daily routine; for if it had been he would surely have been arrested on the spot. Thus those who saw it, and those who heard about it, would have known that it was a gesture intended to make a point rather than to have a concrete result; that is, they would have seen the action as symbolic.

The discussion of whether or not Jesus succeeded in interrupting the actual functioning of the temple points us in the right direction for seeing what the action symbolized but did not accomplish: it symbolized destruction. That is one of the most obvious meanings of the action of overturning itself. Some have seen this, but the force and obviousness of the point are obscured as long as we continue to think that Jesus was demonstrating against the Sadducees for profiting and in favour of purifying the temple of externalism.[59] Had Jesus wished to make a gesture symbolizing purity, he doubtless could have done so. The pouring out of water comes immediately to mind. The turning over of even one table points towards destruction.

Professor Moule has proposed to me that overturning one or more tables is not an entirely self-evident symbol of destruction. He quite correctly points to the broken pot of Jer. 19.10. Would breaking something not have been a better symbol? Perhaps so. I must leave to others the assessment of 'overturning' as a self-evident symbol of destruction, though it appears to me to be quite an obvious one. My view, however, depends in part on further considerations.

Let us continue by pursuing the question of how the action would have been understood by others. The import to those who saw or heard of it was almost surely, at least in part, that Jesus was attacking the temple service which was commanded by God. Not just priests would have been offended, but all those who believed that the temple was the place at which Israel and individual Israelites had been commanded to offer sacrifice, to make atonement for their sins. Further, it is hard to imagine how Jesus himself could have seen it if not in these terms. We should suppose that Jesus *knew what he was doing*: like others, he regarded the sacrifices as commanded by God, he knew that they required a certain amount of trade, and he knew that making a gesture towards disrupting the trade represented an attack on the divinely ordained sacrifices. Thus I take it that the action at the very least symbolized an attack, and note that 'attack' is not far from 'destruction'.

But what does this mean? On what conceivable grounds could Jesus have undertaken to attack – and symbolize the destruction of – what was ordained by God? The obvious answer is that destruction, in turn, looks towards restoration.[60] This will be better seen when we consider the sayings about the destruction of the temple, which complement and help us understand the action.[61]

The sayings about the destruction of the temple

The first form in which the reader of the Gospels meets a saying about the destruction of the temple is in the form of a simple *prediction*, with no implication of a threat:

> As he was leaving the temple, one of his disciples exclaimed, 'Look, Master, what huge stones! What fine buildings!' Jesus said to him, 'You see these great buildings. Not one stone will be left upon another; all will be thrown down.' (Mark 13.1f.)

To this prediction all three synoptists append the 'little apocalypse'. It is likely that the saying was originally independent of this entire context (both the introduction, which, as Bultmann observed, seems designed to elicit the saying,[62] and the attached apocalypse), but it would seem likely that Jesus said something of the sort and applied it to the temple. For one thing, other traditions contain the charge that he *threatened* the temple. One of these is the trial scene:

> And some stood up and bore false witness against him, saying, 'We heard him say, "I will destroy this temple that is made with hands, and in three days I will build another, not made with hands." ' (Mark 14.57f.)
> At last two [false witnesses] came forward and said, 'This fellow said, "I am able to destroy the temple of God, and to build it in three days." ' (Matt. 26.6of.)

The reports of what was said at the trial scene are notoriously difficult to verify. In fact, it may even be wondered whether or not the entire 'trial' before the high priest and others is largely fictional.[63] Even if the entire scene were composed after Easter, however, it would still seem likely that this specific accusation is based on an accurate memory of the principal point on which Jesus offended many of his contemporaries. One can imagine a subsequent Christian penning *de novo* the scene in which Jesus is charged with blasphemy for claiming to be the Son of God (Mark 14.61–64), but it is hard to imagine a purely fictional origin for the accusation that he threatened to destroy the temple. For one thing, it leads nowhere. According to the evangelists, the testimony of the witnesses as to what Jesus said did not agree, and the charge was apparently dropped. For another, the implication of physical insurrection which the charge seems to contain would scarcely have been something that a Christian author would spontaneously have thought of. Luke drops the charge from the trial scene, and Matthew and Mark characterize it as false. Mark's contrast 'made with hands', 'not made with hands' may also be an attempt to water down this implication.[64]

Most striking, however, is the reappearance of the charge in other traditions. In the crucifixion scene both Matthew (27.40) and Mark (15.29) (but again not Luke) depict the crowd as calling Jesus 'the one who would destroy the temple and rebuild it in three days'. According to Acts 6.14 the charge against Stephen was that he said – even after Jesus' death and resurrection – that 'this Jesus of Nazareth will destroy this place' (the temple). If we could be absolutely sure of the historicity of this charge against Stephen, it would be clear that Jesus had spoken so firmly that Christians continued to expect the imminent destruction of the temple. It is noteworthy that the author of Acts says that the charge against Stephen was brought by false witnesses (Acts 6.13). This is further evidence of early Christian reluctance to admit the accusation, and it helps confirm that Jesus actually said something which was taken as a threat.

Finally, we should quote John 2.18–22:

> The Jews then said to him, 'What sign have you to show us for doing this?' Jesus answered them, 'Destroy this temple, and in three days I will raise it up.' The Jews then said 'It has taken forty-six years to build this temple, and will you raise it up in three days?' But he spoke of the temple of his body. When therefore he was raised from the dead, his disciples remembered that he had said this; and they believed the scripture and the word which Jesus had spoken.

In John's account, this exchange immediately follows the 'cleansing' of the temple. This passage is especially striking. We see here the characteristic Johannine device of having Jesus say something which his interlocutors understand on one level, which gives the evangelist the opportunity of explaining the true meaning, which resides on another level. For our purposes, however, the statement of John 2.19 shows how deeply embedded in the tradition was the threat of destroying and the promise of rebuilding the temple. It was so firmly fixed that it was not dropped, but rather interpreted. John, it is to be noted, does drop the threat, 'I will destroy', in favour of the second person statement which implies a condition, '[If] you destroy'. The change is necessary for the evangelist's explanation that the temple is Jesus' body. Jesus could not have said that he would destroy his own body.[65] It is reasonable to see the change in subject as John's and to suppose that John had the tradition contained in Mark 14.58, Matt. 26.61, Mark 15.29, Matt. 27.40, and Acts 6.14: Jesus threatened the destruction of the temple (and perhaps predicted its rebuilding after three days).

We seem here to be in touch with a very firm historical tradition, but there is still uncertainty about precisely what it is. Did Jesus *predict* the destruction of the temple (Mark 13.1f. and parr.) or *threaten* it (Mark 14.58 and elsewhere)?[66] Did he mention destruction and rebuilding, or only the former? The christological use of the prediction that it would be rebuilt after three days is evident, but even so Jesus may have predicted just that, for the application to the resurrection is not always explicit (e.g. Mark 15.29 and par.). If Jesus either threatened or predicted the destruction of the temple and its rebuilding after three days, that is, if the saying in any of its forms is even approximately authentic, his meaning would be luminously clear: he predicted the imminent appearance of the judgment and the new age.

The saying and the deed would then correspond. Both point towards the destruction of the present order and the appearance of the new. We should probably think that his expectation was that a new temple would be given by God from heaven, an expectation which is not otherwise unknown during the period, even if it may not have been universal.[67] In this case the characterization of the temple as 'made without hands' could be original, rather than a spiritualizing interpretation. But if (following Mark 13.1f.; Acts 6.14) there was no prediction of a rebuilding, the meaning would be only slightly less concrete. Jesus either threatened or predicted that *God* would put an end to the present temple: that is, that the end was at hand. If he said 'I will destroy', he saw himself as God's agent.

We have thus far not attempted to determine the original form of the saying, nor is it likely that this can be done with certainty. Some possibilities, however, can be excluded. We should first observe that the existence of the threat form ('I will destroy', Mark 14.58; implied by Mark 15.29 and Acts 6.14, and probably by John 2.19) makes it virtually incredible that the entire saying could be a *vaticinium ex eventu*, a 'prophecy' after the event.

After the temple was in fact destroyed by the Romans in the year 70, the Christians would not have composed a threat by Jesus that he would destroy it, nor would they have turned an existing prophecy that the temple would be destroyed into such a threat. If we had only the prediction, we could believe it to be a *vaticinium*, though perhaps not a very likely one,[68] but we cannot explain the origin of the double form in this way. One would then have to suppose that the prediction was composed after it was fulfilled in 70, that an evangelist or someone in the pre-Gospel tradition creatively turned the prediction into a threat and made it the object of a charge before the high priest which failed for lack of agreement in the testimony, that one of Luke's sources for the early chapters of Acts independently arrived at the same charge (for Luke can scarcely have composed it, having twice dropped it in the Gospel), and that the fourth evangelist found the threat form of the saying to be so well known that it had to be taken account of. All of this, especially the change from a prediction based on facts to a threat which became the object of a charge, strains the imagination too much. It is better to believe that Jesus said something which lies behind the traditions. But did *he* predict a military disaster? It is not inconceivable that as a sagacious man he saw where zealotism would lead the nation one generation later, but there is no reason to think that this sort of commonplace observation (if you fellows keep up your trouble-making, it is bound to lead to disaster) lies behind the double tradition of prediction and threat as we have it. Even if we push the prediction back to Jesus, it is still unlikely that the threat form derived from a simple prediction of disaster. It seems far better to suppose that Jesus either threatened the destruction of the temple, with himself playing a role, *or* predicted its destruction in such terms that the prediction could be construed as a threat, than that he made a general prediction that foreign arms would some day take Jerusalem and destroy the temple. It is hard to know how such a prediction could have led to the traditions in the Gospels and Acts.

If Jesus did not predict the conquest of the temple by foreign arms, and if he himself was not planning armed insurrection, then it follows that he must have either predicted or threatened the destruction of the temple *by God*. In this case there would still be the question, though it probably cannot be resolved, of his own role in the destruction. Mark 13.1f. and parr. give him no role, while the other passages, including John 2.18f. by inference, do. Even if he said 'I will destroy', however, he could only have meant that he would act as God's agent and do so in the context of the arrival of the eschaton.

Finally, we can note that whatever Jesus said became public in some way or other. Mark has the prediction of destruction made to one disciple (13.1), while Matthew has 'his disciples' (24.1). Luke gives the saying a wider setting (21.5). Here as elsewhere we must suppose that the settings are secondary. The public nature of the statement is implied by its being used in charges against Jesus and Stephen.

Thus we conclude that Jesus publicly predicted or threatened the destruction of the temple, that the statement was shaped by his expectation of the arrival of the eschaton, that he probably also expected a new temple to be given by God from heaven, and that he made a demonstration which prophetically symbolized the coming event.

Roloff took the 'cleansing' of the temple and the prediction of its destruction to be 'obviously contradictory' to each other in a way suitable to the words and deeds of a prophet. Jesus *both* saw the temple as the place of God's presence which should be purified for present use *and* predicted its destruction.[69] Others have interpreted the action as 'cleansing' and have then allowed this meaning to submerge the force of the saying about destruction. Thus Bornkamm wrote that the temple 'cleansing' is 'more than an act of reform to restore the temple service to its original (sic!) purity'. Jesus was also 'cleansing the sanctuary for the approaching kingdom of God'.[70] Here the threat to destroy is dropped and thus the radical connection with eschatology.

On the hypothesis presented here the action and the saying form a unity. Jesus predicted (or threatened) the destruction of the temple and carried out an action symbolic of its destruction by demonstrating against the performance of the sacrifices. He did not wish to purify the temple, either of dishonest trading or of trading in contrast to 'pure' worship. Nor was he opposed to the temple sacrifices which God commanded to Israel. He intended, rather, to indicate that the end was at hand and that the temple would be destroyed, so that the new and perfect temple might arise.[71]

Our hypothesis receives partial confirmation from the embarrassment of Matthew and Mark about the threat to destroy and the embarrassment of all three synoptists about the action in the temple. Matthew and Mark explain that the threat to destroy was testified to only by false witnesses (Matt. 26.59f; Mark 14.56f); and all three synoptists, by use of the quotation about a 'den of robbers', make it appear that Jesus was quite reasonably protesting against dishonesty (Mark 11.17 and parr.). They attempt to make the action relatively innocuous, and they deny the force of the saying – while reporting both. Despite their efforts, we should take both the action and the saying at full value. We see immediately behind the surface of the Gospels that Jesus threatened (or predicted) the destruction of the temple and that he acted to demonstrate it.

Our interpretation has the additional advantage of making sense of the acceptance of temple worship by the early apostles (Acts 2.46; 3.1; 21.26). They did not think that Jesus had considered it impure, but only that the days of the present temple were numbered.

The only question which remains outstanding at this point is whether or not Jesus' contemporaries would have clearly understood the prophetic symbolism. I have previously urged that pious Jews, not just the supposedly profiteering priestly class, would have been offended at the action in the temple. This follows both from intrinsic probability and from the sequel – Jesus was put to death, apparently with the approval of many in Jerusalem. But would the crowd have understood without ambiguity that Jesus intended to symbolize the impending eschatological act of God? We recall here the question of whether or not the meaning of the symbolic action was self-evident. To this question no certain answer can be given.[72] The chapter which immediately follows argues that there was current in some circles the expectation of the destruction and rebuilding of the temple. Thus it is at least reasonable that the intent of Jesus' action was clear to his contemporaries. Even if he was understood, however, the action and saying were still highly offensive. Jesus still attacked the functioning temple, where the sins of Israel were atoned, and the crowd could simply have disbelieved his eschatological prediction or resented his personal self-assertion. To attempt a real answer to the question posed in this paragraph, however, would be to press hypothetical reconstruction too far. In the subsequent chapters supporting evidence for the interpretation of Jesus' word and deed will be presented. I doubt that we can ever securely know how well Jesus was understood by how many of his contemporaries.

Our discussion of the temple starts two lines of enquiry which must be pursued: to what degree Jesus is to be fitted into Jewish views of the end of the age and the restoration of Israel, and what was Jesus' stance towards other institutions, groups and realities within Judaism. The two prongs of our enquiry have been often studied and, furthermore, are interrelated. It has often been proposed, for example, that he opposed the Pharisaic interpretation of the law and even 'abrogated' the law in principle in the name of the coming kingdom of God. For the present, however, we shall follow each path separately, beginning with other evidence that bears on the question of Jesus' relationship to the hope for restoration. We must first, however, turn to Jewish literature to see what the ramifications of an expectation of a new temple might be expected to be.

2

NEW TEMPLE AND RESTORATION IN JEWISH LITERATURE

I have proposed that the best explanation of Jesus' demonstrative action in the temple and his saying against the temple (whether a prediction or a threat) is to be found in his eschatological expectation. The kingdom was at hand, and one of the things which that meant was that the old temple would be replaced by a new. This explanation of Jesus' word and deed could be countered if the proposed meaning were to have no context in contemporary Judaism; that is, if there were currently no expectation that the eschaton would bring a new temple. On the other hand, evidence that a connection between eschaton and temple was current would serve to buttress the position which has just been proposed.

In 1969 and 1970 two major investigations of the place of the temple in Judaism were published.[1] Lloyd Gaston's work *No Stone on Another* directly focused on the connection between temple and eschaton in Jewish thought. His position, if sustained, would mean that the eschatological significance which I have thus far proposed for Jesus' action in the temple area would not have been perceived.

> We find no background in Jewish apocalyptic before 70 A.D. for the statement 'I will destroy this temple and in three days I will build it.' The future salvation was couched in terms of the new Jerusalem, even if the temple should occasionally be presupposed as a part of this (Tobit, Jubilees). (p. 119)

Gaston grants that the occasional expectation of a new temple might reasonably imply the destruction of the old one (p. 112), but argues that it is significant that destruction and rebuilding are never explicitly connected (p. 119). The discussions in Jewish literature of cleansing and purifying the temple, on the other hand, do not have a setting in eschatological expectation, but stem 'more from historical profanations' (p. 119). He sorts the evidence out like this:

> While there is evidence that some groups expected a new temple in the age to come, this idea is not nearly as important as that of the new Zion, and such an expectation is never connected with the idea of the destruction of the old temple. And while other groups were so opposed to the Jerusalem temple as to hope for its destruction, this opposition is motivated by the concept of a cult without sacrifices, and there is no question of rebuilding the temple. (p.162)

Approximately the opposite case was argued by R. J. McKelvey in *The New Temple*. He pointed out, quite correctly, that in the Bible 'Zion' was sometimes equated with Jerusalem or used in place of 'Jerusalem' (Isa. 1.26f.; more clearly 60.14). At other times the word 'Zion' is virtually equated with the temple (Jer. 50.28; 51.10f.). Thus it could be said that God dwells in Zion (Isa. 8.18; Jer. 8.19 and elsewhere). In Isa. 40–66, according to McKelvey, there is only one explicit reference to the rebuilding of the temple (Isa. 44.28), although other passages imply it (56.5, 7; 60.7; 66.20; 60.13) (p. 11 nn. 1, 2). One could add that the last passage cited explicitly refers to the physical improvement of the temple. His more general case, however, is this: 'The descriptions of the New Zion presuppose a new temple, for no good Israelite could think of one without the other' (p. 11 n. 2).

McKelvey's statement reflects the natural assumption: 'New Jerusalem' implies 'New Temple', and this can be seen in part by the use of 'Zion' to refer either explicitly to the temple or more generally to Jerusalem. But even if this is granted, especially in interpreting the expectations of prophets of the exilic period, the problems raised by Gaston must be carefully considered. While *a* temple stood and was in use was there still a general expectation of a new and more glorious temple? Did those who opposed the Jerusalem temple or its priesthood expect a new temple? Answers to these questions should throw light on one of the questions of the previous chapter: whether or not a prophetic gesture implying destruction would be understood to demonstrate the expectation of a new temple.

The hopes expressed by the prophets before the building of the second temple are not in dispute.[2] It will be useful, however, in abbreviated form to set out some of the key passages which are often pointed to as providing the terms and the framework of Jewish eschatological expectation in the first century.

Isa. 49.5f.: God will restore 'Jacob' or 'the tribes of Jacob' through his servant, and his salvation will reach the end of the earth.

Isa. 56.1–8: God will gather 'the outcasts of Israel' (*niḏḥe Yisra'el; tous diesparmenous*) and, in addition, foreigners who accept him and who keep the sabbath and the covenant. Even they can make sacrifices on the altar, 'for my house shall be called a house of prayer for all peoples' (*'ammim; ethnē*).

Isa. 60.3–7: Nations (*goyim; ethnē*) will come to Israel's light; her sons and daughters shall come, as will 'the wealth of the nations'. Sacrifices will be brought, 'and I will glorify my glorious house'.

Isa. 60.10–14: Foreigners will rebuild the walls of Jerusalem; Israel will receive 'the wealth of the nations'; Gentiles who do not submit will be destroyed. The temple will be beautified.

Isa. 66.18–24: God will gather 'all nations and tongues'; further, he will send survivors to declare his glory 'among the nations' (*goyim, ethnē*); the Jews dispersed among the nations will be brought 'as an offering to the Lord', and some will become priests and Levites. God will make a new heaven and new earth, which will remain, as will 'your descendants and your name'.

Micah 4: In the latter days 'the mountain of the house of the Lord' will be made the highest mountain, where many nations will come to learn the law, the word of the Lord. God will assemble the lame, who will be the remnant. Israel will defeat opposing nations 'and shall devote their gain to the Lord, their wealth to the Lord of the whole earth'.

These passages reflect the overlapping of themes which also are attested separately: the rebuilding of the temple (also Isa. 44.28; Ezek. 40–43); the restoration of dispersed Israel (Ezek. 34, 37, under the leadership of 'David'; 47.13–48.29, the division of the land among the twelve tribes); the submission of the Gentiles (cf. Isa. 54.3; 60.16; 61.6, and often). These passages and others have often been gathered and studied,[3] and the influence of several of them on the early Christian movement is well known. The present question is this: does the complex of themes represented above constitute a known and identifiable unity in the post-biblical period?

That question has often been answered in the affirmative. Nickelsburg puts it this way:

The destruction of Jerusalem and the Exile meant the disruption of life and the breaking up of institutions whose original form was never fully restored.

Much of post-biblical Jewish theology and literature was influenced and sometimes governed by a hope for such a restoration: a return of the dispersed; the appearance of a Davidic heir to throw off the shackles of foreign domination and restore Israel's sovereignty; the gathering of one people around a new and glorified Temple.[4]

It is important to note the phrase 'was never fully restored'. It is all the more true that the more grandiose visions of Isaiah, Micah and Ezekiel were not realized. 'Jacob' (the twelve tribes) was not brought together again. The restoration of Jerusalem did not cause the walls to be built with jewels; the wealth of nations and kings did not pour in to adorn Jerusalem and the temple; the Davidic boundaries were not, until the Hasmoneans, recovered; and then not for long. Phrases such as 'new heavens and new earth' (Isa. 66.22), coupled with the degree to which reality fell short of more modest predictions, could easily lead to the view that those prophecies were about a still more distant time. It would be comprehensible as a first-century view that the time would yet come when the dispersed of Israel would be restored, when a Davidic king would arise, when Jerusalem would be rebuilt, when the temple would be beautified, and when the nations would submit to Israel's God.

But reasonableness is not proof. Gaston, we have seen, has objected to the 'new temple' part of this composite description of what Jews might reasonably be expected to have hoped for, and in any case the question of whether or not one feature of restoration implies another requires careful consideration. We shall begin by surveying the relevant passages from Jewish literature during the period of the second temple, that is, excluding material from after 70 CE.

The full complex of themes mentioned above (except for the Davidic king) is visible in Tobit. The date of the work is uncertain, but it must be after Nehemiah and is probably before the Maccabean revolt. In Tobit's prayer of rejoicing at the conclusion of the story, he predicts that although God will afflict Israel, he will 'gather us from all the nations among whom [we] have been scattered' (Tob. 13.5). 'Many nations (*ethnē*) will come from afar . . . bearing gifts in their hands' (13.11[13]). Jerusalem will be rebuilt with precious stones and metals (13.16–18; cf. Isa. 54.11f.). The author takes account of the discrepancy between the prophetic predictions which he repeats and the reality of the second temple:

> . . . they will rebuild the house of God, though it will not be like the former one until the times of the age are completed. After this they will return from the places of their captivity, and will rebuild Jerusalem in splendor. And the

house of God will be rebuilt there with a glorious building for all generations
for ever, just as the prophets said of it (14.5).

This prediction is followed by the statement that 'all the Gentiles will turn
to fear the Lord God . . .' (14.6f.). Thus in at least this instance the Isaianic
prophecies, which the rebuilding of the temple did not fulfil, were applied to
the end-time.

In the preface to his abbreviation of Jason of Cyrene's history of the
Maccabean revolt and the purification of the temple, the epitomizer also
reveals a feeling that the restoration has not been completed. Jeremiah, he
writes, hid the tent, the ark, and the altar of incense and predicted that
'The place shall be unknown until God gathers his people together again
and shows his mercy' (II Macc. 2.7).

The vision in I Enoch 24–25 is primarily concerned with the tree of life,
but significantly it is said that the tree will be transplanted 'to the holy
place, to the temple of the Lord, the Eternal King' (I En. 25.5). The
temple is presumably the throne of God, where he will sit 'when he shall
come down to visit the earth with goodness' (25.3). Charles remarks that
'we cannot tell whether the author intended here the New Jerusalem' of
90.29 or not. 'It is, at all events, a Jerusalem cleansed from all impurity,
and that is probably all that the author meant.'[5]

More to the point, although challenged by Gaston, are portions of I En.
89–90. We first read that the offerings were polluted:

> They reared up that tower . . . ; and they began again to place a table before
> the tower, but all the bread on it was polluted and not pure (89.73).

The result is that the temple was taken away and replaced:

> And I stood up to see till they folded up that old house; and carried off all
> the pillars, and all the beams and ornaments of the house were at the same
> time folded up with it, and they carried it off . . . . And I saw till the Lord
> of the sheep brought a new house greater and loftier than that first, and set
> it in the place of the first . . .: and its pillars were new, and its ornaments
> were new and larger than those of the first . . . , and all the sheep were
> within it (90.28f.).

In 90.30 the sheep not taken away, as well as the 'beasts' and the 'birds',
then do homage to 'those sheep'; i.e., the Gentiles obey the faithful of
Israel. Here Gaston argues that, since the 'new house' is large enough to
contain all the sheep, it must be Jerusalem, not just the temple.[6] That is
plausible. The vision in fact does not distinguish city from temple, but
seems to refer to both. The pillars and ornaments more naturally refer to

the temple than to the city. Further, the earlier mention of pollution of sacrifices (89.73) indicates that temple concerns are present. This encourages the inference that a new temple would be included in the new city.

In the Apocalypse of Weeks there is a direct reference to an eternal temple: In the eighth week 'there shall be built the royal Temple of the Great One in His glorious splendour, for all generations forever' (I. En. 91.13). The eighth week belongs to the end-time, and thus here we have a clear reference to the building of an eschatological temple.

Jub. 1.15–17 predicts that Israel will turn to God with heart, soul and strength. He will gather them from among the Gentiles. 'And I will build My sanctuary in their midst, and I will dwell with them . . .'. Later in the same chapter God instructs the angel of the presence: 'Write for Moses from the beginning of creation till My sanctuary has been built among them for all eternity.' God will prove himself to be father of all the children of Jacob (thus implying the restoration of the twelve tribes) (1.28), and he will dwell with Israel 'throughout eternity' (1.26).

The Testaments of the Twelve Patriarchs can be used with less confidence than other works counted among the Pseudepigrapha,[7] but for the sake of completeness we shall quote one passage, T. Benj. 9.2. According to it, despite sin

> the temple of God shall be in your portion, and the last (temple) shall be more glorious than the first. And the twelve tribes shall be gathered there, and all the Gentiles, until the Most High shall send forth His salvation in the visitation of an only-begotten prophet.

In the Psalms of Solomon 17 several of the prophetic themes appear. The king, the son of David (17.23) will purge Jerusalem of the Gentiles (17.25). He will gather 'a holy people', and 'he shall judge the tribes of the people that has been sanctified by the Lord his God' (17.28). This apparently refers to the regathering of a purified, refined Israel. The Gentiles will serve him, and 'he shall glorify the Lord in a place to be seen of all the earth' (17.32). This apparently refers to an exalted Mount Zion and to the temple. The Gentiles shall come 'to see his glory, bringing as gifts her sons who had fainted' (17.34). Here the regathering of the dispersed is clearly meant.

The interpretation of the Dead Sea Scrolls with regard to the issue of temple and eschaton is crucial to Gaston's case, for here we have a community to which cultic terminology and concepts were highly important, which was led by priests, and in which the members saw themselves as living in the last days.[8] Gaston argues that there is no clear indication that the anticipated sacrifices will be offered in the Jerusalem temple. The document which seems most clearly to indicate that the sect's priests will offer sacrifices in the temple is 1QM, the War Scroll. Here Gaston grants that sacrifices are mentioned, but points out that Jerusalem is not. He argues as follows:

> The War Scroll is no exception to the general rejection of the Jerusalem temple. Even if the last battles occur before Jerusalem (I, 3; III,11; XII, 17) and people *leave* Jerusalem to join the camps (VII, 4), there is no indication that the sacrifices mentioned will be offered in the Jerusalem temple. On the contrary, as the camp was organized according to the pattern of the holy wars of pre-Davidic Israel, the assumption is that sacrifices will be offered on the battlefield.[9]

The argument is not persuasive. As Gaston notes, the general regulations for how to conduct a battle presuppose that the sect occupies Jerusalem. Thus 1QM 7.4: 'No young boy and no woman shall enter their encampments when they go forth from Jerusalem to go to battle, until their return.' The sectarians, then, leave Jerusalem only for the explicit purpose of fighting. When the priests go forth to join the battle formation, they are instructed to wear special garments for war, garments which they may not bring into the sanctuary (*ha-miqdash*) (1QM 7.10). Since the priests leave Jerusalem and go onto the field of battle wearing garments which cannot be brought into the sanctuary, Gaston's proposal, that the sanctuary is on the battlefield, seems excluded. The only sound construction of 1QM 7.4–10 is that the sanctuary is in Jerusalem. Having come to this conclusion with regard to column 7, it is then easy to accept the reference to sacrifices in 1QM 2.5f. as referring to real sacrifices offered at the temple, not to the sacred meal, as Gaston proposes.[10] The text refers to the rotating courses of priests (1QM 2.1–4), who offer whole burnt offerings ('*olot*), animal sacrifices (*zebaḥim*) and the fragrant incense offering on the 'table of glory' (2.5f.). It is more than precarious to suppose that the 'table' is the table of the common meal rather than the Jerusalem altar.[11] Even when, in 1QS 9.5, prayer is compared to a fragrant (*niḥoaḥ*; cf. 1QM 2.5) offering, during the period of exile when literal sacrifices cannot be made, the terms for the whole burnt offering and the animal sacrifice are reserved for those literal sacrifices (1QS 9.4). The discussion of the meal, on the other hand, does not use sacrificial terminology (1QS 6.2–5). Thus from every point of view it seems best to accept the commonly received explanation early enunciated by Yadin: at the time of the final war, the sect would occupy the temple and re-establish the sacrifices according to its own laws. It was only during the exile that prayer and the like substituted.[12] Gaston's general view, that once the community and prayer were seen as substituting for the temple and sacrifices (so 1QS), interest in the physical temple waned,[13] is not upheld by 1QM.

Gaston does, however, have a valid objection to taking 4Qflor. 1.1–13 as containing a certain reference to the expectation that God would build a new physical temple at the eschaton.[14] The phrase *miqdash adam* (1.6) is, as Flusser noted, difficult, and the possibility that it means 'sanctuary among mankind'[15] cannot be decisively excluded. The other option, however, and in some ways the simplest one, remains: to follow Gaston and see in this entire passage the identification of the sanctuary with the community.[16] Thus Vermes' translation of 1.6f.: 'He has commanded that a Sanctuary of men be built for Himself, that there they may send up, like the smoke of incense, the works of the Law.' It is evident here that the works of the law substitute for sacrifices, and this equation may determine the meaning of the entire passage. In any case, I consider the interpretation of 4Qflor. in this regard to be too precarious to build on.

There is a further passage from the Dead Sea Scrolls which Gaston failed to note, from the commentary on Ps. 37. I give it in Vermes' translation:

> Interpreted, this [Ps. 37.21f.] concerns the congregation of the Poor, who [shall possess] the portion of all . . . . They shall possess the High Mountain of Israel [for ever], and shall enjoy [everlasting] delights in His Sanctuary [*qodsho*]. [But those who] shall be *cut off*, they are the violent [of the nations and] the wicked of Israel; they shall be cut off and blotted out for ever (4QpPs37 3.11).

The context is clearly the eschaton: described here are the redemption and reward of the sectarians and the final destruction of all their enemies. At the eschaton, then, the sectarians will possess Mount Zion and enjoy the luxuries of the temple. In this passage, as in 1QM, a *new* temple is not specified, and there may here be a divergence of view from Jubilees, Tobit and the Temple Scroll (to be cited below). It is more likely, however, that the author simply does not bother to say that at the time of judgment the Lord will renew the earth, Jerusalem and the temple for the righteous, who will inhabit them for a thousand generations (for 'a thousand generations', see 4QpPs37 3.1).

The Temple Scroll now adds another important piece of evidence that indicates that at least some expected a new temple to be built by God at the eschaton. For the present purpose we do not need to come to a decision as to whether or not the Scroll is a sectarian document in the narrow sense, as distinct from being a valued work kept in the sectarian library. The pertinent facts can be quickly sketched. The Temple Scroll deals in great detail with the conduct of worship in an idealized temple, the temple which should exist in Jerusalem. Thus Herman Lichtenberger describes it:

> There is a real temple described in the Temple Scroll. The priests perform real sacrifices. We find minute details for these sacrifices, regardless of whether they are daily sacrifices or special sacrifices for festival days. The ritual for the Day of Atonement is described in detail. In comparison with the Pentateuch, the rituals here are more elaborate. New festival days have been added together with their respective sacrifices.[17]

The striking point, however, is that this idealized temple, run the way God always intended the temple to be operated, is itself not the final temple. God is described as speaking in the first person:

> I shall sanctify my sanctuary with my glory: I shall cause my glory to dwell upon it until[18] the Day of Blessing, [at which time] I myself shall create ['ebra'] my sanctuary, establishing it for myself for ever, like the covenant which I made with Jacob at Beth-El (11QTemple 29.8–10).[19]

The passage just quoted, besides being one more bit of evidence for the expectation of a new temple at the eschaton, helps to demonstrate the naturalness of the connection between expecting a new temple and supposing that the old one will be destroyed. Gaston made rather a lot of the fact that even the unquestionable new temple passages did not explicitly mention the destruction of the old: thus the saying attributed to Jesus he regarded as without context. The passage from the Temple Scroll does not contain the word 'destruction'; but, by limiting the time during which God's glory will abide on the temple – 'until the Day of Blessing' – , distinctly implies it. The connection between 'new temple' and 'destruction of the old', like the proposed connection between 'new Jerusalem' and 'new (or renewed) temple', was perhaps too obvious to require explicit statement.

Our last evidence, though slight, is important. It is from the Greek Diaspora. The Sibylline Oracles contain references to a new temple and to other aspects of Israel's restoration. In 3.294 the seer states that 'the temple shall be again as it was before'.[20] In the eschatological section we read that 'all the sons of the great God shall live quietly around the temple', and that this will lead the Gentiles to worship God (3.702–20). In 3.772–4 the offerings of the Gentiles are described. In 5.414–33 a 'blessed man' from heaven destroys the wicked, rebuilds Jerusalem so that it is 'more radiant than the stars and the sun and the moon', and makes a temple which is many furlongs in size and which has a giant tower 'touching the very clouds and seen of all'.[21] Then 'east and west' hymn forth the glory of God.

Philo, despite his allegorizing, maintained the traditional hope for the restoration of Israel, as is clear in *De praemiis et poenis* 94–7; 162–72. He depicts the return of the Israelites captive in the dispersion (164f.), once they, instructed by chastisement, repent and turn to virtue (163). He predicts that 'the cities which but now lay in ruins will be cities once more' and that 'all the prosperity of their fathers and ancestors will seem a tiny fragment, so lavish will be the abundant riches in their possession' (168). There is no mention of the temple, although it does not seem far-fetched to think that the rebuilding of the cities will include Jerusalem and that Jerusalem includes the temple.

As the last sentence indicates, I think that McKelvey should be followed when he proposes that the expectation of a new Jerusalem implies a new temple. One further bit of evidence may be cited. There is a detailed description of the new Jerusalem in Rev. 21.9–22.5. Most noteworthy for our purpose is 21.22: 'And I saw no temple in the city, for its temple is the Lord God the Almighty and the Lamb.' This is clearly a polemic against the normal expectation of Judaism. Just as the people in Asia Minor who call themselves Jews and attend the synagogue are not, in the view of the author of the Apocalypse, true Jews (2.9), so the real new Jerusalem – unlike the one of Jewish expectation – will have no temple. This section of the Apocalypse contains a fairly traditional end-time expectation. The Gentile kings will make pilgrimage to Jerusalem (Rev. 21.24). In this context the author's statement about the temple seems to indicate a desire to counter the natural assumption that 'new Jerusalem' means 'new temple', and to do so on the basis of Christian theology: the place of atonement for the sins of Israel is not needed.

This rapid survey of passages does not lead to the conclusion that all Jews everywhere, when thinking of the future hope of Israel, put foremost the building of a new temple.[22] Further, when the temple is explicitly mentioned, it is not depicted in a uniform manner. To be more precise, sometimes it is not *depicted* at all (II Macc. 2.7; Jub. 1.17, 27; 11QTemple 29.8–10), and sometimes it appears that the present second temple is in mind (I En. 25.5; II Macc. 2.7). Sometimes the new temple is modestly expected only to be larger and grander than the present temple (Tob. 14.5, 'glorious'; I En. 90,28f., 'greater and loftier'; T. Benj. 9.2, 'more glorious than the first'), in which case it will be built by human hands (see Tob. 14.5); but sometimes the extravagant language of Micah 4 and Isa. 2 is recalled (Ps. Sol. 17.32; Sib.Or. 5.425). In some instances it is definitely said or clearly implied that God will build or provide a new temple (I En. 90.28f,; Jub. 1.17; 11QTemple 29.8–18), and in Sib.Or. 5.425 the builder is a 'blessed man from heaven'. Thus we can speak of neither a universal expectation nor of a clear and consistent one.[23]

We have had before us two questions: (1) whether or not a complex of prophetic themes (the gathering of dispersed Israel, the rebuilding of the temple, and the entry of the Gentiles) continued in the post-biblical period; (2) whether or not a word and gesture indicating the destruction of the temple would imply the expectation of renewal. The first question will be discussed more fully in the next chapter, but here it may be noted that all the main themes of prophetic expectation continued, though they do not constitute a fixed and unvarying complex. Eschatological expectation is not generally clear and consistent, and there certainly is not any one combination of various hopes which constitutes a set theology. The hope that seems to have been most often repeated was that of the restoration of the people of Israel. Even so there is by no means uniformity. Some had the original twelve tribes explicitly in mind, while others spoke more generally. Nevertheless, the restoration of Israel is a major theme. At the other extreme the Davidic king is mentioned infrequently. We return to both points below. Here we must note that the temple (whether new, improved, or only restored 'as it was before'; whether built by God or by human hands) is, in the extant literature, somewhat less prominent than restored Israel, appreciably more prominent than the Davidic king.

Thus our answer to the second question must be cautious.[24] Gaston goes too far in arguing that a statement predicting the destruction and rebuilding of the temple would have no context in Judaism before 70. There is enough evidence of the expectation of a new (or renewed) temple to make such a prediction – that is, one which included rebuilding – entirely comprehensible. We shall consider the 'destroy' part of the saying immediately below. Here we should pay heed to both the fragmentary character of the remaining material and also to the various circles in which – even while the second temple was standing – future hopes included a new or restored temple. There is little to be said about the accident of survival. I am told that newspaper editors assume that, for every letter to the editor expressing a given opinion, a certain number of others also hold it. We do not know the multiple which should be applied to surviving references to a given theme or idea, but we should assume that each expression of a view represents numerous people who held it.[25] More important is the fact that the theme of a new temple appears in several different places. Tobit shows that, before the Hasmonean conquest, there was a realization that the predictions of the prophets were not actually fulfilled by the construction of a second temple. Jubilees, Enoch and the Dead Sea Scrolls show that apocalyptic or eschatological writers might think of God as building a new temple at the end of days. It is important to observe that this expectation was not one of the ideas peculiar to the Qumran community; rather, it is one which they shared with other circles. It is relevant here to note that the War Scroll had a pre-sectarian form.[26] The Sibylline Oracles (and possibly Philo) show that the hope for a new temple existed in the Greek Diaspora. The idea of a new Jerusalem with a new temple coming down out of heaven was common enough to require being denied by the author of Revelation.[27] We must assume then, that an explicit statement about the temple would have been understood very well.

At least that is true if the statement referred to both destruction and rebuilding. We have seen above that the threat (or prediction) of destruction almost certainly goes back to Jesus. The prediction of rebuilding is subject to some doubt because it may be understood as John interpreted it, as referring to the resurrection. The connection with the resurrection is not always explicit, however, and it would go beyond the evidence definitely to attribute the 'I will rebuild' statement to the post-Easter church. On balance, I would rank that part of the statement as 'probable'. Even without the 'rebuild' part of the saying, however, it is plausible that a threat of destruction would have been understood by many of Jesus' contemporaries as meaning that the end was at hand and thus that redemption was near. It is, to be sure, unusual for the weight to be put on destruction. I En. 90.28f. says that 'the old house' was carried off and a new one brought, but the Temple Scroll and Jubilees mention God's building a new temple without saying that the old one will be destroyed. If Jesus said only 'I will destroy' (or by implication 'God will destroy'), the emphasis would be odd but the statement would nevertheless be comprehensible. Perhaps, like a later Jesus, he would have been regarded as merely a crier of doom;[28] but the connection between disaster, God's chastisement, and the subsequent redemption of a remnant was so firmly fixed in Judaism that we should assume that even a bare statement of destruction would not be altogether misunderstood.

In fact, as we shall see, Jesus himself had provided a context in which the destruction of the temple can be understood as a meaningful part of God's redemptive action. But even on the most astringent view of the evidence, accepting only the bare statement of destruction, we can think with some confidence that Jesus would have been understood as saying that the final hour had come.

But what of the prophetic action of overturning the tables? How would it have been understood? Since the 'cleansing' interpretation of the action has been so predominant – it goes back to the synoptics, where 'den of robbers', etc. is already added as an interpretative comment – we should give further attention to it. If Jesus' action were understood as a symbol of cleansing, he would probably have been seen as favouring a reform of the priesthood. Gaston has correctly observed that in Jewish literature the theme of cleansing the temple is not an eschatological one, but refers to actual historical profanations.[29] These are to be corrected by changing or reforming the priesthood, not by awaiting the end. Even in Qumran, where the end was expected and the priesthood was accused of immorality and impurity, the two are not connected. Pollution of the sanctuary is not cited as a sign of the end. In the Testament of Moses there are numerous complaints about the iniquity of the priests. In this case the resolution of iniquity is neither punishment by enemies nor the separation of the pious. At the end of the work, at least in its present form, Israel is exalted to the heaven.[30] But even though impure sacrifices were part of the problem which required a radical solution (the dispersion of the twelve tribes was another major problem), they are not said to be an eschatological sign. Thus Gaston is correct to object to a causal connection between the impurity of the temple, its need of cleansing, and the eschaton.

I earlier argued that the saying about the temple and the action should be taken together, and that both point towards 'eschaton', not 'purity'. The point may now be broadened. A prophetic gesture, in order to be fully understood, needs some sort of setting, preferably verbal interpretation. Once we deny to Jesus the saying in Mark 11.17 and parr., we have no saying attributed to him which indicates dissatisfaction with the current priesthood. The evangelists provide us with none of the traditional charges of sexual immorality and halakic impurity. Nor is there any indication that Jesus favoured the replacement of the present priests with others. A preference for another line (as in Qumran), or a charge of sexual immorality and impurity (Psalms of Solomon, Qumran) would place Jesus' action in a setting in Judaism which would help us interpret it. It is in some ways surprising that no such saying is attributed to Jesus. A criticism of the priesthood – but not of the religion itself – would have fitted Jesus into a well-known type, and depicting him as urging the cleansing of worship would probably have been much more comfortable for his followers than preserving the more radical saying about destruction. This depiction is partially, but only partially achieved by the addition of the saying 'house of prayer', 'den of thieves'. Much more could have been accomplished along this line. This observation serves to highlight the fact that there is no clue that the symbolic action in the temple should be put in the setting of criticism of the priests and the Levites, or of their conduct of the temple.

If on other grounds we thought that Jesus was in favour of a programme of religious reform, or that he sided with a party in opposition to the current priesthood, we might make out a case for understanding the gesture as symbolizing cleansing. But in fact on other grounds we can see that Jesus' work fits into eschatological expectation, not reform. Thus there is *no* context for understanding the symbolic action as 'cleansing'. Contemporary Judaism would not expect 'cleansing' from an eschatological prophet or teacher; and nothing which is reliably attributed to Jesus points towards cleansing.[31]

On the other hand we have from Jesus a saying about the destruction of the temple, and the gesture itself – overturning tables – points naturally towards destruction. Further, the prediction of destruction is well situated in contemporary Jewish eschatological expectation; and we do best to understand both the saying and the action in this context.

We now turn directly to the other themes which appear in the literature which looks forward to the restoration of Israel.

3

OTHER INDICATIONS OF
RESTORATION ESCHATOLOGY

From John the Baptist to Paul

Two of the things which are most securely known about Jesus are the beginning and the outcome of his career, and these are also two illuminating facts. Jesus began his public work, as far as we have any information at all about it, in close connection with John the Baptist, probably as a disciple.[1] Following his death and resurrection there was a movement which hailed him as Messiah, which spawned a Gentile mission, and which was – at least some times in some places – subject to 'persecution'.

The rise of the church has often been seen as being in distinction from, in fact in opposition to the intention of Jesus: Jesus proclaimed the coming of the kingdom, but it was the church that arrived. For the moment, we fix on only the point at which the church and John the Baptist, one pointing backward and the other forward, tell us the same thing about the life and work of Jesus: they were set in a framework of Jewish eschatological expectation.[2]

The reason for regarding Jesus as having been closely connected with John, perhaps dependent on him at the outset, has been often given: The Gospels and Acts strive to put John in a self-assigned subordinate role to Jesus; and the effort is so pronounced that it leads one to suppose that the opposite was the case, that Jesus began as a follower of the Baptist. The depiction in the Gospels should not, however, be so completely reversed that all connection is denied (as Enslin proposes), but should rather be seen as an admission of an ineradicable connection. The Christian need to relegate John to a subordinate place is seen most clearly in the Fourth Gospel (especially John 1.20, 'He confessed, he did not deny, but confessed, "I am not the Christ" '; 1.34,' "I have seen and borne witness that this [Jesus] is the Son of God" ';3.30, ' "he must increase, but I must decrease" ') and Acts (18.24–26, the baptism of John is inferior). In one respect, however, the Gospel of John points more clearly than do the synoptics to Jesus' actual discipleship under John. John has Jesus draw his first disciples from the ranks of the Baptist's followers (John 1.35–40). In John 3.22–24 and 4.1–3 Jesus is depicted as carrying out a mission which, while independent of that of the Baptist's, is similar in nature and near in locale.[3]

That John himself was an eschatological prophet of repentance is clearly implied in Josephus's account.[4] Further, the depiction of John and his message in the Gospels agrees with Josephus's view: the preaching in the desert; the dress, which recalled Elijah; the message of repentance in preparation for the coming judgment.[5] These features correctly pass unquestioned in New Testament scholarship.

The Gospels emphasize differences between John the Baptist and Jesus. They are presented as in some ways polar opposites. John was an ascetic (predicted in advance, Luke 1.15; cf. Mark 1.6 and parr.; Matt. 11.18//Luke 7.33), and his mission was to separate the wheat from the chaff (Matt. 3.12//Luke 3.17). He and his disciples fasted, while Jesus and his disciples did not (Mark 2.18f. and parr.). Jesus was known as 'a wine-bibber and a glutton' (Matt. 11.19 and par.), and his mission was to include sinners (ibid.). While it is possible that these contrasts have become schematized, there is no particular argument to be brought against any of them, and they probably point to remembered differences between the two men who stood in close agreement on the main task. There is in any case no reason to doubt the depiction of John as an eschatological preacher.[6]

For our purposes it is not necessary to try to decide what recognition, if any, John accorded Jesus.[7] It is more important, for the task of understanding Jesus, to discover how he saw his own work in relation to that of John. Matthew and Luke provide us with material designed to answer that question. Regrettably, it answers it too well. The prophets and the law held good until John the Baptist, who was in fact Elijah (Matt. 11.13f.). John here is given his customary role as the precursor of Jesus. More likely to be authentic is Matt. 11.11//Luke 7.28: No one born of woman is greater than John; but 'the least in the kingdom' is greater than he. As O'Neill points out, 'Jesus is not contrasting all begotten of women, with John at their head, and some other group of men, the least of whom is greater than John; he is contrasting the present state of the greatest of men with the future state of the least in the coming Kingdom.'[8] Later

Christians could have understood the saying to mean that the least member of the church is greater than the greatest non-member, but O'Neill's interpretation gives a plausible interpretation for the meaning of the saying in Jesus' own lifetime. God's kingdom, which will transform the state of things, is at hand. If John the Baptist was great, all the greater will be those who share in the fullness of the kingdom.[9] It follows that Jesus saw his own work as being the proclamation of the kingdom, which, it would appear, he regarded as the next and final step in God's plan of redemption. If Jesus considered John to be the greatest human in history, he probably thought that he himself was engaged in the final act of history (not necessarily that he himself was of a different order).

Of primary importance for our enquiry are the simple facts that Jesus started his public career in close relationship to John the Baptist and that the Baptist was an eschatological prophet who called Israel to repent in view of the coming kingdom. If it is true that Matt. 11.11 gives Jesus' estimate of John, then we may conclude that he saw his own work as being of final significance.

The letters of Paul provide abundant evidence that Jewish eschatological expectation stands at the conclusion as well as at the beginning of Jesus' career. There is, first of all, the expectation that the end of all things was near.[10] This can hardly be Paul's peculiar contribution to Christian self-understanding. It seems to be shared by the entirety of the early Christian movement, and Paul characterizes as 'the word of the Lord' the promise that those who are still alive when the Lord returns will not precede those who have already died (I Thess. 4.15).

But Paul's understanding of his own role in the final stage of history, which emerges especially in Romans, allows us to be more specific about what the expectation was. Paul describes himself as engaged in the mission to the Gentiles. He is an apostle of the last days, preparing 'the offering of the Gentiles' so that it may be acceptable (Rom. 15.16). Further, he is taking up a collection, which, besides being intended to relieve the poor, was probably understood symbolically as representing the tribute from the Gentiles. The expected scheme, however, has gone awry. Israel is not established and victorious. By and large, in fact, Israel has rejected Jesus as Messiah. Paul thus must revise the scheme: first the Gentiles will come in, and then, as a result of the Gentile mission, Israel will be saved (Rom. 11.13–16; 11.26f. ['thus']; 11.30f.). The revision of the scheme proves its existence and establishes beyond question the eschatological setting of the work of the apostles.

Paul, to be sure, revised Jewish eschatological expectation in other,

more far-reaching ways. Gentiles, he held, were on equal footing with
Jews. More radically yet, he argued that Jews must themselves join the
messianic movement. Even they were not members simply by being
obedient to the law.[11] But we may leave aside Paul's peculiar contributions
to Christian self-understanding and focus on the presupposition: the
Messiah has come; the whole people of God, Jew and Gentile alike, is
being gathered; the end is at hand.

Before Paul the new movement already stood out as distinct within
Judaism. It was identifiable and subject to 'persecution' (a subject to which
we shall have to return). Further, it had already started a Gentile mission.
Just as we may doubt the view of the author of Acts that Paul was primarily
apostle to the Jews of the dispersion,[12] so we may doubt that it was Peter
who first admitted Gentiles to the new movement (Acts 10). But it is
certain that the other Jerusalem apostles approved of their admission.
Peter visited a mixed church in Antioch (Gal. 2.11–14), and that church
had apparently been founded before Paul's conversion. Peter, James and
John did not immediately draw the same conclusions as did Paul about
the conditions on which Gentiles should be admitted – without requiring
circumcision and the rest of the law – and the lack of precision in the
prophetic predictions on this point left room for disagreement. It may be,
as Munck proposed, that they thought that Gentiles would be admitted
only after Israel had been established and thus had not thought about the
matter at all.[13] But the success of Paul and other missionaries to the
Gentiles (e.g., to Rome) certainly pushed the matter to the attention of
the 'pillars' in Jerusalem. And, according to Paul, they explicitly agreed
that Gentiles could be admitted to the eschatological people of God
without formal acceptance of the law (Gal. 2.6, 'they added nothing'), thus
endorsing what Paul, and probably others before him, had been doing.

Peter's withdrawal at Antioch (Gal. 2.12) probably tells us all we need
to know about his position. He approved of the Gentile mission and was
willing to eat with Gentiles who had entered the messianic movement; but
there were limits to his own participation with them, since he could not
afford to have his apostleship to the Jews fall into disrepute.[14]

Thus Peter and the others in Jerusalem saw the Gentile mission as
appropriate, though they themselves did not actively engage in it.[15] In case
there were any doubt about it, this puts Peter, James and John squarely in
the context of Jewish eschatological expectation. The movement which
they countenanced (Gal. 2.9) did not require full conversion to Judaism.
It thus did not fall within the context of normal efforts towards proselytism.
Its admission of the Gentiles, therefore, is to be seen as a natural result of

eschatological expectation, according to which Gentiles would turn to the God of Israel.[16] We should also recall the urgency with which Paul (and, presumably, the other missionaries) worked. His concern was to 'complete' the full 'circle' of the Gentile world, so that before the end 'the complete number' of Gentiles would have been admitted (Rom. 15.19, 'complete the gospel' 'in a circle'; 11.25, 'complete number of the Gentiles'; 13.11f., nearness of the end).

This leads us to one more important inference. A teacher and healer who is executed and believed by his followers to have been raised does not, simply on the basis of those facts, account for the rise of a movement which in a very short period of time starts the activity which characterizes the last act of an eschatological drama, the introduction of Gentiles. The first disciples must have been living already in the world of eschatological hope if they so readily countenanced the Gentile mission. Peter and the others, then, must already have been led to see Jesus' ministry as a key event in the fulfilment of the prophecies of the restoration of Israel and the submission of the whole world to the God of Israel. This leads us from the frame of Jesus' ministry directly to his own career.

The twelve tribes

Having noted the beginning of Jesus' ministry in adherence to the movement of John the Baptist (a movement which had as its aim the purifying of Israel in view of the coming judgment) and the outcome of his career (especially the mission to the Gentiles), it is natural to ask about Jesus' own stance on the restoration of Israel and the admission of the Gentiles. We defer the question of the Gentiles to a later chapter, and consider here the restoration of Israel.

We said above that the motif of the restoration of Israel figures more prominently in Jewish literature than that of the restoration or reconstruction of the temple.[17] It will be helpful to give fuller consideration to the theme, paying particular attention to two points: the relationship between the expectation of the restoration of all Israel and the survival of a remnant; the degree to which there was a definite expectation of the reassembly of 'the twelve tribes', as distinct from more general hopes for the freedom of Jews from foreign dominion (whether in the diaspora or in the land).

The remnant theme is a large one, and simply to quote all the relevant biblical passages would noticeably enlarge the size of the present work.[18] It is perhaps most prominent in such passages as Amos 3.12: the Lord will punish Israel for iniquity and will save only a remnant. Those who are to be saved are often described as the people who are 'humble and lowly', while the proud and mighty are destroyed (Zeph. 3.11–13). The remnant, however, can still constitute all Israel: 'I will surely gather *all* of you, O Jacob, I will gather the *remnant* of Israel; I will set them together like sheep in a fold' (Micah 2.12); God will 'assemble the outcasts of Israel, and gather the dispersed of Judah from the four corners of the earth', specifying the area embraced by Assyria, Ethiopia, and the Aegean coast (Isa. 11.11f.). The references in Micah to 'Jacob' and in Isaiah to both 'Israel' and 'Judah' point to the fact that all twelve tribes are in mind.

In the post-biblical literature the theme of a threatened punishment which will leave only a remnant recedes. Remnant terminology, especially various terms designating the survivors as 'poor' and 'lowly', is often retained; but the emphasis is on reassembly, freedom from oppression and foreign dominion, punishment of the Gentiles and the like, not on the further winnowing of Israel.[19] The same tendency is seen in the liturgy of the synagogue.[20] Some have proposed that remnant theology remained strong, and that all the parties and sects of Jesus' day saw themselves as the remnant,[21] the 'true Israel'. But it is a striking fact that, in the surviving literature, no group applies either title to itself during its own historical existence.[22] Even those who thought that they were the only true followers of Moses, or the only ones who knew the correct interpretation of the covenant and its laws, nevertheless did not think of God's *reducing* Israel to coincide with their group, but rather of the reassembly of Israel under the covenant rightly understood.[23]

Before citing evidence I shall offer another generalization. Although there are numerous references to the reassembly or gathering of Israel which are very general, the expectation of the restoration of the twelve tribes is frequent and widespread.

Many of the passages which illustrate the hope for restoration have been listed in ch. 2, and I add here a supplementary collection which bears on the points just discussed.[24]

Baruch 4–5: Israel has been chastised by being given over to her enemies. What lies ahead is the punishment and subjugation of the nations. Israel will be regathered 'from east and west' (4.37; 5.5).

Ben Sira 36: The author calls on God to crush and destroy Israel's enemies, to 'gather all the tribes of Jacob', and to 'give them their inheritance, as at the beginning' (quotations from 36.11).

Ben Sira 48.10: Elijah is ready to 'restore the tribes of Jacob'.

II Macc. 1.27f.: Jonathan prays to God to 'gather our scattered people', to 'set free those who are slaves among the Gentile', to 'look upon those who are rejected and despised', and to 'afflict those who oppress and are insolent'.

II Macc. 2.18: 'We have hope in God that he will soon gather us from everywhere under heaven into his holy place.'

Ps. Sol. 11 deals exclusively with the gathering of Israel from east, west and north, as well as 'from the isles afar off'. This shows that God has had pity on Israel.

Ps. Sol. 17.28–31: God will gather 'a holy people' and 'divide them according to their tribes upon the land'.

Ps. Sol. 17.50: 'Blessed be they that shall be in those days, in that they shall see the good fortune of Israel which God shall bring to pass in the gathering together of the tribes.' Cf. 8.34: gather the dispersed.

T.Mos: The twelve tribes are explicitly in mind in the early sections (see 3.4; 4.9). In the resolution of the work as it now stands, however, only 'Israel' is mentioned without further specification (10.7, punishment of Gentiles and happiness of Israel).

1QM: The twelve tribes will be represented in the temple service (2.2f.); all the tribes will supply troops (2.7f); the army is marshalled by tribes (3.13; 5.1). It is noteworthy that the *conquering* Israelites are called 'the poor' (*ebyonim*, 11.13; 13.13f.).

11QTemple 18.14–16: Twelve loaves of wheat bread are offered by the heads of the tribes. Cf. 57.5f.: a thousand from each tribe, thus twelve thousand.

The expectation that all twelve tribes will be assembled is continued in the post-70 period: see T. Sanh. 13.10 (R. Eliezer) and Rev. 21.12.

In general terms it may be said that 'Jewish eschatology' and 'the restoration of Israel' are almost synonomous. The idea that Israel will need to be purged of sinners is common enough in the post-biblical literature (e.g. Ps. Sol. 17.26), and even where it is not expressed it can hardly be ruled out. Will God save those who reject him? But the overwhelming emphasis is on the reassembly and redemption of Israel, not on its further reduction to a remnant. The Dead Sea Scrolls are, to be sure, notable for their hard line. In 1QM the final war (in which all twelve tribes will be represented) is against both the Gentiles and the 'wicked of the covenant' (1QM 1.2). The general thrust of the commentary on Habakkuk seems to be that the 'breakers of the covenant' (1QpHab. 2.6) will be destroyed. Much of the text is damaged, but the hatred of the 'Wicked Priest' and the 'Spouter of Lies' is so intense that it seems to require the assumption that the author or authors of the Scroll looked forward to the final destruction of their Jewish enemies. This seems to be predicted, for example, in 10.3–5 and 10.9–13. In light of this it is probably best to take 8.1–3 to refer to the salvation of some Jerusalemites ('those who do the Torah in the House of Judah'), who will be saved even when Jerusalem ('the House of Judgment') is destroyed, because of their loyalty to the Teacher of Righteousness.

Even in the Scrolls the hard line is not uniform. 1QSa 1.1–3 looks forward to the entry of other Israelites into the covenant in the last days, and one interpretation of 1QpHab. 5.3–6 would mean that the suffering of wicked Israelites, if in their distress they keep the commandments, would atone.[25]

We should finally note that in the Scrolls nothing is said about the Jewish Diaspora, which generally figures large in the hopes for the end-time restoration. The sectarian consciousness is here as elsewhere determinative. Yet even the Scrolls maintain the motif of 'the twelve'. Thus we see all the more that in the first century Jewish hopes for the future would have included the restoration of the twelve tribes of Israel. It is, as is widely acknowledged, against this background that we are to understand the motif of the twelve disciples in the Gospels. If not every text which looks forward to the vindication of Israel explicitly mentions the number twelve, it is nevertheless true that the expectation of the reassembly of Israel was so widespread, and the memory of the twelve tribes remained so acute, that *'twelve' would necessarily mean 'restoration'.*

The twelve disciples

The earliest evidence for the tradition that there was a special group of Jesus' followers called 'the twelve' is I Cor. 15.5, 'he appeared to Cephas, then to the twelve'. This is generally taken to mean that he appeared to Cephas alone, then to the twelve as a group (including Cephas).[26] A few manuscripts correct the reading to 'eleven', doubtless with an eye on the tradition of Judas's death,[27] but it is precisely this which confirms the reading 'twelve'. Scribes who were perfectly well aware of that tradition would not have corrected 'eleven' to 'twelve', thus the notion of 'twelve' is a fixed part of a pre-Pauline tradition. The second bit of firm evidence is Matt. 19.28, 'you yourselves will be seated upon twelve thrones judging the twelve tribes of Israel'.

The reasoning which allows us to consider the saying about 'the twelve' in Matt. 19.28 to go back to Jesus himself is the same as that which permits a clear judgment on the reading of I Cor. 15.5: it is unlikely that, after the betrayal by Judas, the church would have had Jesus include him as one of those who would sit on a throne judging Israel. If the betrayal is a historical fact, it is unlikely that the church would have moved from 'betrayal by a disciple' (a fact) to 'appearance to the twelve' (I Cor. 15.5), to 'betrayal by one of the twelve' (all four Gospels and Acts), and then to the creation of a saying by Jesus which 'enthrones' the betrayer. Thus we see that, *after* the story of Judas's betrayal became fixed, the number twelve would not have been introduced in Matt. 19.28, just as the church would not have invented the appearance to the twelve (I Cor. 15.5).

But is it not possible that the number twelve and the betrayal by one of them are both inventions, with the tradition of the twelve being created first? One could, with Vielhauer, argue thus: There was no circle of twelve around Jesus. A disciple did betray him. The church, living out of eschatological expectation, first fixed the number twelve for the disciples (I Cor.15.5) and subsequently, from another theological motive, created the legend of the betrayal.[28]

As is the case with most speculative hypotheses, such a view as this cannot be disproved. One can look only for probability, and in this case the cogency of the hypothesis depends on the strength of the theological motive for the creation of the legend of betrayal by one of the twelve. The betrayal argues decisively in favour of the authenticity of the twelve unless the betrayal itself is inauthentic. Vielhauer proposed that the church's creation of the legend of the betrayal was based on Ps. 41.9 (Heb. 41.10; LXX 40.10), which mentions betrayal by a table-companion. This verse is alluded to in Mark 14.18.[29] It is true that 'the church', in general, was interested in finding connections between Jesus' passion and biblical 'prophecies' and may well have created some traditions about the former in order to increase the number of echoes of Scripture. Yet this particular case is a very weak one. 'The church', as represented by Matthew (26.20–25) and Luke (22.21–23), who do not have the tag from the Psalm, does not seem to have been very interested in the connection. It is especially striking that Matthew, who best represents the tendency to create agreements between Jesus' life and teaching and the Bible, does not call attention to this one. Mark, in fact, does not call attention to it, and we cannot even speak of an actual quotation. Nevertheless, the theme of the passage as a whole (Mark 14.17–21 and parr.) may reasonably be held to emphasize, in accord with the Psalm, that it is a table-companion who betrays Jesus. But even if this be granted, it is still difficult to see that the concern to connect 'eating' and 'betrayal' in accord with the Psalm could have led to the assertion that one of the twelve, rather than some slightly more remote follower, betrayed Jesus. Vielhauer's proposal requires us to think that the presence of 'twelve' at the final meal (Mark 14.17 and parr.) is an invention, as is the betrayal by one of them. This double invention was, however, an embarrassment for the church, and it seems unlikely. Further, Vielhauer's view does not really account for the saying in Matt. 19.28. He regards it as inauthentic, but does not say why the church would have invented a saying which supposes the continuing existence of the twelve. One would have to find a third theological motive to account for the creation of this saying, and none seems to be forthcoming.

The embarrassment was handled differently by the evangelists. The later Christians had to explain that Jesus knew all along, or at least in advance, that Judas would betray him (Matt. 26.25; John 6.64, 71 and frequently in John).[30] Matthew also restricts the resurrection appearance to eleven disciples (28.16), while Luke attributes Judas' membership in 'the twelve' to the necessity to fulfil Scripture (Acts 1.16–20). Judas's action is conformed to prophecy in Matt. 26.15 (quoting Zech. 11.12), and the reminiscence of Psalm 41 in Mark 14.18 probably shows the same tendency: a fact is 'explained' by quoting Scripture, not invented on the basis of it. It is probably also embarrassment about the betrayal which led Luke to omit the word 'twelve' before 'thrones' in his parallel to Matt. 19.28 ('you will be seated upon thrones judging the twelve tribes of Israel', Luke 22.30). Goguel regarded this reading as rendering Matt. 19.28 dubious, and thus as constituting an objection to the use of the 'twelve tribes' saying to support the early tradition of 'the twelve',[31] but it is better to attribute it to Luke's editorial work. He and Matthew handle the embarrassment caused by Judas's defection differently, Matthew attributing foreknowledge to Jesus and restricting the number of those who saw the resurrection, Luke simply deleting the damaging part of the one saying which presupposes the continuation of the twelve around Jesus.

Thus the simplest and most probable explanation of the traditions about the twelve and Judas is that the church was faced with two facts: the existence of the twelve as a group (I Cor. 15.5; Matt. 19.28) and the betrayal by one of them. The rest of the references to Judas, including the echo of Psalm 41 in Mark 14.17–21, are readily explained as attempts to accommodate these two facts and to deal with the embarrassment caused by the defection of Judas. Just as we should not suppose that the church's attribution of an inferior role to John the Baptist indicates that there was no connection at all between the Baptist and Jesus, so we should not suppose that the theological/biblical explanations of Judas's betrayal mean that there was no betrayal by one of the twelve.[32]

Although I have included the existence of the twelve among the (almost) indisputable facts about Jesus, his career and its aftermath, it must be granted that it is the weakest item in the list. We have thus far not dealt with the fact which most raises doubt about Jesus' call of the twelve: the lists of names are not identical (Matt. 10.2–4; Mark 3.16–19; Luke 6.14–16; Acts 1.13).[33] This immediately raises the question of whether or not there were twelve identifiable special disciples. We should immediately note, however, that the slight variations in the lists are not readily explicable as a later creation. Why should the church invent the number twelve and then produce lists of names which disagree? The disagreements (it is noteworthy that they appear at the end of the lists) seem to point rather to the fact that the conception of the twelve was more firmly anchored than the remembrance of precisely who they were. As Gaston and Meye have pointed out, the disagreement about the names of some of the minor figures counts for, rather than against, the existence of a *group*, said to number twelve, during Jesus' ministry.[34]

We should here recall that Paul, quoting established tradition, used the number twelve when, if the betrayal is historical, there could not have been twelve. Vielhauer took the reference to twelve in I Cor. 15.5 and the story of the betrayal by one of the twelve to be flatly contradictory. He sought the solution, as we have seen, in a complicated theory of Christian inventiveness: the church created 'twelve' in the list of resurrection appearances and then the legend of betrayal by one of them. He was doubtless correct in seeing behind the number in I Cor. 15 an important symbol. It is likely, however, that the symbol was important to Jesus and did not first come into being after the resurrection. The variations in the names point in the same direction. It was Jesus who spoke of there being 'twelve', and the church subsequently tried to list them.

We encounter here historicity of a curious kind: the historicity of a symbol. In the earliest period (evidenced by I Cor. 15.5) noses were not counted. That it was some time before they started being counted is clear from the lists of names. 'Twelve' is a fixed number pointing to a group, and it was precisely the number which was remembered, whether or not it was strictly applicable, and even though it created several difficulties. 'The twelve' went by that title whether or not there were twelve of them.

The use of a symbolic number by Jesus himself saves all the evidence. Both of the difficulties which we have considered – the apparent contradiction between I Cor. 15.5 and the betrayal, and the variations in the lists of names – are explained if Jesus himself used 'twelve' symbolically. The number was not a subsequent creation, nor was the betrayal by one who, on any count, was one of the inner circle. The church followed Jesus in speaking of 'twelve' even when there could not have been twelve (I Cor. 15.5). One branch of it preserved a saying which predicted a future for the twelve (Matt. 19.28). It tried to tidy up the number in various ways (the change from 'twelve' to 'eleven' in some mss. of I Cor. 15.5; the lists of names; most elaborately Luke's story of the election of a new twelfth member, Acts 1.21–26), and it sought ways of avoiding the embarrassment which the betrayal created (it was predicted by Jesus; it was to fulfil Scripture; cf. also Luke's omission of 'twelve' in 22.30). All this shows the church struggling to accommodate a number which was ineradicable.

It seems to me quite reasonable to think that Jesus used the number 'twelve' symbolically, without anyone then, any more than later, being able to count precisely twelve. Symbolic numbers have to be thought up by someone, and they may or may not rest on precise enumeration (cf. Matt. 1.1–17). It seems to me more likely that Jesus employed the number than that the church first invented it and then had all sorts of difficulty with it, including naming the twelve. The twelve disciples are in one way like the seven hills of Rome: they are a little hard to find, although the idea is very old. In the case of the seven hills we cannot say that the founders of Rome created the idea, since the foundation of Rome was presumably not a single historical event; and if it were it would in any case be lost in the mists of time and legend. It is here that Jesus and the twelve are unlike Rome and its seven hills. The group around Jesus is not that remote, and their conviction that the kingdom was at hand and that the eschatological drama was unfolding is quite tangible. They got the general idea from somewhere, and the specification of 'the twelve' seems to go to the same source: Jesus.

The reason for dwelling on a point which is generally accepted is twofold. There is, first, the need to establish this and the other few facts on which our study is based 'beyond reasonable doubt'. Second, there is a need to question all the evidence, because of a growing tendency to accept the historicity of material which was once regarded as open to question, a tendency which has developed without firm warrant. I pointed out in the Introduction the growing confidence of scholarly assertions about Jesus, and perhaps it is time to remind ourselves that the confidence rests on neither new evidence nor new methods of establishing authenticity. The severe scepticism of the 1920s and 1930s has passed, but this is not justification for considering things which fifty or so years ago were held to be in doubt now to be among the firm results of scholarship.

The tradition of the twelve, to repeat, is the least firm of the facts on which this study rests. Yet even here we can say that the number indicates a concept which is very old and which probably goes back to Jesus. Other information about the disciples – their call, their prior histories,[35] a precise list of names (if there ever was, even during Jesus' lifetime, an invariable group of twelve) and their activity as followers of Jesus – cannot, in my view, be recovered. Almost everyone says that they did not represent a closed community,[36] a point which shows that the arguments of early scholars, such as Goguel and Guignebert, which were mostly directed against the idea of an apostolate,[37] were not altogether ineffective. It goes beyond our evidence to say that among the twelve were to be found representatives of the various movements in Judaism (strict Pharisees, 'zealots', tax collectors, Hellenistic Galileans and the like).[38] We do not know what activities they performed. The apostles subsequently both preached and performed 'wonders',[39] but that cannot be said with certainty of the disciples in Jesus' lifetime.[40] In particular, apart from what we learn from the symbolic nature of the number twelve, we do not know Jesus' purpose in calling them. Mark 3.14 says that it was for them 'to be with him', and that has recently been taken to be a plain statement of fact.[41] But Mark cannot have known what was in Jesus' mind. The call of the early disciples, so forcefully presented in the synoptics (Matt. 4.18–22//Mark 1.16–20; Luke 5.1–11), is intended for the edification of the church[42] and gives us no knowledge about how Jesus gathered about himself a small group of followers, at least some of whom turned out to be devoted to him after his death.

The question of what Jesus had in mind in gathering a special group of twelve shows once more the difficulty of recovering historical information on the basis of precise exegesis of individual passages in the synoptic Gospels. I have just indicated that I regard Matt. 19.28 as on the whole authentic. If it is authentic, it confirms the view that Jesus looked for the restoration of Israel. We would also learn that restoration includes judgment. But what if it is not authentic? Trautmann discusses the text and the Lucan parallel at length[43] and finally offers a reconstructed saying (p. 196), which, however, she does not trace back to Jesus (pp.197–9). She argues as follows: (1) The formation of the twelve by Jesus for the purpose of judging their own people at the eschaton would have been, in view of Jesus' own efforts on behalf of Israel, 'a contradiction in itself'. (2) Further, one must deny that the circle of Jesus' followers was limited to the twelve, which is what the saying in Matt. 19.28 presupposes (p. 199). Trautmann thinks, however, that the sending of the twelve to Israel (Matt. 10) is historical (pp. 200–25), and she argues for the authenticity of Matt. 10.6, 'go to the lost sheep of the house of Israel', which, she urges, could derive neither from contemporary Judaism nor from the early church (pp. 224f.). The 'lost sheep' stand for all Israel, and thus Jesus' calling and sending of the twelve symbolizes God's will to include all Israel in the eschatological kingdom (p. 228).

Trautmann's arguments about Matt. 10.6 and 19.28 seem to me not to hold good. I do not know why the judgment of Israel is excluded by Jesus' own efforts on behalf of Israel. Salvation of 'all' and punishment of some are not mutually exclusive, nor are redemption and judgment (see Ps. Sol. 17.28f.). I also do not see that the saying about the twelve judging the twelve tribes presupposes that Jesus had only twelve followers, any more than would a tradition that he sent out twelve. On the other hand, there is good reason to doubt the authenticity of Matt. 10.6. I shall argue below that the basic theme of Jesus' mission to the 'sinners' ('the lost sheep') is authentic, but that not all passages which repeat that theme go back to Jesus. To name an obvious example, the inclusion of tax collectors and sinners in Luke 15.1 is editorial. Trautmann's argument from double dissimilarity points only to the authenticity of the theme of the inclusion of 'the lost sheep', not to the historicity of the mission of the twelve to them. It would not have pushed Christian creativity very hard to attribute to the disciples the goal assigned to Jesus.

Thus we disagree completely on how to evaluate Matt. 19.28 and 10.6. Further, I doubt that the theme of the 'sinners' and the 'lost sheep' points necessarily to the inclusion of all Israel. Nevertheless, we agree that the twelve symbolize the inclusion of all Israel in the coming (Trautmann, 'inbreaking') kingdom. The fact is that the number twelve itself, *apart from the details of any individual saying*, points to 'all Israel'. *All we have to know is the fact* that Jesus thought of, and taught his followers to think of, there being 'twelve'.[44] We do not have to know that the same individuals were always meant, nor even that the followers of Jesus at any given time could name the twelve. We do not have to know that he sent twelve on a special mission, nor even that he said that the twelve would one day judge the twelve tribes. The more we know, the more precise our understanding will be, but we can see that Jesus fitted his own work into Jewish eschatological expectation if we know only that he *thought* of there being twelve around him.

It would, however, be helpful to know more, and we should consider two further arguments which attempt to specify more particularly the role of the twelve in Jesus' work and thought. O'Neill has argued that Jesus gave them authority,[45] and Jeremias that he sent them out with the admonition not to work.[46] In both cases, as is quite correct, evidence from Paul is important in the argument. O'Neill understands II Cor. 2.10 as stating that Paul can forgive 'in the person of Christ' (*en prosopōi Christou*), and he relates this to the saying about 'binding and loosing' in Matt. 16.19.[47] He also points to I Cor. 9.12–15 and Gal. 1.17f.; 2.2.[48] The former passage discusses the 'rights' or 'authority' (*exousia*) of the apostles, the latter indicates that even Paul granted to Peter a kind of primacy. These points correlate with Matt. 16.19 and 18.18, and together they support the view that Jesus himself gave the twelve authority.

·Jeremias combines I Cor. 9.14 ('the Lord commanded that those who proclaim the gospel should get their living by the gospel') with Matt. 6.25–33 (do not be anxious about what you eat and drink) to conclude that the disciples were sent out with the prohibition to do no work but to bear the message (cf. Matt. 10.10).[49]

It is beyond doubt, as Gal. 1–2; I Cor. 9.5; and I Cor. 15.5 show, that Peter occupied a prominent place in the early Christian movement. Precisely what this tells us about Jesus' view of Peter is rendered a bit difficult because of the role of James, both in I Cor. 15 and in Gal. 2. It appears that, if Jesus gave Peter 'authority', he did not do so in such an unambiguous way that it could not be shared with James. The brothers of the Lord also complicate the question of the right not to work, since Paul assigns them the same privilege as the apostles (I Cor. 9.5). The brothers of the Lord are emphatically excluded from Jesus' own followers in the Gospel accounts (Mark 3.31–35; cf. 6.3). Further, the privileged people in Paul's view are, besides the brothers of the Lord, the apostles, not the twelve. The twelve, apparently with Peter at their head, are distinguished from the apostles, possibly with James at their head, in I Cor. 15.5, 7. Gal. 1.19 also puts James among the apostles, and Paul apparently considered Barnabas as an apostle (I Cor. 9.6). It is possible, though not certain, that Andronicus and Junia count as apostles (Rom. 16.7).[50] In short, the evidence from Paul opens up numerous lines of inquiry, but does not deal with 'the twelve', or with Jesus' followers more generally, in such a way as to allow us to enlarge on our few fixed points. It may well be that Jesus gave the twelve authority and told them that they need work only for the gospel, and that in Paul we see these rights being extended beyond the original circle, to include other apostles and the brothers of the Lord; but here we move beyond reasonable certainty to 'it may be'.

Thus I must conclude that we do not have completely firm evidence which would allow us to say more about what Jesus thought of the twelve and their task. What seems virtually certain is that the conception of 'the twelve' goes back to Jesus himself (though his closest companions at any given moment may not have consisted precisely of twelve men). His use of the conception 'twelve' points towards his understanding of his own mission. He was engaged in a task which would include the restoration of Israel.

Repentance

One of the themes of passages in Jewish literature which look forward to the restoration of Israel is the need for repentance, and the same theme appears often in connection with the inclusion of the Gentiles. Classical Hebrew has no word which is translated 'repent', 'repentance'. The prophets frequently called for errant Israel to 'return' (*shub*), and the verb occurs frequently in the great text on individual repentance, Ezek. 33.7–20 (translated in the LXX as *apostrephō*). I shall not attempt here a history of the development of the noun *teshubah*, 'repentance', which became standard in Rabbinic Hebrew, nor of the verb and noun *metanoeō* and *metanoia*, which are so common in the New Testament.[51] Nor shall we consider the use of 'turn' and 'repent' for the correction of intra-covenantal sins. Our purpose instead is to note the way in which the concept of repentance is frequently tied to the restoration of Israel and the entry of the Gentiles.

In Isa. 44, which concludes with the prediction of the rebuilding of Jerusalem and the temple, God assures Israel that he will not forget them (44.21):

> I have swept away your transgressions like a cloud,
> and your sins like mist;
> return to me, for I have redeemed you (Isa. 44.22).

Similar is Isa. 55. After the promise to make with Israel 'an everlasting covenant' (55.3), Israel is urged to 'return':

> Let the wicked forsake his way,
> and the unrighteous man his thoughts;
> let him return to the Lord, that he may have mercy on him,
> and to our God, for he will abundantly pardon (55.7).

In Baruch 2.32f., looking forward to the restoration of Israel, the author predicts that 'they will remember my name, and will turn from (*apostrephō*) their stubborness and their wicked deeds'. Then God will 'bring them again into the land . . . ' (2.34). In 4.28 the author urges Israel to 'return (*epistrephō*) with tenfold zeal to seek him'. Similarly in Tobit 13.5f. we read: 'If you turn (*epistrephō*) to him with all your heart and with all your soul . . . then he will turn to you.' The passage concludes with the prediction of the glorious rebuilding of Jerusalem (13.16f.). In Ps. Sol. 18.4–7 God's chastisement produces the return (*apostrephō*) of Israel, and God then cleanses them 'against the day of mercy and blessing'. In Jubilees the redemption of Israel from Gentile captivity is to be preceded by their turning to the Lord:

> And after this they will turn to Me from amongst the Gentiles with all their heart and with all their soul and with all their strength, and I will gather them from amongst all the Gentiles. . . . (1.15).

> And after this they will turn to Me in all uprightness and with all (their) heart . . . , and I will circumcise the foreskin of their heart and the foreskin of the heart of their seed, and I will create in them a holy spirit, and I will cleanse them so that they shall not turn away from Me from that day unto eternity (1.23).

The motif is repeated in the eschatological section, ch. 23:

> And in those days the children shall begin to study the law,
> And to seek the commandments,
> And to return to the path of righteousness (23.26).

In the Dead Sea Scrolls, 'turn' is used for conversion to the sect:

> The group was called, among other things, 'those who turned from (repented of) iniquity',[52] and the covenant was a 'covenant of repentance' (CD 19.16). As the psalmist puts it, 'There is hope for those who turn from transgression and for those who abandon sin' (1QH 6.6).[53]

Finally, we may note that in Philo repentance immediately precedes the restoration of dispersed Israel. Those who have gone astray, writes Philo, will be punished. If, however, they accept punishment as chastisement from God, and 'reproach themselves for going thus astray, and make a full confession and acknowledgement of all their sin', they will be restored.

> For even though they dwell in the uttermost parts of the earth, in slavery to those who led them away captive, one signal, as it were, one day will bring liberty to all. This conversion [*metabolē*] in a body to virtue will strike awe into their masters, who will set them free . . . (*De Praemiis* 162–5).

Terminology which indicates repentance also appears in connection with the Gentiles. According to Jer. 3.17f., when 'all nations shall gather' to Jerusalem, 'they shall no more stubbornly follow their own evil heart'. 'Turn to me and be saved' the Second Isaiah cries to the Gentiles on behalf of God (Isa. 45.22). The author of the Jewish Sibylline Oracles depicts the Gentiles as crying, 'Come, let us all fall upon the earth and supplicate the Eternal King . . . . Let us make procession to His Temple' (Sib. Or. 3.716f.).

It cannot be said that there is anything like a strict correlation between the language of repentance and either the assembly of Israel or the entry of the Gentiles. Not only does repentance have a much wider range (being used for the individual correction of transgression), but also many of the predictions of end-time salvation focus on God's action rather than the human attitude which accompanies it. Thus in Jer. 33.7f., where God predicts the restoration of the fortunes of Judah and Israel, the accent is on 'I': 'I will restore . . . I will rebuild . . . I will cleanse them from all the guilt of their sin . . . '. Ps. Sol. 17 puts the emphasis on the action of the Davidic King: 'He shall not suffer unrighteousness to lodge any more in their midst' (17.29). We thus cannot say of repentance, as we said of the twelve, that the theme itself signals the redemption of the end-time.[54] On the other hand, it would be very surprising for a herald of the eschaton not to invoke the mighty theme of the nation's need to turn to God. If this were combined with the prediction of God's coming to cleanse, purify, and heal, both sides of the repentance/cleansing scheme would be present. An individual's message might emphasize one more than the other; but it is also fair to say that one implies the other.

General books and articles about Jesus or Jesus' teaching generally posit as a major and distinctive aspect his message of repentance and forgiveness.[55] An appreciable amount of the evidence comes from his reputation for consorting with 'tax-collectors and sinners'. This topic and certain allied ones we leave aside for the present; they will be returned to in the next part, on Jesus' conception of the kingdom. We may remark here that, if repentance characterized Jesus' message, it would not have distinguished it from others. There is no theme which is more common in Jewish literature, and repentance is also a major element in some presentations of the early Christian message.[56] What is of interest at the moment is the observation, which may be surprising, that there is very little evidence which connects Jesus directly with the motif of collective, national repentance in view of the eschaton.

This is, of course, the major theme in what the Gospels narrate about John the Baptist. Matt. 3.2 depicts him as saying, 'Repent; for the kingdom of heaven is near', and in the material which is approximately parallel (Mark 1.4//Luke 3.3), he is said to have proclaimed a baptism of repentance unto forgiveness of sins. Those who came out to hear him were baptized 'confessing their sins' (Matt. 3.6//Mark 1.5). In the most substantial body of sayings material attributed to him, he is said to have urged his hearers to bring forth 'fruit worthy of repentance' (Matt. 3.8//Luke 3.8). There is an apparently editorial addition in Matt. 3.11 which reiterates that his baptism was 'unto repentance'. In Acts 13.24 the author attributes to Paul the statement that John 'preached a baptism of repentance to all the people of Israel', and a similar statement is attributed to Paul in Acts 19.4.

Thus it seems that virtually everything which the early church remembered about John had to do with repentance and forgiveness.[57] This picture, we noted above, is confirmed by Josephus (*AJ*. XVIII.116–19). From the Gospels we also learn that the motive for the call to repentance was that 'the kingdom is near' and that 'already the axe is laid to the root of the tree' (Matt. 3.10//Luke 3.9).

The material attributed to Jesus which connects repentance to the nearness of the kingdom is, relatively speaking, slight. There is, of course, the summary statement in Matt. 4.17//Mark 1.15 that Jesus preached repentance in view of the nearness of the kingdom. This, however, seems to be misleading as a pointer to the thrust of Jesus' message.[58] There are otherwise only three substantial passages in which Jesus is depicted as calling for repentance on a wide scale: the woes against Chorazin, Bethsaida and Capernaum (Matt. 11.21–24//Luke 10.13–15); the favourable comparison of Nineveh, which repented at the preaching of Jonah, with 'this generation', which has not repented (Matt. 12.38–42//Luke 11.29–32); and Luke 13.1–5 ('unless you repent you will all likewise perish').

The parables about God's seeking the lost (Luke 15.3–6; 15.8f.), once the Lucan conclusions are removed (Luke 15.7, 10), are seen to be focused not on repentance, but on God's action. Another Lucan saying, that one should forgive one's brother who repents (Luke 17.3f.), is not evidence of a call for the return of Israel. The other sayings about repentance appear either to be editorial (the summary in Mark 6.12; Luke's addition 'unto repentance' in 5.32); or they otherwise give signs of lateness (Luke 16.30: 'If someone goes to them from the dead they will repent'; Luke 24.47, which is attributed to the risen Lord). It should be added that the early speeches in Acts emphasize repentance (Acts 2.38; 3.19). The second passage is connected to the expected parousia.[59]

In line with our general principle of not having this treatment depend on balancing the arguments for and against the authenticity of sayings, I do not want to spend much space on assessing the reliability of the three principal passages which call for general repentance. It is worth noting, however, that not one of them looks very sturdy. Bultmann quite correctly considered together Matt. 11.21–24 (woes on the Galilean cities) and Matt. 12.41f. (this generation and the Ninevites). He observed that in both cases Gentiles are contrasted with unrepentant Israel, that both have the same structure, and that in both there is 'a refrain-like repetition of the reproach'. His conclusion was in agreement with that of Fridrichsen: 'the impression is given that both passages have been constructed according to "a scheme of early Christian polemic".'[60] Luke 13.1–5 he dismissed even more quickly: it shows dependence on Josephus, *AJ* XVIII.87.[61] Others have found authentic bits in these passages,[62] and the saying about Jonah has produced a good deal of debate; but the uncertainty that hangs over the saying is well expressed by Perrin:

> What did this [the sign of Jonah] mean in the teaching of Jesus? The answer to this question is simply that we do not know, because we do not know what Jesus and his contemporaries would have understood by the phrase . . . [63]

The result of all this is that there is not a single solid piece of information about Jesus that indicates that he was what Matthew and Mark, at the outset of their Gospels, depict him as being: one who called for *general* repentance *in view of* the coming kingdom. Even Jeremias, who regards all three passages as authentic in whole or in part, regards Luke 13.1–5 as the only passage which indicates that Jesus preached the same message as John the Baptist.[64] Schlosser, on the other hand, is of the view that only Mark 1.15 explicitly connects repentance and the coming kingdom.[65]

Scholars often, to be sure, claim that the call to repentance was central to Jesus' message. Riches states that 'at the heart of Jesus' ministry and preaching lie his sayings about the Kingdom and repentance'. He adds that 'such a message sets him clearly in the ranks of those who sought a renewal and restoration of Judaism'.[66] He is certainly correct that the expectation of restoration would typically be coupled with a call to repentance. The problem comes in asserting that the connection is made in the teaching of Jesus. Riches' footnote to the statement about repentance indicates that he is aware of the problem, for he can refer only to statements about 'watchfulness'. Further, his subsequent summary of sayings which fit 'all the known prophetic types' does not have a section on 'repentance',[67] which should have struck him as odd if Jesus' message in fact had at its core a call to repentance.

We can see the situation even more clearly by considering the list of passages cited by Charlesworth as showing the 'permeating plea for repentance that is preserved in many of Jesus' parables'. He refers to the Sheep and the Goats (Matt. 25.31–46); the Lost Sheep (Matt. 18.12f. and par.); the Sower (Matt. 13.1–9 and parr.); the Unrighteous Steward (Luke 16.1–13); and the Great Supper (Matt. 22.1–14).[68] This is an interesting list, and it serves nicely to show that 'repentance', particularly a call for national repentance, with which we are here concerned, must be read into the message of Jesus. Matt. 18.12f. does have to do with repentance, but apparently individual repentance. The other passages do not mention the subject. Matt. 25.31–46 is focused on the admission of the Gentiles (see 25.32) and can hardly be authentic. In any case, repentance is not mentioned, but rather good deeds. There is no repentance in Matt. 13.1–9 or Luke 16.1–13. Matt. 22.1–14, far from being a call to repentance, threatens destruction of the wicked. Charlesworth, in the course of his article, argues that the apocalypticists threatened destruction rather than called for repentance, and that the theme of repentance distinguishes Jesus from them.[69] Here we have, however, destruction but not a call to repentance in a parable attributed to Jesus.

Other scholars take the theme of the separation of the righteous from the wicked in sayings of Jesus to constitute a call for repentance. Thus Conzelmann refers to the parables of the Tares and the Fishnets, both parables of separation, as showing that Jesus preached repentance.[70] It could be argued that the distinction of the righteous from the wicked, coupled with a threat of the destruction of the latter, implies a demand for repentance, and it may well do so. In this case, however, the same implication should be found in the apocalyptic passages to which Charlesworth refers. The situation is this: there is not a significant body of reliable sayings material which *explicitly* attributes to Jesus a call for *national* repentance. If sayings about the separation of the righteous and the wicked and the destruction of the latter imply such a call, they would serve to fit Jesus into the mould of eschatological preachers.

Sayings concerning forgiveness have, as might be expected, little eschatological thrust. The disciples are to pray for forgiveness (Matt. 6.12, 14//Mark 11.25//Luke 11.4). It is emphasized that Jesus has the power to announce the forgiveness of an individual's sins and thus to heal him (Matt. 9.2–6//Mark 2.3–11//Luke 5.18–24). Blasphemy against the Holy Spirit will not be forgiven (according to Matthew, either in this age or in the one to come [Matt. 12.31f.//Mark 3.28f.//Luke 12.10.]). Matt. 18.21f.//Luke 17.3f., as already noted, has to do with one individual's forgiving another. Luke 7.47–49 concerns the individual forgiveness of the woman who anoints Jesus. According to Luke 23.34 Jesus prays for the forgiveness of his executioners. Mark 4.12 ('unless they turn and be forgiven') is too enigmatic to be helpful. The story of the father with two sons (Luke 15.11–32), though it lacks the words, is clearly a story of repentance and forgiveness; and it makes the same point as the related parables in Luke 15.3–10: there is more joy over a repentant sinner than over the righteous who have no need of repentance. Luke also emphasizes the efficacy of the repentance of the unrighteous in the parable of the Pharisee and the tax-collector (Luke 18.9–14).

One saying which would be very important, if we could have confidence in its reliability, is Matt. 26.28, 'the blood of the covenant poured out for many for forgiveness of sins'. If authentic, the passage could mean that at his last meal, after which he would not eat or drink again until the kingdom arrived, Jesus looked for wholesale repentance and forgiveness. The phrase, 'for forgiveness of sins', however, is missing in all the parallels (including I Cor. 11.23–25), and it is best taken as an editorial addition.

Without doing an analysis to sort out authentic traditions from additions, we may nevertheless observe that national forgiveness is even less in view than national repentance. We do not have the equivalent material to what we find, for example, in Baruch 2 and Tobit 13 (cited above): if Israel will turn to God, he will restore their fortunes.

I am not arguing that Jesus did not 'believe in' repentance and turning to God. I presume that, as a good Jew, he did so. The theme of the inclusion of the lost (ch. 6 below) points to his deep belief in reconciliation between sinners and God. I am not, in short, proposing that Jesus suffered from some deficiency in his commitment to cherished religious abstractions. We are now considering Jesus against the backdrop of standard Jewish expectations and hopes for restoration. In this connection I am arguing (1) that there is no firm tradition which shows that he issued a call for national repentance in view of the coming end, as did John the Baptist; (2) that 'forgiveness' in the message of Jesus does not take on the tone of eschatological restoration; (3) but that, if Jesus had called for national repentance, or if he had promised national forgiveness, he would fit quite comfortably into the category of a prophet of Jewish restoration.

There is a surprising element in the material which we have just briefly surveyed. The gathering of the twelve, the start under John the Baptist, the post-resurrection activity of the apostles, and the action in and saying about the temple clearly point to the well-known eschatological expectation that God would renew his worship, save those who turned to him, and reassemble Israel. One would have expected, accompanying these clear signs, an emphatic call to all Israel to repent in view of the coming end and the explicit promise that God's forgiving mercy would be extended in saving and restoring his people. But the emphatic call and the explicit promise are missing. New Testament scholars have not, I think, sufficiently registered surprise over this situation. Most, in fact, would deny that it exists. But there it is. The great themes of national repentance and God's forgiveness, shown in restoring his repentant people, are prominent in all the literature which looks towards Jewish restoration. Jesus fits *somehow* into that view of God, the world and his people; but his message curiously lacks emphasis on one of the most important themes in the overall scheme.

The evangelists, in fact, seem to have felt the lack of emphasis as a deficiency. They add sayings about the need to repent (Mark 6.12; Luke 5.32; especially Matt. 4.17//Mark 1.14f.). Luke also, we have noted, links the need for repentance with the parousia in Acts 3.19. Thus the relative lack of material cannot be attributed to the evangelists' reluctance to include it. On the contrary, they felt it necessary to remedy the paucity of sayings. Jesus *must* have called on Israel to repent (Mark 1.14f.), and he *must* have told his disciples to preach the same gospel (Mark 6.12); and so the sayings were added. We should, however, take it to be a fact that a call to all Israel to repent did not figure prominently in Jesus' message.

Judgment

We saw above, in discussing the theme of the reassembly of the twelve tribes, that in the post-biblical literature there is not the same emphasis on the sifting or winnowing of Israel which one sees in some of the biblical prophets. That is not to say, however, that the themes of judgment and punishment for transgression recede. What recedes is the theme that Israel as a nation needs the sort of punishment which leads to the survival of a faithful remnant. The belief in judgment and punishment, which was intimately tied to the view that God is just, remained undiminished. Belief in the punishment or destruction of the wicked, and just retribution against even the righteous for their transgressions, is so common that it is almost unnecessary to give examples.[71] I offer three, however, the first two from different sections of I Enoch, the third from the Psalms of Solomon. They illustrate the continuing belief in the judgment of both groups and individuals.

I En. 25.3f.: God's 'true judgment' condemns the 'accursed', while the righteous bless God 'for the mercy in accordance with which He has assigned them (their lot)'.

I En. 90.26: At the judgment the blinded sheep are 'judged and found guilty and cast into [the] fiery abyss'.

Ps. Sol. 9.9f.: 'He that doeth righteousness layeth up life for himself with the Lord;/And he that doeth wrongly forfeits his life to destruction;/For the judgment of the Lord are (given) in righteousness to (every) man and (his) house.

The synoptic Gospels attribute to Jesus a rich variety of sayings and parables which threaten or imply judgment and punishment. Riches has recently proposed that Jesus deleted the standard theme of vengeance in his teaching about the kingdom,[72] but that statement, to be maintained, requires the deleting of a great number of passages. Bultmann lists fourteen sayings about judgment, and he adds that other sayings can be 'classed as Warnings', the first of which is the saying that the first shall be last and the last first (Matt. 19.30; Mark 10.31; Luke 13.30).[73]

Some of the threats or sayings implying damnation are seen to be Christianized, such as Mark 8.38//Luke 9.26: The Son of man will be ashamed of whoever is ashamed of 'me and *my words*'. The Christianization seems to point to an earlier form, and there is another version of the saying in Matt. 10.32f.//Luke 12.8f., where Jesus is depicted as saying that the one who denies him will be denied by him (Luke, by the Son of man). One may, to be sure, doubt the authenticity of this form as well, and in fact most of the sayings given by Bultmann in this section may be queried on some ground or other. I previously proposed that the woes against the Galilean cities (Matt. 11.12–24//Luke 10.13–15) reflect the Gentile mission, as does the saying about this generation and the Ninevites (Matt. 12.41f.//Luke 11.31f.). The other sayings against 'this generation' of Israel probably also mirror the Jewish rejection of the gospel (Matt. 23.34–36//Luke 11.49–51; cf. Luke 23.28–31; Luke 13.28//Matt. 8.12).

Schlosser has recently canvassed the material on judgment, and he has concluded that at least two sayings are genuine: Mark 9.47//Matt. 18.9 (better to enter with one eye than to be cast into Gehenna with both); Luke 12.5//Matt. 10.28 (fear the one able to cast you into Gehenna).[74]

Scholars give higher marks to the parables. There is one parable of destruction, Luke 13.6–9, on cutting down the barren fig tree. Other parables imply destruction by affirming selection: the parable of the Tares (Matt. 13.24–30); the parable of the Drag-net (Matt. 13.47–50). One supposes that the final verse of the second parable (furnace of fire, weeping and gnashing of teeth) is Matthew's contribution, since the phrases appear predominantly in Matthean material (Matt. 8.12; 13.42; 22.13; 24.51; 25.30; also Luke 13.28); but there is no reason to reject the parables as such.[75]

I have already argued that Matt. 19.28, which assigns the judgment of Israel to the disciples, is authentic. That there was a very early expectation that Jesus' followers would participate in the judgment receives confirmation from I Cor. 6.2: 'Do you not know that the saints will judge the world?' While Matt. 19.28 indicates that Jesus expected a judgment, however, it does not point to a message to Israel along those lines. It is not a call to Israel, but a communication to the disciples about their role, and it should be considered in the context of such passages as the Dispute about Greatness (Matt. 18.1–5 and parr.; cf. Matt. 20.20–28 and par.), as bearing on Jesus' expectation and that of his disciples (see ch. 8). It appears that the disciples expected judgment of others, selection of some and rejection of the rest, and even distinction by rank among themselves. Jesus' teaching may have included all these aspects. What is surprising is that the evidence for a *message* about the coming judgment of Israel is so slight.

Thus our evidence is this: Jesus was not opposed to the idea of judgment. He expected there to be a selection, which implies a judgment. He did not, however, address a message to Israel to the effect that at the end there would be a great assize at which Israel would be vindicated and the nations rebuked and destroyed; and it seems that he did not make thematic the message that Israel should repent and mend their ways so as to escape punishment at the judgment.

We noted above that the parables of selection may reasonably be taken as implying a call to repentance, but that there is no explicit evidence that Jesus was a preacher of national repentance. Our discussion of judgment points in the same direction. If the two parables of selection constitute the only public teaching or proclamation about judgment which goes back to Jesus (which may be the case), there is a clear implication that hearers can act in such a way as to be among the select group – i.e., repent. But there is equally clearly the implication that the selection will be of individuals. It is conceivable that the person who directed such parables to hearers as individuals could also, on other occasions, have fixed his view on the direct action of God, who alone is able to bring about wholesale redemption. The twelve tribes – that is, the Israel of standard expectation – cannot be assembled by waiting for individual commitment, but it is perfectly possible for Jesus to have talked about both individual change and group redemption. The problem is that we do not find teaching material or proclamation which calls on all Israel to repent and which looks for the redemption of the Jewish people. As a corollary to this, we now observe that there is no explicit teaching material about a judgment which would weed out the unworthy from Israel.

We shall return to the question of Jesus and the Jewish people in the conclusion to this chapter and at other points in our study. Here I note that the authentic sayings which imply judgment raise questions about Jesus as a prophet of the eschatological restoration of Israel, the same question which is raised by the study of repentance. We find, as we would expect, the theme of judgment, but we do not find teaching or proclamation which depicts or predicts the impending judgment of the nation of Israel. We would have expected such a message to accompany the expectation that Israel would be restored.

Conclusion

We have been enquiring about the degree to which Jesus' work can be seen as pointing towards Jewish restoration. That the question of 'restoration' was in the air is indicated by the appearance of the verb 'restore' in the Gospels: 'Elijah must first restore all things' (Matt. 17.11//Mark 9.12; cf. Mal. 3.24 [ET 4.5]). The full phrase is in Acts 1.6, 'Will you at this time restore the kingdom to Israel?' The exchange in Matthew and Mark relates Jesus positively to the hope for restoration, by identifying John with Elijah, while the question in Acts is turned aside by the risen Lord, and the general implication is negative: the kingdom will not be 'restored' to Israel according to the flesh. Modern scholarship has also seen Jesus' work in both ways.

That Jesus intended to restore Israel in some sense has been often said (e.g. by Caird),[76] just as it has been said that 'not a word does he say either to confirm or renew the national hopes of his people' (Bornkamm).[77] Can the issue be decided? I think that the study of three of our themes thus far (the temple, the context between John and Paul, and the twelve) settles the matter in broad terms: Jesus intended Jewish restoration. One must still ask in what sense he did so. Nuance, as always, is less certain than the broad picture.[78] Most scholars will agree that Jesus did not have in view military victory and political autonomy along the lines of Ps. Sol. 17. It at first appears that, when he denies that Jesus was concerned with 'the national hopes' of his people, Bornkamm means to deny only this sort of national hope.[79] The emphasis in his discussion does seem to fall there, and one must observe that it is inadequate to define the national hope in terms of a Davidic Messiah, which is one of the least frequent themes in Jewish literature. Bornkamm, however, proceeds to argue that at least implicit in Jesus' parables is a form of universalism, and in this context he cites the saying from Matt. 8.11 about many coming from east and west.[80] Thus he apparently wishes substantially to deny that Jesus intended anything that could fall under the term 'Jewish restoration'. We shall have occasion to consider the saying in Matt. 8.11 later, but here it should be noted that, if it is authentic and refers to Gentiles, it need not push Jesus' message beyond the framework of Jewish restoration. The hope of restoration generally included the theme of the inclusion of Gentiles.

It is not surprising that Caird sees Jesus as intending the restoration of Israel and Bornkamm does not, for the former emphasized such *facts* as Jesus' baptism by John and the call of the twelve, while the latter followed the majority procedure of focusing on Jesus' *teaching*. The large outline, which includes the principal facts about Jesus' career and its aftermath, points towards his being a prophet of the restoration of all Israel; but the sayings material does not fit entirely comfortably into that scheme.[81] The teaching attributed to Jesus is markedly *individualistic*, as we have seen in discussing repentance.[82] If one takes the right selection from it, one can say with Breech that there is no reason for thinking that Jesus shared any of the religious ideas of his contemporaries.[83] Bornkamm takes a larger selection, but sees nothing to convince him that Jesus looked for national restoration.

It was, in fact, precisely when we turned to sayings material that the picture of Jesus as one who would restore Israel began to blur: it appears that he did not, at least as a major theme, call for national repentance. We must doubt the authenticity of most of the passages that depict him as doing so, either because they conform his message to that of John the Baptist (e.g. Mark 1.15 and par.), or because the condemnation of Israel and praise of Gentiles makes one suspect the activity of the later church (Matt. 11.21–24; 12.41f.). We have also seen that sayings about judgment (except for Matt. 19.28) do not have a national scope.

Part of this argument is reminiscent of that of Ernst Bammel, who pressed it much further. On the basis of a source analysis of the sayings material, he proposed that one should doubt the eschatological thrust of Jesus' message. The theme of the nearness of the kingdom was imported, he argued, from the preaching of John the Baptist.[84] Bammel's analysis of the sayings about the kingdom deserves careful consideration, but the facts keep us from accepting his far-reaching conclusion.

I would reply similarly to the arguments of C. E. B. Cranfield about eschatology in the New Testament. He proposes that passages which indicate that the end is near did not mean 'in a few years or decades', but more generally that the life, death and resurrection of Jesus mark the beginning of the end-time, which might last for an extended period.[85] Here I would first disagree about the interpretation of the principal passages in Paul, which seem to mean 'in our lifetime' (e.g. I Thess. 4.16f.). In the present context, however, I must urge that the facts about Jesus, his predecessor and the Christian movement indicate that he himself expected the kingdom to come in the near future. In ch. 8 I shall argue that Jesus and his disciples even expected to play a role in the kingdom, obviously in the very near future.

Barry Crawford has recently stated the matter precisely: the sayings often regarded as establishing Jesus' expectation that the kingdom would arrive in the near future may not go back to him, though other evidence may establish that he held this view.[86] I think that we have such evidence in hand.

The situation with regard to Jesus' hope for the restoration of Israel is comparable. Here the importance of deciding on the right method is clearly seen. We know with a good deal of certainty that Jesus was baptized by John, thought of there being 'twelve' with him, acted against the temple, and predicted or threatened its destruction. That his followers worked within the framework of Jewish eschatological expectation is indisputable. We must doubt that a major aspect of his preaching was a call for national repentance, but we must also be less certain about his preaching than about these five facts. What we know with almost complete assurance – on the basis of facts – is that *Jesus is to be positively connected with the hope for Jewish restoration*. The fact – as it now becomes in our study – must set the framework and the limits of our understanding of him. Whatever else we say about him, whatever modifications are necessary, the basic framework of his ministry must be respected. Despite the observation that the teaching and preaching material may not be just what we would expect of a prophet of restoration, and despite the reluctance of many scholars to identify Jesus with Jewish hopes for restoration, the facts compel us to fit him into that context.

The reluctance to think that Jesus hoped for the restoration of Israel has often been connected with the view that such a hope is narrow and unworthy. Jesus is frequently depicted as breaking out of the confines of the national religion, which obviously must include his being opposed to nationalism itself. It is easy to show that Jesus did not look for a political and military restoration, and this can be used as an argument against his having thought in terms of national restoration of any sort. I do not wish to enter into a debate on the merits of Jewish nationalism, although I shall offer the remark that, for the most part, the literature in which hopes for restoration are expressed focuses on the action of God and puts foremost the need of repentance and righteousness. Our concern must be only to describe as precisely as the evidence allows the view which is to be attributed to Jesus. I have argued that the themes of *national* repentance, forgiveness and judgment are largely absent from the sayings material. I do not, however, take it that this proves that Jesus opposed Jewish nationalism. There are, on the contrary, clear and undeniable indications that he expected the restoration *of Israel*; temple and twelve are national symbols. In this context it is noteworthy that his message largely omits the typical *means* for the achievement of restoration. That Jesus did not think that national restoration would be achieved by arms is not especially surprising.[87] What is surprising is that, while looking for the restoration of Israel, he did not follow the majority and urge the traditional means towards that end: repentance and a return to observance of the law.

We have not yet achieved precision and nuance in understanding just how Jesus thought of restoration and what it would involve, but we have begun to see that his thinking differed from that of John the Baptist. It is now time to turn more fully to the teaching material.

PART TWO

THE KINGDOM

4

THE SAYINGS

When broaching a topic which cannot be conveniently handled, scholars often indicate their own coming difficulties by saying that it is one of the 'most difficult' and 'most discussed' problems of scholarship. The present author is no exception, and I have used that formula more than once. We are now at a point where the apology is fully justified. There are several main problems: What is the basic conception of the kingdom in the message of Jesus? If that can be settled, what else can one say? What is its range of meaning? When is it to come, or if it has already come, in what sense? What is the relationship between Jesus and the kingdom which he proclaimed? In theory, the answers to these questions require one to have at hand a reliable solution to the source problem, a complete form-critical analysis of most of the pericopes in the synoptics, and a set of criteria to establish the authenticity of the sayings material. As I have pointed out before, it is partly the degree of uncertainty in all these regards that has led me to seek an alternative way of describing Jesus' intention and his relationship to his contemporaries. Nevertheless, we must now pay attention to the sayings material – although the attention which will be paid to it will not be that most common in New Testament scholarship. After a short prologue, I shall offer an example to illustrate the reasons for which the questions have proved hard to answer, and then proceed to a more substantial consideration of the problems involved in the study of 'Jesus and the kingdom'.

The kingdom as eschatological reality

As every student who has taken an introductory course in New Testament knows, Johannes Weiss 'discovered' that the kingdom of God in the message of Jesus was eschatological: it is a supernatural event which Jesus expected to occur in the immediate future.[1] Albert Schweitzer lent force to this discovery principally by a brilliant account of nineteenth-century, largely German New Testament scholarship, showing that each person's view of the message of Jesus was determined by his own predilections and philosophical stance and, most of all, by the horizons of the modern world-view.[2] The distinctiveness of the first-century Jewish world-view then sprang to life with marvellous clarity: that world-view was eschatological (or apocalyptic),[3] and Jesus obviously shared it.

Schweitzer's own reconstruction of the ministry of Jesus was, among other things, highly arbitrary, and it is easily dismissed. Further, Schweitzer was not a scholar of Jewish literature, and he largely depended on collections and studies which were easily accessible – that is, in German – at the time he wrote.[4] Some of the misconceptions of his treatment of Jesus arose from his falsely attributing 'dogmas' to first-century Judaism. The most obvious example is one which is a keystone of his argument: suffering *must* precede the coming kingdom.[5] It is difficult to find that view in material which can be dated before 135 CE.

Glasson has offered a more complete criticism of Schweitzer's view: his eschatological scheme did not exist at all. Glasson focuses on one of Schweitzer's main themes, that a heavenly figure (the 'Son of man') would come and that the kingdom would involve the end of the present world.

> Messianic beliefs become more and more diversified, and there is nothing resembling the scheme put forward with such definiteness by the Schweitzer/Bultmann school. When a Messiah is mentioned he is of the warrior type. There is no transcendent figure descending in glory to conduct the last judgment.[6]

Glasson's statement is quite true. The picture of the Son of man coming to judge, and the like, is derived from the synoptic Gospels.[7] We have observed earlier that a Messiah is not common in material which reflects eschatological expectation. Yet there *was* eschatological expectation: the hope that God would vindicate and restore Israel.[8] Since the motifs which cluster around that great theme vary (son of David, new temple, admission of the Gentiles), we might speak of various restoration theolog*ies*. It seems to correspond better to the evidence, however, to think of a *common* (presumably not universal) *hope for the restoration of Israel* which could embrace a variety of themes. We might particularly note Glasson's argument against the expectation of an otherworldly kingdom. That is an aspect of Jewish eschatological hope which is by no means always made clear. Even in literature which has an otherworldly solution to the problem of Israel's subjection, as does the Testament of Moses, it can be argued that the transcendent aspect is only a figure for a worldly victory.[9] We shall return to the question of Jesus' own expectation in this regard, and we shall find the same problem of interpretation. For now, however, it must be emphasized that in Judaism there was widespread hope for future, decisive change – whether of an earthly or an otherworldly character. As we have seen in our study thus far, Jesus shared that hope. The framework of his career is eschatological, and we have already seen firm evidence that he himself looked for the restoration of Israel.

Glasson's article is praiseworthy because he responds to Schweitzer's view in a scholarly way, on the basis of historical research, rather than by evading the obvious by the semantic device of denying that by 'kingdom' Jesus meant 'kingdom'.[10] Further, Glasson is correct about the particular points on which he focuses. Yet the general point, that Jesus expected a kingdom and that his expectation can be understood in the context of the expectations and hopes of his contemporaries, still stands. Weiss and Schweitzer hit upon something, even if they got some of the details wrong, and Schweitzer in particular forced into the limelight a real problem.

Before taking up the principal responses to Schweitzer, we should note a recent development in works on the kingdom, the assertion that it is a symbol rather than a concept or idea. Later in this chapter we shall turn often to two works by Norman Perrin which nicely represent mainline, consensus scholarship. Here, however, we should note the different stance which he took in one of his last works, *Jesus and the Language of the Kingdom*, 1976. He argued that it is not 'legitimate to think of Jesus' use of Kingdom of God in terms of "present" and "future" at all'.[11] The reason for the 'illegitimacy' of this distinction is that 'kingdom of God' is not a conception, but a symbol, consciously employed by Jesus 'because of its evocative power'. Jesus intended by using it to challenge his 'hearers to take the ancient myth [of the kingdom] with renewed seriousness, and to begin to anticipate the manifestation of the reality of which it speaks in the concrete actuality of their experience'.[12]

Bernard Scott wishes to take this view further and criticizes Perrin only for not completely denying conceptual content to the word 'kingdom'. It is a symbol to the *exclusion* of concept.[13] Jesus 'experienced Kingdom',[14] but the experience could not be expressed in discursive speech.[15] He employed 'kingdom' as a symbol to express his experience.

To no small degree both Perrin and Scott regard it as an 'insight' that 'kingdom' is a symbol rather than a concept, and the case is simply asserted more than it is argued.[16] There are, however, arguments. We have just noted one, that Jesus did not (add: as far as we know) define 'kingdom' in discursive speech. The second is that the meaning of 'kingdom', if it were a concept, could not have been self-evident (as Schweitzer, for example, assumed), since the term could have meant different things to Jesus' audience. This point is buttressed by the observation that scholars have difficulty retrieving a self-evident meaning of the word.[17]

These observations are at least partly accurate, but they do not constitute persuasive arguments. Both statements could be made about 'kingdom' in Paul's letters. He did not define 'kingdom' in discursive speech, and it presumably had an appreciable range of meaning for his audience. The meaning of the term in Paul's letters is not especially difficult, but nevertheless a certain vagueness is observable if one asks just when it appears and what its nature is or will be. It is future, as the verb 'will inherit' indicates (I Cor. 6.9f.; 15.50; Gal. 5.21). Further, 'flesh and blood' will not inherit it (I Cor. 15.50), and it will be handed over by Christ to God (I Cor. 15.24). Thus it is also otherworldly. On the other hand, I Cor. 4.20 shows that it is present: 'For the kingdom of God does not consist in talk but in power.' From this we could conclude that the 'kingdom' is present wherever and whenever God's power is active. This gives a vaguer definition than is implied by 'kingdom' in I Cor. 15, where it is a future reality which will exist after the total elimination of hostile forces. Thus we see that 'kingdom' can only with some difficulty be given a precise definition even in material which is much easier to handle than that of the synoptic Gospels. We should not, however, conclude from this that the word had no conceptual content.

It is my own view that we can know the meaning of 'kingdom' in the teaching of Jesus with something close to the same degree of certainty as is possible with Paul. That is, we can know in general what is meant, although we can be sure neither of every nuance nor of the full range of meaning. The scholarly disagreements to which Scott appeals, in fact, have to do precisely with nuance and range. We should all agree that 'kingdom' is a concept with a known core of meaning: the reign of God, the 'sphere' (whether geographical, temporal or spiritual) where God exercises his power.[18] If the kingdom 'comes', the result which is asked in the Lord's prayer, the opposition to God is eliminated. For Paul, this will be a cosmic event: Christ will hand over the kingdom and God will be all in all (I Cor. 15.24–28). Thus Paul expected a real future event, an event which could be called 'the kingdom', but he neither defined the term in discursive speech, nor did he always use it in the same way. Just as the lack of explicit definition and the variety of meaning do not lead to the conclusion that, in Paul's usage, 'kingdom' is a conceptionless symbol, they should not do so in the case of Jesus. We have, in any case, already gathered enough evidence to know that Jesus had *ideas*. Presumably some of them contributed meaning to one of the chief words in his vocabulary.

We do not have in the teaching of Jesus anything quite as explicit as I Cor. 15.24–28, 50 – which we would not have if the Corinthians had not had a problem with the resurrection. The closest approximation in the Gospels is the reply to the Sadducees (Mark 12.18–27 and parr.). We cannot simply use this passage to give more precise definition to Jesus' conception of the kingdom, since we do not know that it is authentic. Our constant worries about authenticity, however, also do not constitute evidence that Jesus had no conception of the kingdom. On the contrary, I propose that *we know perfectly well what he meant in general terms: the ruling power of God*. This part of our study will seek to demonstrate that, but will primarily be concerned with probing for nuance, range and precision.

From a different stating point, James Breech reaches conclusions which are in part complementary to the view that 'kingdom' in the teaching of Jesus did not express a concept.

> Judging from the core sayings and parables, there is absolutely no basis for assuming that Jesus shared the cosmological, mythological, or religious ideas of his contemporaries. The core sayings and parables are absolutely silent about such concepts as heaven and hell, resurrection of the dead, the end of the world, the last judgment, angels, and the like. Thus we cannot approach Jesus as a 'historical personage' . . . .

Breech continues by stating that the sayings and parables do not point to history as the locus of activity, that the parables 'do not teach or illustrate ideas', and that neither sayings nor parables 'reflect any relationship with either traditional Jewish canons of conduct (the Law) nor of Graeco-Roman ideals of man or the moral personality'.[19] The dislike of common first-century Jewish hope and thought, which marks much of New Testament scholarship in a more disguised way, could hardly be more clearly expressed.

I doubt that many will be persuaded by Breech's aggressive ahistoricism, but I shall nevertheless raise a few points which count against his view. This will also lead to further criticism of Scott and the late Perrin, and finally back to our more general problem, the use of the sayings material.

First, we should note that the list of elements which, in Breech's analysis, the sayings material does not contain is entirely dependent on the passages which are assigned 'core' status. A large number of sayings, at least some of which I regard as authentic, do have history as their locus. We have already discussed the saying about the judgment of the twelve tribes (Matt. 19.28), and we shall have occasion to consider the saying about drinking wine in the kingdom (Mark 14.25 and parr.). Different scholars will have their own lists, but I doubt that many will completely exclude such common ideas as that God acts in history. Secondly, Breech – here sharing what I regard as a common failing – derives information only from sayings and parables. Thirdly, the fact that parables do not refer to history is not surprising. Parables are not historical analogies, nor (replying here to Scott) are they discursive speech. Their failure to be what they are not does not prove much of anything – certainly not that Jesus had no conception of the kingdom, nor that he had no ideas in common with his contemporaries. Were we to read through all the Tannaitic parables, and apply the reasoning of Scott and Breech, we would conclude that the Rabbis of the Tannaitic period had no interest in present or future history, though a little in *Heilsgeschichte*; that they were not concerned with purity; that they cared not a whit for precise definition and application of the law; but that they had experiences of God's grace which they could not express directly. Any genre of speech or literature imposes certain limitations, and for that reason one should not limit one's information about people or groups to what can be learned from one genre, if that can be avoided. We should not look for legal detail in prayer, nor for personal piety in law codes. Generations of New Testament scholars have been misled about Rabbinic religion, in no small part because they took the Mishnah, a document largely occupied with legal detail, to *be* the religion of the Rabbis. The blatant methodological error of equating a piece of literature with a world-view also governs the latest description of the thought-world of the Mishnaic Rabbis, that of Jacob Neusner.[20] Neusner's work is influenced in part by structuralism, as is Scott's. Users of the method should remember that it is deliberately ahistorical, and that historical results cannot be immediately attained by structural analysis of a given body of literature, especially when it is dominated by one genre. One must hope that the recent healthy interest in literary criticism, which mostly centres on the parables, will not mislead New Testament scholars into thinking that the parables and some closely allied sayings, and nothing else, provide us with Jesus' 'world'.

The fourth point is addressed equally to the views of Perrin, Scott and Breech. It is our standard point that we should look at the results. It is perfectly apparent that Jesus' followers ended up with ideas about God and the kingdom. To suppose that their ideas were based on a total misunderstanding is to recreate in modern form the Marcan apologetic theme of the incomprehension of the disciples. The Pauline letters show us that the apostles and brothers of the Lord (I Cor. 9.5) were acting as leaders of a Jewish eschatological movement. Unless the entire scheme – which is a complete scheme, including a Messiah and extending to the final act, the inclusion of the Gentiles – was imparted via the resurrection appearances, where did it come from? One must doubt that the resurrection appearances implanted that many *ideas* in the minds of the disciples. Presumably they were already thinking along those lines while they were following Jesus. Breech and Scott seem to think that Jesus fooled everybody and was totally enigmatic.[21] There is every reason to think that he was partially enigmatic, but it is extremely unlikely that the disciples completely misunderstood. It is best to continue to suppose that Jesus, like other people, had ideas and that those ideas had some relationship to first-century Judaism.[22]

I do not doubt that those who find the teaching attributed to Jesus in the synoptics to be rich, nuanced, subtle, challenging and evocative are finding something which is really there. Further, in view of the apparent inability of early Christians to create such material,[23] I do not doubt that the teaching of Jesus contained some or all of these attributes. In short I do not doubt that he was a great and challenging teacher. The insight that Jesus was an evocative teacher helps to explain his following, and we shall presently attempt to assess the significance of that. For the present we focus on the sayings material with a view to understanding the questions with which we began: Jesus' relationship to his contemporaries, his intention, the causes of his death, and his role as originator of what became a distinct movement within Judaism. Admiration for sayings which are profound and multivalenced, correspondingly, will play a minor role. Our interest must be fixed on what Jesus said, thought and did which bore on the hopes of his people and which had results. This means that we should stay with the kingdom as an idea with identifiable content.

Present and future: the problem of the sayings material

In protesting against the views that Jesus' teaching reflects a conceptionless, symbolic use of 'kingdom', or was unrelated to the thinking of his contemporaries, I do not wish to argue that information of historical importance about him is easily and certainly to be derived from a study of the sayings material.[24] On the contrary, the difficulty of that material is one of the reasons for the strategy of the present study. If ahistorical methods of studying the sayings reflect frustration at the difficulty of deriving clear and unambiguous meaning, one may well sympathize.

We can exemplify the problems involved in using the sayings material and also press ahead with the question of the eschatological character of Jesus' message by returning to one aspect of the theme of the kingdom which was brought to the fore by Weiss and Schweitzer and which has continued to dominate most discussions: the question of the coming or the time of the kingdom.

Here as elsewhere Schweitzer had a perfectly clear position: the kingdom would be a cataclysmic event, one which Jesus first expected in his own lifetime. It would coincide with the harvest.[25] His disciples were to go out and suffer, (suffering being the pre-condition of the arrival of the kingdom),[26] and the kingdom would come with Jesus as its Viceroy.[27] The disciples went forth, but they did not suffer, and the kingdom did not come. Jesus took the matter of suffering into his own hands, thinking thereby to force God to bring in the kingdom.[28] He died, but dying saw that his expectation was to be disappointed: 'My God, my God, why hast thou forsaken me?'

Two of the most notable works of the two most notable scholars of twentieth-century New Testament research are attempts to respond to Schweitzer. The response is acknowledged in the case of Dodd, unacknowledged but nevertheless perfectly apparent in the case of Bultmann.[29] At first it appears that Bultmann accepted Schweitzer's basic definition: 'There can be no doubt that Jesus like his contemporaries expected a tremendous eschatological drama.'[30] Further, it was the standard drama of Jewish expectation: 'He took for granted as did his contemporaries that *the Kingdom of God was to come for the benefit of the Jewish people.*'[31] But one does not read much further before discovering that this has been conceded on one level only to be retracted on another, the level of meaning: 'The coming of the Kingdom of God is therefore not really an event in the course of time, which is due to occur sometime and toward which man can either take a definite attitude or hold himself neutral.'[32] We shall not digress from the problem of understanding Jesus to the problem of understanding Bultmann, a task which itself has created an appreciable body of literature.[33] It is evident, however, that in terms of common speech the first and third statements quoted above are, *if* they refer to Jesus, simply self-contradictory. If Jesus 'like his contemporaries' expected an eschatological drama, then it would have been 'an event in the course of time' which he expected.

Dodd's approach was very different. His response to Schweitzer was not hermeneutical and semantic, but exegetical:

> This declaration that the Kingdom of God has already come[34] necessarily dislocates the whole eschatological scheme in which its expected coming closes the long vista of the future. The *eschaton* has moved from the future to the present, from the sphere of expectation into that of realized experience. It is therefore unsafe to assume that the content of the idea, 'The Kingdom of God,' as Jesus meant it, may be filled in from the speculations of Apocalyptic writers. They were referring to something in the future, which could be conceived only in terms of fantasy. He was speaking of that which, in one aspect at least, was an object of experience.[35]

The point of rehearsing this history, which is well known to most of the readers of the present work and is in any case already sketched in part in the Introduction, is to come to the following point: readers of Dodd almost universally agreed that he had a point, but overplayed it.[36] Ever since, scholars have been trying to discover how to strike the balance between Weiss and Schweitzer on the one hand and Dodd on the other. This, in turn, has thrown the problem into the hands of the exegetes, who have thought that the balance could be struck if only it were possible to decide on the authenticity of each saying, the original wording of it (i.e., the underlying Aramaic), and its original setting and connotation. Kümmel put the matter precisely:

> This great divergence between the conceptions proves that not only the exegesis of several ambiguous passages is disputed, but that the sum total of the original evidence for Jesus' eschatological message is appraised entirely differently, and that therefore a correct decision can be obtained only by examining the complete record of Jesus' preaching.[37]

This view, that a sufficiently careful exegesis of the sayings material will lead to 'a correct decision', has led many a New Testament scholar into a quagmire from which he has never emerged. The quagmire is produced by treating the synoptic Gospels as if they were the letters of Paul (or the work of any single author writing in his own language): as if by sufficiently careful attention to what they say one can discover with precision and nuance what Jesus thought. This is, of course, in theory possible. If one could hit on the passages which report accurately what Jesus said, if one could rediscover the setting in which he said it (one of the first rules of exegesis is that meaning depends on context), and if one could then correlate sayings on a given topic with others on the same topic but in a somewhat different context, one could presumably discover what Jesus basically thought on that subject and what nuances there were to his thought. That is a great goal, and the theoretical possibility of achieving it by studying the sayings material leads to ever more involved exegetical efforts, and often to over-exegesis: hammering away at a saying in the hope that it will tell us more about Jesus than can reasonably be expected from a small piece of evidence.

The real situation should be faced more frankly. We can seldom recover original context, and thus understanding of the nuance and range of a conception is very difficult to achieve. It will help if we make an analogy (or rather contrast) between 'Jesus and the kingdom' and 'Paul and the law'. In the case of Paul, we know what law he was talking about, we have statements about it in different contexts which are subject to fairly successful reconstruction (e.g. the polemical situation of Galatians and the parenetic situation of Rom. 13), and it is possible to determine his fundamental stance and variations on it which derive from changed contexts. That is, of course, just what scholars have tried to do with 'Jesus and the kingdom'. We start off on good ground: we know basically what 'kingdom' he was talking about. But then the contrasts set in. It is as if an author or authors had written a composite work called 'the Gospel of Paul' and set into diverse new settings such passages as Rom. 2.13; Gal. 2.16; Rom. 3.21; Rom. 8.4; II Cor. 3.6; then added some more sayings of their own; made the material available for use in preaching and teaching; and finally translated it into another language where it underwent still further adaptation and alteration. If Paul's letters had been treated in such a way, what chance would we have of understanding his view(s) of the law? Do we have a better chance of understanding Jesus' view of the kingdom *if all our information must come from sayings?* It will prove to be hard enough to establish the main lines, and nuance and precision will remain elusive. Just establishing the main thrust of Jesus' message about the kingdom will require the separation of sayings which have an authentic kernel from those which are entirely later products – a by no means certain enterprise. Nuance will depend on reconstructing both the authentic bits of the sayings material and the original contexts. The chances of making enough correct reconstructions to give both precision and nuance to Jesus' conception of the kingdom are, to understate the case, very slight. Worse, if anyone were to accomplish it, the rest of us would not know it.

Although the difficulty and uncertainty of reconstruction may have led some to pursue ahistorical means of studying the Gospels, others have insisted that exegesis must be done more carefully. Thus Martin Hengel has argued that 'progress in Synoptic research to a great extent depends on ... detailed analysis of small units', which is exemplified by his own treatment of Matt. 8.21f.//Luke 9.59f.[38] Every passage must be studied individually, employing 'redaction and form criticism, plus *Religions-geschichte*'.[39] It is hard to argue with Hengel's view, in light of the dazzling success of its application. I think that Hengel's book is a masterpiece, possibly the best single treatment of a synoptic pericope ever done. He sheds real light on how we should understand Jesus, and his conclusions are convincing. Why, then, do I remain sceptical about learning about Jesus by the precise exegesis of passage after passage? Hengel's remarkable success, unfortunately, does not show that the method will continue to pay off as one goes through the synoptics. Hengel picked the right passage. Others have not been and, in my view, will not be explored with even approximately equal results. The history of scholarship since Bultmann's *History of the Synoptic Tradition* seems to prove that to be the case. Passage after passage has been subjected to detailed analysis, but knowledge about Jesus does not move swiftly forward. The effort has not been entirely futile; or, put another way, it has been necessary to examine each passage in order to see what can and cannot be known. I regard most of the exegetical efforts of the last decades as proving a negative: analysis of the sayings material does not succeed in giving us a picture of Jesus which is convincing and which answers historically important questions.

For an example, we may turn to one of the most-discussed passages in the synoptics, Matt. 12.28//Luke 11.20. This is a verse which has for years loomed large in the discussion of Jesus and the kingdom. Matthew's wording is this: 'If I by the Spirit of God cast out demons, then the kingdom of God has come (*ephthasen*) upon you.' Luke's version is identical, except that it reads 'by the finger of God' instead of 'by the Spirit of God'. Dodd seized vigorously on *ephthasen*, and argued that it means that 'the "Eschatological" Kingdom of God is proclaimed as a present fact', and he extended this same understanding to *engiken* ('has drawn near') in Mark 1.15.[40] Bultmann read the same verses and concluded that the kingdom is like the dawn which is breaking but has not arrived, or is like a train coming into the station which has not arrived at the platform.[41] Perrin read the verse and pronounced quite confidently that it shows that Jesus thought that his exorcisms were a 'manifestation of the kingdom of God in the present'.[42] He went further: the verse shows that '*the experience of the individual has become the arena of the eschatological conflict*'.[43]

It is of course true, and must be immediately said, that each scholar thought that he had corroborating evidence for his interpretation. But even granting this, we must note that Matt. 12.28//Luke 11.20 is the linchpin of the argument.[44] Yet there are problems. The passage itself, 'the Beelzebub Controversy', is both complex and unusual.[45] One may read numerous attempts to analyse it.[46] The saying in Matt. 12.28 itself presents a puzzle, one which is often overlooked: has the kingdom of God 'come upon' Jesus' opponents and not upon those whom he healed?[47] We stay, however, with the common view of the verse:[48] (1) it is a detached saying which has come into the tradition without a context; (2) it is authentic; (3) it shows that Jesus thought that the presence of the kingdom was attested to by his exorcisms. Why are these things so? (1) It is detached because, if it went originally with the preceding verse ('If I cast out demons by Beelzebub, by whom do your sons cast them out?'), the meaning would be 'that the Jewish exorcists would also prove by their actions that the Kingdom of God had come',[49] and Jesus could not conceivably have thought that of the work of 'Jewish exorcists'. (2) It is authentic because 'it is full of that feeling of eschatological power which must have character-ized the activity of Jesus'.[50] (3) It means that the kingdom is present because *ephthasen* undoubtedly means 'has come'.[51]

I must confess that I do not find all this convincing and that I can imagine other possibilities. Even if we accept without debate the authenticity of the verse, we may still doubt that the prevailing opinion about its meaning is absolutely secure. In the first place, it seems to me obviously dubious to lean so heavily on the meaning of the verb *ephthasen*.[52] How can we know that the Greek verb accurately captures not only something which Jesus said but also the nuance which he intended to convey? Clearly we cannot. If, however, we must decide its precise meaning, we shall discover that it frequently means 'came' in the sense of 'the coming was determined', not 'the coming was accomplished'. When the author of the Testament of Abraham wrote that the 'cup of death' came (*ephthasen*) to Abraham (T.Ab. A 1.3), the patriarch still had more than nineteen chapters to live.[53]

Secondly, I do not know in advance (that is, unless this verse tells me so) that Jesus held the view that the casting out of demons was the expression of the appearance of the kingdom of God and that only the possessor of the end-time Spirit could do it: or perhaps that only his doing it really counted. The arguments for isolation, authenticity and significance are in part circular. They depend on a conclusion about how Jesus saw the relationship between his exorcisms and the eschaton, but the conclusion depends to no small degree on the saying in question. In part, however, the position attributed to Jesus – that his exorcisms were signs of the kingdom – is based on the view that the Messiah (or his herald) was expected in Judaism to overcome the demonic world and to demonstrate this victory miraculously by exorcisms.[54] If this were so, the probability that Jesus and others saw his exorcisms in that light would be enhanced. But in fact that view is hard to find. The evidence usually cited is T.Mos. 10.1 and T.Levi 18, only the second of which says just that;[55] and this hardly counts as evidence for a view common in Judaism. One suspects that the true source of scholarly belief in this supposed Jewish eschatological view is Matt. 12.28 – considered in isolation from 12.27. The entire argument about the isolation and significance of this verse for understanding Jesus' view of his work, it appears to me, depends more on circular reasoning than on anything else.[56]

Thirdly, it is not difficult to find evidence which leads one to attribute to Jesus another view of his exorcisms. Perhaps he thought that other people could cast out demons and that his doing it was no more proof of an alliance with Satan than was the same activity in the case of others. That is, after all, the major point made in Matt. 12.27f. as the passage now stands. What forces vv. 27 and 28 apart except the presupposition that Jesus *must* have been conscious of unique power and *could not* have ascribed the same power to others?[57] On this point, in fact, we have the curious double tradition about other exorcists, one passage saying that those not against Jesus are for him (Mark 9.38–41//Luke 9.49f.), the other that those not with Jesus are against him (Matt. 12.30//Luke 11.23). If either of those sayings is authentic and originally referred to other exorcists,[58] we have evidence in addition to Matt. 12.27//Luke 11.19 that Jesus did not consider his own exorcisms as unique. Further, the Marcan form (9.38–41) supports holding Matt. 12.27 and 28 together, for it positively allies other exorcists with Jesus.

If, then, we fixed our attention not on Matt. 12.28//Luke 11.20 in isolation, but on Matt. 12.27f.//Luke 11.19f., and on Mark 9.38–41//Luke 9.49f., we would come to a view appreciably different from that of Bultmann, Perrin and numerous others: namely, that Jesus attached the same significance to his own exorcisms and those of others. Can we be sure beyond reasonable doubt that one interpretation is true and the other false?

One will immediately say that there is other evidence that Jesus attached special significance to his ministry. That I shall by no means contest. But does the special emphasis fall on his ability to exorcize demons? Can his conception of the arrival of the kingdom be determined with nuance on the basis of Matt. 12.28//Luke 11.20? Those things do not seem to me in the least clear.

Let me repeat the decisions that scholars have to come to in order to derive from Matt. 12.28 information which allows them meaningfully to explain Jesus' understanding of the kingdom. One must first decide on the setting of the verse. In its transmitted setting, for the reason given by Kümmel, it is relatively innocuous. Once it is made an isolated saying, it must be argued that it is authentic. When that is decided, it must be supposed that in it Jesus *intended* to offer his own *decisive* interpretation of his exorcisms. Then one must presume that the wording has been carefully maintained in Aramaic, precisely translated, and carefully transmitted in Greek. Finally one must decide on the nuance of the principal verb: does it mean 'proleptically' present? virtually on top of us? fully arrived in all its force and glory? These exercises then must be repeated simply dozens of times and the results correlated before one can pronounce on the full meaning of 'kingdom of God' in the message of Jesus. And at the end, to repeat, no one will know whether or not all the decisions were right ones and all the synthesizing judgments sound.

I have deliberately picked on the strongest case in the arsenal of those who explain Jesus by interpreting the sayings in order to show the severe limitations of the method. There probably is no other verse in the Gospels about which there is so much unanimity. I do not hold the deep conviction that the common opinion is wrong. But I do not think that we shall actually move towards 'assured results' along the path which I have briefly traced. We shall return in the next chapter to the question of exorcism and other miracles. Here I wish to push further the point about what cannot be securely known about the kingdom of God in the teaching of Jesus.

We may profitably dwell for a moment on one of the other passages which supports the view that the kingdom is already present in Jesus' words and deeds: Jesus' response to the question of the Baptist, Matt. 11.2–6//Luke 7.18–23.[59] As has been often observed, the passage presents difficulties. Bultmann regarded the principal part of Jesus' reply, Matt. 11.5f. ('the blind receive their sight ... '), to have been an originally independent element. 'In all probability the Baptist's question is a community product and belongs to those passages in which the Baptist is called as a witness to the Messiahship of Jesus.'[60] The point of the core saying ('the blind see', etc.) 'is intended simply to take the colours of (Second) Isaiah and use them to paint a picture of the final blessedness which Jesus believes is now beginning, without any need to relate particular statements with particular events that have already happened.'[61] Bultmann did, however, regard the saying in Matt. 11.5f. as authentic.[62] Dunn's discussion makes it clear that the pericope is difficult to accept as an account of an interchange between John and Jesus, but he concludes by accepting it and offers a setting for it: it would have occurred 'as soon as the note of imminence characteristic of John's preaching was supplanted by or at least supplemented by the note of fulfilment characteristic of Jesus' preaching'.[63] But where does one hear that note of fulfilment which is 'characteristic' of Jesus' preaching? In Matt. 12.28 and 11.5f. And how do we know that that note is characteristic? In Bultmann's words, already referred to above in connection with Matt. 12.28: 'It is full of that feeling of eschatological power which must have characterized the activity of Jesus.'[64] When we recall the chain of assumptions and arguments (some circular) which were required to single out Matt. 12.28 as Jesus' decisive interpretation of his activity, especially the isolation of Matt. 12.28 from 12.27 and the efforts to find the precise nuance of *phthanein* – as if Jesus used the word – , it may begin to appear that scholars have become too confident about making 'fulfilment' and 'presence' the decisive and controlling characteristics of Jesus' message.

One of the principal things which is at stake in the labour expended on Matt. 12.28 and 11.5f. (and a few other passages which can be called in as support) is the distinctiveness of Jesus over against other Jewish prophets and exorcists, especially John the Baptist.[65] In order to maintain that the kingdom was 'somehow'[66] present in Jesus' words and deeds, especially in the exorcisms, and that these supposedly eschatological miracles set Jesus apart from others, the case has to be made, implicitly or explicitly, that Jesus was unique. Occasionally, I assume by an unfortunate choice of words, someone will seem to suggest that miracles were signs of the kingdom and that, since Jesus performed them, he brought the kingdom.[67] We must assume that Jesus was not the only miracle worker of his day, and I think that no one will seriously champion the view that he was. Recently Harvey has presented the argument that Jesus was unique in the *kind* of miracles which he performed, and that just these indicated the arrival of the time foretold by the prophets. This is an interesting proposal, but I think that it will not carry the day; it is returned to in the next chapter. Usually weight falls on the *uniqueness of Jesus' self-consciousness or claim*. 'Nowhere does John refer to any casting out of demons (as Jesus does), as a token that "the kingdom of God is upon you".'[68] 'There was something wholly distinctive, indeed *unique* about this consciousness of power' (referring to Matt. 12.28//Luke 11.20).[69] 'John believed that the end-time was at hand; Jesus believed that the shift in the aeons had already taken place' (referring to the two passages we have considered and one or two others).[70] According to Trautmann, nowhere in ancient Judaism does one find that a human act of exorcism brings about the inbreaking of the eschaton in the present world, that in a human deed God's kingdom breaks through.[71]

Thus we see that, in order to derive meaningful information about Jesus from such passages as Matt. 12.28, scholars must suppose not only that they can reconstruct precisely what Jesus said and precisely what he meant by it, but also that they can eliminate the possibility that anyone else held such views. This enormously increases the dubiousness of the method, which already requires hypothesis upon hypothesis. How can one argue historically that a certain attitude or conception is unique? A sober estimate in accord with the normal canons of the writing of history can go no farther than 'otherwise unattested'. But can 'otherwise unattested' on such a point as self-claim become decisive for understanding Jesus? We have virtually no evidence about what other first-century Jewish healers and preachers thought about the significance of their own work. We do have, of course, some information about John the Baptist, but it can hardly be thought that we know the full range of what he thought and said. Can we be sure that neither Theudas (Josephus, *AJ* XX.97–9) nor the Egyptian (*AJ* XX.168–72; *BJ* II.261–3) thought that the kingdom was breaking in with him as God's viceroy? I do not think that we can. In fact, it seems to me likely that such prophets thought that God was at work in them and would bring in his kingdom through them. To refer again to Trautmann's statement that nowhere else in Judaism, except in the Gospels, do we find that God's kingdom 'breaks through' in a human deed, we must say not only that our knowledge is severely limited, but also that it is entirely likely that the Jewish 'sign prophets'[72] thought precisely that. If one wishes to say that other prophets who might have thought that were *wrong*, and that in Jesus God's kingdom *really did break through* – and this often seems to be the intention[73] – then we have to note that the discussion no longer has to do with history, but with theological evaluation.

If the case is pressed that Jesus must have been unique because, among Jewish healers and preachers, only he left disciples who formed a major religious body (a point which will be returned to later), we must still admit that we cannot know that it was Jesus' consciousness that the kingdom was present in his words and deeds that accounts for the survival of Christianity. It is a fact that Christianity was uniquely successful, but that does not tell us what it was that made it so.

It will be helpful here to give a lengthy quotation from Kümmel, in which he applies Matt. 11.5f. to the questions of the meaning of Jesus' proclamation and its definitive characteristics. In it he indicates that we know the answers to questions which I think are unresolved.

So Jesus' reply to the Baptist's question claims that the acts and the message are to be regarded as a proof of the beginning of the Kingdom of God, and it sees this beginning taking place exclusively in Jesus and his activity. It is shown once more that the proclamation of the good news of the future coming of the Kingdom of God, which was Jesus' task, receives its particular and decisive character through the fact that the person of Jesus by his actions brings about already now what is expected from the eschatological future; thus the real meaning of the eschatological preaching lies just in this, that it points to the actual presence of him who will bring about salvation in the last days. Again attention has been turned away from the How and When of God's eschatological coming to the present messenger of this eschatological consummation.[74]

The case that is being proposed here is that we cannot, by analysing the sayings material, really know that such passages as those which we have been considering reveal 'the particular and decisive character' of Jesus' preaching of the kingdom, nor that 'the real meaning of the eschatological preaching' is that the one who will bring salvation in the last days is already present. We do not know, or at least not yet, what was 'expected from the eschatological future', which Kümmel here takes to be the things specified in Matt. 11.2–6. This last matter is deferred to the next chapter.

I am not arguing that Jesus did not attach special significance to his own ministry, nor that Matt. 12.28; 11.2–6 and the related passages can be proved to be inauthentic. I am not even arguing that we can know that Jesus did not think that in his words and deeds the kingdom was breaking through. The first concern is to assess the evidence, to distinguish what is beyond doubt from what is probable, and what is probable from what is possible. It follows from this that I do not wish to urge a negative case – for example, that Jesus did not see his miracles as signs of the kingdom – , since a negative can seldom be proved. What I propose is that we do not *know* things which we are often said to know. I would arrange conclusions about the material which has been discussed thus far as follows:

It is beyond doubt that Jesus proclaimed the kingdom. We know this not from analysing any one saying or group of sayings, but from noting the ubiquity of the theme 'kingdom'. We should especially note that (as we shall specify later in this chapter) the word 'kingdom' is applied to a large range of conceptions in the sayings material attributed to Jesus. Often the ideas are not novel, though the use of the word 'kingdom' may be. Expressions to the effect that the kingdom is near constitute such an instance.[75] That 'the day', or 'the end', is near would not be an unusual saying. The material attributed to Jesus stands out from contemporary Jewish and subsequent Christian usage in part because of the word 'kingdom' itself. It stretches credibility too much to imagine that the prominence of the term was invented, and the presence of the theme 'kingdom' is to be given the highest rating: beyond doubt.

It is also beyond doubt that Jesus attached special significance to his own career and saw it as intimately connected to the kingdom of God. This is seen from the demonstration against the temple and the call of the twelve. We need add to those two facts only the bare fact of the theme 'kingdom' in order to draw our conclusion.

It is possible – no more – that Jesus saw the kingdom as 'breaking in' with his own words and deeds.

It is conceivable – weaker than possible – that the wording of Matt. 12.28//Luke 11.20 and Matt. 11.5f. gives us his own precise interpretation of his work.

Of recent years this last point has been promoted to the status of one of the assured results of scholarship, and scholars have repeated again and again that Jesus thought that his exorcisms showed that the kingdom of God was present (Matt. 12.28),[76] as did his healings and preaching in general (Matt. 11.2–6). To conclude this discussion I shall here summarize the reasons for which I think it necessary to demote this view to only 'conceivable'. The third and fourth reasons, however, will not be fully presented until we have looked at more material about the kingdom.

1. The principal sayings which support the view that the kingdom was present in Jesus' work are not absolutely firm, either with regard to their original context or their precise wording – both of which are essential to the arguments based on them. It would, in fact, be impossible for us to know the precise wording of anything said by Jesus with sufficient assurance to place on it the weight which scholars lately have put on *ephthasen* in Matt. 12.28//Luke 11.20.

2. Even if we were to assume that Jesus held the view which we have been considering, we could not say that such a view was distinctively characteristic of him, since we do not know everything that John the Baptist thought about his own mission, and nothing about what other prophets before the first revolt thought about theirs. The fact that Theudas and the Egyptian thought that they could produce mighty signs (the parting of the river and the collapse of the walls of Jerusalem), however, indicates that they attributed considerable importance to their own roles in the divine scheme.

3. It is easily possible to offer a hypothesis in which other aspects of

Jesus' work and words are seen as 'central' and 'determinative' and in which the motif of the present dawning of the kingdom plays a subsidiary role. (For this hypothesis, see the conclusion to this chapter and ch. 8.)

4. The outcome of Jesus' career does not lend much support to seeing Matt. 12.28 and related passages as central to his own understanding of the kingdom and his role in it. (See below, p. 152 no. 2.)

The problem of diverse meanings

In making the analogy between 'Paul and the law' and 'Jesus and the kingdom',[77] there was the clear implication that the sayings about the kingdom which are attributed to Jesus are not all of a piece. That of course is the case, and it is what would be expected if he said very much about it.[78] There are various ways of categorizing the 'kingdom' sayings. The following sixfold one seems most helpful:[79]

1. 'Kingdom' in the sense of 'covenant', a usage which is well known from Jewish literature.[80] I put this first partly because it generally plays little role in discussions of Jesus' distinctive meaning,[81] and partly because I once erred by relegating this use of 'kingdom' to a footnote.[82] This meaning should be rescued from relative obscurity. A good example of the usage from Rabbinic literature is this:

> R. Joshua b. Karḥa said: Why does the section *Hear, O Israel* (Deut. 6.4–9) precede [the section] *And it shall come to pass if ye shall hearken [diligently to my commandments]?* – so that a man may first take upon him the yoke of the kingdom of heaven and afterward take upon him the yoke of the commandments (Berakoth 2.2).

In other passages Israel is said to have accepted the 'kingdom of God' at Mount Sinai.[83] Here 'covenant' could be used in place of 'kingdom' were it not for the Rabbinic tendency to restrict 'covenant' (*berith*) to mean 'circumcision'; that is, the covenant with Abraham. 'Accept the kingdom' may refer either to a daily renewal of commitment to God's covenant with Israel (as it does when one says the *Shema*‵), or to the fresh commitment which one makes at the point of entry into the covenantal community. There are also Rabbinic parables in which God is king, and in which his kingly role is that of the maker and maintainer of the covenant with Israel.[84] Although the phrasing is different, this meaning of 'kingdom' seems to be the one which is uppermost in the Gospel material which has to do with *entering* the kingdom. The parallel is not exact. The Gospel passages stress the individual's attainment of eternal life, while the Rabbinic passages are focused on commitment to the God who has redeemed and who will save Israel. But there is a general sense in which the sayings about 'entering the kingdom' are illuminated by the Rabbinic use of 'kingdom': there is a stipulation of commitment and obedience on the human side and the promise or implication of saving mercy on God's side. Some of the more interesting examples are these:

Matt. 7.21: 'Not everyone who says to me, "Lord, Lord, " will enter into the kingdom of heaven, but the one who does the will of my father in heaven.' The next verse speaks of 'that day' and thus ties in this usage with the eschaton.

Matt. 18.3//Mark 10.15//Luke 18.17: 'Unless you turn and become as children, you shall not enter into the kingdom of heaven.'

Matt. 19.23//Mark 10.23//Luke 18.24: It is hard for the rich (or those who have possessions) to enter the kingdom of heaven.

2. Closely related to this there is the thought of the kingdom as still to be fully established: 'Thy kingdom come!' (Matt. 6.10), a usage which has well-known parallels in Jewish literature.[85]

3. The kingdom will come as an otherworldly, unexpected event in which the righteous will be separated from the wicked. This differs from the preceding category because of the dramatic imagery which is employed. One of the major expressions of this view is found in material which is largely but not entirely peculiar to Matthew and in which the distinctive phrases are 'the consummation of the age' and 'angels'. An example is found in the Matthaean 'Interpretation of the Parable of the Tares': 'thus will be the consummation of the age: the Son of man will send forth his angels and they will gather all *skandala* and all those who do evil, and cast them into the furnace of fire' (Matt. 13.40–42). No one, I think, will maintain the authenticity of this pericope, but the language occurs elsewhere, among other places in one of the parables which immediately follow in Matthew (from which it may have come into the 'Interpretation'): 'The kingdom of heaven is like a net cast into the sea . . . . Thus it will be in the consummation of the age: the angels will come and separate the evil from the righteous' (Matt. 13.47–50).[86] The language also occurs in the 'little apocalypse', although the most precise verbal parallels are again with the Matthaean version: 'When will be . . . the consummation of the age?' (Matt. 24.3//Mark 13.4//Luke 21.7). The Son of man will appear (Matt. 24.30//Mark 13.26//Luke 21.27), 'and he will send his angels with a great trumpet and they will gather up his elect from the four winds . . . ' (Matt. 24.31//Mark 13.27). There are two further Matthaean repetitions of two parts of this language: 'When the Son of man comes in his glory,

and all his angels with him, then he will sit upon the throne of his glory'
(Matt. 25.31); 'Behold I am with you all days until the consummation of
the age' (Matt. 28.20). And, finally, there is a triple tradition passage within
an apparently composite pericope:

Matt. 16.27	Luke 9.26
The Son of man is about to come in the glory of his Father with his angels, and then he will repay to each according to his deeds.	Whoever is ashamed of me and my words, the Son of man will be ashamed of, when he comes in his glory and that of his Father and the holy angels.

Mark 8.38

Whoever is ashamed of me and my words in this adulterous and sinful
generation, also the Son of man will be ashamed of him when he comes in
the glory of his Father with the holy angels.

Of these slightly varying forms, the Matthaean seems earliest. The
evangelist Matthew would have had no reason to omit 'ashamed of me and
my words' (cf. Matt. 10.22, 'for my name's sake'), and the Marcan
accusation of 'this generation' is similar to the criticism of Matt.
12.39–41//Luke 11.29f., a criticism which Matthew repeats in 12.45.[87]

This category of sayings material has been presented at some length for
several reasons. In the first place, the general tendency of recent scholarship
has been to give it little weight in depictions of Jesus. This can be done by
simply not mentioning it, or by denying its authenticity, or (most frequently)
by subsuming it under the general category of 'future expectation', which
is then defined in less lurid colours.[88] It is not my intention to argue that
it must be given prominence (as will shortly be explained), but I fear that
it has receded in importance not so much because it has been proved to
have played a small role in Jesus' message as because of scholarly
preference for less dramatic material.

The second point of interest is its special, and in fact peculiar relationship
to the Gospel of Matthew. It has a place of prominence there, and the
wording of the passages is more harmonious in that Gospel than in the
others, but we cannot suppose that it was all composed by the evangelist
Matthew. To sort through this body of material properly, one would have
to solve the synoptic problem and also do a redactional study of Matthew.
Let me instead sketch a conceivable (and I think not unlikely) scenario.
The evangelist Matthew penned Matt. 28.20. That verse picks up the
phrase 'consummation of the age' and shifts it off safely into the indefinite
future. An intermediate redactor or author is responsible for the 'Interpretation of the Parable of the Tares'. The same person could have written

the judgment scene in Matt. 25. The evangelist Matthew, however (in this scenario), is not the author of these two passages. His mind, rather, is fixed on an extended mission and the *individual* entry of followers of Christ 'into the kingdom of heaven'.[89] In any case, the Gospel of Matthew has picked up an unusual amount of the material connected by the themes 'Son of man coming to judge', 'angels', and 'consummation of the age'. It may be that we see here the interest of an intermediate redactor.

Our third observation, and the one of most importance for the present study, is that the general theme of a heavenly figure who comes with angels is very early and quite possibly goes back to Jesus. The earliest evidence is I Thess. 4.15–17. Paul writes that it is 'a word of the Lord' that

> We who are alive, who are left until the coming of the Lord, shall not precede those who have fallen asleep. [16]For the Lord himself will descend from heaven with a cry of command, with the archangel's call, and with the sound of the trumpet of God. And the dead in Christ will rise first; [17]then we who are alive, who are left, shall be caught up together with them in the clouds to meet the Lord in the air . . . .

It is not clear that the 'word of the Lord' includes vv. 16 and 17, but the conclusion in v. 18, 'comfort one another with these words', makes it probable. In any case, the similarities between this passage and the synoptic depictions of the Son of man coming with angels, accompanied by the sound of a trumpet, while some are still alive (Matt. 24.30f. and parr.; Matt. 16.27f. and parr.), are so close that it is difficult to avoid the conclusion that both reflect a tradition which, before Paul, was already attributed to Jesus.[90] The similarities between Paul and Matthew are most striking, for only Matthew has a trumpet (24.31). But even without this phrase the relationships are close.

The verses in Paul are regarded by many scholars as among the 'words of the Lord' which were spoken through a prophet by the risen Lord: i.e., as not authentic.[91] This hypothesis I regard as possible but not provable one way or the other. I take it, however, that the saying is at least pre-Pauline.

The second best evidence is Matt. 16.27, which was quoted above with the Marcan and Lucan parallels. The saying virtually never gets discussed, since mechanical observance of the two-source hypothesis makes it secondary to Mark 8.38, which itself has evidently been Christianized.[92] It is, however, only the part of Mark 8.38 which Matthew does not have which shows the influence of Christian redactional activity. The saying in Matthew, as I observed above, has neither the implied equation between

Jesus and the Son of man which marks Luke and Mark, nor the theme of 'being ashamed' of the Son of man (= Jesus). Matthew was fully in agreement with Mark and Luke that those who denied the Son of man = Jesus would be denied by him in heaven (see Matt. 10.22, 32), but he has here a different saying, one focused entirely on the coming of the Son of man and one which closely agrees with I Thess. 4.16. It is more likely that Matthew is following another tradition than that, reading the saying which we have in Mark 8.38, he rejected it and composed his own.

The third bit of evidence is the other principal saying regarding the coming of the Son of man, Matt. 24.30f.//Mark 13.26f. This saying is ordinarily dismissed, the only debate being whether it is a Jewish eschatological tradition which has found its way into the synoptics or a Christian creation.[93]

Thus I Thess. 4.16 is generally assigned to a Christian prophet, Matt. 16.27 to the evangelist Matthew, and Mark 13.26f. to a non-Christian source or a Christian prophet. It seems to correspond better to the evidence to see this as a triply attested saying, one which goes back at least to a pre-Pauline 'prophet' and quite possibly back to Jesus. I shall not attempt to reconstruct the saying, but we may note the following parallels:

I Thess. 4.15–17	*Matt.* 16.27f.	*Matt.* 24.30f.
we who are left alive/ Lord descends, archangel cries, trumpet sounds/ with them on the clouds	Son of man comes with angels/ Some will not taste death	Son of man comes on clouds with angels and sound of trumpet

It is conceivable that Jesus did not think in these terms, but that the expectation originated very early in the church and has been preserved in various ways. Ordinarily, however, this kind of attestation counts in favour of authenticity.[94]

This is one of those instances in which agreement between synoptic sayings material and early Christian belief supports, rather than argues against, the Gospel material: the principle of dissimilarity here does not work. Paul's expectation of the coming of the Lord (see also I Cor. 15.23) is not his own creation, but was doubtless held in common with other Christians. The early teachers and apostles changed the expectation of the Son of man coming with his angels to the *return* of the Lord, just as in the synoptic tradition they identified the Son of man with Jesus; but the *general* expectation probably goes back to Jesus.

It seems, then, that the tradition contained in this group of passages is old, and very possibly authentic, at least in general terms. Here as elsewhere I do not feel confident of our ability to assign certain phrases to Jesus, some to the Gospel writers, and some to intermediate redactors; but it would be rash to deny to Jesus this complex of ideas (a cataclysmic end in which a heavenly figure sends angels to separate the just from the unjust).

The reader will have observed that in this instance I have not been able to resist offering my own assessment of authenticity. The argument in favour of an authentic saying which connects a heavenly figure with angels and probably with judgment, and which lies behind I Thess. 4.16f.; Matt. 16.27; and Matt. 24.30and parr., seems quite strong, though it has been overlooked. Nevertheless, I must note that the most general point – that Jesus expected a future cosmic event and a future judgment – can be affirmed by those who do not regard these three passages as worth discussing. Perrin, for example, dismissed these passages, but argued for the general point. That Jesus expected the 'apocalyptic Son of man' he took to be shown by other passages, such as Matt. 24.27 par.; 24.37, 39 par.; 24.44 par., while the theme of judgment is confirmed by the parables of the Tares and the Fishnet (Matt. 13.24–30; 13.47f.).[95] Some, to be sure, deny the authenticity of all the Son of man sayings,[96] and many will doubt the parable of the Tares. In general, however, this category of kingdom sayings seems at least as secure as any other.[97]

4. The kingdom will involve a decisive future event which will result in a recognizable social order involving Jesus' disciples and presumably Jesus himself.

There are here only a few passages to be listed: the prediction of a new temple (see ch. 1 above); the twelve disciples as the judges of the tribes of Israel (Matt. 19.28//Luke 22.28–30) (ch. 3); the question of who would sit at Jesus' right hand in the kingdom (Matt. 20.20–28//Mark 10.35–45; cf. Matt. 18.1 and parr.);[98] the saying to Peter (Matt. 16.18f.); the saying about drinking wine in the kingdom (Mark 14.25 and parr.).

Again, in a test of authenticity not many would give high marks to much of this material (the most notable exception being Mark 14.25); or at least would not place emphasis on it in assessing Jesus' view of the kingdom. I shall shortly return to the question of emphasis. With regard to authenticity, I think that something can be said in favour of even the passages most frequently doubted. If one doubts that Jesus said that he would build his church on the Rock, Peter (Matt. 16.18f.), one must still grant that *someone* gave Simon the name 'Kepha' (in Greek 'Petros'). The significant point is that, when the name passed into Greek, sometimes the Aramaic was retained (several times in Galatians and I Corinthians), but often the word was translated rather than transliterated, thus putting the emphasis on the meaning, 'Rock', as in Gal. 2.7f. and throughout the rest of the New

Testament (in John 1.42 the Aramaic is used and translated). It does not seem in the least unlikely that the 'someone' was Jesus; and if Jesus called Simon 'Rock', he must have meant that he was the Rock of something, even if not of 'the church'.[99] His later position as the leader among the former followers of Jesus (I Cor. 15.5), whose authority was rivalled only by James, the Lord's brother (Gal. 1.18f.; 2.9), probably reflects the fact that he was singled out by Jesus.

The passage about James and John also raises interesting questions. Mark 10.38f., which apparently refers to their martyrdom, is often taken to have been written after the event.[100] The tradition of their joint martyrdom, however, is not reliable; and that of John's is uncertain.[101] Mark 10.38f. and par., which has James and John say that they will drink the cup which Jesus drinks, *may* be a *vaticinium ex eventu*, though one wishes that one knew more about the event of John's martyrdom. The request to sit at Jesus' right and left hand, which he says he cannot grant (Mark 10.37, 41), however, is difficult to explain in this way. We know from Galatians that, at the time of Paul's second trip to Jerusalem, John occupied a position of prominence in the early Jerusalem church (Gal. 2.9). Paul saw neither of the brothers at the time of his first trip (Gal. 1.19). The request to be elevated by Jesus does not reflect the fact that John lived to be a 'pillar' of the church in Jerusalem while James did not. The saying also does not reflect another fact of early Christian history, one just mentioned: Peter's early position as leader. It is hard to imagine a circle which would create a question and answer about first and second place, but which simply ignored Peter's rank. Thus we cannot easily assume that the passage was written after the fact.

There are other indications of authenticity. As Taylor noted, Jesus' saying that it did not fall to him to assign places in the kingdom agrees with the saying in Mark 13.32, that he knows neither the day nor the hour, which many hold to be authentic.[102] Finally, we note that the exchange is a bit discreditable to James and John, which would count against its composition in the church. It seems to me quite probable that the two disciples made the request to sit at Jesus' side in the kingdom (Mark, 'in your glory'), and that it was turned aside by Jesus.

The passage which has attracted most attention is Mark 14.25, which has a very close parallel in Matt. 26.69 and a less precise parallel in Luke 22.18. We have been fairly consistently citing Perrin as representing mainline scholarship on the sayings about the kingdom, and so we should note that he regarded the saying as inauthentic, attributing it to the 'risen Lord'.[103] Schlosser observes, however, that most scholars have viewed the saying about not drinking from the fruit of the vine until the kingdom comes as authentic, the only problems being the precise wording and, of course, the meaning.[104] Does it indicate that Jesus thought that the disciples would constitute a group which would survive his death and endure until the eschaton, or that the kingdom would arrive immediately, with no interval? Is the kingdom this-worldly or otherworldly? We find here the uncertainty which generally characterizes discussions which attempt to specify the precise meaning of the sayings material.

I am content to conclude that we have a group of sayings of possible (in some cases probable) authenticity which, at face value, imply a social order. One may say, to be sure, that such sayings are necessarily figurative and tell us nothing about Jesus' view of the kingdom, except in the most abstract terms. Thus Perrin:

> The imagery of the Messianic Banquet . . . teaches that it [the kingdom] will mean a perfect participation in the ultimate blessings of God; and the imagery of the New Temple . . . which . . . is a regular apocalyptic symbol for the final blessed state, describes the community of the redeemed as enjoying a perfect sacral relationship with God.[105]

It is perhaps noteworthy that Perrin could not avoid the word 'community', even while proposing that we learn nothing this definite from sayings of the sort being considered here.

5. There are sayings which imply or seem to imply that the kingdom is present in the words and deeds of Jesus. We have already discussed the two most important passages, Matt. 12.28//Luke 11.20 and Matt. 11.5f. Some include in this category Matt. 11.11//Luke 7.28 (the least in the kingdom is greater than John the Baptist); Luke 17.20f. (the reign of God is among or within you); and the summary in Mark 1.14f. and parr.[106] Dodd considered that Luke 10.23f. and 11.31f. (blessed are your eyes; a greater than Solomon is here) also pointed to the presence of the kingdom.[107] Müller considers Luke 10.18 (I saw Satan fall) to be a key passage in this category.[108]

By no means all these passages are to the point. The saying about John the Baptist does not seem to imply that the kingdom is present, but rather that it is future. When the kingdom comes, the least in it will be greater than the greatest figure in this age.[109] Those who urge that the saying implies that the kingdom is present do not explain just where that leaves the Baptist.[110] Does Jesus claim that the least of his followers is greater than John? That the least person who 'opens himself to the kingdom' is greater than John?[111] Surely John was 'open to the kingdom'. We gain a better meaning if we suppose that Jesus contrasts the least in the future kingdom with the greatest in the present age.

Two of the passages cited by Dodd (Luke 10.23f. and 11.31f.) affirm only that Jesus' ministry is important. The claim that 'greater than Solomon is here' is strikingly ambitious; but these passages do not say precisely that the kingdom is present, but rather that something of unparalleled importance is under way. They do not allow us to define what 'unparalleled importance' means. It could, as far as I see, mean that Jesus' ministry is of unparalleled importance because it constitutes the last hour before the coming kingdom.

Of the various passages which are held to show that the kingdom, in Jesus' view, was present, Luke 17.21 is the one which actually says so. As it presently stands, it is a reply to a question discussed elsewhere – just when will the kingdom come and how will one know? In the passage on the day of the Son of man, which immediately follows in Luke, there is the warning not to heed those who will say 'he is here' or 'he is there' (Luke 17.23//Matt. 24.26). The latter passage continues to the effect that the Son of man will come from heaven with cosmic signs. In Luke 17.21a, in contrast, Jesus says that people will not say that the kingdom is 'here' or 'there', because it is 'in your midst' or 'within you' (17.21b). The contrast between 'they will not say' (v. 21a) and 'they will say' (v. 23a) indicates that the saying in v. 21, and possibly that in v. 22, has been added to the passage on the day of the Son of man. Schlosser proposes that the saying in v. 21b should be detached not only from the passage which follows, but also from 21a. He would connect it directly with v. 20b: 'The kingdom of God does not come with observation, (for) behold! it is in your midst.'[112]

We have here a standard difficulty. In order to make sense of a saying we must detach it from its context, delete part of it, and reconstruct a hypothetical original. The results of this sort of work can never rate higher than 'possible'. Thus we can conclude only that Jesus may have said that the coming of the kingdom will not be a visible event, since it is present.

The real difficulty is what sort of weight to give this possible saying in an overall reconstruction of Jesus' thought. If we stress the negative thrust of v. 20b – 'not with observation' – we might conclude that Jesus thought that nothing concrete would happen in the future. This, however, flies in the face of so much evidence that we must hesitate. Can we draw from a possible saying a far-reaching conclusion which contradicts hard evidence? I think not. It is methodologically wrong to build very much on the possible saying in Luke 17.20f., and at most we should take it to mean that Jesus may have thought that the kingdom was 'in some sense' present.

6. There is a large amount of material which describes the character of the kingdom or of the king, God. Most of the parables fit here in some way or another. In many of them, as is well known, there is a 'reversal of values'.[113] Labourers who work a short period of time are rewarded as much as those who work all day (Matt. 20.1–16); repentant sinners are more highly regarded than those who are always righteous (Luke 15.3–7; 15.8–10; 15.11–32). This material is the best known and has most frequently been studied, and, further, we shall return to aspects of it in a subsequent section. Here it is necessary only to recall its existence.

Conclusion

There are basically two ways of responding to the diverse sorts of sayings about the kingdom; either to focus on one type to the complete or virtually complete exclusion of the others, or to attempt a harmony among them.[114] Of recent years most scholars have followed the second path. Norman Perrin's work on *The Kingdom of God*, which has been so often referred to in this discussion, argued forcefully in favour of a harmony[115] and more or less epitomizes efforts towards a harmonization. No group of sayings is ruled out entirely, and the problem is how to hold them in balance (in his terms, 'tension'). In the latter pages of the book Perrin simplifies the problem by speaking of only two motifs: the kingdom as present and as future. The difficulty caused by the diversity of expression, imagery, and, indeed, conception among the sayings generally classified as 'future' disappears behind the general category. One does not see immediately, for example, how my categories 3 (future cataclysmic event) and 4 (a recognizable social order) fit together. In the former the judgment is accomplished by the angels of the Son of man, in the latter by the twelve disciples; and, in general, the conceptualizations are different. But even after having somewhat simplified the task, Perrin still comes down on one side. Here is the key sentence: 'So the tension between present and future is a tension, above all, within human experience, and this is most evident in the Lord's prayer.'[116] Here 'present' wins out because, by putting the tension within human experience, the kingdom as an actual future event becomes of little moment.

We should note that it is not at all difficult to reconcile the general idea of 'present' with that of 'future'. What is difficult is to regard *the same thing* as both present and future. G. B. Caird very neatly cuts through a lot of turgid and agonizing attempts to maintain 'present' and 'future' at the same time, or to decide between them:

> The debate between those who hold that Jesus declared the kingdom of God to have arrived and those who hold that he declared it to be imminent is reducible to its simplest terms when we recognise that the parties to the debate have differently identified the referent. If Jesus was referring to the final vindication of God's purposes in the reign of justice and peace, where the righteous are to banquet with Abraham, Isaac and Jacob (Matt. 8.11; Luke 13.28–29), it is mere nonsense even to suggest that this was present on earth when Caiaphas was High Priest and Pilate Governor of Judaea. On the other hand, if Jesus was referring to the redemptive sovereignty of God let loose into the world for the destruction of Satan and all his works (Matt. 12.28; Luke 11.20), it makes nonsense of the whole record of his ministry to argue that for him this lay still in the future.[117]

Thus there is no difficulty at all about having 'kingdom' in some sense present and in another sense future.[118] What is a surprise is to have the same word used over such a wide range of meanings as is the case in the synoptic Gospels.

We gain perspective by again considering Paul on the question of 'present' and 'future'. It is well known that he regarded Christians as already experiencing something and as still awaiting something. He could write that Christians were 'justified' (Rom. 5.1); that they were a 'new creation' (II Cor. 5.17); that they were 'being changed' (II Cor. 3.18) and 'being renewed' (II Cor. 4.16). 'Salvation' itself, however, he put in the future (Rom. 5.9f.; 10.13; and often). This presents no difficulty, partly because in some places, for example Rom. 8, he distinguished perfectly clearly between the present state and the future and described the former as one of awaiting fulfilment and consummation. Thus Rom. 8.23: 'We . . . , who have the first fruits of the Spirit, groan inwardly as we wait for adoption as sons, the redemption of our bodies.'

There are, however, passages in which Paul puts in the future what he elsewhere puts in the past. Thus 'righteousness' (usually represented by the passive verb, 'being justified' or 'righteoused'), which is ordinarily past, is sometimes future (Rom. 2.13; Gal. 5.5). The same is true of 'sonship' (compare Rom. 8.23, future, with Gal. 4.6, present), and, as we noted earlier, of 'kingdom' (compare I Cor. 15.50, future, with Rom. 14.17, present). What if Paul had had no terms which he consistently used for the present existence of the Christian (e.g., Spirit) and for the future state (salvation)? What if he had always used 'righteousness', 'sonship' and 'kingdom', varying their reference between present and future? We could still figure out his basic thought – the Christian possesses the first fruits while awaiting consummation – because we have his letters. We would be unable, however, to give a single meaning to either 'kingdom', 'righteousness' or 'sonship'.

I suspect that this is part of the problem with the sayings of Jesus. He used the word 'kingdom' an overwhelming number of times in comparison with other terms, and it was forced to carry a very wide range of meaning. We have no sayings which allow us to come to the clarity which we can achieve with Paul, thanks to our having such passages as Rom. 8.23. 'Future' and 'present' in the teaching of Jesus have constituted a worrisome problem because we cannot say clearly what is present – nor even precisely what he thought of as future, whether a new order or a cosmic cataclysm. He may well have thought that 'the kingdom' in the sense of 'the power of God' was at work in the world, but that the time would come when all opposing power would be eliminated, and the kingdom of God in a somewhat different sense would 'come' – be ushered in. The surviving sayings material does not allow us to offer this as being definitely Jesus' view, but it seems the most probable supposition.

If, however, we have to choose between 'present' and 'future' as emphases in Jesus' message, we must, on the basis of present evidence, put the emphasis on the kingdom as immediately future.[119] The evidence is this: (1) A future emphasis corresponds to Jesus' early association with John the Baptist. (2) The behaviour of the apostles indicates that they expected a dramatic event in the near future. Paul, to be sure, thought of the kingdom as present, but this depends on his doctrine of the Spirit and his sacramental/mystical theology of being 'in Christ', not (as far as we can tell) on knowledge of Jesus' own view. It appears that what the followers of Jesus learned from him was that the kingdom was at hand. Others than Paul experienced the *presence of Christ* (see Matt. 18.20; 28.20), and doubtless devout members of the Christian movement felt themselves to be in the *presence of God* – as did other devout Jews. But this in no way indicates that they learned from Jesus that the *kingdom* of God was *fully* present in his words and deeds. The Christian movement was differentiated from the rest of Judaism by the conviction that the Lord would soon return, and this is to be seen as a transformation of Jesus' view that the kingdom of God was near. (See further ch. 8). This fact, more than any other single one, shows where the emphasis lay in Jesus' own message. (3) The prediction of the destruction of the temple shows that a future event was expected. (4) The expectation of the arrival of the kingdom is well grounded in the Judaism of Jesus' day.

It is also true that, in addition to the saying about the temple, there are numerous sayings which point to a future act of God; but study of the sayings material does not, by itself, determine Jesus' own emphasis. The temple saying stands out because it points to a concrete future event, and it also correlates with a prophetic action. But the determining evidence is not analysis of the sayings material, which, as I have argued throughout, leads to no more than possibility.

We are not yet in a position to attempt to describe what sort of event Jesus expected. This effort will be made in ch. 8. Some elements, however, are clear. Jesus looked for the imminent direct intervention of God in history, the elimination of evil and evildoers, the building of a new and glorious temple, and the reassembly of Israel with himself and his disciples as leading figures in it. This list partially harmonizes our categories 3 and 4 (cataclysmic ending and new order); but the harmony is not perfect, for there is still a conflict on the judgment. Category 3, as we noted above, has judgment (or selection) take place at the time of the coming of the heavenly figure and the angels (Matt. 16.27 end; 24.31 and par.). Matt. 19.28, which goes in category 4, assigns judgment to the disciples. We cannot know that one person could not have said both, since apparent contradiction of this sort not infrequently marks the statements of people who think in images. The pictures called up by Matt. 24.31 on the one hand and 19.28 on the other are quite different, and they serve to show that seeking a harmony does not lead to logical consistency. There is no reason, however, to reject completely one or the other.

Jesus also thought that the power of God was present. Just how fully it was present, in his view, depends on sayings such as Matt. 12.28 and 11.5f., which were discussed at such length early in this chapter. We can, however, on the basis of more secure evidence, say some things about what Jesus thought about the present power of God. The demonstration in the temple shows that he thought that the power of God was active in him: he was God's spokesman, God's agent. The temple demonstration goes a long way towards proving what many people have argued on the basis of shakier evidence, such as Jesus' view of his exorcisms. Many of the sayings which some have seen as pointing to the presence of the kingdom actually point to Jesus' view of his own importance: 'greater than Solomon is here', 'blessed are the eyes which see what you see' (Luke 10.23f.; 11.32f.).

Thus there is no doubt that Jesus thought of the present as an important moment – apparently the most important moment of all time. This does not allow us, however, to shift the emphasis of his view of the *kingdom* from 'future' to 'present'. The two were, we must assume, linked. But if Jesus truly expected God to act decisively in the future, we must also assume that this expectation dominated and controlled his activity and message and that the future event is what primarily defines Jesus' view of 'the kingdom'. The future, climactic action of God must be more important than the present manifestation of his power.

Just as we cannot yet say precisely what Jesus thought would happen in the future, so also we cannot say just what he thought was taking place in the present. Our study of sayings confirms general points – Jesus looked for a future event and saw his own work as important – but does not precisely define them. It does, however, offer some possibilities and exclude others. Possibly the future event will involve a cosmic drama, possibly a social order. Excluded seems to be the existentialist view that 'future' and 'present' in Jesus' message refer to tension within individual, present human experience.

I think that there are two explanations of the fact that so many scholars emphasize the presence of the kingdom in the teaching of Jesus, while acknowledging that he thought of it as a future reality.[120] One is simply theological. In that way the message of Jesus is made more relevant, and the problem of his mistake about the immediate future is muted.[121] The second explanation is that people wish to emphasize whatever is regarded as distinctive. It is thought to be the notion of the presence of the kingdom which sets Jesus apart from Jewish eschatology, including first and foremost John the Baptist.[122] In order to make Jesus' message truly distinctive, however, he must be said not only to have proclaimed that the kingdom was 'in some sense' present, but to have proclaimed that it was present in something approaching the power of the end-time itself; for the idea that God reigns in the present is by no means distinctive. Simply to say that God is king (in the present tense) would be a Jewish commonplace. O'Neill puts the common view quite accurately:

> Judaism confessed that God was King of all men, whether or not they acknowledged him to be such; many Jews believed the time would come when all men would be openly under his sovereignty, when the Kingdom of the world would become the Kingdom of our Lord . . . . [123]

Dodd saw this clearly: 'Any Jewish teacher might have said, "If you repent and pledge yourself to the observance of Torah, then you have taken upon yourselves the Kingdom of God." ' He continued,

> But Jesus says, 'If I, by the finger of God, cast out demons, then the Kingdom of God has come upon you.' Something has happened, which has not

happened before, and which means that the sovereign power of God has come into effective operation. It is not a matter of having God for your King in the sense that you obey His commandments: it is a matter of being confronted with the power of God at work in the world.[124]

He concludes, 'It [the kingdom] is not merely imminent; it is here.'[125]

This puts us back where we started. Will Matt. 12.28//Luke 11.20 (supplemented by Matt. 11.5f.; Luke 17.20f. and a few other verses) bear this much weight? That is, will they allow us, with Dodd, to shift the emphasis to the present; to say that Jesus thought that the kingdom was present in some *extraordinary* sense, in its *full end-time power*, and to find in this *conception* what distinguishes Jesus from all others? I do not think so. The passages are just not clear enough to allow us to think that Jesus claimed that the kingdom which was present was the same as the kingdom which he expected to come, nor can they overcome the firm evidence that he expected a future kingdom. It is better to distinguish the referents of the word 'kingdom'.

We can put this another way. Dodd, in common with many subsequent scholars, emphasized both the boldness of Jesus' claim and the uniqueness of his conception of the kingdom. In this view, not only did Jesus claim that God was active in his own work, but he asserted an idea which is striking and distinctive: that what was generally thought to be future had become fully present. It is this second point about which, I think, we cannot be sure. It is beyond doubt that he thought that the 'kingdom', whether present or coming or both, was intimately tied to himself and his work. He knew, he claimed, whom God would include in the kingdom and who would take leading places in it. What seems to me dubious is the scholarly view that Jesus was also distinctive because he defined 'kingdom' in a curious way and considered the same thing to be both present and future.

In broad terms, there is not much dispute about what Jesus thought. He thought that the kingdom would come in the near future and that God was at work in a special way in his own ministry. We can classify these two statements as 'beyond reasonable doubt'. Yet we could doubtless say the same things of John the Baptist, and probably of Theudas and the Egyptian. It is entirely understandable that scholars seek for nuances and emphases which will set Jesus apart. The results of his work stand apart – even though the followers of John the Baptist did, at least for a time, continue loyal to him – , and the normal expectation is that Jesus himself should have been unique in his proclamation and view, as he was in his effect.

Thus far, we are all agreed. I hesitate to follow the majority, and to see Jesus' *sense* or *idea* of the presence of the kingdom as what distinguished him, because the sayings which are appealed to cannot carry the burden which is put on them. They do not allow us to determine the relative weight of 'the kingdom would come in the near future' and 'God was at work in his own ministry'. Nor do they enable us to say with certainty what was the precise meaning in Jesus' own mind of 'at work in a special way in his own ministry'.

This is almost necessarily the case. The nature of the sayings material will not allow us to be certain about the precise nuance which Jesus wished to give such a large concept as 'the kingdom of God'. We can see that 'kingdom' has a range of meanings in the synoptics, but we cannot see just how much emphasis should be placed on each meaning. We never have absolute certainty of authenticity, and we probably have the original context of any given saying seldom, if ever. Facts allow us to be fairly sure that Jesus looked for a future kingdom. But to some degree conclusions about nuance and emphasis still rest on analysis of sayings, and since this analysis will always be tentative, some things about Jesus' view of the kingdom can never be known with certainty.

As we proceed to the study of other material, we must bear in mind the most secure conclusions: Jesus expected the kingdom in the near future, he awaited the rebuilding of the temple, he called 'twelve' to symbolize the restoration of Israel, and his disciples thought about the kingdom concretely enough to ask about their place in it. Thus we cannot shift the normal expectations of Jewish restoration theology to the periphery.

5

MIRACLES AND CROWDS

In this and the following chapter we extend the study of 'kingdom' by considering the miracles and the recipients of Jesus' ministry, who, according to the Gospels, were 'the crowds', the possessed, the ill and handicapped, and the sinners. There is agreement on the basic facts: Jesus performed miracles, drew crowds and promised the kingdom to sinners. It is a natural assumption that miracles and the inclusion of sinners are intimately tied to Jesus' conception of the kingdom and of his own mission. Thus far most scholars will agree. When, however, we explore the question of just how to relate miracles and proclamation to sinners to each other and to Jesus' conception of the kingdom and his own task, we find commonly held opinions which should be queried. These opinions have served to explain the meaning in Jesus' career of the miracles and the offer of the kingdom to sinners, and they have done so with such success that they have prevented further exploratory efforts. The opinions are these:

1. Exorcisms were generally regarded as a sign of the kingdom.[1] They are thus to be subsumed under the proclamation of the kingdom as signs of it.

2. Forgiveness of sinners was also regarded in Judaism as one of the promises of the eschaton.[2] Therefore Jesus' offer of salvation to sinners had basically the same meaning to his audience as the exorcisms: the kingdom is *present*.

3. Jesus himself saw his exorcisms and healings as a manifestation of the presence, or at least imminence, of the kingdom.

4. Jesus was primarily a teacher and preacher. Crowds flocked to him to hear his word, and he also healed some among them.

Of these, I regard the first two as simply erroneous. The first point, that exorcisms would generally have been taken to indicate the presence of the kingdom, we discussed above.[3] The question of the repentance and forgiveness of sinners will be considered in the next chapter. The third view, that Jesus himself saw his work as demonstrating the inbreaking of the kingdom, is possible but not provable. Proof would depend on such sayings as Matt. 12.28//Luke 11.20 and Matt. 11.5f., which we discussed in the previous chapter. That Jesus thought that his own work was intimately connected with the arrival of the kingdom should not be contested; but the precise view that he saw the proof of the *presence* of the kingdom in his exorcisms and table fellowship with sinners is not certain.

The fourth assumption – that Jesus was first and foremost a teacher – is seldom explicitly stated. One discerns it simply by reading books about Jesus.[4] The assumption itself I regard as uncertain and in need of examination. Our present tasks are to explore the interrelationships among miracles, teaching and crowds, and to examine the possible significance of the miracles for our understanding of Jesus. We shall have before us four questions:

1. Can we learn anything from the *fact* of miracles about what Jesus thought of himself and how his followers regarded him? I have rejected the sayings in Matt. 11.5f. and 12.28 as providing certain information, but can a more general study of the miracles cast light on this question?

2. Can we learn something of importance for understanding the outcome of Jesus' career?

3. How was Jesus seen by others, those not his followers?

4. Does Jesus fall into a general social and religious type? This involves a consideration of the relationship between teaching and performing miracles.

Miracles, teaching and crowds in the Gospels

The natural assumption, to repeat, is that there probably was an interrelationship among preaching, healing, and the crowds. One readily assumes, that is, that Jesus saw himself as having a mission to people, and that it involved both preaching and healing. It is true that this is not self-evident on the basis of simply reading the Gospels; in the passages in which crowds are present, proclamation and miracle do not always appear together. But it is intrinsically improbable that, in a short period of time, and in the confines of a small geographical area, Jesus sometimes drew crowds by healing and sometimes by preaching.[5]

The evangelists do not make much of an effort to explain the crowds; they are on the whole taken to be always present, and Jesus has occasionally to escape the press of people. A consideration of the first chapters of Mark is instructive in this connection. Jesus preached in the synagogue (1.21), and while there he exorcized a demon (1.23–26). The *exorcism* led the onlookers to comment on his *teaching* first and then on his ability to exorcize (1.27).[6] Then the result is given: 'And at once his fame spread everywhere through all the surrounding region of Galilee' (1.28). We next meet the crowds ('the whole city') apparently accompanying those who bring to him the sick and the possessed (1.32f.). In a lonely place, however, Jesus confided to Simon that he wished to go to another city to preach; that, apparently, was his mission (1.35–39). Despite this intention, he healed a leper (1.40), and his fame spread again, with the result that he could not even enter a city, but had to stay in the country. The crowds, however, pursued him even there (1.45). He was finally able to go back to Capernaum, and many gathered, so many as to block the door. He preached to them, and despite the press of people the friends of a paralytic managed to get the afflicted man to Jesus, who healed him (2.1–5). After that, at least in this section of the narrative, the crowds are assumed to be present except when Jesus withdraws (2.13; 3.7; 4.1). In 3.9f. this press of people is attributed to his fame as a healer.

It is not to be supposed that Mark or any of the other evangelists knew the actual interconnections among Jesus' fame, his intention, his healing and his preaching. Nor could we suppose that they would have cared about cause and effect in the modern sense of the term (a point to which we shall eventually return).[7] Further, it can by no means be assumed that even a modern reporter, had there been one, would have been able to describe all that we want to know. Did Jesus, with what he regarded as a divinely inspired message already in mind, deliberately set out to attempt cures in the hope of attracting crowds so that he could then preach to them? Did he discover more or less by accident that he could heal and, as a development from that, come to think that he had a special message to deliver? Even if those questions had been posed directly to him, could he have given a single, clear and unambiguous answer? Putting the matter in this way will make it evident that there is a level to which we cannot penetrate.

I do not mean that we can never recover cause and effect, nor even intention. At a later chronological point in Jesus' career (some aspects of which we have already discussed), things begin to get clearer. Observable events begin to accumulate in such a way as to allow reasonable inference as to their cause or causes. But some things about the beginning of Jesus' public career can never be known.

The Gospels, in this respect as in most others, were not written to answer our questions. They cannot tell us what was in Jesus' own mind as he began his career, nor precisely what hopes and expectations he aroused among the people of Galilee. We thus far have no more than our opening assumption, that Jesus saw himself as having a mission with regard to the kingdom of God, and that he employed both deeds and words. The Gospel accounts about Jesus' activities among 'the crowds' do not tell us even this in so many words. Do they contain other evidence which will allow us to press further?

Motive

If we could determine Jesus' motive in healing, we would be on the way to understanding just what he considered his task to be. But the answer to the question of motive is by no means self-evident, once one drops the idea that exorcisms necessarily implied to Jesus' audience the presence of the reign of God, and that in performing them Jesus was, in effect, proclaiming that presence. Two other answers come immediately to mind: he healed for reasons of compassion or in order to authenticate himself and his mission.[8] What evidence is there? There are, of course, editorial explanations, especially in Mark. It is almost amusing to see scholars seriously pondering the verb 'he was moved with compassion' (Mark 1.41 and elsewhere) as possibly offering the motive for healing.[9] I would not wish to deny that Jesus was a compassionate man, but the editorial introduction to healing stories will hardly supply us with useful information about Jesus' own view of what he did.

The question of using miracles for authentication is more complicated, and it will be necessary to introduce some comparative material before we can properly address it. We note now simply that Jesus is reported to have refused a sign to opponents who asked for one (Matt. 16.1–4 and par.; Matt. 12.38f. and par.), and to have offered his miracles as signs to the Baptist (Matt. 11.2–11 and par.). We leave this matter for the present, and turn to two recent attempts to explain the significance of miracles for understanding Jesus, and especially his intention and 'type'.

Harvey has recently made a truly interesting proposal for understanding Jesus' view of the significance of his miracles. He observes that the stories of exorcism occupy a prominent place among the miracles. That agrees with other stories (the temptation) and several sayings which represent 'Jesus as engaged, and victorious, in a contest with the devil'.[10] Exorcisms, however, may – and in Jesus' case did – give rise to the charge that the exorcist 'had more knowledge and experience of the world of evil spirits than would be possible for anyone who did not himself dabble dangerously in the black arts'.[11] Harvey continues,

> Jesus evidently opted for a type of miraculous healing which was bound to be dangerously ambiguous; but, at least according to the records, he carried it out with the absolute minimum of those technical procedures which would most surely have aroused suspicion about his true credentials and motives.[12]

His next principal point is that there is considerable congruence between miracles attributed to Jesus (those for which he 'opted') and those predicted in Isa. 35.5f. Matthew, he observes, in one of his summaries (Matt. 15.31) 'makes the connection explicit'. He proceeds:

> Such cures were not merely unprecedented; they were characteristic of the new age which, as we have seen, was expected one way or another by the majority of the contemporaries of Jesus. To use the jargon of New Testament scholarship, they were eschatological miracles.[13]

His conclusion is that Jesus' healings (not exorcisms) conform in general to the prophecies in Isaiah about the new age, while the exorcisms (which would not be expected on the basis of Isaiah) point to the relief which Jesus' contemporaries would have expected when the new age arrives. Demonic possession was not part of Isaiah's world-view, but in first-century Judaism it was perceived to be part of the human predicament. Thus both the cures and the exorcisms point in the same direction: the new age.[14]

Harvey grants that not all the miracles fall into one pattern,[15] but his argument is that Jesus 'opted' to perform primarily those miracles which, to his contemporaries, would hold out the promise of a new age. With regard to Jesus' healing 'those ailments which we call congenital', Harvey remarks: 'If a prophet were to inspire genuine hope of a new age in store for mankind, he must offer an assurance that this intolerable constraint on human dignity and freedom would, in God's good time, be removed.'[16] And by his exorcisms, as well as by the sayings 'in which he proclaimed his superiority' to the demonic powers,

> Jesus seemed to demonstrate the possibility of final victory over this demonic constraint. Indeed we may say that such was the sense of enslavement to the spirit-world felt by so many of his contemporaries that Jesus could hardly have been acknowledged as their saviour had he not seemed to have struck a decisive blow against this redoubtable enemy.[17]

The argument that Jesus consciously performed cures which, while 'completely without precedent in [his] own culture',[18] were modelled on

Isa. 35.5f., is complementary to his later argument that Jesus' career was in important respects modelled on Isa. 61.1.[19]

Harvey's argument deserves careful evaluation. His claim for the uniqueness of Jesus' miracles is different from the claim that we earlier considered, which was that Jesus had a unique *consciousness* of eschatological power.[20] Harvey's claim of uniqueness is subject to empirical testing – at least in theory. The recording angel has not left us a list of all the miracles ever done in Palestine. At any rate, this is Harvey's fullest statement:

> . . . most of the miracles performed by Jesus consisted on the one hand of cures of the blind, the lame, the deaf and the dumb (cures which had virtually no precedent in his culture) and on the other hand of exorcisms (which laid him open to the charge of sorcery).[21]

This is a careful statement. Josephus claims that Jews were especially adept at exorcism,[22] and Harvey brackets that off as being not unique but dangerous (though if Jews were famous for it, how dangerous could it be?). And it is true that reports from Judaism of recent cures of the blind and others similarly afflicted are hard to find. One wonders why Harvey did not discuss the Elisha cycle, where there are stories of cures which parallel those attributed to Jesus, such as the cure of a leper (II Kings 5.1–14; cf. Mark 1.40–45 and parr.) and the raising of a dead child (II Kings 4.32–37; cf. Mark 5.21–43 and parr.). These may be excluded because they are remote in time, but they nevertheless reduce the uniqueness of the miracles attributed to Jesus.

But does the claim for uniqueness, even leaving the Elisha stories aside, count for much in providing the clue to Jesus' own intention? Such cures, as Smith has made abundantly clear, were common enough in the Mediterranean,[23] and it seems to be a very tenuous argument to suppose that Palestine was so isolated that the scantiness of attestation of such miracles in Palestinian Jewish literature prior to Jesus means that Jesus and his contemporaries saw such healings as unique.[24]

Part of Harvey's claim for the uniqueness of Jesus, not contained in the quotation just given, is that foreknowledge, common stock-in-trade of magicians, is not attributed to Jesus.[25] One must assume that he rules out as inauthentic a lot of passages.[26] But even so the denial is in error, unless he intends to make so fine a distinction as to make the point worthless. He defines foreknowledge as based on 'a close observation of present phenomena'. This, one supposes, suffices to exclude the prediction about the colt tied (Mark 11.2–6), the attribution to Jesus of knowledge of distant events (e.g. Mark 7.29), Jesus' ability to read minds (Mark 10.33–35), and other forms of preternatural knowledge (which side of the boat the fish were, Luke 5.4–7; the coin in the fish's mouth, Matt. 17.27).[27] Here Harvey should grant Smith's case: the Gospels ascribe to Jesus some of the traits of a magician.[28]

But the greatest difficulty with Harvey's argument is that he considers the *selection* of miracles to reflect Jesus' intention: 'what was his motive and intention in choosing this singular range of options?'[29] – as if Jesus had at his disposal any number of miracles that he could perform and selected just those which pointed to the coming new age, either because they coincided with Isa. 35, or because they responded to contemporary hopes.[30] It seems much more likely that Jesus performed those miracles which came to hand.[31] Once one grants that Jesus healed, the prominence of cures of the lame, the dumb and the blind is not surprising. Those diseases respond to faith-healing, and they are quite frequent in pagan sources. One cannot say that they absolutely predominate in the stelae found at Epidauros, but they are certainly common enough.[32] And, further, they are not overwhelmingly predominant in the Gospels. There one finds nature miracles, the raising of the dead, mind reading, and other things which, as Harvey grants, do not fit the list in Isa. 35.5f.

Harvey's attempt to draw inferences from the miracles about Jesus' intention, his own view of his mission, is the most sustained and reasonable one that I know. He does not, for example, fall into the common error of supposing that in Judaism exorcisms would necessarily imply eschaton – a supposition which has kept scholars from looking much further in assessing their significance. Nor does Harvey try to make his case, as have so many, by hammering away at Matt. 12.28 and 11.5f. in the hope that one or two verses would reveal what Jesus thought of himself. His argument is a great deal subtler and also better than that. Nevertheless, the argument fails to carry conviction. The miracles will not tell us what Jesus had in mind. I hasten to add that I do not think that the search for enlightenment from Jewish eschatological expectation is pointless – on the contrary! Harvey's careful argument and its failure, however, help to persuade me that Isa. 35 is not much help. Jesus' miracles are too diverse to allow us to put much weight on the partial correspondence between them and that prophecy. And I continue to bear in mind that subsequent Jewish literature does not indicate that Jews habitually looked for miracles as a sign of the coming end. Our quest for the significance of the miracles in Jesus' own view still finds no certain answer.

Miracles, proclamation and crowds

Can we, however, determine the relative importance of miracles and proclamation in the general view of Jesus? If we have to arrange them in order, then the obviousness of Morton Smith's case, it seems to me, will win out. The miracles attracted the crowds, to whom Jesus proclaimed the good news of salvation for 'sinners'.[33] I do not want to be understood to be saying that Jesus was not a compelling speaker or that his message would not have attracted hearers. But if it is true that large crowds surrounded him in Galilee,[34] it was probably more because of his ability to heal and exorcize than anything else. One could argue as follows: Jesus thought that he had a special role to play in the kingdom whose imminence John had proclaimed; he then decided to cast his own activity according to a group of Isaianic prophecies; he did so by healing the kinds of illness mentioned in Isa. 35.5f. and by proclaiming the message of Isa. 61.1f. This view (which follows from Harvey's discussion) is not impossible. The more natural one seems to be that Jesus found that he could heal; that he thus attracted crowds and special followers; that he complemented his healing of the needy in Galilee by promising the kingdom to the poor and the outcasts. The influence of Isaiah need not be excluded from this picture, but it would be, at least at the outset, more coincidental than determinative.

The principal significance of Smith's argument about miracles, crowds and preaching, however, is not chronological. His observations serve principally to clarify our understanding. He puts it this way: 'The rest of the tradition about Jesus can be understood if we begin with the miracles, but the miracles cannot be understood if we begin with a purely didactic tradition.' One can move from *miracles* to *crowds* to *teaching* to *tumult* to *death* much more easily than from a *teacher* of law to a *miracle worker* to a *prophet* whose passion for sanctity irritated the authorities in Jerusalem.

> Teachers of the law were not, in this period, made over into miracle workers. Neither were the authors of apocalyptic prophecies; we have a dozen, and their authors are wholly anonymous. But a miracle worker could easily come to be thought a prophet and an authority on the law.[35]

We spent some time in the Introduction dwelling on the lack, in much of New Testament scholarship, of sustained attempts to show a relationship between what is usually regarded as Jesus' main activity and the consequences. He is often held to have been primarily a teacher of the law who debated with the Pharisees, and his execution as a trouble-maker is not intrinsically connected to the main thrust of his career and his message. One of the merits of Smith's case is that he makes a positive connection between what he regards as Jesus' principal activity (miracles) and the consequences (crowds, tumult and death).

Magic

But Smith's view of the role of miracles in Jesus' career is more far-reaching. We best understand Jesus, he argues, by thinking of him as a magician.[36] Part of the evidence is a list of parallels between Jesus' miracles and those of pagan magicians, Apollonius of Tyana in particular.[37] More important, numerous parallels between the Gospel accounts and the Greek Magical Papyri are cited, and these include whole stories, types of miracles and formulae.[38] Naturally not every parallel is equally close, but Smith has offered us a kind of Strack-Billerbeck to the miracle stories, with the *PGM* taking the place of the Talmud and Midrash. This material, to give one of Smith's striking points, may explain the use of the title 'Son of God' for Jesus, which occurs, among other places, in stories of exorcisms.[39] He proposes that 'Son of God' (or 'son of god'; following Smith, I have a hard time knowing when to use capitals) means simply 'god'. With regard to the story of the baptism and Jesus' reception of the Spirit (Matt. 3.13–17//Mark 1.9–11//Luke 3.21f.), he argues that it is really a story of Jesus' deification. But this is only the beginning:

> . . . the gospel story still has to be explained: It tells of a man made a god by a rite of purification followed by the opening of the heavens and the coming of the spirit. Where do we find such stories? In the magical papyri.[40]

The first of several passages which are cited is this one, in which a magician is speaking:

> 'Open to me, heaven! . . . Let me see the bark of Phre descending and ascending . . . for I am Geb, heir of the gods; I make intercession before Phre my Father. . . .

The quotation continues and more, some closer to the baptismal story in the Gospel, are to follow.[41]

Smith points out that the Gospels themselves contain evidence that Jesus was a magician.[42] There is the Beelzebub story, in which Jesus is reported to answer the charge that he casts out demons by the prince of demons. We have discussed this passage before, and now I should state that I find the fact that Jesus was charged with the practice of magic a more telling one than part of the reported answer, Matt. 12.28//Luke 11.20, to which New Testament scholars have attached so much weight. I am not sure, that is, that Matt. 12.28 shows that Jesus thought that the kingdom was breaking in with his exorcisms, although that may be the case. But that Jesus was charged with the practice of magic seems indisputable. Why answer a charge that was not levelled? We see a similar charge in John 8.48.

The most striking Gospel account, in my view, is Mark's version of the story, Mark 3.20–30. Mark does not have a parallel to Matt. 12.28, and his story ends with what appears to be another version of a defence against the charge of healing with the aid of a demon.

> 'Whoever blasphemes against the Holy Spirit never has forgiveness, but is guilty of an eternal sin' – for they had said, 'He has an unclean spirit.' (3.29f.)

The nature of the charge against Jesus is even clearer in Mark's introduction:

> Then he went home; and the crowd came together again, so that they could not even eat. And when his family heard it, they went out to seize him, for people were saying, 'He is beside himself.' (3.19b–21)

Smith comments:

> From this it seems that Jesus' exorcisms were accompanied by abnormal behaviour on his part. Magicians who want to make demons obey often scream their spells, gesticulate, and match the mad in fury.[43]

Smith's precise explanation is not the only one available, and the verse might be taken to indicate that Jesus was a visionary or one given to trances.[44] But the report that Jesus was regarded as 'beside himself' or as one who 'had lost his senses' (so Bauer)[45] points to something that is not explained by the depiction of Jesus as a teller of parables and a teacher who entered into legal debate with the Pharisees.[46]

Smith offers an entire theory to account for the Jesus of the Gospels – and for subsequent points in Christian development. His fame as a magician led the crowds to think of him as Messiah and made him a threat to the authorities.[47] And he perceptively comments, though he does not elaborate on the point, that his healings correspond to the sayings which promise salvation to the poor.[48] I do not propose here to offer a point-by-point critique of Smith's work. I am in the course, in fact, of developing a different hypothesis. And, as we observed many pages back, the only way to proceed in the search for the historical Jesus is to offer hypotheses based on the evidence and to evaluate them in light of how satisfactorily they account for the material in the Gospels, while also making Jesus a believable figure in first-century Palestine and the founder of a movement which eventuated in the church.[49] Here I shall only comment on the hypothesis as such that it ought not to be dismissed out of hand because it is unpalatable and extreme. It does not proceed from some unsupported first assumption as do many total hypotheses. It deals seriously with the evidence, there are no blatant instances of leaping to grand conclusions from a slender base, and it introduces a wealth of material to fit Jesus into the world of antiquity – or into an aspect of it. There are, naturally, explanations which are not self-evident on the basis of simply reading the Gospels; the explanation of Mark 3.19b–21 is such a case. But Smith's explanation of that passage is plausible once one has found grounds to start looking for vestiges of magic.

Nor should Smith's hypothesis be dismissed because the parallel material is too remote from first-century Palestine. Philostratus's life of Apollonius was written well after Apollonius's death, but there is no reason to think that it was entirely based on a third-century rather than a first-century point of view. A similar comment would apply to the magical papyri. Geographical distance does not mean that the parallels are necessarily inapplicable. We have all learned by now that Palestine was not an island. I earlier compared Smith's parallels to those of Billerbeck, which scholars have used for decades. I do not know that one is more remote than the other. Further, I have appreciably more confidence in Smith's reading of the *PGM* than in Billerbeck's interpretation of Rabbinic religion.

It may help us to get some perspective on Smith's view of Jesus' miracles by considering a recent discussion by Ramsay MacMullen about conversion. MacMullen describes what it took in the ancient world shortly after the period of the Gospels (he deals with approximately the period 100–300)[50] to convince someone to change his mind about a god, to 'convert'.

> Converts sought reality, they sought truth, and the definition of what they sought can be seen in what produced a change in their allegiance. There are plenty of explicit descriptions of the moment.[51]

After giving examples, some pagan, some Christian, he continues:

> Their point in common was of the simplest: announcement of supernatural powers new in the world it would be quite irrational to credit, without proof

of their efficacy before one's own eyes. *That* was what produced converts. Nothing else is attested. . . .

True divinity . . . will prove itself by its wide or long-lasting impact on the human scene. Therein lies a further test by which mere magicians and manipulators of minor, dark spirits can be distinguished . . . . And still further: the divine is beneficent. . . . Finally: the divine has no needs, or different needs, compared with humankind. Its working can be judged, and its prophets known apart from frauds, through their superiority to material things. Asceticism will mark them. . . .

To credit the divinity behind a name newly presented to one, a person had to discover the qualities generally thought to belong to a god. Of course. Those qualities were: a constitution and substance somehow different and above material nature; the ability to do things humans could not do; and the applying of this ability in ways helpful and desirable to worshippers, indeed, helpful to everyone.[52]

I have presented verbatim so much of MacMullen's discussion because his definitions are so succinct and are useful in evaluating Smith's proposals, and consequently in attaining a clearer view of what people in the first century might have made of Jesus. We note at first that he does not fit very well any of the roles in MacMullen's brief discussion of new gods and conversion to them. As a god, Jesus fails MacMullen's test. He did not, during his lifetime, have wide impact, and he had human needs. He lacked asceticism, one of the marks of a prophet. MacMullen's statement appears to imply that magicians not only used evil spirits, but did so for evil ends; the divine, by contrast, is beneficent. In this case, based on present knowledge, Jesus would be disqualified as a magician.[53]

Granted that they are not discussing precisely the same subject, nevertheless Smith and MacMullen differ on two points: the definitions of a god and of a magician. In Smith's view, but not in MacMullen's, a magician could be called a god.[54] Smith's evidence is from the magical papyri, while MacMullen is discussing publicly proclaimed deities. Thus the difference is in the audience and the scope of the word 'god'. In MacMullen's terms, a magician has human needs and relatively restricted impact, and so could not be a god. Smith shows, however, that a magician could privately or in the circle of his disciples or fellow-magicians say that he was a god. He notes that Jesus is generally called 'Son of God' in connection with the miracles, and he proposes that the connection is causal.[55]

MacMullen's definition, then, does not serve to refute Smith's proposal for the origin of the title 'Son of God'. We should ask, however, whether miracles could have evoked that title from a Jewish audience. Even if in pagan circles magic could lead to the title 'son of god', could it do so in Jewish Galilee? We do not know how strictly and thoroughly monotheistic the ordinary people of Galilee were. In Smith's view, many Galileans were recent, forced converts, and their conversion may have been only skin-deep.[56] But even if, following Freyne, we assume that they were loyal Jews of long standing,[57] we still cannot know that for them monotheism excluded use of the phrase 'Son of God', or 'son of god', for one who had extraordinary power. We should recall that even such a self-conscious and sophisticated monotheist as Philo could point out that Moses, like God, was called 'god and king of the nation' (*Moses* I.158; Philo has biblical support: see Exod. 4.16; 7.1). Philo is perhaps further from the Galilean peasantry than are the Greek magical papyri, and neither gives direct evidence about possible meanings of 'god' among Galilean peasants. The present point must remain general: we cannot know that even in Jewish circles a person could not be called 'god'. Smith's proposal remains as a possibility.

The second question – whether or not a magician could do good deeds and still be a magician – is an interesting one, since it raises the question of what deeds prove about the doer. We shall return immediately to this as a general question. With regard to the strict definition of a magician, however, it would seem that Smith is correct. The implication of the Beelzebub controversy, as it now stands in the Gospels, is that Jesus was accused of employing an evil spirit to perform exorcisms and was himself therefore allied with evil. This seems to mean that, although he did good deeds, he could be accused of not being a good person – in effect, of being a magician. We must assume that this made sense to the evangelists and their readers, and thus that Jesus, while doing good deeds, could have been thought of as a magician.

Just as we earlier observed that Smith's argument cannot be brushed aside as relying on evidence too remote from first-century Palestine, we must now observe that MacMullen's observations about gods and miracles in the ancient world do not lead to the dismissal of Smith's view. As I proposed above, his hypothesis as a whole is unsatisfactory because it leaves largely out of account the persuasive evidence which makes us look to Jewish eschatology as defining the general contours of Jesus' career.[58] That his miracles exemplify some of the traits of magic need not be denied.

Conclusion

We have dealt principally with two recent attempts to make the fact of miracles provide a definition of who Jesus was, or at least of what *sort* of figure he was. Harvey, with others, has proposed that the miracles were eschatological and agree with other evidence that Jesus saw himself as being a, or the, end-time figure. Smith has proposed that Jesus' miracles bear some of the marks of magic and that Jesus was a magician who moved upward to holy man and god on the strength of his ability to work wonders. There have been other proposals, for example that of Vermes, that Jesus fits the type of a Galilean charismatic such as Honi.[59] It is my own judgment that we learn nothing this definite from the fact of the miracles.

The problem is indicated by the Beelzebub controversy. We see there that miracles would indicate different things to different people, depending on their point of view.[60] Even if Jesus, in performing miracles, sometimes employed some of the devices of a magician (e.g., imitating the madness he was trying to heal), and thus may be said to have practised 'magic',[61] we cannot, from that possibility, conclude that he *was* a magician. The Essenes, Josephus informs us, were adept at magical practice (*BJ* II.159), but we do not understand them adequately by calling them 'magicians'. Nor do we understand Jesus by calling him 'a magician'. There is too much evidence in hand which inclines us to call him an eschatological prophet to permit us to dismiss it and to allow our title for his 'type' to be determined only by his miracles.

We are in part here debating two closely related questions, one of emphasis, the other of what categories provide helpful labels. I shall reserve full comments on Jesus' religious and social 'type' for ch. 8, and here make only preliminary remarks. Smith and I – and more or less everyone else – think that Jesus claimed to be a spokesman for God and performed what were viewed as miracles. The questions are whether we should (1) emphasize the miracles and (2) derive from them the basic label for Jesus. I propose that Smith presses beyond what is helpful in categorizing Jesus as 'a magician'. 'Prophet', at least thus far, is probably to be regarded as the better term. The importance of this distinction will be seen immediately below.

But the miracles themselves, as I have more than once observed, do not push us further towards the view that Jesus was an eschatological prophet. There is nothing about miracles which would trigger, in the first-century Jewish world, the expectation that the end was at hand.

That is not to say, however, that an eschatological prophet – or, for that matter, any prophet – would not be asked for a 'sign'. Quite the contrary. Anyone who made a claim to have inside knowledge about God's intention would probably be asked for a sign, just as would be the proclaimer of a new god.[62] Here the evidence of Josephus is clear.[63] In retelling the story of Moses, he follows the Bible fairly closely, but the treatment of 'signs' seems to reflect his own view as well. Moses accepted God's word as God's word because it was accompanied by such great signs (*AJ* II.275), and he employed signs to attempt to persuade Pharaoh. The signs were rejected by Pharaoh as 'juggleries and magic' (II.284), which shows that miracles cannot be self-authenticating. But Moses persevered and attempted, though without success, to persuade Pharaoh by still greater signs that it was 'from no witchcraft . . . , but from God's providence and power', that his signs proceeded (II. 286). At a period contemporary with Josephus we note that Theudas promised to part the river Jordan, that unnamed people promised marvels and signs to those who followed them into the desert, and that the Egyptian claimed that the walls of Jerusalem would collapse at his command.[64] We cannot be sure just what these people claimed to be. According to Josephus, Theudas and the Egyptian claimed to be prophets, and that will do as a general designation. Their promised signs were doubtless intended to prove *that they were who they said*, and that *God truly acted through them*. The signs promised by Theudas and the Egyptian, which recalled the Exodus and the conquest, were almost certainly intended to be eschatological signs.[65] The deeds promised were proferred as signs of the kingdom, not because miracles themselves point to the eschaton, but because of the events which they recalled. Whether Theudas and the Egyptian thought that the kingdom was future, or was 'breaking in' in their deeds, we have no way of knowing. But generically, these signs, like others, were intended to prove that the doer of them spoke the truth and acted with power given by God. It is also clear that not everyone believed. Signs and wonders, whether performed or only promised, do not necessarily convince all and sundry that the person who performs them speaks and acts for God.

Josephus clearly signals his own view of Theudas (informed by hindsight) by calling him a *goēs*, a magician or deceiver (*AJ* XX.97).[66] The title is intended pejoratively. Theudas considered himself a prophet; Josephus called him a magician. Had Theudas's sign worked, had the Romans been put to rout, or had something approaching 'the kingdom' arrived, Josephus doubtless would have found another title. Similarly Philostratus termed Apollonius a 'sage' and defended him against the charge that he was a 'sorcerer' (*magos*) (*Life of Apollonius* I.2). The terms distinguish point of view more than activity.

We can now see the situation in the Gospels clearly. Jesus, we read, was asked for a sign, and we may be reasonably sure that the report is accurate. According to Matt. 12.38–42 and par.; Mark 8.11f. and par., he refused. Matt. 11.2–6, however, depicts John the Baptist as asking if Jesus is 'the one to come', and in his reply Jesus is said to offer signs. I share the general opinion that the pericope as such does not describe an actual event, but it does show the naturalness of appealing to signs for authentication. But whether or not Jesus offered his miracles as signs that he spoke for God, they convinced some that he did so, and they considered him a special figure in God's plan. They also probably asked just who he was (cf. Matt. 11.3; Mark 8.27 and parr.), and they gave him favourable titles (Mark 8.28f. and parr.), probably even 'Son of God' (Mark 3.11 and elsewhere). Others were unpersuaded. They very likely called Jesus a 'magician' or 'deceiver'.

In any case, the miracles by themselves do not suffice to tell us what was Jesus' religious 'type'. I am inclined to put him closer to Theudas than to Honi or to the magicians of the *PGM*,[67] but that is because there is other evidence which leads us to think of Jesus as an eschatological prophet, not because the miracles make him one. Miracles were sufficiently common, sufficiently diverse, and sufficiently scattered among holy men, messianic pretenders, magicians and temples that we cannot draw firm inferences from them in order to explain what social type Jesus fits best or what his intention really was.

While the miracles themselves do not dictate their own meaning, it is entirely reasonable to assume that Jesus' following, and perhaps Jesus himself, saw them as evidencing his status as true spokesman for God, since that sort of inference was common in the Mediterranean. We cannot say that Jesus proferred his miracles to his audience as bearing this significance – even though it is reasonable that he saw them in this way – because of the tradition that he refused to give a sign. According to the Gospels, the miracles show that Jesus spoke and acted with divine authority, and some saw it that way, though others doubted. They depict Jesus himself as not appealing to the miracles as establishing his authority except in replying to John. It turns out that we cannot go much behind their view of the matter. The miracles constitute a fact about Jesus' career, but they do not tell as much as could have been desired.

At the beginning of the chapter we posed four questions which should be considered in studying the miracles and what they tell us about Jesus, his intention, and the significance of his career. Let us now offer summary answers:

1. We do not learn with certainty what Jesus thought of himself, although it is reasonable to think that he, as well as his followers, saw his miracles as testifying to his being a true messenger from or agent of God.

2. The miracles, as Smith proposed, doubtless contributed greatly to his ability to gather crowds, and they thus help explain why he was executed. It was not just that his words, abstractly considered, were challenging to the authorities, but that he attracted attention and commotion.

3. 'Outsiders' probably regarded Jesus as a charlatan, a magician.

4. Jesus cannot be considered simply a teacher. The miracles do not require us to think that he was an eschatological prophet, but they are compatible with that view.

We earlier noted Smith's proposal that Jesus' miracles correspond to his proclamation to the 'poor'.[68] There is no explicit connection made in the literature, but the Gospels lead us to see his followers as being religiously the 'sinners' and socially the lame, halt and blind: that is, as being on the fringes of society for one reason or another. This leads us to the question of Jesus and the 'sinners'.

6

THE SINNERS

The one distinctive note which we may be certain marked Jesus' teaching about the kingdom is that it would include the 'sinners'. Even if we grant that Jesus may have held the view that the kingdom was breaking in with his own words and deeds (Matt. 11.2–6; 12.28), we must also note that such a view is very difficult to find in the didactic material which is attributed to him. Thus the opening sentence: the promise of salvation to sinners is the undeniably distinctive characteristic of Jesus' message. Everyone agrees that this is at least one of the characteristic traits, but we may nevertheless ask how such happy concord is reached. There are three considerations. (1) The material which conveys that message is large in extent. (2) It reaches us in many diverse forms – parables, other sayings, flat declarations of purpose, reports of Jesus' activity, and reported accusations against him.[1] (3) A high tolerance for sinners was not a characteristic of the early church, as far as we can know it. The description of Jesus' group as 'sinners' probably originated, as Jeremias and others have suggested, as an accusation.[2] That Jesus' group was said to consist of (or at least include) sinners has the same probability of authenticity as has the accusation that he exorcized by a demon. This is one of the instances in which the usual criteria for authenticity really work.

Of the material which conveys the promise of salvation to sinners, I, with others, would single out 'flat declarations of purpose' as having the slightest claim to authenticity.[3] Jesus may have said 'I came not to call the righteous, but sinners' (Mark 2.17) and 'I was sent only to the lost sheep of the house of Israel' (Matt. 15.24; the same restriction is laid on the disciples in 10.6), but all the 'I came' and 'I was sent' passages are under the suspicion of being creations of the later church.[4] If these statements are such, however, it would appear that the church expanded an authentic motif.

Passages about the 'sinners' show us again how tenuous it is to rely on the authenticity of any individual saying. What I am proposing is this: (1) The church would not have created the description of Jesus' proclamation as being directed towards 'sinners'. (2) Nevertheless some of the summary statements (especially Matt. 9.11–13//Mark 2.16f.//Luke 5.30–32, Jesus came to call sinners, not the righteous) were probably created in the early church. Here as elsewhere we can rely on general probability more than on the analysis of any individual passage.[5] It is unlikely that the church created from nothing the charge that Jesus associated with sinners; but once that charge was fixed in the tradition, it would appear that further sayings could be generated. The saying in Mark 2.16f. and parr. seems to have an apologetic thrust, since it partially protects the righteous: they are all right, yet Jesus' special mission was to call sinners. Luke heightens the apologia by adding 'unto repentance' (Luke 5.32). It is also quite possible that the first statement, 'that he eats with sinners and tax collectors' (Mark 2.16a), is an addition. Matthew and Luke elsewhere have no objection to incorporating that description. Similarly Luke 15.1f. (as we shall see below) is almost certainly an editorial creation; and I would regard the parable of the Pharisee and the Tax Collector (Luke 18.9–14), with its heavy accent on breast-beating and repentance, as a Lucan (or pre-Lucan) creation.[6] The story of Zacchaeus, who in public promised restoration of all that he had unfairly gained, is also peculiar to Luke (Luke 19.1–10).[7] One may also note as dubious Luke's conclusion to the parable of the Lost Sheep (joy over one sinner who repents, Luke 15.7), which is an edifying remark not present in the Matthaean parallel (Matt. 18.10–14).[8] Luke concludes the parable of the Lost Coin in the same way (Luke 15.10).[9] We shall return to the question of repentance, noting here only that Luke was concerned to emphasize that the disreputable people with whom Jesus associated were moved to repentance and reformation. At any rate we see that the theme of Jesus' concern for the 'sinners', once it was embedded in the synoptic tradition, could be expanded, especially if a moral could be attached.

The authentic material, which we shall discuss shortly, will turn out to be slight in comparison to the elaborations and enhancements of the theme. The distinctiveness and importance of the topic, however, as well as the difficulty of giving it a meaningful setting, require an extended treatment. The question becomes what we can learn from the *fact* that Jesus was accused of associating with 'tax collectors and sinners'. The answer to this question is, I think, harder to discover than is usually thought to be the case, and we shall have to spend some time evaluating the predominant view.

The sinners, the wicked, the poor and the 'amme ha-arets

Jeremias presents under the heading 'the poor' the position that several terms in the Gospels are synonymous; more precisely, that they refer to the same group.[10] He proposes that the reader of the Gospels sees this group from two perspectives, that of Jesus' opponents and that of Jesus himself. The former called his followers 'tax collectors and sinners' or 'sinners', as well as other derogatory names – 'the little ones' (Mark 9.42 and elsewhere) or 'the simple ones' (Matt. 11.25). About the terminology for Jesus' group as seen by his enemies (here tacitly assumed to be the Pharisees), Jeremias says this:

> Summing up, then, we can now say that Jesus' following consisted predominantly of the disreputable, the 'ammē hā-'āreṣ, the uneducated, the ignorant, whose *religious* ignorance and *moral* behaviour stood in the way of their access to salvation, according to the convictions of the time.[11]

From Jesus' own point of view, this group was called 'the poor' (a well-known term to mean 'our group, presently out of power', the biblical background of which Jeremias concisely presents). The term occurs in Matt. 11.5//Luke 7.22; Luke 4.18; 6.20. An alternate phrase is 'those who labour and are heavy laden' (Matt. 11.28).[12]

Jeremias's position, then, is that Jesus' opponents could call his followers *either* 'sinners' *or* 'amme ha-arets (or words equivalent to it) with no clear distinction of meaning. This position I believe to be incorrect, though many accept the equation of the 'poor', the 'little ones', the 'sinners' and the common people.[13] There are, in fact, several views about Jesus, the sinners, the 'amme ha-arets and the Pharisees which are widely held, but which I think can be shown to be completely wrong.[14] Principal discussion of the Pharisees as Jesus' opponents will occupy us in ch. 10, but we may here lay out the complex of interrelated views which dominate New Testament scholarship and begin to evaluate the evidence. The views are these: (1) That 'Pharisees', 'ḥaberim', and 'Rabbis' are more or less equivalent terms. (2) That in Jesus' day the Pharisees (= the ḥaberim) controlled Judaism. (3) That the term 'sinners' includes the ordinary people, those called 'amme ha-arets in Rabbinic literature. (4) That the leaders of Judaism (believed to be the Pharisees) successfully made these people feel excluded. (5) That Jesus' uniqueness consists in part in his offering forgiveness to repentant sinners (= common people). (6) That Jesus offended the Pharisees by associating with the common people and offering them forgiveness. The association, in the form of table-fellowship, is held to have transgressed the Pharisaic purity code. (7) That Jesus' behaviour was so offensive as to account, in no small part, for his execution.

The discussion which immediately follows will focus on the first, third, fourth, fifth and sixth points, but aspects of the second and seventh will also be considered. The discussion will be a bit involved, and I have resorted to an enumeration scheme to keep the points straight. We shall begin with terminological points (under 1) and proceed to the common people and salvation (under 2). Finally, we shall offer a new proposal about the significance of Jesus' inclusion of the 'sinners' (under 3). Since most discussions of the sinners and the *'amme ha-arets* rely on Rabbinic literature to define Pharisaic opinions, our discussion will include the Rabbis. I shall, however, try to distinguish the situation before 70 from that after 70.

1. *Terminology*

1.1. *The sinners.* Many scholars have recognized that the inclusion of the common people under the term 'sinners' is not correct,[15] but it still seems that the erroneous view is popular enough, and is contained in sufficiently important books, to require one more refutation. There should be no confusion about the basic meaning of the term 'sinners' in the Gospels. The word in English versions of the Bible translates the Greek word *hamartōloi*. Behind *hamartōloi* stands, almost beyond question, the Hebrew word *resha'im* (or the Aramaic equivalent). The Semitic languages have other words which are used in parallel with *resha'im*, but it is the dominant term. *Resha'im* is virtually a technical term. It is best translated 'the wicked', and it refers to those who sinned wilfully and heinously and who did not repent.[16] It is often said that the wicked were 'professional sinners', and Jeremias has collected lists of such from here and there in Rabbinic literature.[17] Certainly the term would include professional sinners, such as usurers, who in their daily business transgressed Lev. 25.36–38:

> Take no interest from him [your brother who becomes poor] or increase, but fear your God; that your brother may live beside you. You shall not lend him your money at interest, nor give him your food for profit. I am the Lord your God, who brought you forth out of the land of Egypt to give you the land of Canaan, and to be your God.

The clear implication of the passage is that those who renounce the commandment not to charge interest also renounce the Lord God, who brought them out of the land of Egypt: they renounce the covenant. These are, in later Jewish terminology, 'the wicked'. The Rabbis understood the implication very well, and Rabbinic literature spells it out, dealing with this and other similarly weighted injunctions in detail.[18] There is every reason to think that this understanding of the 'wicked' prevailed also before 70.[19] How can one read the biblical passage and not see the point? Those who fear God do not charge interest; those who charge interest do not fear God.

Jeremias, in making a basically correct point, follows the late Rabbinic homiletical exaggeration in making all sorts of trades the equivalent of usury.[20] These lists and similar ones have an observable tendency to lengthen,[21] and we should not follow Jeremias to the bottom line of the latest list; but the general point is correct.

The wicked need not be involved in a profession which requires renunciation of the God who redeemed Israel. There are other ways of renouncing the covenant. The apocryphal story about Elisha b. Abuya makes the point perfectly well. He rode his horse in front of the temple site on the Day of Atonement when it fell on a Sabbath.[22]

Thus we know in general terms who the wicked were, and we can readily understand why 'tax collectors' and 'sinners' go together in several passages in the Gospels: they were all traitors. Tax collectors, more precisely, were quislings, collaborating with Rome. The wicked equally betrayed the God who redeemed Israel and gave them his law. There was no neat distinction between 'religious' and 'political' betrayal in first-century Judaism.

There are two principal passages in the Gospels in which Jesus is said to have been criticized for eating with the tax collectors and the wicked. One is a triple tradition passage, usually called 'The Call of Levi' (Matt. 9.9–13//Mark 2.13–17//Luke 5.27–32). Jesus calls a tax collector to follow him, and he does so. They enter a house to eat and are joined by other 'tax collectors and sinners'. The Pharisees, ever on the look-out for Jesus' table companions, since they are constantly concerned with the question of with whom Jesus eats, ask the disciples why Jesus eats with tax collectors and sinners. This serves to introduce the statement which we earlier mentioned, 'I came not to call the righteous, but sinners.' The story as such is obviously unrealistic. We can hardly imagine the Pharisees as policing Galilee to see whether or not an otherwise upright man ate with sinners. But the charge, I think, is authentic, and we shall eventually come back to it.

The second story is more realistic. The passage in Matthew (11.16–19) is set in a context of accusations against 'this generation'. Jesus complains that they rejected John, and now they reject him. They call him 'a glutton and a wine-bibber, a friend of tax collectors and sinners' (Matt. 11.19; cf. Luke 7.34). This has the ring of authenticity.[23] Jesus is in something like despair: nothing works, neither John's asceticism and austerity, nor his own different tactic.

But we do not need to try to prove that the passage is a verbatim account. As we said above, the general charge that Jesus associated with tax collectors and sinners is very likely one that was actually levelled against him, even though none of our accounts may be verbatim reports. Thus here I can happily join the consensus and agree that Jesus associated with the wicked and was criticized for it.

The wicked (more precisely, the lost) appear prominently in three consecutive parables in Luke, and these parables, if authentic, indicate Jesus' view of them. The parables are the Lost Sheep, the Lost Coin, and the Prodigal Son (Luke 15.1–32).[24] I do not wish to allegorize the parables,[25] but it is hard not to see the Lost Coin and the Lost Sheep as corresponding to the tax collectors and sinners that Jesus associated with. If we can make this equation, then we can note that they are called 'the lost' (Luke 15.4, 6, 9, 32), and the prodigal son characterizes himself as one who has 'sinned' (Luke 15.18). Luke's setting in 15.1f. (tax collectors and sinners were near Jesus, and the Pharisees and scribes said that Jesus eats with sinners) is of course his own contribution, as are the concluding summaries to the first two parables ('more joy in heaven over one sinner who repents', Luke 15.7, 10).[26] But Luke seems to have been on the right track. Jesus was concerned with 'the lost'.

Thus, to conclude this sub-section: Jesus saw his mission as being to 'the lost' and the 'sinners': that is, to the wicked. He was doubtless also concerned with the poor, the meek and the downtrodden, and in all probability he had a following among them. But the *charge* against him was not that he loved the *'amme ha-arets*, the common people. If there was a conflict, it was about the status of the *wicked*. It is a mistake to think that the Pharisees were upset because he ministered to the ordinarily pious common people and the economically impoverished.[27] To drive this point home, we should now turn to the relationship – or lack thereof – between the wicked and the common people.

1.2. *The wicked and the 'amme ha-arets.* The problem with Jeremias's position is that the term 'the wicked' (in Greek, 'sinners') – which is used with complete consistency in the Gospels and in Jewish·literature from Ben Sira to the close of the Mishnah, a period of 400 years – does not include the *'amme ha-arets*. Rabbinic literature is the only source to which one may look for traces of Pharisaic attitudes towards the ordinary people. I maintain that there is absolutely no passage in the entirety of that literature – which is large enough to contain some element of virtually every known attitude and emotion – which in any way supports the assertion that the scrupulous and learned regarded the ordinary people as 'the wicked', those who flagrantly and persistently disobeyed the law. Earlier Jewish literature generally uses the term 'wicked' and the like for the powerful who oppress the 'pious'.[28] In short, I know of no passage in Jewish literature which indicates that any group which can reasonably be connected with the Pharisees considered the common people as beyond the pale.[29]

There is one passage in the New Testament which attributes to the Pharisees the view that 'this crowd, who do not know the law, are accursed' (John 7.49). Further, the parable of the Pharisee and the Publican may be read as attributing to the Pharisees the view that *all* others are 'extortioners, unjust, adulterers' and the like (Luke 18.9–14). (The note on the latter passage in the New Oxford Annotated Bible describes these faults as being ritual failures. This indicates very well how deeply committed New Testament scholarship is to the view that the Pharisees were interested only in ritual and trivia.) Neither passage can be regarded as actually indicating the views of Pharisaism before 70,[30] and the second may reflect nothing other than Luke's anti-Pharisaism.[31] At a maximum, they might be taken as reflecting one side of the hostility between the learned and the unlearned which sometimes appears in Rabbinic literature.[32] It is not unreasonable to think that both before and after 70 there was some hostility between the learned and the scrupulous (the *ḥaberim*, scribes and Pharisees), on the one hand, and the common people on the other. But we must remember that feelings of hostility and despite do not add up to a fixed view on the part of the Pharisees or the *ḥaberim* that those less learned and scrupulous were cut off from access to salvation, as many would have it. We shall later note the significance of the fact that the hostility was mutual.

In Rabbinic literature the term *'am ha-arets* is used in two contexts: they are contrasted with the *ḥaberim* and with the *ḥakamin*.

1.3. The *'amme ha-arets* are contrasted with the *ḥaberim*, the 'associates'. These took upon themselves the obligation to observe some of the priestly laws of purity (e.g. Demai 2.3; T. Demai 2.2). The relationship between accepting special laws of purity and undertaking to be 'trustworthy' in tithing is difficult to sort out, but it would appear that originally these were two separate obligations.[33] In any case we concern ourselves here only with the matter of purity. It is usually said that the motive of the *haberim* was to treat the world like a temple, the sanctuary where God dwells.[34] This is the most likely general explanation, though it is to be noted that they accepted for themselves a lower standard of purity than that which governed priests (e.g. Demai 2.3). This and other considerations have led Solomon Spiro to conclude that, prior to 70, the *haberim* played a distinctive role in the socio-economic order: 'The *haberim* . . . were expected to observe those laws of ritual purity which are associated with heave offerings and tithes because they were occupied with these two essential agricultural contributions to the religious state. They collected them.'[35]

This does not mean that we should surrender the view that they took upon themselves special obligations out of piety. Others who undertook special obligations probably did so from pious motives, at least in part. The ancient equivalents of modern morticians, for example, undertook a special task which required *impurity*; and since care of the dead was a religious obligation, we should assume for them the attitude of offering service to God.[36] Similarly with the *haberim* who accepted a high standard of purity: as Neusner and others have proposed, doubtless they did see themselves as living in a sanctified universe.

I have neither the need nor the competence to sort out, on the basis of the complicated evidence in the Mishnah and Tosefta, the history of groups which accepted special obligations of purity and tithing. It is generally granted on all hands, and it should be accepted, that before 70 there were *haberim* – lay people who maintained themselves in a relatively high state of ritual purity. What is important to note is that such groups were small, voluntary associations which accepted special rules for special reasons. They may have thought that others should be like them. There is absolutely no reason, however, for supposing that such people – whether before or after 70 – thought of themselves as 'the righteous' and of the rest of Israel – the *'amme ha-arets* – as 'the wicked'. The supposition so often held by New Testament scholars, that the *haberim* considered all others to be 'cut off' from God, Israel and salvation, is totally without foundation.

Finkelstein put the matter with complete clarity:

The *'am ha-arez* did not accept the Hasidean norm requiring even profane food to be kept pure so far as possible and to be consumed only in a state of purity. The Hasideans themselves admitted that these norms were not 'biblical' in the usual sense of the term; but regarding the world as a Temple they insisted that all normal life should be in a state of purity. . . . [The person violating this view] might not be a *ḥaber*, but neither was he a transgressor.[37]

The common people were not irreligious. They presumably kept most of the law most of the time, observed the festivals, and paid heed to 'some of the more serious purity regulations'.[38] It was only the special purity laws of the *ḥaberim* which they did not observe. We should pause to consider those which they probably did observe – or were generally expected to observe.

1.3.1. *Biblical purity laws.* Purity laws are strange to most of us in the West, and confusion seems to settle like a cloud around the heads of New Testament scholars who discuss Jewish purity laws. Some clarification may be useful.[39] There are biblical laws concerning purity which all who counted themselves as at all observant would have kept. Most purity laws, however, are not prohibitions; they do not require people to avoid impurity. They regulate, rather, what must be done after contracting impurity *in order to enter the temple.* Josephus put it very well: in several instances the law prescribes purification 'in view of the sacrifices': 'after a funeral, after childbirth, after conjugal union, and many others' (*Ap.* II.198; cf. II.103f.; *BJ* V.227). Purity is related to the temple and the sacrifices, and impurity does not limit ordinary associations, except for very short periods of time (*AJ* III.261f.).

As Josephus indicated, the most pervasive laws concerning purity are corpse uncleanness (Num. 19), menstruation, intercourse and childbirth (Lev. 12.1–8; 15.16–24). Care for the dead was and is considered a firm religious duty, and contracting corpse-uncleanness was therefore required in a family in which there was a death. Childbirth and intercourse are good, and menstruation is natural. The impurity which is incurred by childbirth, until it is removed, prevents a woman from touching 'any hallowed thing' (that is, something intended for use in the temple) and from entering the temple itself (Lev. 12.4). Luke describes Mary and Joseph (depicted as good *'amme ha-arets*) as observing the purity laws regarding childbirth (Luke 2.22f., 39). In such matters the rule is that people who have contracted impurity should not defile the temple (Lev. 15.31). Similarly the warning about corpse-uncleanness is not to defile 'the tabernacle' (Num. 19.13). Most people had corpse-uncleanness a lot of the time; and, since the rite of purity requires the ashes of the red heifer, purification has been impossible since shortly after the destruction of the temple. There is nothing wrong with such people; they are only forbidden by biblical law to enter the temple area. People in a state of impurity according to these and similar laws – the laws which were presumably accepted by all – were not sinners, nor had they done anything which made them inappropriate companions for 'table fellowship'.[40]

There are also prohibitions related to purity, such as those against eating or touching certain unclean creatures (Lev. 11; cf. *AJ* III.259f.). These convey impurity which is removed by washing and the setting of the sun (see e.g. Lev. 11.28). There are a few prohibitions which involve the transgressor in sins, such as the eating of certain fats or blood. For these, the penalty is 'cutting off' (Lev. 7.22–27). In the later Rabbinic interpretation, 'cutting off' puts the transgression strictly between human and God, and it is atoned for by repentance.[41] The same penalty is prescribed for those who, while impure, eat sacrificial food (Lev. 7.20f.).

This discussion has by no means dealt with all aspects of the purity laws, but I shall attempt some generalizations. (1) Most impurities do not result from the transgression of a prohibition, although a few do. Purification in either case is necessary before entering the temple or otherwise contacting something holy, and it is accomplished by washing and the setting of the sun (or, in the case of corpse-uncleanness, a more complicated variant of the procedure: Num. 19.1–13). In neither case is the impure person a sinner. A substantial sin is committed only if someone while impure eats holy food or enters the temple. (2) A few purity transgressions, such as eating blood, are in and of themselves sins; that is, they require atonement. (3) Contact between an impure person and a pure person is not ordinarily considered a sin, although such contacts may have been avoided to keep impurity from spreading and ultimately touching something connected with the temple. In one important instance contact with an impure person involves both parties in a sin: sexual intercourse with a menstruant. The Bible (Lev. 20.18) specified 'cutting off' as the punishment, while the Rabbis required a sin-offering (Niddah 2.2). (4) But, as a general rule, those who became impure, either because they should do so (e.g. to care for the dead and bear children), or because they touched something forbidden (e.g. vermin), did not, as long as they lived their ordinary lives, *sin*. Normal human relations were not substantially affected. Recourse to the immersion pool (see just below), and waiting for the sun to set, cleansed most impurities.

˙ It should be emphasized that observation of the biblical purity laws was not a special concern of the Pharisees. Westerholm, who in general understands the topic of purity very well, nevertheless has some curious statements. He writes that 'in O.T. times, it was clearly the priests' responsibility to define the areas of clean and unclean, and to teach the observance of these distinctions to the people', while 'in the N.T. period, Pharisees observed distinctions in this area drawn by scribes'.[42] We should first note that the prescriptions for cleansing before entering the temple could not be enforced by anyone, but lay on each person's conscience. But since the biblical laws principally have to do with the temple, it was still in Jesus' day the priests' responsibility to teach them.[43] There is no reason to believe that they had surrendered this prerogative to the Pharisees, or to secular scribes who taught them to Pharisees.

The biblical laws seem to have been widely observed. Westerholm calls attention to the passage in Josephus which describes resistance in the days of Herod Antipas to settling in Tiberias, which overlay a burial ground (*AJ* XVIII.36–38).[44] Living in such an area would make one always impure. We may now also point to the numerous ritual baths (*miqvaot*) which archaeology has brought to light in houses in Jerusalem during the Herodian period. There were also *miqvaot* to the south and west of the temple area. With one exception (to my knowledge) these are not equipped with a pipe connecting the bath water to a cistern containing rain or spring water,[45] which is virtually required in cities by later Rabbinic rule, and probably also by the Pharisees.[46] We know that at least some of those most zealous for the law and Israel built such *miqvaot* before 70.[47] The houses in west Jerusalem, a prosperous area of the city, may have been occupied by priests or others who worked for or in the temple. We may attribute the number of *miqvaot* partly to prosperity, and perhaps also partly to respect for Jerusalem as a holy city: observance of ritual purity may have been higher there than elsewhere. But we see in any case that it was widely observed, and observed by people of different classes and halakic orientations. The well-to-do inhabitants of West Jerusalem, probably Sadducees if anything, did not observe it because the Pharisees and scribes demanded it, but because the Bible does.[48]

One should ask what was the situation of a person who disregarded the purity laws and did not use the immersion pool, but remained perpetually impure. Here it would be reasonable to equate being impure with being a 'sinner' in the sense of 'wicked', for such a person would have taken the position that the biblical laws need not be observed. All the laws of purity and impurity are to be voluntarily observed. If, for example, a husband and wife agreed not to observe the prohibition of intercourse during menstruation, no one would ever know unless they announced the fact. If the woman never used the immersion pool, however, her neighbours would note that she was not observant (unless she could afford a private pool). *Not intending* to be observant is precisely what makes one 'wicked';

but the wickedness comes not from impurity as such, but from the attitude that the commandments of the Bible need not be heeded.

Thus these biblical purity laws, which most people seem to have observed, did not lead to a fixed view that the common people were sinners.

1.3.2. *Handwashing.* Handwashing is an entirely different matter. It appears from the Gospels that some lay Jews (either in Jesus' day or later) washed their hands before eating (Mark 7.2f. and par.). One assumes that these were the *haberim*, who might see this as a way of pursuing their programme: of living life as in the temple. What we do not know about the practice of handwashing, however, exceeds what we do know. We do not know, for example, that the priests washed their hands before eating. It is not a biblical requirement, though it appears in the Mishnah. According to Yoma 3.2 a priest in the temple must wash his hands and feet after urinating, and Zabim 5.12 lists the hands as rendering heave-offering invalid. In Yadaim 2.2 handwashing is also connected with eating heave-offering. In these and other cases purification by handwashing is not argued, but presupposed, and this may incline one to the view that the practice was older than the Rabbis who discuss it. Even so, however, we cannot say that the priests in the temple followed what later Rabbinic law regards as obvious, although they may have done so.

The origin and development of the rules about handwashing by the laity are even more obscure.[49] The Mishnah itself says that unwashed hands do not defile common food (Parah 11.5). Further, according to the same mishnah, a person impure 'according to the words of the Scribes' but not according to the law (the category with which we are dealing), could, without immersion, enter the temple without being guilty. That is, he was not truly impure. The authors of the Mishnah took handwashing seriously: in various tractates they gave elaborate details about when it is to be done, how it is to be done, the effect of doing it, what happens if one hand is washed and the other not, and so on. But they knew that it was not an area in which one who did not follow their rules was guilty of a sin. We do not know the precise chain of tradition from those who practised handwashing in Jesus' day (I assume that some did) to the Mishnah. Perhaps in the days of Jesus some were more rabid on the subject. We have no reason, however, to think that it was an area of serious controversy.

Having granted that we do not know the actual history of handwashing either by the priests or the laity, I shall propose a probable understanding of it. Many Jews in the time of Jesus thought that priests should wash their hands before eating heave-offering. The priests may or may not actually have done so, and all my proposal requires is a lay perception that they did or should. Some laypeople undertook to be 'trustworthy' purveyors of food to the priests, and in this connection they washed their hands before handling heave-offering.[50] They also, perhaps motivated by the desire to live as did priests in the temple, adopted the practice of eating even common food in a state of purity. This involved, among other things, washing their hands. These were – my proposal continues – the *haberim*.

Although there are some uncertainties about the history of the rules on handwashing, some things are clear. It is not a biblical purity law (1.2.1), but a practice which, in Jesus' day, was probably developing among certain groups. It is best, at least for the present purpose, to presume that those who practised it were *haberim*, to whom can be attributed concern for special purity rules. Mark says that 'the Jews' washed their hands before eating (7.3), but in Jesus' day it would have been a small number of them. The Rabbis eventually made handwashing 'normative', and it is worth noting that it is one of the very few practices of ritual purity which have continued. But before 70 the common people did not accept the practice. That is so by definition: had they done so they would have met one of the requirements of the *haberim*. But their failure to be *haberim* in this way, as in others, did not make them sinners. That is true even if we were to assume that the laws of the Mishnah governed the *haberim* in Jesus' time.[51]

1.3.3. *Purity: Conclusion*. The reason for making these simple observations is that, as I said above, confusion seems to surround the subject. Thus Braun takes Mark 7.6–9 (on handwashing) to be an instance in which Jesus castigated 'specific abuses in the Jewish practice of his time'.[52] Braun, we must assume, did not know the religious motive behind the programme of the *haberim* (to sanctify daily life), and characterizes it as 'abuse'. But the particular point here is that he regards the handwashing code as a Jewish practice, when in fact it was limited to a small group. Similarly Aulén, summarizing recent New Testament scholarship, writes that Jesus' view was that prescriptions in the law of Moses, 'for example those concerning the Sabbath and purity', must give way when they come into conflict with the love commandment.[53] But handwashing is the only purity issue discussed in the synoptics, and it is not a prescription of 'the law of Moses'. Prescriptions in the law which deal with purity cannot, in any case, be held to conflict with the commandment to love one's neighbour, since they do not affect inter-personal relationships.[54]

To reiterate: the purity laws which governed everybody did not affect 'table-fellowship', but principally access to the temple. Incurring impurity by the biblical code usually did not make a person a 'sinner'. Failure to abide by the special laws of the *haberim*, which did govern eating, only made one a non-*haber*, that is, an *'am ha-arets*.

Thus when scholars focus on *purity* as constituting the issue behind the criticism that Jesus *ate* with 'sinners', what they are saying, sometimes without knowing it, is that the *haberim* accused Jesus of eating with the *'amme ha-arets*, *not* that Jesus associated with those who transgressed the biblical law.[55] Making *purity* and *table-fellowship* the focal points of debate trivializes the charge against Jesus. It becomes a dispute between the *haberim* and the *'amme ha-arets*, and Jesus strikes a blow against the minutiae of the former. One then misses the point of the charge: that Jesus was accused of associating with, and offering the kingdom to those who *by the normal standards of Judaism* were wicked. They were doubtless also impure, but it was not impurity as such which made them wicked, nor can Jesus' inclusion of them be construed as defiance primarily of the laws of ritual purity.

1.3.4. *Haberim and Pharisees.* Before 70, the *haberim* were almost certainly a very small group, and it is dubious that *haberim* and Pharisees were identical. The case for identity can be made if one assumes a direct equation between the Pharisees and the Rabbis; for the Rabbis certainly thought that the laity (or at least some of them) should eat food in a state of semi-priestly purity. But the equation of 'Pharisees' and 'Rabbis' is itself precarious. And, once we turn to Rabbinic literature, we find further complications. One Rabbi proposed that no *haber* should touch a corpse (the *haber* should become in this way too like a priest).[56] If all Rabbis were *haberim*, and if the opinion that *haberim* should not touch a corpse were to carry the day (it did not), then who would tend the dead? Neither the Rabbis, nor their wives, nor anyone who followed their rules. Thus it is doubtful that even all the Rabbis were *haberim*. Before 70, there was probably an appreciable overlap between Pharisees and *haberim*; and after 70 the Rabbis accepted the main point of the *haberim*. But these connections do not amount to an equation.

People who have learned who the Pharisees were by reading Jeremias, supposedly a reliable authority, will find these terminological distinctions puzzling. That is because Jeremias, obviously thinking that all Pharisees were *haberim* and all *haberim* Pharisees, simply wrote the word 'Pharisees' when he was discussing a text which contains the word *haberim*. Thus, for example, he wrote that 'A Pharisee does not dwell with them [the *'amme ha-arets*] as a guest' as his translation of Demai 2.3;[57] but 'Pharisee' does not appear in the text: it reads *haber*. When one adds the assumption (which was long held, and which Jeremias shared with many) that the Rabbis perfectly represented the Pharisees, the use of 'Pharisee' for '*haber*' in translating Rabbinic texts resulted in the simple equation of *haber*, Pharisee and Rabbi which we noted above, and naturally gave the impression – in fact seemed to prove conclusively – that Pharisaism in the period before 70 was defined by insistence that the laity observe the priestly laws governing handling and eating food. But that is just what we do not know. All that we hear about Pharisaism from people who were actually Pharisees before 70 is that the party was defined by its zeal for the knowledge of the law, belief in the resurrection, and acceptance of the tradition of the elders.[58] Did the tradition of the elders insist that lay people act like priests? Not that we know of. It is noteworthy that Josephus makes a point of the fact that the Essenes would not eat other people's food (*BJ* II.143f.), but says nothing about the Pharisees' observing special food laws which set them off from other Jews.

Neusner in recent years has argued in favour of the view formulated by Jeremias and others -- that the Pharisees were a small purity sect – , but his analysis of the Rabbinic texts is unpersuasive and is made especially dubious by the evidence from Josephus.[59]

Josephus's descriptions of the Pharisees, as we shall see later in this chapter and also in ch. 11 are suspect in one regard: the great influence which he attributes to them in the *Antiquities*. But he would have had no reason for concealing their peculiar food and purity laws, had such laws defined them. He appears to have found ascetic and rigidly scrupulous practice attractive, as did many, and he gives numerous such details about the Essenes, covering not only food but sex (e.g. *BJ* II.160f.). He unvaryingly characterizes the Pharisees as 'exact' with regard to the law, and there is every reason to think that the Pharisees tried to have their views of the law carry the day. He exaggerates only their success. They do not emerge from his pages as a 'small, retiring group of purity-observers', and it is probably wrong to stress too much the dominance of the *haberim* among them. In Josephus, the Pharisees are lay interpreters of the law.[60]

1.4. *The 'amme ha-arets and the hakamim*, the learned, are also contrasted in Rabbinic literature (Horayoth 3.8). In this context the meaning is 'uneducated', that is, by the Rabbinic standard.

2. *The 'amme ha-arets and salvation*

Now we come to the important point, which justifies the terminological discussion. Jeremias wrote that the *'amme ha-arets* (hereafter, now that the terminological clarification is complete, the common people) were, in the

accepted view of their day, excluded from salvation.[61] That this is incorrect
might be seen simply from the preceding terminological discussion: since
the term 'wicked' did not include the common people, and since the latter
are to be characterized simply as neither *haberim* nor *hakamim*, it should
follow that no one thought that the common people were excluded from
salvation. Here, however, we must not only clear out some terminological
underbrush, but fell a large tree; for we are up against a dearly cherished
view: the Pharisees, who dominated Judaism, excluded everyone but themselves from salvation, and Jesus let the common people in. Gustaf Aulén,
who in theory knew that 'the sinners' were not the same as 'the common
people',[62] nevertheless accepted the view which is expressed by Jeremias:

> Table fellowship with 'sinners' was not a simple breach of etiquette on the
> part of the individual, it was clear defiance of both the regulations concerning
> purity and the ordinances which prescribed the penance required of such
> violators of the law for restoration into the religious and social community.[63]

In this passage Aulén, having said that the 'sinners' were not the common
people, describes 'the sinners' as not obeying the 'regulations concerning
purity' which govern 'table-fellowship' – that is, whether he knew it or not,
as being common people. Further, he evidently thought that those who
were impure had transgressed the law, were required to do penance, and
were not fit associates for others. All these suppositions are wrong. We
have seen that impurity may be incurred by obeying the law as well as by
certain sorts of disobedience, that acts of penance are not required for
most forms of impurity, and that association with others is not forbidden.
The statement that the sinners needed to repent in order to be restored
to the community is correct with regard to the wicked, but not with regard
to those who were only impure. Aulén followed standard definitions and
ran the two together. He also saw Jesus' offence as being that he *ate* with
the impure and that this offended the Pharisees.[64] By putting the emphasis
on purity and eating, he in effect agrees with Jeremias's view that the issue
was between a small purity group – called by Jeremias, Aulén and others
'Pharisees' – and Jesus, who favoured including those who did not accept
special purity regulations, that is, the common people.

Since this position is here under attack, I should explain why I have
quoted a distinguished bishop and theologian who, in his nineties, wrote
a remarkably good book about recent research on the life of Jesus. It is
precisely because he was not a professional New Testament scholar and
certainly not one who claimed expertise in pre-70 Judaism. On such a
point as this he could do nothing other than repeat the opinion prevailing

among supposed experts. It is not difficult to compile a very long list of New Testament scholars who hold or have held the view just quoted from Aulén's book. But the fact that Aulén wrote that sentence shows more clearly than any such list how common are the opinions which we listed at the beginning of the chapter. In Aulén's discussion we see virtually the entire package of erroneous views on the significance of Jesus' going to the sinners. Since he thought that the issue had to do with eating with the impure and that the opponents were the Pharisees, we see two equations: (1) Those who had special laws governing eating were 'Pharisees'; therefore 'Pharisees' were *haberim*. (2) The people with whom this special group would not eat were 'sinners'; therefore the common people were sinners and outcasts. (See above, pp.176f. nos. 1 and 3.) Since Aulén thought that the impure were outside the community, he must have thought (3) that the 'Pharisees' controlled Judaism and could make those with whom they disagreed feel excluded (nos. 2 and 4 above). (4) He saw Jesus' association with the impure as offending the Pharisees (no. 6 above). This is all incorrect.

Our understanding of the situation will be better if we consider the common people under the two headings which characterize them: lack of education and non-observance of special purity laws.

2.1. *The uneducated and salvation.* I shall take first the question of the uneducated. Did the sages (before or after 70, though we have opinions only from Rabbinic literature) consider the uneducated to be necessarily condemned sinners? It has been often said that the unlearned *must* have been considered sinners, since they could not understand, much less do the law.[65] Thus Nolan speaks of the 'laws and customs' as being 'so complicated that the uneducated were quite incapable of understanding what was expected of them'.[66]

We may ask, first, if that was the Rabbinic view. It was not. The Rabbis had a strong sense of diminished responsibility. The common people were not expected by the learned to know and do everything which they (the learned) did. The light sins of the learned count as the heavy sins of the unlearned; and the heavy sins of the unlearned as the light sins of the learned.[67]

Secondly, we may observe that Josephus deals with the question explicitly and elaborately, and argues that Jews were different from others because they knew their own laws. Others employ 'professional legal experts'. 'But, should anyone of our nation be questioned about the laws, he would repeat them all more readily than his own name' (*Ap.* II.177f.). Josephus, throughout this section, engages in obvious and easily comprehensible exaggeration. In the same section he exaggerates Jewish loyalty to the law (see ch. 9 n. 4). In these and related cases, however, the exaggeration seems to rest on common observations which would ring true to Gentile readers: the Jews really did stand out in Graeco-Roman culture because of their knowledge and observance of the law. On such a point we cannot assume that Josephus speaks for the sages, but he probably represents common opinion.

Thirdly, we should apply common sense. It will help us to get rid of nonsense. Jewish law, as I have written elsewhere, looks hard to modern Christians, not to ancient Jews.[68] And, besides, we can look around. Is it true today that the uneducated cannot observe the law? Is there a high correlation between the uneducated and those who break the traffic code (a very detailed bit of law)? Or those who are guilty of tax frauds (the modern equivalent in complexity to the laws of purity, except that the latter, in comparison, are quite simple)?

It may help us, in evaluating the claim that the Pharisees viewed the uneducated as excluded from Israel, and thus from salvation, to put the matter in human terms; and to do so we may take the case of Jo in Dickens' *Bleak House*. Jo is not only completely illiterate, he also has what we would now call a very low IQ. But he knows enough to attend an inquest and to be prepared to answer questions (though the coroner disdains to put them). He knows that he must 'move on' when told by a constable to do so. He even knows that it is appropriate (though not required by law) to tend a lonely and derelict graveyard. He perseveres through a short life without committing a crime. Ah, someone will say, Jo only avoided transgressing the negative commandments; he could not have *known*, let alone obeyed, the positive commandments. Which ones? He had no mother or father to honour, but he was completely loyal to the few people who were even passingly kind to him. He very likely observed 'the Sabbath' (that is, in Victorian England, Sunday) by necessity. His 'job', sweeping a corner, would not have paid on Sunday.[69] Had income tax forms been invented, he would not have had to fill them out. In Rabbinic terms, he would not have been a *ḥaber* and would not have needed to know their purity code. Where are those Pharisees who would look at a first-century equivalent of Dickens' Jo and say, 'You are an accursed sinner; and those who associate with you are outside the religious and social community'? Had belonging to such a religion as Judaism, which is alleged to inculcate unremitting severity, deprived the Pharisees of all semblance of humanity? Will those who earnestly believe that to have been the case please produce one scrap of evidence?

2.2. *Non-ḥaberim in Rabbinic literature.*

2.2.1. *The non-ḥaberim and salvation in Rabbinic literature.* Nor can it be said that those who did not observe the priestly purity laws were considered beyond the reach of God's mercy. After 70 the Rabbis certainly did not think that. Rabbinic statements on the *'amme ha-arets* explicitly include them among those who have a share in the world to come.[70]

2.2.2. *Non-ḥaberim, sin and atonement in Rabbinic literature.* There is a simple test to determine whether or not the post-70 Rabbis considered the *'amme ha-arets* condemned sinners: Did they appoint means of atonement for them? They did not. Reading the Mishnah makes it clear that the Rabbis did not think that failing to observe the purity code of the *ḥaberim* was a sin. Thus (despite Aulén's statement above)[71] there is no *penance* for the kind of impurity which separates *ḥaber* from *'am ha-arets*.

2.2.3. *Social exclusion in Rabbinic literature.* By quoting such a passage as Demai 2.3 (a *ḥaber* may not be the guest of an *'am ha-arets*, nor receive him as a guest in his own raiment), Jeremias gives the impression of a rigid exclusivism. In Aulén's words, the ritually impure are outside the 'religious and social community'. Certainly social and business intercourse were restricted by the *ḥaberim*. But the exclusion was not complete: note the exception to the rule in the Mishnah just quoted: A *ḥaber* may serve as host to an *'am ha-arets* if the latter changes his garment. In Demai 2.2 R. Judah offered the opinion that one who is trustworthy in tithes may be the guest of an *'am ha-arets*. Other aspects of the Mishnah's tithing and purity laws envisage various forms of contact. Demai 4.2, for example, has further rules for eating with an *'am ha-arets*, and Makshirin 6.3 allows certain purchases of food from an *'am ha-arets*. Certainly there were restrictions (even assuming that all the Mishnah's rules were obeyed), but the usual depiction of complete avoidance is exaggerated.[72]

2.3. *Exclusion from the social and religious community before 70.* Before 70 we have no literary evidence for the attitude of the *ḥaberim* towards other Jews, but we can settle the question without it. In the first place, the Rabbinic discussions of the *ḥaberim* make it clear that they took upon themselves a special vow which they did not expect others to take. They were more scrupulous than others, but they did not exclude them from anything but certain of their own activities – certainly not from the religious and social life of Judaism.

Secondly, we can draw a strong inference from the fact that neither the *ḥaberim* nor the Pharisees withdrew from Jerusalem. As long as they lived there and continued to worship at the temple, they clearly did not think that other people were 'cut off'. If they had come to the view that the common people were not truly in Israel, they would have had to reach the same conclusion about the priests; for the priests accepted the standard of piety of the 'amme ha-arets (see below). Further, the surviving attacks on the priests (e.g. Ps. Sol. 8) show that they were subject to criticism from the especially strict and scrupulous. The Dead Sea Sect – in contrast to the ḥaberim, the Pharisees and later the Rabbis – did consider everyone else to be outside the body of the truly elect. They applied this to the common people, to the Pharisees and to the priests. The other groups of superior piety – by whatever name they go – , by staying in Jerusalem and accepting the common worship, show that they did not consider the less strict to be outside the covenant.

There is, thirdly, a decisive argument against the view that the ḥaberim (equated, in the scholarly discussion of the point, with the Pharisees) excluded the common people from the social and religious community. They did not control it. Saying that *lay* people who transgressed the *priestly* purity code were considered outside 'the religious and social community' is nonsense, just as is saying that it was 'the conviction of the time' that the 'amme ha-arets did not have access to salvation. The notion that the ḥaberim or Pharisees could, in Jesus' day, effectively exclude others from the religious community attributes to them a power which they did not have and seems to rest on a retrojection of the kind of dominance which Rabbis in orthodox communities eventually came to possess. We should recall that in the Rabbinic passages which express hostility between the learned and the common people the hostility is mutual.[73] The common people thought that they were *right*, and there is no reason to think that, when they were in the vast majority, they felt excluded and were therefore awaiting a prophet to admit them to the kingdom. If they had considered themselves cut off from salvation for not washing their hands before eating, they could have started washing them. We should remember that, before 70, the 'amme ha-arets were primary members of 'normative Judaism', along with the priesthood.[74] According to the dominant 'conviction of the time', that of the common people and the priesthood, the former were worthy members of Israel. Both groups doubtless thought that, as long as people participated in the worship of the temple, repented on the Day of Atonement, and did the other things prescribed in the Bible for the correction of sin and the removal of impurity, they were fully members of the social and religious community.

To return to our illustration from *Bleak House* above: The coroner who refuses to hear Jo testify may reasonably be said to have held him to be a non-citizen, one unworthy to take his place in civilized society, despite his desire to do so. Let us say that there were, in Judaism before 70, some *haberim* who held this attitude towards the common people. Did they occupy places in Jewish society analogous to that of the coroner in Dickens' novel? Could the *haberim* have effectively excluded the common people from the religious and social life of Judaism? It appears not. If any one group had that power, it would have been the priesthood. Their responsibilities included 'general supervision, the trial of cases of litigation, and the punishment of condemned persons'.[75]

We should briefly consider the probable attitude towards the common people of those who actually ran the 'religious community' (that is, the national religion). If a man had transgressed a law which required a sacrifice, and brought that sacrifice, the priest would not ask him if he, though a lay person, observed the priestly purity code. He would ask him if he repented. When the sacrifice was accepted (as it would be, if accompanied with a prayer of repentance), the person who brought it would hardly feel outside the religious community just because some petty and legalistic group of *haberim*, crouched in their conventicle, having table-fellowship with one another, would not eat with him. Why would he want them to? The mind boggles. He may have resented their self-assigned superiority, but would have had no discernible reason for feeling excluded from Judaism. Another modern analogy may be helpful. An eighteenth-century Anglican, in communion with the church, would not, on leaving the church, have felt excluded from the religious and social community just because the Methodists, in their small conventicles, thought that, instead of taking sugar in his tea, he should have given the money to the poor. He might have resented the Methodists' superior righteousness, but enough eighteenth-century English literature survives to show that non-Methodists did not feel excluded.

Yet it may be argued that the Pharisees controlled public opinion and could thus effectively exclude those who disagreed with them from the religious life of Judaism. Those who think that the Pharisees were *haberim* may thus persist in thinking that the common people were outcasts. This requires us to pause for a moment to consider the power of the Pharisees.

2.3.1. *The role of the Pharisees in Judaism before 70.* We must now pay attention to one of the basic assumptions of those who hold the view which is here under attack, or some variant of it: the Pharisees governed Judaism. This view is an important one, and it informs discussions not only of 'Jesus and the sinners', but also of 'Jesus and the law' and 'the cause of his death'. Common views about the Pharisees (here including some already mentioned and some yet to be discussed) are these: that the Pharisees attacked Jesus for association with those who transgressed *their* purity laws; that these people were considered by them to be 'sinners'; that the debates on the law also brought Jesus into conflict with its guardians, the Pharisees; and that Jesus' challenge to the Pharisees on these two counts (purity and the sinners; the law) was a major factor in bringing him to the cross. We shall have to come back to aspects of this view in several connections. Here I wish to comment on the basic supposition which gives this view, or collection of views, apparent explanatory power: before 70 the Pharisees dominated Judaism. We read of the 'ruling Pharisaic piety'[76] and that they were the 'leaders'[77] of Judaism and a 'new ruling class'.[78] When Jeremias wrote that it was 'the conviction of the time' that the common people were excluded from salvation, he obviously meant that it was the conviction of the Pharisees, who are thus implicitly understood as controlling 'Judaism'.[79] That was not, I have argued, the Pharisaic opinion. But in any case they could not dictate 'convictions'. I have just offered an alternative – that the priests 'controlled' Judaism, to the extent that anyone did, and (following Morton Smith) that 'normative Judaism' consisted of whatever the priests and the masses found religiously adequate, which in most cases was simply the biblical law. One aspect of this debate, Jewish self-government and the role of the Pharisees in the Sanhedrin, becomes much more pressing when we turn to the question of Jesus' execution, and I shall take it up then. We should here take account of the view, especially as put forward by Jeremias, that the Pharisees controlled the religious opinions of the masses. On that supposition rests the view that the Pharisees could effectively exclude those who did not follow their rules.

From ancient sources scholars who hold this view can cite Josephus. He calls the Pharisees the leading party in *BJ* II.162, and they are given an even more dominant role in *AJ* XIII.298: they have the 'support of the masses'. According to *AJ* XVIII.12–15, everyone followed the Pharisees' views on prayer and worship, while *AJ* XIII.288 says that 'even when they speak against a king or high priest, they immediately gain credence'. Their small number (Josephus, *AJ* XVII.42, fixes it at 6,000) can be discounted as not reflecting their popular support – Josephus himself implies.

We must, however, doubt that Pharisees controlled the view of the masses in the way stated in *AJ* XVIII.12–15 and XIII.288, 298. Morton Smith, followed by Shaye Cohen, has correctly pointed out that this view of the Pharisees in the *Antiquities* is determined by Josephus' desire to enhance the reputation of the party which, in the nineties, had become predominant and which he wished to support.[80] The Pharisees do not play a prominent role in the *War*, nor in Josephus's accounts of particular events, as we shall show below (ch. 11). Cohen puts the case strongly: Josephus's 'Pharisaism is of the most dubious variety, and he did not discover it until the nineties of our era. In the sixties he was a Jerusalem priest and, in all likelihood, not a Pharisee.'[81] It is not necessary to accept this proposal, though it seems to me quite possible, to see that in his later works Josephus exaggerates the role of the Pharisees and that before 70 they 'had no real hold either on the government or on the masses of the people.'[82]

The opposite view, which was argued for by Jeremias and has been explicitly or implicitly accepted by many, is that 'as a whole the people looked to the Pharisees, in their voluntary commitment to works of supererogation, as models of piety, and as embodiments of the ideal life which the scribes, these men of divine and secret knowledge, had set before them'.[83] The Pharisees, argued Jeremias, were 'the people's party'. 'Their much-respected piety and their social leanings towards suppressing differences of class, gained them the people's support and assured them, step by step, of the victory.'[84]

This view, which a critical reading of Josephus throws into question, is difficult to maintain for a second reason – it conflicts with the exclusivism and hatred of the masses which Jeremias also attributes to the Pharisees.[85] The latter, according to Jeremias, side by side with championing the common people, despised and excluded them. They introduced a 'caste distinction', and some of the masses showed 'evidence of an intense desire to throw off the yoke of a contempt based on religious superiority'. It was these to whom Jesus appealed, and Jesus literally put his life in jeopardy by calling them to repentance.[86]

I submit that this both contradicts the evidence and does not make sense. Jeremias needs to make the Pharisees an extremely narrow and bigoted group in order to make an innocuous action – associating with common people – offensive. He needs to make the Pharisees influential with the masses in order to give them a major role in Jesus' execution. I think that neither point is correct, but that in any case one cannot have it both ways. The path by which this position was reached is worth pointing out, since Jeremias is representative of a general line of scholarship, and others need to avoid the same sequence of suppositions. Jeremias first assumed that the Pharisees were *ḥaberim* – a small group focused on purity. He then assumed that the *ḥaberim* = Pharisees wanted to impose their view on all Israel. Both points, as we saw above, are improbable. There was then added to this the common Christian denigration of 'late Judaism': it was based on merit-seeking legalism and led to *Heilsegoismus* and *ängstliche*

Religiosität. Finally, Jeremias switched to Josephus's exaggerations of Pharisaical dominance for the view that they controlled Judaism. Thus he reached a false construction, based on dubious assumptions and an even more dubious conflation of them: the Pharisees were bigots who both wanted and were able to exclude those who did not follow their laws, and to have a man who accepted the common people executed.

There is a third and fatal objection to the view that the Pharisees dominated the religious life of Judaism: when one forgets theological abstractions (the masses loved their commitment to works of supererogation) and thinks concretely, one sees that the Pharisees did not dominate any of the centres of Jewish religious life.

They did not, in the first place, control access to or the service of the temple. Even Rabbinic literature, which goes further than Josephus in assigning the Pharisees religious dominance, shows how little they affected this, the primary focus of Jewish religious life. According to Rabbinic literature, the debates between the Pharisees and the Sadducees about the temple had to do with such things as whether or not the incense which was taken into the Holy of Holies on the Day of Atonement was to be lit before or after entry (see Yoma 19b; cf. Parah 3.7). Whether or not the *'amme ha-arets* could offer sacrifices is not an issue. The special laws of the *ḥaberim* (even assuming that the Pharisees as such held to them) have nothing to do with access to or worship in the temple, but rather concentrate on secular life. We must assume that the Pharisees never proposed that temple worship was invalid or that those who participated in it were nevertheless cut off from Judaism. The Rabbinic tractates on the Day of Atonement and other passages on the efficacy of sacrifice, which probably reflect views commonly held before 70, point in the opposite direction: the sacrificial service was accepted.[87] Thus we have no reason to think that the Pharisees engaged in even theological polemic against the temple service as such.

When one asks about actual physical control, the possibility of Pharisaic influence disappears entirely. I referred above to the non-Rabbinic, and thus arguably non-Pharisaic construction of the *miqvaot* outside the temple walls. They help us think concretely, as do the great gates and broad steps by which the people entered the temple, which are now visible on its south side. One must contrast the great concourse of people entering and leaving, supervised only by the dozens of Levites and priests,[88] with the relatively few learned and scrupulous men who made up the Pharisaic party, most of whom earned their living outside the temple area, to see the lack of reality which has dominated discussions of the religion of Judaism. There were vastly more temple 'employees' – priests, Levites, other guards, treasurers, musicians and servants – than there were Pharisees;[89] and, later, thousands would demonstrate their loyalty to the high priest and the official government of the temple by dying for them (*BJ* IV.313). The Pharisees controlled nothing about the temple. It was run by the priests and used by the people.

Similarly, we hear nothing about the exclusion of the *'amme ha-arets* from worship in the synagogues. It may in fact be doubted that the Pharisees played a large enough role in Galilee during Jesus' career to affect synagogue worship one way or the other.[90] But even if they did, we have no reason to think that they controlled the synagogues and excluded the common people from worship and learning. I do not wish either to deny or minimize the importance of the lay interpreters of the Bible, who by Jesus' time had attained appreciable influence. These are usually called 'scribes' by scholars, though Josephus called them 'Pharisees' (*BJ* II.162).[91] One must certainly grant them some influence. The present points are: (1) that they did not control the institutions of Judaism, and certainly not the Galilean synagogues; (2) that nothing presently known about either the Pharisees or the *haberim* indicates that they aimed at the exclusion of the common people from worship or study.

It is frequently said that temple and synagogue were the two foci of Jewish religious life. There was, however, a third: the home. The normally pious common people doubtless kept Passover, Sukkoth and other festivals, and we should presume that they saw themselves as participating fully in the national religion.

Thus we must conclude that the Pharisees neither did nor could exclude non-Pharisees from the social and religious life of Judaism.

2.4. *Conclusion: Jesus, the Pharisees and the common people.* Many scholars, not just Jeremias, observing that in the Gospels there are passages which mention the 'poor', presumably the ordinary people of Galilee, and others which contain the word 'sinners', slide them together. They then combine two other facts – that the *haberim* had special purity rules and separated themselves in certain ways from the common people, and that all observant Jews, not just the Pharisees, considered the wicked to be 'cut off' – to make it appear that the powers of the Jewish hierarchy (believed, in this construction, to be the Pharisees) considered the *common people* to be *cut off* on the grounds of impurity and ignorance. Jesus then becomes the champion of plain folk against an intolerant bunch of bigots.

I believe this view to be incorrect in all its parts. I have argued that associating with sinners – the actual charge against Jesus – has nothing to do with associating with the common people, though I presume that Jesus did associate with them and was one of them. His appeal to sinners and outcasts, however, cannot be understood as an appeal to the common people. Secondly, it is incorrect to make purity the issue between Jesus and his critics. Thirdly, the point of offence could not have been that he included ordinary people in the kingdom. The Pharisees – at least those who were *haberim* – may have held aloof from the ordinary people, but they did not control the religious life of Judaism in such a way as to make non-Pharisees feel excluded and grateful for the offer to join the kingdom of God. All the evidence, further, is against the assumption that the Pharisees would feel hostile to including ordinary people in the kingdom.

One of the regrettable aspects of the view which has been widely accepted is that it has prevented exploration of what it would have meant to offer the kingdom to the *wicked*. It debases and falsifies Judaism, and it trivializes Jesus, to understand the issue of 'Jesus and the sinners' as if it were 'Jesus and the common people *versus* the narrow, bigoted but dominant Pharisees'. We must understand the conflict on some other basis.

Before turning to the question of what the actual significance of Jesus' proclamation to the sinners was, I wish to make one last observation in aid of the effort to eliminate from scholarship the view that Jesus was criticized for association with the common people. The notion that the learned and scrupulous considered the less learned and scrupulous to be sinners beyond redemption, and that the former made the latter feel excluded, is actually determined by religious propaganda. This view does not offer a serious historical explanation of a first-century conflict. Doubtless without knowing it, its proponents have been carrying on theological polemic: we have love, mercy, repentance, forgiveness, and even simple decency on our side, and that is why our religion is superior to its parent. This, however, is not historical thinking: it focuses on religious abstractions and it floats into the realm of unreality. Scholars who have written, write, and will write in that way lack historical imagination. They cannot imagine the crowded streets of Jerusalem, the villages of Galilee, the farms in the valley of Jezreel. If they did, they would know that no small group of super-pious, super-educated bigots (in case there were actually such a group) could in any way effectively exclude from religious and social life those who did not meet their standards; much less would such a group have any reason for taking umbrage at a wandering Galilean healer and preacher who associated with the common people, nor would they be able to coax or coerce the Roman government into killing him.

3. *Jesus and the sinners*

But, if the significance of Jesus' proclamation to the wicked is not
that he promised membership in the kingdom of God to the common
people, who were excluded by the iniquitous Pharisees, what is the
point? Why do the 'sinners' loom so large in the Gospels? I think that
absolute clarity is not possible, although we can narrow the options. It
will be helpful here to turn to Norman Perrin as representing consensus
scholarship.

3.1. *Was the offence forgiveness?* Perrin, unlike his teacher Jeremias, did
not confuse the ordinary Jews who sinned with 'the sinners'.[92] His own
proposals, however, about how to understand Jesus' inclusion of the
sinners are at least equally off-target. Thus he states that the Jews longed
for ultimate, end-time forgiveness, not being able to receive it within the
daily framework of Judaism. The Day of Atonement, other rituals, and
works of supererogation, he assures us, 'were of limited effectiveness'.
'So, God himself must ultimately forgive sin . . . '.[93] It is noteworthy that
Perrin leaves repentance, which is crucial to the Jewish conception of
atonement, out of his list. Besides, one may ask, who, in the normal Jewish
view, forgives sins on the Day of Atonement? There is no justification, in
a supposedly historical description of Jewish views, for Perrin's separation
of the Day of Atonement and other sacrificial occasions from what 'God
himself' does. Put in the terms used earlier, I doubt very much that ordinary
Jews, who brought sacrifices for occasional sins and prayed and fasted on
the Day of Atonement, felt the need of some further, eschatological
forgiveness. We may reasonably think that many would expect the coming
of the end to be signalled by large-scale repentance (above, ch. 3 section 4),
and Perrin may have misunderstood this as meaning that people generally
thought that true forgiveness could be attained only at the eschaton.
But whatever the source of his confusion, his view has no basis whatever.

He continues by attaching even more significance to what he regards as
Jesus' novel view that sinners could be forgiven. The real 'sinners', he
states, were equivalent to Gentiles.[94] But then he shows again his lack of
understanding of normal Jewish theology: 'Such Jews were widely regarded
as beyond hope of penitence or forgiveness . . . '.[95] Jesus offered forgiveness
to them, and thus 'confronted' Judaism with 'a crisis' (p. 97).

> Here was a situation in which the reality of God and his love was being
> revealed in a new and decisive way, and in which, therefore, the joys of the
> salvation time were suddenly available to those who had longed for them
> for so long and so earnestly (ibid.).

Jesus' promise of forgiveness to such people gave 'very grave offence . . . to his contemporaries' (p. 102). His disputes about the law were not especially offensive, and the cleansing of the temple will not explain his execution (ibid.). He was killed, rather, because he offered sinners forgiveness.

> To have become such an outcast [as were the tax collectors] himself would have been much less of an outrage than to welcome those people back into the community in the name of the ultimate hope of that community. Intense conviction, indeed, is necessary to explain such an act on the part of Jesus, and such an act on the part of Jesus is necessary, we would claim, to make sense of the fact of the cross (p. 103).

Perrin's statement of the case that Jesus offended his contemporaries by offering forgiveness to sinners is extreme, but I have presented it at such length because it is a clear statement of a widely held view. It was *grace* that offended the Pharisees, who were committed to merit and unremitting punishment for transgression. Perrin here echoes Jeremias, who wrote that Jesus took an 'unparalleled risk' when he struck against the Pharisees by calling sinners to repentance, 'and this act brought him to the cross'.[96]

Riches' view is equally clear-cut. He tries to answer the question 'why Jesus believed so strongly in the mercy and forgiveness of God when many contemporaries held such widely differing views', and he depicts Jesus' commitment to a kingdom of love, mercy and grace as leading to 'deep resistance' on the part of the leaders of Judaism.[97]

Two of the leading members of the 'new quest' maintained the connection between Jesus' favouring grace and his being executed. Thus Käsemann:

> the hate of the Jewish religious leaders goes back to Jesus' attitude to the Law and to his understanding of grace and the fellowship with sinners which derives from it, so that activity and fate can, historically speaking, hardly remain unconnected.[98]

According to Fuchs, the men of Jerusalem killed Jesus because 'they could not tolerate his claim to assert through his own conduct that God's will was a gracious will'.[99]

Finally, we note that the view is embedded in the standard New Testament reference works. Behm, in writing on 'repentance', bitterly protests Montefiore's saying that Jesus did not go beyond the Rabbis. Jesus, Behm assures us, was in fact in 'mortal conflict with the Pharisees' on this point.[100]

We see in such proposals the laudable desire to find links between Jesus' teaching and activity, on the one hand, and his death, on the other. Further, we see the desire to give Jesus a setting in first-century Jewish Palestine and to derive from that context information for understanding his career. Regrettably, it all goes astray because of three interrelated factors: the persistent refusal to do research into Jewish views; the preference for deriving 'historical' information from another source (theological commitment);[101] and the deep-rooted Christian desire to have Jesus die for the truth of the gospel: for his belief in grace.

The link between Jesus' gospel and his death is made in various ways. Sometimes the causal chain runs from eating with sinners, to opposition by the Pharisees, to crucifixion,[102] while others make this point by fixing on the parables instead of the act of eating. In the parables Jesus proclaimed grace to sinners and thereby offended the righteous. 'Jesus goes to the cross because he clings to the word of grace.'[103] It was those against whom Jesus told the parables who killed him: 'He dies for the truth of his parables.'[104] The position is basically this: *We* (the Christians, or the true Christians) believe in grace and forgiveness. Those religious qualities *characterize* Christianity, and thus could not have been present in the religion from which Christianity came. Otherwise, why the split? But the Jews, or at least their leaders, the Pharisees, did not believe in repentance and forgiveness. They not only would not extend forgiveness to their own errant sheep, they would kill anyone who proposed to do so.

The position is so incredible that I wish it were necessary only to state it in order to demonstrate its ridiculousness. But thousands believe it, and I shall try to show what is wrong with it. Let us focus first on the *novelty* of an offer of forgiveness. The tax collectors and sinners, Perrin assures us, 'responded in glad acceptance' to Jesus' saying that they would be forgiven.[105] But was this news? Did they not know that if they renounced those aspects of their lives which were an affront to God's law, they would have been accepted with open arms? Is it a serious proposal that tax collectors and the wicked longed for forgiveness, but could not find it within ordinary Judaism? That they thought that only in the messianic age could they find forgiveness, and thus responded to Jesus 'in glad acceptance'?[106] Perrin, citing only irrelevant evidence, asserts that the 'sinners' 'were widely regarded as beyond hope of penitence or forgiveness',[107] and thus he denies one of the things about Judaism which everyone should know: there was a universal view that forgiveness is *always* available to those who return to the way of the Lord.[108]

Secondly, he presents an extraordinary picture of the tax collectors and sinners: they *wanted* forgiveness but did not know how to obtain it. I think that a quick chat with any religious leader – that is, a priest – would have clarified the issue: God always accepts repentant sinners who turn to his way.

Thirdly, it is inaccurate to say that Jesus welcomed people 'back into the community'.[109] Jesus did not control access to the temple. We must continue to try to think realistically. It is quite possible (in fact, as will soon appear, quite likely) that Jesus admitted the wicked into *his* community without making the normal demand of restitution and commitment to the law. That might give his followers *a* sense of community; but it is not accurate to say that 'he welcomed those people [the sinners] *back* into *the* community'. They all would have known perfectly well what to do if they wished to be considered members of the covenant in good standing.

Fourthly, we should remember that Jesus himself was not primarily a preacher of repentance. We earlier observed that there is scant material which depicts Jesus as calling Israel to repent. The parables about God's seeking the lost (Luke 15.3–6; 15.8f.), once the Lucan conclusions are removed (Luke 15.7, 10), are seen to be focused not on repentance but on God's action.[110] The latter may imply the former, but it is difficult to show that Jesus was a spokesman for a return of the sinners to *the* community. The story of Zacchaeus (Luke 19.1–9) brings home the curiosity of the reported charge that Jesus ate with tax collectors and sinners and promised them a place in the kingdom. This story was, as I proposed above, created by Luke (or possibly a pre-Lucan writer) to emphasize repentance and *reform*.[111] It emphasizes these qualities so effectively that their scarcity elsewhere becomes striking. Jesus doubtless believed in reconciliation between the wicked and God, but the absence of passages which call for repentance and restitution shows at least that he did not aim at restoring the wicked to *the* community. If Jesus, by eating with tax collectors, led them to repent, repay those whom they had robbed, and leave off practising their profession, he would have been a national hero.

This leads us to the fifth and most decisive point. No one would have been offended if Jesus converted quislings. The case with other 'sinners' is similar. Let us take the case of a professional sinner, an usurer. If such a person were led by Jesus to repay the interest which he had accepted, and to turn to a life in accord with the law, who would have objected? Those who needed to borrow money, for example farmers who borrowed each year against the next harvest, would be inconvenienced if their accustomed usurer quit his profession. But presumably there would be someone from whom to borrow, and the defection of one usurer from the money market would not seriously affect the economy. Those who were zealous for the law, such as the Pharisees, would rejoice. The notion that the conversion of sinners was offensive to the Pharisees is, when thought about concretely, ridiculous.

3.2. *The offence.* As I said earlier, it is hard to establish with certainty what was offensive about Jesus' behaviour. This has not been problematic to scholars as long as they could think that the offer of *forgiveness to repentant sinners* was unique and would have been offensive to the leaders of Judaism. Jesus proclaimed that the wicked who repented would share in the kingdom, and the Pharisees were led thereby to a fatal enmity. But once we see (1) that everybody (except the Romans) would have favoured the conversion of tax collectors and other traitors to the God of Israel and (2) that Jesus' message in any case was not primarily orientated around a call to repentance, the significance of the charge that Jesus was a friend of tax collectors and the wicked becomes difficult to determine. The success of the explanation that conversion was offensive, however, has kept other proposals from being brought forward, and we do not have a rich array of alternative possibilities.

There is one other which should be mentioned. The controversy has sometimes been held to be that Jesus offered forgiveness (inclusion in the kingdom) *before* requiring reformation, and for this reason he could be accused of being a friend of tax collectors and sinners. Had they already reformed, they would not have been sinners. That is one of the ways in which Jeremias stated the case: Judaism offers forgiveness only to those who are righteous. They had first to become righteous to be forgiven.[112] Jesus' offer in advance is sometimes called *unconditional forgiveness*.[113] But what precisely does this mean? The intended contrast is, of course, with Judaism, where conditional forgiveness was offered. Quite apart from the fact that Jeremias has caricatured Judaism by dividing up chronologically reformation of life and forgiveness, we must still press the question: are we dealing with a significant contrast? We should, once more, think concretely. If the result of Jesus' eating with a tax collector was that the tax collector, like Zacchaeus, made restitution and changed his way of life (we recall that Jeremias accepts the story), Jesus' proclamation of forgiveness was not unconditional. The condition of its effectiveness was obviously the conversion. I submit that the distinction proposed is too small to create much of a dispute. For clarity, I shall repeat the proposed distinction. It is this: Jesus said, God forgives you, and now you should repent and mend your ways; everyone else said, God forgives you if you will repent and mend your ways.

Modern theologians find here a significant difference, and perhaps rightly so. It is a profound insight that the gift should precede the demand, and putting the two clearly in that sequence is satisfying theologically. It can also be effective in human relations. But is it a matter of offence? How large would this theological distinction have loomed in the first century? For, it must be emphasized, we can be discussing only a theological distinction. Jesus did not tell sinners that, before purifying themselves, and without bringing a sacrifice and a prayer of repentance, they could enter the temple. Urging and acting on this view would certainly have been fatal. But I cannot see that the same could be said for Jesus' symbolic action of eating with sinners. He may have intended to symbolize thereby the priority of grace to repentance, but in the eyes of pious outsiders he would simply have been joining the ranks of the ungodly. They might regret it, but they would not have killed him for it. In their effort to have Jesus die for the truth of the gospel, modern scholars who find here the crucial point of offence go even beyond the evangelists in creating plots by the Pharisees.

I doubt that tax collectors and usurers walked round Galilee in such a state of anxiety about forgiveness that the distinction between 'if you repent' and 'assuming that you subsequently repent' was a burning issue. Likewise I doubt that the formulation attributed to Jesus ('assuming that you subsequently repent') would have offended anybody. I can well imagine that saying to a tax collector that he would enter the kingdom ahead of the righteous (Matt.21.31) would have been irritating to the latter; but not that the righteous would have conceived a deadly enmity for Jesus for putting grace before repentance – *if his aim was in fact reformation*. We must look elsewhere.

We may gain a clue to the meaning of the theme of the sinners by considering further repentance and forgiveness. It is an interesting and somewhat curious fact that most scholars who write about these themes in the Gospels do not say just what they have in mind. Jeremias's view is clear: he accepts the story of Zacchaeus. But Perrin, for example, wrote page after page on repentance and forgiveness without ever saying whether or not repentance, in Jesus' view, required restitution.[114] Westerholm has an interestingly ambiguous paragraph: Jesus' view was that all were on the same footing; all needed to repent. Some

> ... seized gratefully the chance to enter in. For others, however, the undiscriminating nature of the message proved offensive .... Clinging to

their claim to be righteous, they refused to enter a kingdom ... where 'sinners' and 'righteous' sat together at a table spread by God.[115]

Westerholm's depiction of the banquet seems to imply that the sinners admitted by Jesus remained sinners, but he does not spell this out. On the contrary, he, like others, writes about their repentance. We see here a typical lack of clarity about the meaning of 'sinners', 'repentance' and 'forgiveness'. If the sinners had repented, they would not have been sinners.

Let me say clearly what 'repentance' would normally have involved. By ordinary Jewish standards offences against fellow humans required restitution as well as repentance (see e.g. Lev. 6.1–5 [Heb. 5.20–26]; Num. 5.5–7; cf. Baba Kamma 9.6 and Baba Metzia 4.8 for the Rabbinic interpretation). Other offences were atoned for by repentance alone. While the temple stood – that is, in Jesus' time – repentance would be demonstrated by a sacrifice (see the same passage in Leviticus).[116]

My proposal is this: it may have been just these requirements that Jesus did not make of his hearers. He may have offered them inclusion in the kingdom not only *while they were still sinners* but also *without* requiring repentance as normally understood, and therefore he could have been accused of being a friend of people who indefinitely *remained* sinners.[117] Here at last we see the full implication of the repeated observation that Jesus did not issue a call for repentance and that it was Luke who emphasized the reform of the wicked who accepted him.

Some support for this view comes from considering, again, the relationship between John the Baptist and Jesus. It appears that John's message was distinguished from Jesus' on the question of repentance and the sinners (Matt. 21.32; 11.18f.). One might argue that the distinction between them was that John called for national repentance while Jesus sought individuals who were lost, but that both equally hoped for conversion and righteousness. But this is not likely. We must remember that it was an *accusation* against Jesus that he associated with sinners, while John came in the way of righteousness. This points to a more fundamental difference than those of tactics and audience. John, the preacher of repentance, was not accused on the grounds that Jesus was. It appears that John was the spokesman for *repentance and righteousness ordinarily understood*. Jesus, equally convinced that the end was at hand, proclaimed the *inclusion of the wicked who heeded him*.

There are three further passages which point in this direction: the Call of Levi//Matthew (Matt. 9.9–13//Mark 2.13–17//Luke 5.27–32); the

Question about Fasting (Matt. 9.14–17//Mark 2.18–22//Luke 5.33–39); and the story of the would-be follower who wished to bury his father (Matt. 8.21f.//Luke 9.59f.). The last passage will be discussed more fully later, and here I shall only indicate that it puts following Jesus above obeying the fifth commandment. The authenticity of the other two passages is less certain, but each seems to rest on a reliable kernel. Jesus probably did have a tax collector among his followers – even though later his name was not securely remembered – and it is probably this fact which gave immediate substance to the charge that he ate with tax collectors. The Gospel tradition subsequently expanded this point ('many tax collectors and sinners', Mark 2.15 and parr.), but we can safely assume that there was at least one.[118] It is noteworthy that this one is not said to have repented, repaid those whom he had robbed, and assumed a life conformable to the law. What he did was 'follow' Jesus.

The Question about Fasting makes basically the same point: some of the traditional practices of Judaism may be foregone by those who follow Jesus. The saying that the 'sons of the bridechamber do not fast while the bridegroom is with them' (Mark 2.19 and parr.), were it to be given general application, would be the clearest indication in the Gospels that Jesus put 'following' him above observing the law; for at least the fast of the Day of Atonement (Lev. 16.29) was emphatically observed. The passage in its present form seems to have in view some lesser fast or fasts not observed by everyone and not commanded in the Torah. We regrettably cannot recover the original application of the saying, but it harmonizes well in the present context.[119]

The only passage which might count against the view proposed here is Mark 1.44 and parr., where Jesus tells the cleansed leper to show himself to the priest and to make the required offering. This curious passage – which in any case does not deal with a transgression – actually highlights the lack of any such statement to the tax collectors and other sinners who accepted him. Even in the Lucan story of Zacchaeus the tax collector was not required by Jesus to make restitution, and no sacrifice is mentioned.[120]

I propose, then, that the novelty and offence of Jesus' message was that the wicked who heeded him would be included in the kingdom even though they did not repent as it was universally understood – that is, even though they did not make restitution, sacrifice, and turn to obedience to the law. Jesus offered companionship to the wicked of Israel as a sign that God would save them, and he did not make his association dependent on their conversion to the law. He may very well have thought that they had no time to create new lives for themselves, but that if they accepted his message they would be saved. If Jesus added to this such statements as that the tax collectors and prostitutes would enter the kingdom before the righteous (Matt. 21.31), the offence would be increased. The implied self-claim, to know whom God would include and not, and the equally implied downgrading of the normal machinery of righteousness, would push Jesus' stance close to, or over, the border which separates individual charisma from impiety.

I realize that my proposal will not be a popular one. Surely Jesus desired the conversion of sinners. But if that were all he sought, what was controversial about him?

Speculative as this proposal is, I consider it much more likely than the popular one: Jesus called sinners to repentance; and therefore mainline Judaism, being opposed to repentance and forgiveness, sought to kill him.

But before we can conclude our discussion of Jesus and those who would be included in the kingdom, there is one last topic to be considered.

Table-fellowship

'Table-fellowship' has loomed large in recent discussion of Jesus. His eating with tax collectors and sinners has, probably correctly, been seen as a proleptic indication that they would be included in the kingdom: the meal looks forward to the 'messianic banquet', when many would come from east and west and dine with the patriarchs (Matt. 8.11).[121] Several parables tell us that the kingdom is like a banquet, to which many are called. And, most tellingly, before his death Jesus looked forward to drinking the fruit of the vine in the kingdom of God (Mark 14.25//Matt. 26.29//Luke 22.18).

Thus it would appear that Jesus' eating with 'tax collectors and sinners' promised, as clearly as words, that they would inherit the kingdom; and thus it is likely that Jesus saw his eating with tax collectors and sinners as promising membership in the coming kingdom. But did it work out that way? Did Jesus' table-fellowship with sinners help prepare the way for the church which, instead of the kingdom, followed his ministry? There is an obvious drawback to this proposal. Those who had table-fellowship with Jesus did not, with the exception of Peter and John, become major figures in the church. One need mention only James (the Lord's brother), Paul and Barnabas to make the point clear. It would be nice to think that Jesus bound his companions to him in such a way that they could do no other than carry on his work after his death.[122] But in fact at least three of the principal leaders of the early Christian movement were not disciples – and many of the disciples drop from view. And, as we observed at the outset, 'sinners' are hard to find in the early church. It would appear that the force which welded together the early Christian movement was not Jesus' table-fellowship with tax collectors and sinners.

Conclusion

One prevalent view of the significance of Jesus' appeal to sinners is wrong on all counts. The view is that Jesus was criticized by the Pharisees for breaking their purity code by eating with common people and for offering them forgiveness, and that the common people responded with joy to his readmission of them to Judaism, from which their ritual impurity had cut them off. This is against all the evidence: (1) The term 'wicked' or 'sinners' does not include the common people. Neither the *haberim* nor the Pharisees considered the ordinary people to be condemned sinners. (2) Jesus' going to the wicked did not have primarily to do with his willingness to break purity laws. Most forms of impurity do not result from sin, nor is wickedness primarily a state of impurity – though it is also that. (3) In any case Jesus' eating with the sinners probably did not involve him in a dispute with a super-scrupulous group (whether called *haberim* or Pharisees). (4) Even if it had, it would not have thrown him into conflict with the leading powers in Judaism. The *haberim*, even if the same as the Pharisees, did not control Judaism. Neither the common people nor the priests accepted the special rules of the *haberim*. Had Jesus opposed them, he would simply have sided with the majority and with commonly accepted practice. (5) It is incorrect to say that the issue was *re*admission to Judaism. (6) The offence was not that Jesus favoured repentance and forgiveness.

Even if the prevalent view is modified by recognizing that the sinners of the Gospels cannot be simply the common people, it still will not stand. Some scholars who know that 'sinners' are not *'amme ha-arets* nevertheless maintain that Jesus offended the *Pharisees* by *eating* with sinners and that the offence had to do with the transgression of ritual *purity*. This in effect makes the dispute the sectarian one between the *haberim* and the *'amme ha-arets*. No gain in understanding is made by recognizing that sinners are not common people if the dispute is still understood as having to do with eating, purity and the Pharisees. Those who hold this view are, without knowing it, simply embracing the identification of 'sinners' and *'amme ha-arets*, while in theory rejecting it.

I have proposed that there is no evidence that the significance of Jesus' eating with sinners has to do primarily with purity, nor any that the ground of offence was his transgression of the purity code. New Testament scholars with remarkable consistency put the offence just there. Purity laws are considered trivial and externalistic, and Jesus is thus made to oppose Jewish trivialization of religion. But from the point of view of Judaism, everyone, except the priests, often lived in a state of ritual impurity, which was removed only for entry to the temple or (in the case of the menstruant) for intercourse. The *ḥaberim* handled and ate food in ritual purity, but they did not think that failure to do so was a *sin*. Laity who were not themselves *ḥaberim* forfeited the right to eat with *ḥaberim* (in case they wished to do so), and the rules of the *ḥaberim* imposed certain restrictions on trade. In Jesus' day, however, the economy was not governed by the *ḥaberim*, and we do not know whether or not their self-imposed rules were damaging to the common people. Thus I do not doubt that Jesus ate with people who were ritually impure, both by the standards of the priesthood and those of the *ḥaberim*. But we cannot find, in the question of ritual purity, the source of a conflict with Jewish leaders.

It seems to be the case, rather, that Jesus offered the truly wicked – those beyond the pale and outside the common religion by virtue of their implicit or explicit rejection of the commandments of the God of Israel – admission to *his* group (and, he claimed the kingdom) *if* they accepted him. Putting the matter this way explains the connection between tax collectors and sinners in the Gospels (complete outsiders), attributes to Jesus a distinctive view of his own mission and the nature of the kingdom, and offers an explanation of what in Jesus' message was offensive to normal piety – not just to trivial, externalistic super-piety.

Our study of the 'sinners' has highlighted some problems, one or two of which had already appeared.

1. What is the significance of the relative paucity of the theme that Israel should repent? (See also ch. 3 above.). To this I have proposed a partial answer: Jesus did not call sinners to repent as normally understood, which involved restitution and/or sacrifice, but rather to accept his message, which promised them the kingdom. This would have been offensive to normal piety.

2. If Jesus regarded the sinners who accepted him as candidates for membership in the kingdom, even though they did not reform their lives according to the law, should we attribute to him a sectarian purpose? We noted in chs. 3 and 4 that the sayings material is individual in tone. Should we add together the individualism of the sayings, the lack of a call to Israel to repent, and the promise to sinners, and then conclude that Jesus, after all, was not a prophet of national eschatological salvation?

3. Did Jesus' stance on the sinners throw him into conflict with his contemporaries about the law? We turn directly to this question in ch. 9.

4. How are we to understand Jesus' call of sinners in light of the fact that the church seems not to have continued the practice of admitting them?

These problems and others will be addressed in subsequent chapters. First, however, we have to consider one last question under the topic of 'the kingdom': Jesus and the Gentiles.

7

THE GENTILES

We saw above that one of the surest proofs that Jesus' career is to be seen within the general context of Jewish eschatological expectation is that the movement which he initiated spawned a Gentile mission.[1] The question of his own attitude towards the inclusion of the Gentiles in the kingdom naturally arises in a study which has identified him with the hope for the restoration of Israel. The topic has received appreciable attention,[2] and we may most conveniently begin our discussion by considering two books which deal with it, one a classic focused on the Gentiles and the other a recent work on Jesus and Judaism.

In his monograph devoted to Jesus and the Gentiles (*Jesus' Promise to the Nations*),[3] Joachim Jeremias argued that Jesus limited his own mission (and that of his disciples during his lifetime) to Israel (Matt. 10.5f.), but that he predicted the proclamation 'to all the world' at the end: not by human missionaries, but by God's angel (Mark 14.9//Matt. 26.13; Matt. 24.14//Mark 13.10).[4] He took Matt. 8.11f.//Luke 13.28f. to show that Israel (at least the present generation) would be excluded from the kingdom, while Gentiles would enter.[5] Jesus was in accord with the biblical view of the ingathering of the Gentiles at the last hour[6] and opposed to contemporary Judaism, which almost universally took a negative view towards the Gentiles.[7] Finally, he argued, the purpose of Jesus' proclamation and death – that is, his own intention – was to provide for the incorporation of the Gentiles.[8]

Recently John Riches, apparently independently of Jeremias's book, has put forward a similar case.[9] Judaism in the time of Jesus uniformly regarded God as one who would destroy all those who were impure and disobedient,[10] and that includes the Gentiles. Jesus deleted the note of vengeance and destruction from the idea of the kingdom[11] and thus 'transformed' Judaism by introducing the idea of God as 'a loving and forgiving father rather than

. . . a God who will have dealings only with the pure and the righteous and who will exact retribution from the impure and the wicked'.[12] Such a God is God of both Jews and Gentiles.[13] The idea of a universal God of love is completely opposed to the views of Jesus' contemporaries. Riches even finds here the point of conflict between Jesus and others: they resisted the idea of a God of love.[14]

We shall now evaluate these positions, beginning with a discussion of the Gentiles in Jewish literature.

Jewish views of Gentiles

Riches' generalizations about Jewish views are aided by his failure to discuss texts, except a few from the Dead Sea Scrolls, which, one supposes, he takes to represent universal Jewish thinking.[15] Jeremias, on the other hand, gives long lists of passages in building the biblical picture of the pilgrimage of the nations and the depiction of 'late Judaism' as 'uncompromisingly severe'.[16] Jeremias's conscientiousness in listing passages, in fact, puts his own view in jeopardy. In his summary on pp. 40f., he states that the view of late Judaism towards Gentiles was thoroughly negative. On p. 61, however, he notes the 'constantly recurring theme' of the entry of the Gentiles in post-biblical literature. As he remarks on the same page, this leaves only Rabbinic literature to represent the 'uncompromisingly severe' attitude of 'late Judaism'. Thus, as happens so often, it is the Rabbis – whose views, as I shall show, are misrepresented – who constitute the regrettable religion which serves as a foil for Christianity, and it is the Rabbis who are usually in mind when the summary phrase 'late Judaism' is used. It is obvious that neither Jeremias nor Riches provides us with a reliable summary of the evidence from Judaism, and I shall offer my own.

A full study of Jewish attitudes towards Gentiles from the inside would have to take account of the shifting political fortunes of Judaism in a predominantly Gentile world and also of differences among different groups at the same time. Such a study will not be attempted here. We should note, however, that reading the Bible (accepting Jeremias's point that it should not be read through the eyes of modern critics)[17] does not produce such a uniformly favourable view as he asserts and that attitudes towards Gentiles in post-biblical literature are much more variegated than either Jeremias or Riches allows.

There are at least six discernible (although often overlapping) predictions about the Gentiles in the end-time within the biblical prophets, all of which are repeated somewhere or other in later Jewish literature. It is perhaps worth noting that four of these occur in Second Isaiah. The lists are not intended to be exhaustive:

1. The wealth of the Gentiles will flow into Jerusalem: Isa. 45.14; cf. Isa. 60.5–16; 61.6; Micah 4.13; Zeph. 2.9; Tobit 13.11; 1QM 12.13f.

2. The kings of the Gentiles will bow down, and the Gentile nations will serve Israel: Isa. 49.23; cf. 45.14, 23; Micah 7.17 (lick the dust); I En. 90.30; 1QM 12.13f. (quoting Isa. 49.23).

3. Israel will be a light to the nations; her salvation will go forth to the ends of the earth: Isa. 49.6; cf. Isa. 51.4; Isa. 2.2f.; Micah 4.1. It accords with this that the Gentiles may be added to Israel and thus be saved: Isa. 56.6–8; Zech. 2.11; 8.20–23; Isa. 45.22; Tobit 14.6f.; I En. 90.30–33. Here we should include also the one passage which predicts a mission *to* the Gentiles, Isa. 66.19.[18]

4. The Gentiles will be destroyed. Their cities will be desolate and will be occupied by Israel: Isa. 54.3; cf. Ben Sira 36.7, 9; I En. 91.9; Baruch 4.25, 31, 35; 1QM 12.10.

5. As a supplement to the theme of destruction we may add predictions of vengeance and the defeat of the Gentiles: Micah 5.10–15; Zeph. 2.10f.; T.Mos. 10.7; Jub. 23.30; Ps. Sol. 17.25–27.

6. Foreigners will survive but will not dwell with Israel: Joel 3.17; Ps. Sol. 17.31.

This sort of list naturally obscures nuances and complexities. Some of the complexities will be noted by observing that the same or closely related passages from the same book occur in more than one category. Isa. 45.22f. promises salvation to all who turn to God and adds that 'to me every knee shall bow', which sounds very much like submission. Zeph. 3.8 (which is not listed above) combines the threat to judge and destroy the nations with the promise to convert them. For an instance of complex or, better, multivalenced attitudes, one may cite Sib.Or. 3.489–808, which deals successively with the historical vicissitudes of empires, with the messianic era, and with the final consummation. There are dire predictions of the destruction of Gentiles because of their idolatry and sexual immorality (e.g. 3.517f.; 669–72; 761), coupled with the hope that many will turn to God, worship him, and share Israel's salvation (3.616: 'to God the Great King, the Eternal, they shall bend the white knee'; 716–18: 'Come, let us all fall upon the earth and supplicate the Eternal King . . . . Let us make procession to his Temple'; 752f.: 'from every land they shall bring frankincense and gifts to the house of the great God').

Our purpose, however, is not to try to explain complexities and ambiguities in the attitudes of individual authors towards the Gentiles, but to undermine the uniformity and clarity of Jeremias's presentation. He took our category 3 above to be 'what Jesus read in his Bible'.[19] But the Bible contains Micah 5 as well as Micah 4, and there are also harsh statements in Second Isaiah. Some of the passages which Jeremias listed as indicating the salvation of the Gentiles in fact refer to their military defeat and subjugation.[20] And Jesus would also have read predictions of their destruction.

Jeremias's selection of passages and restatement of what they say serve a definite end: the Bible promised the salvation of the Gentiles. 'Late Judaism' (that is, the Rabbis), on the other hand, picked up the few, minor statements in the Bible which predicted their destruction and was overwhelmingly negative towards the Gentiles. Jesus, who predicted the salvation of the Gentiles and the destruction of Jews, 'was not influenced by late Jewish exegesis, but by the Old Testament itself'.[21]

But the above lists also show that in post-biblical literature Jewish attitudes towards Gentiles are not all negative. This would also be true if we were to extend our survey, as Jeremias purported to do, to post–70 literature. He wrote this: 'The exclusively nationalistic conception of the Messianic age which envisaged the destruction of the Gentiles had completely prevailed after the destruction of the Temple in A.D. 70.'[22] Part of the evidence is the saying attributed to R. Eliezer the Great that there are no righteous Gentiles.[23] But the point of the Rabbinic passage is to pair that saying with the opposite one by R. Joshua, to the effect that there are righteous Gentiles who will share in the world to come. Jeremias's misrepresentation of Rabbinic views proceeds beyond citing only half of a passage: he cites no favourable sayings about the Gentiles from Rabbinic literature, when in fact they predominate.[24]

Despite this effort to rectify the balance, it should be noted that, just as the theme of the deserved punishment of Israel recedes in post-biblical literature,[25] that of the punishment of the Gentiles increases. As Israel's punishment at the hands of the nations stretched on, there doubtless seemed less reason for God's spokesmen to say that Israel's sins required punishment.[26] Correspondingly, the Gentiles, as various foreign powers continued to hold Israel in subjugation, were continuously visible as the enemies of God's people. Thus the caricatures presented by Jeremias and Riches (and others), while they are hardly models of scholarly thoroughness and balance, do not come simply out of thin air. First-century Jewish Palestine was not a good nursery for the development of Helleno- or Romano-philism.[27] And after the horrors of the first revolt, R. Joshua's saying that there are righteous Gentiles must have taken some moral courage.

But what, one may ask, has the question of general attitude to do with eschatological expectation?[28] A Jew need not have been an admirer of Gentiles in the present in order to think that at the end, when Israel would be restored and victorious, Gentiles would repent and turn to God. This points to another, in some ways more serious distortion in Jeremias's description of late Judaism as represented by Rabbinic literature. None of the Rabbinic discussions about 'the righteous of the nations of the world' has to do with whether or not they will turn and be saved in the day of the Lord, which is the topic of Jeremias's book and of this chapter. It is well known that, presumably because of the two revolts, early Rabbinic literature is silent about the triumph of the God of Israel in the last days.[29] The Rabbinic discussions such as T.Sanh. 13.2 have to do with whether or not, in the ordinary course of affairs, it is possible for Gentiles who do not become proselytes to be righteous. In this connection, apparently at a later date, arises discussion of the Noachian commandments.[30] The Rabbinic view on that topic is that God does not expect the Gentiles to obey the full law.[31] The question then becomes whether or not any obey enough of those parts of the law for which they can reasonably be held accountable to deserve to be called 'righteous'. The prevailing attitude, as I have indicated, is that it is possible. Jeremias cited a minority opinion (that of R. Eliezer) on this topic as representing the view of 'late Judaism' on the salvation of the Gentiles. Citing the exceptions to the rule on a different subject hardly suffices to determine common Jewish opinion.

It is, however, difficult to establish what the view of any given group in Jesus' day would have been. Were we to have to infer the views of the Pharisees from Rabbinic literature, I would guess that they would have hoped for the conversion of Gentiles. If, after 70, they were prepared to grant that some are righteous day by day, why would they not, before 70, have thought that, at the time of Israel's vindication, many Gentiles would turn to the true God?

If we ask for direct evidence, we encounter the well-known scarcity of Palestinian Jewish literature for the period between the conquest of Pompey and the destruction of Jerusalem. Josephus and the Dead Sea Scrolls are not very helpful for the present topic – whether or not Jews who expected eschatological victory, could, during a time of actual subjugation, envisage the conversion of their oppressors. Josephus is not helpful because he has too many axes to grind. One is that Jews, except for a fanatical fringe, were loyal to Rome when monotheism and its corollaries were not in question.[32] Another is that only a few, all quickly dispatched by Rome's firm hand, looked for redemption. Thus one cannot find out from him what followers of the Egyptian and other 'sign prophets' thought about Gentile conversion.[33] The Qumran covenanters, though free to write what they thought, must be regarded as atypical. They thought that all who did not align themselves with their covenant, under their leaders, would be destroyed. One reads in the Dead Sea Scrolls as little about the reassembly of the Jewish diaspora as about the conversion of Gentiles. Yet the expectation that the diaspora would be gathered is the most stable and consistent point in Jewish eschatological expectation. We must regard the Scrolls' narrow soteriology as unrepresentative.

Just above I called it a guess that Pharisees would have thought that, at the end, many Gentiles would turn to the God of Israel. The guess was based on the fact that after 70 many Rabbis were prepared to think that some Gentiles were righteous in the course of ordinary life. We do, however, have one bit of first-hand evidence. There is one person whom we can *know* to have been a Pharisee who expresses himself about the Gentiles and the eschaton: Paul. During his career as apostle to the Gentiles in preparation for the coming end, he evidently thought that they could turn to the God of Israel and be saved. Yet we see in Paul's own usage a strong disparagement of Gentiles: they are 'sinners' (Gal. 2.15), and they notoriously commit all kinds of sexual transgression (Rom. 1.18–32; I Thess. 4.5). It seems likely that Paul represented a common view in thinking that Gentiles in their day-to-day life were sinners, but that at the end many of them would turn to God from idols (I Thess. 1.9) and conform their behaviour to the normal requirements of the law (Rom. 13.8–10). We can see the same combination of views in Sib.Or. 3, discussed above. Paul also thought, of course, that Gentiles should not accept those parts of the law which distinguish Jew from Greek, especially circumcision, if doing so was understood as necessary for membership in the people of God. This last view distinguished him from others. Very likely the general expectation of Gentile conversion at the end was common.

A similar attitude towards the Gentiles appears in another one of the very few passages which come from the period before 70 and which deal with the eschaton and with Gentiles: Ps. Sol. 17. The emphasis is on the defeat of the nations that trample down Jerusalem (17.25), the gathering of the tribes and the punishment of sinners within Judaism (17.28f.), the exclusion of Gentiles from the land (17.31), and their submission (17.32). The psalmist also says, however, that Jerusalem, apparently especially the temple, will be made glorious 'so that nations shall come from the ends of the earth to see his [God's] glory, bringing as gifts her sons who had fainted, and to see the glory of the Lord' (17.34f.). The theme of the acknowledgment of the God of Israel and of worship at the temple is not far from the conversion and pilgrimage (with inferior status, expressed or implied) that we find, for example, in Second Isaiah. Thus even in this psalm, which so emphasizes Israel's triumph over the Gentiles and separation from them, room is left for them to turn and worship – or at least admire – the one God.

The purpose of this exercise, which I repeat is a long way from the full study which the subject deserves, has thus far been to show that the stark good-bad-good pattern which informs the work of Jeremias, Riches, and many others will not hold as historical description. It is a pattern which springs from and serves theological interests: the biblical religion, at least in the great prophets, was good; late Judaism was a bad religion;[34] Jesus reformed late Judaism, in part by harking back to the prophetic tradition. On the question of attitudes towards the Gentiles (assuming that favourable attitudes mark a good religion!), I have argued that the good-bad contrast in the history of Judaism rests on a distortion and over-simplification of the evidence. The evidence does not permit a precise account of the views of Jesus' contemporaries about Gentile conversion at the end-time. It would be very surprising, however, if that hope had generally been abandoned in favour of a view like that at Qumran. It seems far more likely that most Jews who thought about the matter one way or the other would have expected many Gentiles to turn to the Lord when his glory was revealed.

Jesus and the Gentiles

The pertinent synoptic passages are well known.[35] They are the two forms of the banquet parable (Matt. 22.1–10; Luke 14.16–24), in which the 'highways and hedges' of Luke 14.23 and the 'thoroughfares' and 'streets' of Matt. 22.9f. may not unreasonably be taken as referring to Gentile lands; Matt. 8.11f.//Luke 13.28f. (many will come from east and west and the sons of the kingdom will be cast out); Matt. 10.18 (in being punished the disciples will bear testimony before the Gentiles); Mark. 13.10//Matt. 24.14 (the gospel must be preached to all the Gentiles); Mark 14.9 (the gospel will be preached in the whole world). Against these passages, which point towards the inclusion of the Gentiles and even a mission to them, are generally set those in which Jesus is said to limit his activity or that of the disciples to Israel: Matt. 10.5, 23 (which seems not even to allow time for a Gentile mission); Matt. 15.21–28 (the healing of the Canaanite woman's daughter, where Jesus is reported to have said 'I was sent only to the lost sheep of the house of Israel'); Matt. 8.5–13 (another healing at long distance). The last two passages, by their reticence, count against Jesus having seen himself as having a mission to Gentiles. The evangelists all favoured the Gentile mission, but the tradition about Jesus had to be stretched in order to have him come into contact with Gentiles at all. Here Jeremias's conclusion seems well founded:

> If we leave out of account quotations, summaries, and allegorical interpretations of parables, we find that Matthew yields the same result as Mark and Luke: the only solid evidence for Jesus' activity among the Gentiles consists of the accounts of the two cases of healing at a distance (Matt. 8.5–13 and parallel; Mark 7.24–30 and parallel), alongside of which the story of the Gadarene demoniac may perhaps be placed. That is all.[36]

This is one of the numerous instances in which the policy of relying more on general considerations than on the painstaking and always tentative assessment of the authenticity of one or more sayings will stand us in good stead. The assumption that Jesus' attitude can be recovered by applying various criteria to the sayings material has, as is to be expected, led to very different results in assessing his attitude towards the Gentiles. Jeremias's view was briefly recounted at the beginning of the chapter: Jesus limited his own activity to Israel, but predicted the inclusion of Gentiles to the exclusion of the present generation of Jews. Bosch, investigating the same passages, accepted as authentic Mark 13.9b, 10; Matt. 10.18; 24.14; Luke 21.12f. and, following Beasley-Murray, offered a reconstructed logion, based on those passages, as a saying of Jesus:[37]

> They will hand you over to sanhedrins,
> And you will be beaten in synagogues,
> And you will stand before governors and kings
> For [my name's] sake
>
> [It will be] as a testimony to you.
> And [it will be testified] before the Gentiles.
> First it is necessary for the gospel to be preached
> [Before the coming] of the end.

One could imagine still other combinations of the potentially authentic bits in the passages cited above. One of them I regard as not unlikely: In Matt. 8.11f. it could readily be argued that the note about the sons being cast into outer darkness is Matthaean and that only the 'many will come from east and west' part is authentic.[38] If Matt. 8.12 is dropped, 8.11 itself need not refer to Gentiles, but could refer to the Jewish dispersion, as do similar sayings in Isa. 49.12; 43.5; Ps.107.1–3 (LXX 106.1–3); Baruch 5.5; Ps. Sol. 11.3–7. Thus, for example, Baruch 5.5:

> Arise, O Jerusalem, stand upon the height
>   and look toward the east,
> and see your children gathered
>   from west and east. . . .

If Matt. 8.11 were held not to refer to the ingathering of the Gentiles, it seems to me that the arguments in favour of Mark 13.10 and similar passages (the gospel must be preached to the Gentiles before the end comes), already very dubious, would simply collapse.

It would be equally possible to argue that all the synoptic references to the mission to the Gentiles, or even the statements of their eventual inclusion, come from after the time that the Gentile mission was started; while the restriction of the mission of the disciples to Israel (Matt. 10.5f., 23) comes from a section of the Palestinian church which itself opposed the Gentile mission.

In either of these two cases, both of which seem to be at least as probable as the reconstructions of Jeremias, Bosch and others, the result would be that there are substantially *no* authentic materials on the subject at issue. There would be left only the references to the banquet guests, the meaning of which is vague, and the healings at long distance, which, besides being possibly tendentious (Jesus must have had *some* favourable relationship with Gentiles), do not tell us anything about his view of the entry of Gentiles into the kingdom at the eschaton.

What, at the end of it all, can we *know*? Pretty well what we knew at the outset, the information which can be inferred from the post-resurrection activity of the disciples, and especially from Galatians. The leaders among Jesus' own followers (Peter and John, plus James the Lord's brother)[39] were conducting a mission to prepare Israel for the coming of the kingdom.[40] They were not engaged in the Gentile mission, but they regarded it as an entirely appropriate activity. As far as we can see from Galatians, as I have pointed out before, no Christian group objected to the Gentile mission; they disagreed only as to its terms and conditions. Matt. 10.5f. could conceivably show that there was a hard-line group not mentioned in Galatians, one which positively opposed a Gentile mission.[41] But the overwhelming impression is that Jesus started a movement which *came to see the Gentile mission as a logical extension of itself.*

Saying that it *came* to this view means that Jesus did not consciously 'delete' from his disciples' expectation the uniform view of contemporary Judaism that all Gentiles would be destroyed, which is what Riches has proposed. Had that been the uniform expectation, and had Jesus consciously 'transformed' it, the early disciples would probably have had a clearer view about what to do about the mission to the Gentiles. They seem to reflect what is more likely to have been the common Jewish view: in the last days the Gentiles can be admitted to the kingdom on some condition or other. Enthusiasm for their admission would have varied from person to person, as did the view of what admission requirements should be imposed. We understand the debates in early Christianity best if we attribute to Jesus no explicit viewpoint at all. To understand the controversy which is reflected in Galatians, we actually need to have before us only the biblical and post-biblical passages on the entry of the Gentiles. Most of the early Christians, it appears, followed what I believe to be the majority of Jews in thinking that, at the end, some Gentiles would be admitted to the people of God. They disagreed precisely where the biblical and other passages become vague – whether or not such Gentiles should become proselytes.[42] We need not think that Jesus imparted to his disciples any view at all about the Gentiles and the kingdom.

I have left out of discussion in this section one of the traditional topics which comes up in trying to assess Jesus' attitudes towards the Gentiles: the cleansing of the court of the Gentiles and the saying attributed to him in Mark 11.17, 'a house of prayer for all the Gentiles.'[43] I argued in ch. 1 that 'cleansing' is not the correct interpretation of Jesus' demonstration in the temple; and in any case the quotation of Isa. 56.7 in Mark 11.17 is not likely to be an authentic saying. The simple fact that the action may have taken place in the court of the Gentiles does not seem to bear the weight that some have put on it.

8

THE KINGDOM: CONCLUSION

The facts and the sayings: all Israel or a little flock

Most of the things which we know about Jesus with virtually complete certainty fit him rather neatly into the category of a prophet of Jewish restoration. (1) He began his career as a follower of John the Baptist, who called on all Israel to repent in preparation for the coming judgment. (2) His call of twelve disciples points to the hope for the restoration of the twelve tribes. (3) His expectation that the temple would be destroyed and rebuilt corresponds to a known, if not universal, expectation about the restoration of Israel. (4) After his death and resurrection the disciples worked within a framework of Jewish restoration expectation. Thus our list of facts, including the behaviour of the early Christians, points towards an 'orthodox' eschatological movement whose peculiar characteristic is that it continued, flourished, and even followed out the natural momentum of a realized Jewish eschatological movement by admitting Gentiles.

Yet the sayings material, viewed as a whole, is not what we would expect of a prophet of Jewish restoration. It is not focused on the nation of Israel. Jesus is not depicted (except in the opening summaries in the synoptics) as calling all Israel to repent, there is no teaching material about the reassembled twelve tribes (Matt. 19.28 cannot be considered 'teaching'), and in the material which can reasonably be considered authentic there is no prediction of a general judgment cast in terms of groups (leaving Matt. 25 out of account as inauthentic).[1] The sayings material is markedly individual in tone, and when collective terms are used they do not imply 'all Israel': 'little flock', the 'poor', and the 'sinners'.

The absence of terminology which points to 'all Israel' is so striking that one might suppose that Jesus had a sectarian interest.[2] Did he think that *only* the sinners who accepted him would be in the kingdom? What about those normally counted as righteous? The ambiguity of Jeremias's position is instructive and indicates the existence of a problem. He proposed that Jesus intended to include only his followers, the 'poor', in the kingdom, to the exclusion of the scribes and Pharisees. He then curiously argued that this shows that Jesus did not intend to found an exclusivist sect, but to call all Israel.[3] It points, rather, to a discrepancy between the intention to summon all Israel, which firm evidence leads us to attribute to Jesus, and the thrust of much of the sayings material, in which there might be found a sectarian implication. I do not suppose that Jesus intended to found a real sect, complete with its own interpretation of the covenant and the law. I intend, rather, to indicate that the problem which we first noticed in discussing 'repentance' is a substantial one.

I do not think that I am making too much of the absence of expected themes. The call to repent and the threat of a general judgment were prominent in John's message, and they were very likely part of early Christian preaching. The evangelists were not adverse to them. The thinness of the material which attributes these motifs to Jesus must be accounted for, and that thinness has sometimes been seen as noteworthy by other scholars.[4] Further, Martin Hengel, treading a different path, reached a similar point. He argued that Jesus called only select individuals to follow him, though he wanted a message directed to all Israel.[5] The individualism of Jesus' call to follow him, he pointed out, 'eliminates any interpretation of Jesus as a "popular messianic leader" like Judas the Galilean or Theudas' (p. 59). On the other hand, the instituting of the twelve 'points to [his] openness for all Israel', and it shows that he did not intend to found 'a community of the "holy remnant" sealed off from the outside world' (p. 60; cf. p. 68). That is, there is evidence which points to an ambition which includes all Israel, but other evidence which indicates that he did not appeal directly for their support, as did others. I add to Hengel's point that Jesus differed from John the Baptist as well as from Judas and Theudas: he did not call for public repentance.

The discrepancy between two sets of data may be seen also if we contrast Jesus' execution with his teaching. Jesus was executed by the Romans as would-be king, that is, as a messianic pretender (see below, ch. 11). Not only the Romans, but probably also the 'crowds' and the disciples so saw him.[6] Yet if all we had were his parables and related sayings, we would not expect this to have been the result of his career. Nothing about his teaching is adequate to account for his execution on the grounds of implied insurrection. The characterization of the kingdom as including a 'reversal of values' and his inclusion of the sinners might have been offensive to some of the pious, but they do not explain the Roman execution. The call to follow him at great cost and to love one's neighbour does not lead us to see him as a threat to the established order. The forced efforts of some to find in Jesus' teaching the cause of his death show the point. Some have had to make the promise of forgiveness lead to his execution, and Riches has recently proposed that the conflict was over love, mercy and grace.[7]

Hengel proposed a solution for our problem. Jesus, he argued, did not call all to *follow* him, but he did expect all to repent (*Charismatic Leader*, p. 61; cf. p. 62).[8] It was the mission of the disciples to convey that message to 'all Israel'. It was they who 'proclaimed the message of repentance or of the immediate proximity of the rule of God' (p. 73). Hengel is aware that in the passages which portray the mission of the disciples later materials have been 'fused almost indissolubly . . . with the inherited older traditions' (p. 74), but he regards the mission as actually having taken place. He poses a challenge to others:

> That Jesus did send forth the disciples can hardly be doubted in principle, even if it is no longer possible to reconstruct the circumstances in detail. Anyone who considers the tradition of a Mission to be unhistorical in principle must adequately explain why it was that Jesus called individuals to follow him in such an incomparably rigorous way although he did not wish to found either a royal 'messianic' household or the esoteric nucleus of a community (p. 74).

Hengel's point is well made. If we are to attribute a purpose to Jesus in calling disciples, we must be able to say what it was. It is reasonable to say that he wanted them to complement his work by addressing a wider audience. There is, however, a consideration which makes us hesitate for a moment. Hengel later argues that the disciples themselves did not fully understand Jesus' mission. They read it, 'as did the mass of his Galilean audience, in terms of traditional Jewish national messianic hopes'. He continues,

> It is therefore entirely possible that because the disciples were caught up in apocalyptic and national notions, the service he had in mind for them as their specific personal vocation, was as a whole ineffective (p. 79).

We shall presently return to the question of the disciples' misunderstanding, and I shall propose an alternative to Hengel's view; but for the present we may enquire where we are led by the theory that almost everyone – the Romans, the crowds and the disciples – misunderstood Jesus' intention. If it was a misunderstanding which led to the crucifixion, the implication is that Jesus' intention was innocuous. And so it was, in

Hengel's view. Jesus proclaimed repentance and the nearness of God (p. 73). The masses, followed by the Romans, 'could not understand anyone proclaiming charismatically the nearness of the Rule of God without at least hidden political goals' (p. 59), and on the basis of that misunderstanding Jesus was killed. Only the Sadducees, Hengel acutely remarks, did not misunderstand. They 'subsequently promoted the persecution under Herod Agrippa I and still later saw to the execution of James, the Lord's brother' (p. 40), and the charges against James were similar 'to those with which they had promoted the trial of Jesus some thirty years earlier' (p. 42).

There are obviously difficulties with this view. How could the Sadducees have understood what the disciples did not? This difficulty in Hengel's view points to a difficulty in the evidence. The sayings and parables about the kingdom, as they are usually evaluated, do not lead to the results. The teaching material is taken to represent Jesus' view (which was innocuous), while the results reflect others' assessment of him (a threat). Thus the theory of misunderstanding. Hengel is too good an historian, however, not to see that other *facts* show that the same or a similar result continued even when a military threat was clearly not feared. The disciples, at least some of them, were persecuted, at least some of the time – but not by the Romans. James the brother of the Lord was finally executed – but not by the Romans. The Romans (in the person of Albinus) were angered by the execution of James, and Agrippa II thought it expedient to depose the high priest who had it carried out.[9] Thus Hengel finds a link from Jesus' execution to that of James in the attitude of the Sadducees, and he must accept that they did not misunderstand Jesus, but nevertheless opposed him and his followers after him. I think that he is right on both points. But his correct perception about the Sadducees (or the Jerusalem aristocracy: we do not know that they were all Sadducees) makes one wonder about the theory of misunderstanding on the part of the disciples and the Romans.

Further, the clarity of Hengel's argument reveals another problem. If Jesus taught one thing about the kingdom, but was understood by even his disciples as meaning something else, it follows that he could not communicate effectively, or else had too little time to do so (too little time: Hengel, pp. 79f.). Yet the ideas, as Hengel sketches them, would not take long to convey. The theory of misunderstanding leads us to ask ourselves whether or not Jesus did in fact have a clear conception of his goal and a plan for attaining it. In the Introduction I partly supposed and partly argued that it is reasonable to think of him as having a plan, an intention which links his principal activities and the outcome.[10] If the theory of misunderstanding is correct, it follows that he could not have had a plan which was complete at the level of strategy. He had no effective way of clarifying for the masses his convictions about the kingdom, and his effort to do so by employing the disciples (still following Hengel) failed.

With or without the theory of misunderstanding, however, we must doubt the effectiveness of Jesus' tactics if he intended to be widely accepted. He was able to arouse the interest of the masses and to attract a following, and he was certainly capable of binding his close followers to him in a dedicated way (though even they stopped short of following him to the death). He had a message which he was convinced was of importance for all Israel, but no effective way of making it persuasive. If he sent out disciples to supplement his own activity, he seems not even to have conveyed to them clearly what, if anything, distinguished his message from that of others (see the next subsection). And if he did not send them, he calculated even less how to make the impact which he apparently desired.

We often read that Jesus 'shook the foundations' of Judaism.[11] It is clear, however, that Judaism was not very severely shaken,[12] although Jesus was probably an irritating presence, as were his followers after his death. There was, however, at the time of his execution, no rounding up of the disciples, nor was it necessary to suppress crowds of rioters. It is likely that, during his lifetime, Jesus made a smaller impact than had John the Baptist.[13] Often people who see themselves as acting for God do not worry much about numbers or about realistic strategy. Paul and Peter appear to have divided up the world into the circumcised (to be won by Peter and his colleagues) and the uncircumcised (to be won by Paul and his) without counting noses. When he wrote Romans Paul considered the work of the Gentile mission to be almost over, though he had not been to North Africa. Peter's mission to Jews likewise did not include Egypt. Scholars still debate who was supposed to win the Jews even in Paul's geographical area, and there may well have been lack of clarity on the point.[14] There is, in all this, a lack of calculation which is reminiscent of Jesus. All these people (Jesus, Paul, Peter, James and others) had *plans*, but the means which they could bring forward for their accomplishment were not commensurate with the task. They doubtless left part of the work to God.

I propose, then, that part of the solution to our puzzle is that Jesus may not have had a completely worked out plan which would convey his hope and expectation to 'all Israel', even though he saw his work as bearing on the fate of Israel as a people.

It must be emphasized that the discrepancy between the data which point to 'all Israel' and those which point to a 'little flock' goes back to

Jesus himself. He it was who called twelve disciples and who looked for God to destroy the old temple and bring a new one. His kingdom was surely intended, therefore, to include all Israel. Yet it was also he who, accompanied by a few followers, led the life of an itinerant healer and preacher, who concentrated on the outcasts to the virtual exclusion of the rest, and who did *not* follow John in encouraging a display of mass repentance. He may not have had a clear programme for making a bridge between 'the little flock', the special recipients of his message, on the one hand, and 'all Israel', on the other. He communicated the significance of his message for all Israel well enough, however, for at least some to see him as constituting a threat to peace and public order. And at the end of his career he made two symbolic gestures for all who could to read: he entered Jerusalem on an ass (see ch. 11 below), and he overturned the tables of the money-changers in the temple.

There is one other proposal which may stand as a partial explanation of how the many and the few were related in Jesus' view. We return to the fact that he started under John and that John made a clearly public display of the need of repentance in view of the coming judgment. It may well be that, in Jesus' view, he did not himself have to do it *all*. Although we all know that we should not follow the Gospels and relegate John to the status of an intentional forerunner of Jesus, we often fail to explore the possibilities inherent in Jesus' positive relationship to John. He may have seen himself as supplementing and thus completing John's work. John had called on Israel to repent and had warned of a coming general judgment, but too few had responded. Jesus then set out to promise inclusion to the most obvious outsiders. It is not that he did not 'believe in' repentance and a general judgment, but that he left the basic proclamation of them to his great predecessor. This suggestion gains some support from the Parable of the Banquet (Matt. 22.1–10; Luke 14.15–24): those first called – we add, 'by John' – did not come in, and so others were invited.

This part of our answer to the puzzle is obviously speculative, but it seems to be required by facts which are virtually certain: (1) Jesus followed John and saw his own work in relation to John's. (2) John proclaimed the coming judgment and the need for repentance. (3) In general Jesus stood firmly in the tradition of Jewish restoration eschatology. (4) After his death Jesus' followers worked within the same framework. (5) Jesus himself, however, did not stress the two aspects of restoration eschatology which formed the heart of John's message. (6) His special mission was to promise inclusion in the coming kingdom to the outsiders, the wicked, if they heeded his call.

If these six statements are true, it seems reasonable to suppose that Jesus thought of someone else, John, as having called all Israel to repent.

The nature of the kingdom

Before we return to the issue of the misunderstanding of Jesus, we must resolve a difficult question: Just what did he expect to happen? What sort of kingdom did he look for, and what did his hearers understand him to be promising?

Hengel, as we noted above, has made one difference between Jesus and other would-be leaders of Israel completely clear. Jesus did not, as did Theudas and the Egyptian, expect all Israel to *follow* him.[15] This difference, however, may be one only of style and tactics. Was the kingdom itself different? There is an initial clue that it may have been. In the case of Theudas and the Egyptian, the Romans attacked the followers.[16] This points to the probability that the Roman rulers did not understand Jesus and his followers to have posed the sort of threat which a later generation saw in the activities of Theudas and the Egyptian.[17]

The question of just what Jesus expected is hard to answer, for obvious reasons. Here, if anywhere, the crucifixion and the resurrection would have influenced the expectations of Christians after Jesus' death, and consequently may have affected the evidence. We must, however, assess it as best we can.[18]

Paul gives it as 'a word of the Lord' 'that we who are alive, who are left until the coming of the Lord, shall not precede those who have fallen asleep.' He continues:

> For the Lord himself will descend from heaven with a cry of command, with the archangel's call, and with the sound of the trumpet of God. And the dead in Christ will rise first; then we who are alive, who are left, shall be caught up together with them in the clouds to meet the Lord in the air; and so we shall always be with the Lord (I Thess. 4.15–17).

The modification of the hope which he had first imparted to the Thessalonians consists in including those who have died. It apparently is not a new point to say that the redemption would take place 'in the air'. The cosmic and spiritual nature of the expectation is also clear in I Cor. 15.20–28. Further, on this point there is no indication that Paul's expectation was different from that of the Jerusalem apostles. His belief that, when the offering of the Gentiles would be complete (Rom. 15.16; 11.25), the Redeemer would come (Rom. 11.25f.), is not his innovative contribution to Christian thought. What marked off his position as distinctive was the insistence that the Gentiles need not become proselytes to Judaism. He, Peter, James, John, and even the 'false brethren' (Gal. 2.4) agreed that the Gentile mission was part of the unfolding messianic drama, and they doubtless also agreed on the nature of the kingdom. Paul was not preaching a kingdom to be consummated 'in the air' while Peter and the others were awaiting a political victory. And they all thought that Jesus was the Christ.

Paul's evidence is the best on this point because he can hardly be suspected, as can the Gospels, of having disguised the Christian expectation in order to keep the real intentions of the movement secret from the Roman government. His letters were not intended to be read outside the circle of initiates. We find in Rom. 11 and 15, as in I Cor. 15 and I Thess. 4, what he really expected to happen.

There is, of course, supporting evidence from the Gospels. The prophecy of I Thess. 4.15–17 is paralleled closely in Matt. 24.31//Mark 13.27: the Son of man will send his angels, with the sound of a trumpet (Matthew only), and they will gather up the elect from the four winds. As I argued above, this is quite possibly a genuine saying of Jesus which Paul already knew. But even if it is not, it represents the common primitive Christian expectation. The saying of Jesus at the Last Supper points in the same direction. Doubtless with the prospect of death already before him, Jesus said that he would drink wine again 'in the kingdom' (Matt. 26.29//Mark 14.25//Luke 22.18) – apparently not the present world order. And Paul thought that the Eucharist was a meal held until Jesus' return (I Cor. 11.25) – obviously not with arms.

There is other evidence which points to the expectation of an otherworldly kingdom in a different sense: one on an earth renewed by God's hand. Most telling is the expectation of a new temple. Whether or not Mark's phrase 'without hands' (14.58) is authentic, the idea would have to be supplied. Jesus and his disciples did not envisage a new temple built by stonemasons, but they probably also did not expect a new temple 'in the air'. The idea of a new temple points towards an expectation of a kingdom on earth in which there are analogies to present life. We note also in this connection other evidence of an expected social order. The twelve disciples would judge the twelve tribes (Matt. 19.28), and it was possible to discuss who would be at Jesus' left hand and right (Matt. 20.21//Mark 10.37), as well as who was greatest in the kingdom (Matt. 18.1//Mark 9.34//Luke 9.46; cf. Matt. 11.11//Luke 7.28).

The expectation of the re-establishment of the twelve tribes also points to the same kind of otherworldliness. That Israel will be restored is not the view of a realistic political and military strategist. The theory that the British are the lost ten tribes had not yet been invented, and the hope that the tribes could be reassembled shows that a miracle was expected. Conceivably one could vaguely connect the actual Jewish dispersion with the vanished tribes, but it is far more likely that the expectation that Israel would be restored points to the hope for a fundamental renewal, a new creation accomplished by God.

We should add here, finally, Jesus' prohibition of divorce (I Cor. 7.10f.; Matt. 5.31f. and par.; Matt. 19.1–9 and par.). The saying will be discussed in ch. 9, and there I shall propose that it is authentic and may reflect the eschatological view that the end is like the beginning. In any case it points to a new order which is analogous to the present one (there is marriage), but not just like it (there is no divorce). This probably reflects the expectation of a real change in the world, and is not just a strict 'interim ethic'. The church quickly found the rule difficult and impracticable, as is shown by Paul's further discussion of when divorce is and is not advisable (I Cor. 7.12–16) and the incredulous remark of the disciples in Matt. 19.10 and the reply: one must be given the ability to keep the commandment (that is, not to remarry) (v. 11). It is conceivable that the commandment was intended by Jesus to apply to the present order and to be kept by means of earnest endeavour assisted by grace. It seems more likely that he expected a changed state.

Paul's view, that the kingdom would be 'in the air', can readily be explained as resulting from the crucifixion and resurrection, which required it if hope in Jesus' victory was to be maintained. It seems quite likely that the exclusive concentration on the redemption as taking place in another sphere, not on this world at all, may indeed be the result of the resurrection experiences. The hope for a renewal of the created order, however, is not readily to be explained in the same way. It is not at all difficult to think that, before the crucifixion, Jesus' disciples expected his kingdom to be on a renewed earth, in a transformed situation, and that the hope was shifted from 'renewed world situation' to 'in the air' by the resurrection.

We return now to the question of the misunderstanding of Jesus. A few may have taken him to have been promising political deliverance from Rome. The defection of Judas may have stemmed from disappointment when it became evident that no such victory was in the offing, and there may have been other defections. Another nine of 'the twelve' are hard to trace. Possibly they remained in Jerusalem (were some of them the 'false brethren' of Gal. 2.4?), or possibly they conducted missions elsewhere.[19]

Possibly some defected. Here we enter into pure speculation. I am not, however, persuaded that in general Jesus' disciples misunderstood him as predicting the sort of kingdom which the Zealots subsequently looked for. It is hard to imagine that many of those who followed Jesus around Galilee, saw and tried to imitate his miracles, heard him speak about the wicked and the poor, and counted his followers, first expected military victory and then lost heart when it became apparent that there would not be even a guerilla attack, only to come forth with a drastically revised expectation after the resurrection appearances. We must remember that the disciples almost immediately started a movement which (1) was identifiable as a separate entity within Judaism; (2) regarded Jesus as the Messiah; (3) expected him to establish a kingdom on a different plane from those of this world. We must also bear in mind (4) the apolitical nature of Jesus' work as healer and preacher. *It would be hard to account for these facts if the original expectation were fundamentally different from the post-Easter one.* People who had followed Jesus because they were attracted to his pleasant ideas about love and grace, but who had never expected anything but revised self-understanding, would have had no reason, after the crucifixion and resurrection, to call him 'Messiah' or to form a movement with a definite programme.

The point may be pressed further. It is now virtually universally recognized that there is not a shred of evidence which would allow us to think that Jesus had military/political ambitions, and (5) the same applies to the disciples. As I just proposed, they knew, in wandering around Galilee, that an army was not being created, and their expectation after the resurrection was not that Jesus would return leading a heavenly army, a host of angels. The expected *something*, but not a conquest. Thus, except for the especially dense, *their expectation throughout must have been for a miraculous event which would so transform the world that arms would not be needed in the new kingdom.* Finally, we note (6) that the disciples were not rounded up and executed, which indicates that *no one regarded Jesus' movement as posing an actual military threat. Thus some form of 'otherworldliness' must be attributed to Jesus and his disciples even before the crucifixion, and it would appear that neither the Jerusalem aristocracy nor the Romans understood Jesus' hope differently.*

I think, then, that we must grant an element of continuity between what Jesus expected and what the disciples expected after the crucifixion and resurrection. It appears that the latter originally expected something which was *transformed* by the resurrection appearances, but which was not as completely different as is often thought. The resurrection did not change political, military and nationalistic hopes (based on misunderstanding) into spiritual, heavenly ones, but otherworldly-earthly hopes into otherworldly-heavenly. What the disciples originally expected, I propose, was a kingdom which did not involve a military revolt, but which was a good deal more concrete than either a collection of nice thoughts about grace and forgiveness, or a *message* about God's love for sinners and his being near.

The evidence points to the conclusion that Jesus and his followers expected a renewal reminiscent of some aspects of the War Scroll and the Temple Scroll from Qumran. It is a renewal which includes known social elements and institutions, but one which cannot be achieved without a direct intervention of God which actually changes things. The War Scroll, for example, supposes that the army will be divided according to the twelve tribes. The Temple Scroll looks forward to a time when the temple not only will be run correctly, but also will differ physically from the one built by Herod. The similarities cannot be pushed much further. Jesus did not expect an eschatological war, nor did his disciples. More generally, these two scrolls describe the future with a wealth of detail which is nowhere attributed to Jesus. Jesus' expectation, though it did not remain entirely in the realm of religious abstractions, as is often thought, was nevertheless not nearly so concrete and explicit as the expectation of the authors of these two scrolls.

Thus the kingdom expected by Jesus is not quite that expected by Paul – in the air, and not of flesh and blood –, but not that of an actual insurrectionist either. It is like the present world – it has a king, leaders, a temple, and twelve tribes – but it is not just a rearrangement of the present world. God must step in and provide a new temple, the restored people of Israel, and presumably a renewed social order, one in which 'sinners' will have a place.

The proposed solution has numerous advantages, some of which have already been indicated.

1. It does not force us to think that Jesus failed entirely to communicate his own vision of the future. Most people understood it well enough.

2. We can hold together the facts that Jesus was executed by the Romans, that his followers were not pursued and killed, and that subsequently they did not expect a legion of heavenly warriors. The expectation of an otherworldly kingdom explains all these points. It may not be immediately evident that it explains the crucifixion; and so, although I here transgress on the subject of later chapters, I shall say something about that point. John the Baptist, we recall, was executed, as was, years later, James, the Lord's brother. Neither can be thought to have posed a threat as a leader

of an army. Neither was killed by the Romans, but we nevertheless see that religious spokesmen could pose a threat without drawing a sword. The Romans did, however, kill other prophets who, 'under the pretence of divine inspiration', fomented changes (*BJ* II.259f.). Stirring up people's hopes and dreams could result in death.[20]

3. We can understand better how the disciples could so readily shift their hopes to awaiting the return of the Lord from heaven. If they had always expected an eschatological miracle, it is easy to understand the role of the resurrection appearances in the creation of Christian belief in a heavenly kingdom.

4. The present proposal saves evidence which ordinarily plays little role in explaining the message of Jesus and the rise of the Christian movement, but which is hard to explain as having been created after Jesus' death. (a) There is, first of all, the material about the temple. I think that Jesus expected a new temple, and the present explanation takes that fully into account. But even if one continues to think that Jesus 'cleansed' the temple, he presumably did so for a purpose. It is often said that he did so in order to prepare it for the coming kingdom,[21] but then the fact is dropped and plays no role in defining what sort of kingdom Jesus expected. It is best to think that he expected one in which a temple, whether new or cleansed, would be useful. (b) The passages about the role of the disciples in the kingdom are also taken account of. I argued extensively above in favour of the authenticity of Matt. 19.28 (the twelve judging the twelve tribes) and less extensively, but nevertheless with conviction, for the request by James and John to sit at either side of Jesus in the kingdom (Mark 10.37 and par.).[22] Neither passage is likely to have been created. The passage about James and John can hardly have arisen after Peter gained the ascendency which we see in Paul's letters, and that, in turn, goes back to the ministry of Jesus. Further, it is likely that Jesus himself was the one who named Simon 'Rock', which we might take to be the second part of his reply to the request of James and John. There is every reason to think, then, that there was discussion about who would hold what place in the kingdom. These passages about the disciples traditionally, however, play no role when Jesus' conception of the kingdom is discussed. I think that they should be taken seriously as indicating what Jesus' disciples thought, and I then note that such discussions go back to the lifetime of Jesus and that the disciples did not misunderstand their master entirely. (c) The expectation of the reassembly of the twelve tribes becomes a true expectation, not just a vague symbolic reminiscence of Israel's history. (d) The prohibition of divorce and remarriage also assumes a place in an overall

world-view. It can be understood not as interim ethic nor as an ideal goal which will never be reached, but as a serious decree for a new age and a new order.

5. Finally, we can comprehend why it was that the disciples thought of Jesus as Messiah. It has often been observed that a crucified man who becomes a heavenly redeemer does not easily qualify for the title. On the hypothesis proposed here, the disciples already thought of Jesus as 'king' – or, better, as viceroy under the true king, God. If Jesus taught his disciples that there would be a kingdom and that *they* would have a role in it, he certainly, at least by implication, gave himself a role also. 'Messiah' will do perfectly well for the person who is superior to the judges of Israel, even if he was not a warrior. As long as they expected him to return and establish 'his' kingdom (Matt. 20.21), the disciples could think of Jesus as Messiah.

Once we accept that Jesus was not misunderstood, a different light is shed on the question of how his view of the kingdom differed from that of others. It may not have differed very much. The notion of an eschatological miracle is by no means unknown in the literature. I have already pointed to parallels at Qumran, and elsewhere one can see that there was an expectation of a new heaven and a new earth. Such a view is implied, for example, whenever the temple is depicted in terms which surpass the ordinary.[23] Prophetic or oracular exaggeration cannot be ruled out in such cases, but it is also easy to move from verbal exaggeration to grandiose conception.

Theudas as well as others unnamed expected an eschatological miracle.[24] Unfortunately we do not know what they expected next. In the case of the Egyptian, who apparently created a more serious disturbance than did the others, we can make a good guess. He probably promised a miracle and expected it to be followed by a military defeat of the Romans. (This assumes that there is some truth to each of Josephus's two accounts.)[25] But the others, to whom Josephus attributes no military action in either the *Antiquities* or the *War*, may have expected only a miracle and not have thought that a mighty sign would cause all Israel to gather behind them to defeat the Romans. They may have thought that God would continue to intervene miraculously and that he would bring back into being the twelve tribes of Israel and create his own glorious temple. Perhaps they expected a new heaven and a new earth, in which there would be no hunger or sorrow, and in which people would study war no more. The possibilities could go on and on.

The point is that Jesus was not the only one who read the great prophets, and we cannot *know* that his conception of the kingdom was more spiritual than that of others, or that he assigned a higher place to love of God and neighbour. Here as elsewhere we do best not to base our view of Jesus on the assumption that he believed in religious abstractions which others denied.

We can, however, see a distinction in Jesus' *style*. He did not make grand gestures or promise grand events which were designed to convince all. *There are prophetic and symbolic actions, but they are not miracles, and the miracles were not put forward as substantiating his claim.*

We can go further. He deliberately demonstrated, by riding on an ass, that the claim to a special role in God's kingdom was being made by one who was 'meek and lowly'.[26] It is Matthew, of course, who has looked up the passage and quoted the words 'humble and riding on an ass' (Matt. 21.5, quoting Zech. 9.9), but the action speaks for itself. Jesus saw himself as one who was a servant of all (Matt. 20.28a//Mark 10.45a), not their glorious leader in a triumphal march through parted waters.

We earlier observed that, if Jesus was misunderstood, that would be evidence that he did not have a clearly thought-out strategy for getting his message across. Now it appears, however, that he was not all that much misunderstood. His self-assertion is appreciably different from that of Theudas or the Egyptian, but the view that God would bring in the kingdom miraculously was the same. This gives us a better way of understanding that Jesus did not have a plan which included practical strategy. He did not need one, since he looked to God for the vindication of his message and his claim. When he decided to go to Jerusalem and to offer symbolic gestures to indicate what was to come (the replacement of the temple) and his own role in it (a king, but one who rides on an ass), it is unlikely that he realistically thought that the leaders and aristocrats would be convinced that the kingdom was at hand and that he was God's last envoy before the end. He performed the prophetic actions, and they were understood, but even they do not count as being part of an orchestrated effort to convince. He doubtless knew that their minds were hardened. Thus we see that Jesus had a plan, including the device of an effective means of communication, but that he did not have a long-range policy which would win the Jerusalemites over to his conviction. It is in this sense that we can say that he did not have a programme which could bridge the gap between those who accepted him (some of the poor and outcast of Galilee) and the leaders in Jerusalem.

I have, at last, been led to lay emphasis on one group of sayings about the kingdom, those which depict the coming kingdom as having aspects of a social order. If the only evidence about Jesus were a collection of sayings – and many scholars write about him as if this were the case – we would not necessarily be led to make this group of sayings determinative (see the end of ch. 4). We have been pushed to do so by the need to explain history and to account for facts. After Jesus' death the disciples formed a group which had concrete expectations and which was not just an assembly of people committed to the same abstractions. Jesus doubtless believed in love, mercy and grace, and so did the disciples, but those beliefs would not lead to their becoming an identifiable group within Judaism.[27] Further, we must account for the fact that Jesus was executed but that his disciples were not. Their ideas about the kingdom, though concrete, were not expected to be realized by force of arms.

Still further: two of our basic facts themselves imply an otherworldly kingdom with analogies to the present order: The demonstration against and saying about the temple, which point to a new – or, at a minimum, purified and renewed – temple; the calling of twelve disciples, which prefigures the re-establishment of twelve tribes.

It remains the case, however, that we still have no grounds for ruling out in principle any of the other groups of sayings about the kingdom. Those which we have thrust into prominence in this chapter might seem to exclude those which predict a cosmic cataclysm, since both include sayings about the judgment, and it is not reasonable to think that the judgment could, in Jesus' view, be carried out both by angels at the coming of the Son of man (Matt. 24.31 and elsewhere) and by the twelve disciples seated on twelve thrones (Matt. 19.28). The principle of coherence might seem to require us to deny the authenticity of the saying about angels and the Son of man. The problem is that we cannot know just how hard to press the principle of coherence. In mentioning this point earlier, I observed that people who think and talk in pictures may use apparently self-contradictory ones, and that observation still stands.

All the other groups of sayings blend happily enough with our conclusion about Jesus and the kingdom. Those sayings and parables which speak of or imply a reversal of values cohere with the expectation that Jesus and his followers would take leading places in the kingdom and that it would include 'sinners'. Those which speak of the kingdom as present, or which use it as a word to mean 'covenant relation with God', offer little difficulty for any particular hypothesis, and certainly not for the one argued for here. One need realize only that 'kingdom' does not always carry precisely the same meaning. The kingdom in the full eschatological sense could not be present, nor could it be entirely entered into by individuals, but the meaning of the word can be stretched so that one can talk of the kingdom, in the sense of God's power, as present and as extended to individuals in the present.

We have, in fact, explained the hardest group of sayings, and those which were least likely to be created or to be supplemented by similar ones. That, to repeat, is one of the virtues of our proposal. After Peter became recognized as the foremost of the former disciples, and especially after the disciples began to die, sayings about which of them would occupy which place in the kingdom are unlikely to have come into being. Jesus may have turned such questions aside by saying that he could not assign places (Matt. 20.23 and par.), or he may have pointed to the children as typifying members of the kingdom (Matt. 18.2–5 and parr.) – or such answers may be a later rebuke, designed to turn the ambition of the disciples into stories with a moral pointing to the virtue of humility. But whether the answers are authentic or not, the question probably was really posed.

The proposal that Jesus had in mind an otherworldly-earthly kingdom does not involve the denial that he expected there to be a resurrection. I see no way of coming to a hard decision about the authenticity of a debate on the resurrection (Mark 12.18–27 and parr.), but we should accept that Jesus 'believed in' resurrection. It is often emphasized that the Pharisees did so, but we should probably turn the phrasing around: everyone did, except the Sadducees.[28] Those who care for system can quite readily put 'new order' or 'messianic age' chronologically before 'resurrection'. Some Rabbis eventually made such an arrangement, and one can see a two-stage eschatology in the Temple Scroll.[29] Jesus and his followers could readily have done the same. There is no firm evidence that they did so, nor need we suppose that they did. Many people have combined a belief in personal and individual immortality with belief in a general resurrection, without sitting down and working out just how the two are related. Possibly Jesus thought of 'the kingdom' in two ways and never brought the two into a systematic relationship. I see no evidence, however, which allows us to move beyond possibility.

Jesus as religious type

We should now draw together those points of our discussion which bear on the question of what sort of figure Jesus was. This can be done very briefly, for here I think that Hengel's case is persuasive. Hengel compares Jesus to leaders of 'prophetic-charismatic movements of an eschatological

stamp' (*Charismatic Leader*, pp. 2of.), and he settles on the term 'eschatological charismatic' as best giving Jesus' type (e.g. pp. 44, 48, 63, 68). It does
not lie outside the scope of such a person to teach, and Hengel points to
Josephus's description of Judas the Galilean as a *sophistēs* (pp. 23f.). Besides
Judas, the others who are closest to Jesus, and whose names we have, are
Theudas and the Egyptian (pp. 20–24), who have been so often mentioned
in this chapter. There were still others, unnamed by Josephus. Hengel
explores other possibilities, chiefly that of Rabbi (pp. 42–50), with largely
negative results.

Jesus, however, he argues, is not to be understood entirely within the
limits of the type. He is best described by the category 'eschatological
charismatic', though he goes 'far beyond anything that can be adduced as
prophetic prototypes or parallels from the field of the Old Testament and
from the New Testament period' (p. 68). Hengel is apparently ready to
follow Fuchs in speaking of Jesus as standing in God's stead (ibid.), and
he adds:

> He shatters the power of the evil one, invites sinners to the messianic
> banquet, makes the claim that his message of the nearness of salvation and
> of God's judgment is binding without reserve on all Israel, including the
> Holy City and The Temple (ibid.).

This claim was unique. It was an 'unique, underivable claim to authority,
grounded in God himself' (p. 69).

> Quite certainly Jesus was not a 'teacher' comparable with the later rabbinical
> experts in the Law, and he was a great deal more than a prophet.
> Even within the characterization we have preferred, of an 'eschatological
> charismatic', he remains in the last resort incommensurable, and so basically
> confounds every attempt to fit him into the categories suggested by the
> phenomenology or sociology of religion (ibid.).

We may recall here Morton Smith's view. He agrees that Jesus conforms
to a general type represented by Judas the Galilean and Theudas. The
former was 'a legal teacher who started a resistance movement against
Roman control', and 'comparison with him places Jesus in the category of
revolutionists and/or messiahs'. Theudas, on the other hand, was a *goēs*,
a 'magician' or 'deceiver'. 'Comparison with him reflects Jesus' reputation'
as miracle worker.[30] Smith, while affirming that in some ways Jesus
was connected to would-be political messiahs, sees him primarily as a
magician.[31] Smith's observations, however, are in need of refinement.
Theudas, according to Josephus, called himself a *prophet*, and that presumably was how his followers saw him. Josephus called him a *goēs* in the sense

of 'deceiver' (*AJ* XX.97). Whether he worked any miracles we do not know. Jesus was apparently seen by his opponents as both a 'deceiver' and a 'magician', but he was crucified as would-be 'king'. 'Magician' does not do justice to the implicit claim to be spokesman for God, and thus a 'prophet'; and the comparison with Theudas also points towards considering him a prophet, and a prophet of a certain kind: that called by Hengel an 'eschatological charismatic'.

This is not a novel conclusion. Many scholars have agreed that, of various roles which we can identify, Jesus best fits that of 'prophet'. It is also generally recognized that Jesus' repute as a miracle worker must be taken into account in defining him. Thus not infrequently one will read that he combined styles or types.[32]

We have, then, fairly wide agreement on a general category, but it is a category which contains people who differed from one another in substantial ways.[33] I shall offer a list, emphasizing factors which distinguish one from another.

1. John the Baptist may be considered a prophet. From what we know of him, he had a message with one basic thrust: to repent in view of the coming judgment. He had disciples, but they were not viewed as potential insurgents. He seems to have confined his work to a remote area near the Jordan. (In addition to the Gospels, see *AJ* XVIII.116–19.)

2. Judas the Galilean and his successors were true insurgents. Judas taught, but he did not perform miracles or promise a great eschatological sign. (See *BJ* II.118, 433.)

3. Theudas (and the unnamed others) offered a miracle which recalled the exodus. We do not know that any of them had previously performed miracles, nor that any expected an armed uprising. Josephus's account in the *War* seems to show that they probably did not, for there he does attribute a military attack to the Egyptian. (See *BJ* II.258–60; *AJ* XX.97f., 167f.)

4. The Egyptian wanted to overthrow the Roman garrison and establish himself as king (*BJ* II.261–63). There was probably the promise of an eschatological miracle, and it is this point which Josephus fixes on in the *Antiquities* (*AJ* XX.169–72).

5. Jesus, unlike any of the others – as far as we know – , gained fame from miracles. As Smith points out, the taunt against him that he saved others but could not save himself reflects this.[34] Further, like Judas, he was a teacher. Unlike the Egyptian, but like John, Theudas and the unnamed others, he did not expect armed revolt. He differs from Theudas and the others, however, in not promising an eschatological miracle. As I

pointed out before, the symbolic gestures pointing to the eschaton were not miracles. Further, he may not have sought a mass following at all, and thus would be unlike all the others. We shall examine the question of numbers more closely in ch. 11, and here it is necessary only to recall Hengel's point that he did not call all Israel to follow him.

And so, among the main representatives of a very broad type, Jesus can be distinguished. I do not doubt that in the ways just indicated he was unique; in some way or other everyone is unique. I do not know, however, that he was unique because he claimed more authority than did Theudas and Judas (so Hengel, p. 69), just as I do not know that he went beyond them in hoping for a kingdom in which outcasts received God's love. Their followers came from somewhere, and probably not from aristocratic circles. Quite likely they were not all pious – and perhaps some were sinners. They were at least 'poor'.[35] 'Renewal movements' (Theissen's term) appeal to outsiders. How much authority Theudas and the Egyptian claimed we cannot know, but we do know that some of their followers, unlike Jesus', paid for their devotion with their lives. The oft-repeated claim that Jesus 'put himself in the place of God' is overdone. He is often said to have done so in forgiving sins;[36] but we must note that he only pronounced forgiveness, which is not the prerogative of God, but of the priesthood. I do not know of any other instance in which it can reasonably be said that Jesus put himself in God's place.[37] In short, I must doubt many of the claims for Jesus' uniqueness.

I do not wish to minimize Jesus' self-claim. Obviously it was great indeed. He claimed to know that the kingdom was at hand and to be in a position to say who would be in it. He even knew that he and his disciples would be main figures in it, though he apparently declined to designate precise places. It is by no means unlikely that he thought of himself as viceroy-to-be. But I worry a bit about the word 'unique'. Others also thought that they spoke for God and were appointed directly by him to lead his people into the kingdom.

What is unique is the result. But, again, we cannot know that the result springs from the uniqueness of the historical Jesus. Without the resurrection, would his disciples have endured longer than did John the Baptist's? We can only guess, but I would guess not.

In parts of this conclusion to the study of the kingdom, we have had to get ahead of our story, and the question of the execution has had to figure in the discussion. It is now time to return to the proper sequence, and to take up points where there may have been opposition and the groups from which it may have come.

PART THREE

CONFLICT AND DEATH

9

THE LAW

General considerations

The question of 'Jesus and the law' is twofold. One must inquire whether or not Jesus took an attitude towards the law which was in any way negative. If he did so, was it one of the factors which helps to explain his crucifixion and the rise of the Christian movement? The answers are not self-evident. As A. E. Harvey has recently pointed out, people generally do not have an *attitude*, much less a negative one, towards the law as such.[1] Does this apply to first-century Jews? We can see that at least some Jews, during crisis periods especially, had to adopt a general attitude towards the law. In the early stage of the Maccabean revolt the leaders had to decide not to obey the Sabbath law if doing so meant losing battles and men.[2] During the persecutions which followed the second revolt against Rome, the Rabbis specified that only three laws need be maintained if keeping the law would lead to execution.[3] Paul and the other leaders of the Christian movement, in a quite different kind of crisis, had to think about the status of the law. Josephus tells us that Jews were generally loyal to the law,[4] and self-consciousness about observing it would be sharpened by the intermixture of cultures. Jews in the diaspora must have been conscious of being different from Gentiles, but the situation in Roman-governed Palestine could hardly have been different – as, again, is seen in Josephus's accounts of hostility and strife between Jews and their overlords.

There is thus some reason to think that Jews in general in the first century may have been more conscious of living under 'a law' than are most moderns, who tend to think only about particular laws. Besides, it may be urged, Jesus, no less than Paul, saw himself as living at a time of crisis, with the eschaton near at hand. Thus the circumstances were right for a consideration of the law as law.

Perhaps most readers will think that general considerations such as these are not needed. There are several passages in the Gospels in which Jesus is depicted as being challenged about the law, and such conflicts would have necessarily pressed him to consider what he thought about it. Of recent years many New Testament scholars have shown themselves willing to accept these passages more or less at face value, and they have concluded that Jesus explicitly and consciously opposed the law.[5] Kümmel, further, has argued from Jesus' execution to the probability that he offended some of the leaders of Judaism by openly opposing the law.[6] The fact that the trial narratives do not mention Sabbath, food and the like need not be taken as conclusive; and the argument may be pressed that general hostility towards Jesus needs to be accounted for, and that the passages describing debate on the law help to do so. Still others, without taking this precise line, see Jesus as having been consciously and deliberately anti-Torah in sweeping terms.[7]

Yet, as we saw in the Introduction, a major line of New Testament research has held that Jesus did not take a negative attitude towards the law. Bultmann and others have granted that some historicity attaches to at least some of the passages in the Gospels which show a conflict. They have argued, however, that, though he opposed the law on some points and thus now can be seen to have opposed it in principle, he was unaware of having taken such a stance. This is, in effect, the view that he had no attitude towards the law other than that of the normally observant Jew: it represents the will of God.

This view results from trying to hold together two types of evidence. One I have just mentioned, the pericopes which show Jesus in conflict with others about the law. The other is the difficulty about the law in the early Christian movement. We move here into the question of whether or not Jesus' own attitude towards the law helps account for the results. As usual, we find ourselves thinking backwards, from the result to its cause. The result was not a clear position which held that the law could readily be set aside; therefore, the argument runs, Jesus could not have taken an unambiguously negative stance towards the law in general, nor towards the parts later debated, such as the food laws.[8] It seems to me that this argument is fatal to the view that Jesus openly and blatantly opposed the law. The theory of explicit opposition may make hostility towards Jesus easier to account for, but it makes the controversies in the early church incomprehensible. We must still consider, however, the position that, although Jesus opposed parts of the law, he did not intend to oppose it in principle.

A recent thesis has argued in favour of such a position. Banks proposes that Jesus took up no attitude towards the law, but simply bypassed ('surpassed') it.[9] He regards Jesus as having adopted a position which was not in conscious relation to the law one way or another, although opposition to the law was *latent* in his position.[10] One of his formulations is noteworthy: 'Jesus neither moves out from the Law in making his own demands nor relates those requirements back to it.'[11] The first clause seems to be a useful generalization and a true one. Jesus was not, as far as we can tell from the surviving material, a midrashist. He did not develop his own statements as exegetical comments on the Torah.[12] I am not, however, persuaded of the accuracy of the second clause, that Jesus did not relate his own requirements back to the law. This point requires testing.

It must be asked of those who propose such views how it could be that Jesus opposed aspects of the Mosaic legislation but did not take up a negative stance towards the law as such. The view that the law is unitary – it was all given by God to Israel, and all parts are thus equally binding – was so common in Judaism[13] that Jesus must have known it and, moreover, daily encountered others who accepted it as obvious and who would have brought home to him the implications of his actions. It is thus hard to see that Jesus could have opposed aspects of the law without seeing the implications for the law as a whole.

There is a line of defence. One can argue that he opposed individual laws but not the law as such if one can show that he made a conscious distinction within the law. A recent thesis by Westerholm, which is valuable in several ways, shows how this sort of argument can be developed.

Westerholm discusses Jesus' attitude towards 'scribal authority', which turns out to include most of the things generally covered under the heading of 'Jesus and the law'.[14] The learned of Israel thought of Scripture as essentially containing statutes, while Jesus did not. Westerholm deduces from the divorce pericope, for example, that Jesus' view was that 'scripture is not statute; the will of God may be sought in what scripture reveals of his purposes; divorce is opposed to that will.'[16] Although I shall disagree with aspects of Westerholm's view, I think there is a fair bit of truth to this formulation. Just as I above agreed with Banks that Jesus was not a midrashist, I can here agree with Westerholm that he was not a halakic midrashist. His occupation was not taking up scriptural statutes and interpreting them (the partial exception is, again, the pericope on divorce).

What I have called a 'line of defence' involves an appreciable shift in position. A view such as Westerholm's allows one to cope with the anti-Torah evidence of the Gospels and the fact that the disciples did not know that Jesus had broken with the law. It does not, however, require him to be unconscious of the implications of *de facto* transgression or opposition. On the contrary, it attributes to him a distinct and well-thought-out position which distinguishes truth from error, or profound meaning from superficial observance, within the law itself. Thus when Westerholm proposes that Jesus did not agree with the position of the Torah on divorce, he does not mean that Jesus opposed the law but was not conscious of the implication. In Westerholm's view, Jesus deliberately challenged the authority of the law as it was understood, as containing statutes.[17]

Many others have proposed that Jesus made a distinction between the ceremonial or ritual law, which he opposed or held to be superficial and unnecessary, and the moral law, which reflects the will of God.[18]

It should be emphasized that this sort of defence is necessary if one is to maintain that Jesus broke the law on certain points and even debated about it, but did not oppose the law itself. It can hardly be maintained that he did not know at all what he was doing, and so it must be held that he knew and had thought it out. This line of defence, however, is difficult to maintain. There are two points to consider.

The first is that we cannot find, in the Judaism of Jesus' day, any precedent for making the sort of distinction within the law which is attributed to him. From Philo we learn that some Jews allegorized parts of the law and did not keep it all literally.[19] Later, in Rabbinic Judaism, we can observe that some aspects of the law were interpreted away, though not by allegory. One may reasonably attribute this practice to the Pharisees and others of Jesus' day. The clearest example is the deletion of one part of the law with which the Rabbis strenuously disagreed, the statement that those who take the name of the Lord in vain cannot be acquitted (Exod. 20.7; Deut. 5.11).[20] It appears that different Rabbis got around that part of the law in different ways, but not by explicitly saying that 'the law here is wrong'. Citing one passage against another in order to justify ignoring or disbelieving an unpalatable part of the Torah is also known. The Rabbis did not agree with another major aspect of the ten commandments: that God visits 'the iniquity of the fathers upon the children to the third and the fourth generation' (Exod. 20.5). Against that view they could appeal to Ezekiel (Ezek. 18.1–20).[21]

These interpretations, even though the result is to oppose the obvious meaning of a scriptural law, were not considered by those who practised them to be denials of the law, nor to call into question its *adequacy*. The Pharisaic/Rabbinic concept of 'oral law' shows that they wanted to assert that the law given to Moses was adequate in all respects – even when they were in fact adding to it, deleting from it, and otherwise altering it. Similarly in 1QS a distinction is made between the 'hidden things' in the law, which are known only to the sect, and the rest (1QS 5.11f.). Entrants to the community pledge to keep 'every commandment of the Law of Moses in accordance with all that has been revealed of it to the sons of Zadok' (1QS 4.8f.). Thus the sect's special rules were formally considered to be in 'the law of Moses', though from our point of view they are additions and modifications.

Did Jesus change or avoid the law by interpretation? Individual cases will be discussed below, but here it may be noted that, apart from the pericope on divorce, the material in the synoptics is not readily amenable to this interpretation.

The frequent proposal that Jesus opposed the cultic aspects of the law recalls the Rabbinic distinction between 'commandments which govern relations among humans' (*mitsvot ben adam le-adam*) and 'commandments which govern relations between humans and God' (*mitsvot ben adam le-Maqom*).[22] This is not the same as the distinction between ritual and moral aspects of the law – which is, in fact, anachronistic – but in any case the distinction was not made for the purpose of relegating some part of the law to a secondary place. The Rabbis used this distinction to specify what should be done to atone for transgression. Transgression of commandments governing relations among humans requires compensation as well as repentance to God.[23]

Thus we know of various ways in which people could avoid the obvious meaning of the law without, however, admitting that they opposed it. Further, we see that some could make distinctions within the law. What is lacking from ancient Judaism is a parallel to the attitude attributed to Jesus: that he saw himself as sovereign over the law and as being able to decide that parts of it need not be obeyed.

The unparalleled character of this view does not, to be sure, trouble a great many scholars. On the contrary! Here can be seen a novel point and one that distinguishes Jesus from others. He was conscious of unparalleled sovereignty, and rightly so.[24]

There is, however, a second difficulty. We must face, again, the evidence from early Christianity. The parts of the law which are most prominent in the Gospels are Sabbath and food, and those who hold the view that Jesus himself distinguished aspects of the law which need not be observed from the rest of it, or from the will of God reflected in it, must put these two parts of the law in the group which he was willing to break. Yet these are two of the three major points of law in Paul's letters (the third being circumcision). If Jesus had declared all foods clean, why did Paul and Peter disagree over Jews eating with Gentiles (Gal. 2.11–16)? Or, put in terms of Acts rather than Galatians, why did it take a thrice-repeated revelation to convince Peter (or, rather, to leave him puzzled and on the way to conviction) (Acts 10.9–17)? And if Jesus consciously transgressed the Sabbath, allowed his disciples to do so, and justified such action in public debate, how could Paul's Christian opponents in Galatia urge that the Sabbath be kept (Gal. 4.10)?

The discussion thus far has followed a chain of questions, proposals, and counter-arguments. I shall recapitulate: (1) Did Jesus have an attitude towards the law? (2) If he did, was it negative, and did it help lead to his death and the rise of the Christian movement? (3) Some have answered yes. (4) Others have argued that he had no clear and unambiguously negative stance, but that he opposed the law in some specific details. (5) This view comes about by combining pericopes in the synoptics which describe conflicts with the fact that early Christianity did not easily dismiss the law. (6) The early Christian debates about the law show that one cannot maintain position 3 above – that Jesus took an unambiguously negative stance towards it. (7) Against position 4, one may urge that he could not have opposed the law in detail without seeing the implications. (8) In defence it is argued that he himself distinguished parts of the law which could be disregarded from the parts which must be kept, or from the will of God itself. (9) Against this it may be urged that such a distinction is unprecedented. (10) Proponents of position 8 accept Jesus' uniqueness. (11) But against position 8 it may nevertheless be urged that his followers did not know that he had 'abrogated' *just those parts of the law* which are most prominent in the synoptics and which constitute the details which he is held to have set aside.

The history of the early church poses difficulties for any view which holds that Jesus opposed the law. The question then becomes how firm are the passages which depict him in opposition to it.

The question is not so much whether or not we can find a record of some *de facto* disobedience of the obvious meaning of the Scripture – which in and of itself would be only moderately interesting – but whether or not there is evidence that Jesus *consciously challenged the adequacy of the Mosaic dispensation*.

The temple and the law

It is one of the curiosities of research on the question of Jesus and Judaism that Jesus' sayings and actions with regard to the temple are often separated from his attitude towards the law.[25] We have seen above that some regard Jesus as having opposed *not only* the law *but also* the cult, while numerous others propose that Jesus changed opponents in Jerusalem: from the Pharisees, whom he offended by not observing the law (at least as they understood it), to the priests, whom he offended by threatening their revenue.[26] As Schürmann puts it, Jesus opposed the legal interpretation of the Pharisees and the cultic piety of the Sadducees. [27] We shall return to Jesus' opponents, but here it may be remarked that it was surely not the case that only the Pharisees were interested in maintaining the law, nor that only the Sadducees were interested in the temple. But we let this point pass for the present, and concentrate on the view of many scholars that Jesus' attitude towards the law can be separated from his attitude towards the temple.

This understanding, or misunderstanding, is seen in an extreme form in Banks' recent investigation of Jesus and the law. He mentions the temple only in passing, and even then it is only Mark 11.16 (passing through the temple area while carrying vessels) that is in view.[28] He later concludes that Jesus' remarks on this score show only that he did not affirm oral tradition.[29] It seems not to have occurred to Banks, as it has not occurred to numerous others, that Jesus' attitude towards the temple cannot be dissociated from his attitude towards the Torah, nor can his attitude towards law be studied without dealing with the traditions on the temple; for *the temple rites were based on the Torah*. It is hard to conceive that Jesus could have had fundamentally different attitudes towards the temple and towards other points of the Mosaic legislation.

If it be true that Jesus' action against the temple informs us about his view of the entire Mosaic dispensation, we have the possibility of reaching at least a partial conclusion. It would seem that Jesus did not regard it as inviolate. I have previously argued that the action and the saying are eschatological, that is, they point to the end of the old order and the coming of the new, and we see that, in this conviction, Jesus could strike a physical blow at the existing temple sacrifices.[30] As we have seen in chs. 1 and 8, the gesture cannot be taken as simply negative. It is probable that the prediction that the temple would be rebuilt (Matt. 26.61//Mark 14.58) is authentic. But even if it is not, we should connect the apparently negative action and saying with Jesus' positive view of the coming new age. We thus cannot say that the passages about the temple show that he opposed the law. They demonstrate, however, *his view that the current dispensation is not final.*

Let the dead bury the dead

It was, as far as I have noted, Schlatter who first observed how the commandment to a would-be disciple to 'Let the dead bury their dead' would have sounded to Jewish ears: a wanton act of blatant transgression ('*ein schlechthin schändender Frevel*').[31] Wilder also noted that the saying violates not only filial duty but the fifth commandment (honour of father and mother). He draws from the violation, however, only the conclusion that Jesus felt his 'errand' to be urgent. The saying should not be generalized in its application.[32] Despite the relative neglect of the pericope, I regard it as being the most revealing passage in the synoptics for penetrating to Jesus' view of the law, next only to the conflict over the temple. Among recent scholars, it is primarily Martin Hengel who has seen the force of the saying, at least as far as its negative implications go, and what follows will be seen to be in close agreement with his position.[33] We should begin by briefly sketching the most pertinent points concerning form and authenticity.

In Matthew (8.21f.) the passage is the second of two concerning those who would follow Jesus, in Luke (9.59f.) the second of three. The arrangement is presumably the result of collecting and redactional activity, but there is widespread agreement on the authenticity of the passage.[34] It is also generally agreed, correctly it seems to me, that the introduction in Luke is the more original, while Matthew has the original ending.[35] The passage would thus read as follows:

> Jesus said to another: 'Follow me.' He said: 'Let me first go and bury my father.' But Jesus said to him: 'Follow me, and leave the dead to bury their dead.'[36]

This is one instance in which the 'criteria of dissimilarity' stand us in good stead. As Schlatter's remark makes clear, the saying is not conceivable as coming from any part of Judaism known to us. Further, it is not comprehensible as a creation of the early community.[37] Hengel has also shown that there are no true parallels to the saying 'Let the dead bury their dead' in the Graeco-Roman world.[38] It counters not only the Mosaic legislation as it was understood throughout Judaism, but also normal and common Graeco-Roman piety.[39] There is one final remark about authenticity: the saying presupposes the question.[40] It would not be imaginable that the request to go and bury one's father first was created as a frame for the saying to let the dead bury their dead.

But what does the exchange mean? It will be useful to dwell for a moment on the severity of the requirement to honour one's parents by burying them. The obligation to bury dead relatives is first indicated in Gen. 23.3f., Abraham's request for a burial place for Sarah, and common Jewish interpretation understood it to be implied by the fifth commandment. The seriousness of the obligation to care for dead relatives is most clearly seen in Berakoth 3.1, where it is said to override even the obligation to recite the *Shema*[c] and wear phylacteries. Similarly in Tobit, Tobias protests against marrying a woman who had lost seven husbands on her wedding night, on the ground that if he, Tobias, were killed by the demon who jealously guarded the woman, the tragedy would also bring his parents to the grave, and 'they have no other son to bury them' (Tobit 6.13–15). Here the obligation to bury one's parents is the ground for backing out of a betrothal. It thus becomes clear that the requirement to care for dead relatives, especially parents, was held very strictly among Jews at the time of Jesus. In addition to the obligation to bury one's parents, the general obligation to care for the dead was very strong. According to later Rabbinic opinion, even the High Priest and a Nazirite, ordinarily forbidden to contract corpse-uncleanness, should do so in the case of a neglected corpse (Nazir 7.1).

The saying 'Follow me, and leave the dead to bury their dead' has a double impact, and a double impact which has not, as we noted above, been widely recognized. The positive thrust – a call to discipleship which is urgent and which overrides other responsibilities – has been generally appreciated. Dibelius, for example, commented that it is 'not as if Jesus' message forbade the fulfilling of the obligations of filial reverence, but because the decision for the Kingdom of God cannot be postponed'.[41] Similarly Schweizer interpreted the passage to mean that 'discipleship excludes all other ties'.[42] What is striking about this sort of interpretation is the lack of realization of what the negative implication of the passage is: Dibelius has it apply only against the 'obligations of filial reverence', without noting that the obligation was imposed by God in the Torah, and Schweizer against 'other ties', again without noting that the duty is one commanded by God. Disobedience of the requirement to care for one's dead parents is actually disobedience to God.

Banks, while noting the strictness of the requirement to bury dead relatives in Judaism, has nevertheless proposed a different meaning for the passage from the one suggested here: 'It is far more likely that, as in the surrounding pericopes, it is the priority of discipleship over domestic responsibilities that is at stake rather than an issue relating to oral or written Law and that the reply of Jesus is a purely proverbial one with no actual referent(s) in view.'[43] Both halves of this proposal are unlikely, though on different grounds. We have already noted that Banks' general position with regard to Jesus and the law is that he did not specifically relate to it one way or another; he surpassed it but never directly countered it. In the present case Banks supposes that Jesus had in mind the positive call for discipleship but did not see it as being opposed to Torah obedience. What is unlikely about this view with regard to the particular case, as with regard to Jesus' attitude towards the law in general, is that it is simply hard to believe that any first-century Jew who dealt with matters covered by the Torah would not have consciously realized that he was either accepting it as binding or rejecting it. It is hard to believe that Jesus saw the requirement to bury dead parents as only a 'domestic responsibility' and did not know that it was a commandment from God. With regard to the second half of Banks' proposal, that the saying is proverbial without any direct referent to a real case,[44] one must rather follow Hengel: the attitude indicated is so shocking, not only in Judaism, but in the entire Graeco-Roman world, that the saying 'Let the dead bury their dead' could hardly be a general proverb. This would require the question concerning the would-be disciple's father to be a later creation to particularize the proverb, but it is extremely unlikely that the later church would have created a setting which made Jesus sound so impious. The only realistic reading of the passage is to consider both the question and the answer as authentic. This means that they apply to a real situation: the man's father is actually dead, and Jesus actually requires that the man follow him rather than bury his father. Any other reading requires that the saying be either proverbial or metaphorical, and we have seen these to be unlikely possibilities.

In chs. 6 and 8 we noted the positive thrust – the requirement to follow Jesus at all costs. What is important here is to see the force of the negative thrust: Jesus *consciously* requires disobedience of a commandment understood by all Jews to have been given by God. Should this be generalized, or should we take it to be a rare, perhaps unrepeated instance in which Jesus put the call to follow him above even the law? That must depend on the assessment of other evidence. It is probable that Jesus did not expect all who heeded his message to *follow* him (see ch. 8), in which case the urgent requirement of this passage may not reflect a *consistent* and *general* view of the relative value of his own work and of the law. Even after we have fully registered the shocking character of the demand, we must still hesitate before drawing far-ranging conclusions as to Jesus' attitude towards the law.

We should briefly mention here another passage about a would-be disciple, the rich man of Matt. 19.16–30//Mark 10.17–31//Luke 18.18–30 (he is young in Matt. 19.22 and a ruler in Luke 18.18). He is told, in addition to observing the law, to sell all that he has and to follow Jesus. It is tempting to combine the two stories and conclude that the requirement laid on would-be disciples was to surrender whatever was precious to them, which would lead to the inference that it is not the law as such which is at stake in Matt. 8.21f. One might also say that, in both stories, the law is held not to be adequate. This may point us in the right direction, although we can by no means be sure that the story of the rich man is authentic.

A modest conclusion about the pericope on burying the dead is in order. At least once Jesus was willing to say that following him superseded the requirements of piety and the Torah. This may show that Jesus was prepared, if necessary, to challenge the adequacy of the Mosaic dispensation.

The sinners

We should return to our proposal about Jesus' view of the inclusion of the 'tax collectors and sinners'. If what I earlier suggested is true – that he thought that accepting him would ensure them a place in the kingdom even if they did not repent and make restitution according to the normal requirements of the law – then he obviously called into question the adequacy of the law. This would not have been precisely *opposing* it, but rather acting on the premise that it need not be applied to those who followed him. Here would be a point of real offence, not just to the Pharisees, but to all who thought that the wicked should repent and make restitution. The case of the wicked would then be roughly parallel to the case of the would-be disciple who wanted to bury his father, but it would have been blatant and publicly obvious. If Jesus' public following included notorious sinners who had not repented and made restitution, and if Jesus publicly proclaimed that they would precede the righteous in the kingdom – even those righteous who had been persuaded by John to repent – then public indignation may well have been pronounced.

Divorce

The historicity of Jesus' prohibiting divorce is confirmed by Paul's giving it as a commandment, not from himself but from the Lord, that neither the wife should divorce the husband nor the husband the wife. He adds that in case a wife does divorce, she should remain single or be reconciled to her husband (I Cor. 7.10f.). Paul proceeds to give his own divorce rules, which are not based on the view that remarriage constitutes adultery, but rather deal with whether or not believers should divorce unbelieving spouses (I Cor. 7.12–14). Finally, he urges believing spouses not to oppose a divorce sought by an unbelieving partner (7.15).

All the synoptic passages on divorce (Matt. 5.31f.; Luke 16.18; Matt. 19.3–9//Mark 10.2–12), while there are interesting differences among them, are determined by the view that divorce leads to adultery.

Naturally a great deal of exegetical work has been done on these passages.[45] One of the principal problems has been whether or not Matthew's allowing of divorce in case adultery had already been committed goes back to Jesus. A second is raised by the fact that Mark, Luke and Paul deal with a woman's divorcing her husband as well as a man's divorcing his wife, while Matthew does not.[46] The third principal problem is that neither Paul nor Luke attributes to Jesus scriptural warrant for his view, while Matthew and Mark do (Matt. 19.4–6//Mark 10.6–8). The argument is based on Gen. 1.27 and 2.24: 'he made them male and female'; 'the two shall become one flesh'.

There are obviously many other issues which may be discussed: the form-critical analysis of the passages; the examination of Rabbinic views on divorce; and of course the earliest form of the prohibition. There is also the interesting question of why Paul, having prohibited divorce in the name of the Lord, proceeds to discuss when it is and is not appropriate. But our needs are limited to two points:

1. In forbidding divorce Jesus did not directly defy the Mosaic law. It is a general principle that greater stringency than the law requires is not illegal. The *ḥaberim* and the Essenes, to name two obvious groups, took on themselves stringent requirements not in the Mosaic law, and they doubtless did so on religious grounds. Those of the *ḥaberim* are obvious: they intended 'to elevate everyday Jewish life as a whole, and in its minute details, to the sphere of cultic worship'.[47]

We can put this matter another way. It is not the case in Jewish law that everything not forbidden is required. Moses did not *command* divorce, he permitted it; and to prohibit what he permitted is by no means the same as to permit what he prohibited. Westerholm, who employs this passage in his argument that Jesus did not deal with the law as statute, does not adequately explain what is and is not a statute in the Mosaic law. Since the point seems to be often misunderstood we should briefly consider it. In Deut. 24.1–4 there is a clear statute: a man may not remarry a wife whom he had divorced if she subsequently was married to somebody else. This applies even if her second spouse died. There is also an implied ordinance: a man who divorces a wife should write her a bill of divorce. Divorce itself is not a statute: it is neither forbidden nor required.[48] In the New Testament passages, Jesus forbids divorce. He cannot be said here to be refusing to deal with the law as statute. In fact, it would seem that he introduces a statute where there was none: he forbids divorce.[49] This makes two other statutes pointless (those requiring a legal bill and prohibiting certain remarriages), but only by the standard legal device of excluding the situation in which they were relevant.

Westerholm, to be sure, principally wants to argue that Jesus was not interested in halakic definitions, and one may certainly agree. In this particular case, we do not need to debate further whether or not he intended his view to be interpreted by his followers as a statute. It is enough that we see that he does not say anything which would lead to disobedience of the law, and he cannot be said to be opposing it.

2. The long form of the tradition about divorce, which includes the appeal to Gen. 1.27 and 2.24 (Matt. 19.3–9//Mark 10.2–12), or something very like it, represents Jesus' original saying. It is likely on intrinsic grounds that Jesus gave a religious reason for his limitation. Further, a similar passage in the Covenant of Damascus (or the Zadokite Document) is so closely related to our passage that it becomes overwhelmingly probable that Jesus' original ruling cited Scripture. The passage in CD is worth examining in some detail.

The author's presentation is a little confused, and there are also some uncertainties of punctuation. The author first says that Israel is ensnared in three 'nets of Belial' which are set up as 'three kinds of righteousness'. The first is sexual immorality, the second wealth, and the third making the temple impure (CD 4.14–18). The general point is that in three areas laws ('righteousness') are followed which are in fact wrong ('nets of Belial'). The profanation of the temple is caused because the priests (apparently) 'lie with a woman who sees her menstrual blood' (5.6f.). This is a standard charge against the priesthood, known also from the Psalms of Solomon and Rabbinic literature (Ps. Sol. 8.13; Niddah 4.2), and it probably reflects a halakic dispute on the time which must elapse before a woman is

considered pure. The point apparently is that the Sadducean[50] interpretation of the law ('a kind of righteousness') is wrong.

The author eventually, after a good deal of other material, gets around
to wealth, the second 'net', although the word 'net' does not recur: the
members of the covenant (that is, the Covenant of Damascus) 'shall keep
away from the unclean riches of wickedness acquired by vow or anathema
or from the Temple treasure' (6.15f.).[51] One will here, of course, recall
Mark 7.11//Matt.15.5. By a legal device, money vowed to God can be
kept for one's own uses.

The author has much more to say about the first 'net', sexual immorality.
Israel (more precisely, 'the builders of the wall', identified as those who
'follow after Precept') is ensnared *bishtayim bizenut* (4.20). It is difficult to
know just how to construe this phrase and the words following it. Vermes
translates 'shall be caught in fornication twice by taking a second wife. . .'.
Lohse has 'They are caught in two ways: in fornication, that they take two
wives. . .'. Rabin reads 'caught in two kinds of fornication: (first) to take
two women. . .'.[52] It seems best to follow Rabin and read 'in two kinds of
sexual immorality', and also to follow him in introducing at that point a
colon. In this case a second charge of sexual immorality can be found in
5.8–11,[53] which illogically comes *after* the charge of priestly impurity
(5.6f.). The second kind of sexual immorality in this understanding is that
Moses forbade a man to marry his mother's sister, while the forbidden
degrees should be extended to prohibit analogous marriages between
uncle and niece (5.8–11).

Now for the immediately relevant parallel, which is the first of the two
types of sexual immorality: It is immoral for men to take two wives in their
– the men's – lifetimes. 'The foundation of creation is "male and female
he created them"' (4.21). The author has further arguments, and the issue
seems to have been important: (1) 'Those who entered the Ark went in
two by two.' (2) Deut. 17.17 forbids the king to multiply wives – although
David is excused, since he could not have read Deuteronomy, which had
been sealed up (5.1–6).

The prevailing interpretation of the passage in CD and also of the
synoptic pericope on divorce is well stated by Dungan: The argument of
both the Zadokite Document and Jesus is based on

> the expectation of the imminent return of the Time of Creation, the
> primordial age of perfection soon to manifest itself through God's direct
> intervention. Indeed, the time is felt to be so close at hand as to provide a
> basis for opposition to the polluted legal traditions of men . . . . This
> particular point of similarity between the Damascus Document and Jesus'

appeal to the age of Creation establishes the thoroughly apocalyptic horizon of Jesus' answer.[54]

I have presented the argument of the Zadokite Document in such detail because it is important not to rush to a conclusion. Dungan, for example, does not cite the further biblical arguments in CD. The Zadokite author's argument in this entire section is by no means dominated by eschatological expectation and the view that *Endzeit* should equal *Urzeit*. Although we know from the Temple Scroll that at least some at Qumran expected a new temple, our particular author is not concerned about that. He is concerned about profanation of the present temple and about whether or not money vowed to the temple is turned to private use. In the case of his position against taking two wives he has three scriptural arguments, and only one of them is an appeal to the order of creation. The eschatological key does not open every door.

When we return to the argument attributed to Jesus (Matt. 19.3–9 and par.), we note that there are two scriptural arguments, one of which is an appeal to the order of creation. The other is based on another principle: 'the two become one flesh', and this one, furthermore, is elaborated: 'so that there are no longer two but one' (Matt. 19.8//Mark 10.8). This line of argument is followed by Paul in his discussion of employing a prostitute: 'Do you not know that he who joins himself to a prostitute becomes one body with her? For, as it is written, "The two shall become one flesh"' (I Cor. 6.16).

Jesus, Paul, and the author of the Covenant of Damascus all shared the view that they lived in the last days (for the view of CD, see 4.4). But eschatology does not necessarily explain everything. Paul's statement about divorce and marriage *are* based on eschatology: see I Cor. 7.24–31. But his statement about prostitution, where he quotes Gen. 2.24 (I Cor. 6.16), does not seem to depend on eschatology.

I am not attempting to prove definitively that Jesus' prohibition of divorce did *not* flow from his view that at the end there would be a reversion to the time before the fall. It may have done so, and the fact that both CD and the synoptic pericope put Gen. 1.27 first may point in that direction. But I do not think that we can be sure. The saying on divorce does not *prove* that Jesus' world-view was determined by eschatological expectation. On other grounds I think that he saw himself as a prophet of the coming reign of God, and it is reasonable to interpret the saying on divorce as springing immediately from his eschatological expectation, but I do not think that we can tie the two together with absolute certainty.

Anyone who accepted Jesus' prohibition of divorce would not thereby become a transgressor of the law, and in that sense Jesus' saying is not against the law. Yet we do see here the view that the Mosaic dispensation is not adequate. The prohibition shows that Jesus expected there to be a better order. That this was based on the view that the new age would duplicate in some ways the original creation is possible but not certain. Yet the implied expectation of a new and better order is itself eschatological.

Other antitheses and related sayings

In Matthew the saying on divorce, besides appearing in the long form in 19.3–9, appears as one of the antitheses (Matt. 5.21–47; the divorce saying is 5.31f.). It has been common to identify some of the antitheses as authentic and to take them as showing that Jesus intentionally broke with the law.[55] The opposite case has also been made out. They are not infrequently combined with Matt. 5.17 ('I have come not to destroy but to fulfil') to show that Jesus radicalized rather than abrogated the law.[56]

Of these two tacks, it is the second which catches the spirit of the antitheses, whether one isolates two or three or takes them in their present context. We should repeat here what was said in discussing the pericope on divorce: it is not against the law to be stricter than the law requires. Only those who think that it is can readily harmonize the antitheses with the view that Jesus opposed aspects of the law.[57] I shall leap ahead to a passage not yet considered to make the point. Let us assume that Mark 7.15 is authentic, that Jesus actually said that *not* what goes into a person, but what comes out, produces defilement. The simplest meaning of the saying would be that unclean food does not defile, and consequently that, in the opinion of the speaker, it may be eaten. That would permit what Moses forbade and would be directly against the law. If, however, Jesus said 'not *only* what goes in defiles, but even more, what comes out', the law would be maintained and radicalized, but not opposed. One would assume that the speaker was pointing to a different type of impurity from that forbidden by the dietary code, but not that the validity of the law was being denied. The antitheses, except for the saying on divorce, are 'not only . . . but also' sayings. They affirm the law, but press beyond it. If authentic they would be further indications that Jesus did not oppose the Mosaic code, but did find it to be inadequate.[58]

There are, however, doubts about their authenticity. The principal problem is that they are part of a general depiction of Jesus which must be doubted. There is a layer of material, primarily in Matthew, which presents us with a Jesus who defines his own position *vis à vis* the Pharisees, but not by including those whom the Pharisees exclude. His distinction is that he calls his followers to be more righteous than the Pharisees *by the same standard*. The Pharisees have the right idea, but they do not follow it well enough or far enough. We see this Jesus in Matt. 5.17–20, 43–8; 6.1–8, 16–18; 18.15–18; 23.5–7, 23–6.[59] This Jesus is one who proclaimed a super-righteousness of both outer and inner perfection (5.48), who said that not one bit of the law could be relaxed (5.19), and who urged his disciples to be more righteous than the Pharisees (5.20).

The Jesus of this material approves of external 'minutiae', such as fasting and tithing, but objects to Pharisaic obviousness. His followers are to do the same things, but with a better appearance, not making a show (Matt. 6.1–8, 16–18; 23.5f.). This Jesus, in short, requires super-strict observance of every particular of the law – and then some. He calls outsiders 'Gentiles and tax collectors' (*ethnikoi, ethnikos*: Matt. 5.47; 6.7; 18.17; 'tax collectors' used pejoratively: Matt. 5.46; 18.17). This, I think, is not the historical Jesus, who was a friend of tax collectors and sinners and who did not make entrance into the kingdom dependent on being better at Pharisaism than the Pharisees themselves. Further, the evidence from the early church counts strongly against accepting the Jesus of Matt. 5.17–20 (and related material) as the historical Jesus. We have previously observed (and we shall have to observe again) that explicit anti-law statements are hard to accept in view of the conflicts over the law after Jesus' death. *But the same argument applies to explicitly pro-law statements.* If Jesus was really on record as saying that absolutely all the law must be kept, Paul could hardly have persuaded James and Peter to sanction his mission.

There are two sorts of reply that can be made by those who wish to maintain the authenticity of this material. One is to argue that Jesus said some of the things attributed to him in these sections, but that they did not originally mean what they now appear to mean. Thus 5.48 ('be perfect') and 5.17 (I came to fulfil the law) in their present context mean 'be perfectly observant of the higher as well as of the lower law'; but they can be abstracted from it and defined to mean 'bring the law to eschatological fulfilment', which might conceivably include breaking or altering some of it.[60] Or one might separate 5.17 from its sequel in 5.18f. (every bit of every single law) and combine it with Mark 2.17 (I came to call sinners), which conceivably could yield the meaning that Jesus saw his mission to sinners as being fulfilment of the law (interpreting one 'I came' saying by another). Such exercises can never be proved to be wrong, but we cannot build on them.

Matt. 5.17 reminds us again of how little we can know of the nuances of Jesus' teaching and of how little can be proved by combining sayings from here and there. Jesus may have said something like Matt. 5.17. He surely thought of himself as fulfilling God's plan and thus, in a sense, the law and the prophets. The problem is that, unless we know in advance what the saying must have meant in order to be judged authentic, we cannot use it. And if we know that in advance, we do not need it. This saying, like any other, must be set in a framework of evidence which makes sense of it and which also makes sense in the general depiction of Jesus. In its present setting 5.17 points to a strict legalism which no one will attribute to Jesus. Can the saying be preserved by creating for it a new setting or combining it with other sayings? It is my own judgment that we cannot be confident of reconstructed settings which provide new meanings. I shall offer, once more, an analogy with 'Paul and the law'. The reader of Galatians is perhaps surprised to find Paul saying, in Rom. 3.31, that he 'uphold[s] the law'. Since we have the two letters, however, the apparent contradiction can be explained, first of all by noting context. In Romans Paul is in part reacting to a charge of antinomianism (3.8), which he is at pains to correct (cf. also 6.1, 15). Thus we can understand that he himself did not intend his negative statements about 'righteousness by the law' to mean the wholesale abandonment of the law and that he wished to rectify the balance. Thus far, I think, all will agree. Precisely how all Paul's statements about the law can be held together, however, is a question which produces a torrent of different answers – even though we have the letters. What chance, then, do we have with a saying such as Matt. 5.17? None, I think. If Jesus did say that, or something like it, we will never know it. We cannot, as things stand, use the statement as a pillar of our reconstruction of Jesus and Judaism. If we had original sayings by Jesus on the law in their original context, we could possibly provide a nuanced understanding of how he saw his work in relation to the Mosaic dispensation. But, I fear, we shall never be able to obtain such material.

The same argument applies to the antitheses. Can they successfully be lifted out of their present context? Matt. 5.17–20, 48; 6.1–8, 16–18 point strongly in the direction of a super-legal Jesus, and the antitheses (5.21–47) fit well in that context. If they are removed, however, they could be read as pointing to a different kind of righteousness, one of the heart and mind instead of just the deed. They might then mean not 'do all the law to its most minute detail and more', but 'real fulfilment of the law resides in the heart'. Such an interpretation would not put the antitheses in direct contradiction to the dominant picture of Jesus, who did not found his ministry on requiring super-strict obedience to the law. The problem, again, is that such reconstructions must be based on prior knowledge and can only supplement it – and do so hypothetically at that.

There is another way of harmonizing the Jesus of Matt. 5, 6 and 23 with the one who accepted sinners. It may be proposed that he made the moral requirements more stringent, but relaxed the external ones.[61] The relaxation of external requirements allowed him to associate with the wicked, while he demanded that his followers observe the highest of moral standards. The first problem with this proposal is that the Jesus of much of Matt. 5, 6 and 23 is not depicted as relaxing the external requirements. His disciples are still to tithe mint, dill and cummin (23.23) and to fast (6.16–18).[62] The followers of the other Jesus did not fast during his lifetime (Mark 2.18–22 and parr.), and his credentials could be questioned because he did not keep the ascetic discipline which fasting represents ('a wine-bibber and a glutton', Matt. 11.19 and par.). As long as one remains in the realm of theory, it is perhaps possible to combine a piety of superior stringency with the view that certain religious practices can be relaxed. But when it comes to the same issue, and when the issue is a matter of practice, as is fasting, the combination is not possible.

The second objection to this harmony is that the 'heroes' of much of the Gospel tradition, the tax collectors, are treated as outsiders in Matt. 5.46.

Since negatives are so difficult to prove, I do not wish to argue that we can know that Jesus said none of the things attributed to him in the sections under consideration. I am inclined to reject the entire section, Matt. 5.17–6.18, except for the prayer (6.9–13). Even the saying on divorce is probably preserved in a form closer to the original in Matt. 19.3–9. If, however, some or all of the antitheses were regarded as authentic, we would learn in somewhat more detail what we have already learned: that Jesus did not oppose the Mosaic law, but held it in some ways to be neither adequate nor final.

To summarize the results of our discussion of the statements in the Sermon on the Mount which bear on the law: Except for the pericope on divorce, they are of dubious authenticity. Even if some of them are authentic, they do not help us much in our present endeavour. They will still be controlled by facts and one's reconstruction of cause and effect. Unless we are prepared to think that Jesus fell foul of the authorities for being too strict about the law and that the 'false brethren' (Gal. 2.4) were following Jesus in insisting that the law had to be completely fulfilled, we must conclude that they had no immediate result. If they are true or even partially true, then they would of course mean that Jesus did not reject the Jewish law. But that, surely, would not in any case be a serious proposal. His whole work, and that of his disciples, is set, as we have frequently repeated, in the frame of Jewish eschatology. We do not need Matt. 5.17 to persuade us that Jesus did not dismiss the Scriptures of his people.

Sabbath, handwashing and food

I shall deal with these points of law, about which Jesus is depicted as coming into direct conflict with the Pharisees, with extreme economy. Some scholars have found in Jesus' supposed violation of the laws of Sabbath and food the clue to the conflict which resulted in his death (as, in fact, is proposed by Mark 3.6).[63] More, though finding here no fatal conflict, have seen these points of law as defining Jesus' conflict with his contemporaries.[64] Opinions range from this extreme all the way to another: there is no violation of the law at all, or none worth much attention.[65] In this case, one of the extremes must be judged to be correct: the second one.

I shall not discuss each pericope in detail, and consequently shall make relatively little reference to the special exegetical treatments of them. A fair range of opinions has been given in the Introduction. The position which is taken here can be supported, I think, largely on the grounds of general observations.

Before dealing with the passages, we should make the preliminary observation that the issues of food and Sabbath would loom much larger in churches which contained Gentiles than they would in pre-Christian Judaism. In a Jewish environment, observance of the Sabbath and the consumption of kosher food are largely matters of routine.[66] That food and Sabbath were issues in the Gentile churches is shown by the letters of Paul, where they are the only two items other than circumcision which require special treatment (Gal. 2.11–14; 4.10; Rom. 14.1–6). Thus it is very probable that the issues of food and Sabbath are so prominent in the Gospels because of the importance which they assumed in the church. That is not to say, of course, that it can be proved that Jesus never debated such issues. This is another negative which cannot be proved. But that they *defined* his relationship to his contemporaries is most unlikely.

We must then note that this means that debates with the Pharisees recede in importance. I am one of a growing number of scholars who doubt that there were any substantial points of opposition between Jesus and the Pharisees (that is, with the Pharisees in particular, as distinct from the rest of Jewish Palestine). Again, a negative cannot be proved. But all the scenes of debate between Jesus and the Pharisees have more than a slight air of artificiality. We consider this question further in the next chapter.

Bultmann and many others have pointed out the unrealistic ('imaginary')[67] character of the scenes. Just *how* incredible many of them are, however, seems not to be realized by many. Harvey, for example, seriously discusses the story narrated in Mark 2.23–26 as representing a real *event* in which Jesus transgressed the law by allowing his disciples to pluck grain on the Sabbath.[68] Similarly he seems to think that Pharisees really did go to Galilee in order to inspect Jesus' disciples' hands (Mark 7.2).[69] In the latter case, and also in discussing Mark 2.18, Harvey does not note that it is not Jesus who is said to have been accused, but his disciples.[70] In taking the stories at face value he also seems to deny what he had just accepted as an 'assured result' of form criticism, namely, that the conflict stories were composed in the light of debates between Christianity and Judaism.[71]

The extraordinarily unrealistic settings of many of the conflict stories should be realized: Pharisees did not organize themselves into groups to spend their Sabbaths in Galilean cornfields in the hope of catching someone transgressing (Mark 2.23f.), nor is it credible that scribes and Pharisees made a special trip to Galilee from Jerusalem to inspect Jesus' disciples' hands (Mark 7.1f.). Surely stories such as these should not be read as describing actual debates between Jesus and others.

It may be argued, to be sure, that 'where there is smoke there is fire'; that is, that the accounts of disputes do not *describe* debates between Jesus and the Pharisees, but that they preserve the memory that Jesus fell into conflict with the Pharisees on the law.[72] On the face of it, this is a reasonable, but unprovable proposal. I think that further consideration of the evidence, however, will lead to the conclusion that there was no substantial conflict between Jesus and the Pharisees with regard to Sabbath, food, and purity laws.

Even if we accept all the stories as depicting things that really happened (though with artificially contrived introductions), it must still be noted that there is no actual transgression of the law on the part of Jesus. In the passage on handwashing (Matt. 15.1–20//Mark 7.1–23)[73] it is the disciples who are accused. I have been at pains previously to point out that 'handwashing' is not a biblical requirement for the laity. While the *haberim* undertook to observe special purity rules, there is no evidence that they thought that those who did not do so were sinners, and there would certainly be no reason to single out Jesus' disciples for criticism. Jesus and his disciples were obviously not *haberim*, but that put them in the vast majority.

The handwashing dispute, at least in Mark, slides into a discourse on food, which is quite a different matter in Jewish law.[74] The artificiality of the connection is evident. Thus, after the dispute on handwashing, Mark introduces what is clearly a second topic: 'And again calling the crowd he said to them' (Mark 7.14). Which crowd? The one always around Jesus' door? In any case, the topic changes to 'what defiles', and the general point of Jesus' discourse is that a person is defiled not by what goes into his mouth, but by what comes out. Mark (not Matthew) applies this explicitly to the food laws (7.19). Even so, there is no indication that Jesus and his disciples did not eat kosher food,[75] although the importance of Mark's comment for churches which included Gentiles is obvious.

The saying in Mark 7.15 ('not what goes in defiles . . . ') is often taken as the most secure bit of the whole passage,[76] and it is sometimes understood to be a reply to a question like that of Mark 7.5, which concerns handwashing.[77] That, however, can hardly be the case. 'What goes in' must surely be the food itself – nothing else goes in and comes out – ,[78] and the statement does not respond to the question of whether or not Jesus' disciples should become *haberim*, laypeople who accept special purity rules. The point of the saying, in fact, is so clear that the positions of the 'false brethren', Peter and James become impossible to understand if the saying be considered authentic.[79]

It is very likely that the entirety of the pericope on plucking grain on the Sabbath (Matt. 12.1–8//Mark 2.23–28//Luke 6.1–5) is a creation of the church. Bultmann long ago observed that the disciples (that is, the church) are criticized, not Jesus, and the passage represents a Christian response to Jewish criticism.[80] If there is a historical kernel, I do not see how it can be recovered,[81] except possibly for the concluding sayings (on which more below).

The stories of healing on the Sabbath (the Man with the Withered Hand, Matt. 12.9–14//Mark 3.1–6//Luke 6.6–11; the Woman with a Spirit of Infirmity, Luke 13.10–17; the Healing of a Woman with Dropsy, Luke 14.1–6) also reveal no instance in which Jesus transgressed the Sabbath law.[82] The matter is quite simple: no work was performed.[83] If Jesus had had to remove a rock which was crushing a man's hand, there would have been a legal principle at issue: was the man's life in danger, or could the work have waited for the sun to set? But the laying on of hands (Luke 13.13) is not work, and no physical action of any kind is reported in the other stories.[84]

It is not impossible that authentic sayings of Jesus have been incorporated in one or more of the stories which we have considered. This has often been proposed for Mark 7.15, but as the saying now stands it can hardly be authentic. As we noted, it must refer to food, and it probably never had any setting outside the church's rejection of the food laws. It is different, however, with the saying that the Son of man is Lord of the Sabbath (Matt. 12.8//Mark 2.28//Luke 6.5). The saying is used in the Gospels to justify transgression of the Sabbath, but if it is older than its current setting it could not have been intended this way originally. The church took some while to come to the position that the Sabbath need not be kept, and it is hard to think that Jesus explicitly said so. I have no new proposal as to what the saying may originally have meant. The Son of man saying, of course, introduces us into one of the most uncertain aspects of the study of the Gospels, and one which, as far as I can tell, we do not need to enter.[85]

Conclusion

We have found one instance in which Jesus, in effect, demanded transgression of the law: the demand to the man whose father had died. Otherwise the material in the Gospels reveals no transgression by Jesus. And, with the one exception, following him did not entail transgression on the part of his followers. On the other hand, there is clear evidence that he did not consider the Mosaic dispensation to be final or absolutely binding. He spoke of and demonstrated the destruction of the old temple and the coming of the new, he admitted sinners to the kingdom without requiring the lawful signs of repentance, and he issued at least one law for a new order: the prohibition of divorce.

Thus one can understand why scholars speak of Jesus' 'sovereign freedom' over the law. He apparently did not think that it could be freely transgressed, but rather that it was not final.

This attitude almost certainly sprang from his conviction that the new age was at hand. The saying about the temple is completely unambiguous, and we best explain the other points as well by appealing to Jesus' expectation of the eschaton. The prohibition of divorce, as we saw, need not have been based entirely on the view that *Endzeit* equals *Urzeit*, but in any case it points to a new order. The kingdom into which the sinners were admitted is, of course, the coming kingdom. It was Jesus' sense of living at the turn of the ages which allowed him to think that the Mosaic law was not final and absolute.

The disciples did not gain the impression that the Mosaic dispensation was valueless and had already passed away. I think that we can rely on Acts as showing that they felt that the temple was a fit place of worship (e.g. Acts 3.1; 21.23–26). They may have thought that it was doomed, but not that it was impure or had already been superseded.

We have again and again returned to the fact that nothing which Jesus said or did which bore on the law led his disciples after his death to disregard it. This great fact, which overrides all others, sets a definite limit to what can be said about Jesus and the law.[86] I wish, however, to call attention to a curious aspect of the fact. Even when we know or have good reason to believe that we have a saying which touches on the law and which goes back to Jesus, we can also tell that the saying did not entirely determine early Christian behaviour and attitude. The saying on divorce is secure and is attested to by Paul – who quotes it, attributes it to the Lord, and proceeds to give his own rules independently. These neither spring from nor totally agree with the saying attributed to 'the Lord' (I Cor. 7.10–16). The saying to let the dead bury the dead seems to have had no repercussion at all. It is unlike anything known from early Christianity, and this helps support its authenticity; but it also means that it was without influence. The Jesus of Matt. 15.4//Mark 7.10 and of Matt. 19.19 and parr. repeats the commandment to honour father and mother as if it is to be accepted without reservation. If one or other of these sayings, as well as Matt. 8.21f., is authentic, we would have to conclude that one nuances the other: Even though in Matt. 8.21f. Jesus says something which seems clearly to imply disregard of the commandment, his acceptance of it elsewhere shows that this was not his intention. In any case, the disciples did not take the saying in Matt. 8.21f. and par. as permission to disobey the law.[87]

Should we follow this line and conclude that, after all, Jesus may have opposed the law directly in other instances? That possibly he did intend to oppose Sabbath, food and other 'ceremonial' laws, but that the disciples did not get it? I do not think so. These are matters of concrete behaviour which the disciples could not have missed. If we were to suppose that, as in the case of divorce, there were clear traditions about these matters, but that they were disregarded by the apostles, we could not explain why Paul does not even appeal to them. He at least quotes a version of the saying on divorce, even though he does not regard it as a binding precept, and we cannot suppose that he would have failed to refer to traditions about the Sabbath and food which supported his own case.

It is only the action and saying against the temple which had ascertainable results: probably the crucifixion as well as Stephen's speech. We gather, however, that the action was not construed to mean, and probably did not mean, that Jesus objected to the sacrifices instituted by God. Stephen appears to have taken a more negative stance than did Jesus. Jesus himself looked to a new age, and therefore he viewed the institutions of this age as not final, and in that sense not adequate. He was not, however, a reformer. We find no criticism of the law which would allow us to speak of his opposing or rejecting it.

10

OPPOSITION AND OPPONENTS

Opposition

The implications of what has been argued thus far about Jesus, the sinners, the law and the temple for understanding the opposition to him should be reasonably clear, but I shall briefly lay them out.

Jesus did come into fundamental conflict with 'Judaism'; that is, with views, opinions and convictions which were probably shared by most. He made a threatening gesture, and added a threatening statement, against the temple. He was doubtless seen as having attacked it. In this case not just the priests, but most Jews, probably even those only marginally observant, would have been deeply offended. If we read Josephus and Philo, we surely cannot think that a thrust against the temple would have been offensive only to the priestly hierarchy. A true threat to the temple would raise the spectre of a world-wide revolt. A minor gesture would generate strong hostility.[1] An attack on Parliament would not be resented only by Members, nor an attack on the White House only by the President and his Cabinet. The temple was the pride and joy of Jewry, both at home and abroad.[2] Lots of people criticized the priesthood.[3] They, like politicians today, were fair game. High priests in particular would come and go and would be replaced by secular rulers. Many were unworthy of the office. Even so, merely donning the robes gave them prestige and authority in the eyes of others.[4] Further, many of the priests were worthy. Josephus has a lengthy panegyric on Ananus, the high priest at the time of the revolt (*BJ* IV.318–25). The thousands who died defending him and the temple against the Zealots and Idumeans testify to the devotion inspired by the cult (IV.313). Josephus also tells us of priests who preferred to die rather than to forsake their sacred duties (*BJ* I. 148).

Thus, even though there were some doubts about the qualifications of some of the priests, normal reverence for the temple was not affected. On the contrary, criticism of priestly practice 'is itself a sign that the Temple matters'.[5] The temple was ordained by God, and any threat against it would have been deeply offensive.

Secondly, Jesus claimed to be spokesman for God. The priests were the official spokesmen, but there was considerable readiness on the part of the people to credit others. Scholars sometimes say that prophecy was regarded as having ceased in Israel,[6] but quite evidently that was not the case. John the Baptist preceded Jesus, and other spokesmen followed him. They were all prophets, or claimed to be, and they all had followings. Jesus' claim to be spokesman for God was not, like the attack on the temple, generally offensive. The official spokesmen – in effect the Jerusalem aristocrats – cannot have been pleased by the claims of others. Yet they evidently did not have the policy of repressing this sort of dissent. There were, for one thing, lay interpreters of the scripture who challenged the priestly prerogative (see *BJ* I.110). These stayed safely in Jerusalem, survived all kinds of tumult, and eventually emerged as the leaders of Judaism. Further, the history of the deaths of other prophets does not indicate that the priests systematically had them eliminated. None was executed as the result of a trial at which the chief priests may have played a part.[7]

A central aspect of Jesus' message, however, was probably more widely offensive: the claim that sinners would be in the kingdom. Jesus apparently did not require them to make restitution and to indicate their repentance by offering sacrifice. If he did not do so, he was probably seen as having challenged the adequacy of the Mosaic covenant, not because there was some part which he explicitly opposed, but because he thought that its requirements could be waived for those who accepted him. This means, secondly, that he displayed an egocentricity which must have struck many of his contemporaries as impious.[8] Thirdly, anyone even normally pious might have been offended at his saying that tax collectors and harlots would precede the righteous in the kingdom (Matt. 21.31).

We must reserve the discussion of how these points of opposition led to his execution, and we should now review other issues which many think represent opposition to Jesus.

Aulén has a useful summary of four areas of conflict:

1. Violation of the law, not only the Pharisaic interpretation, but the law itself.
2. 'The driving out of evil spirits by Beelzebul.'
3. 'His association and table fellowship with ostracized people, "sinners and publicans".'

4. 'His blasphemy in claiming to bestow the forgiveness of sins, something reserved to God alone.'[9]

To Aulén's list we should add:

5. Jesus attacked Jewish or Pharisaical legalism and this roused opposition to him.

We take the points in turn.

1. In common with several scholars, but against the mainstream, I find no definite violation of the law. This has been a topic which has been more than usually subject to fads among scholars. Within the fairly recent past, as we noted in the Introduction, Christian scholars seem to have become progressively more confident that Jesus openly defied the law. This view is especially associated with the 'New Quest'. Thus, for example, Käsemann understands Mark 7.15 as decisive: Jesus overthrows ancient religion.[10] Bornkamm makes 'open conflict with the law' the key point which led to the hostility of the scribes and Pharisees.[11] Bornkamm has to retract his 'open conflict with the law' statement by a clever piece of writing, and he concludes that Jesus gauged the law by the Scripture itself, which contains the will of God.[12] If it be true that Jesus criticized the law on the basis of the law (the one clear example is the issue of divorce), then he showed himself to be a good Jewish teacher. Citing Scripture was the acknowledged way to emend statements in Scripture or to alter practice. This is not a device that Jesus invented. As I have indicated already, I think that most of the 'conflict with the law' passages are later creations. But even if they be taken at face value, they reveal no open transgression.

2. That Jesus was accused of driving out evil spirits by the help of his own familiar spirit (Beelzebul) seems to be true. We do not know enough about Jewish healers in first-century Palestine to be able to assess how serious this matter was. There is no evidence that the Jewish leaders regularly sought the death penalty of those whose healings and other miracles were suspect. Thus, while we can agree that Jesus was accused of black magic, we cannot make this accusation pivotal. It does not reappear in the passion narratives.[13]

3. Jesus' association with 'tax-collectors and sinners' seems to have been offensive. The only problem here is understanding wherein the offence lay. Despite Jeremias, Perrin and others, the offer of forgiveness to *repentant* sinners could not conceivably have been offensive. As I wrote above, anyone who convinced tax-collectors to repent, repay those whom they had defrauded, and thereafter live blameless lives would have been a hero. It is simply inconceivable that Jewish leaders would have been offended if people repented, and this is a cliché which should be dropped from

Christian scholarship. Jesus' position on the sinners does seem to have been genuinely offensive, however, for reasons which are sketched immediately above. It should only be added that he might have been dismissed as a crank for holding so eccentric a view, except for his following, which made him a public figure.

4. That Jesus put himself in the place of God by forgiving sins has often been repeated.[14] It goes without saying that if Jesus claimed to have divine authority to forgive he would have been considered egocentric and impious. But I cannot find the passages in which he claims to take God's place in forgiving sins. If Jesus actually said to a paralytic, 'My son, your sins are forgiven' (Mark 2.5; cf. Luke 7.47f.), he was presumably speaking for God (note the passive),[15] not claiming to be God. The reaction which Mark attributes to the scribes does not correspond to the saying attributed to Jesus. The scribes are said to ask, 'Who can forgive sins but God alone?' (Mark 2.7), and this question appears to have misled some scholars into reading the passage in light of it. They accept it as a strict account of Pharisaic opinion. Thus, for example, Dupont-Sommer observes that the members of the Dead Sea community thought that exorcists and others could forgive sin, and he states that they here disagreed with the Pharisees, who gave God alone that power. The evidence for the Pharisaic view is the verse in Mark.[16] But the Pharisees, to repeat a point already made, did not leave Jerusalem and continued to believe in the sacrificial system, in which the priests speak for God. We have no reason to think that the Pharisees thought that the priests could not announce forgiveness on God's behalf. For, it should be emphasized, that is what Jesus is depicted as doing. The saying attributed to him – even assuming its authenticity – does not mean that he forgives sins. He merely announces that they are forgiven.

Some scholars, in attempting to make this deeply offensive, go to the extreme of saying that in Judaism 'no one had the right to announce the will of God on his own account'. But that is not true. To speak for God was not forbidden, and it certainly was not considered blasphemy.[17] No prophet – by definition a spokesman for God – was, as far as our knowledge goes, accused of blasphemy. A prophet might be considered wrong in interpreting God's will, but making the effort was not blasphemous. The priests also represented God in more ways than just in the temple service. According to Josephus, commenting on the role and position of the high priest: 'any who disobey him will pay the penalty as for impiety towards God Himself' (*Ap.* II.194). If Jesus claimed to know whose sins were forgiven, he might have been seen as arrogating to himself the prerogative of the priesthood. He would have been seen in any case as claiming to be spokesman for God, and that would have been resisted by those who were not convinced. It goes too far, however, to say that Jesus, in claiming to speak for God, was guilty of blasphemy.[18]

5. There is a remarkably persistent tendency in Christian scholarship to fix on 'externalism' and 'legalism' as lying at the root of Jesus' difficulty with his contemporaries. The same conflict, of course, is posited in the study of 'Paul and Judaism' and 'Christianity and Judaism' as well. C. K. Barrett states the view very succinctly: Although Jesus was executed by Pilate, the important opposition was between Jesus and his contemporaries in Judaism. '. . . It was the question whether grace or legalism represented the truth about God, whether true and final dominion belonged to the Torah or to the Son of man.'[19] Here the Son of man apparently represents grace, the Torah legalism. Barrett attaches a footnote:

> It is not suggested that Judaism is intrinsically legalistic, still less that Christian thought has never been corrupted by legalism. But there certainly was a marked legalistic development in first-century Judaism which went far beyond mere faithfulness to Torah, and it was against this that Jesus (and Paul) reacted, and on this issue that conflict arose.[20]

I take one more example. John Reumann writes that 'what Karl Barth called [Jesus'] "attack of grace" mobilized the defenders of Jewish law against him.'[21] Further: what Jesus opposed were 'legalism and pettifogging rules and practices'.[22] Curiously he supports this by citing Matt. 5.21–6.18 and 23.1–36,[23] just those sections of Matthew where Jesus is portrayed as preaching a super-piety which is even more rigorous than that of the scribes and Pharisees. The requirement to anoint one's head while fasting (Matt. 6.16–18) sounds uncommonly like a pettifogging rule.[24]

In the study of Jesus externalism and legalism are usually seen as being at issue in three connections: the temple, the sinners and the law. We read that Jesus wanted to cleanse the temple of corrupt practice and restore 'pure' worship, that he associated with sinners in spite of their being ritually impure, and that he opposed the Pharisees on the law because by casuistry they used it to their own advantage or incorrectly (!) read it as consisting of statutes. In the chapters on each point I have argued that what was at stake was something other than externalism or legalism. The demonstration against the temple was not based on a preference for worship which had no external rites; the primary fault of the 'sinners' was not that they were ritually impure, and saying that they would be included in the kingdom was offensive because they were blatant transgressors, not because they failed to wash their hands before eating; there is no substantial conflict over the law, and what discussions there are do not focus on legalism.

The view that Jesus criticized externalism and legalism, best exemplified by the purity code (the pettifogging practice *par excellence*), generally is accompanied by the view that his main opponents were the Pharisees.[25] We shall discuss opponents more fully later in this chapter, but something should be said here. Even if externalism and legalism were at issue, that would not mean that the basic conflict was with the Pharisees. *Judaism* requires some external acts (e.g. circumcision) and forbids others (e.g. the eating of certain meats). Others, while not wrong in themselves (e.g. contact with the dead or with menstrual blood), produce impurity which, in turn, is removed by an external act. The Pharisees did not invent these laws, nor were they the public guardians of them. Most are not enforceable, but in any case the official keepers of the law were the priests. Josephus sometimes exaggerates the degree to which the priests could enforce the law, but the exaggeration nevertheless shows that it was their responsibility.[26] As I wrote above, we err in thinking that only the Pharisees were concerned to keep the law.[27] That they were especially zealous for the law cannot be contested,[28] but Josephus tells us that the Sadducees also observed the law.[29] We also saw above that the laws of purity were widely observed.[30] External observance, I think, was not at issue between Jesus and his contemporaries. But if it had been, it would have brought him into conflict with the public (most of whom kept many of the external laws) and with the responsible officials, the priests, not only with the Pharisees.

The idea that Jesus and Paul opposed Jewish legalism is both widely and deeply held, and it will not be corrected by only summarizing the exegetical results of previous chapters. Numerous opinions about Judaism, Paul and Jesus interlock in such a way as to offer a coherent picture of a continuing strife between grace and legalism. Decades of scholarship stand behind this view, and it is perceived to rest on evidence.[31] In broad terms the view contains these elements:

1. At least one strand of Judaism, Pharisaism, has been shown by the study of Rabbinic material to have been dominated by legalism.
2. Paul attacked Judaism for being legalistic.
3. Jesus fell into conflict with the Pharisees over legalism and externalism. He opposed their self-righteous reliance on their own merit and offended them by offering grace and forgiveness to sinners. He opposed their legalistic interpretation of the law as statute and saw the Torah as revealing the naked will of God.

4. Points 2 and 3 support 1.
5. Christianity is different from Judaism, and at its heart lies reliance on grace and rejection of legalism.

This section of the chapter actually need do no more than summarize my comments on point 3, but it is clear that for a response to be effective one must be able to reply to the other points as well. I shall attempt to do so briefly.

1. A reading of Jewish material which is more or less contemporary with Jesus (that is, give or take 200 years) does not reveal the legalistic, externalistic Judaism which Jesus and Paul are believed to have criticized. I say no more about this here, having written enough about it elsewhere.

2. After the publication of *Paul and Palestinian Judaism*, one scholar told me that he accepted the demonstration that legalism does not characterize Rabbinic literature. But why, he asked, if the Pharisees were as good as I implied, did Paul criticize them so? The answer is that he did not. But others have urged on me the position that Judaism must have been legalistic because Paul criticized it under the heading 'righteousness by works of law', which means legalism. But that is not the meaning of that debate. Paul first uses that phrase in the midst of debate with other Jewish Christians, not Judaism, and it refers to the problem of whether or not Gentile converts to Christianity must become Jewish. He opposed the position that people must be Jewish to belong to the people of God. His opponents thought that circumcision, Sabbath observance and following the dietary code were required conditions for membership in God's people – not that enough good works merit salvation. Paul's counter argument, when pressed further, especially in Romans, does finally touch Judaism. When it does so, it implies a rejection of the election of Israel, a rejection which is occasionally made explicit. Thus we do not learn from Paul that Judaism was legalistic, but that it was based on the election, the same thing that we learn from studying Jewish literature.[32]

3. But it may be different in the case of Jesus. Here we have Matt. 23, and if the accusations in that chapter go back to Jesus, he accused the scribes and Pharisees of hypocrisy and legalism – the preference of trivia to matters of more substance (still not, however, of seeking salvation by compiling merit). The refrain of 'scribes and Pharisees, hypocrites' and the saying in 23.23 show that somebody accused the Pharisees of hypocrisy and legalism, but it was not, I think, Jesus. With regard to these sayings, as with almost all others, complete agreement will never be achieved. But here the negative argument seems quite strong. As I argued in the preceding chapter, the Jesus of Matt. 23.5–7, 23–26 is not the historical

Jesus. He is one who objects to the Pharisees because they are not righteous enough, and he favours a higher righteousness according to the law, while not denying any of the law, even its minutiae (see also Matt. 5.17–20, 43–8; 6.1–8, 16–18).[33] Further, the charges of Matt. 23 are related to the use of 'tax collector' to mean 'outsider', which I take not to be an authentic saying of Jesus. The criticism of the Pharisees for making a show in the synagogues (23.5f.) is related both thematically and terminologically to the criticism of hypocrites on the same ground in 6.2, 5.[34] These latter passages, in turn, are only one side of a single coin, and the other side has on it Matt. 5.46f. The followers of Christ are urged in 5.46f. to be superior to the Gentiles and the tax collectors and in 6.1–8 to be superior to the hypocrites. We can be certain that Jesus did not use 'tax collector' as it is used in Matt. 5.46, and this counts against the authenticity of the passages on the hypocrites (6.1–4, 5–8, 16–18), and consequently against the authenticity of the charges against the Pharisees in Matt. 23. As I argued in ch. 6, Jesus promised the tax collectors and sinners admission to the kingdom without requiring strict obedience of the law. The church, as a social institution greatly concerned with behaviour, emphasized their reform (especially Luke); and at least one section of it, that represented by these groups of material in Matthew, urged the disciples of Christ to obey the letter of the law in all particulars, and to go beyond the strict requirement of the law in various ways.[35] In doing so, this section of the church had to insist that, despite the policy of strict observance, it was still distinctive, it was not just Pharisaic Judaism. This, it appears, is the *Sitz im Leben* of the criticisms of Pharisees in Matt. 23.[36]

Thus exegesis of the material convinces me that in the case of Jesus, as in the case of Paul, the criticism of contemporary Jewish faith and practice was not directed against some gross and obvious fault which riddled the entire structure and made it an easy mark for anyone who believed in love, mercy and grace.

But can it be that, although Pharisa*ism* was a decent enough movement, and Juda*ism* a decent enough religion, Jesus accused *some* Pharisees of hypocrisy and offended *some* by offering grace to sinners? In every religion, one may urge, there are legalistic, externalistic bigots.[37] Jesus may have opposed these and been killed at their instigation. Not infrequently legalistic bigots head up religions.

The first answer is to repeat our observations about Matt. 23. But the one who proposes that at least some Pharisees were legalists, and that Jesus opposed them, can point out that other material in the synoptics attacks self-righteousness. There is the Lucan parable of the Pharisee and the Tax Collector (Luke 18.9–14) and the Lucan passage on the Pharisees who justify themselves before men (16.14f.). The hypothetical interlocutor might also follow Jeremias in interpreting the parables, and he would then take many of them as being attacks on the Pharisees for being opposed to repentance and forgiveness.[38]

One can continue to reply exegetically, which would require a demonstration of Luke's special form of anti-Judaism[39] and of the way in which Jeremias simply accepted Luke's settings of the parables.[40] One soon realizes, however, that there is more to the question of Pharisaic legalism and Jesus' supposed attack on it than exegesis. Exegesis here runs against an enormous but mostly submerged rock: the assumption that, in discussing Jesus or Paul, we are discussing what is religiously true.[41] This assumption has as its corollaries the further assumptions that they must have favoured whatever is religiously true and opposed what is false and deplorable in religion. The sin of self-righteousness on the part of the religious is well known. Religious truth, in all times and places, must therefore oppose self-righteousness, i.e. legalism. Jesus (and Paul) spoke religious truth. Therefore they must have opposed legalistic self-righteousness. And, if they opposed it, someone must have been guilty of it. Christian scholars who think this way are unanimous in nominating the Pharisees for the role.

One sees what is really going on in this sort of writing when one reads that Jesus 'meant the end of Judaism', 'destroyed Pharisaism', 'shattered the law', and 'put an end to legalism'. One must ask what sort of statements these are. Though they appear in the midst of supposedly historical and exegetical accounts, it is clear that they are neither history nor exegesis. Judaism, Pharisaism, the law and even legalism live on (though one should deprecate the implied equations). Such statements are comprehended when we add an understood phrase: 'for us who believe in him'; that is, Jesus destroyed the law and legalism for confessing Christians, and we are reading nothing other than confessions of faith disguised as historical descriptions.[42] Once we see the confessional context, the situation becomes quite clear. The Christian gospel is defined as renouncing achievement, it is assumed that Jesus *must* have proclaimed that gospel, and so theology provides historical information: Jesus attacked legalism. It is then a short and all-too-familiar step to equating Judaism, or at least Pharisaism, with legalism.

Though theology provides most of this sort of 'information' about Jesus, scholars naturally tend to justify this way of thinking by appealing to passages. They will fasten on to such a passage as Luke 18.9–14 and make it determinative for the issue 'Jesus and Judaism', and they will turn a redactional setting, Luke 15.2 (he told parables of forgiveness against the Pharisees and scribes), into the issue which led to Jesus' crucifixion.[43] A reasonable assessment of cause and effect is surrendered in favour of having the issue of Jesus' life and death hinge on what is now perceived to be religiously true, and in fact of primary importance in religious life – a renunciation of achievement and a surrender to grace.[44]

Christians who are not scholars are often more forthright. I have occasionally complained about the singing of anti-Jewish songs in church, or the expression of denigrating comments in sermons, to be told that by 'Jews' and 'Pharisees' one should understand not those people, but religious people in general and many of today's church members in particular. The clergy need Jesus to have opposed Pharisaic self-righteousness so that they can preach against that sin as manifested not historically in the Jews, but in their own parishioners.

Here, I think, we have the explanation of why scholars, when faced by overwhelming evidence which shows that Pharisaism and Judaism were not as such legalistic, fall back on the argument that some individuals must have been legalistic. They can then still maintain that the opposition between Jesus and his compatriots had to do with their (all too human) reliance on legalism and his devotion to grace. Jesus' message then becomes immediately relevant in today's churches.[45]

I shall reply at the same level, that of religious significance. I think that such a view trivializes Jesus and, when it is extended to cover Paul and the early church, trivializes the eventual Christian divorce from Judaism. If all that was at stake was what scholars often call the 'abuse' of Jewish institutions on the part of a few, not much was at stake. We would be dealing only with a particular instance of a universal situation: people often do not live up to their ideals, and they are sometimes criticized for the failure.

Further, it is unlikely that a major step in religious history – more accurately, in world history – was taken because of a dispute over religious *abstractions*. Most important disagreements, even though they are sometimes couched in abstract terms, are about specific points. Paul and his opponents in Galatia did not disagree about 'faith' and 'works' abstractly conceived, though some of the terminological argument might make it appear as if they did, but only about particulars. All parties to the dispute favoured trusting in God and doing good deeds. The question was *what* deeds must be done to maintain membership in the people of God. It was more particular yet: must Gentiles do the deeds which separate Jew from

Gentile in order to inherit the blessing of Abraham?[46] We face an analogous situation with Jesus. He did not disagree with his contemporaries over whether or not God is gracious and forgiving. All could cheerfully have sat down and drawn up a list of religious abstractions on which they agreed: love, mercy, charity, justice and the like. They would also have agreed on many particulars: the God of Israel is the one God of the world; he has been active in the history of Israel; he speaks through prophets. To this day Jews and Christians can agree on these and other points (replying to no. 5 on p. 276 above). Where did Jesus and his contemporaries disagree? On specifics. (1) If Jesus was of the view that accepting his message meant that one need not repent and make restitution according to the law, the conflict was not over the abstract value of grace versus works, but over the concrete manifestation of grace and the precise condition attached to its offer: Not whether or not God would be merciful and forgiving, but *to whom* and *on what condition*: to sinners on the condition of their accepting Jesus and his message? or to those who indicate their intention to remain within the covenant by doing what the law requires?[47] (2) Was Jesus being a spokesman for God, or impious, when he threateningly predicted the destruction of the temple?

Perhaps I will be permitted one more analogy between Paul and Jesus: both were arguing uphill. Paul thought that circumcision was not necessary for membership in the people of God. His argument, against the obvious meaning of Gen. 17, is a desperate one, and his commentators frequently apologize for aspects of it (especially Gal. 3.16).

Jesus' case – briefly put, that he was God's spokesman, knew what his next major action in Israel's history would be, and could specify who would be in the kingdom – put him equally obviously against any reasonable interpretation of the scripture. If we give full weight to Jesus' extraordinary statements about the kingdom and about the role of his disciples – and thus, by implication, about himself – we have no trouble seeing that his claims were truly offensive. We do not need the hypocritical bigots of Matt. 23 to stand as his unworthy opposition. He had real opposition, and there is no reason to doubt the motives of his opponents.

I have drifted from the broad consideration of what sort of issues important battles are fought over, back to the exegesis of the texts and the particular issues which brought Jesus into conflict with others who spoke for God and the nation. That is as it should be. First and last my viewpoint is shaped by exegesis and historical analysis. I am inclined to look for basic disagreement, beginning even with Jesus, as the source of the Jewish-Christian split; but I would not insist on it if the evidence pointed to a shallow, trivial disagreement, such as the accusation that *some* Pharisees were hypocrites. But exegesis indicates that there were *specific issues* at stake between Jesus and the Jewish hierarchy, and that the specific issues revolved around a *basic question*: who spoke for God? The hypothesis offered here satisfies everything that I can require of a reconstruction: it takes account of what is in the primary material; it posits a basic disagreement as the occasion of a momentous moment in history; it offers a religious debate fought over specific issues, not abstractions; it traces a causal connection from early events to later ones.

Did Jesus oppose self-righteousness at all? I think that he had his mind on other things than the interior religious attitudes of the righteous. The parables are about God, who seeks and saves sinners, not primarily about elder sons, who resent them. His message in general was about God and the kingdom, and it was not a critique of problems which develop within a religious community, such as self-righteousness. To say that we have no material against self-righteousness which goes back to Jesus, however, one would have to show that Luke 15.25–32 (the second half of the Parable of the Prodigal Son); Luke 16.14f.; and Luke 18.9–14 are inauthentic. I harbour doubts about all these passages,[48] but I do not wish to undertake a decisive argument. I am content to say that Jesus did not focus on the interior attitudes of the righteous and that the opposition to him did not spring from his criticism of self-righteousness. Those who need texts on which to base criticism of religious hypocrisy and self-righteousness still have them. Matt. 6.1–8, 16–18; 23; Luke 15.2; 15.25–32; 18.9–14; 16.14f. are still in the canon. They do not, however, serve to explain Jesus' conflict with Judaism.

Persecution

One of the facts on which the study is based is that Jesus' disciples, after his death and resurrection, formed a group which was identifiable and which was persecuted, at least some of the time in some places. Does the persecution of the early Christian movement shed light on the opposition to Jesus?

The earliest and best evidence about persecution comes from Paul, but it points to 'circumcision' as the cause of punishment; that is, to the Torah-free Gentile mission.[49] Thus in Gal. 5.11 he asks why, if he is still preaching circumcision, he is still persecuted. His opponents, he charges, preach circumcision 'in order that they may not be persecuted for the cross of Christ' (Gal. 6.12). The issue is the admission of Gentiles to the new movement without requiring them to become proselytes. It is noteworthy that at Paul's time the apostles in Jerusalem were not being persecuted. Both his letters and Acts depict him as visiting them with no difficulty.[50] They are also not engaged in the admission of Gentiles without requiring circumcision, since he has to justify his mission to them (Gal. 2.1–10).[51] This fits with the rest of the evidence from Paul's letters: persecution has to do with not requiring circumcision. The Jerusalem apostles did not admit uncircumcised Gentiles, and they were not being persecuted.

There obviously was persecution before Paul started his own mission. He himself conducted some of it (Gal. 1.13, 23; Phil. 3.6; I Cor. 15.9), and he refers to persecution of the movement in Judea in I Thess. 2.14–16. But here again the question of the Gentiles appears: the Jews 'killed both the Lord Jesus and the prophets, and drove us out, and displease God and oppose all men by *hindering us from speaking to the Gentiles* that they may be saved'. It is, to be sure, possible that, in the final clause, Paul speaks only of the reason for which he was given difficulty, while the persecution of the churches in Judea had a different cause. But if so, we cannot recover it from Paul's letters. His punishment at the hands of his compatriots (II Cor. 11.24) seems to have resulted from his mission to the Gentiles, and it is probable that his own activity as persecutor was directed against missionaries who preceded him in admitting Gentiles. Antioch, we must remember, was a mixed church and was not founded by Paul.

Persecution of the early Christian movement on the grounds that some of them admitted Gentiles to 'the Israel of God' without requiring circumcision does not explain the opposition to Jesus. It is worth remarking, however, that in two respects there is material agreement between Paul and Jesus on this point. There is, first, the agreement on the plan of God and the task which this imposes, to which we pointed many pages back.[52] Both Jesus and Paul (and Jesus' other followers) thought that the end was at hand, and they therefore constituted a Jewish eschatological movement. Paul (and other missionaries to the Gentiles) were simply carrying out the last expectation of Jewish eschatology. Thus the issue that led to Paul's being punished (II Cor. 11.24) directly *stems from* Jesus' eschatological expectation, even though Jesus himself appears not to have dealt substantially with the question of Gentile membership in the kingdom.

There is material agreement of a different sort between Paul and Jesus when we look at the content of their respective messages. Jesus proclaimed that the wicked (at least those who accepted him) would be included in the kingdom. His message apparently did not require them to make restitution and repentance in accordance with the law. Paul thought that

Gentile sinners (Gal. 2.15) would be saved if they accepted Christ, even though they did not become members of the people of God in the way required by the law. Paul does not appeal to Jesus' activity as justification for his own stance. It is very likely that he did not know about it. There is a puzzle with regard to Jesus' view of the sinners: we do not know just how he expected them to live after their acceptance of his message. It is impossible to find the 'tax collectors and sinners' in early Christianity. In a church dominated by James, the brother of Jesus, they probably disappeared or became blameless according to the law. Paul had a good deal to say about how his Gentile sinners should live once they are admitted 'apart from the law': they are to be blameless and to keep the whole law (I Thess. 3.13; 5.23; Phil. 1.10; Gal. 5.14; Rom. 13.8–10). Thus Paul and Jesus took the same stance on admission, and they faced the same question with regard to behaviour. We can be sure of how Paul, but not Jesus, answered the question of behaviour (though Paul's own converts were sometimes puzzled). We cannot say, however, that the agreement on admission stems from Paul's following the teaching of Jesus. In fact, we see that persecution of the early Christians did not result from their repeating the peculiarity of his message, that God would include the wicked of Israel in the kingdom, though that may have been irritating to his contemporaries.

This issue has been introduced here because of its connection with persecution. Both Paul and Jesus were persecuted for their activity. There is even material agreement on the activity. But Paul was not persecuted simply because he followed Jesus. He was persecuted because of the way in which he carried out the *next* stage of the eschatological drama, the admission of Gentiles.

If Paul was not persecuted simply because he followed Jesus, were others? It has sometimes been held that persecution was directed against the preaching of faith in Jesus, a condemned criminal, as Messiah.[53] Thus the persecution is held to have resulted from Christian faith itself. If persecution were simply the result of faith in the cross of Christ, it would tell us nothing about the reason for opposition to Jesus. There must be, however, appreciable doubt about this as a ground of persecution. If it were, it should follow that Christianity was persecuted and hounded wherever there were enough Jews to give the followers of Christ a hard time. Yet, to repeat, it is clear from Paul's letters that the leading Jerusalem apostles were not persecuted, at least during his career, even though they believed that Jesus was the Messiah. Their relative immunity indicates that it was not belief in the cross of Christ which differentiated those persecuted from those not. Yet there is evidence of persecution apart from the issue of 'circumcision'. Can we determine its cause? We shall briefly rehearse the accounts in Acts and Josephus.

According to Acts 4.5–22 Peter and John were arrested by the Jewish leaders (specifically by the chief priest and other members of the high-priestly family, 4.6) on the ground of healing a man 'by the name of Jesus Christ of Nazareth' (4.10). They were charged 'not to speak or teach at all in the name of Jesus' (4.18). According to 5.17–42, the high priest and his colleagues (that is, Luke tells us, Sadducees) arrested the apostles. After an escape and another arrest, they were beaten by the order of the Sanhedrin and 'charged not to speak in the name of Jesus' (5.40). Stephen was charged for speaking against the temple and the law (6.13). His speech (7.2–53) indicates that the charge was at least partly justified, and he was stoned (7.57–60). Finally, we learn that Herod Agrippa I killed James, the son of Zebedee, and, finding that it pleased 'the Jews', also arrested Peter (12.1–3).

There is one concrete piece of information about persecution in Josephus. When there was no procurator in Jerusalem, the high priest had James, the brother of Jesus, executed. This was clearly against Roman policy, and the high priest was subsequently deposed (see *AJ* XX 199–203).

We can accept without argument the reason given for Stephen's death: he spoke against the temple, and consequently against the law, which establishes it. In the other cases, however, we cannot be sure what the complaint was. The early Christians *saw themselves* as being persecuted 'for the sake of Christ', or 'for his name's sake'. The problem is that we cannot be sure just what it was that the *other side*, those inflicting the punishment, found offensive. The early Christians saw all their deeds as being done 'for the sake of his name'. In his name they prophesied, cast out demons and performed other miracles (Matt. 7.22; Luke 10.17; Mark 9.38f.//Luke 9.49; Acts 4.10); in his name they accepted children, gave a cup of water to the thirsty, and gathered together (Matt. 18.5//Mark 9.37//Luke 9.48; Mark 9.41; Matt. 18.20). For his sake, or for his name's sake, they left house and family (Matt. 19.29//Mark 10.29). And so naturally it was for his name's sake that they were hated (Matt. 10.22; Matt. 24.9//Mark 13.13//Luke 21.17) and tried and flogged (Matt. 10.18; Mark 13.9//Luke 21.13; Acts 5.40f.). From *their* point of view they were following their master and doing what God commanded them (Acts 5.29), and they were being persecuted simply for that; i.e., 'for his name's sake'. That does not, however, tell us how the Jewish leadership saw the matter.

Three things are clear. One is that the persecution in Jerusalem stopped after a while, to flare up one more time, when James the brother of the Lord was killed.[54] The arrest of Paul, on his last trip to Jerusalem (Acts 21.28), is the exception which proves the rule. Paul, according to this passage, was accused of opposing the law and the temple, the same charge which was brought against Stephen. Other members of the Christian movement were not bothered.

The second clear point is that the harassment of the Christians was at the instigation of the Jewish leadership. Throughout Acts the emphasis is on the chief priests and the Sadducees (Acts 4.5f.; 5.17; 7.1). A Pharisee is once said to speak in favour of leniency (5.34–9).[55] The Sanhedrin is named several times (Acts 4.15; 5.21, 27, 34, 41; 6.12, 15); but, as we shall see in the next chapter, Luke shares our ignorance about its composition. The one actor who remains involved throughout is the high priest. The enmity of the chief priesthood is clear also in Josephus's story about the execution of James. Further, it is evident in all this that the Romans were not involved. The passages in the synoptics sometimes mention Gentiles and their rulers (Matt. 10.18; Mark 13.9; Luke 21.12); but, at least in Judea, the Romans played no role in the persecution of the movement after the death of Jesus.[56] The evidence from Josephus confirms the view of Acts. The results point in the same direction: had the Romans wished to eliminate all the leaders of the new movement, Peter, John and James could not have remained active in Jerusalem.

That the latter were not substantially molested is the third point of clarity. Acts here, perhaps against the will of the author, who wishes to present a general picture of survival despite persecution, confirms the information from Paul. Peter and John, according to Acts, were arrested (4.3), and 'the apostles' were arrested and even flogged (5.40). But even at a time of supposed 'violent persecution' the apostles were excepted and did not have to scatter (8.1). How are we to explain *sporadic* persecution by *Jewish leaders* which left the *principal apostles free* to go about their task?

It appears that in the case of Stephen and Paul, Luke had accurate information. In his other accounts of punishment and interrogation, the Christians are not charged with speaking against the law and the temple, and such charges would have been hard to make out. The conflict between Peter and Paul at Antioch shows that James, at least, was careful not to allow the movement to be accused of having non-observant leaders (Gal. 2.11–14). James was subsequently accused by the high priest of breaking the law, but those who were strict with regard to the law took offence (*AJ* XX.200f.), which probably shows that the charge was trumped up. In all probability a reasonable charge of being against the law could not have been levelled at the Jerusalem apostles, and Luke's silence on the motive for punishment probably indicates ignorance. All he knew about the persecution was the Christian perspective: it was for the sake of Jesus. He did not know just wherein the offence lay from the perspective of the Jewish leaders. We can of course speculate. The proposal earlier mentioned, that the offence lay in proclaiming a condemned criminal as Messiah, is a speculation. As a specific charge it is not, as I pointed out, entirely convincing, since it does not explain the sporadic nature of the persecution.[57] I do not have another speculation which will explain everything, but I shall offer an explanation of a general sort. The Christians may have been right in seeing their persecution as being for the sake of Christ: that is, they may have been persecuted simply because of their continuing loyalty to a leader who was, in the eyes of the Jewish leaders, discredited and who had been objectionable. Stephen carried on Jesus' attack against the temple and was killed. The others did not themselves do anything which merited death or which could be put to the Romans as grounds for execution. The Jewish leaders were not in a position to carry out a thorough and systematic persecution of the followers of Jesus. There was an early burst of persecution which is probably echoed in different ways by Paul (I Thess. 2.15, they drove us out) and Matthew and Mark (the disciples went to Galilee). The leaders of the new movement, however, soon established themselves in Jerusalem, amidst some lingering hostility: James was finally executed when the coast was clear. But mass execution could not be justified to the Romans, and the Christian leaders who did not themselves break the law or speak against the temple were allowed to continue their work unmolested.

This brief account of the persecution of the Christian movement does, finally, pay off for understanding the causes of Jesus' death. It supports the Gospels in their depiction of the Jewish leaders, expecially the chief priests, as being the ones who pressed for his execution. If the primary conflict had been between Jesus and the Romans, Jesus and the Pharisees, or Jesus and the crowds, we could not explain subsequent events. (See the next chapter.) The enduring hostility was that of the chief priests against the followers of Jesus, and that supports the view that they were the prime movers in the death of Jesus.

This is not overturned by the fact that Paul, a Pharisee, was one of the persecutors of the Christian movement. The Pharisees were not an opposition party, required to present an alternative to government policy at every point. They had their own programme for inculcating a life of piety and learning among the laity. They seem not to have disputed the priests' role as the official leaders and spokesmen of Judaism, as we shall see in the next chapter. If the chief priests were against Jesus and his followers, many loyal Jews, including Pharisees zealous for the law, may well have followed their lead. If Paul in fact persecuted only Jewish Christians who admitted Gentiles without requiring observance of the law, he was striking against something which threatened Jewish identity, not just the principles of Pharisaism or Sadduceanism. His own position on the Gentiles, when he became an apostle of Christ, struck at the doctrine of the election, which was common to all groups of Jews,[58] and thus led to his being repeatedly punished. The study of persecution does not point us in the direction of seeing either Jesus or his followers as being opposed to aspects of party platforms, but as threatening values and commitments common in Judaism. We must now, however, take further the question of the identity of Jesus' opponents.

Opponents

We now return to the points of opposition which we outlined at the beginning of this chapter and ask who would have taken offence.

One issue would have led to opposition from many: the action and saying against the temple. No matter how positively the action was meant, it must have struck numerous people as impious. The prediction or threat of destruction would hardly have improved matters. In order to see the offence, we need not suppose either that Jesus was misunderstood or that his word and deed created any real apprehension for the physical safety of the sacred place. Only those who believed that he really knew what God was about to do and that he spoke for God could have heard him predict or threaten the destruction of the temple without a feeling of dismay at least. Such words incite emotions of various kinds, even though all and sundry could see that he was not able actually to demolish the temple. If he excited feelings of alarm in the populace, we can understand with no difficulty why steps were taken against him. But even if he attracted relatively little notice, it is still easy to see why he may have been regarded as a potential threat to peace and order. We cannot say precisely how broad the opposition to him was, because we do not know in general what public impact he had (see further below), but threatening the temple must have offended *many*.

His self-claim to be spokesman for God – in effect, to be a prophet – may have met with some public approval (at least until the temple incident), but it can hardly have endeared him to the *normal leaders* of Judaism, the chief priests and the 'powerful' among the laity.[59] Presumably such people looked upon demagogues and would-be demagogues with distrust, and they doubtless did so for the standard reasons: a combination of self-interest and sincere disagreement. Josephus's stories about prophets, to which we have so often referred, show that demagogues could be dangerous. The Jewish leaders could reasonably oppose a charismatic leader even without fearing for the security of their own positions. They might wish only to save their people from direct action by the Romans. (John 11.50 gives this reasoning perfectly.) In the general category of 'charismatic leaders', Jesus obviously was considerably less of a threat than the Egyptian was to be, but anyone who claimed to speak for God and who attracted a following would alarm those who wanted to maintain the somewhat precarious *status quo* with Rome. The leadership would be alarmed even if they did not suspect the principal figure of secretly raising an army and having a store of arms. Talk of a 'kingdom' might excite a crowd, and mass excitement could be dangerous. The execution of John the Baptist makes the point admirably. He posed no military threat, but he did stimulate popular excitement. That was enough.[60]

Jesus' message to sinners presumably further discredited him in the eyes of the *normally pious*. If his hearers understood him to be challenging the adequacy of the law, the offence may have been general. The inclusion of sinners in the kingdom, though it denies the value of obedience to the law, is also more theoretical than the gesture against the temple, and by itself probably would not have been fatally offensive. It may be that because of the theological significance of this point we are ready to credit it with too much importance as an issue between Jesus and others. I think that it is safe to say that the pious would have been irritated at having a self-proclaimed spokesman for God say that they would be preceded in the kingdom by gross sinners: irritated but not threatened. They would not, after all, suppose that Jesus actually knew. The proclamation to sinners also, however, highlights his self-claim. It appears that Jesus did not go to the extreme of saying that only those who *followed* him would be in the kingdom,[61] but he nevertheless proclaimed not only that he spoke for God, but that God would reverse the present order. Those now ranked last would be first. If in the name of God he had proclaimed only a standard message (e.g., that the wicked should repent, make restitution, and live a life conformable to the law) the offence of his self-claim would probably have been reduced.

Thus we can name as Jesus' probable opponents the pious, the leaders and the populace. It is frequently said that Jesus earned the opposition of all groups.[62] My proposal differs from that formulation in two ways. In the first place, I do not propose that we pair up issues with opponents: Jesus offended the Pharisees by disputing the oral law, the Sadducees by attacking the temple, and so on. This pairing results from an oversimplification of both the parties and the issues, and it obscures the historical situation. We should presume that many Sadducees as well as Pharisees were pious and would have resented being told that the wicked would precede them in the kingdom. 'The pious', in fact, presumably included people who did not think of themselves as 'belonging' to a 'party'. Most people could not be identified with a party, and surely some of these 'independents' were pious. In any case there is no reason to limit 'the pious' to the Pharisees.

Secondly, we must be prepared to see a degree of popular rejection of Jesus, especially after the incident in the temple, and possibly more generally from the populace of Jerusalem. 'The crowds' in the Gospels and Acts serve the convenience of the narrators. One day they hail Jesus, another demand his execution, and another protect Peter and the others from being severely persecuted.[63] We cannot know, from these reports, how to gauge their reaction to Jesus. I suggested above that Jesus may have had a smaller public impact than John the Baptist, and certainly smaller than a temporarily successful demagogue like the Egyptian.[64] This is the impression which one gains from reading Josephus, although certainty cannot be attained, thanks to the corruption of his passage on Jesus.[65] The impression is confirmed, however, by the fact that Jesus' disciples were not executed. Further, there is the intrinsic probability that anyone who spoke or acted against the temple in any way would have provoked the Jerusalemites.

Thus I do not think it to be the case that Jesus was someone who gained truly massive support from the populace and who was executed because he posed a real threat to the Jerusalem leaders. On the other hand, we cannot say that all Jerusalem was against him. He doubtless had a following of Galileans, but we do not know enough to be able to say that the populace of Jerusalem opposed him because he was a Galilean.[66] We cannot, then, say that the issue was either 'the masses versus the leaders', nor 'the Galileans versus the Jerusalemites'. Jesus seems to have offended many from various walks of life.

When, however, one asks whether or not it is possible to single out some opponents as more important than others, the answer is affirmative. The last subsections pointed clearly to the priestly aristocracy as the prime movers behind Jesus' execution. This identification is confirmed by several strands of evidence, of which the last will be discussed in the next chapter: (1) The Gospels themselves, despite making the Pharisees the primary enemies during most of Jesus' career, depict the Jewish leadership in Jerusalem as being actually responsible for his death. (2) The persecution of Jesus' followers after his death, such as it was, came from this circle. (3) The chief priests were the intermediaries between the Jewish people and the Romans. They were thus in a position to represent him to the Romans as dangerous.

Many scholars, even while saying that Jesus offended many parties and groups and granting that it was the attack on the temple which immediately led to his death, nevertheless make the Pharisees his prime opponents. The Pharisees, as we noted above, tend to crop up in scholarly discussions along with the position that a main issue in Jesus' life and death was a conflict between 'grace' and 'legalism'. The Pharisees, along with legalism, occur in three contexts: purity, the law and the sinners. A collection of common views, which I have more than once sketched and argued against, would go like this: Jesus opposed the Pharisees by going to the sinners, who were excluded by their purity laws from life in Judaism; he also fell foul of them with regard to other points of the law; they were the true leaders of Judaism; basic to the conflict was Jesus' view of grace and their view of justification by works; a conflict with the Pharisees helps account for Jesus' execution.

In part those who hold such views are simply following the Gospels themselves, who have the Pharisees (sometimes accompanied by scribes)[67] appear when Jesus or his disciples do something on the Sabbath (e.g. Mark 2.23–3.6), or when the disciples eat without washing their hands (Mark 7). Luke also has Jesus tell the parables about the lost against the Pharisees and scribes (Luke 15.2). In part scholarly agreement with these depictions in the Gospels rests on the complex of views which we discussed above when considering 'legalism' as an issue between Jesus and others.

The desire to make a theology of grace versus legalism the issue which led to Jesus' death, and to have the Pharisees bear the principal responsibility, sometimes leads to self-contradiction. I have cited above Jeremias's view that it was declaring the forgiveness of sinners which was at issue between Jesus and the Pharisees and that Jesus' view led to his death.[68] In other places Jeremias more reasonably adopted the position that Jesus came into conflict with all groups.[69] And, of course, he knew that he was executed by the Romans on a political charge. Similarly Reumann finds the chief issue to be legalism or grace, and he quotes apparently with approval an extraordinary statement by Ethelbert Stauffer on what would have happened if Jesus had fallen into the hands of the Qumran sect: ' "They would have murdered him as ruthlessly as did the Pharisees." '[70] But Reumann, like Jeremias, finds opposition with all parties,[71] and he too knows that the Pharisees did not murder Jesus.

But leaving such exaggerations of the role of the Pharisees aside, can we determine whether or not they constituted a significant element in the opposition to Jesus? Our discussions of the sinners, the law, purity and legalism all point towards finding little contact, either hostile or cordial, between Jesus and the Pharisees. The reader will have learned that I think that each of the common generalizations just above is wrong. The Pharisees did not dominate Judaism. If Jesus disagreed with them over laws of purity which were peculiar to them, he would have been only one more *'am ha-arets* among many. He seems not to have committed any substantial breach of the law. But, if he did, there is no reason to think that only the Pharisees would have been offended. Thus I find no substantial conflict between Jesus and the Pharisees.

It is noteworthy that several recent works have sharply diminished or even eliminated the role of the Pharisees as substantial opponents of Jesus.[72] The arguments are in large part exegetical and simply draw further conclusions from the earlier form-critical insights about the imaginary settings of the conflict pericopes. The trend to reduce the role of the Pharisees can be seen even among those who are not sceptical as I am about the historicity of the debates about the Sabbath and food.

Harvey, for example, who accepts such passages as Mark 2.23–26; 7.2; and 2.18 as representing actual debates with opponents, nevertheless sees that controversies with the Pharisees were magnified by the early church. He proposes that there were fewer points of contact and less sharp disagreement between the Pharisees and Jesus than the Gospels suggest.[73] Baumbach has expressed some doubts about the Pharisees as Jesus' opponents,[74] and Schürmann has proposed that we should not think that Jesus was in opposition to any particular group within the Judaism of his time.[75]

Some press further. Berger, in a detailed and often convincing study of the history of the traditions in which Jesus is depicted as interpreting or debating the law, makes some telling observations about the Gospels' characterizing Jesus' opponents as Pharisees. In a series of pericopes, he proposes, the oldest tradition is a contrast-logion. In the following list the basic logion is placed in brackets: Mark 2.16–17 (17a); 2.18–20 (19); 2.23–28 (27); 3.1–4 (4b); 7.1–23 (15); 10.1–12 (9); 12.13–17 (17). These pericopes, he argues, stem from Christian tradition and have been made 'biographical' by placing 'Jesus' and 'the Pharisees' in opposition. Apart from these pericopes 'the Pharisees' appear in Mark only in 8.11, 15; 9.11. Berger regards the Jesus/Pharisees opposition as a schematizing of opposition between the early Christian community and their Jewish opponents. 'The Pharisees are, apparently, opponents of the early liberal community practice, projected back into the life of Jesus.'[76]

Cook is also cautious about identifying Jesus' opponents as Pharisees and correctly points out that the evangelists may not have had a clear idea of who constituted the various groups.[77]

Hultgren, in a detailed form-critical study of the conflict pericopes, argues that the earliest stage of the conflict stories which are now in Mark 2.1–3.6 and parallels probably did not contain references to scribes and Pharisees. Mark 3.6 is an addition by a pre-Marcan compiler which has led to the identification of the Pharisees as the opponents for the whole collection.[78] Mark 3.6, in fact, caused difficulty for the final evangelist, who felt compelled to reintroduce the Pharisees in 12.13, where they do not fit.[79]

Morton Smith, arguing less as a form-critic and more as a historian, calls into question the authenticity of most of the passages which depict Jesus as in debate with the Pharisees. The term 'Pharisees', he proposes, reflects the disputes between church and synagogue in the 80s. He makes a more telling point: 'There is strong evidence that there were practically no Pharisees in Galilee during Jesus' lifetime.'[80]

Of these scholars Harvey, the least extreme, is also the least convincing. As I pointed out in the chapter on the law, he misses the basic form-critical observation that in two of the passages which he accepts, Mark 2.23–28 and Mark 7.1ff., it is not Jesus who is criticized, but the disciples, apparently standing in for the early church.[81] He basically falls back on the theory that 'where there is smoke there is fire': 'It is hardly conceivable that the whole picture of an on-going controversy between Jesus and the sages of his time is fictional.'[82]

It is, I think, quite conceivable. Several of us conceive it. On the other hand the 'where there is smoke there is fire' view cannot be positively disproved. I shall be contented here to reiterate the view to which I have come: we *know* of no substantial dispute about the law, nor of any substantial conflict with the Pharisees.

Conclusion

Jesus offended many of his contemporaries at two points: his attack on the temple and his message concerning the sinners. On both points he could be said to be challenging the adequacy of the Mosaic dispensation, and both are large-scale, sweeping and blatant. His presuming to speak for God was certainly approved by those who became convinced that he did so, and it was probably not generally offensive. It may have become so, however, when the spokesman for God turned on the temple. He pressed this, the most offensive point, in Jerusalem at Passover time, so that it could not be overlooked. We add to these considerations only that he had a noticeable following, and we need look no further to understand why he was executed.

At this level of offence, we do not need to find a group which opposed Jesus and which aroused the Romans to execute him. At another level, however, a reasonable inference about the instigators of his death may be made. He was executed by the Romans, and if Jews had anything to do with it – that is, if he were not executed simply because he caused public disturbance – the instigators of his death would have been those with access to Pilate. Chief among these were the leaders of the priesthood.[83]

11

THE DEATH OF JESUS[1]

The firm facts

We should begin our study with two firm facts before us: Jesus was executed by the Romans as would-be 'king of the Jews',[2] and his disciples subsequently formed a messianic movement which was not based on the hope of military victory.

The difficulty of explaining how to hold these two facts together is the fundamental problem involved in attempting to understand the death of Jesus. The problem of his execution is neatly put by Harvey:

> We are apparently faced with a contradiction. On the one hand, the events and legal procedures leading up to Jesus' death can be established with reasonable certainty as implications of the bare statement that he was crucified; and the charge upon which he was crucified is given by a report which, again, seems highly reliable: King of the Jews. On the other hand, it seems incredible that the person condemned on this charge was Jesus of Nazareth.[3]

The reason the facts seem incredible is that everything we know about Jesus indicates that he sought no secular kingship.[4] Harvey argues that 'The royal pretender must have attracted sufficient support to be capable of offering a real threat to the Roman government'; i.e., to be executed as would-be king he must have had an army.[5]

But this statement of wherein the problem lies is not complete. It is crucial to remember that the disciples formed a *messianic* group, one which claimed Jesus as Messiah and expected his return, and one which was steadfastly *apolitical. Thus not only was Jesus executed as would-be king even though he had no secular ambitions, his disciples also combined the same two points: Jesus was Messiah, but his kingdom was 'not of this world'.*

In explaining Jesus' death, we must simply accept these facts. The last statement quoted from Harvey must be questioned, as I argued above. Jesus' execution as 'king' does not show that he had an army, nor that the Romans thought he had. We can understand it simply by knowing that he spoke of a kingdom and stirred the hopes of the people.[6] His miracles also produced excitement, and excitement carries its own dangers. The explanation of Jesus' death must follow what at first appears to be a very narrow path between the fact that he was executed as 'king' and the fact that neither he nor his disciples were perceived to constitute any real threat to Rome: they were not rounded up and executed. I think in fact that the path is not all that narrow. A man who spoke of a kingdom, spoke against the temple, and had a following was one marked for execution; but no one need have regarded him as a military leader.

Dogmatic positions have obscured the obviousness of the explanation. Winter and many others, because of fixed views of what a 'messiah' must be like, have not seen the force of the most obvious facts. Thus Winter wrote that, since Jesus lived on as *Christos*, at least some of his followers must have pursued political ends, since 'the word denotes a worldly ruler'.[7] But Christianity is living proof that it need not do so.

In general terms, our task is already accomplished. Jesus and his followers thought of there being a kingdom in which Jesus was the leader, and he was executed as 'king of the Jews', while his disciples went free. This shows that the Romans regarded him as dangerous at one level but not at another: dangerous as one who excited the hopes and dreams of the Jews, but not as an actual leader of an insurgent group.

But, as always, we need to see how much more can be known. Can this general picture be made clearer and sharper? In particular, what role did Jewish leaders and opponents play?

As we saw in the previous chapter, the real conflict was between Jesus and his contemporaries in Judaism. The Romans did not act entirely on their own initiative. We could know this to be the case without accepting as authentic a single one of the conflict stories in the Gospels. Here, as so often, the facts speak for themselves. The disciples continued as an apolitical group which was persecuted, at least sporadically, by the Jewish leadership and which was tolerated, perhaps even protected, by the Roman government. This points to an original conflict between Jesus and the Jewish leaders, and we shall now investigate what can be known about how that led to his death.

The cause of the execution

It should be noted that, once one turns to an internal conflict within Judaism as the principal cause of Jesus' death, it is incorrect to make a rigid distinction between 'religious' and 'political' reasons.[8] The question is whether the primary conflict was with the Romans or with other Jews.[9] I have used the term 'apolitical' to means 'not involving a plan to liberate and restore Israel by defeating the Romans and establishing an autonomous government'. If Jesus claimed that those who followed him, even though sinners by the standard of the law, would be first in the kingdom, and demonstrated the nearness of a new order by his gesture against the temple, he would have been seen as presenting a challenge to the rest of Judaism in a way that cannot be called just 'religious' or 'political'.[10] If he claimed, in effect, that he, rather than the acknowledged leaders of Israel, spoke for God, he challenged the leadership in all respects. A blow against the temple, even if a physically minor one, was a blow against the basic religio-political entity: Israel.

We have examined above in some detail the reports in the Gospels about opponents and points of opposition. Our task now is simply to focus on those which the Gospels directly claim to have played a role in Jesus' execution.

In Matthew and Mark a plot to put Jesus to death starts after the healing of the man with a withered hand on the Sabbath. Mark names the plotters as the Pharisees and the Herodians, Matthew simply as the Pharisees (Matt. 12.14//Mark 3.6). According to all three synoptic Gospels the Parable of the Wicked Husbandmen inspired plots against Jesus.[11] Matthew names the chief priests and the Pharisees, and Luke the scribes and the chief priests (Matt. 21.45f.//Luke 20.19). Mark does not name the plotters at this point (12.12), and for a subject for the verb 'they sought' in 12.12 we have to go back to 11.27: chief priests, scribes and elders. Plots, unspecified as to cause, continue in Matthew (22.15; 26.3–5). Mark, but not Matthew, says that the chief priests and scribes planned Jesus' death after the temple event (Mark 11.18). According to Luke the chief priests, scribes and 'principal men' tried to destroy Jesus while he was teaching in the temple (Luke 19.47), but we are not told precisely why. In John the plot to kill Jesus originates with the chief priests and the Pharisees after the resurrection of Lazarus (John 11.45–53).

Most to the point, Matthew and Mark, and to some degree Luke, but not John, offer a trial scene in which a serious religious charge is said to have been sustained: blasphemy (Matt. 26.57–75//Mark 14.53–72; the word 'blasphemy' is in Matt. 26.65//Mark 14.64). In Luke's account (22.71) the word 'blasphemy' may be avoided simply in order to eliminate the explicit statement that Jesus was found guilty of irreligion.[12]

There are well-known difficulties with accepting this scene as accurately revealing the actual point of dispute:

1. It is prepared for only by the 'Triumphal Entry', which presents its own problems (see below). There is nothing in the *public* teaching attributed to Jesus in the synoptic Gospels to explain the reported question of the High Priest: 'Are you the Christ, the Son of God?' (Mark, 'Son of the Blessed') (Matt. 26.63//Mark 14.61).[13]

2. The Gospels are surprisingly reluctant to have Jesus admit to the supposed charge, though doubtless all the evangelists believed that he was the Christ and also the Son of God. Matthew has Jesus answer: 'So you say. But on the other hand (*plēn*) I say, "From now you will see the Son of man . . ."' (Matt. 26.64). Luke separates the titles 'Christ' and 'Son of God' and presents them as two separate questions. In reply to the question of whether he is the Christ, Luke has Jesus answer evasively and refer to the Son of man. In reply to the question whether he is Son of God Luke's Jesus responds, 'You say that I am' (Luke 22.67-70). Only Mark attributes to Jesus an unequivocal 'yes' to the question of whether he claims to be the Son of God (Mark 14.62).[14] It is striking that John, who earlier had written that 'the Jews' sought to kill Jesus because he 'called God his own Father, making himself equal with God' (John 5.18), nevertheless includes no such charge in his story of Jesus' appearances before Annas and Caiaphas (John 18.19, 24).[15] It is of course possible that all the evangelists, not just Luke, wanted to protect Jesus from being guilty of the supposed charge, even though they all believed that he was the Son of God. It is more likely, however, that the charge of blasphemy was not firmly rooted in the tradition.[16]

3. The exchanges between the high priest and Jesus in the synoptic accounts, especially in Matthew and Mark, do not carry conviction. We are first told that a charge was brought which was almost certainly true, that of speaking against the temple; but the Gospels indicate that Jesus was not convicted of that charge. Mark explicitly states that those who testified to Jesus' threat against the temple did not agree (Mark 14.59). Matthew implies that all the witnesses were false witnesses (Matt. 26.59), but he simply runs the charge that Jesus threatened the temple into the question of the high priest, and it receives no explicit counter. The issue which in Matthew and Mark is said to lead to the charge of blasphemy, Jesus' being Christ (Messiah) and Son of God, is not compelling. For one

thing, the combination of the two appellations looks more like a Christian one than a Jewish one: outside the Christian movement there is no evidence for the combination of 'Messiah' and 'Son of God'. Further, as is widely recognized, neither phrase points towards blasphemy. We need not accept the Rabbinic definition of blasphemy (pronouncing the explicit name: Sanh. 7.5) in order to rule out 'Messiah' and 'Son of God' as blasphemous claims. Subsequent would-be Messiahs were not charged with blasphemy, and 'son of God' might mean almost anything. All Israelites can be said to be 'sons of God' (see e.g. Rom. 9.4), and it is only the subsequent Christian claim that Jesus himself was divine that clearly constitutes blasphemy.

It seems to me quite conceivable that speaking and acting against the temple could have been considered blasphemous, but according to the Gospels that charge did not lead to the sentence of blasphemy. Thus there is a charge which might constitute blasphemy but which is said to lead nowhere, and a combination of titles which is both unlikely and unblasphemous which is said to have resulted in the sentence 'blasphemy'. The trial scene is unlikely on all counts.

4. It is hard, though not impossible, to imagine a chain of transmission which would have passed on the exchanges of the supposed trial.

5. It is hard to believe that a formal court actually convened on the first night of Passover, as Matthew and Mark have it. Luke, we should note, states that Jesus was taken to the Sanhedrin only after daybreak (Luke 22.66). John does not depict a trial before the Sanhedrin at all.

6. It is even harder to believe that Matthew and Mark are correct in depicting two trials, one in the night and one the next morning.[17] It has long been noted that the night trial (Matt. 26.57–75//Mark 14.53–72) looks like an expansion of the short report to the effect that there was a trial in Matt. 27.1//Mark 15.1.[18]

7. The Gospels are all influenced by the desire to incriminate the Jews and exculpate the Romans. The insistence of the crowd that Jesus be killed, despite Pilate's considering him innocent (Matt. 27.15–26//Mark 15.6–15//Luke 23.18–23; cf. John 18.38), shows this clearly enough. The elaborate Jewish trial scenes in the synoptic Gospels also tend to shift responsibility to Judaism in an official way and help serve the same purpose.[19]

These difficulties with the trial scene are not new ones. Some, to be sure, still defend the scene as being an authentic portrayal.[20] Many more scholars recognize that the earliest Christians knew only the general course of events (a Jewish interrogation, the handing over to Pilate, the crucifixion), but not the details.[21] Yet many of these carry on doing word-for-word exegesis of statements which cannot be direct quotations. Thus, for example, Reumann concludes that details which go beyond the summary of Mark 15.1 are difficult to recover, but he immediately states that 'the trial was marked by the appearance of false witnesses (Mark 14.55–56)'.[22] He later expresses uncertainty about how 'the exact question' of Matt. 26.63//Mark 14.61//Luke 22.67, 70 was worded. [23] Similarly Harvey correctly grants that the evangelists had only a bare outline of facts. He considers a meeting of the Sanhedrin, but not necessarily a trial, to be an unquestionable fact. Later he states that Jesus' supposed answer to the high priest is 'manifestly unhistorical'. Subsequently, however, he offers it as a fact that Jesus was arraigned on a charge of blasphemy and that the blasphemy consisted of his using the term 'son of God' in answering a charge of blasphemy.[24] I do not see how, having said that the evangelists knew only a bare outline of facts and that Jesus' answer to the question 'Are you the Christ?' is unhistorical, he can then offer a detailed interpretation of the other half of Jesus' reported answer to the high priest.

All we need do is to accept the obvious, that we do not have detailed knowledge of what happened when the high priest and possibly others questioned Jesus. We cannot know even that 'the Sanhedrin' met. Further, I doubt that the earliest followers of Jesus knew. They were not privy to the membership list; if people hurried into the high priest's house at night there was no one to identify them and tick their names off. I do not doubt that Jesus was arrested on the orders of the high priest and interrogated. But we cannot know much more. Scholars will continue to dissect the accounts of the 'trial', but I fear that our knowledge will not be greatly advanced.

I am not proposing that the evangelists have deliberately deceived us. It seems quite clear that they did not know why Jesus was executed from the point of view of the Jewish leaders. We shall see, in fact, that they were ignorant even about the composition of a Jewish court. New Testament scholars all tell themselves, one another and their students that the Gospel writers were not historians in the modern sense, but we do not apply this fact rigorously enough. One of the aspects of a course of events on which ancient writers in general are weakest is cause and effect. Thus when the empire flourished, Roman historians would say that it was because the emperor was virtuous and just. Ramsey MacMullen put it this way:

Vegetius and Jerome, discussing matters that seem to require the drawing of parallels to their own times from the 200s A.D., go back instead to the 200s B.C. They are not ignorant. They have their books. History is spread out before their eyes, but they see only events and persons floating loose in a timeless past, without caused links between them – a gallery of isolated portraits and anecdotes made classical by remoteness.

He continues, 'It had always been thus.'[25]

I think that this describes our Gospel writers very well. Luke, who made most of being an accurate historian, is most easily shown to have shared the failings of his contemporaries. All one has to do is examine him on the census and on Theudas and Judas the Galilean. Quirinius, Theudas, Judas, a census – all are floating around back there somewhere, and Luke puts them in his story. But he does not really know how, or whether, they fit.[26] Why should it be otherwise when it comes to the motives of the Jewish leadership, details such as the composition of the Sanhedrin, and the events which actually caused Jesus' death? And in fact, as we see from the conflicting evidence and the unpersuasive accounts, it is not otherwise.

It will of course be urged that the passion narrative originates from a time very close to the events. This is doubtless true, but proximity in time does not necessarily give the authors of it any insight into cause and effect and the inner workings of events. There is a general impression of a confused night, and this is probably accurate (as I shall argue below). *That anyone, even someone close to the scene, knew precisely who did what is unlikely.* That the *internal motives* of the actors were known by those on whom the evangelists drew seems impossible.[27]

The unlikeliness of the charge of blasphemy has led some to search the trial scene and Jewish law for evidence of a formal charge on which Jesus was convicted at the supposed Sanhedrin trial. Those who follow this course hold that there was a formal trial and a conviction under Jewish law, as the synoptic Gospels have it, but that the charge was not 'blasphemy'. Bowker has proposed that Jesus was convicted of being 'a rebellious elder',[28] and others have proposed 'false prophet' or 'deceiver' (*mēsît*).[29] It seems to me, however, that once we grant that we do not know what went on inside – that is, when we admit that the long trial scene of Matthew and Mark is not historical – then we must also grant that we do not know (1) if there was a trial; (2) if the whole Sanhedrin actually convened; (3) if there was a formal charge; (4) if there was a formal conviction under Jewish law. There are a lot of possibilities. I earlier said that the attack on the temple could be considered blasphemy. I presume that it could also be considered the act of a 'rebellious elder', and that the prediction of the temple's destruction could be the words of a 'false prophet'. But the truth is that we do not know the answers to any of the questions just itemized. We share the ignorance of the evangelists. If, as seems highly probable, they were wrong about Jesus' being convicted by a formal Jewish court for blasphemy, we can hardly prove, on the basis of their accounts, that some other charge was sustained. Other sources can hardly put us closer to the events. The best that we can hope to achieve is a general view of cause and effect, based on incidents which surely preceded the execution (the action of the temple being the most important) and the outcome (the continuation of Jesus' disciples as an identifiable group within Judaism).[30]

Other 'religious' grounds for seeking Jesus' death have already been dealt with. Despite the great popularity of the view, it is not reasonable to think that Jesus was killed because he believed in mercy and forgiveness.[31] Debates on the law – if there were any – are too insubstantial to have led to a fatal enmity. Jesus' stance towards the wicked might have been irritating, but it does not linger in the Gospels as having had anything to do with his death.

The last point, however, deserves additional comment. If it be true that Jesus said that those who followed him, but did not repent and make restitution according to the law, would be included in the kingdom, he challenged the adequacy of the law of Moses.[32] The priests (as we shall see) were the administrators of the law, and also those who were authorized to say whether or not atonement had been made or purity achieved. If Jesus pronounced forgiveness of sins (Mark 2.9–12), he might also have been arrogating to himself the prerogatives of the priesthood.[33] I do not want to argue, however, that the priests actually felt threatened by this Galilean upstart and sought his death – at least not for these reasons. As I pointed out above, the priests did not systematically have executed all who claimed to speak for God, nor did the Romans oblige them by killing everyone who irritated them.

Thus we still must seek the immediate cause of Jesus' death, one which did not publicly and obviously implicate him and his followers as rebels against Rome, but one which could be presented to the Procurator as meriting death.

The one point that will not go away is the attack (both by word and deed) against the temple. The threat to destroy the temple is swept under the rug by Matthew and Mark in the trial scene, and Luke omits it. It crops up, however, later (Matt. 27.40//Mark 15.29; cf. Acts 6.14). Mark links the decisive plot to kill Jesus to the action (not the saying) (Mark 11.18). There is no reason to suppose that he here had access to the thinking of the Jewish leaders, but this time (unlike Mark 3.6), he seems to have hit it right. As we shall see more fully below, the temple scene is the last public event in Jesus' life: he lived long enough for it, but not much longer. In this case it seems entirely reasonable to argue *post hoc ergo propter hoc.*

This means that we should make a connection between the threat of destruction and the gesture against the temple (as I argued extensively in ch. 4 above). The connection is not made in the Gospels. According to Mark Jesus' enemies plot against him because of the prophetic action, and he is accused because of the verbal threat, but the two are not connected. Mark, in fact, understood the action in the way followed by modern scholars: it was a cleansing to prepare the temple for the worship of the Gentiles (Mark 11.17). We should make an inference as to the inner connection of events and cause and effect which the evangelists had neither the ability nor the interest to make. Jesus probably did not *do* one thing in the temple and *say* another about it during the same brief period without there being some interconnection. We can also see that the action and the threat (or prediction) were both offensive. *Even if Jesus understood himself to be cleansing the temple for the Gentiles* – which I do not for a moment believe – *the action would certainly have been seen as hostile.* When the action and the saying came to the attention of the Jewish leaders, they surely saw them both as arrogant and wicked.

We shall return later to the *dramatis personae.* Here it should be repeated that both the word and deed would have been offensive to most Jews. The gesture, even if it did not raise much tumult, could readily have led the Romans to think that Jesus was a threat to public order. In particular the physical demonstration against the temple by one who had a noticeable following looms as so obvious an occasion for the execution that we need look no further.

The phrases 'physical demonstration' and 'noticeable following' constitute important points. Simply speaking against the temple – prophesying its destruction – would lead to punishment and at least the threat of death. We see this earlier in Israel's history in Jer. 26, where Jeremiah is threatened with death for predicting the destruction of the temple and the city. Later, just before the outbreak of the first revolt, there is a story of another solitary woe-sayer: A man named Jesus went through the streets crying.

> A voice from the east, a voice from the west, a voice from the four winds; a voice against Jerusalem and the sanctuary, a voice against all the people.

He was 'chastised' by some of the leading citizens of Jerusalem and scourged to the bone by the Romans, but was finally released to continue his cry of woe.[34] He did not have a following, he did not physically touch one of the holy things in the temple, and he was obviously regarded as a more or less harmless, though irritating, eccentric. We do not have to add much to such stories to set the conditions for execution: a physical action, even though very minor, and a noticeable following.

We cannot say just how noticeable a following had to be in order to provoke the secular ruler to act without urging. Herod the Tetrarch, according to Josephus, acted quickly to execute John because his preaching excited the populace – we do not know how many of them.[35] It appears that the 'sign prophets' 'were not insignificant cranks with one or two followers'.[36] Josephus says that Theudas persuaded 'the majority of the crowd' (*AJ* XX.97). According to Acts 5.36 the number was four hundred. The unnamed sign prophets were followed by 'the crowd' or 'many' (*AJ* XX.167f.). The Egyptian led either 'the populace' (*AJ* XX.169) or thirty thousand men (*BJ* II.261) or four thousand (Acts 21.38).

Putting down the Egyptian, it appears, required a pitched battle. Josephus (*BJ* II.263) specifies the use of *hoplites*, armoured infantry. Pilate used both cavalry and *hoplites* against the Samaritans. Some were killed in the battle, and he later executed several of the leaders (*AJ* XVIII. 85–89). Theudas and the others may have been suppressed by something closer to police action, and for Theudas Josephus specifies a squadron of cavalry (*AJ* XX.98). There is probably a rough correlation between numbers and the outcome. Solitary prophets might escape with only flogging, those with thousands of followers would lead not only themselves but their followers into battle and death. (Though the wily Egyptian escaped.) I think that we can take the stories in Josephus as giving approximate parameters within which we can understand the execution of Jesus. He, like John the Baptist, falls in between the solitary woe-sayer and the Egyptian. The leader is executed but not the followers. There were enough followers, however, to make it expedient to kill Jesus, rather than simply flog him as a nuisance and release him.

These observations about numbers are in general supported by evidence from the New Testament. The general impression given by the Gospels is that Jesus had a small band of actual followers. We recall the point that he did not call all Israel to follow him, but only a select few, and that his message was generally individualistic and was not couched in the terms of national repentance and restoration which might have attracted a large following of people who expected dramatic results (ch. 8). We recall, further, that John the Baptist appears to have attracted greater public attention and that he was killed by Herod the Tetrarch without priestly urging. One piece of information points to an appreciable number of followers of Jesus, Paul's mention of five hundred who saw the resurrected Lord (I Cor. 15.6). The ancients cannot be relied on to give accurate estimates of a crowd. Paul's figure is as good as we can do. We can take it that 'the whole crowd' did not actually hail Jesus as king or marvel at his teaching, nor did the whole populace of Jerusalem subsequently support Peter and the others (see Matt. 21.8; Mark 11.18; Acts 5.26). It is probably not true that the popular support for Jesus was so great that the priests and Romans were afraid to act against him (e.g. Mark 12.12). The evidence points the other way: if support had been this massive, more than just Jesus would have fallen. I am not accusing the Christian authors of being either uninformed or dishonest. They report according to the conventions of the day. It is also not true that an actual majority of the people followed Theudas, and Josephus's other references to 'the populace' and 'the crowd' are just as accurate as are the references in the Gospels and Acts. In defence of the ancient authors, we can observe that the science of estimating crowds is very recent indeed, is still partially unreliable, and in part depends on aerial photography.

The discussion of numbers leads me to emphasize again a point made earlier: no one misunderstood the threat posed by Jesus. Neither the priests nor the Romans thought that a crowd of even five hundred could actually seize control. They would have acted against the leader to prevent widespread excitement, but the leaders of Judaism did not feel that the foundations of their position were being shaken. We can make the present proposal more precise yet by noting those of Smith and Trocmé. Smith proposed that it was primarily the *number* of people who, attracted by the miracles, thought of Jesus as Messiah which led to his execution.[37] Trocmé suggested that Jesus became a public figure only by his action against the temple.[38] The truth seems to lie in between. It was not just the numbers, since a large enough following would have triggered a Roman response without urging from the priesthood. Nor was it just the minor disturbance in the temple. It was the combination of a *physical action* with a *noticeable following* which accounts for and led immediately to Jesus' death. The Jewish leaders could then reasonably and persuasively propose to Pilate that Jesus should be executed. Pilate agreed. It is probable that the Jewish leaders did not see Jesus' followers as posing any threat once their leader was removed. But if they did, they failed to persuade Pilate.

It may be objected that too many chapters intervene between the gesture against the temple and the execution for the former to be the sufficient cause of the latter. But we do not know that the sizeable blocks of material between the events have been put in the right place. Jeremias, among others, has proposed that we 'bracket out' Mark 12 and 13 and parr., and this seems a reasonable proposal.[39] Many have seen the Question about Authority as originally following immediately on the temple account, and that could be correct.[40] There is no particular reason, however, to think that the Parable of the Vineyard (Mark 12.1–12 and parr.), the further disputes with the Pharisees and Sadducees (Mark 12.13–34), the question about David's son (Mark 12.35–40), the story of the Widow's Mite (Mark 12.41–44), or the 'little apocalypse' (Mark 13 and parr.) represent teaching and controversy which actually took place between the events narrated in Mark 11 and Mark 14. We know so little about the relationship between events and the arrangement of material in the Gospels that the material now found between the gesture against the temple and the 'trial' should not prevent us from seeing the temple conflict as the last thing which happened before Jesus' execution, and probably as its immediate cause.

I do not wish to argue that it was only Jesus' action and saying against the temple which offended many of his contemporaries. We have earlier seen that Jesus' presumption to speak for God would have been resented. Even the solitary woe-sayer was resented. Further, Jesus had attracted enough of a following as a healer to be accused of healing by means of an evil spirit. These matters may well have made the Jewish leaders wary and suspicious of him. Also, if the Jerusalem leaders thought that Jesus would attract the hostile attention of Rome, they would have been quick to single him out as an undesirable troublemaker.[41] John attributes to Caiaphas the saying that 'it is expedient that one man should die for the people, and that the whole nation should not perish' (John 11.50). John has in mind Jesus' saving death, but the saying itself doubtless catches the spirit of the Jewish leadership. We should also recall that at Passover the Romans took special preparations to suppress any trouble.[42] Many factors – Jesus' extraordinary self-claim; the gathering he attracted; the nervousness on the part of Jewish leaders not to give the Romans occasion for punishment of the people generally; the Romans' own anxiety about prophets and about crowds at feasts – doubtless help account for the fact that Jesus was crucified. *But he was not crucified until after he had time to make a demonstration against the temple*, and that appears to have been the last thing which he *did* (except for his last meal with the disciples) before he was executed. The gun may already have been cocked, but it was the temple demonstration which pulled the trigger.

Even if this be granted, there are important questions unresolved: why was Jesus executed as *king*? Can the precise role of the Jewish leaders be decided? Though we have touched on both questions, they require further study, and we take them in turn.

The triumphal entry

The Gospels offer us an event prior to the temple action which, were it the unvarnished truth, could well have led to Jesus' execution: the entry into Jerusalem. The claim to be king is explicit only in Matthew and John, who quote Zech. 9.9 (Matt. 21.4f.; John 12.15) and say that the crowds cried not only 'Hosanna', but also 'Son of David' (Matt. 21.9) or 'King of Israel' (John 12.13). But Mark and Luke also portray Jesus as riding on an ass, and plenty of those in Jerusalem would have remembered the prophetic passage, especially if Jesus' followers cried 'Blessed be he who comes in the name of the Lord' (Matt. 21.9//Mark 11.9//Luke 19.38; quoting Ps. 118.26 [LXX 117.26]). Is the story true? Perhaps it is. Jesus was executed as one who claimed to be 'king of the Jews'. The entry and the execution fit each other precisely.[43]

But, as always, there is a problem. The Gospels also put several days between the entry and the execution, during which time Jesus is said to have come and gone without people hailing him as king. If the entry was what we are told it was, why did it take so long for the Romans to execute Jesus? Why were the disciples not rounded up and killed? And why do the Gospels have the Jewish leadership play any role at all? The Romans were not slow to act when sedition threatened, nor, were this a large demonstration, would they have needed a Jewish 'trial' in order to urge them on. Perhaps the event took place but was a small occurrence which went unnoticed. Perhaps only a few disciples unostentatiously dropped their garments in front of the ass (cf. Matt. 21.8//Mark 11.8//Luke 19.36), while only a few quietly murmured 'Hosanna'.[44]

I regard the passage as being one of the most puzzling in the Gospels. If it happened *at all*, surely the disciples were in on the secret and knew that Jesus was claiming to be king. We have seen previously that they very likely did have this understanding, and also that they knew that he was to be a special kind of king. The expectation of a new world order (whether 'in the air' or in a new Jerusalem), in which Jesus and his disciples would be the chief figures, but which would not be established by human might, seems to me the best explanation of the puzzling passage about the 'triumphal' entry. Jesus and his close followers understood that he was entering as 'king', but there was no large public hue and cry about it. It fits into Jesus' last symbolic acts: he entered as 'king', demonstrated the destruction of the present temple, and had a meal with his disciples which symbolized the coming 'banquet'.

The reader will notice that I did not put the Triumphal Entry and the passages about the otherworldly kingdom in the list of things which are unquestionable. In terms of probability, I regard all this as approximately on the same level as the suggestion, several times repeated, that Jesus promised membership in the kingdom to the wicked who followed him but who did not repent and return to the Mosaic law. Let me lay things out in what I regard as the order of probability:

1. Jesus taught about the kingdom (unquestionable).
2. He depicted the kingdom in metaphorical terms, including that of a banquet (almost beyond the shadow of doubt).
3. His disciples never expected the kingdom to be a political one, brought about by the aid of arms, but rather to depend on the future act of God (almost beyond the shadow of doubt).
4. The coming kingdom was symbolized by three gestures, only one of them publicly dramatic:
   a. the temple (certain)
   b. the supper (almost equally certain)
   c. the entry (probable).
5. Jesus gave himself and his disciples a role in the kingdom. His own role was obviously superior to theirs, and his role could be summarized as 'king' (almost certain). This may have led to discussions of him as 'Messiah' in his lifetime (possible),[45] but in any case this is the title which was given him after the resurrection (certain).

The question of Jesus' self-claim has, to understate the case, vexed scholars – it seems to me unduly. Jesus taught about the *kingdom*; he was executed as would-be *king*; and his disciples, after his death, expected him to return to establish the *kingdom*. These points are indisputable. Almost equally indisputable is the fact that the disciples thought that they would have some role in the kingdom. We should, I think, accept the obvious: Jesus taught his disciples that he himself would play the principal role in the kingdom.[46]

There are, it appears, two reasons for hesitating about Jesus' self-claim. One is that there are only two instances in the Gospels in which Jesus accepts the title 'Messiah' (the trial, Mark 14.61f.; Peter's Confession, Mark 8.29f. and parr.), and both are dubious historically.[47] The other is that the title 'Messiah' was used by the early church, and the criterion of dissimilarity therefore excludes it from the ministry of Jesus.[48] I do not think it worthwhile to quibble very much about terms. Let us grant that Jesus did not call himself 'Messiah'. We must still take into account the indisputable or almost indisputable facts outlined above. These focus on 'king' rather than 'Messiah', but they explain why 'Messiah' was *ever* thought to be an appropriate title.[49] If Jesus said to the disciples only 'there will be a kingdom', 'you will have a role in it', and 'I will share the banquet of the new kingdom with you', the disciples would naturally have been as willing as the Romans to think that he considered himself 'king', and they would equally naturally have found the title 'Messiah' an appropriate one.

The point which remains unsolved is *just* how Jesus conceived his own role. I must confess that I have no answer to the question of precisely how Jesus saw the relationship between himself, the Son of man, and the Father. In some passages it is *Jesus'* kingdom, in others *God's*, in others, apparently, the *Son of man's*. Thus Matt. 19.28 mentions 'the new age, when the *Son of man* comes on the throne of his glory', while the parallel, Luke 22.28–30, refers to *Jesus'* kingdom. In the saying about drinking wine again in the kingdom (Matt. 26.29//Mark 14.25//Luke 22.18), all three Gospels refer to the kingdom of *God* (Matthew, 'in the kingdom of my father'). In the story of the request by the two sons of Zebedee (or their mother), both Matthew and Mark refer to *Jesus'* kingdom (Mark, 'glory') (Matt. 20.21//Mark 10.37). The Parousia passage (Matt. 24.30//Mark 13.26//Luke 21.27) refers to the *Son of man* (so also Matt. 16.27 and parr.). I presume that, since they were Jews, Jesus' disciples, when they discussed *Jesus'* kingdom, meant by it 'the kingdom of God with Jesus as his viceroy'. But beyond that I cannot see clearly. I do not consider any combination impossible. It is conceivable that Jesus spoke in different ways: referring to the kingdom of God; or to the messianic feast with himself at the head; or to God's sending the Son of man to see to the establishment of the kingdom, still with Jesus at the head of it; or to his own identity with the Son of man. It is of course the Son of man who makes things difficult. I have no hope of solving a problem which has defeated so many.

To conclude: the entry was probably deliberately managed by Jesus to symbolize the coming kingdom and his own role in it.[50] I account for the fact that Jesus was not executed until after the demonstration against the temple by proposing that it was an intentionally symbolic action, performed because Jesus regarded it to be true (he would be king, but a humble one) and for the sake of the disciples, but that it did not attract large public attention.

The betrayal

The explanation of the *execution* of Jesus as *king* still lacks, however, one important ingredient. We have seen that Jesus' demonstration against the temple (when added to other contributing causes) will account for his execution, and we have seen that he and his disciples very probably thought of him privately as 'king', presumably in the sense of 'viceroy'. But how are the two points related? Schweitzer long ago pointed the way: *what* Judas betrayed (a point on which the Gospels are unhelpful) was that Jesus and his small band thought of him as 'king'.[51] It will remain possible that, at the Entry, someone shouted 'son of David' or 'king' loudly enough to attract attention, and also that what Judas betrayed was simply where Jesus was; but the more obvious explanation is that Judas conveyed Jesus' pretension to the chief priests (Matt. 26.14//Mark 14.10//Luke 22.4). It was the final weapon they needed: a specific charge to present to Pilate, more certain to have fatal effect than the general charge 'troublemaker'.

The role of Jewish leaders

In ch. 10 we saw that the role of the Pharisees as Jesus' opponents has at least been greatly exaggerated in the early chapters of the synoptics and that the principal actors against Jesus were the chief priests. It now remains to examine the explicit statements in the Passion Narratives.

As is well known, the Pharisees as such largely disappear from the last chapters of the Gospels. Their last appearance in Mark is in the passage on Tribute to Caesar (Mark 12.13). Matthew names them there (Matt. 22.15) and also as the adversaries in two of the subsequent passages: the Great Commandment (Matt. 22.34; cf. Mark 12.28: 'one of the scribes'); David's Son (Matt. 22.41; there are no adversaries in Mark and Luke). In Matthew the Pharisees also join the chief priests in petitioning Pilate to guard the tomb (Matt. 27.62). Their last appearance in Luke is 19.39, a passage peculiar to Luke in which the Pharisees are said to tell Jesus that he should rebuke his disciples for hailing him when he entered Jerusalem. According to John 18.3 Judas procured 'a band of soldiers and some officers from the chief priests and the Pharisees' in order to arrest Jesus. The Pharisees otherwise play no role in the trial and execution.[52]

Scribes appear at various points in the last chapters of the synoptics (a chart is given below). If the general opinion that scribes were on the whole Pharisees be followed, it could be maintained that the synoptic Gospels

assign the Pharisees a role in the events leading immediately to Jesus'
death.

The chief priests, however, play the prime role in all the Gospels.[53] This
is very likely historically accurate. But just as we previously doubted that
the evangelists knew the cause of Jesus' death, so we should also doubt
that they had precise knowledge of who did what. Except for the consistent
portrayal of the chief priests as the principal Jewish leaders, the Gospels
present a shifting picture of Jesus' enemies. The following chart will help
make the point clear:[54]

Matthew	Mark	Luke
21.15	11.18	19.47
After the Temple Scene		
chief priests and scribes were indignant	chief priests and scribes sought to destroy him because of influence on the multitude	chief priests and scribes and principal men sought to destroy him but could not because of his popularity
21.45f.	12.12	20.19
After the Parable of the Wicked Husbandman		
The chief priests and Pharisees sought to seize him	'they' (apparently chief priests, scribes and elders: see Mark 11.27) sought to seize him	the scribes and chief priests sought to seize him
26.4f.	14.1f.	22.1f.
Two days before Passover	Two days before Passover	Near Passover
chief priests and elders with Caiaphas planned to kill him by stealth but hesitated to do so during the feast for fear of tumult	chief priests and scribes sought to kill him by stealth to avoid public tumult	chief priests and scribes sought to kill him because they feared the people
26.14–16	14.10f	22.3–6
Judas arranges for betrayal with chief priests	Judas arranges for betrayal with chief priests	Judas arranges for betrayal with chief priests and captains
26.47	14.43	22.47
Judas aids arrest by a crowd from chief priests and elders	Judas aids arrest by crowd from chief priests and scribes and elders	Judas aids arrest by crowd
26.57	14.53	22.54
Jesus led before Caiaphas and high priest, where the elders and scribes assembled	Jesus led before the high priest, where the chief priests, elders and scribes assembled	Jesus led to high priest's house

Matthew	Mark	Luke
26.59	14.55	
chief priests and the Sanhedrin sought false testimony	chief priests and Sanhedrin sought testimony	
26.60–66	14.56–64	
the night 'trial'	the night 'trial'	
27.1f.	15.1	22.66
when morning came, all the chief priests and the elders took counsel against Jesus,	in the morning the chief priests, with the elders and the scribes, and the whole Sanhedrin took counsel,	when day came, the elders, both chief priests and scribes, led him to the Sanhedrin
		22.67–71
		the 'trial'
		23.1
and they delivered him to Pilate	and they delivered him to Pilate	the whole company arose and brought him before Pilate

A study of the chart will show that there is considerable variation in the descriptions of the chief actors in the drama. We may note, for example, that a comparison of Matt. 26.57 with 26.59 and of Mark 14.53 with 14.55 indicates that 'the Sanhedrin' was composed of the 'elders and scribes', while the chief priests are named separately. On the other hand, Mark 15.1 seems to distinguish the 'whole Sanhedrin' from the chief priests, the elders and the scribes at the time of the morning trial. Matthew mentions only the chief priests and the elders at the morning trial, but not the Sanhedrin (Matt. 27.1f.). Luke's view is that the elders, consisting of the chief priests and the scribes, led Jesus to the Sanhedrin (22.66), apparently composed of others (though possibly here a place).

In John it is the raising of Lazarus which leads the chief priests and the Pharisees to gather the Sanhedrin and consider the advisability of putting Jesus to death (11.47). He is arrested by soldiers and officers from the chief priests and the Pharisees (18.3; 18.12), who take him to Annas (18.3). There are vague questions and innocuous answers (18.19–23), and then he is taken before Caiaphas (18.24). He is turned over to the Romans to be executed as an evildoer (18.30).

It seems to be a fair inference that the evangelists did not know who was who, at least not precisely. The high priest and the chief priests stand out, but the precise relationships among the leading priests, the elders, the scribes and the Sanhedrin are not clear.

It is not, however, only the Gospels which are muddy on this point. The evidence from Josephus about Jewish self-government is also unclear. There is, to be sure, a scholarly consensus: There was a body of Jewish leaders who constituted the Sanhedrin, which in turn played an appreciable role in government and which saw to the administration of Jewish law.[55] From the time of Salome Alexandra 'the constitution of the Sanhedrin represented a compromise between the nobility on the one hand – lay and priestly – and Pharisaic learning on the other.'[56] Although the chief priests 'often stand alone as the leading personalities in the Sanhedrin',[57] the scribes 'exercised a considerable influence' in it. They were mostly Pharisees.[58] Thus the Sadducees (most of the chief priests) and the Pharisees (the scribes) sat together on the court. Some scholars insist that the Pharisees came increasingly to dominate the Sanhedrin and that the Sadducees yielded to them on many matters, including those affecting the temple.[59] Others regard the importance of the Pharisees as still under debate.[60]

This general consensus rests on a harmonization of Josephus, the Gospels and the Talmud. Josephus describes the predominance of the Pharisees under Queen Salome Alexandra (78–68 BCE), the Gospels place the scribes in the Sanhedrin, and some passages in Josephus's *Antiquities* and in the Talmud ascribe dominance to the Pharisees.[61] I think that the evidence is a good deal murkier than the scholarly consensus implies. It lies beyond the scope of this study to attempt a full analysis of the evidence, but it will be worth a few pages to present some of the complexities in order the better to evaluate the Gospel accounts of Jesus' trial. We shall examine a few key points in Josephus with regard to the Sanhedrin and the role of the Pharisees.

1. There are two accounts of the position of the Pharisees during the reign of Salome Alexandra: *BJ* I.110–14 and *AJ* XIII.408–18. They are in very close agreement. Alexandra essentially turned domestic policy over to the Pharisees, who were known for their observance of the national religion and their exact interpretation of the law. They could recall exiles and banish their enemies. They killed some, including one Diogenes. The leading citizens (*hoi dokountes*, *BJ* I.114; *hoi dynatoi*, *AJ* XIII.411) turned to Aristobulus for protection.

I do not know why these passages are interpreted as meaning that the Pharisees became a majority of the Sanhedrin.[62] The Sanhedrin is not mentioned, nor is any other assembly, such as a *boulē*, council. Further, the Pharisees are said to have been given full authority: they became absolute rulers, both acting on their own and dictating to Alexandra (e.g. *BJ* I.112). Their opponents, the leading citizens, were dispersed throughout the countryside after Aristobulus's intercession, but not killed or imprisoned (*BJ* I.114; *AJ* XIII.417f.). It is evident that these opponents did not simply assume a minority position in a governing body. Indeed the picture drawn by Josephus seems to exclude the existence of a governing body. The dominance of the Pharisees seems to have come to an abrupt halt with the death of the Queen. They are not given a role in government in Josephus's accounts of subsequent rulers. It is precarious to see the reign of Salome Alexandra as a time from whence the Pharisees assumed a permanent place in the Sanhedrin.

2. The trial of Herod the Great is also in both the *War* (*BJ* I.208–11) and the *Antiquities* (*AJ* XIV.165–84), but this time they are not in close agreement. In the *War* Josephus says that many at court, that is, around the king, Hyrcanus II (*en tois basileiois*) urged him to take steps against Herod. They wanted Herod to appear 'in court' (*epi dikēn*) if in fact he was still subject to the laws of the country. Herod went to Jerusalem with an escort of moderate strength. Sextus Caesar ordered Hyrcanus to acquit Herod, and, 'being inclined to take that course on other grounds', he did so. There is no Sanhedrin, but rather counsellors around the king; there is no court appearance; there is no formal trial, though there is an acquittal.

According to the *Antiquities* the 'principal Jews' (*hoi prōtoi tōn Ioudaiōn*) became alarmed at Herod's power and ambition (*AJ* XIV.165). They urged Hyrcanus to take steps. Sextus, as in the *War*, is said to have ordered Hyrcanus to acquit Herod (XIV.170). Then the account becomes confused. We are first told that Herod appeared before the Sanhedrin with his troops and that no one dared speak except Samaias (according to another passage a Pharisee) (XIV.171f.).[63] Hyrcanus perceived that the Sanhedrin was about to order Herod's execution, and he postponed the trial (XIV.177). He secretly advised Herod to flee (XIV.177f.). According to XIV.182, however, Herod's friends urged him to remember his acquittal.

It seems to me probable that the Sanhedrin, which plays a major role throughout the account in the *Antiquities*, has been added in order to conform the situation to subsequent Jewish law. *AJ* XIV.182 contains a reminiscence of the account in the *War*, which has Herod acquitted – but not by the Sanhedrin.

3. The execution of Hyrcanus II also raises questions about the Sanhedrin. In *BJ* I.434 Josephus simply says that Herod put him to death. In *AJ* XV.165–78 he offers two versions of the execution. According to the first, *a* letter to Hyrcanus from the Arab king, Malchus, came into Herod's hands. It promised aid to Hyrcanus. Herod showed 'the letters'

to the Sanhedrin and had Hyrcanus executed (XV.172f.). According to the second version Herod trumped up a charge that Hyrcanus had accepted a bribe from Malchus and had him strangled. Josephus notes, in support of this second story, that Hyrcanus was eighty-one years old and not likely to have been engaged in an intrigue to overthrow Herod (XV.178). The first story, which cloaks the action as a legal one approved by the Sanhedrin, Josephus derived from Herod's Memoirs (XV.174).

4. In the *Life*, Josephus assigns the Sanhedrin a role in directing the war. He depicts himself as writing to the Sanhedrin in Jerusalem for instructions while he is commanding troops in Galilee (*Vita* 62). We may compare *Vita* 28, where he says that 'the principal men of Jerusalem' sent him and two other priests on a mission.

In the *War*, however, the Sanhedrin plays no role in government. We hear, rather, of various leading groups and of a council, *boulē*. The standard answer to this problem is that the terms are synonymous,[64] and they may well be. Yet even so, in the *War* the *boulē* does not seem to bear the responsibility that is assigned to the Sanhedrin in some passages in the *Antiquities*, in the *Life* and in Rabbinic literature. In order to grasp how, in a time of crisis, 'Jewish self-government' actually worked, it will be helpful to summarize Josephus's description of the last events before the outbreak of the war. I do not wish to claim that the execution of Jesus was a time of equal crisis, but I do think that the sections to be summarized below indicate how Jewish leadership functioned under Roman rule – especially when there seemed to be, or actually was, need for haste.

Florus, seeking vengeance against some who insulted him, called together the *chief priests*, as well as the *powerful* (*dynatoi*) and the *best known of the city*. He demanded that they find those who were guilty (*BJ* II.301f.). The leaders pointed out the impossibility of the task and urged Florus not to press the matter (II.302–304). He ordered the soldiers to sack the market. A massacre followed, during which Jews of even equestrian rank were scourged before Florus's tribunal and crucified (II.305–308). In the tumult of the next day, the *powerful*, with the *chief priests*, tried to prevail on the crowd not to provoke the Procurator (II.316). Florus sent for the *chief priests* and the *best known men* and told them that, to demonstrate their obedience, the people had to go along the road to meet arriving Roman troops (II.318). The *chief priests* urged this action on 'the multitude' in the temple (II.320). The priests temporarily carried the crowd, but the Romans, in response to further outcries against Florus, started another massacre (II.322–29). After the rebels seized the porticoes, Florus sent for the *chief priests* and the *council* (*boulē*), and told them that he intended to quit the city, but would leave them whatever garrison they desired. In reply, they undertook to maintain perfect order and to prevent any revolution, provided that he left them a single cohort . . . . (II.331f.)

It is noteworthy that, although the chief priests and other leaders figured in the tumult as the intermediaries between the Romans and the Jerusalem-ites, the *boulē* appears when Florus is going to do something official: leave a garrison in the control of the responsible Jewish body. Massacres, flogging and execution could take place without the involvement of the *boulē*. But just before quitting the city, Florus summoned them.

From the safety of Caesarea, Florus wrote to the governor, Cestius; and the rulers (*hoi archontes*) of Jerusalem also wrote, putting the blame on Florus (II.333). Cestius now took a direct hand. His emissaries met King Agrippa, who was just returning from Alexandria, at Jamnia. The Jewish leaders – the *chief priests*, the *powerful* and the *council* – also went to Jamnia to seek the king's help (II.333–37).

The story continues, and later we hear about the *chief priests* and the *best known men* trying to persuade the *priests* who were in charge of the offerings not to stop the sacrifices for the Roman rulers (II.410). The priests were not persuaded, and the *powerful* gathered with the *chief priests* and the *best known of the Pharisees* to consider the situation (II.411). In subsequent action the *chief priests* continue to be mentioned as those who sought accommodation with Rome (II.422).

The impression is overwhelming that the chief priests took the lead in mediating between the Romans and the populace: they were held responsible by the Romans, they asserted their authority and prestige in seeking accommodation, and they undertook to speak to the Romans on behalf of the nation. There was a council, but it seems to have met formally only once during the events under Florus. When things reached a disastrous stage, and only then, did the priests assemble 'the best-known Pharisees' to help consider the matter.

5. In the *Antiquities* there are several passages which claim that the Pharisees controlled the masses and played a major role in Jewish affairs at times other than the reign of Salome Alexandra. We earlier discussed these in considering the question of whether the Pharisees controlled the opinions of the populace. We must now ask if they show, as Josephus intends them to do, that the Pharisees were leaders in the government of Israel. We recall that many New Testament scholars regard the Pharisees

as having held real power.[65] It turns out, however, that Josephus's statements to this effect are not convincing.

In *AJ* XIII.288, discussing the reign of Hyrcanus I, Josephus states that the Pharisees were heeded even when they spoke against the king *or* a high priest. As Marcus notes, the statement is anachronistic: it requires a time when the two offices were separated.[66] We read subsequently that the same Hyrcanus left the Pharisees and joined the Sadducees, that the Pharisees had the support of the masses, and that Hyrcanus had a lengthy and peaceful rule (*AJ* XIII.296–300). It is not clear that all these statements hang together. If everyone heeded the Pharisees, why did Hyrcanus join the Sadducees, and why was his reign so peaceful? In *AJ* XVIII.17 Josephus states that whenever a Sadducee assumes some office he submits 'to the [views] of the Pharisees', since 'otherwise the masses would not tolerate them'. This view is reflected also in the Babylonian Talmud;[67] but Josephus gives us no explicit example, and the claim of Pharisaic dominance seems to be contradicted by the facts. As Smith puts it, 'the influence of the Pharisees with the people, which Josephus reports, is not demonstrated by the history he records'.[68] The Hasmoneans (with the exception of Salome Alexandra), the Herods, and the Sadducean high priests seem to have followed their own views. Thus, for example, Josephus writes that the high priest Ananus followed the school of the Sadducees (*AJ* XX.199). Ananus is the high priest who convened the Sanhedrin and had James executed. When King Agrippa learned of it, he deposed Ananus (*AJ* XX.197–203).[69] The real situation is clear: the Pharisees did not dictate policy. The secular ruler held power, and under him the high priest; and they ruled according to their own views, with or without the approval of the Pharisees.[70]

In other summary statements Josephus attributes administration of the laws to the priesthood: The priests exercised 'a strict superintendence of the Law and the pursuits of everyday life; for the appointed duties of the priests included general supervision, the trial of cases of litigation, and the punishment of condemned persons' (*Ap.* II.187). Near the end of the *Antiquities* Josephus writes that after the deaths of Herod and Archelaus 'the constitution became an aristocracy, and the high priests were entrusted with the leadership of the nation' (*AJ* XX.251). This seems to accord with the facts, and the passages which say that the Pharisees governed the nation *de facto* because of their popularity with the masses are probably to be taken as reflecting the subsequent dominance of the Rabbis, whose prestige Josephus, in the *Antiquities*, was eager to uphold.[71] Falk, despite his reliance on Rabbinic literature in describing the Sanhedrin, neatly summarizes the actual situation: After Pompey's conquest

> Political independence was then abolished, although the High Priest was authorised to serve as *prostates tou et[h]nou*, head of the people, on behalf of the Roman government. This authority included judicial autonomy, but not the power to strike coins; this power and the royal crown were given to Herod. After the death of Herod limited autonomy was restored to the High Priest, who acted in political matters and perhaps also in matters of capital offences, under the supervision of the Roman provincial governor or of the king enthroned by the Romans.[72]

I do not wish to insist on any given reconstruction of who held what influence during the period that Pontius Pilate was Procurator. We should, however, be aware that 'trials' and judgments need not have proceeded in the orderly fashion depicted in Mishnah Sanhedrin. There is nothing intrinsically improbable about the account in John, according to which Jesus was interrogated by Annas and Caiaphas, but not 'tried' before the Sanhedrin (John 18.19–28).[73] The accounts in Josephus of the way in which the Romans related to Jewish leaders show that it is by no means impossible that, in such a matter as this, the Romans would have dealt entirely with the chief priests. They constitute the one group which remains constant in all the Gospels, and they also emerge from the pages of Josephus as the natural Jewish leaders and those who had the ear of the Roman rulers.[74] It is also clear from Josephus that whoever was in power – whether a Hasmonean, a Herod or a Roman Procurator – could execute or free whom he wished without a formal trial. It is entirely possible that Hyrcanus freed Herod and that Herod executed Hyrcanus without the benefit of a trial by a court. It is certain that Florus carried out executions on a large scale with no trial, except possibly one before his own tribunal, conducted by himself. The confusion in the Gospels about the events which immediately led to Jesus' execution may well point to the fact that there was no orderly procedure which was noted and remembered.

Conclusion

We should return to our standard attempt to distinguish what is certain from what is not. First, we recall the surest facts: Jesus was executed by the Romans; his disciples were not rounded up and executed. In addition, it is highly probable that he was executed for sedition or treason, as would-be king. As we pointed out in discussing the Triumphal Entry, if he had been publicly hailed as king, he would probably have been killed earlier than he was, and those who proclaimed him would probably have fallen also. Any interpretation of Jesus' death must hold together his own execution as would-be 'king of the Jews' and the survival of his disciples as an apolitical messianic group which was not rooted out and eliminated. The Gospels offer a way of holding the two together: Jesus was tried and convicted by Jewish authorities for blasphemy (Matthew and Mark) or he was turned over to Pilate by the chief priests as an evildoer according to Jewish law (John 18.30; cf. 19.7). We must, I think, accept the view of the Gospels, at least in general terms. He was executed by Pilate at the behest of the Jewish leadership, including at least the chief priests. Had the public tumult been so great that the Romans executed him without being urged, they almost certainly would have killed many of his followers as well.

I think that we cannot *know* that he was formally convicted of a crime under Jewish law.[75] The vaguer account of John seems better to correspond with the way things actually worked. There could have been a hearing before a group which represented others than the chief priests, but I think that we cannot know that to be the case. The situation seems to require only the involvement of the priests, but we cannot definitely exclude the participation of other leaders. The Pharisees cannot be decisively eliminated from participating because it remains possible (though not necessary) that there was a hearing by the Sanhedrin and that scribes were present. We should recall, however, that it is difficult to find any substantial conflict between Jesus and the Pharisees.[76] In any case, the immediate occasion of Jesus' death was the temple scene, which doubtless persuaded the leaders of Judaism that this Galilean, perhaps already an irritating presence, should not be allowed to create further trouble.

CONCLUSION

Results

Jesus saw himself as God's last messenger before the establishment of the kingdom. He looked for a new order, created by a mighty act of God. In the new order the twelve tribes would be reassembled, there would be a new temple, force of arms would not be needed, divorce would be neither necessary nor permitted, outcasts – even the wicked – would have a place, and Jesus and his disciples – the poor, meek and lowly – would have the leading role. He had devoted followers who accepted his expectation, made it their own, and remained committed to a transformation of it after his death and resurrection. Further, he had a following among the masses. They were attracted both by his healings and by his message, which promised them a prominent place in the kingdom. Some, impressed by his message and power, saw him as a great figure from Israel's past, some, possibly, as 'son of God'.

Jesus and his followers were not strange and unique in their expectation of a new age, nor in thinking that it would come without arms. They were not unique because they held out its promise especially to the outcasts. Jesus' promise to the wicked is distinctive and characteristic of his message, but other charismatic leaders also appealed to 'the poor'. New ages by definition must alter the present. Why offer the kingdom to those who are already running it? They have had their reward. Sociologically and psychologically Jesus and his movement are quite comprehensible.

In fact, we cannot say that a single one of the things known about Jesus is unique: neither his miracles, non-violence, eschatological hope or promise to the outcasts. He was not unique because he saw his own mission as of crucial importance, nor because he believed in the grace of God. The combination can doubtless be called 'unique', but that shows that he was an individual and not a two-dimensional representative of a type. His teaching may have been uniquely profound, perceptive and creative. Certainly the parables attributed to Jesus constitute a corpus which is better than that attributed to anyone else. The problem here as elsewhere is that we do not have enough comparative material to allow an absolute judgment. Judas the Galilean, for example, was known as a teacher, and he had a following; but we do not know what he taught or how he taught it. Further, we do not know that all the parables attributed to Jesus were actually told by him. There may have been great tellers of parables in the early Christian movement.

We cannot even say that Jesus was an uniquely good and great man. I agree with John Knox that the church's memory can guarantee his 'personal moral stature', but I also agree with him that critical history will not produce a figure of sufficient moral greatness to satisfy those who have felt their lives to be ennobled and uplifted by him.[1] History, in fact, has grave difficulty with the category 'unique'. Adequate comparative information is never available to permit such judgments as 'uniquely good', 'uniquely compassionate' and the like. It is, rather, a fault of New Testament scholarship that so many do not see that the use of such words as 'unique' and 'unprecedented' shows that they have shifted their perspective from that of critical history and exegesis to that of faith.[2] We can accept without argument Jesus' greatness as a man, but we must stop well short of explaining his impact by appeal to absolutely unique personal qualities.

What is unquestionably unique about Jesus is the result of his life and work. They culminated in the resurrection and the foundation of a movement which endured. I have no special explanation or rationalization of the resurrection experiences of the disciples. Their vividness and importance are best seen in the letters of Paul. They are, to my knowledge, unique in their *effect*. There was a report that Apollonius of Tyana appeared after his death (Philostratus, *Life of Apollonius* VIII.31), and we must remember that the *claim* of resurrection was not unique. But one does not receive from the pages of Philostratus the impression of burning conviction that, in Apollonius, God spoke and acted decisively. Philostratus, of course, was not Jewish, and thus not prepared to think of a single action of God which revealed his will and intention. We must suppose that Jesus' disciples were prepared to receive such a revelation – though not in the form it took. We have every reason to think that Jesus had led them to expect a dramatic event which would establish the kingdom. The death and resurrection required them to adjust their expectation, but did not create a new one out of nothing.

That is as far as I can go in looking for an explanation of the one thing which sets Christianity apart from other 'renewal movements'. The disciples were prepared for *something*. *What* they received inspired them and empowered them. It is the *what* that is unique.

Certainties, possibilities and speculations

We need to consider how certain each element in this depiction of Jesus is, but first I want to recall the strategy and aim of the study. We seem to have reached an impasse in New Testament studies, in which work on Jesus can never be pronounced much more than 'interesting': occasionally provocative, challenging or even illuminating, but usually only 'interesting'. I have attempted to make at least a small hole in the barrier, and to rest the main themes of the study on unassailable data. The full reconstruction, to be sure, involves inference, surmise and conjecture. I hope that these aspects will be at least 'interesting', but for the main themes themselves I have greater ambition: general conviction.

The study has been based on the view that knowledge about Jesus can be stratified, according to its degree of certainty, along the following scale: beyond reasonable doubt (or 'certain'), highly probable, probable, possible, conceivable, unprovable, incredible. The things best known about Jesus are certain facts about him, his career and its aftermath. Chronologically these range from his baptism by John to Paul's view that he was apostle to the Gentiles in the messianic era, and they embrace Jesus' call of disciples, the fact that he healed and preached, his 'attack' on the temple, his execution by the Romans, and the continuation of his disciples as a group which was identifiable, which expected the kingdom to come (but not with arms), and which was persecuted by some within Israel, though not by Rome.

These facts yield *certain* knowledge about Jesus of a *general character*. They allow us to understand him as a figure in religious history. They show that he fits into the general framework of Jewish restoration eschatology, and they identify him as the founder of a group which adhered to the expectations of that theology.

When we return to the first paragraph, in which the kingdom which Jesus expected was characterized, we see that not all the elements in the list are equally certain, and it is quite possible to add to it. The least certain point is that Jesus gave himself a role in the kingdom. The Gospels show him as remarkably reluctant to say who he was, and the proposal that he considered himself 'king' or 'viceroy' rests on inference. The inference is a strong one: he gave his disciples a role, and a teacher is greater than his disciples;[3] further, the disciples immediately gave him a title, 'Messiah', which is compatible with a claim to rulership. The execution of Jesus as would-be 'king of the Jews' shows us that *others* thought that he had claimed to be king. A second line of inference, therefore, is this: despite his reluctance to give himself a title, the Jewish aristocrats and the Romans understood him very well. What he claimed for himself was *tantamount* to claiming kingship. The only direct statement, however, is the symbolic gesture of entering Jerusalem on an ass – and some, quite reasonably, have worries about the authenticity of that story. The hard evidence is this: he talked about a kingdom; his disciples expected to have a role in it; they considered him their leader; he was crucified for claiming to be king.

Everything else in the list of characteristics is as solidly established as historical information of this sort can be. The temple, the twelve, the wicked, prohibition of divorce – all are firm.

It is sometimes possible to press beyond this general portrayal of Jesus. We can know the main themes of his particular message with assurance. They are summarized by the words 'kingdom' and 'the wicked'. How he differed from others who shared his general perspective can be known with only slightly less certainty. The paucity of material which attributes to him aspects of common belief – the coming of a great judgment for which repentance is the preparation – is especially striking. The explanation of the lack of prominence of expected themes is 'hypothetical' in the sense of 'speculative'. I proposed that these themes were largely bypassed by Jesus because he understood that John had taken care of that part of the overall task. Yet even though it is speculative and rests on no direct evidence, this proposal too is supported by inference from facts: Jesus started under John, he generally falls into the same overall perspective, and he did not emphasize the two main themes of John's message. One could, to be sure, infer from this that he omitted them because he came to disbelieve in them, but that seems much less likely. He continued to believe in a judgment (though he did not teach about it),[4] and he certainly believed in reconciliation between sinner and God.

Other things intimately connected with main themes cannot be known with security. The chief one is just what he expected the sinners who accepted him to do. They are invisible in Acts and Paul's letters (where there are Gentile 'sinners', but not Jewish ones). That Jesus came to *call* the wicked was transformed into the belief that he *died to save* sinners from sin and to make them upright. We must here pause to note the strong emphasis in the early Christian material which points to correction of behaviour. We have seen repeatedly that Luke emphasizes repentance and *reform* in his Gospel, and the same theme is prominent in Acts. Matthew has a lot of material stressing perfection of way: virtually all of the Sermon on the Mount (see e.g. 5.20), ch. 23 (e.g. 23.3), and his collection of material about church order and individual behaviour (18.1–22). Paul repeatedly urged his converts to be blameless and to act correctly: Rom. 6.2; I Cor. 6.9–11; Gal. 5.16–24; I Thess. 3.13; 5.23; I Cor. 1.8; Phil. 2.15f.

Thus we can know what the early church made of Jesus' call to sinners: the former sinners should behave uprightly, in fact their behaviour should exceed the normal requirements of Judaism. Did Jesus think the same? There is no good evidence, once we attribute most of the Sermon on the Mount to Matthew or a pre-Matthaean author or editor.[5] It is possible that Jesus imposed a higher righteousness on those who accepted him, though without requiring them to observe the machinery of righteousness according to the law. It seems somewhat more likely that, in view of the eschaton, he simply did not deal in detail with their behaviour, and thus could truly be criticized for including the wicked in his 'kingdom'. I consider this 'probable'.

What survived after Jesus' death and resurrection was a movement which followed more-or-less traditional Jewish expectations about the end. The end was at hand, or was in the process of being realized, and it was time to turn to the Lord and his law. It was therefore also time to start admitting Gentiles – on some conditions or other. The most distinctive aspect of Jesus' own message – the admission of sinners without requiring formal restoration of status within the covenant – seems to have been dropped. We must assume that the church in Jerusalem, apparently dominated by James and influenced by people whom Paul called 'false brethren' (Gal. 2.4), was no more enthusiastic about counting among its membership the wicked of Israel than it was about admitting Gentiles while they were still 'sinners', that is, non-observers of the law. We must also recall, however, that what we know most securely about Jesus are precisely those facts which fit him most comfortably into the category of a prophet of Jewish restoration: his start under John, his call of the twelve, his expectation that the temple would be destroyed and rebuilt (or at least renewed). *Thus most of the securely attested facts about Jesus' career also agree closely with what happened afterwards, and what endured from his work is what his message had in common with Jewish restoration eschatology: the expectation that Israel would be restored.* The inclusion of Gentiles is a natural consequence of Jewish restoration, and this also may have been prepared for by Jesus (if Matt. 8.11 is authentic and originally referred to Gentiles). Jesus was survived by an 'orthodox' Jewish messianic movement, one which expected an imminent end; one which was scrupulous about the law; and one which was pushed towards another stance on the law only by the pressures of the Gentile mission and the efforts of a few creative and remarkable apostles and other leaders (Paul, the Hellenists, the founders of the church at Antioch). The early church was not just a continuation of Jesus' own work. It lacked 'fellowship' with sinners. It appears that at least this one important nuance of Jesus' message, and a point at which he went beyond John the Baptist, was taken over only in a modified form: they should repent and adapt their lives to the requirements of the law. This provision, however, was seldom successfully enforced on Gentile converts, and it was one form of the Gentile mission which finally separated the Christian movement from the law.

The positive relationship between Jesus and the movement which succeeded him can be clearly seen if one examines Bultmann's admirable list of eight points which show that the early Christian movement considered itself 'the Congregation of the end of days'.[6] The list omits the admission of the Gentiles, which I regard as one of the most important facts, but is otherwise convincing. He points to such features as the 'twelve', the communal eschatological meal, and the mission to Israel. I would put these features of the early movement back into the lifetime of Jesus. They constitute the historical connection between Jesus and the movement which succeeded him, and these points of connection are also some of the surest things which we know about him.

Jesus doubtless thought and stood for things which we cannot attribute to him with certainty. The reader may well be surprised that I have said so little about two important topics: titles and how Jesus thought of his death, once it became apparent to him that he would be executed. I have proposed as a strong inference that Jesus thought of himself as 'king' (whether or not he directly used the title), but beyond that everything gets murky. Did he identify himself with the suffering servant?[7] Did he ever call himself 'Messiah'? What are we to make of the enigmatic Son of man?[8] I have no answers for any of these questions. I think that the Last Supper scene indicates that Jesus did not despair of thinking, even when he saw that he was to die, that the kingdom which he had expected would come. He would drink with his followers from the fruit of the vine (Mark 14.25 and parr.). The Christian interpretation of Jesus' death as atoning was so immediate and thorough that one could argue that even here Jesus prepared his followers. On the other hand, the idea that a martyr's death is beneficial for others and that his cause will be vindicated is attested in Judaism and is an obvious explanatory device.[9] It is not necessary to assume that Jesus indicated to his followers that they should think in this way. Once he died, it probably seemed entirely natural to attribute benefit to his death and to look for vindication. We shall return, however, to the question of Jesus' view of his own death.

The things which we do not know should not keep us from seeing and appreciating what we do know. We do know that Jesus gave the lead to his followers – whether directly or only implicitly – to think of him as singled out by God for a special task, in fact for *the most* special task. He may have given himself no title at all, but titles are surely less important than the substantive realities to which they point.

There are numerous other things which Jesus may have thought, though now we can call them only 'possible' or 'conceivable'. One sees this especially in the survey of meanings of the word 'kingdom'. We cannot definitively deny any of the basic usages to Jesus. He may well have thought that the kingdom would be heralded by the appearance of the Son of man on clouds, accompanied by angels; that the individuals who heeded him were being admitted one by one to the kingdom; that the kingdom was present in his words and deeds. Scholars who attribute one or more of these views to Jesus can be criticized only if they elevate to the principal role a point which is not much better than 'possible'. This often happens inadvertently. Someone will start pursuing a point and end by writing a book about it, without ever referring it back to the more secure general outline of Jesus' career.

We see this not only when we look at books about 'kingdom', but also when we consider 'Jesus and the law'. Here the great *fact* is that Jesus' followers did not know that he had directly opposed the law, and in particular they did not know him to have opposed the laws governing *Sabbath, food and purity*. Sabbath and food, which are prominent in the Gospels, are two of the three issues which figure in Paul's letters. In Rom. 14, for example, we see clearly that neither the Roman Christians nor Paul had a tradition from Jesus which clarified the proper stance towards the law on these points. Thus we learn a negative with virtually complete certainty: Jesus did not explicitly oppose these parts of the law, nor did he 'abrogate' the law in general. No study of the synoptic conflict pericopes can ever establish their 'authenticity' if that is taken to involve 'proving' Jesus' explicit opposition to the law. The great fact of Christian behaviour proves otherwise. Opposition to Sabbath, food and purity do not belong to the bedrock of the tradition.

I have several times given various lists of things that are certain and those which are less so. A final list entails repetition, but it may nevertheless be helpful.

I. Certain or virtually certain:

1. Jesus shared the world-view that I have called 'Jewish restoration eschatology'. The key facts are his start under John the Baptist, the call of the twelve, his expectation of a new (or at least renewed) temple, and the eschatological setting of the work of the apostles (Gal. 1.2; Rom. 11.11–13, 25–32; 15.15–19).

2. He preached the kingdom of God.

3. He promised the kingdom to the wicked.

4. He did not explicitly oppose the law, particularly not laws relating to Sabbath and food.

5. Neither he nor his disciples thought that the kingdom would be established by force of arms. They looked for an eschatological miracle.

II. Highly probable:

1. The kingdom which he expected would have some analogies with this world: leaders, the twelve tribes, a functioning temple.

2. Jesus' disciples thought of him as 'king', and he accepted the role, either implicitly or explicitly.

III. Probable:

1. He thought that the wicked who accepted his message would share in the kingdom even though they did not do the things customary in Judaism for the atonement of sin.

2. He did not emphasize the national character of the kingdom, including judgment by groups and a call for mass repentance, because that had been the task of John the Baptist, whose work he accepted.

3. Jesus spoke about the kingdom in different contexts, and he did not always use the word with precisely the same meaning.

IV. Possible:

1. He may have spoken about the kingdom in the visionary manner of the 'little apocalypse' (Mark 13 and parr.), or as a present reality into which individuals enter one by one – or both.

V. Conceivable:

1. He may have thought that the kingdom, in all its power and might, was present in his words and deeds.

2. He may have given his own death martyrological significance.

3. He may have identified himself with a cosmic Son of man and conceived his attaining kingship in that way.

VI. Incredible:

1. He was one of the rare Jews of his day who believed in love, mercy, grace, repentance and the forgiveness of sin.

2. Jews in general, and Pharisees in particular, would kill people who believed in such things.

3. As a result of his work, Jewish confidence in election was 'shaken to pieces', Judaism was 'shaken to its foundations', and Judaism as a religion was destroyed.[10]

Meaning

Some readers will justly wonder how the Jesus who has been described here is relevant to Christian faith and practice. That is a theological problem into which I am not going to venture, at least not here. If my portrayal of Jesus be found convincing, there will be plenty of time to sort out its meaning for contemporary Christianity. Christianity has received a lot of blows in its history – the worst one was that the end did not come in the first generation – and has survived. The discovery that Jesus was a visionary who was mistaken about the immediately future course of events has been made before.[11] One immediately thinks of Albert Schweitzer's Jesus.

Mine differs from his. His Jesus was principally the one of Matt. 10: he expected the end, the end would be a cosmic cataclysm, and suffering must precede it. Schweitzer reasoned like a historian: there must be something which explains the sequence of events. His portrait of Jesus did that in a way that New Testament scholarship has been reluctant to admit.

I think that mine does too. The description offered here has an additional advantage: it is based on an analysis of the evidence which can be separated from the theory that there must be a connecting link from one event to another. Both proposals, however, raise the question of what Jesus really *meant*; and it will be helpful, in evaluating the view advanced here, to recall the objections to Schweitzer and to compare our procedures.

Schweitzer was argued against principally in two ways: exegesis and true meaning. Dodd examined the sayings material, particularly the verbs 'is near' and 'has come' (Mark 1.15; Matt. 12.28), and concluded that Jesus had never actually said 'the kingdom is an imminent future reality', but had said that 'the kingdom is here'.[12] Thus he took 'realized eschatology' to be bedrock. Dodd had a second line of attack. He granted that Jesus spoke in the terms of apocalyptic eschatology, but proposed that he had not really meant that one age would succeed another, but rather employed the language to describe a higher reality: the language sounds temporal and horizontal, but in fact it must be understood as spiritual and vertical.[13]

Bultmann held that Jesus had said and thought that the kingdom would come as a future event, but that the words have another, 'true' meaning: the kingdom is *always* future and *always* determines the present.[14] He accepted Schweitzer's Jesus, but proposed for him a different significance and meaning.

How would the present proposal fare were it to be attacked in these two ways? To respond to this, I shall have to lay out Schweitzer's proposal.

He began with the assumption that there was a well-formulated and universally held system of Jewish eschatology, one which included, among other things, a cosmic Son of man and the requirement of sufferings before the end.[15] He attributed to Jesus this eschatological dogma (p. 350), and then showed that the dogma makes sense of a series of passages:

1. The parables about sowing and harvesting: the end will come at harvest time; John the Baptist sowed the seed which grows of itself (pp. 355–7).

2. The Mission Charge in Matthew 10: the passage is entirely authentic and must go at this spot chronologically. It shows that Jesus sent out the twelve expecting them to suffer, and that he expected the Son of man to come before they completed going to all the cities of Israel (pp. 358–64).

3. The Return of the Disciples and Jesus' decision to escape the crowds (Mark 6.30f., 45): Jesus' expectation was not fulfilled, and he withdrew, apparently to consider his next move (p. 364).

4. The Predictions of the Passion (Mark 8.31–33 and elsewhere): Jesus decided to suffer himself and thus force the eschaton (pp. 370, 387–9).

5. The Transfiguration (Mark 9.2–8): Jesus' identity as Son of man and Messiah was revealed to the three leading disciples (pp. 382–6).

6. The Confession at Caesarea Philippi (Mark 8.27–30): the secret is revealed to the other disciples (pp. 386f.).

7. The Betrayal (Mark 14.10f.): Judas reveals the secret of Jesus' self-claim to the chief priests (pp. 393, 396).

8. The High Priest's Question (Mark 14.61): the high priest was in possession of the secret, and this led to Jesus' condemnation (p. 397).

As has been clear throughout this work, I think that Schweitzer was right to look for an 'inner connection' which ties Jesus' activity to his death and links his own expectation to that of his followers. Further, it is entirely reasonable to seek the inner connection in Jewish eschatology. The particular eschatology which Schweitzer posited did not, we now know, exist as a set system, and perhaps not at all.[16] But here I wish principally to remark on the pillar passages in Schweitzer's theory. Few of them have much to be said on their behalf apart from the eschatological dogma which Schweitzer thought up. The predictions of the suffering of the disciples and of Jesus' own martyrdom are usually, and I think correctly, taken as 'prophecies' after the events. The Confession at Caesarea Philippi is often doubted on the same ground. Doubts about the historicity of the trial, and especially about the high priest's question, were outlined in ch. 11. In short, the passages which are foundational in Schweitzer's theory are, apart from the theory, dubious. It has generally appeared to scholars, as it does to me, that Schweitzer's theory was imposed on the texts and does not arise from them naturally.

I think that the same objections cannot be brought against my view. The foundational passages are not subject to the same degree of doubt, and the essential ones are indisputable. It is really true, for example, that Jesus was executed by the Romans and that the disciples were not, either then or for the next thirty years or so. From this the conclusion seems inescapable that *no one* thought of Jesus as an insurgent. A comparison of Jesus' followers – their number and lack of armour – with the temple and its guards, let alone the Roman troops, would show immediately that Jesus and his group could not take the temple, and certainly not destroy it so that not one stone was left on another. There were thousands of guards, a vast number of priests and Levites, and the stones are enormous. One has been calculated to weigh 80 tons. *No one* could think that the wandering charismatic posed an actual threat to the Jewish government (centred around the high priest), and certainly not to the Roman Empire.[17] *Yet* Jesus talked about a kingdom. *It must then follow* that he talked about another kind of kingdom, not one that depended on force of arms.

Up to this point, I think, everyone must agree. This is the sort of *general* characterization of Jesus which I regard as *certain*. Hereafter disagreements can start. Some will insist that Jesus looked for an inner, spiritual kingdom existing within the normal world, entered by individuals who undertake to live by the Golden Rule. Others will still prefer Schweitzer's cosmic cataclysm. And so forth. It is impossible, however, to suppose that he did not really mean 'kingdom' when he used the term. If he meant it only symbolically (it represents the call to submit oneself to God), then we would have to conclude that he completely deceived his disciples, who continued to expect a kingdom. The view that Jesus was entirely deceptive and misled his disciples into false hopes, while spinning parables which can be unravelled only by twentieth-century literary analysis, must be rejected.

The general framework of Jesus' career, restoration eschatology, also rests on more or less undisputed facts. Virtually no one now doubts that Jesus got his start under John the Baptist, and Paul's letters prove that the movement which succeeded him was carrying out the work suitable to the eschatological period: first the winning of Israel, and then of the Gentiles (to the Jew first, and also to the Greek: Rom. 1.16 and elsewhere; the scheme is reversed in Rom. 11, but that is Paul's own contribution). To pull Jesus entirely out of this framework would be an act of historical violence.

Jesus, of course, made his own particular contributions to Jewish restoration eschatology. I have repeatedly discussed these, and I classify none of them as more than 'highly probable'. Here, too, debate can be joined.

Thus I propose that the fundamental elements of my portrayal, unlike Schweitzer's, can stand entirely on their own, apart from my *particular* reconstruction. Once seen as established, they point *inescapably* to the description of Jesus as connected with hope for the restoration of Israel. This general depiction is not imposed on the texts, but arises naturally from them.

What can be challenged, of course, is the meaning. One can grant that Jesus said the things which I propose he said, that he did the things which I propose he did, and that the early Christians held the views which I have attributed to them, but still deny that the overall portrait is true. This will be done – in fact has already been done – by arguing that the words, deeds and other facts do not mean what I propose. They are not to be taken, as I have taken them, at face value. Rather, they mean something else. Perhaps in the temple scene Jesus meant to offer a symbol in favour of a non-sacrificial and purely inward worship of God;[18] perhaps the prediction of the destruction of the temple was only a figurative way of saying that the old religion would be destroyed and would be succeeded by 'a new way of religion and a new community to embody it'.[19] Perhaps in going to the sinners he meant that even the most desolate and lost human souls could make peace with God if they realized that they had no merit but must accept grace as a gift.[20] Perhaps he prohibited divorce to show the folly of striving to achieve the law,[21] or perhaps the requirement is only a cipher for the absoluteness of God's claim.[22] Perhaps, in short, Jesus intended to establish modern liberal Protestantism.

It is amazing that so many New Testament scholars write books about Jesus in which they discover that he agrees with their own version of Christianity. After Schweitzer's devastating exposé of previous scholarship on just this point, one would think that people would be more sensitive to the issue. But it is seldom raised. We can best get at it by considering the view, to which I have several times referred, that Jesus died 'for the truth of the gospel'.

The 'gospel' for which he died varies from author to author. We can distinguish broad major groups. A large number think that he died because he believed that God mercifully saves sinners. Jesus believed in grace, he opposed the Pharisees for being legalistic and believing in merit and supererogation, and this conflict was a major cause of his execution.[23]

Some find 'the gospel' in another part of the faith formula of Rom. 3.21–26: he died as a sacrifice 'for many', in the belief that life comes only through suffering and death.[24]

A third group have Jesus die for his own christology, either because of his claim to special status (e.g. Messiah), or more generally because he set himself at least by implication above Moses, or because he saw himself as the Suffering Servant.[25]

Many have held, in short, that he died for the Doctrine of Justification by Grace alone without Works of Law, or for the Doctrine of the Atonement, or for some form of a Doctrine of the Person of Christ. It is possible to combine some or all of these variants of 'the gospel'. Jeremias, for example, proposed all three,[26] while Dodd favoured the second and third.[27]

Of these lines, the first should be simply dismissed. I spent appreciable space criticizing the view that Jesus was killed because he believed in grace. That one is manufactured out of whole cloth, but it seems to be the most common. It seems to arise from the following sequence: first Christianity is defined as consisting of a set of religious abstractions (rather than as a community with its own history or as one which is faithful to credal formulations); then those abstractions are denied to its parent; then this supposed theological disagreement is retrojected into the life of Jesus and made the pivot on which the story turns.[28] The view that Jesus died for grace thus ends with sheer invention about what would constitute an issue in first-century Judaism. It is, therefore, not surprising that Käsemann can combine it with the view that Jesus opposed the entirety of the ancient world-view.[29] This line is basically opposed to seeing Jesus as a first-century Jew, who thought like others, spoke their language, was concerned about things which concerned them, and got into trouble over first-century issues.[30] It is thus bad history. Though I am no theologian I suspect that it is bad theology.

The second view, that Jesus *intended* by his death to accomplish his mission, raises as a preliminary question what he thought of his death once he knew that it was inevitable. Here I regard one of the answers as 'conceivable', and perhaps it should be moved up to 'possible'. That is the view that Jesus, when he knew that he was going to die, saw his death as that of a martyr who would be vindicated. The question is, to put it mildly, complicated; and I can best refer the reader to two admirable treatments by C. K. Barrett, who has, I think, done the best job possible in sorting most of it out.[31] My own trial runs at re-examining the evidence do not encourage me to think that publishing them will bring any improvement in understanding. More briefly, I can embrace Moule's view: 'Such evidence as we have suggests that Jesus . . . did not seek death; he did not go up to Jerusalem *in order* to die; but he did pursue, with inflexible devotion, a way of truth that inevitably led him to death, and he did not seek to escape.'[32] One may add the natural conclusion that he saw himself as dying in a good cause, as the agent of God, and thus thought that God would save the cause. Mark 14.25 (he would drink the wine again in the kingdom) may show that he thought that God would restore him at the time of the kingdom, which is a reasonable view for one who believes in bodily resurrection. It could also mean, however, that even that late he hoped for the divine intervention which would establish the kingdom before he died.

Some wish to press further and propose that Jesus intended to die, either because of the general theological principle that life requires death;[33] or because he saw death imposed upon him by the love of God 'which seeks out the sinner', though without defining to himself how that love would use his death;[34] or, most fully, because he conceived in advance the doctrine of the atonement.[35] In its fullest form, that of Jeremias, this last variant of the view requires the conflation of an extraordinary number of passages, the most prominent being the Predictions of the Passion, Mark 10.45 (to give his life as a ransom for many), and Mark 14.24 ('poured out for many').[36] Aspects of Jeremias's view, for example that Jesus identified himself with the Suffering Servant of Isaiah, have been disproved,[37] but there are general objections to the whole line of thought that has Jesus *intending to die for others*, rather than just accepting his death and trusting that God would redeem the situation and vindicate him.

The first and most obvious objection is that all the sayings which attribute to Jesus the will to die correspond so closely with what happened, and with early Christian doctrine, that the case for their creation by the early church is overwhelmingly strong. The criterion of dissimilarity is by no means infallible, but here it must come into play. One might as well attribute to Jesus the doctrine of the Trinity or of the Incarnation.

Further, a historian must be uncomfortable with an explanation which leaves other actors in the drama out of account. When pushed to its limit, this view means that Jesus determined in his own mind to be killed and to have his death understood as sacrificial for others, and it must then imply that he pulled this off by provoking the authorities.[38] It is not historically impossible that Jesus was weird, and I realize that my own interpretation of his views may make twentieth-century people look at him askance. But the view that he plotted his own redemptive death makes him strange in any century and thrusts the entire drama into his peculiar inner psyche.[39] The other things that we know about him make him a *reasonable* first-century visionary. We should be guided by them.

The third view, that Jesus died for his self-claim, is a serious historical possibility. I regard it, in fact, as true in part. There is abundant evidence pointing to self-assertion, which was probably considered by others to be egoism and impiety. These words show why this view can respond to the interests of a historian: it attributes to Jesus a view which would be offensive to others.[40] The first two do not. The first position simply has him espouse things as controversial as motherhood, while the second attributes to him a theology which others would find incomprehensible, but destructive of nothing but himself.

But self-claim, to repeat, is different. It places him in the now familiar world also inhabited by Judas, Theudas and the Egyptian. The last two, to be sure, followed him chronologically, but they show that leaders who favoured God, the poor and Israel could arise and that they would be killed. They were not killed *simply* for their self-claim, simply for saying 'I know a secret about God and I accept followers even though they may not be scrupulous about the law, provided only that they are sufficiently loyal to me.' They had to *do* something to be killed, but so did Jesus. Self-claim is, however, a factor in Jesus' death, although we cannot be absolutely sure that the self-claim was explicit. It was at least implicit.

Thus scholars who propose that Jesus died for the truth of 'the gospel', or to establish their version of Christianity, may or may not be on the right track. Christianity, in assigning Jesus a high role, was apparently being true to him. As long as we stay just with this point, and do not press towards further christological development (atoning death) or the religious abstractions of Reformation rhetoric (justification by faith), we are on safe historical ground.

The relationships between history and theology are very complex, and I shall make no poor effort to delve into a vast and difficult subject here. I have been engaged for some years in the effort to free history and exegesis from the control of theology; that is, from being obligated to come to certain conclusions which are pre-determined by theological commitment, and one sees this effort being continued here. This is a very simple task, but I regard it as essential for a more complex enterprise. I aim to be only a historian and an exegete. But, since I have criticized so many for having their 'history' and 'exegesis' dictated by theology, the reader may well wonder how well 'my' Jesus squares with my theological heritage. I can explain simply: I am a liberal, modern, secularized Protestant, brought up in a church dominated by low christology and the social gospel. I am proud of the things that that religious tradition stands for. I am not bold enough, however, to suppose that Jesus came to establish it, or that he died for the sake of its principles.

The connecting link

There is one vital point, however, at which the results of this study correspond to my own expectations. We went in search of a thread which connects Jesus' own intention, his death and the rise of the movement. We found first a general context which embraces both Jesus and the movement which succeeded him: hope for the restoration of Israel. Second, we found a specific chain of conceptions and events which allows us to understand historically how things came about. Jesus claimed that the end was at hand, that God was about to establish his kingdom, that those who responded to him would be included, and (at least by implication) that he would reign. In pointing to the change of eras, he made a symbolic gesture by overturning tables in the temple area. This is the crucial act which led to his execution, though there were contributing causes. His disciples, after the death and resurrection, *continued* to expect the restoration of Israel and the inauguration of the new age, and they *continued* to see Jesus as occupying first place in the kingdom. Also, as we saw in ch. 8, they *continued* to look for an otherworldly kingdom which would be established by an eschatological miracle, although its locale may have shifted from this world to the heavenly one. The person of Jesus himself was also progressively interpreted: he was no longer seen just as 'Messiah' or 'Viceroy', but as Lord. Some who were attracted to the movement began to win Gentiles to it. The work of the early apostles, which is so well reflected in Paul's letters, fits entirely into known expectations about the restoration of Israel.

Thus I think that the connecting links are really there. Further, they seem so obvious that it is hard to understand why so many have thought that there is no causal chain from Jesus' own view of his mission and the kingdom to his death and then to the church. I must realize, however, that there is a strong tradition of denying causal connections and that some will think that it is I who have spun the thread which stitches together the pieces. Historians should be self-suspecting. I have tried to be so, but I cannot see that there is any other construction which can be given to the most obvious facts about Jesus, his career and the events which immediately followed it.

The setting in Judaism: the New Testament and Jewish restoration eschatology

We have also situated Jesus believably in first-century Judaism. Many who have made this effort have accomplished the task by creating strange myths about Judaism. Some of these myths are supported by quoting passages from the New Testament itself. It is now often said that we must read the New Testament as a source for first-century Judaism, and that is true;[41] but we must exercise the normal caution of historians.

I shall return to statements in the New Testament which should not be taken as evidence for first-century Judaism, but first I shall dwell on 'Jewish restoration eschatology', which is evidenced both from the New Testament and from non-Christian Jewish literature. A review of chs. 1–3 will show that the same main themes – the redemption of Israel (whether politically or in a new world), a new or renewed temple, repentance, judgment, admission of the Gentiles – crop up in numerous places in Jewish literature and in the New Testament. All the main themes do not always appear together. When some are absent they may be presupposed or implied, they may be denied explicitly or implicitly, or they may have been displaced by something else. In Paul, for example, we see first and foremost the admission of the Gentiles (all his extant letters except Philemon) and the interconnection between Jewish salvation and Gentile salvation (Rom. 11). Repentance plays a small role, because (I think) it has been displaced by death to sin. The theme of the new temple, as in 1QS, has been transformed and the language transferred to the people of God. It is noteworthy that this happens in two groups which are cut off from the actual temple. The presence of the main elements of Jewish restoration eschatology in the Gospels has been the subject of most of the book.

Thus the existence of 'Jewish restoration eschatology' is supported by the New Testament, and Jesus fits believably into that world-view.

The hope for restoration presupposes God's loyalty to the covenant with Israel and, in most of the expressions of it which are still available, the expectation that Israel would show its loyalty to God by obeying his law. That is, the theology includes what I have elsewhere called 'covenantal nomism',[42] but extends to embrace a further element: restoration. These three component parts are found very widely in Jewish literature: chronologically from Ben Sira to the Rabbinic material (where, however, future expectation is expressed relatively seldom, though it is prominent in the liturgy), and geographically from Alexandria around the Mediterranean to Asia Minor. We may again refer most readily to Paul. He reflects the common view that God is faithful to his covenant promises in Rom. 9.4; 11.29; the hope for the redemption of Israel is implied throughout Rom. 11 in particular and is precisely enunciated in 11.26. Despite his polemic against the law (rather, against the imposition of parts of it on the Gentiles), we see the common expectation that loyalty to God includes obeying his law: Gal. 5.14; I Cor. 7.19; Rom. 13.8–10. The common expectation that Jews obey the law is clear in Rom. 9.30–10.3. In none of this do I intend to discuss Paul's particular views and characteristic theology, but only the reflection of common opinion.

We can likewise see that Jesus accepted 'covenantal nomism'. His mission was to Israel in the name of the God of Israel. He thus evidently accepted his people's special status, that is, the election and the covenant. I think that it is equally clear that he accepted obedience to the law as the norm. He did not stress or dwell on the 'nomism' part of the scheme. He was not a legal teacher, discussing how to obey the law, how to know when one has satisfactorily obeyed it, and the like. The one law which he discussed concretely is the divorce code, which he short-cut by prohibiting divorce. I doubt the reported debates about the fine points of Sabbath observance. But if he did engage in such debates, it simply proves the present case. To debate details of Sabbath observance presupposes a general acceptance of the law. The final proof that he accepted the law is the fact that there is only one instance in which following him required transgression of it (Matt. 8.21f. and par.). If he had truly opposed the law, we would know it from the history of early Christianity. His eschatological expectation did lead him to think that the Mosaic law was neither absolute nor final. In the new age which was about to dawn, God would go beyond the law: he would admit the wicked. But, in general, it appears that Jesus lived a life of normal obedience.

I continue to regard 'covenantal nomism' as the common denominator which underlay all sorts and varieties of Judaism. Few spent their time proclaiming those two points as a system. Some were principally engaged in discussing the hows and whys of obedience – while praying in the synagogues for God to honour his covenantal promises. Some spent their lives piously conducting the work necessary for sacrifices – sacrifices which are required in the law and which were regarded as a necessary part of Israel's responsibility under the covenant.[43] Some fixed on God's promises and wrote and talked about how they would be kept – that is, they looked for the redemption of Israel. Jesus fits here. Since he did not spend his time discussing the covenant *historically* (why God chose Israel, why he brought them out of Egypt, and the like), nor discussing the fine points of obedience, but rather preparing his followers and hearers for the coming redemption, I have managed to write virtually an entire book without the phrase 'covenantal nomism'. Now at last it comes in, but only to show in one more way that Jesus fits into his milieu.

I now return to the ways in which the New Testament should not be used in describing the Judaism of Jesus' day. Many passages in the New Testament, followed by many New Testament scholars, make it appear that Jesus fits into his context by contrast rather than by agreement: he is to be understood as the antithesis of Judaism, or of its supposedly dominant form, Pharisaism. I recall from ch. 10 the statements to the effect that Jesus 'destroyed Pharisaism', 'put an end to Judaism', or 'shattered the law'. To the slight degree that these are intended as historical statements, they could only mean that he was *opposed to* Pharisaism, Judaism or the law. Our present task is not to appeal once more for realistic and scholarly evaluations, but to point out the character of the New Testament passages which are called in support of such views. They are polemical.

We must, to understand them, pay attention to the standard themes of polemic and what they mean. They ordinarily indicate disagreement and are not truly descriptive. I offer some examples.

1. Paul says that Peter acted hypocritically and did not preserve the truth of the gospel (Gal. 2.13f.). We should not allow this obviously polemical passage to persuade us that Peter was untrue to the gospel and hypocritical. Let us reverse the situation in Antioch. Let us suppose that Peter first would eat only with Jews and then, when Paul sent a message, changed and began to eat with Gentiles. Paul would not have called him a hypocrite, but would have applauded his aligning his behaviour with the gospel. James might then have called him a hypocrite for letting the side down and laying the movement open to the charge of not being upright. If he professed belief in the God of Israel, why not also believe in the importance of the separation of the elect? Why damage his credentials among Jews who might be won?

So, what was Peter really? He was a man torn between two commitments. We understand nothing about him by calling him a hypocrite. We learn something about him and the movement by seeing the conflict in which he was caught – and which also had Paul in its vice. It is Paul who enunciated the principle of living like a Jew to win Jews and living like a Gentile to win Gentiles (I Cor. 9.20f.). To criticize Peter because he could not do both simultaneously shows that he did not, in the heat of the moment, put himself in the shoes of the fisherman.

2. Along the same lines, we should suppose that the false brethren (Gal. 2.4) also acted on principle, that those who preached circumcision had motives other than escaping persecution (Gal. 6.12), and that nobody preached Christ while Paul was in prison simply to harass him (Phil. 1.15). Paul repeatedly attributes bad motives to others. He was engaged in polemic, and polemic usually involves questioning the other's hidden motives. It tells us nothing about what the intentions of the others were from their point of view. The historian must do the best he can to reconstruct them, and that should not involve credulously repeating polemic.

3. Two or three times I have referred to charges that the priests served in the temple when impure because of contact with menstrual blood. We find the charge in the Damascus Document and in the Psalms of Solomon, and it is reflected in Rabbinic literature.[44] What does it mean? If such a charge against the priests were attributed to Jesus, I do not doubt that many New Testament scholars would report it as a fact that the priests regularly had intercourse while their wives were menstruating. But the accusation must rest on disagreement with regard to legal interpretation. Obviously various pious groups wanted to extend the period during which a woman is considered impure. The priests followed biblical law. It is not the case that the pious who made the accusations had private knowledge about the priests' habits in their bedrooms.

I have just said that New Testament scholars are often credulous about statements in the New Testament. We have seen this in different contexts, including many which are not polemical. It is really true, some hold, that Jesus looked around sharply and that his bowels were moved with compassion.[45] Naturally the same credulity extends to polemics, and thus Matt. 23.23 can become a flat statement of fact which describes Pharisees: they were interested only in trivia and neglected matters of religious substance. Not surprisingly, polemical statements composed by redactors are taken as factual: it is really true that the parable of Luke 18.10–14 was told against 'some who trusted in themselves that they were righteous and despised others' (18.9), and thus we learn what Pharisees were like (Pharisees: 18.10).[46] Similarly many would have us believe that scribes and Pharisees really did grumble against Jesus for receiving sinners (Luke 15.1f.).[47] The Gospels also contain editorial remarks about the private motives which animated those who wanted Jesus executed: they wanted to entrap him (Mark 12.13); in his heart Jesus knew their hypocrisy (12.15). With regard to the editorial comments, many of which have to do with motive, it must be realized that the evangelists did not know and could not know. But none of these examples of polemic can be taken as descriptive.

What the historian should do in dealing with motive is to make reasonable assumptions. Motives are usually mixed. People in charge generally think that they are right and should be in charge. They want, of course, their own comfort and authority. But we should not assign to whole groups of people in the ancient world bad motives: The priests intended to oppress and rob the poor; they were usurpers of power; they were not truly devoted to serving God.[48] The Pharisees were motivated by belief in merit and despite of others; they sought the chief place and praise from men; they were avaricious and vain. More reasonable assumptions are that the priests saw their work in the temple as true service of God[49] and that the Pharisees genuinely thought that they knew how to interpret the Scripture. Presumably they also all wanted to come out on top, and they would have taken reasonable action to ensure that.[50]

When we examine more closely the polemic against the Pharisees, we see that a lot of it has to do with motive. They do this or that 'in order to make a show'.[51] I do not think that Jesus said that, but whether he did or not, it tells us – and can in the nature of the case tell us – nothing about their actual motives.

The setting of Jesus' work within Judaism, therefore, is not to be understood as one of polar opposition between a man of good will and men of bad intent. It is not reasonable historical explanation to say that Jesus believed in a whole list of non-controversial and pleasant abstractions (love, mercy and grace) and that his opponents denied them. It is not reasonable to say that he sought the will of God and that they intended only to play with Scripture to turn it to their own advantage. Let us give them all equally good motives – remembering that motives are usually mixed – and then find a setting and reasonable cause of conflict.

We have, I think, done this. Jesus does not 'fit' into Judaism as its moral and spiritual antithesis (as some polemical passages have led some to think). There was, rather, a firm context of agreement, and within that context there was conflict. Many people were dissatisfied with the accommodation with Rome, and this dissatisfaction – doubtless mixed with other frustrations – led to what Theissen has aptly called 'renewal movements'.[52] These took various forms, and there is no single and unified 'type', but Jesus fits into this general context. He differed from others in ways that I have repeatedly emphasized, in part because, it seems, he relied on the work of his great predecessor, John the Baptist. John's proclamation of repentance in view of impending judgment was partly successful. Many repented, and hopes for the kingdom were aroused. But the kingdom did not come. Jesus pushed ahead by initiating the gospel that the wicked would be included in the kingdom, a message which was accompanied by healings and exorcisms. The great symbolic acts of his life show that he stayed within the general framework of Jewish restoration eschatology, though they also show his self-claim and his offence to normal Jewish piety: he called 'twelve' (with himself as their head); he dramatically pointed to the coming of a new or renewed temple; and perhaps he rode into Jerusalem on an ass. Finally, he symbolized the coming kingdom in a banquet shared with the 'twelve'.

He went to his death. His followers, by carrying through the logic of his own position in a transformed situation, created a movement which would grow and continue to alter in ways unforeseeable in Jesus' own time, but in progressive steps, each one explicable in its own historical context.

BIBLIOGRAPHY

1. TEXTS AND REFERENCE WORKS CITED OR QUOTED

Bauer, Walter, *A Greek-English Lexicon of the New Testament and other early Christian literature*, 2nd English ed. (revised and augmented by F. Wilbur Gingrich and Frederick W. Danker), Chicago 1979.

The Apocrypha and Pseudepigrapha of the Old Testament in English, 2 vols., ET (ed. R. H. Charles) Oxford 1913 (repr. 1963).
The Old Testament Pseudepigrapha I: Apocalyptic Literature and Testaments, ET (ed. James H. Charlesworth), New York 1983.
The Book of Enoch or I Enoch, translated from the editor's Ethiopic text, R. H. Charles, Oxford ²1912.

The Dead Sea Scrolls in English, ET Geza Vermes, Harmondsworth 1962.
Megillat ha-Miqdash, 3 vols. (ed. Yigael Yadin), Jerusalem 1977.
The Scroll of the War of the Sons of Light against the Sons of Darkness (ed. Yigael Yadin), ET, Oxford 1962.
Die Texte aus Qumran, Hebräisch und Deutsch (ed. Eduard Lohse), Darmstadt ²1971.
The Zadokite Documents (ed. Chaim Rabin), Oxford 1958.

Sishah Sidre Mishnah (*The Six Orders of the Mishnah*) (ed. Chanoch Albeck), 6 vols., Jerusalem and Tel Aviv 1958–1959.
The Mishnah, ET Herbert Danby, Oxford 1933.

Josephus (trans. and ed. by H. St J. Thackeray [vols. 1–5], Ralph Marcus [vols. 5–8] and Louis Feldman [vols. 9 and 10]), the Loeb Classical Library, London and Cambridge, Mass. 1926–1965.
Philo (trans. and ed. by F. H. Colson [vols. 1–10] and G. H. Whitaker [vols. 1–5]), 10 vols., The Loeb Classical Library, London and Cambridge, Mass. 1929–43.

2. GENERAL

Abrahams, I., *Studies in Pharisaism and the Gospel*, First and Second Series, Cambridge 1917, 1924 (repr. New York 1967).

Alon, Gedalyahu, *Jews, Judaism and the Classical World*, ET Jerusalem 1977.

Aulén, G., *Jesus in Contemporary Historical Research*, ET London and Philadelphia 1976.

Avigad, Nahman, *Discovering Jerusalem*, New York 1983.

Bailey, J. A., *The Traditions Common to the Gospels of Luke and John*, NovT Suppl 7, Leiden 1963.

Bammel, Ernst, 'Erwägungen zur Eschatologie Jesu', *Studia Evangelica* 3, part II (ed. F. L. Cross), TU 88, Berlin 1964, pp. 3–32.

— ' "John Did No Miracle" ', *Miracles, Cambridge Studies in their Philosophy and History* (ed. C. F. D. Moule), London 1965, pp. 181–202.

— ed., *The Trial of Jesus: Cambridge Studies in Honour of C. F. D. Moule*, SBT II 13, London and Nashville 1970.

Banks, Robert, *Jesus and the Law in the Synoptic Tradition*, SNTSMS 28, Cambridge 1975.

Barbour, R. S., *Traditio-Historical Criticism of the Gospels*, Studies in Creative Criticism 4, London 1972.

Barnett, P. W., 'The Jewish Sign Prophets—A.D. 40–70—Their Intentions and Origin', *NTS* 27, 1981, pp. 679–97.

Barrett, C. K., 'The Background of Mark 10:45', *New Testament Essays, Studies in Memory of Thomas Walter Manson* (ed. A. J. B. Higgins), Manchester 1959, pp. 1–18.

— 'Cephas and Corinth', *Essays on Paul*, London and Philadelphia 1982, pp. 28–39.

— *Jesus and the Gospel Tradition*, London 1967, Philadelphia 1968.

Bartsch, H. W., *Jesus. Prophet und Messias aus Galiläa*, Frankfurt, a.M. 1970.

Baumbach, Günther, *Jesus von Nazareth im Lichte der jüdischen Gruppenbildung*, Berlin 1971.

Baumgarten, A. I., 'The Name of the Pharisees', *JBL* 102, 1983, pp. 411–28.

Baumgarten, Joseph M., Review of Yigael Yadin, *The Temple Scroll*, *JBL* 97, 1978, pp. 584–89.

Beasley-Murray, G. R., *A Commentary on Mark Thirteen*, London and New York 1957.

— *Jesus and the Future*, London and New York 1954.

Behm, J., 'μετανοέω, μετάνοια in Hellenistic Jewish Literature', *TDNT* IV, pp. 989–95.

— 'Conversion in Rabbinic Literature', ibid., pp. 995–9.

— 'μετανοέω and μετάνοια in the New Testament', ibid., pp. 999–1006.

Beilner, W., *Christus und die Pharisäer*, Vienna 1959.

Berger, Klaus, *Die Gesetzesauslegung Jesu. Ihr historischer Hintergrund in Judentum und im Alten Testament*, Teil I: *Markus und Parallelen*, WMANT 40, Neukirchen 1972.

Betz, Otto, 'Das Problem des Wunders bei Flavius Josephus im Vergleich zum Wunderproblem bei den Rabbinen und im Johannesevangelium', *Josephus-Studien. Untersuchungen zu Josephus, dem antiken Judentum und dem Neuen Testament. Festschrift Otto Michel* (ed. Otto Betz, Klaus Haacker and Martin Hengel), Göttingen 1974, pp. 22–44.

— *What Do We Know about Jesus?*, ET London and Philadelphia 1968.

Bickerman, Elias, *Studies in Jewish and Christian History* II, AGAJU 9, Leiden 1980.

Blinzler, Josef, *The Trial of Jesus*. ET of 2nd Edition, Westminster, Maryland 1959.

Boismard, M.-É., *Synopse des quatre Évangiles en Français* II, *Commentaire*, Paris 1972.

Bokser, Ben Zion, 'Jesus: Jew or Christian', *Jewish Expressions on Jesus* (ed. Trude Weiss-Rosmarin), New York 1977, pp. 201–29 (repr. from *Judaism and the Christian Predicament*, New York 1967).

Boring, M. Eugene, *Sayings of the Risen Jesus*, SNTSMS 46, Cambridge 1982.

Bornkamm, G., *Jesus of Nazareth*, ET London and New York 1960.

Bosch, David, *Die Heidenmission in der Zukunftsschau Jesu*, ATANT 36, Zürich 1959.

Bousset, W., *Die Religion des Judentums im späthellenistischen Zeitalter* (ed. H. Gressmann), HNT 21, Tübingen ³1926 (repr. 1966).

— *Jesu Predigt in ihrem Gegensatz zum Judentum*, Göttingen 1892.

— *Jesus*, ET (ed. W. D. Morrison) London and New York ²1911.

— *Kyrios Christos* (1913), ET Nashville and New York 1970.

Bowker, J., *Jesus and the Pharisees*, Cambridge 1973.

Brandon, S. G. F., *Jesus and the Zealots*, Manchester 1967.

Braun, H., *Jesus of Nazareth: The Man and his Time*, ET Philadelphia 1979.

— *Spätjüdisch-häretischer und frühchristlicher Radikalismus*, 2 vols., Tübingen 1957.

Breech, James, *The Silence of Jesus. The Authentic Voice of the Historical Man*, Philadelphia 1983.

Brown, Raymond, *The Gospel according to John*, Vol. I, I–XII, The Anchor Bible 29, New York 1966, London 1971.

— *The Gospel according to John*, Vol. II, XIII–XXI, The Anchor Bible 29A, New York 1970, London 1971.

Büchler, Adolf, 'The Law of Purification in Mark vii. 1–23', *ExpT* 21, 1909–10, p. 40.

— *Das Synedrion in Jerusalem und das grosse Beth-Din in der Quaderkammer des jerusalemischen Tempels*, Vienna 1902.

Büchler, Adolf, *Studies in Sin and Atonement in the Rabbinic Literature of the First Century*, London 1928, reissued New York 1967.
— *Types of Jewish-Palestinian Piety from 70 BCE to 70 CE. The Ancient Pious Men*, London 1922, reissued New York 1968.
Buehler, William W., *The Pre-Herodian Civil War and Social Debate. Jewish Society in the Period 76–40 B.C. and the Social Factors Contributing to the Rise of the Pharisees and the Sadducees*, Basel 1974.
Bultmann, R., *Die Geschichte der synoptischen Tradition*, Göttingen ⁷1967. *Ergänzungsheft* (ed. Gerd Theissen and Philipp Vielhauer), Göttingen ⁴1971.
— *The History of the Synoptic Tradition*, ET Oxford and New York 1963.
— *Jesus and the Word* (1926), ET New York 1958.
— *Primitive Christianity in Its Contemporary Setting*, ET London and New York 1956.
— *Theology of the New Testament* I, ET New York and London 1954.
Butler, B. C., *The Originality of St Matthew*, Cambridge 1951.
Cadbury, Henry J., *The Peril of Modernizing Jesus*, New York 1937, reissued London 1962.
Caird, G. B., *Jesus and the Jewish Nation*, London 1965.
— *The Language and Imagery of the Bible*, London, 1980.
— *Saint Luke* (Pelican Gospel Commentaries), Harmondsworth 1963.
Calvert, D. G. A., 'An Examination of the Criteria for Distinguishing the Authentic Words of Jesus', *NTS* 18, 1971–72, pp. 209–19.
Carmignac, J., 'Qu'est-ce que l'apocalyptique? Son emploi à Qumrân', *RQ* 10, 1979, pp. 3–33.
Catchpole, David R., 'The Answer of Jesus to Caiaphas (Matt. xxvi. 64)', *NTS* 17, 1971, pp. 213–26.
— 'John the Baptist, Jesus and the Parable of the Tares', *SJT* 31, 1978, pp. 557–70.
— 'The Problem of the Historicity of the Sanhedrin Trial', *The Trial of Jesus* (ed. E. Bammel), SBT II 13, London and Nashville 1970, pp. 47–65.
— *The Trial of Jesus*, Leiden 1971.
— 'The "Triumphal" Entry', *Jesus and the Politics of His Day* (ed. Ernst Bammel and C. F. D. Moule), Cambridge 1984, pp. 319–34.
Charlesworth, James, H., 'The Historical Jesus in Light of Writings Contemporaneous with Him', *ANRW* II.25.1, Berlin 1982, pp. 451–76.
Chilton, Bruce D., *The Glory of Israel. The Theology and Provenance of the Isaiah Targum*, JSOT Suppl. 23, Sheffield 1983.
— *God in Strength. Jesus' Announcement of the Kingdom*, SNTU 1, Freistadt 1979.
Cohen, Shaye J. D., *Josephus in Galilee and Rome. His Vita and Development as a Historian*, Columbia Studies in the Classical Tradition VIII, Leiden 1979.
Collins, John J., ed., *Apocalypse: The Morphology of a Genre*, Missoula 1979.

Collins, John J., ed., *Between Athens and Jerusalem. Jewish Identity in the Hellenistic Diaspora*, New York 1983.

Conzelmann, H., 'Current Problems in Pauline Research', *Interpr* 22, 1968, pp. 171–86 (= *Der Evangelische Erzieher* 18, 1966, pp. 241–52).

— *Jesus*, ET (ed. J. Reumann), Philadelphia 1973.

— *An Outline of the Theology of the New Testament*, ET London and New York 1969.

— *The Theology of St Luke*, ET London and New York 1960.

Cook, Michael J., 'Jesus and the Pharisees—the problem as it stands today', *Journal of Ecumenical Studies* 15, 1978, pp. 441–60.

— *Mark's Treatment of the Jewish Leaders*, NovTSuppl 51, Leiden 1978.

Cope, O. Lamar, *Matthew: A Scribe Trained for the Kingdom of Heaven*, CBQMS 5, Washington, D.C. 1976.

Cranfield, C. E. B., 'Thoughts on New Testament Eschatology', *SJT* 35, 1982, pp. 497–512.

Crawford, Barry S., 'Near Expectation in the Sayings of Jesus', *JBL* 101, 1982, pp. 225–44.

Creed, J. M., *The Gospel According to St Luke*, London 1960.

Dahl, N. A., *The Crucified Messiah and Other Essays*, Minneapolis 1974.

Dalman, Gustaf, *The Words of Jesus*, ET Edinburgh 1902.

Davies, W. D., *The Gospel and the Land. Early Christianity and Jewish Territorial Doctrine*, Berkeley and Los Angeles 1974.

— 'Matthew 5:17, 18', *Christian Origins and Judaism*, Philadelphia and London 1962.

— *The Setting of the Sermon on the Mount*, Cambridge and New York 1964.

Derrett, J. D. M., 'The Zeal of thy House and the Cleansing of the Temple', *Downside Review* 95, 1977, pp. 79–94.

Dibelius M., *From Tradition to Gospel*, ET of 2nd ed., London 1934, New York 1935.

— *Jesus* (1939), ET Philadelphia 1949.

Dodd C. H., *According to the Scriptures*, London 1952, New York 1953.

— *The Founder of Christianity*, New York 1970, London 1971.

— *The Parables of the Kingdom* (1935), rev. ed. London and New York 1961.

Donohue, J. R., *Are You the Christ?*, Missoula 1973.

Downing, F. G., *The Church and Jesus*, SBT II 10, London and Nashville 1968.

Drane, J. W., *Paul: Libertine or Legalist? A Study of the Theology of the Major Pauline Epistles*, London 1975.

Dungan, David, *The Sayings of Jesus in the Churches of Paul: The Use of the Synoptic Tradition in the Regulation of Early Church Life*, Philadelphia and Oxford 1971.

Dunn, James, D. G., *Jesus and the Spirit*, London and Philadelphia 1975.

— *Unity and Diversity in the New Testament*, London and Philadelphia 1977.

Dupont-Sommer, A., *The Essene Writings from Qumran*, ET Oxford and New York 1961.

Easton, B. S., *Early Christianity: The Purpose of Acts and other Papers* (ed. Frederick C. Grant), New York 1954, London 1955.

Edelstein, E. J. L. and L., *Asclepius: A Collection and Interpretation of the Testimonies*, 2 vols., Baltimore 1945.

Edersheim, Alfred, *The Life and Times of Jesus the Messiah*, 2 vols., Grand Rapids 1936.

Ellis, E. Earle, 'Gospels Criticism. A Perspective on the State of the Art', *Das Evangelium und die Evangelien. Vorträge vom Tübinger Symposium 1982*, ed. Peter Stuhlmacher, WUNT 28, Tübingen 1983, pp. 27–54.

Enslin, Morton Scott, *Christian Beginnings*: Parts I and II, New York and London 1938, reissued Harper Torchbook 1956.

— 'John and Jesus', *ZNW* 66, 1975, pp. 1–18.

Falk, Ze'ev W., *Introduction to Jewish Law of the Second Commonwealth*, 2 vols., AGAJU 11, Leiden 1972, 1978.

Farmer, W. R., 'An Historical Essay in the Humanity of Jesus Christ', *Christian History and Interpretation: Studies Presented to John Knox* (ed. W. R. Farmer, C. F. D. Moule, and R. R. Niebuhr), Cambridge 1967, pp. 101–26.

— *Jesus and the Gospel*, Philadelphia ³1982.

Fiedler, Peter, *Jesus und die Sünder*, Frankfurt a.M. 1976.

Finkel, A., *The Pharisees and the Teacher of Nazareth*, Leiden 1964.

Finkelstein, L., *The Pharisees* II, Philadelphia ³1962.

Fitzmyer, Joseph, *The Gospel According to Luke, I–IX*, The Anchor Bible 28A, New York 1981.

Flender, H., *Die Botschaft Jesu von der Herrschaft Gottes*, Munich 1968.

Flusser, David, 'Two Notes on the Midrash on 2 Sam. vii', *IEJ* 9, 1959, pp. 99–109.

Fridrichsen, A., *Le Problème du Miracle*, Paris 1935.

Freyne, Sean, *Galilee from Alexander the Great to Hadrian: 323 B.C.E. to 135 C.E. A Study of Second Temple Judaism*, Notre Dame 1980.

Fuchs, E., 'Jesus and Faith' (1958), ET, *Studies of the Historical Jesus*, SBT 42, 1964, pp. 48–64.

— 'The Quest of the Historical Jesus' (1956), ibid., pp. 11–31.

Funk, Robert W., *Language, Hermeneutic, and Word of God*, New York and London 1966.

Gärtner, Bertil, *The Temple and the Community in Qumran and the New Testament*, SNTSMS 1, Cambridge 1965.

Garland, David E., *The Intention of Matthew 23*, NovTSuppl 52, Leiden 1979.

Gaston, Lloyd, *No Stone on Another. Studies in the Significance of the Fall of Jerusalem in the Synoptic Gospels*. NovTSuppl 23, Leiden 1970.

Geller, Markham J., 'Jesus' Theurgic Powers: Parallels in the Talmud and Incantation Bowls', *JJS* 28, 1977, pp. 141–55.

Gerhardsson, Birger, 'Der Weg der Evangelientradition', *Das Evangelium und die Evangelien. Vorträge vom Tübinger Symposium* 1982, ed. Peter Stuhlmacher, WUNT 28, Tübingen 1983, pp. 79–102.

— *Memory and Manuscript: Oral Tradition and Written Transmission in Rabbinic Judaism and Early Christianity*, ET, Acta Seminarii Neotestamentici Upsaliensis 22, Uppsala 1961, 1964.

— *The Origins of the Gospel Traditions*, ET Philadelphia 1979.

— Review of R. Riesner, *Jesus als Lehrer*, in *TLZ* 108, 1983, cols. 500–3.

— *Tradition and Transmission in Early Christianity*, Coniectanea Neotestamentica XX, Lund 1964.

Glasson, T. Francis, 'Schweitzer's Influence—Blessing or Bane?', *JTS* n.s. 28, 1977, pp. 289–302.

— 'What is Apocalyptic?', *NTS* 27, 1980, pp. 98–105.

Goguel, Maurice, *Jesus and the Origins of Christianity*, vol. I, *The Life of Jesus*, ET London and New York 1933, reissued 1960.

Goppelt, Leonhard, *Jesus, Paul and Judaism. An Introduction to New Testament Theology*, ET New York 1964.

Goulder, Michael, *Midrash and Lection in Matthew*, London 1974.

— 'On putting Q to the test', *NTS* 24, 1978, pp. 218–34.

Guignebert, Ch., *Jesus*, ET London and New York 1935.

Güttgemanns, Erhardt, *Candid Questions concerning Gospel Form Criticism. A Methodological Sketch of the Fundamental Problematics of Form and Redaction Criticism*, ET Pittsburgh 1979.

Hahn, Ferdinand, *Mission in the New Testament*, ET, SBT 47, London and Nashville 1965.

Harvey, A. E., *Jesus and the Constraints of History*, London and Philadelphia 1982.

— *Jesus on Trial. A Study in the Fourth Gospel*, London 1976.

Heinemann, Joseph, *Prayer in the Talmud. Forms and Patterns*, ET Berlin and New York 1977.

Helfgott, B. W., *The Doctrine of Election in Tannaitic Literature*, New York 1954, London 1955.

Hengel, Martin, *Nachfolge und Charisma, Eine exegetisch-religionsgeschichtliche Studie zu Mt. 8.21f. und Jesu Ruf in die Nachfolge*, BZNW 34, Berlin 1968; ET *The Charismatic Leader and His Followers*, Edinburgh 1981.

— Review of S. G. F. Brandon, *Jesus and the Zealots*, *JSS* 14, 1969, pp. 231–40.

— *Was Jesus a Revolutionist?*, ET Philadelphia 1971.

Hill, David, *New Testament Prophecy*, London and Atlanta, Ga., 1979.

Hirsch, Emil G., 'Sacrifice', *JE* 10, p. 615–28.

Hoheisel, K., *Das antike Judentum in christlicher Sicht*, Wiesbaden 1978.

Hooker, M. D., 'Christology and Methodology', *NTS* 17, 1970–71, pp. 480–87.

— 'On Using the Wrong Tool', *Theology* 75, 1972, pp. 570–81.

Hooker, M. D., *The Son of Man in Mark*, London and Montreal 1967.

Horbury, William, 'New Wine in Old Wine-Skins: IX. The Temple', *ExpT* 86, 1974–75, pp. 36–42.

— 'The Passion Narratives and Historical Criticism', *Theology* 75, 1972, pp. 58–71.

— Review of Geza Vermes's *Jesus the Jew*, *Theology* 77, 1974, pp. 227–32.

Huebsch, Robert, *The Understanding and Significance of the 'Remnant' in Qumran Literature: Including a Discussion of the Use of this Concept in the Hebrew Bible, the Apocrypha and Pseudepigrapha*, McMaster University thesis, 1981.

Hultgren, Arland J., *Jesus and His Adversaries. The Form and Function of the Conflict Stories in the Synoptic Tradition*, Minneapolis 1979.

— 'Paul's Pre-Christian Persecutions of the Church: Their Purpose, Locale, and Nature', *JBL* 95, 1976, pp. 97–111.

Hunzinger, Claus-Hunno, 'Fragmente einer älteren Fassung des Buches Milhama aus Höhle 4 von Qumran', *ZAW* 69, 1957, pp. 131–51.

Jackson, B. S., 'Jésus et Moïse: le statut du prophète à l'égard de la Loi', *Revue historique de droit français et étranger* 59, 1981, pp. 341–69.

Jeremias, J., 'Zwei Miszellen: 1. Antik-Jüdische Münzdeutungen. 2. Zur Geschichtlichkeit der Tempelreinigung', *NTS* 23, 1977, pp. 177–80.

— 'Der Gedanke des "Heiligen Restes" im Spätjudentum und in der Verkündigung Jesu' (1949), *Abba. Studien zu neutestamentlichen Theologie und Zeitgeschichte*, Göttingen 1966.

— *Jerusalem in the Time of Jesus*, ET London and Philadelphia 1969.

— *Jesus' Promise to the Nations* ET, SBT 24, London and Nashville 1958.

— *New Testament Theology I: The Proclamation of Jesus*, ET London and New York 1971 (cited as *Proclamation*).

— *The Parables of Jesus*, rev. ET (of 6th ed., 1962) London and New York 1963.

de Jonge, M., ed., *Studies on the Testaments of the Twelve Patriarchs*, Leiden 1975.

Juel, Donald, *Messiah and Temple: The Trial of Jesus in the Gospel of Mark*, SBLDS 31, Missoula 1977.

Kadushin, M., *The Rabbinic Mind*, New York ²1965.

Käsemann, E., 'Blind Alleys in the "Jesus of History" Controversy', *New Testament Questions of Today*, London and Philadelphia 1969, pp. 23–65.

— 'The Problem of the Historical Jesus' (1953), *Essays on New Testament Themes*, ET, SBT 41, London and Nashville 1964, pp. 15–47.

Keck, L., *A Future for the Historical Jesus*, Nashville, New York and London 1971.

Kee, Howard Clark, *Miracle in the Early Christian World*, New Haven 1983.

Kelber, Werner, *The Oral and the Written Gospel*, Philadelphia 1983.

Kittel, G., *Jesus und die Rabbinen*, Berlin-Lichterfelbe 1914.

Klausner, J., *From Jesus to Paul*, ET New York 1943, London 1944.

Klausner, J., *Jesus of Nazareth*, ET London and New York 1925.

Klijn, A. F. J., 'Scribes, Pharisees, Highpriests and Elders in the New Testament', *NovT* 3, 1959, pp. 259–67.

Klinzing, Georg, *Die Umdeutung des Kultus in der Qumrangemeinde und im Neuen Testament*, SUNT 7, Göttingen 1971.

Knox, John, *The Church and the Reality of Christ*, New York 1962.

— *Jesus: Lord and Christ*, New York 1958.

Koch, K., *The Rediscovery of Apocalyptic*, ET, SBT II 22, London and Nashville 1972.

Kümmel, W. G., 'Äussere und innere Reinheit des Menschen bei Jesus', *Das Wort und die Wörter. Festschrift G. F. Friedrich* (ed. H. Balz and S. Schulz), Stuttgart 1973, pp. 35–46.

— *Promise and Fulfilment*, ET, SBT 23, London and Nashville 1957.

— *Theology of the New Testament*, ET, New York and London 1974.

Lambrecht, Jan, 'Jesus and the Law. An Investigation of Mk 7, 1–23', *ETL* 53, 1977, pp. 24–83.

Leivestad, Ragnar, 'Das Dogma von der prophetenlosen Zeit', *NTS* 19, 1973, pp. 288–99.

Lührmann, Dieter, 'Markus 14.55–64. Christologie und Zerstörung des Tempels im Markusevangelium', *NTS* 27, 1981, pp. 457–74.

Maccoby, Hyam, 'Jacob Neusner's Mishnah', *Midstream* 30, 1984, pp. 24–32.

MacMullen, Ramsay, *Paganism in the Roman Empire*, New Haven 1981.

— *Roman Government's Response to Crisis A.D. 235–337*, New Haven 1976.

Manson, T. W., *Servant Messiah: A Study in the Public Ministry of Jesus*, Cambridge and New York 1953.

— *The Teaching of Jesus. Studies in its form and content*, Cambridge. ²1935, reissued 1963.

Mazar, Benjamin, 'Herodian Jerusalem in the Light of the Excavations South and South-West of the Temple Mount', *IEJ* 28, 1978, pp. 230–37.

McArthur, H. K., 'Basic Issues: A Survey of Recent Gospel Research', *Interpr* 18, 1964, pp. 39–55.

McEleney, Neil J., 'Authenticating Criteria and Mark 7:1–23', *CBQ* 34, 1972, pp. 431–60.

McKelvey, R. J., *The New Temple. The Church in the New Testament*, Oxford and New York 1969.

McNeile, A. H., *The Gospel according to St Matthew*, London 1915, reissued 1961.

Mealand, David L., 'The Dissimilarity Test', *SJT* 31, 1978, pp. 41–50.

Merkel, Helmut, 'Jesus in Widerstreit', *Glaube und Gesellschaft. Festschrift für W. F. Kasch*, ed. K. D. Wolf, Bayreuth 1981, pp. 207–17.

Meye, Robert P., *Jesus and the Twelve. Discipleship and Revelation in Mark's Gospel*, Grand Rapids 1968.

Meyer, B. F., *The Aims of Jesus*, London 1979.

Moore, G. F., 'Christian Writers on Judaism', *HTR* 14, 1921, pp. 197–254.

— *Judaism in the First Centuries of the Christian Era: The Age of the Tannaim*, 3 vols., Cambridge, Mass. 1927–30.

Morgan, Robert, 'Günther Bornkamm in England', *Kirche. Festschrift für Günther Bornkamm zum 75. Geburtstag* (ed. Dieter Lührmann und Georg Strecker), Tübingen 1980, pp. 491–506.

— *'Non Angli sed Angeli:* Some Anglican Reactions to German Gospel Criticism', *New Studies in Theology* I (ed. Stephen Sykes and Derek Holmes), London 1980, pp. 1–30.

Moule, C. F. D., *The Birth of the New Testament*, London and San Francisco ³1981.

— *The Origin of Christology*, Cambridge 1977.

— *The Phenomenon of the New Testament*, SBT II1, London and Nashville 1967.

— 'Some observations on *Tendenzdritik*', *Jesus and the Politics of His Day* (ed. Ernst Bammel and C. F. D. Moule), Cambridge 1984, pp. 91–100.

Müller, Ulrich B., 'Vision und Botschaft', *ZTK* 74, 1977, pp. 416–48.

— 'Zur Rezeption Gesetzeskritischer Jesusüberlieferung im frühen Christentum', *NTS* 27, 1981, pp. 158–85.

Munck, Johannes, *Paul and the Salvation of Mankind*, ET London and Richmond, Va. 1959.

Neusner, Jacob, *From Politics to Piety*, Engelwood Cliffs, N.J. 1973.

— *The Idea of Purity in Ancient Judaism*, Studies in Judaism in Late Antiquity 1, Leiden 1973.

— 'Josephus's Pharisees. A Complete Repertoire', *Formative Judaism: Religious, Historical and Literary Studies. Third Series: Torah, Pharisees, and Rabbis* (Brown Judaic Studies 46), Chico 1983, pp. 61–82 = 'Josephus' Pharisees', *Ex orbe religionum oblata. Studia Geo Widengren* I (ed. J. Bergman and others), Leiden 1972, pp. 224–44 = 'Josephus's Pharisees: "The Real Administrators of the State" ', *From Politics to Piety*, pp. 45–66.

— *Messiah in Context* (forthcoming).

— *The Rabbinic Traditions about the Pharisees before 70*, 3 vols., Leiden 1971.

Nickelsburg, George W. E., *Jewish Literature between the Bible and the Mishnah*, Philadelphia and London 1981.

Nolan, Albert, *Jesus before Christianity. The Gospel of Liberation*, Cape Town 1976, London 1977 (repr. 1980).

O'Neill, J. C., *Messiah. Six Lectures on the Ministry of Jesus*, Cambridge: Cochrane Press 1980.

Pamment, Margaret, 'The Kingdom of Heaven according to the First Gospel', *NTS* 27, 1981, pp. 211–32.

Perrin, N., *Jesus and the Language of the Kingdom*, London and Philadelphia 1976.

Perrin, N., *The Kingdom of God in the Teaching of Jesus*, London and Philadelphia 1963 (cited as *Kingdom*).

— *Rediscovering the Teaching of Jesus*, London and New York 1967.

Pesch, R., 'Das Zöllnergastmahl (Mk 2, 15–17)', *Mélanges Bibliques en hommage au R. P. Béda Rigaux* (ed. A. Deschamps and others), Gembloux 1970, pp. 63–87.

— 'Der Anspruch Jesu', *Orientierung* 35, 1971, pp. 53–6, 67–70, 77–81.

Przybylski, Benno, *Righteousness in Matthew and his World of Thought*, SNTSMS 41, Cambridge 1980.

Räisänen, Heikki, 'Zur Herkunft von Markus 7,15', *Logia. Les Paroles de Jésus—The Sayings of Jesus. Mémorial Joseph Coppens* (ed. J. DeLobel), BETL LIX, Louvain 1982, pp. 477–84.

— 'Jesus and the Food Laws: Reflections on Mark 7.15', *JSNT* 16, 1982, pp. 79–100.

Reicke, Bo, 'Judaeo-Christianity and the Jewish Establishment, A.D. 33–66', *Jesus and the Politics of His Day* (ed. E. Bammel and C. F. D. Moule), Cambridge 1984, pp. 145–52.

Remus, Harold, 'Does Terminology Distinguish Early Christian from Pagan Miracles?', *JBL* 101, 1982, pp. 531–51.

Rengstorf, K. H. 'ἀπόστολος', *TDNT* I, pp. 407–47.

Reumann, John, *Jesus in the Church's Gospels. Modern Scholarship and the Earliest Sources*, Philadelphia 1968.

Riches, John, *Jesus and the Transformation of Judaism*, London 1980.

Riesner, Rainer, *Jesus als Lehrer. Eine Untersuchung zum Ursprung der Evangelien-Überlieferung*, WUNT 27, Tübingen 1981.

Rivkin, Ellis, 'Defining the Pharisees: The Tannaitic Sources', *HUCA* 40–41, 1969–71, pp. 234–38.

— *A Hidden Revolution*, Nashville 1978.

Robinson, James M., *A New Quest of the Historical Jesus*, SBT 25, London and Nashville 1959.

Robinson, John A. T., *Redating the New Testament*, London and Philadelphia 1976.

Rohde, Joachim, *Rediscovering the Teaching of the Evangelists*, ET London and Philadelphia 1968.

Roloff, J., *Das Kerygma und der irdische Jesus*, Göttingen 1969.

Rowland, Christopher, *The Open Heaven. The Study of Apocalyptic in Judaism and Early Christianity*, London and New York 1982.

Safrai, S., 'Jewish Self-Government', *The Jewish People in the First Century* I (ed. S. Safrai and M. Stern), Assen 1974, pp. 377–419.

Sanday, W., *The Life of Christ in Recent Research*, Oxford 1907, New York 1908.

Sanders, E. P., 'The Argument from Order and the Relationship between Matthew and Luke', *NTS* 15, 1969, pp. 249–61.

— 'The Genre of the Palestinian Jewish Apocalypses', *Apocalypticism in the*

Mediterranean World and the Near East (ed. D. Hellholm), Tübingen 1983, pp. 447–59.

Sanders, E. P., 'New Testament Studies Today', *Colloquy on New Testament Studies. A Time for Reappraisal and Fresh Approaches* (ed. Bruce C. Corley), Macon, Ga. 1983, pp. 11–28.

— 'The Overlaps of Mark and Q and the Synoptic Problem', *NTS* 19, 1972, pp. 453–65.

— *Paul, the Law, and the Jewish People*, Philadelphia 1983.

— *Paul and Palestinian Judaism*, London and Philadelphia 1977.

— 'Puzzling Out Rabbinic Judaism', *Approaches to Ancient Judaism* II (ed. William Green), Brown Judaic Studies 9, Chico 1980, pp. 24–32.

— *The Tendencies of the Synoptic Tradition*, SNTSMS 9, Cambridge 1969.

— and W. D. Davies 'Jesus: from the Semitic Point of View', *The Cambridge History of Judaism* II (forthcoming).

Sanders, Jack T., *Ethics in the New Testament. Change and Development*, Philadelphia 1975.

— 'The Parable of the Pounds and Lucan Anti-Semitism', *Theological Studies* 42, 1981, pp. 660–68.

— 'Tradition and Redaction in Luke XV.11–32', *NTS* 15 1969, pp. 433–38.

Schäfer, Peter, *Die Vorstellung vom heiligen Geist in der rabbinischen Literatur*, SANT 28, Munich 1972.

Schenk, W., 'Gefangenschaft und Tod des Täufers. Erwägungen zur Chronologie und ihren Konsequenzen', *NTS* 29, 1983, pp. 453–83.

Schiffman, L. H., 'At the Crossroads: Tannaitic Perspectives on the Jewish-Christian Schism', *Jewish and Christian Self-Definition II: Aspects of Judaism in the Graeco-Roman Period*, ed. E. P. Sanders, A. I. Baumgarten and Alan Mendelson, London and Philadelphia 1981, pp. 115–56.

Schlatter, A., *Der Evangelist Matthäus*, Stuttgart ⁵1959.

Schlosser, Jacques, *Le règne de Dieu dans les dits de Jésus*, 2 vols., Paris 1980.

Schmiedel, P. W., 'Gospels', *Encyclopaedia Biblica* II, ed. T. K. Cheyne and J. S. Black, London and New York 1901, cols. 1765–1896.

Schoeps, H.-J., *Paul: The Theology of the Apostle in the light of Jewish Religious History*, ET London and Philadelphia 1961.

Schottroff, L., 'Das Gleichnis vom verlorenen Sohn', *ZTK* 68, 1971, pp. 27–52.

Schürer, Emil, *The History of the Jewish People in the Age of Jesus Christ*, rev. ET (ed. Geza Vermes, Fergus Millar and Matthew Black), Edinburgh, vol. I 1973, vol. II 1979, vol. III forthcoming.

Schürmann, H., 'Der Jüngerkreis Jesu als Zeichen für Israel', *Das Geheimnis Jesu. Versuche zur Jesusfrage*, Leipzig 1972, pp. 126–53.

— 'Die Symbolhandlungen Jesu als eschatologische Erfüllungszeichen', ibid., pp. 75–110.

— 'Wie hat Jesus seinen Tod bestanden und verstanden?' *Orientierung an*

Jesus. Zur Theologie der Synoptiker. Festschrift Josef Schmid (ed. P. Hoffmann and others), Freiburg 1973, pp. 325–63.

— 'Zur aktuellen Situation der Leben-Jesu-Forschung', *Geist und Leben* 46, 1973, pp. 300–10.

Schwartz, D. R., 'Josephus and Nicolaus on the Pharisees', *JSJ* 14, 1983, pp. 157–71.

Schweitzer, A., *The Mysticism of Paul the Apostle*, ET London and New York 1931, reissued 1956.

— *Paul and His Interpreters*, ET London 1912, reissued London 1950, New York 1951.

— *The Quest of the Historical Jesus*, ET London 1910, New York 1922, ³1956.

Schweizer, E., *Jesus*, ET London and Richmond, Va. 1971.

— *Lordship and Discipleship*, ET, SBT 28, London and Nashville 1960.

Scott, Bernard Brandon, *Jesus, Symbol-Maker for the Kingdom*, Philadelphia 1983.

Sloyan, G., *Jesus on Trial; the Development of the Passion Narratives and their Historical and Ecumenical Implications*, Philadelphia 1973.

Smith, Morton, 'A Comparison of Early Christianity and Early Rabbinic Traditions', *JBL* 82, 1963, pp. 169–76.

— 'The Dead Sea Sect in Relation to Ancient Judaism', *NTS* 7, 1960–61, pp. 347–60.

— *Jesus the Magician*, New York and London 1978.

— 'Palestinian Judaism in the First Century', *Israel, Its Role in Civilization* (ed. Moshe Davis), New York 1956, pp. 67–81 (= *Essays in Greco-Roman and Related Talmudic Literature* [ed. Henry A. Fischel], New York 1977, pp. 183–197.

— 'The Reason for the Persecution of Paul and the Obscurity of Acts', *Studies in Mysticism and Religion presented to Gershom G. Scholem* (ed. E. E. Urbach, R. J. Zwi Werblowsky, Ch. Wirszubski), Jerusalem 1967, pp. 261–8.

— *Tannaitic Parallels to the Gospels*, JBLMS 6, Philadelphia 1951.

Spiro, Solomon J., 'Who was the Ḥaber? A New Approach to an Ancient Institution', *JSJ* 11, 1980, pp. 186–216.

Stanton, G. N., *Jesus of Nazareth in New Testament Preaching*, SNTSMS 27, 1974.

Stauffer, E., *Jesus and His Story*, ET London 1960.

— *Jesus and the Wilderness Community at Qumran*, ET Philadelphia 1964.

Stern, M., 'Aspects of Jewish Society: the Priesthood and other Classes', *The Jewish People in the First Century* II (ed. S. Safrai and M. Stern), Assen 1976, pp. 561–630.

Strobel, August, *Die Stunde der Wahrheit: Untersuchungen zur Strafverfahren gegen Jesus*, WUNT 21, Tübingen 1980.

Suhl, A., *Die Funktion der alttestamentlichen Zitate und Anspielungen im Markusevangelium*, Gütersloh 1965.

Sweet, J. P. M., 'The Zealots and Jesus', *Jesus and the Politics of His Day* (ed. Ernst Bammel and C. F. D. Moule), Cambridge 1984, pp. 1–9.

Taylor, Vincent, *The Gospel According to St Mark*, London and New York 1959.

Theissen, Gerd, *The First Followers of Jesus. A Sociological Analysis of the Earliest Christianity*, ET London 1978 (= *Sociology of Early Palestinian Christianity*, Philadelphia 1978).

Tiede, David L, *The Charismatic Figure as Miracle Worker*, SBLDS 1, Missoula 1972.

Trautmann, Maria, *Zeichenhafte Handlungen Jesu. Ein Beitrag zur Frage nach dem historischen Jesus*, Forschung zur Bibel 37, Würzburg 1980.

Trocmé, É., 'L'expulsion des marchands du temple', *NTS* 15, 1968, pp. 1–22.

— *Jesus and his Contemporaries*, ET London 1973 = *Jesus as seen by his Contemporaries*. Philadelphia 1973.

Tuckett, Christopher, 'On the Relationship between Matthew and Luke', *NTS* 30, 1984, pp. 130–42.

Urbach, E. E., *The Sages*, ET Jerusalem 1975.

Vermes, G., *Jesus the Jew*, London 1973, New York 1974.

Vielhauer, Philipp, 'Gottesreich und Menschensohn in der Verkündigung Jesu', *Festschrift für Gunther Dehn* (ed. Wilhelm Schneemelcher), Neukirchen 1957, pp. 51–79.

Volz, Paul, *Die Eschatologie der jüdischen Gemeinde im neutestamentlichen Zeitalter*, Tübingen 1934.

Weiss, Johannes, *Die Predigt Jesu vom Reiche Gottes*, Göttingen 1892 (ET *Jesus' Proclamation of the Kingdom of God*, Philadelphia and London 1971).

Weiss-Rosmarin, Trude, ed., *Jewish Expressions on Jesus. An Anthology*, New York 1977.

Westerholm, Stephen, *Jesus and Scribal Authority*, Lund 1978.

Westermann, Claus, *Isaiah 40–66. A Commentary*, ET, Old Testament Library, London and Philadelphia 1969.

Wilder, A., *Eschatology and Ethics in the Teaching of Jesus*, New York ²1950.

Wilson, W. R., *The Execution of Jesus*, New York 1970.

Wink, Walter, *John the Baptist in the Gospel Tradition*, SNTSMS 7, Cambridge 1968.

Winter, Paul, *On the Trial of Jesus*, Berlin 1961; rev. ed. (ed. T. A. Burkill and G. Vermes), Berlin 1974.

Yadin, Y., *Masada. Herod's Fortress and the Zealots' Last Stand*, London and New York 1966.

Zahrnt, H., *The Historical Jesus*. ET London and New York 1963.

Zeitlin, Solomon, 'Jesus of Nazareth' and 'Jesus and the Pharisees', *Jewish Expressions on Jesus* (ed. T. Weiss-Rosmarin), New York 1977, pp. 116–47, 148–58 (repr. from *The Rise and Fall of the Second Judaean State* I, Philadelphia 1962).

NOTES

INTRODUCTION
The Problem

1. 'Relationship to his contemporaries in Judaism' is the correct way to phrase the matter, but I shall sometimes use the abbreviation 'Jesus and Judaism'. The short phrase is not intended to cast doubt on the fact that Jesus was thoroughly Jewish.

2. These questions have lately received more attention than they did for some decades after the rise of form criticism. They are explicitly posed, for example, by C. K. Barrett in *Jesus and the Gospel Tradition*, 1967.

3. Paul Winter, *On the Trial of Jesus*, 1961; rev. ed. (ed. T. A. Burkill and G. Vermes), 1974. Page numbers refer to the revised edition.

4. See, for example, Ernst Bammel (ed.), *The Trial of Jesus: Cambridge Studies in Honour of C. F. D. Moule*, 1970; D. Catchpole, *The Trial of Jesus*, 1971.

5. Martin Hengel, *Nachfolge und Charisma*, 1968; ET *The Charismatic Leader and his Followers*, 1981.

6. Joachim Jeremias, *New Testament Theology I: The Proclamation of Jesus*, ET 1971.

7. Eduard Schweizer, *Jesus*, ET 1971, esp. pp. 13–51.

8. C. H. Dodd, *The Founder of Christianity*, 1970.

9. G. Vermes, *Jesus the Jew*, 1973.

10. J. Bowker, *Jesus and the Pharisees*, 1973.

11. B. F. Meyer, *The Aims of Jesus*, 1979.

12. A. E. Harvey, *Jesus and the Constraints of History*, 1982.

13. See, for example, Dodd, *Founder*, p. 36.

14. On the shift towards confidence that Jesus' ministry can be accurately described, see also Gustaf Aulén, *Jesus in Contemporary Historical Research*, ET 1976, pp. viii, 3; H. Schürmann, 'Zur aktuellen Situation der Leben-Jesu-Forschung', *Geist und Leben* 46, 1973, pp. 300–10, here p. 300.

15. On the problem see recently W. G. Kümmel, *Theology of the New Testament*, ET 1974, pp. 24–7; L. Keck, *A Future for the Historical Jesus*, 1971; H. Zahrnt, *The Historical Jesus*, ET 1963, chs. 1–7, esp. pp. 14, 109.

16. E. Käsemann, 'The Problem of the Historial Jesus' (1953), *Essays on New Testament Themes*, ET 1964, pp. 15–47. Cf. Keck (*Future*, p. 20) on the motive for the new quest. Note James M. Robinson's chapter on the theological legitimacy of a quest for the historical Jesus in *A New Quest of the Historical Jesus*, 1959, ch. 4. The question of 'legitimacy' continues to be raised by at least some who wish to seek historical information. Note J. Roloff's defence of the 'legitimacy' of finding historical material in the Gospels: *Das Kerygma und der irdische Jesus*, 1969, e.g. p. 74.

17. E. Käsemann, 'Blind Alleys in the "Jesus of History" Controversy', *New Testament Questions of Today*, ET 1969, pp. 23–65.

18. Ibid., pp. 51, 56.

19. Ibid., p. 51: 'The hate of the Jewish leaders goes back to Jesus' attitude to the Law and to his understanding of grace and the fellowship with sinners which derives from it. . . .'

20. See for example the remarks on Bornkamm, below, p. 29.

21. Cadbury argued against attributing to Jesus a programme, but for different reasons. His position is discussed below.

22. E.g. by Bousset, whose view is described in the next section.

23. On the depiction of the Judaism of Jesus' day as a debasement of the older Israelite religion, see E. P. Sanders, *Paul and Palestinian Judaism*, 1977, pp. 419f.; K. Koch, *The Rediscovery of Apocalyptic*, ET 1972, p. 37.

24. See e.g. J. Klausner, *From Jesus to Paul*, ET 1943, pp. 4, 441, 514f., 582; cf. H. Conzelmann, 'Current Problems in Pauline Research', *Interpr* 22, 1968, p. 172.

25. J. Klausner, *Jesus of Nazareth. His Times, His Life and His Teaching*, ET 1925, p. 369.

26. A good example is G. B. Caird, *Jesus and the Jewish Nation*, 1965.

27. Cf. Kümmel, *Theology*, p. 26.

Method of proceeding

1. The almost exclusive concentration on Jesus as a teacher will be familiar to most readers. For two recent examples, see Bernard Brandon Scott, *Jesus, Symbol-Maker for the Kingdom*, 1983 (see esp. p. 153); James Breech, *The Silence of Jesus. The Authentic Voice of the Historical Man*, 1983. Some exceptions to the rule will be discussed below.

2. See the works of Scott and Breech, just cited.

3. E. Fuchs, 'The Quest of the Historical Jesus' (1956), *Studies of the Historical Jesus*, ET 1964, pp. 21f.

4. See Graham Stanton, *Jesus of Nazareth in New Testament Preaching*, SNTSMS 27, 1974, pp. 137–52; cf. p. 175.

5. M. Smith, *Jesus the Magician*, 1978, p. 17.

6. Ibid., p. 5.

7. Harvey, *Constraints*, pp. 5f.

8. Ibid., p. 6.

9. Smith, *Magician*, pp. 11, 14.

10. Scott, *Symbol-Maker*; Breech, *Silence*.

11. Breech, *Silence*, p. 218.

12. Scott, *Symbol-Maker*, p. 11. Scott, however, is aware of the problem. He comments (pp. 165f.) that any interpretation must make sense of the execution. He proposes that Jesus 'burlesques and pokes fun; his images are daring and at times scandalously inappropriate . . . . The healing power of his images was what was terrifying to his opponents and therefore they perceived him as demonic' (p. 166). We can safely say that he does not, in fact, explain opposition and execution.

13. See, for example, the comments on Eduard Schweizer, below, pp. 39f.

14. Morton Smith, *Tannaitic Parallels to the Gospels*, JBLMS 6, 1951, p. 136. Cf. further parallels to lines in the Lord's prayer cited by Smith on p. 137.

15. Harvey, *Constraints*, p. 7.

16. Harvey's list of facts is given on his p. 6, quoted just above. My list is given immediately below. I do not regard conflict about the law as being on the same plane of certainty as crucifixion by the Romans. See further below, ch. 9. Elsewhere in his book, Harvey counts additional things as indisputable facts, such as the accusation that

Jesus committed blasphemy. It is 'one of the most securely attested facts about him' (p. 171). Elsewhere, however, he shows that he knows that in fact we cannot be sure of this charge. See pp. 31f.

17. See especially his ch. 4, e.g., pp. 67, 71–7, and ch. 5.

18. Ernst Käsemann, 'The Problem of the Historical Jesus', p. 37.

19. I do not regard any items in the following as dubious, but some may. Those on which the present interpretation hinges are discussed and justified in the chapters which follow. There are other facts about Jesus about which I have no doubts (e.g. that he had a brother named James) but which are not relevant to the present discussion.

20. The very fact that the execution was by the Romans seems to have been determinative for several scholars, such as Winter and Brandon, whose views are discussed below. N. A. Dahl argued that the starting point for the study of the life of Jesus is his death, specifically his death as king of the Jews. See *The Crucified Messiah and Other Essays*, 1974, pp. 10–36, 68, 72–4.

21. Also in favour of beginning with the temple controversy is R. Pesch, 'Der Anspruch Jesu', *Orientierung* 35, 1971.

22. Robert Morgan, '*Non Angli sed Angeli*: Some Anglican Reactions to German Gospel Criticism', *New Studies in Theology* I (ed. Stephen Sykes and Derek Holmes), 1980, pp. 1–30, here pp. 7, 14f. Cf. 'Günther Bornkamm in England', *Kirche. Festschrift für Günther Bornkamm zum 75. Geburtstag* (ed. Dieter Lührmann and Georg Strecker), 1980, pp. 491–506, esp. p. 499.

23. John Knox, *Jesus, Lord and Christ*, 1958, p. 115. On Knox's position, see E. P. Sanders, 'New Testament Studies Today', *Colloquy on New Testament Studies* (ed. Bruce C. Corley), 1983, pp. 11–28, here pp. 11–14, 20.

24. 'From Rawlinson to Moule': see Morgan, '*Non Angli*', pp. 14f.

25. Morgan, 'Günther Bornkamm', pp. 500–2.

26. On J. B. Lightfoot, see Morgan, '*Non Angli*', p. 4.

27. See especially Gal. 5.1; 6.12; cf. I. Thess. 2.16. See E. P. Sanders, *Paul, the Law, and the Jewish People*, 1983, pp. 190–92; pp. 204f. n. 77.

28. There is now available a rich and illuminating body of literature on the criteria for assessing authenticity. I have found the following to be the most useful: M. D. Hooker, 'Christology and Methodology', *NTS* 17, 1970–71, pp. 480–7; 'On Using the Wrong Tool', *Theology* 75, 1972, pp. 570–81; R. S. Barbour, *Traditio-Historical Criticism of the Gospels* (Studies in Creative Criticism 4), 1972; F. G. Downing, *The Church and Jesus*, SBT II 10, 1968, esp. ch. VI; D. G. A. Calvert, 'An Examination of the Criteria for Distinguishing the Authentic Words of Jesus', *NTS* 18, 1971–72, pp. 209–19; David L. Mealand, 'The Dissimilarity Test', *SJT* 31, 1978, pp. 41–50.

29. The clearest statement of the position is by Hooker, 'Christology and Methodology', pp. 484–7; cf. Barbour, *Traditio-Historical Criticism*, p. 11.

30. The word 'authenticity' is used as a convenient short term. An 'authentic' saying is one which we have good reason to believe is as close to something that Jesus said as we can hope for.

31. So Hooker, 'Christology and Methodology', p. 485.

32. Cf. Downing, *The Church and Jesus*, pp. 108f.; Hooker, 'Christology and Methodology', p. 480.

33. Especially Rainer Riesner, *Jesus als Lehrer. Eine Untersuchung zum Ursprung der Evangelien-Überlieferung*, WUNT 27, 1981. See Gerhardsson's review in *TLZ* 108, 1983, cols. 500–3. While generally appreciative, Gerhardsson thinks that Riesner has gone too far in affirming the reliability of the synoptic tradition.

34. B. Gerhardsson, *Memory and Manuscript: Oral Tradition and Written Transmission*

in Rabbinic Judaism and Early Christianity, ET 1961, 1964. Note his nuanced and convenient restatement in *The Origins of the Gospel Traditions*, ET 1979.

35. In addition to Morton Smith's well-known review ('A Comparison of Early Christianity and Early Rabbinic Traditions', *JBL* 82, 1963, pp. 169-76), see the more sympathetic assessments by W. D. Davies (*The Setting of the Sermon on the Mount*, 1964, pp. 464-80); Downing (*The Church and Jesus*, pp. 105-9), and E. P. Sanders (*The Tendencies of the Synoptic Tradition*, 1969, pp. 294-6).

36. B. Gerhardsson, *Tradition and Transmission in Early Christianity*, 1964.

37. B. Gerhardsson, 'Der Weg der Evagelientradition', *Das Evangelium und die Evangelien*. Vorträge vom Tübingen Symposium 1982 (WUNT 28; ed. P. Stuhlmacher), Tübingen 1983, pp. 79-102.

38. Ibid., pp. 80, 87.   39. Ibid., p. 83.

40. Ibid., p. 87.   41. Ibid., pp. 87f.

42. Ibid., p. 93. In this essay Gerhardsson still does not say how much of the material he has in mind. On p. 93 he writes that the church needed 'Jesus-traditions' – with neither an article nor a modifying adjective – in the same way as it needed scriptural texts. On p. 10, however, he writes of *the* sayings material (excluding the parables) that its archaic character is best explained by the hypothesis that, from the time before Easter, it was transmitted with precise wording and with little re-working.

43. Gerhardsson's examples (ibid., p. 80) are I Cor. 11.23-25; Acts 20.35; I Cor. 15.3-8.

44. Ibid., pp. 94f.   45. Ibid., pp. 82, 83, 89, 100, 102.

46. Cf. Stanton, *Jesus of Nazareth*, esp. pp. 172-7. Stanton is also dissatisfied with form criticism's attribution of material to diverse settings, and he proposes that historical remembrances about Jesus were included in missionary preaching. See also the admirable treatment of this and other matters of synoptic research by E. Earle Ellis, 'Gospels Criticism. A Perspective on the State of the Art', *Das Evangelium und die Evangelien* (n. 37), pp. 27-54.

47. Sanders, *Tendencies*. Of the supposed tendencies, the one which has remained in use, despite numerous criticisms, is that of decreasing Semitism. See, for example, Neil J. McEleney, 'Authenticating Criteria and Mark 7:1-23', *CBQ* 34, 1972, pp. 431-60. On p. 437 he cites and agrees with my view of Semitisms (that they do not help establish authenticity), but he uses them on pp. 438-40.

48. This point is now frequently made. The most thorough presentation is Downing's in *The Church and Jesus*.

49. E.g. the present form of the passion predictions.

50. Cf. Downing, *The Church and Jesus*, pp. 108f.

51. Cf. Gerhardsson, 'Der Weg der Evangelientradition', p. 98.

52. Sanders, *Tendencies*, pp. 14-21, 146f. n. 3.

53. The difficulties in using the sayings material are given in more detail at the beginning of ch. 4. For other discussions of the limitations of form-criticism, see Erhart Güttgemanns, *Candid Questions concerning Gospel Form Criticism*, ET 1979; Werner Kelber, *The Oral and the Written Gospel*, 1983, ch. 1.

54. The first formulation of the test, as far as I know, is R. Bultmann's in discussing parables (*Gleichnisse*) and related materials: *Die Geschichte der synoptischen Tradition*, [7]1967, p. 222; *The History of the Synoptic Tradition*, ET 1963, p. 205. It has been widely used and often discussed. See, for example, N. Perrin, *Rediscovering the Teaching of Jesus*, 1967, pp. 39-43 (it is 'the basis for all contemporary attempts to reconstruct the teaching of Jesus'). For a rigid application of one-half of what became of the double test, see P. W. Schmiedel, 'Gospels', *Encyclopaedia Biblica* II, 1901, cols. 1765-1896,

esp. 1881–3: five passages could not have been invented by the post-resurrection church.

55. Some would shift the outside dates for the composition of the Gospels earlier, for example to 66 and 90. The present point, which is that they were written during a 'tunnel' period, about which we have little knowledge, is not affected. I must with some regret leave aside the proposals of John A. T. Robinson (*Redating the New Testament*, 1976) to press the dates of composition earlier yet. His analysis of the weakness of some of the traditional arguments, while usually penetrating, does not lead to the radical revision which he proposes.

56. On multiple attestation, see Calvert, 'An Examination of the Criteria'; Barbour, *Traditio-Historical Criticism*, pp. 3f.

57. Cf. Barbour, *Traditio-Historical Criticism*, p. 18: if one starts with individual sayings it is necessary, after testing each one, to try to work it 'into an overall hypothesis'. See also Meyer, *Aims*. p. 19. Bruce Chilton puts the point sharply: 'It may be questioned whether or not the application of *a priori* criteria to data constitutes historical knowledge at all' (*God in Strength. Jesus' Announcement of the Kingdom*, 1979, p. 20; cf. p. 288).

58. N. A. Dahl, 'The Problem of the Historical Jesus' (1962), *The Crucified Messiah*, 1974, pp. 48–89, here pp. 68f.

59. *Paul and Palestinian Judaism*.

60. Ibid., pp. 157, 232, 275–8, 389, 397f. Contrast J. Jeremias, *Proclamation of Jesus*, p. 2: the idea of God's love for sinners was 'so offensive to the majority of his contemporaries that it cannot be derived from the thinking current in his environment'.

61. W. Bousset, *Jesus*, ET (ed. W. D. Morrison) 1911, p. 44.

62. See *Paul and Palestinian Judaism*, pp. 33–59.

63. There are a few exceptions. See the discussion above of Breech, *Silence*.

64. See, for example, R. Bultmann, *Theology of the New Testament* I, ET 1954, pp. 42f.; H. Conzelmann, *An Outline of the Theology of the New Testament*, ET 1969, p. 32: the church 'was assembled as a community through the appearance of the risen one . . .'.

65. H. J. Cadbury, *The Peril of Modernizing Jesus*, 1937, reissued 1962.

66. It is often difficult to distinguish the *ḥaberim* from the Pharisees. I discuss the problem below, in ch. 6. Here I assume that the Dead Sea Scrolls represent the views of at least some Essenes.

67. See Emil Schürer, ed. Geza Vermes and others, *The History of the Jewish People in the Age of Jesus Christ* (revised ET), vol. II, 1979, p. 388, n. 16, citing especially the work of Jacob Neusner.

68. *Paul and Palestinian Judaism*, pp. 244–7; Robert Huebsch, *The Understanding and Significance of the 'Remnant' in Qumran Literature*, PhD thesis, 1981.

69. Israel and secondarily the Gentiles: note 'to the Jew first and also the Greek', Rom. 1.16 and elsewhere; full number of the Gentiles: Rom. 11.25; imminent return of the Lord: I Thess. 4.16f.; cf. I Cor. 15.23; Phil. 3.20f.

70. Cf. Smith, *Magician*, p. 5; similarly Mealand, 'The Dissimilarity Test', pp. 44f. In favour of a connection between Jesus' teaching, his death, and the church can now be cited several scholars. See, for example, Catchpole, *The Trial of Jesus*, pp. 107–12, 271.

71. So also N. A. Dahl, 'The Problem of the Historical Jesus', pp. 72–4.

72. Bousset, Bultmann, Klausner, Winter and Vermes, all discussed below, have presented this view or some variation of it.

State of the Question

1. Readers who wish to read other recent reviews of research on Jesus may see N. Dahl, 'The Problem of the Historical Jesus', pp. 50–63; Aulén, *Jesus in Contemporary Historical Research*; Meyer, *Aims*, pp. 25–54.

2. For the view that Jesus reformed crass opinions see A. Schweitzer, *The Quest of the Historical Jesus*, ET 1910, ³1956, pp. 196f. (Strauss), p. 203 (Holtzmann), p. 205 (Weisse, Holtzmann, Schenkel and Weizsäcker), p. 215 (Hase) and elsewhere.

3. Schweitzer, *Quest*, ch. 19.

4. Ibid., pp. 371f., 387f.

5. See Glasson's criticism, below, ch. 4.

6. Schweitzer, *Quest*, p. 257: 'On which of the two presuppositions, the assumption that His life was completely dominated by eschatology, or the assumption that He repudiated it, do we find it easiest to understand the connexion of events in the life of Jesus, His fate, and the emergence of the expectation of the Parousia in the community of His disciples?' Cf. pp. 350, 395.

7. Cf. A. Schweitzer, *Paul and His Interpreters*, ET 1912, reissued 1950, p. ix: 'The teaching of Jesus does not in any of its aspects go outside the Jewish world of thought . . ., but represents a deeply ethical and perfected version of the contemporary apocalyptic.'

8. These are principally two: W. Bousset, *Jesu Predigt in ihrem Gegensatz zum Judentum*, 1892, and *Jesus*. We shall quote from the latter book, which repeats Bousset's views in a convenient form. On the earlier work, see Schweitzer, *Quest*, pp. 242–50; G. F. Moore, 'Christian Writers on Judaism', *HTR* 14, 1921, pp. 241–3.

9. On W. Bousset, *Die Religion des Judentums im späthellenistischen Zeitalter* (ed. H. Gressmann), ³1926 (reissued 1966) as a standard text, see *Paul and Palestinian Judaism*, pp. 55f.

10. Here Bousset has this footnote: 'It is to be assumed that from the average here considered an exception must be made in favour of a few celebrated and really pious rabbis, such as Hillel, Gamaliel, and some others.' The same view of the Rabbis and the same contrast with Jesus are seen in Kittel, *Jesus und die Rabbinen*, 1914, pp. 9f.

11. Most recently, see E. E. Urbach, *The Sages*, ET 1975, p. 6.

12. Since I have now twice offered a lengthy criticism of aspects of Bousset's work, and since I regard him as an important scholar, a more general evaluation should be made. I regard his programme of research, as indicated for example in *Kyrios Christos* (1913), ET 1970, and his separate volumes on Gnosticism and Judaism, as admirable and worthy of emulation. Many of his insights and analyses are provocative and helpful and may still be read with profit. Further, his view of Judaism, especially Rabbinic Judaism, was in no way remarkable. It was not, in fact, his own, but was largely derivative. The view of Judaism cannot be simply regarded as a period piece and passed over, however, for two reasons: (1) the use of a denigrating view of Judaism to set off Christianity as superior, which is so clear in Bousset, has continued; (2) his depiction of Palestinian Judaism is still cited as authoritative and 'standard' (n. 9 above).

13. Moore, 'Christian Writers', pp. 242f. Recently, note the remark of Keck, *Future*, p. 122: In some presentations, 'Jesus increases "in stature and wisdom and in favor with God and man" in direct proportion to the extent to which his contemporaries decrease – that is, they are invariably portrayed as narrow-minded legalists (Pharisees), fanatical nationalists (Zealots), sophisticated sceptics (Sadducees), esoteric sectarians (Essenes), and persons devoid of religious sensitivities altogether ('Am ha-arez). When Jesus is played off against such a milieu, his appeal is purchased too cheaply. The error

of the old liberal lives of Jesus lay precisely here – they lionized Jesus by playing him off against both Christian theology and the Judaism of which he was a part in order to present an appealing hero of liberal religion and ethics. As we saw in the previous chapter, the same error is made by Fuchs and Bornkamm; Jesus "brings God to speech" in a culture existentially devoid of God.'

The best recent description of Judaism as seen in New Testament scholarship is that of K. Hoheisel, *Das antike Judentum in christlicher Sicht*, 1978.

14. Bousset, *Jesus*, pp. 38f. The emphasis is mine.

15. Cf. Sanday, *The Life of Christ in Recent Research*, 1907, p. 44: Steinmann 'shows an almost nervous dread of anything in the least degree external in religion. The tendency is common in Germany . . .'.

16. Originally published in 1926. Page references are to the Scribners' paperback ed. of the ET (R. Bultmann, *Jesus and the Word*, 1958).

17. C. H. Dodd, *The Parables of the Kingdom*, 1935; rev. ed., 1961.

18. See Dodd's 'Preface' to *Parables*.

19. Note Bultmann's passing reference to Schweitzer's history of research, with no mention of Schweitzer's own view, in *Jesus and the Word*, pp. 8f.

20. Johannes Weiss, *Jesus' Proclamation of the Kingdom of God* (1892), ET 1971.

21. 'The coming of the Kingdom of God is therefore not really an event in the course of time . . .'. *Jesus and the Word*, p. 51.

22. Ibid., p. 218.

23. Ibid., p. 131; cf. p. 52.

24. When Bultmann raises the question of the relation between Jesus' teaching on the law and the demand of God, on the one hand, and his eschatological message, on the other, it is not to offer a connection between teaching and death, but to explain the unity of eschatology and ethics. See *Jesus and the Word*, pp. 121ff.

25. See Bultmann, p. 9; Bousset, *Jesus*, p. 17.

26. For Bultmann's view of the failure of Judaism to fulfil its own promise, and Jesus' success, see, e.g., pp. 72–9.

27. Not only in *Jesus and the Word*, but also in *Theology of the New Testament* (Vol. I, ch. 1) and *Primitive Christianity in Its Contemporary Setting*, ET 1956 (p. 71), Jesus is placed within Judaism. As is well known, this was a controversial step, and Bultmann was criticized for it: he did not make Jesus a Christian, but a Jew! It was indeed bold in the context in which Bultmann wrote, and his having Jesus deal with the potentialities of Judaism might have opened the way for a more positive evaluation of Judaism. But for Bultmann, Jesus seems to have been the only Jew to seize Judaism's positive potentialities, and the rest of Judaism remained mired in legalism, in which even repentance was a deed of works-righteousness (*Primitive Christianity*, p. 71). Thus, from my point of view, he did not succeed in breaking with the prevailing stereotype of Judaism.

28. For discussion of the pros and cons, see *Paul and Palestinian Judaism*, pp. 212–15.

29. Günther Bornkamm, *Jesus of Nazareth*, ET 1960.

30. Morgan, '*Non Angli*', p. 22; 'Günther Bornkamm', p. 494.

31. See n. 13 above.

32. M. Dibelius, *Jesus* (1939), ET 1949.

33. Principally to be noted from this period, although omitted from this survey, is M. Goguel, *La Vie de Jésus*, 1932. (The ET appeared in 1933.)

34. 'The Problem of the Historical Jesus', pp. 37–45.

35. Cf. Bousset, *Jesus*, pp. 139–43 ('freedom based on moral conviction' *versus* 'the legal and casuistic world of the Pharisees'); Bultmann, *Jesus and the Word*, pp. 68, 76f.

36. 'The Quest of the Historical Jesus', pp. 11–31.

37. Fuchs elsewhere ('Jesus and Faith' [1958], ET, *Studies of the Historical Jesus*, 1964, p. 61) characterizes the association with sinners, in Jewish eyes, as 'blasphemy and treachery to Israel'.

38. Cf. ibid., p. 62: 'Thus the words of the Lord's Supper which are a later ecclesiastical formulation, and also the prophecies of suffering which are similarly a later formulation, both express Jesus' self-understanding.'

39. See N. Perrin, *The Kingdom of God in the Teaching of Jesus*, 1963, pp. 109, 126; Robinson, *A New Quest of the Historical Jesus*, pp. 14–16, 113–15 (on p. 114, however, Fuch's statement of Jesus' intention to suffer is discussed); Keck, *Future*, pp. 30f.

40. In his *Theology of the New Testament*, Kümmel's most distinctive view is that Jesus himself anticipated a short lapse of time between his death and return. See his earlier *Promise and Fulfilment*, ET, SBT 23, 1957, and pp. 85–90 of his *Theology*. This point is not dealt with in the present survey.

41. Kümmel's statement that Jesus, in combining the two love commandments, intended to say *all* that one should do may also be criticized as ignoring the context of such statements in Judaism. When Hillel said that the 'love thy neighbour' commandment was 'the whole Torah', there was no intention to imply that the rest of the Torah should be ignored. See Shabbath 31a.

42. Kümmel does not intend to account for how it was that Jesus, being non-violent and apolitical, was crucified as a 'political pretender', although he takes it that this is why he was executed, at least from the Roman point of view. See pp. 85f. But whatever the Romans thought they were doing, Kümmel intends to describe why Jesus died from *his own* point of view.

43. A. Schweitzer, *The Mysticism of Paul the Apostle*, ET 1931, reissued 1953, pp. 334–39.

44. Schweizer, *Jesus*.

45. C. F. D. Moule, *The Birth of the New Testament*, ³1981.

46. Dodd, *Founder*.

47. Thus Dodd maintains the position on the coming of the kingdom for which he argued in *Parables*: it is 'realized' and *not* future.

48. Jeremias, *The Proclamation of Jesus*.

49. The quotation is from O. Betz, *What Do We Know about Jesus?*, ET 1968, p. 74.

50. Demai 2.3. The Mishnah does not actually mention 'a Pharisee', but 'a *haber*', 'associate'. Jeremias habitually but incorrectly equates the two. See *Paul and Palestinian Judaism*, pp. 152–57; below, ch. 6.

51. See *Paul and Palestinian Judaism*, pp. 152–55, and immediately below.

52. Below, ch. 6 at nn. 103, 104.

53. See *Paul and Palestinian Judaism*, pp. 250f. and n. 35.

54. On sin as rebellion in Rabbinic Judaism, see 'Denial of God' in the index to *Paul and Palestinian Judaism*. Jeremias always discusses the Pharisees on the basis of Rabbinic literature, so that my discussion of sin in the view of the Rabbis is an appropriate response to his view of sin in Pharisaism.

55. *Paul and Palestinian Judaism*, pp. 183–98.

56. See *Paul and Palestinian Judaism*, p. 61 n. 12; p. 153 n. 34.

57. Ibid.

58. See Bowker, *Jesus and the Pharisees*, pp. 13f.; *Paul and Palestinian Judaism*, pp. 153f. The point is that *perushim* is used exegetically, almost lexicographically, in Rabbinic literature, especially Sifra, to define what *qedoshim* means: to be holy means to be separate. Thus where Lev. 11.44 says, 'be holy (*qedoshim*). . . you shall not defile

yourselves with any swarming thing that crawls', Sifra comments that 'holy' means 'separate' (*perushim*), i.e., do not touch swarming things that crawl; they confer ritual impurity. This is just sound exegesis. The exegesis probably comes from the school of R. Akiba in the second century, and there is no reason to see here a proof of sectarian self-definition by the Pharisaic party before 70. Jeremias, for example, takes such passages to mean that the *perushim* = Pharisees understood themselves to be the only holy people of God: *Jerusalem in the Time of Jesus*, ET 1969, pp. 247, 249, following Baeck. Bowker's interpretation is more to the point: 'All Jews must be *perushim* in order to be Jews' (p. 14). Here *perushim* does not mean the pre-70 Pharisees. There is no reason, however, to follow Bowker in supposing that separateness is a special key for understanding what he calls the *hakamic* movement. One might better stay with the word *ts-d-q* for this purpose, for it is far more frequent in Rabbinic literature, it occurs very frequently in other post-biblical literature (the Dead Sea Scrolls are a partial exception, but even so *ts-d-q* is more common than *p-r-sh*), and it too is urged as characteristic behaviour of Jews: 'Be *tsaddiq* as I am *tsaddiq*' (Sifre Deut. 49).

59. Bowker, p. 45, quoted above. Ch. I of *Paul and Palestinian Judaism* is devoted to demonstrating that this is the correct understanding of the relationship between the Torah and the covenant in Rabbinic literature.

60. For a thorough canvassing of Jewish scholarship on Jesus, especially on the trial scenes, see Catchpole, *The Trial of Jesus*. There is a valuable collection of essays in *Jewish Expressions on Jesus. An Anthology* (ed. Trude Weiss-Rosmarin), 1977.

61. Klausner, *Jesus of Nazareth*.

62. These include the commandments concerning idolatry and the Sabbath, which can hardly be covered by the trivializing term 'ceremonial'.

63. See Klausner, *From Jesus to Paul*, pp. 441, 528–36, 580–90.

64. G. Vermes, *Jesus the Jew*.

65. So also Solomon Zeitlin, 'Jesus and the Pharisees', repr. in Weiss-Rosmarin, ed., *Jewish Expressions*, pp. 148–56 (= *The Rise and Fall of the Second Judaean State* I, 1962); Ben Zion Bokser, 'Jesus: Jew or Christian?', *Jewish Expressions*, pp. 201–29 (= *Judaism and the Christian Predicament* [ed. B. Z. Bokser], 1967); A. Finkel, *The Pharisees and the Teacher of Nazareth*, 1964. See also Helmut Merkel, 'Jesus im Widerstreit', *Glaube und Gesellschaft. Festschrift für W. F. Kasch*, 1981, pp. 207–17. Merkel disputes the view of P. Lapide, who has frequently argued that Jesus did not break the law, and concludes that Jesus in fact directly contradicted Moses on the questions of Sabbath, purity and divorce. Both are simply repeating positions which we have sketched already.

66. E. Stauffer, *Jesus and His Story*, ET 1960, pp. 149–59. Cf. H.-J. Schoeps, *Paul: The Theology of the Apostle in the Light of Jewish Religious History*, ET 1961, pp. 160–62.

67. Above, p. 34, on Käsemann.

68. *Paul and Palestinian Judaism*, chs. I-III.

69. See the discussion of how the clear intent of Exod. 20.7 is avoided by different Rabbis in *Paul and Palestinian Judaism*, pp. 159f.

1. JESUS AND THE TEMPLE

1. Bultmann (*History*, p. 36): Mark 11.15, 18f. come from the editor; v. 17 is an added saying which has replaced another, which may be preserved in John 2.16. One may conjecture that 11.27–33 followed 11.16 immediately, though probably not as part of the same unit. Roloff (*Der irdische Jesus*, p. 93): the oldest form of the narrative was Mark 11.15f., 18a, 28–33. Vincent Taylor (*The Gospel According to St Mark*, 1959, p. 461): the original unit is 11.15b–17. Mark added vv. 15a, 18f. Boismard (*Synopse*

des quatre Évangiles en Français II: *Commentaire*, 1972, pp. 334–6): Mark 11.27–33 originally followed the 'cleansing' scene. Verses 17f., 19 are later insertions. The casting out of the vendors (11.15) was originally followed by a saying better preserved in John 2.16b. Note also Goguel's view, n. 4 below.

It should be noted that Mark 11.16, absent from both Matthew and Luke, plays little role in these analyses. It is my own view that this sort of general prohibition (see I. Abrahams, *Studies in Pharisaism and the Gospels* I, 1917, reissued 1967, pp. 84f.) does not accord well with overthrowing tables and the like and is probably a later addition, even though it usually passes unquestioned. It may also be doubted that the admonition is appropriate to the temple at Jerusalem, in view of the placement of the gates. In any case, it plays no role in our analysis.

2. For a list of scholars regarding Mark 13.2 as inauthentic (because a weakened form of 14.58, which was embarrassing), see G. R. Beasley-Murray, *A Commentary on Mark Thirteen*, 1957, p. 23. The passage is often accepted as authentic, however, it being noted that in fact the temple was destroyed by fire (see Taylor, *St Mark*, p. 501). Lloyd Gaston (*No Stone on Another*, 1970, pp. 12f., 65, 244, 424f.) has correctly noted that only the redactional framework of Mark 13.2 and parallels mentions the temple, and he proposes that the prophecy of destruction is found in its original form in Luke 19.44, where it refers to the destruction of Jerusalem. He gives (p. 65 n. 1) a bibliography of scholars who combine Mark 13.2 with 14.58 and 15.29 and consider that Jesus did predict or threaten the destruction of the temple – the view taken here. Gaston's view is discussed further in n. 5 and in the next chapter.

3. For both views, that Mark 14.58 is authentic and that it is inauthentic, see Taylor, *St Mark*, p. 566. Taylor regards the passage as authentic.

4. M. Goguel, *Jesus and the Origins of Christianity*, vol. I, *The Life of Jesus*, pp. 412–15, argued that the act and the saying do not form a unity (cf. n. 1), but he proposed that the saying against the profanation of the temple was authentic and that the act of overthrowing the tables was unhistorical and had been created on the basis of the saying. Scholarship has not, however, followed Goguel's proposal. The action against the buyers and sellers and the frequent accusation that Jesus threatened to destroy the temple are mutually supportive.

5. See the survey of opinions by W. D. Davies, *The Gospel and the Land. Early Christianity and Jewish Territorial Doctrine*, 1974, pp. 349–52, nn. 45 and 46.

We should note in addition the intriguing proposals of Lloyd Gaston in *No Stone on Another*. He considers that the origin of the threat to destroy the temple is actually to be found in Stephen's position and does not come from Jesus. Jewish opponents of Christianity picked up Stephen's threat and employed it against the Christian movement. Mark 14.58 and 15.29 (and parallels) are then considered to be a defence against Jewish accusations. He believes that the accusation that Jesus threatened to destroy the temple is no more historical than the accusation that Jesus committed blasphemy by claiming to be Son of God (Mark 14.61–64 and parallels); that is, both accusations are later Jewish accusations against the church (pp. 65–9). The two halves of Mark 14.58 and 15.29 (the threat to destroy and the promise to rebuild) are to be taken separately. The threat to destroy goes back only to Stephen (p. 161), while the promise to rebuild the 'temple' goes back to Jesus but refers to the founding of the eschatological community as the 'temple of God' (pp. 226f., 241, 243). It was only the opponents of Christianity who combined the two traditions, and they appear together in the Gospels because it was necessary to answer the charge (pp. 145f., 162). Gaston considers it conceivable that 'a saying against the temple was important in Jesus' condemnation' (p. 68), but is more impressed by the absence of the charge in Luke and John (p. 68 n.

4). Jesus' own attitude towards the temple as a place of cult was one of indifference (pp. 102, 240f.). I shall argue that the threat of destruction appears in too many strata and coheres too well with the 'cleansing' of the temple to be denied to Jesus, and I follow the majority of scholars in taking the multiple attestation to indicate authenticity. It should be noted that Gaston finds no background in contemporary Jewish thought for the expectation of the destruction and renewal of the temple, and this buttresses his view that the threat is inauthentic. We shall see in the next chapter that the threat and implied renewal do have a setting in Jewish thought.

6. There is some debate about what took place within the temple precincts and what was relegated to the area outside. According to J. Klausner (*Jesus of Nazareth*, p. 314), the Pharisees would have permitted no selling or money-changing in the temple, although the Sadducees, then in charge, may have permitted the use of the outer court. See also Abrahams, *Studies*, pp. 86f.: commercial money-changers would not have been allowed in the temple precincts, but those who turned the profits over to the temple would have been permitted inside for one week, from 25 Adar to 1 Nisan. The buying and selling of sacrificial victims ordinarily took place outside. We cannot settle the question of precise location, but we may assume that trade was allowed only in the court of the Gentiles – if anywhere in the temple confines. To the degree to which the view that there was never any exchange of money in the temple precincts rests on Berakoth 9.5 (and parallels), it may now be dismissed. Jeremias has better explained that mishnah as applying to visitors to the temple area (tourists and the like), who are prohibited from carrying money, not to those who came to offer sacrifice. See J. Jeremias, 'Zwei Miszellen: 1. Antik-Jüdische Münzdeutungen. 2. Zur Geschichtlichkeit der Tempelreinigung', *NTS* 23, 1977, pp. 179f.

7. Edersheim, *The Life and Times of Jesus the Messiah* I, 1936, p. 370.

8. Ibid.: 'Most improper transactions were carried on, to the taking undue advantage of the poor people.'

9. Abrahams, *Studies* I, p. 87.

10. Ibid., p. 88.

11. Ibid., p. 84.

12. Cf. Klausner, *Jesus of Nazareth*, p. 314: the money-changing was necessary (he compares the sale of candles by Christians), 'though such behaviour arouses indignation in the truly devout'.

13. Roloff, *Der irdische Jesus*. p. 89, citing H. Braun, *Spätjüdisch-häretischer und frühchristlicher Radikalismus* II, 1957, p. 12.

14. Roloff, p. 89, citing A. Suhl, *Die Funktion der alttestamentlichen Zitate und Anspielungen im Markusevangelium*, 1965, p. 143.

15. Roloff, p. 95.

16. Ibid., p. 96.

17. Roloff, p. 97. One may note here Bousset's view (*Jesus*, pp. 105f.): Jesus attached no value to any outward forms. In exerting himself 'for the holiness and purity of the Temple service' he still did not give it any true value. The action just shows his dislike of 'pseudo-holiness and hypocrisy'. Roloff agrees on what Jesus did: *purify* the service; but he assigns real value to it in Jesus' eyes.

18. Jeremias, *Proclamation of Jesus*, p. 145. It should be noted that Jeremias accepts Mark 11.17 as authentic, and thus his critical view corresponds to the motive which he attributes to Jesus.

19. Aulén, *Jesus*, p. 77.

20. E. Trocmé, *Jesus as seen by his Contemporaries*, ET 1973, p. 118. Again, compare Davies' analysis of divergent views, *The Gospel and the Land*, p. 349 n. 45, item 2.

21. Harvey, *Constraints*, p. 15.

22. Ibid., p. 131.

23. Ibid., p. 129.

24. Note the argument by Robert Banks (*Jesus and the Law in the Synoptic Tradition*, 1975, p. 208) that an inner/outer distinction is anachronistic (discussing Matt. 5.17).

25. Most explicitly, Bornkamm speaks of the action as 'more than an act of reform to restore the temple service to its original purity' (*Jesus of Nazareth*, pp. 158f.), which means that it was also that.

26. I believe the best treatment of the particular point at hand to be that of Abrahams, *Studies* I, pp. 82–9. For a general account of the priesthood and the temple service, see Emil Schürer, ed. Vermes, *The History of the Jewish People in the Age of Jesus Christ* II, pp. 237–308.

27. On the 'Tyrian' coinage accepted by the temple, see Abrahams, p. 83, where there are references to further literature. See also Bekhoroth 8.7 on the requirement of 'Tyrian' coins.

Here and elsewhere I take the Rabbinic discussions of the temple, the trade, the temple tax, and sacrifices to be somewhat idealized but basically to reflect common thought and practice before 70. Most of the Rabbinic statements about these matters are not peculiarly Pharisaic, and many are confirmed by Josephus and the New Testament. See the discussion of the views of Jacob Neusner and J. N. Epstein in *Paul and Palestinian Judaism*, pp. 63f.

28. See Matt. 17.24–7; Shekalim 1.3 (on taking pledges from those who have not paid).

29. That the temple tax was paid follows from the fact that the Romans, after the fall of the temple, assigned the payment to the capital. According to Josephus (*BJ* VII.218), this resulted in a levy on all Jews, no matter where resident. See further Thackeray's notes in the Loeb edition of Josephus. For Rabbinic theory about how the tax was collected, see Shekalim 1.3 and 2.1.

30. See Shekalim 1.6.

31. Hirsch ('Sacrifice', *JE* 10, p. 617) summarized the uses of the pigeon and turtledove in sacrifices thus: they 'served for burnt offerings and sin-offerings in cases of lustrations. They were allowed as private holocausts, and were accepted as sin-offerings from the poorer people and as purification-offerings . . .' So Josephus, *AJ* III.230. Thus numerous unblemished birds were required.

32. Ps. Sol. 17.6–8. See Adolf Büchler, *Types of Jewish-Palestinian Piety from 70 B.C.E. to 70 C.E.*, 1922, pp. 170–4.

33. T.Mos 6.1; Büchler, ibid.

34. CD 5.7; Ps. Sol. 8.13; cf. Niddah 4.2. See *Paul and Palestinian Judaism*, p. 404.

35. For the criticism of the cult on the grounds of different halakah, see Yigael Yadin, *The Scroll of the War of the Sons of Light Against the Sons of Darkness*, 1962, pp. 198f.

36. Yoma 19b; *Paul and Palestinian Judaism*, p. 151.

37. Nahman Avigad, commenting on a discovery of what he believes to have been a workshop which supplied incense and the like to the temple, describes the owner as having 'usurped' the privilege for his own gain. Such information does not come from archaeology, but from applying a generalization to a particular person. The priests in general, he writes 'abused their position . . . through nepotism and oppression' (*Discovering Jerusalem*, 1983, pp. 130f.).

38. Gaston (*No Stone on Another*, p. 85) gives a bibliography of those who see Jesus as a religious reformer and appropriately comments: 'In contrast to the manner in

which the Essenes would have cleansed the temple, beginning with the High Priest and continuing with a reform of the whole cult, Jesus cannot be seen here as a religious reformer, cleansing the temple of abuses.'

39. We noted above (n. 18) that Jeremias, for example, accepts Mark 11.17 as giving Jesus' motive. Cf. also Albert Nolan, *Jesus before Christianity*, 1980, p. 102: the issue was only the 'abuse of money and trade'. Nolan continues by stating that there is evidence for fraud and theft, citing Jeremias, *Jerusalem in the Time of Jesus*, pp. 33f. Those pages, however, contain no such evidence, nor do I know of any.

40. See above, n. 1; further the *Ergänzungsheft* to Bultmann's *Geschichte*, ed. G. Theissen and Philipp Vielhauer, ⁴1971, p. 29. The authenticity of Mark 11.17 is doubted also by Georg Klinzing, *Die Umdeuteung des Kultus in der Qumrangemeinde und im Neuen Testament*, 1971, p. 209. Note also the view of Maria Trautmann, *Zeichenhafte Handlungen Jesu*, 1980. She never doubts that 'cleansing' is the right term, though she argues persuasively against the authenticity of Mark 11.17 (pp. 87–90).

41. Roloff, *Der irdische Jesus*, p. 93.

42. Harvey, *Constraints*, p. 132 and notes.

43. For references, see W. D. Davies, *The Gospel and the Land*, p. 349 n. 45 item 1 See especially the sensitive treatment by Moule, *Birth*, pp. 21–5.

44. Davies, loc. cit.

45. For the sake of argument, we presently accept the view that the trade, or part of it, was conducted in the court of the Gentiles. See n. 6 above and Davies' defence of this location, *The Gospel and the Land*, pp. 350f.

46. Compare, however, the argument of J. D. M. Derrett, 'The Zeal of thy House and the Cleansing of the Temple', *Downside Review* 95, 1977, pp. 79–94. He proposes that the casting out of merchants is something to which the prophets looked forward, citing Zech. 14.21 and other passages which do not appear to be directly relevant.

47. One could conceivably think that Jesus wanted to purify the temple, but simultaneously to redefine purity in such a way as to eliminate the standard distinction between sacred and profane. The redefinition would involve purging externals (sacrifice) in favour of internals (prayer). One may think, for example, of Käsemann's view that this is what Jesus did in Mark 7.15: it is not food which makes impure, but what comes out of the heart (see the Introduction, p. 34). I have not noted that anyone explicitly argues this case with regard to the temple, but the widespread discussion of Jesus' action in the temple as cleansing or purifying the service may rest on such a view. I would regard such a proposal, were it to be made, as being too improbable to discuss. Cf. the comment on the inner/outer distinction in the next note.

48. I am not arguing that *no* Jew of Jesus' day could have made the inner/outer distinction which is often attributed to him. On the contrary, Philo's writings contain this sort of distinction, and it may also be seen in Rom. 2.28f. It is more than slightly difficult, however, to find this kind of distinction in literature of Palestinian provenance. Most to the point, I know of no clear example in the synoptic Gospels.

49. S. G. F. Brandon, *Jesus and the Zealots*, 1967. See Davies, *The Gospel and the Land*, pp. 349f. n. 45 item 4.

50. Davies, *The Gospel and the Land*, pp. 350f. n. 46. So also Dodd, *Founder*, p. 147; Pesch, 'Der Anspruch Jesu', p. 56. According to the latter, the key passage is the quotation of Isa. 56.7 in Mark 11.17, but we have already seen that the verse is most probably a later addition.

51. Trade in the court of the Gentiles: see above, nn. 6 and 45.

52. Davies, *The Gospel and the Land*, p. 351.

53. See especially Hengel, *Was Jesus a Revolutionist?*, ET 1971.

54. Gaston (*No Stone on Another*, p. 87) has strongly objected to drawing far-reaching conclusions from the possibility that the 'cleansing' took place in the court of the Gentiles.

55. Trautmann, *Zeichenhafte Handlungen*, pp. 120–22.

56. Examples are given throughout the section on the 'State of the Question' in the Introduction. Recently see Jeremias, *Proclamation*, p. 145; Meyer, *Aims*, p. 238; H. W. Bartsch, *Jesus. Prophet und Messias aus Galiläa*, 1970, p. 48; Boismard, *Synopse* II, p. 408: it was the sacerdotal caste which became exasperated at seeing Jesus pose as a religious reformer with regard to cultic practice.

57. Thus, for example, Roloff, *Der irdische Jesus*, p. 95; Brandon, *Jesus and the Zealots*, p. 338; cf. Meyer, *Aims*, p. 170: 'Jesus' act was symbol-charged'; Gaston, *No Stone on Another*, p. 86: the action was symbolic.

58. Hengel, *Was Jesus a Revolutionist?*, pp. 16f. Cf. Dodd, *Founder*, pp. 144f. 'The force which effected it was simply the personal authority which made itself felt when Jesus confronted the crowd.'

59. See the next note.

60. In favour of this interpretation of the action, see for example R. J. McKelvey, *The New Temple. The Church in the New Testament*, 1969, p. 66 ('it points to the coming of the kingdom of God'); pp. 71f. ('The new age would have its temple . . .'); James D. G. Dunn, *Unity and Diversity in the New Testament*, 1977, p. 324 (Jesus' disciples understood the action as pointing towards 'eschatological renewal centred on Mount Zion and on an eschatologically renewed or rebuilt temple'); Trautmann, *Zeichenhafte Handlungen*, pp. 124, 126f., 129, 386. On p. 130 she argues that the action was not 'prophetic', since there was no appeal to the Lord, which I take to be a distinction without much of a difference. Trautmann's position is interesting, since she holds that Jesus intended to purify the temple of present corrupting practice, but yet manages to see that the action points towards a new temple. The real force of the event stands out even more sharply when it is not confused with another, competing interpretation.

61. Note the setting of Jer. 19.10 in a lengthy spoken prediction of destruction.

62. Bultmann, *History*, p. 36.

63. See ch. 11 below.

64. The principal alternative for understanding Mark's meaning has been well argued by Donald Juel, *Messiah and Temple: The Trial of Jesus in the Gospel of Mark*, 1977. His chief conclusion is that the author of Mark had in mind the Christian community as the temple not made with hands (see, for example, pp. 168f.). See also Dodd, *Founder*, pp. 89f.; Klinzing, *Umdeutung*, pp. 202f. (with bibliography). Klinzing (p. 204) also argues that the phrases 'made with hands' and 'not made with hands', absent from Matthew, are secondary additions.

65. Cf. Gaston, *No Stone on Another*, p. 71.

66. Thus Bultmann: a saying about the temple goes back to Jesus, but we must remain uncertain about the form (*History*, pp. 120f.; *Ergänzungsheft*, pp. 46f., with bibliography). In the *Ergänzungsheft* he corrected his earlier view that the saying has a mythological basis and correctly placed it in the framework of Jewish apocalyptic (in the sense of eschatology). Dieter Lührmann's discussion of the sayings is quite instructive. He points out that Mark regarded the threat of Mark 14.58 as inauthentic, but accepted the prediction of 13.2. One can be certain that there was *a* saying and suspect that the version in 14.58 is closer to the original. See Lührmann, 'Markus 14.55–64. Christologie und Zerstörung des Tempels im Markusevangelium', *NTS* 27, 1981, pp. 457–74, here 466–9.

67. See the next chapter.

68. Gaston (*No Stone on Another*, p. 45) cites a true *vaticinium ex eventu* on the destruction of Jerusalem from Lactantius, *Divine Institutions* IV.21. It is much more explicit and detailed than anything in the Gospels.

69. *Der irdische Jesus*, p. 97; cf. Meyer, *Aims*, p. 170.

70. Bornkamm, *Jesus of Nazareth*, pp. 158f.

71. The view that Jesus expected a new, end-time temple is by no means unique, although, as I have indicated, it is often mixed – I think uncomfortably – with the interpretation of the action as cleansing (e.g. Trautmann and others, cited in n. 60; Roloff and Meyer, cited in n. 69). For the view that Jesus expected a new temple, see recently Klinzing, *Umdeutung*, p. 205 (citing further literature); Meyer, *Aims*, pp. 168-70; 181-5; 197f.

72. Harvey (*Constraints*, pp. 133f.) proposes that the action was not immediately understood, but that it would have been at least seen as a claim to authority.

2. NEW TEMPLE AND RESTORATION IN JEWISH LITERATURE

1. Lloyd Gaston, *No Stone on Another*, 1970; R. J. McKelvey, *The New Temple*, 1969. The standard older works on Judaism, such as those by Billerbeck, Bousset and Volz, have treatments of the theme (lacking, of course, the important evidence of the Dead Sea Scrolls), but Gaston has adequately taken account of them. The most important recent works which deal with aspects of thought about the temple, though not so specifically with temple and eschaton as do Gaston and McKelvey, are these: Gärtner, *The Temple and the Community in Qumran and the New Testament*, 1965; Klinzing, *Die Umdeutung des Kultus in der Qumrangemeinde und im Neuen Testament*, 1971; Juel, *Messiah and Temple*, 1977.

2. Claus Westermann (*Isaiah* 40-66, ET 1969, p. 296) dates Trito-Isaiah (chs. 56-66) around 530 BCE. The temple was dedicated in 515.

3. See McKelvey, *New Temple*, pp. 12-17. Joachim Jeremias brought these and similar passages to prominence in New Testament studies (*Jesus' Promise to the Nations*, ET 1958).

4. George Nickelsburg, *Jewish Literature Between the Bible and the Mishnah*, 1981, p. 18.

5. Charles, *I Enoch*, p. 53.

6. Gaston, *No Stone on Another*, p. 114.

7. See M. de Jonge, *Studies on the Testaments of the Twelve Patriarchs*, 1975, p. 189: 'The very fact that Jewish traditions were taken over by Christian groups with or without alterations, and that Jewish documents were used for and adapted to Christian purposes makes it wellnigh impossible to distinguish exactly between Jewish and Christian elements in the Testaments.'

8. There is no conflict between the view that the sect substitutes for the temple (1QS) and the expectation of a future temple, as some propose (e.g. Klinzing, *Umdeutung*, pp. 89-93). See Joseph Baumgarten, Review of Yadin, *The Temple Scroll*, *JBL* 97, 1978, p. 589.

9. Gaston, *No Stone on Another*, p. 126.

10. Ibid.

11. Ibid.

12. Yadin, *The Scroll of the War*, pp. 198-201.

13. Gaston, p. 162; see the summary quotation above, p. 78.

14. See Gaston, ibid., pp. 127f.; 164. There is a careful consideration of the difficulties of the passage from 4Qflor. in Klinzing, *Umdeutung*, pp. 80-87. Klinzing

favours the view that the passage refers to the future temple to be built by God. Cf. Juel, *Messiah and Temple*, pp. 172–79; McKelvey, *New Temple*, p. 51.

15. David Flusser, 'Two Notes on the Midrash on 2 Sam. vii', *IEJ* 9, 1959, p. 102 n. 11.

16. Gaston, *No Stone on Another*, pp. 127f., 164.

17. Quoted from a paper read in June, 1978, at Brown University. I am grateful to Dr Lichtenberger for sending a copy of the typescript.

18. The word '*ad*, 'until', is smeared in the fragments, but Yadin seems sufficiently certain of the reading that he does not bracket it.

19. Yigael Yadin, *Megillat ha-Miqdash* II, 1977, pp. 91f.

20. In the outline of world history which this oracle contains, the reference in Sib.Or. 3.294 is to the building of the second temple after the Exile. We nevertheless see how natural was the connection between restoration and new temple. On this section of the Sibylline Oracles, see John Collins, *Between Athens and Jerusalem*, 1983, pp. 66–8.

21. For 'seen of all', cf. Ps.Sol. 17.32; Isa. 2.2; Micah 4.1 ('highest of the mountains').

22. See the comments on the Testament (Assumption) of Moses below.

23. I do not take up here the standard question of whether the *Messiah* would be expected to build the new temple. Here there is really no evidence which can be firmly dated to the time of Jesus or shortly before. See Gaston, pp. 147–54, and now the very careful and nuanced work of Juel, *Messiah and Temple*, ch. 9. Cf. also Dieter Lührmann, 'Markus 14.55–64', p. 465.

24. Klinzing (*Umdeutung*, pp. 86f.), who thinks that the expectation of a new temple was very widespread in Judaism, may overstate the case, just as Gaston seems to understate it. There is a similar overstatement in G. Baumbach, *Jesus von Nazareth im Lichte der jüdischen Gruppenbildung*, 1971, pp. 65f.

25. Cf. Ramsay MacMullen, *Paganism in the Roman Empire*, 1981, p. 14.

26. Claus-Hunno Hunzinger, 'Fragmente einer älteren Fassung des Buches Milhama aus Höhle 4 von Qumran', *ZAW* 69, 1957, pp. 131–51.

27. I transgress here the rule of not citing evidence from after 70 CE. In fact some of the post-70 Jewish apocalypses do not explicitly mention the temple (4 Ezra; Apocalypse of Abraham), and it is not unreasonable to see Revelation countering a general and continuing expectation of a new temple rather than explicitly post-70 hopes.

28. Josephus, *BJ* VI.300–305, on Jesus son of Ananias.

29. Gaston, *No Stone on Another*, p. 119.

30. For 'iniquity of the priests', see T.Mos. 5.3. This reference is apparently to the pre-Maccabean priests. Hasmonean priests are referred to in 6.1 (they also work iniquity). The exaltation of Israel is in 10.9. Nickelsburg (*Jewish Literature*, pp. 18, 213) points out that chs. 6 and 7 have been added to an earlier work.

31. An interpretation which combines cleansing and reform with restoration would fit perfectly well into the overall depiction of Jesus which will be offered here. Thus Meyer, *Aims*, p. 170; cf. p. 198. But I think in fact that the evidence for reform is quite weak.

3. OTHER INDICATIONS OF RESTORATION ESCHATOLOGY

1. That Jesus was baptized by John is now virtually unquestioned. See, for example, Bultmann, *History*, p. 247, answering Eduard Meyer's more sceptical view. Ch. Guignebert, who was prepared to be sceptical about more things than is customary

today (usually with just cause; he had a clear eye for what he called the hagiographical aspects of the Gospels), had some doubts, but concluded that the church's evident embarrassment about the baptism renders it on the whole probable (*Jesus*, ET 1935, pp. 147, 157). For the view that the paths of John and Jesus never crossed, see Morton Scott Enslin, *Christian Beginnings*: Parts I and II, 1938, reissued 1956, p. 151; 'John and Jesus', *ZNW* 66, 1975, pp. 1–18.

2. Cf. James D. G. Dunn, *Jesus and the Spirit*, 1975, p. 42: 'To set a non-apocalyptic Jesus between an apocalyptic John the Baptist on the one hand and an apocalyptic primitive Christian community on the other, is to strain the "criterion of dissimilarity" beyond breaking point.' Jack T. Sanders (*Ethics in the New Testament*, 1975, p. 5) points out that the strongest proof that Jesus expected an imminent end is his endorsement of John the Baptist, Matt. 11.7–11a, 16–19 and par.

3. For a hypothetical reconstruction of a source behind the Fourth Gospel's portrayal of Jesus' continuation with the Baptist, see Goguel, *Jesus*, pp. 269–75. He took his study to show that Jesus worked for a while 'on lines similar to those of the Baptist' and that the two separated after a disagreement.

4. Josephus, *AJ* XVIII.116–119. According to Josephus, John's baptism was not for the eradication of sins, but required prior cleansing by right behaviour. The need for repentance is in any case clear. That John was an eschatological prophet is less clear in Josephus, who here as elsewhere probably downplays eschatological features. Nevertheless, he writes that Herod had him executed because he feared that trouble would result. Baptism and piety do not account for that reaction, and a message of national redemption is thus made probable.

5. The evangelists call attention to Isa. 40.3 (Mark 1.3 and parr.). On the desert as a place for the restoration of Israel's true worship, see Hos. 2.14–20 (Heb. 2.16–22); cf. 12.9(10). On John's dress (Matt. 3.4), see II Kings 1.8: Elijah on his return is recognized by his clothing. (The clothing could be worn by false prophets: Zech. 13.4) Goguel (*Jesus*, p. 276) called the expectation that Elijah would precede the Messiah 'widespread'. He cited as primary evidence Ben Sira 48.10f., where, however, there is no Messiah. Mal. 4.5 appears not to have been very influential, and this aspect of 'Jewish messianic dogma' is less well attested than even the expectation of a Davidic king, which itself cannot be called 'widespread'. But whether or not the expectation was widespread, the conscious recollection of Elijah is clear enough in the Gospel accounts. See on this Hengel, *Charismatic Leader*, p. 36 n. 71.

6. Among recent works on Jesus which aim at a more detailed account of the Baptist, one may consult Jeremias, *Proclamation*, pp. 43–9, and especially the careful and critical account in Meyer, *Aims*, pp. 115–22. There is also, of course, a body of literature which focuses on the Baptist himself. See for example Walter Wink, *John the Baptist in the Gospel Tradition*, 1968. Most of Wink's work deals with the evangelists' use of the traditions about John, but he sees clearly that the theological use of the Baptist depends on a 'historical fact, that through John's mediation Jesus perceived the nearness of the kingdom and his own relation to its coming' (p. 113, emphasis removed).

7. There is an interesting, though not entirely convincing argument in favour of such recognition in J. C. O'Neill, *Messiah. Six Lectures on the Ministry of Jesus*, 1980, pp. 2–8.

8. O'Neill, *Messiah*, pp. 10f.

9. On Jesus' frequent use of arguments *a fortiori (qal vahomar)*, see Cadbury, *The Peril of Modernizing Jesus*, pp. 58–63.

10. This is present over the whole chronological range of Paul's letters. His view of the end, and of the probability that he would live to see it, may have changed somewhat,

but the expectation that it was near did not. See I Thess. 4.15–17 (we who are left); I Cor. 15.51f. ('we shall not all sleep'); I Cor. 7.29 and Rom. 13.11f. (both to the effect that the end was near). See also II Cor. 4.14; II Cor. 5.1–10; Phil. 1.19–26.

11. Sanders, *Paul, the Law and the Jewish People*, pp. 171–79.

12. Ibid., pp. 179–90.

13. Johannes Munck, *Paul and the Salvation of Mankind*, ET 1959, pp. 119f.

14. The motive behind Peter's withdrawal is hypothetical, but it is the most reasonable one that can be advanced. See *Paul, the Law and the Jewish People*, pp. 19; 50 n. 13 (further literature).

15. We cannot be certain that Peter never baptized a Gentile, just as we cannot be certain that Paul never baptized a Jew. The intention here is to describe the main lines of apostolic endeavour. Peter was basically an apostle to the circumcision (Gal. 2.9). His position on the Gentiles was 'moderate'. Paul distinctly separates him from those who wished to require circumcision of the Gentiles. Further, Peter visited Gentile churches, not only in Antioch, but apparently elsewhere (I Cor. 1.12; perhaps also 9.5).

16. See above, p. 79. Proposals that the expectation of the conversion of Gentiles had greatly declined are discussed below, ch. 7.

17. Above, p. 87. T. F. Glasson, who is generally sceptical about eschatology as dominating the period, nevertheless correctly notes that all the Jewish literature of the period includes 'the national hope': 'What is Apocalyptic', *NTS* 27, 1980, p. 100.

18. See Huebsch, *The Understanding and Significance of the 'Remnant' in Qumran Literature*.

19. The end of punishment – which has been more than enough – is proclaimed in Isa. 40.2; but this turned out to be premature. See, for example, Dan. 9. There is no effort here to fix a point at which the theme of a remnant which survives Israel's well-deserved punishment disappears. I intend only to point to a general tendency in the later period.

20. See J. Heinemann, *Prayer in the Talmud. Forms and Patterns*, ET 1977, pp. 35f.

21. Especially Jeremias, *Proclamation*, p. 48; 'Der Gedanke des "Heiligen Restes" im Spätjudentum und in der Verkündigung Jesu' (1949), now in *Abba*, 1966. Note Meyer's caution on the Pharisees: *Aims*, p. 234.

22. Thus 1QH 6.7f.: 'Thou *wilt* raise up . . . a remnant'. 1QM 13.8f.; 14.8f. are best taken as referring to the eschatological period. See Huebsch, *The Understanding and Significance of the 'Remnant' in Qumran Literature*; *Paul and Palestinian Judaism*, pp. 250f. and n. 35.

23. See the discussion on the Dead Sea Scrolls immediately below.

24. From the biblical passages in ch. 2, note for example Isa. 49.6 ('the tribes of Jacob') and 56.8 ('the dispersed' without specifying the tribes).

25. For various interpretations, see *Paul and Palestinian Judaism*, pp. 253f.

26. Note also I Cor. 9.5, where Cephas is named alongside the apostles and the brothers of the Lord. He receives separate mention, but is one of the apostles. See C. K. Barrett, 'Cephas and Corinth', *Essays on Paul*, 1982, pp. 30f.

27. Matt. 27.3–10; Acts 1.18f. The stories are legendary; but, as I shall argue below, the betrayal and defection are historical. See below on the church's embarrassment about Judas's inclusion in the twelve.

28. See Phillip Vielhauer, 'Gottesreich und Menschensohn in der Verkündigung Jesu', *Festschrift für Gunther Dehn*, 1957, pp. 62–4. For the criticism of Vielhauer's position, cf. Robert Meye, *Jesus and the Twelve*, 1968, pp. 206f.

29. See Vielhauer, 'Gottesreich und Menschensohn', p. 63.

30. Cf. Jeremias, *Proclamation*, p. 234.

31. Goguel, *Jesus*, pp. 340f. Jeremias (*Proclamation*, p. 232 n. 3) proposes that Luke has simply abbreviated the saying.

32. For discussions of more scholarly positions about the twelve, see Meye, *Jesus and the Twelve*, pp. 192–209; Trautmann, *Zeichenhafte Handlungen*, p. 168 and notes; Dunn, *Spirit*, p. 25. A vast majority of scholars is in favour of the basic historicity of the twelve as Jesus' chosen followers.

33. In these lists Matthew and Mark have a Thaddeus and Luke and Acts a Judas, son of James. John gives no list of names, though he does call the disciples 'the twelve' (John 6.67; 20.24). In John 1.40–51 we find the names Andrew, Simon (Peter), Philip and Nathanael. The last name is not in the other lists. In John 20.24 Thomas is called one of the twelve.

34. Cf. Gaston, *No Stone on Another*, p. 417: 'the very fact that the various lists in the gospels do not completely agree is a sign of the institution of the Twelve not by the church but by Jesus'; so also Meye, *Jesus and the Twelve*, pp. 200f.

35. It may well be that, as John 1.25–40 has it, some of Jesus' disciples were originally disciples of John the Baptist. Cf. Raymond Brown, *The Gospel According to John*, 1966, p. 77.

36. E.g. Kümmel, *Theology*, pp. 37f.; Bornkamm, *Jesus of Nazareth*, p. 150; Dunn, *Spirit*, p. 81.

37. Especially Guignebert, *Jesus*, pp. 219–23; cf. Goguel, *Jesus*, pp. 340f.

38. H. Schürmann, 'Symbolhandlungen Jesus als eschatologische Erfüllungszeichen', *Das Geheimnis Jesu. Versuche zur Jesusfrage*, 1972, p. 89; Pesch, 'Anspruch', p. 68.

39. Cf. II Cor. 12.12; Acts 3.5–7.

40. As does Trocmé, *Jesus*, pp. 37f.

41. Schweizer, *Jesus*, p. 41. Schweizer here as elsewhere turns the lack of evidence for a more ambitious programme into an argument that Jesus had nothing in particular in mind (cf. pp. 42f.).

42. Cf. Goguel, *Jesus*, p. 335; Guignebert, *Jesus*, pp. 217f.

43. Trautmann, *Zeichenhafte Handlungen*, pp. 190–99. Further page references are given in the text.

44. Cf. Moule, *Birth*, p. 54: 'The very number twelve bears witness to the Israel-consciousness of Jesus.' See also H. Schürmann, 'Der Jüngerkreis Jesu als Zeichen für Israel', *Das Geheimnis Jesu*, 1972, pp. 126–53; 'Die Symbolhandlungen Jesu als eschatologische Erfüllungszeichen', esp. pp. 89f.

45. O'Neill, *Messiah*, pp. 90–3.

46. Jeremias, *Proclamation*, p. 236.

47. O'Neill, p. 90, citing also Matt. 18.18 ('bind and loose') and John 20.23.

48. Ibid., p. 92.

49. Jeremias, loc. cit.

50. On 'apostle' in Paul, see the fine survey by K. H. Rengstorf, 'ἀπόστολος', *TDNT* I, pp. 407–47.

51. One can see the beginnings of the later terminology by comparing the Hebrew and Greek in Jer. 8.6 and Ben Sira 48.15. There is further information on the history of the terms in J. Behm, 'μετανοέω, μετάνοια in Hellenistic Jewish Literature' and 'Conversion in Rabbinic Literature', *TDNT* IV, pp. 989–99. The classical treatment of repentance in Rabbinic literature, however, remains that of G. F. Moore, *Judaism in the First Centuries of the Christian Era: The Age of the Tannaim*, 3 vols., 1927–30; see the index s.v. Repentance. A collection of passages from a wider range of material will

be found under the same index heading under *Paul and Palestinian Judaism*. See also the passages from the post-biblical period cited by Jacques Schlosser, *Le règne de Dieu dans les dits de Jésus*, 1980, I, pp. 101–3.

52. See CD 4.2; 6.4f.; 8.16; 20.17; 1QS 10.20; 1QH 2.9; 14.24; cf. 4QpPs37 3.1.

53. *Paul and Palestinian Judaism*, p. 270.

54. See below, ch. 4 n. 44; ch. 6 section 3.1.

55. See, for example, Perrin, *Rediscovering*, pp. 90–102; H. Braun, *Jesus of Nazareth: The Man and his Time*, ET 1979, pp. 44–52; Jeremias, *New Testament Theology I*, pp. 152–58; Hans Conzelmann, *Jesus*, ET 1973, pp. 19, 78; James Charlesworth, 'The Historical Jesus in Light of Writings Contemporaneous with Him', *ANRW* II.25.1, 1982, pp. 451–76.

56. It is major in Luke-Acts, substantial in Hebrews, peripheral in Paul and absent from John.

57. As in the first section of this chapter, I here leave aside studies which try to distinguish original material about John from later accretions. See, for example, Bultmann, *History*, pp. 245–47 (he suspects a Christian addition, for example, in the reference to Isa. 40).

58. Bultmann (*History*, p. 341), correctly in my view, considered this summary to show 'the influence of the terminology used in Christian missionary preaching'. So also Joachim Rhode (*Rediscovering the Teaching of the Evangelists*, ET 1968, p. 124): 'The words in Mark 1.14, 15 are in fact the beginning of the preaching of the Risen One in the evangelist's view and not a beginning of the preaching of the historical Jesus.' Jeremias (*Proclamation*, p. 42) pointed out that 'until quite recently' Matt. 4.17 'has continually misled scholars into thinking that Jesus made his appearance with a call to repentance.' Herbert Braun, however, considers that the community, in formulating Matt. 4.17, 'correctly caught the meaning of Jesus' message' (Braun, *Jesus*, p. 40). Other scholars who take Mark 1.14f. as a reliable summary of the teaching of Jesus include Charlesworth, 'The Historical Jesus', pp. 458f. and notes, where there is extensive bibliography; Schlosser, *Règne*, I, p. 105 (in Mark 1.14f. the authentic fragments are 'the kingdom is near' and 'repent').

59. I shall return to Luke's role in attributing sayings about repentance to Jesus, pp. 175, 203, 206, 277 below. For the present it is not necessary to debate authenticity, except to note the Lucan conclusions in 15.7, 10.

60. Bultmann, *History*, pp. 112f., quoting A. Fridrichsen, *Le Problème du Miracle*, 1935, p. 49. I do not find the structural argument very persuasive, but the anti-Jewish polemic seems clear enough.

61. Bultmann, *History*, pp. 54f.

62. See e.g. Jeremias, *New Testament Theology I*, pp. 135, 156.

63. Perrin, *Rediscovering*, p. 194. He regarded the refusal of a sign and the reference to 'the sign of Jonah' to be authentic, but problematic as to meaning.

64. Jeremias, *Proclamation*, pp. 156f.

65. Schlosser, *Règne* I, p. 103. He thinks that these two points are authentic fragments (p. 105.).

66. John Riches, *Jesus and the Transformation of Judaism*, 1980, p. 87.

67. Ibid., pp. 87–90.

68. Charlesworth, 'The Historical Jesus', p. 472.

69. Ibid.

70. Conzelmann, *Jesus*, p. 78.

71. Numerous passages from a wide range of Jewish literature are collected in *Paul and Palestinian Judaism*, pp. 117–25; 350f.; 352; 355–8; 360; 366f.; 391–4.

72. Riches, *Jesus and the Transformation of Judaism*, pp. 99–106, 168.

73. Bultmann, *History*, pp. 111–18.

74. Schlosser, *Règne*, pp. 632f.

75. They are accepted, for example, by Conzelmann, above, n. 70.

76. Caird, *Jesus and the Jewish Nation*, p. 16; Meyer, *Aims*, passim, e.g., p. 223; Dunn, *Spirit*, p. 81.

77. Bornkamm, *Jesus of Nazareth*, p. 66.

78. Davies (*The Gospel and the Land*, pp. 336–54) seeks a nuance between Caird and Bornkamm: Jesus was concerned not with the *nation* of Israel, but with the People of God (p. 349).

79. Bornkamm, *Jesus of Nazareth*, p. 66.

80. Ibid., pp. 77f.

81. Caird accepts as authentic material about which I am dubious, such as the mission to the cities of Israel (Luke 10.1–12; he regards the number seventy [or seventy-two] as Lucan), and the woes against the Galilean cities (Luke 10.13–15). He would not, I think, grant the distinction between facts, which point to the theme of 'all Israel', and the sayings, which are individualistic. The saying of woe on the Galilean cities he takes to show that Jesus looked for 'a corporate rather than an individual response'. See G. B. Caird, *Saint Luke*, 1963, pp. 142–44.

82. Martin Hengel (*The Charismatic Leader and His Followers*, p. 59) points to a similar problem. Jesus called only select individuals to *follow* him. He was thus not a ' "popular messianic leader" '. Hengel thinks that Jesus' message was one of repentance (p. 61), but he nevertheless sees the same general problem ('all Israel *or* individualism) which we have found. I return to Hengel's solution in ch. 8.

83. Breech, *Silence*, p. 218.

84. Ernst Bammel, 'Erwägungen zur Eschatologie Jesu', *Studia Evangelica* 3, 1964, esp. pp. 8f., 18. Accepted by W. Schenk, 'Gefangenschaft und Tod des Täufers', *NTS* 29, 1983, pp. 455f.

85. C. E. B. Cranfield, 'Thoughts on New Testament Eschatology', *SJT* 35, 1982, pp. 497–512.

86. Barry S. Crawford, 'Near Expectation in the Sayings of Jesus', *JBL* 101, 1982, pp. 225–44.

87. Freyne has shown that the revolutionary atmosphere in Galilee has been greatly exaggerated. This renders even less surprising the fact that Jesus thought of restoration without recourse to arms. See Seán Freyne, *Galilee from Alexander the Great to Hadrian: 323 B.C.E. to 135 C.E.*, 1980, pp. 208–55.

4. THE SAYINGS

1. Johannes Weiss, *Jesus' Proclamation of the Kingdom of God* (1892), ET 1971.

2. Schweizer, *Quest*.

3. Schweizer used the word 'eschatology'; but, because of the long-standing definition of apocalyptic literature as including an urgent expectation of the end, 'apocalyptic' and 'eschatological' have often been used more or less interchangeably. See for example Kümmel, *Promise and Fulfilment*, pp. 88f. ('the question arises whether Jesus' eschatological message must not be simply fitted into this late Jewish apocalyptic'); though Kümmel goes ahead to say that Jesus rejected many of the features of apocalyptic. In recent years a concern has arisen to define terms more carefully, and definitions have been offered for 'apocalyptic' and 'apocalypse' which do not necessarily include urgent expectation of the end. See J. J. Collins (ed.), *Apocalypse: The Morphology*

of a Genre, 1979; J. Carmignac, 'Qu'est-ce que l'apocalyptique? Son emploi à Qumrân', *RQ* 10, 1979, pp. 3–33; Christopher Rowland, *The Open Heaven*, 1982; E. P. Sanders, 'The Genre of the Palestinian Jewish Apocalypses', *Apocalypticism in the Mediterranean World and the Near East* (ed. D. Hellholm), 1983. Here as elsewhere in this work I use 'eschatology' to refer to the expectation of an imminent end to the current order.

4. Cf. T. Francis Glasson, 'Schweitzer's Influence – Blessing or Bane?', *JTS* n.s. 28, 1977, pp. 289–302, here 296. Schweitzer did not make his limitations clear in his discussion of Jewish apocalyptic literature and Jewish eschatology in *Quest*, pp. 367–70. In the Preface to *The Mysticism of Paul the Apostle*, however, his need to rely on experts (he names Gerhard Kittel and Karl Rengstorf) is expressed.

5. Schweitzer, *Quest*, pp. 371f.; cf. p. 362.

6. Glasson, 'Schweitzer's Influence', p. 299.

7. I share the doubts of Glasson and others about the date of the Similitudes of Enoch, where the Son of man does figure as judge. See *Paul and Palestinian Judaism*, pp. 347f. But even if this section is pre-Christian, we still could not say that the expectation of a heavenly figure coming to judge humanity was widespread in first-century Judaism.

8. Glasson admits the ubiquity of 'the national hope', 'What is Apocalyptic?', p. 100.

9. Glasson ('Schweitzer's influence', p. 299) cites T. W. Manson, *Servant Messiah*, 1953, p. 32.

10. As do, in various ways, Bultmann, Breech and Scott, all to be cited below.

11. Perrin, *Jesus and the Language of the Kingdom*, p. 40.

12. Ibid., p. 43, referring to Luke 11.20.

13. Scott, *Symbol-Maker*, pp. 10f.

14. Ibid., e.g. pp. 12, 29.

15. Ibid., pp. 11f. Scott's point, if I follow it, is that Jesus did not define 'kingdom' in discursive speech (which is true, as far as our limited knowledge goes), but further that, as a symbol, it cannot be so defined. To some degree this is based on the nature of parables, a point which will be discussed more fully just below.

16. Scott, *Symbol-Maker*, pp. 9–11; cf. Perrin, *Language*, pp. 2f.

17. Scott, *Symbol-Maker*, p. 11.

18. This is the core meaning which Bruce D. Chilton assigns the word in the synoptic Gospels and the Targum to Isaiah: *God in Strength. Jesus' Announcement of the Kingdom*, 1979, pp. 89, 285, 287. His phrases are 'God's self-revelation' and 'God come in strength'.

19. James Breech, *Silence*, pp. 218f.

20. See my 'Puzzling Out Rabbinic Judaism', *Approaches to Ancient Judaism* II (ed. William Scott Green), 1980, pp. 65–79, esp. pp. 69–75. The best critical assessment of Neusner's overall programme is that of Hyam Maccoby, 'Jacob Neusner's Mishnah', *Midstream* 30, 1984, pp. 24–32. For the present point see esp. p. 26.

21. See especially Breech, *Silence*, pp. 1–5.

22. Cf. Chilton, *God in Strength*, p. 15: 'We should avoid exegeting "the kingdom of God" from a perspective which would have been esoteric to Jesus' hearers.'

23. See Jacques Schlosser, *Règne*, pp. 42–7.

24. Here and elsewhere I use 'sayings material' as a general term to include sayings proper (*logia*), parables, other forms of teaching, and proclamation. Bruce Chilton has correctly objected to the use of 'teaching' to cover all sayings, including proclamation: *God in Strength*, p. 21.

25. Schweitzer, *Quest*, pp. 357f.

26. Ibid., pp. 360f.   27. Ibid., pp. 365–7.

28. Ibid., pp. 370f.
29. See above, pp. 26f. and notes.
30. *Jesus and the Word*, p. 38.
31. Ibid., p. 43.
32. Ibid., pp. 51f.
33. See, for example, Perrin, *Kingdom*, pp. 115–17.
34. The passages in mind are Matt. 12.28; Mark 1.14f.; Luke 10.23f.; Luke 11.31f.; Matt. 11.2–11.
35. Dodd, *Parables*, p. 34.
36. See Perrin, *Kingdom*, p. 73.
37. Kümmel, *Promise and Fulfilment*, p. 16.
38. Hengel, *The Charismatic Leader*, p. 3 n. 1.
39. Ibid., p. 3.
40. Dodd, *Parables*, pp. 28f. For the development of Dodd's interpretation, see Perrin, *Kingdom*, pp. 58–61.
41. I owe the images to Perrin, *Kingdom*, p. 114. Note also Bultmann, *History*, p. 14: 'has drawn nigh'.
42. Perrin, *Kingdom*, p. 76.
43. Ibid., p. 171. See also p. 199.
44. See above, n. 34, for the passages on which Dodd relied. Perrin (*Kingdom*, pp. 74–6) gives a much longer list. Some are extraordinarily off the mark. It is not true, for example, that forgiveness was reserved for the messianic period (p. 75; see above, ch. 3 at n. 54), and this point excludes several of Perrin's passages. It would be in some ways a useful exercise to go through Perrin's list of passages which he claimed to prove that Jesus regarded the kingdom as present and to show how few of them actually lead to that view. It would deflect us from the present purpose, however, and would be tedious for most readers. Perhaps it will suffice to say that the whole stack of cards would collapse if Matt. 12.28 and 11.5f. were withdrawn. For that reason, and also because I want only to exemplify the problems of the sayings material, I limit the discussion to those two passages.

Schlosser (*Règne*, p. 675) notes that the chief passage in favour of the kingdom as present is Luke 11.20 (which he regards as the more original form), but he discusses three other passages: Mark 1.15; Luke 7.28//Matt. 11.11; Luke 17.20f. (pp. 89–243). Ulrich Müller ('Vision und Botschaft', *ZTK* 74, 1977, pp. 416–48) cites as the pertinent passages Luke 11.20; 10.23f.; 10.18; Mark 2.19a, and focuses his article on Luke 10.18.

45. It is, for example, one of the few passages in which Matthew rather than Mark is the 'middle term', and it is generally considered a 'Mark-Q overlap' (see Sanders, 'The Overlaps of Mark and Q and the Synoptic Problem', *NTS* 19, 1973, pp. 453–65). It is nevertheless difficult to see the passage as resulting from the mechanical copying of alternate verses from Mark and Q, which the Mark-Q overlap theory must assume. For a convincing analysis of the structure of the passage as it stands in Matthew, see Lamar Cope, *Matthew: A Scribe Trained for the Kingdom of Heaven*, CBQMS 5, 1976, pp. 37–40, 46f.

46. In addition to the works cited in the previous note, see, for example, Arland Hultgren, *Jesus and His Adversaries*, 1979, p. 105; B. C. Butler, *The Originality of St Matthew*, 1951, pp. 8–12.

47. O'Neill, *Messiah*, p. 15: Whatever '*ephthasen* upon you' means, it cannot be 'that the Kingdom itself has come, because no one would expect the decision of men who deny God's workings in the world to bring in his Kingdom, much less to *be* his Kingdom.

The words "the Kingdom of God" must therefore stand for something like "the judgment of God which he will pronounce when his Kingdom comes". The saying as a whole means, "If you are wrong about my exorcisms and if I am casting out demons by the finger of God, then you have pronounced against yourselves the judgment God will pronounce when he comes openly to reign".'

48. See recently Schlosser, *Règne*, pp. 130, 134–9. See also Perrin, Bultmann and others cited below.

49. Kümmel, *Promise and Fulfilment*, pp. 105f. So also Bultmann, *History*, p. 14.

50. Bultmann, *History*, p. 162.

51. Perrin, *Kingdom*, p. 87.

52. In addition to Dodd and Perrin, cited above, see David Bosch, *Die Heidenmission in der Zukunftsschau Jesu*, 1959, p. 47: 'The use of *phthanein* in Matt. 12.28 par. in opposition to *engizein* in Mark 1.15 par. can be no accident.' According to Bosch, it proves Jesus' conception of the presence of the kingdom in his exorcisms. Kümmel (*Promise and Fulfilment*, pp. 106f.) in a similar way bases part of his argument on the distinction between the verbs in Mark 1.15 and Matt. 12.28. Cf. the attempt by Schlosser (*Règne*, p. 137) to determine the precise meaning of *ephthasen*. All this I take to be gross over-exegesis. Perhaps one can lean in this way on a turn of phrase or a single word in Paul's letters, but not in the synoptics.

53. O'Neill, *Messiah*, pp. 17f. The same problem with the meaning of the verb is to be seen in the commentaries to I Thess. 2.16.

54. Thus Bosch, *Heidenmission*, p. 49: 'Late Judaism expected the cessation of the rule of the demonic powers at the beginning of the future messianic period.' He concludes by stating that what for Jews remained in the future 'broke in' in Jesus' behaviour, deeds and preaching. Bosch cites other scholars holding the view. Cf. John Reumann, *Jesus in the Church's Gospels*, 1968, pp. 153f.; Perrin, *Kingdom*, p. 166; Ernst Bammel, "John Did no Miracle", *Miracles. Cambridge Studies in their Philosophy and History*, ed. C. F. D. Moule, 1965, pp. 188–91; Howard Clark Kee, *Miracle in the Early Christian World*, 1983, p. 155: 'The miracles . . . are accomplished through [God's] agents, whose exorcisms are seen as signs of the impending defeat of the God-opposing powers.'

55. T.Mos. 10.1: 'And then His kingdom shall appear throughout all His creation, And then Satan shall be no more, And sorrow shall depart with him.' T.Levi 18.12: 'And Beliar shall be bound by him, And he shall give power to His children to tread upon the evil spirits.'

56. That at the eschaton God would destroy evil was of course universally held. But I see no evidence that the sign of the coming kingdom was generally thought to be exorcism; for one thing, there were too many exorcists. Kee (loc. cit., n. 54) draws his conclusion after running through some passages in Jewish literature, none of which leads to it. The only 'signs and wonders' which he can cite as evidence of the coming kingdom are not exorcisms (which Kee claims them to be, p. 155), but the miraculous deliverances of Daniel (Kee, p. 154). The exorcisms (e.g. in the Prayer of Nabonidus) have nothing to do with the arrival of the kingdom. Kee's actually citing passages makes it evident that the conclusion about exorcisms and the kingdom is independent of the evidence from Jewish sources.

57. It is noteworthy that M.-E. Boismard, not usually reluctant to divide passages into component parts, leaves Matt. 12.27 and 28 together: *Synopse* II, pp. 127f.

58. Perhaps needless to say, neither point is by any means sure, but I do not regard the saying in Matt. 12.30 and par. as being much less probable than that in Matt. 12.27 and par.

59. This passage is not infrequently seen as decisive for Jesus' conception of his own ministry, as well as offering support for the view that he believed the kingdom to be 'breaking in' in his words and deeds. See Dunn, *Spirit*, pp. 53f., where there are further references. Harvey, (*Constraints*, pp. 141f.) has offered the suggestive proposal that Jesus' depiction of his ministry in terms of Isa. 61 (which is reflected in Matt. 11.2–6) explains the application to him of the title 'Messiah'.

60. Bultmann, *History*, p. 23.

61. Ibid.

62. Ibid., p. 126.

63. Dunn, *Spirit*, pp. 55–60; the quotation is from p. 59 and is italicized in the original.

64. Bultmann, *History*, p. 162.

65. See, for example, Kümmel, *Promise and Fulfilment*, p. 88; Dunn, *Spirit*, p. 49, 64; John Reumann, *Jesus*, pp. 153f.

66. It is a standard embarrassment for scholars to try to say just how the kingdom was 'breaking in' with Jesus' words and deeds. One may note Bornkamm's efforts: 'This mystery is nothing but the hidden dawn of the kingdom of God itself amidst a world which to human eyes gives no sign of it'; 'God's kingdom comes in concealment, indeed even in spite of failure' (*Jesus of Nazareth*, pp. 71f.). Cf. also Kümmel, *Promise and Fulfilment*, p. 111, quoted below. Perrin recognized the difficulty of saying 'in some sense' (*Kingdom*, pp. 42f.).

67. Reumann, *Jesus*, p. 154: 'It is nowhere recorded that John the Baptist worked miracles, which were signs of the kingdom.'

68. Reumann, ibid.

69. Dunn, *Spirit*, p. 47.

70. Ibid., p. 64.

71. Trautmann, *Zeichenhafte Handlungen*, p. 265. I assume that she means that nowhere else does one find such a claim. The statement may, on the other hand, be simply a confession of faith.

72. P. W. Barnett, 'The Jewish Sign Prophets – A.D. 40–70 – Their Intentions and Origin', *NTS* 27, 1981, pp. 679–97.

73. See, for example, Bornkamm, *Jesus of Nazareth*, p. 62, quoted above, p. 30.

74. Kümmel, *Promise and Fulfilment*, p. 111.

75. See Jeremias, *Proclamation*, p. 32. He does not, however, distinguish between novelty of terminology and novelty of conception.

76. See recently Schlosser, *Règne*, pp. 674f.

77. Above, p. 132.

78. Cf. G. B. Caird, *The Language and Imagery of the Bible*, 1980, p. 11. Bruce Chilton has proposed that the range of meanings of 'kingdom' in the sayings attributed to Jesus has a partial parallel in some of the Targums, particularly Targum Jonathan to Isaiah. See *God in Strength*, esp. pp. 283–6; *The Glory of Israel*, 1983, pp. 77–81.

79. The first two categories especially follow Dodd's arrangement (*Parables*, pp. 21–8). Chilton (*God in Strength*, pp. 11–18) has a helpful discussion of categorization.

80. Perrin (*Kingdom*, p. 25) attributes the identification of this meaning of 'kingdom' to Dalman (*The Words of Jesus*, ET 1902, pp. 96–101).

81. See, for example, Perrin's criticism of Dalman and Manson, *Kingdom*, pp. 25–7; 95 ('the true background to the teaching of Jesus here is the apocalyptic rather than the rabbinical literature').

82. In giving an account of how it can be that the idea of the covenant is prominent in Rabbinic literature, although the word itself is not, I put the most important

observation in the least important place. The observation is that other words substitute for 'covenant'. See *Paul and Palestinian Judaism*, p. 421 and notes.

83. E.g. Sifra Aḥare Mot pereq 13.3 (to Lev. 18.1f.).

84. E.g. Mekilta Baḥodesh 5 (Lauterbach II, pp. 229f.); Mekilta Baḥodesh 6 (Lauterbach II, pp. 238f.). The parables are quoted in *Paul and Palestinian Judaism*, p. 86.

85. See, for example, Dodd, *Parables*, pp. 22–4.

86. David Catchpole ('John the Baptist, Jesus and the Parable of the Tares', *SJT* 31, 1978, pp. 557–70) argues that Matt. 13.47–8 is authentic. Verse 49, which contains the phrase 'consummation of the age', is to be considered an addition. The theme of 'gathering together' in 13.47 is judged authentic, and Catchpole points here to an overlap with the message of John (p. 560, citing Matt. 13.30; 3.12//Luke 3.17).

87. The customary explanation that Matthew, in copying Mark, 'sharpened' the reference to the Son of man (Perrin, *Kingdom*, p. 139) is extraordinarily weak. If Matthew has here copied Mark, he has deleted a saying requiring commitment to Jesus and his words. This is simply another instance in which unwavering allegiance to the two-source hypothesis goes awry.

88. The problem of future expectation is often posed in terms of the difficulty for modern Christians caused by the fact that Jesus expected an imminent end. See, for example, Herbert Braun, *Jesus of Nazareth*, pp. 36–43; Harvey, *Constraints*, ch. 4. Perrin grants that 'Jesus did expect a future eschatological event in which the Son of Man would exercise his function as Judge' (*Kingdom*, p. 139), but this form of the future expectation plays very little role in his general discussions of the kingdom as future (see pp. 83, 147).

89. See Matt. 5.20; 7.21; 19.23; 23.13; 25.21, 23; cf. 'enter into life', 18.8; 19.17. See the illuminating study by Margaret Pamment, 'The Kingdom of Heaven according to the First Gospel', *NTS* 27, 1981, pp. 211–32, esp. 212–16. I do not mean to assert with confidence that the first evangelist created all these sayings, but only that they reflect a prominent motif in the Gospel, one doubtless close to his own interest. For Matthew's emphasis on 'discipleship', see Benno Przybylski, *Righteousness in Matthew and his World of Thought*, 1980, pp. 108–12.

90. Contrast Ulrich B. Müller, 'Zur Rezeption Gesetzeskritischer Jesusüberlieferung im frühen Christentum', *NTS* 27, 1981, p. 158: I Thess. 4.15 has no recognizable synoptic parallel.

91. For the category, see Bultmann, *History*, pp. 127f., referring to Gunkel and von Soden. For the attribution of I Thess. 4.15f. to Christian prophecy, see, for example, Hans Conzelmann, *Theology*, p. 38. This attribution is doubted by David Hill, *New Testament Prophecy*, 1979, pp. 130, 166. Eugene Boring, however, takes the passage as a prime example of a revelation from 'the risen Lord', though still pre-Pauline. See *Sayings of the Risen Jesus*, 1982, pp. 34, 75.

92. See, for example, Perrin, *Rediscovering*, p. 186: Mark 8.38 is secondary to Luke 12.8. Similarly Boring, *Sayings of the Risen Jesus*, pp. 165–7, 183: Mark 8.38 is secondary to Matt. 10.32//Luke 12.8. Matt. 16.27 goes unmentioned.

93. See Perrin, *Rediscovering*, p. 174. Schlosser (*Règne*, p. 362 n. 130; p. 368 n. 187) dismisses the saying even more quickly. See recently Boring, *Sayings of the Risen Jesus*, pp. 186–95: it is a Christian prophecy.

94. Michael Goulder has noted the correspondence between Paul and Matthew, but he considers Matthew's phrase about the trumpet to have been added under Pauline influence. See *Midrash and Lection in Matthew*, 1974, p. 166.

95. Perrin, *Kingdom*, p. 187f.

96. E.g. Vielhauer, 'Gottesreich und Menschensohn'.

97. Cf. Perrin, *Kingdom*, p. 140; Dunn, *Spirit*, p. 42.

98. In both cases the word 'kingdom' occurs only in Matthew. In the passage about James and John, Mark has 'in your glory' (10.37) where Matthew has 'in your kingdom' (20.21). I take this not to be a substantial difference.

99. Cf. the discussion by Meyer (*Aims*, pp. 193–7), who offers a more precise meaning than I would be prepared to do: the *ekklesia* would embrace all Israel, which would be the temple built on the rock – those who, like Peter, recognize Jesus as Messiah. For the common interpretation of the saying as arising from the community, see e.g. Klinzing, *Umdeutung*, pp. 205–7: it refers to the community as temple, but does not go back to Jesus.

100. Bultmann, *History*, p. 24: 'a manifest *vaticinium ex eventu*'.

101. See the summary by Vincent Taylor, *The Gospel According to St Mark*, p. 442. James was executed by Agrippa I (Acts 12.2).

102. Ibid., p. 439; cf. pp. 522f.

103. Perrin, *Rediscovering*, p. 38.

104. Schlosser (*Règne*, pp. 373–417) has a clear and full treatment of problems and solutions. The statement that most scholars accept the authenticity of the saying is on p. 389. Schlosser agrees (p. 398). Cf. Dunn, *Spirit*, p. 36.

105. Perrin, *Kingdom*, pp. 188f. He here includes Mark 14.25, although apparently he later came to regard it as inauthentic (n. 103).

106. See Schlosser, *Règne*. pp. 89–243.

107. See Dodd, *Parables*, pp. 28–33, esp. p. 31.

108. U. Müller, 'Vision und Botschaft'.

109. O'Neill, *Messiah*, pp. 10f., quoting also A. H. McNeile, *The Gospel According to St Matthew*, 1915, p. 154.

110. See, for example, Schlosser, *Règne*, pp. 166f.

111. 'Opens himself to the kingdom': ibid., p. 167.

112. Schlosser, *Règne*, pp. 187f.

113. In *Rediscovering*, p. 83. Perrin gives a classification of the parables, and in *Kingdom*, p. 83, a list of 'reversal' passages. In both cases I would organize the material somewhat differently and retitle some of the categories. It is a task which, however, for the present purpose does not need to be attempted.

114. Cf. Kümmel, *Promise and Fulfilment*, pp. 15f.

115. Perrin, *Kingdom*, p. 159.

116. Ibid., p. 199.

117. G. B. Caird, *The Language and Imagery of the Bible*, p. 12.

118. Cf. Chilton, above, n. 78.

119. For doubts on this, see above, ch. 3 n. 83.

120. Cf. Crawford, 'Near Expectation in the Sayings of Jesus', p. 226 n. 5.

121. Cf. Kümmel, *Promise and Fulfilment*, pp. 144–46.

122. Schlosser, *Règne*, p. 166, citing numerous others. See above, pp. 137–9.

123. O'Neill, *Messiah*, p. 14.

124. Dodd, *Parables*, p. 29.

125. Ibid., p. 33.

5. MIRACLES AND CROWDS

1. Above, pp. 134f. and nn. 54, 56 and 67 to ch. 4.

2. E.g. Perrin, *Rediscovering*, p. 91. See further below, ch. 6, section 3.1.

3. Above, pp. 134f. and esp. n. 56.

4. Most scholars who deal with the quest for the historical Jesus concentrate on the teaching material, thus tacitly assuming that Jesus was principally a teacher. One sometimes finds a direct statement, such as Martin Hengel's: 'The preaching of Jesus, through which alone we can gain a truly reliable picture of his purpose and work . . .' (Review of S. G. F. Brandon, *Jesus and the Zealots*, in *JSS* 14, 1969, pp. 231–40, here 236.)

Birger Gerhardsson has most explicitly attempted to explain Jesus by analogy with Rabbinic teachers. See Gerhardsson, *Memory and Manuscript*. Of recent years Gerhardsson's view is gaining ground in some circles, most strikingly in Tübingen. See recently Rainer Riesner, *Jesus als Lehrer*. See further above, pp. 14–16.

5. Smith (*Magician*) remarks that 'the miracle stories in the synoptics are *not* usually connected with Jesus' teaching, and when they are, the connections are usually secondary. Evidently the traditions were originally separate; this suggests that the activities were' (p. 83). See also p. 115: 'We should not expect the teaching that the gospels attribute to Jesus to be so consistently connected with magic as were the miracles.' Without attempting a statistical analysis, I shall offer the following generalization: the bodies of actual teaching material, most of which are in Matthew and Luke, are not said to have been given in connection with miracles. But the reports which summarize the activities often put them together. The reports are presumably the evangelists' own summaries. The large bodies of teaching material seem to have been transmitted separately from miracle stories. It is my judgment that *both* the separation of the substantive materials and the summarizing connections are the result of redactional activity in the transmission of the material. Thus I fall back on intrinsic probability: miracles, teaching and crowds went together in Jesus' career.

6. There is a punctuation problem in Mark 1.27. The RSV translates: 'What is this? A new teaching! With authority he commands even the unclean spirits. . . .' The Nestle/Aland text reads thus: 'What is this? A new teaching with authority. And he commands the unclean spirits. . . .' Grammatically the Nestle/Aland punctuation is the more natural. Luke 4.36 reads 'What is this word, that with authority and power he commands the unclean spirits . . .?' – a reading which removes any possibility of connecting 'authority' with 'teaching'.

7. See below, on the reasons for Jesus' death, pp. 299f.

8. Harvey (*Constraints*, pp. 111–13) lists compassion and 'acquiring fame, popularity and authority' as the two principal possibilities, both of which he rejects. There is a very careful assessment of the use of miracles to authenticate a message in Guignebert, *Jesus*, pp. 189–92. His conclusion is that all religions can appeal to approximately the same sort of miracles, and that miracles of themselves thus do not 'possess an objectivity capable of convincing . . . the unbeliever' (p. 191).

9. An extreme example is that of Albert Nolan, *Jesus Before Christianity*, p. 28: 'The English word "compassion" is far too weak to express the emotion that moved Jesus. The Greek verb *splagchnizomai* . . .'. But even Harvey seriously considers this editorial description as possibly giving Jesus' motive (*Constraints*, p. 111). He rejects compassion as Jesus' motive because the evangelists themselves do not present it as primary, thus apparently assuming that they knew.

10. Harvey, *Constraints*, pp. 114.

11. Ibid., p. 108.

12. Ibid., p. 109.

13. Ibid., p. 113. Cf. earlier, Kümmel, *Promise and Fulfilment*, p. 111.

14. Harvey, *Constraints*, pp. 116–18.

15. Ibid., p. 116
16. Ibid., p. 117.
17. Ibid., p. 118.
18. Ibid., p. 115.
19. Ibid., pp. 141f.
20. Jesus' unique consciousness: above, p. 137.
21. Harvey, p. 111. By p. 115 'virtually no precedent' has become 'completely without precedent'.
22. Josephus, *AJ* VIII.46.
23. Smith, *Magician*, p. 109 and the notes on p. 195.
24. On the very point as regards magic, see Smith, *Magician*, pp. 68f.
25. Harvey, pp. 105f.
26. E.g. the predictions of the passion, the prediction of the destruction of Jerusalem, and the prediction of betrayal by Judas and denial by Peter.
27. These and other examples can be found in Smith, *Magician*, p. 199, notes to p. 116; see also p. 117.
28. It may be that Harvey did not read Smith, whose book is not referred to. He sometimes seems, however, to have Smith's book in mind (e.g. Harvey, pp. 108f.).
29. Harvey, p. 111. Note also 'opted' (p. 109), 'options' (p. 108). But note also his reservation, p. 105.
30. We are probably in touch here with the undeclared theological agenda of the book.
31. Harvey (p. 111) mentions this possibility, but connects it with the question of whether or not Jesus healed simply on compassionate grounds – which he also, quite correctly, denies. But the two need not go together.
32. See E. J. and L. Edelstein, *Asclepius*, 2 vols., 1945.
33. Smith, *Magician*, pp. 9, 11, 23f. Cf. Hengel, *Charismatic Leader*, p. 66: the miracles awakened 'at least as much attention and enthusiasm as his preaching'.
34. On the crowds: Smith, p. 23.
35. Smith, *Magician*, p. 16.
36. For terms and meanings, see Smith, *Magician*, pp. 68–80.
37. Ibid., pp. 84–93. The parallels have been often discussed. Smith's particular contribution is to describe how 'outsiders' viewed Apollonius and to compare that with the 'outsiders' ' view of Jesus.
38. Ibid., primarily pp. 96–139 and notes.
39. The prominent example in the Gospels is the story of the Gadarene demoniac and the swine, Mark 5.1–20 and parr. See also Mark 3.11. For 'Son of God' in connection with another type of miracle, see Matt. 14.33. On 'Son of God' as a title, see Smith, pp. 100f.
40. Smith, p. 101.
41. Ibid., pp. 102–4.
42. Ibid., pp. 31–6.
43. Smith, p. 32.
44. See Hengel, *Charismatic Leader*, p. 64.
45. Bauer, *Lexicon*, p. 276.
46. Cf. Hengel, *Charismatic Leader*, pp. 64–6.
47. Smith, *Magician*, pp. 16f., 10, 38–44.
48. Ibid., p. 24.
49. Above, pp. 16–22.

50. Ramsay MacMullen, *Paganism in the Roman Empire*. On p. xii he sets the 'spans of time and space' in such a way as to exclude first-century Palestine – barely.

51. Ibid., p. 95.

52. Ibid., pp. 96f.

53. Smith (*Magician*, pp. 1–6) raises the problem of suppressed evidence, but obviously nothing can be said about unreported deeds. As far as we know, all of Jesus' miracles were good.

54. Smith, *Magician*, pp. 101–3.

55. Ibid., pp. 81–4.

56. Ibid., p. 68.

57. Freyne (*Galilee*, pp. 43–5) cogently argues the case against Schürer's widely accepted view.

58. Above, pp. 7f. See immediately below on Theudas.

59. Vermes, *Jesus the Jew*, pp. 69–80.

60. Cf. Markham J. Geller, 'Jesus' Theurgic Powers: Parallels in the Talmud and Incantation Bowls', *JJS* 28, 1977, p. 146: 'These similarities between Jesus' words and conventional exorcisms, however, do not prove *a priori* that Jesus was an exorcist rather than a holy man or charismatic, as Vermes has characterized him. Much depends upon the point of view of the ancient sources.'

61. Cf. David L. Tiede, *The Charismatic Figure as Miracle Worker*, 1972, p. 263: 'Cautious clarifications about what is or is not "magical" were not characteristic of the society that authenticated its charismatic heroes as divine on the basis of their miraculous performances.' Harold Remus has now shown that the terms for miracles in Christian literature do not distinguish the deeds attributed to Jesus and others from pagan miracles: 'The distinctions pagans and Christians draw between miracle claims lie in the eyes of the beholders' (Harold Remus, 'Does Terminology Distinguish Early Christian from Pagan Miracles?', *JBL*, 101, 1982, pp. 531–51, quotation from p. 550).

62. See MacMullen's discussion above.

63. See Otto Betz, 'Das Problem des Wunders bei Flavius Josephus im Vergleich zum Wunderproblem bei den Rabbinen und im Johannesevangelium', *Josephus-Studien* (ed. O. Betz, K. Haacker, and M. Hengel), 1974, pp. 23–44, esp. 25–34.

64. Theudas: *AJ* XX.97–9; unnamed people: *AJ* XX.168; *BJ* II.259; the Egyptian: *AJ* XX.168–72; *BJ* II.261–63.

65. I follow here the account of the Egyptian in the *Antiquities*. For the partial conflict with the story in the *War*, see below, p. 234 and n. 25.

66. On *goes*, see Smith, *Magician*, p. 20.

67. Smith (*Magician*, p. 20) says that Jesus fits the religious and social type of Judas and Theudas, but putting Judas here seems to confuse the issue. See below, pp. 237–40.

68. Smith, *Magician*, pp. 23f.

6. THE SINNERS

1. See Stanton, *Jesus of Nazareth in New Testament Preaching*, p. 146.

2. Jeremias, *Proclamation*, pp. 109–11.

3. See, for example, Peter Fiedler, *Jesus und die Sünder*, 1976, p. 271.

4. See Cadbury, *The Peril of Modernizing Jesus*, pp. 135–45; Hultgren, *Jesus and His Adversaries*, pp. 109–11 (with bibliography). Some favour authenticity, e.g. Trautmann, *Zeichenhafte Handlungen*, p. 157.

5. Cf. Hultgren, *Jesus and His Adversaries*, pp. 109–11; Fiedler, *Jesus und die Sünder*,

p. 271; H. K. McArthur, 'Basic Issues: A Survey of Recent Gospel Research', *Interpr* 18, 1964, p. 48.

6. Cf. Fiedler, *Jesus und die Sünder*, pp. 228–33; 271.

7. Fiedler (ibid., pp. 129–35, 271), correctly in my view, regards the story as a secondary construction.

8. Perrin (*Rediscovering*, p. 99) regards Matthew's version as nearer the original. Jeremias accepted Luke's setting here and elsewhere. This plays a substantial role in incorrectly identifying Jesus' opponents: below, ch. 10 at nn. 38–40.

9. That Luke 15.7 and 15.10 are editorial additions is generally agreed. See, for example, Perrin, ibid., p. 101.

10. For what follows, see Jeremias, *Proclamation*, pp. 108–13.

11. Ibid., p. 112.   12. Ibid., pp. 112f.

13. E.g. Nolan, *Jesus before Christianity*, p. 21.

14. It would require a small dissertation to sort out the views of New Testament scholarship on the relationship of the sinners and the *'amme ha-arets*. The older generation generally accepted the equation without discrimination. Thus, for example, Bousset, *Jesus*, p. 65: the 'sinners' were 'those who had refused in any way to fall in with the forms of the ruling Pharisaic piety'. Many more recent scholars also accept the simple equation: thus Hultgren, *Jesus and his Adversaries*, p. 111: the 'sinners' are the *'amme ha-arets* of M. Demai 2.3. On p. 98 n. 93 he gives a long bibliography. R. Pesch ('Anspruch', pp. 56, 67, 69) also seems to make a flat equation between the 'sinners' and the *'amme ha-arets* in the Pharisaic view. Jesus accepted them and thus overcame Jewish *Heilsegoismus, Selbstgerechtigkeit, ängstliche Religiosität*, etc. (pp. 67f.). Nolan (*Jesus before Christianity*, p. 22), following Jeremias, also informs us that the 'poor' and those of 'low class' were considered sinners by the Pharisees.

Jeremias's view shows that he was caught in a difficult position. When he simply defined the 'sinners' in the Jewish view, he did it accurately enough: they were deliberate and unrepentant transgressors of the law, not simply those who did not follow the purity code of the *ḥaberim* (the *'amme ha-arets*). See, for example, his *Parables of Jesus*, rev. ET, 1963, p. 132. But when he came to write his theology of Jesus' preaching (*Proclamation*), he had to go against his own knowledge, and equate the *'amme ha-arets* with the 'sinners', partly to put all those with whom Jesus was especially concerned under one heading ('the poor'), and partly – at least so it appears – to magnify the supposed opposition between Jesus and the Pharisees: if the Pharisees considered the common people (the *'amme ha-arets*) *sinners*, and if Jesus favoured the inclusion of the common people in the kingdom, the enmity was obvious. Jeremias seems to have reasoned like this: the Pharisees and the *ḥaberim* were identical; the *ḥaberim* would not eat with the *'amme ha-arets*; Jesus ate with them; therefore he offended Pharisaic purity regulations. This is all wrong, as the succeeding discussion will, I hope, show.

Scholars could have learned decades ago that there is no connection in Jewish materials between the common people, the *'amme ha-arets*, and those called 'sinners'. See e.g. Klausner, *Jesus of Nazareth*, p. 276; L. Finkelstein, *The Pharisees* II, [3]1962, pp. 754–61; Abrahams, *Studies in Pharisaism and the Gospels* I, ch. 7, 'Publicans and Sinners'.

Finally, it should be pointed out that some scholars who have in theory learned that the *'amme ha-arets* were not 'sinners' still do not get the point, since they continue to think that those who transgressed the purity code of the *ḥaberim* were considered 'sinners' (see below). In fact, failing to keep the priestly purity code is precisely what defines an *'am ha-arets* – not a sinner.

15. See e.g. Stephen Westerholm, *Jesus and Scribal Authority*, 1978, pp. 69f. See

further the discussion in Fiedler, *Jesus und die Sünder*, pp. 140–44.

16. I have given the terminological information in *Paul and Palestinian Judaism*, pp. 142f.; 203 (n. 119: the wicked do not accept the Torah); 342–5; 351–5; 357f.; 361; 399–405; 414. See also, 'Jesus: from the Semitic Point of View', *The Cambridge History of Judaism*, forthcoming.

17. Jeremias, *Jerusalem in the Time of Jesus*, ch. 14.

18. See *Paul and Palestinian Judaism*, pp. 92–4.

19. See *Paul and Palestinian Judaism*, pp. 243f., 257, 272 (Dead Sea Scrolls), 351 (I Enoch 83–90), 391, 399–406 (Psalms of Solomon).

20. N. 17 above.

21. See *Paul and Palestinian Judaism*, p. 149.

22. PHagigah 77b (2.1).

23. Cf. Hultgren, *Jesus and his Adversaries*, pp. 109–11.

24. Even these parables, usually regarded as sacrosanct, may be questioned. For the sake of the present argument, however, I do not press the doubts. On the dubious character of Luke 15.25–32, see Jack T. Sanders, 'Tradition and Redaction in Luke XV.11–32', *NTS* 15, 1969, pp. 433–38. For the view that the entire parable is Lucan, see L. Schottroff, 'Das Gleichnis vom verlorenen Sohn', *ZTK* 68, 1971, pp. 27–52.

25. See the caution in Perrin, *Rediscovering*, p. 97.

26. See above n. 9; below, ch. 10 at nn. 38–40.

27. Nolan (*Jesus before Christianity*, pp. 96–8) proposes that the Pharisees oppressed the poor and that Jesus attacked them for this. The Gospels do not, however, fit simple socio-economic theories. The 'wicked' – tax collectors and usurers – were not necessarily impoverished!

28. See the Index to *Paul and Palestinian Judaism*, s.v. 'The wicked'.

29. I have proposed before that the view that the Pharisees considered the *'amme ha-arets* cut off from Israel is without foundation (*Paul and Palestinian Judaism*, pp. 149, 152–7). No one has challenged the proposal; but, on the other hand, it does not seem to have been accepted.

30. Jeremias (*Proclamation*, p. 119) seems to accept John 7.49 as evidence of the view of Pharisaism before 70. In *Jerusalem in the Time of Jesus* (p. 266 n. 71) he relies on both John 7.49 and Luke 18.9–14.

31. On the anti-Pharisaic polemic of Luke, see Jack T. Sanders, 'Tradition and Redaction in Luke XV.11–32', esp. p. 438; 'The Parable of the Pounds and Lucan Anti-Semitism', *Theological Studies* 42, 1981, pp. 660–68. Sanders now has in hand a more detailed study of anti-Judaism (including anti-Pharisaism) in Luke.

32. E.g. Pesahim 49b.

33. See recently Solomon J. Spiro, 'Who was the *Haber*? A New Approach to an Ancient Institution', *JSJ* 11, 1980, pp. 186–216, esp. pp. 187–9; cf. p. 211.

34. Jacob Neusner, *The Idea of Purity in Ancient Judaism*, 1973, pp. 65f. See also Vermes and others, eds., *The History of the Jewish People in the Age of Jesus Christ* II, p. 388 n. 16. Neusner speaks of 'the Pharisees', which raises a problem: see 1.2.4 below.

35. Spiro, 'Who was the *Haber*?', p. 208.

36. I am indebted for this point to Hyam Maccoby.

37. Finkelstein, *The Pharisees* II, p. 757.

38. M. Smith, 'Palestinian Judaism in the First Century', *Israel: Its Role in Civilization* (ed. M. Davis), 1956, pp. 74–81 (= *Essays in Greco-Roman and Related Talmudic Literature* [ed. Henry A. Fischel], 1977, pp. 190–7), here pp. 73f. (= 189f.). Cf. Westerholm, *Jesus and Scribal Authority*, p. 65. Cf. Josephus, *Ap.* II.175–8.

39. The biblical purity laws are summarized by Neusner, *The Idea of Purity*, ch. 1. I

shall not discuss the fascinating question of what conception(s) of reality lay behind these laws, but only the question of when impurity involves sin. We enter this discussion under the chapter heading 'The Sinners'. On the use of the *language* of impurity for moral wickedness, see especially Adolf Büchler, *Studies in Sin and Atonement in the Rabbinic Literature of the First Century*, 1929, repr. 1967, pp. 212–69 (the Bible), 270–374 (post-biblical literature). This subject is also left out of account here, though there are short summaries in *Paul and Palestinian Judaism*, see the index, s.v. 'purity'.

40. See the quotation from Finkelstein just above. See also Adolf Büchler, *Types of Jewish-Palestinian Piety from 70 B.C.E. to 70 C.E.*, 1922, repr. 1968, p. 143: 'The common mistaken assumption of modern Christian historians of rabbinic Judaism that the contraction of a levitical defilement implied a sin, is totally foreign to rabbinic law, especially with reference to Temple times. Not even if the high-priest accidentally contracted the gravest defilement from a human corpse, did he incur the slightest sin, unless he, in his defiled state, entered the Temple or handled holy things.'

41. *Paul and Palestinian Judaism*, p. 179.

42. Westerholm, *Jesus and Scribal Authority*, p. 62. Dr Westerholm now informs me that he intended to say that the scribes taught *additional* purity laws.

43. On the priests' responsibility in general, see *Ap* II.187, below, at n. 75.

44. Westerholm, *Jesus and Scribal Authority*, p. 66.

45. For the *miqvaot* in the houses, including one with the connecting pipe, see Avigad, *Discovering Jerusalem*, pp. 139, 142. Those outside the temple area may be inspected, though technical evaluation is difficult. Their existence is noted by Benjamin Mazar, 'Herodian Jerusalem in the Light of the Excavations South and South-West of the Temple Mount', *IEJ* 28, 1978, p. 236.

46. Mikwaoth 6.1, 7f.; cf. 3.2.

47. See Yigael Yadin, *Masada. Herod's Fortress and the Zealots' Last Stand*, 1966, pp. 166f.

48. Note Avigad's slight surprise: Even though the inhabitants of the western hill were probably Sadducees, 'there is no specific archaeological evidence here to indicate any laxity' . . . 'On the contrary, the finds indicate that the laws of ritual purity were kept' (p. 83). He seems to have been influenced by a common view, generally accepted by Christian scholars, that only the Pharisees were concerned about the law, especially laws of purity. Similarly Yadin (loc. cit.) states that the construction of the *miqveh* at Masada shows that the defenders were 'devout Jews'. But so were many of those in Jerusalem who constructed their *miqvaot* differently. We should not equate devotion and piety with agreement with Rabbinic law.

49. See Westerholm, *Jesus and Scribal Authority*, p. 66 and notes; *Paul and Palestinian Judaism*, p. 154 n. 40. To the literature cited there should be added Ch. Albeck, *The Six Orders of the Mishnah, Tohorot*, 1959, pp. 605–7; and the ET of Alon: Gedalyahu Alon, *Jews, Judaism and the Classical World*, ET 1977, esp. pp. 219–23. The problem of the extension of handwashing to the laity has been fully aired, though not resolved, by Büchler and those who have attempted – not, in my judgment, entirely successfully – to refute him. He dated the general extension to the laity ca. 100 CE. It is reasonable to think that the extension of some laws of purity coincided with the elimination of others, when the temple was destroyed.

50. Cf. Spiro, 'Who was the Ḥaber?'

51. The talmudists who have debated the extension of the handwashing code to the laity (see n. 49) have not, as far as I have noted, come to terms with a basic problem: why *hand*washing? My colleague Al Baumgarten remarked to me that the biblical view is 'all or nothing': a person who is unclean should be *immersed* and wait for the sun to

set (see the previous subsection). Büchler pointed out that the simple washing of hands does not remove true levitical (biblical) impurity (Adolf Büchler, 'The Law of Purification in Mark vii.1–23', *ExpT* 21, 1909–10, p. 40), and he therefore proposed that 'handwashing' was not the issue in the Gospels, but 'defilement' (by biblical law) of hands which touched priestly food. For someone to reply, as does Alon, that Judith 11.13 indicates that lay hands could render priestly food impure, and that therefore 'it follows that the washing of the hands for holy things was practised before the time of Hillel and Shammai', (Alon, loc. cit., p. 222 n. 85) is to miss the point. Lay hands may well have been considered *defiled* and not to be cleansed simply by washing. Scholars themselves shift from the biblical purity laws to the scribal ones; we should not be too hard on Mark for not knowing the difference. But I dare say that Jesus and his contemporaries did. In any case, the questions of priestly and lay handwashing, as far as I can see, await solution. They are irrelevant, however, for our present problem. Sin is in no case involved.

52. Braun, *Jesus of Nazareth*, p. 53.

53. G. Aulén, *Jesus*, p. 49.

54. They would of course affect relations with Gentiles (as Gal. 2.11–14 shows). This, however, is not the problem in the material about Jesus.

55. Westerholm, who clearly perceives that the wicked are not the *'amme ha-arets*, nevertheless writes that 'In taking his message to the most notorious sinners, Jesus indicated that the matter of ritual purity was at best a very subordinate consideration' (*Jesus and Scribal Authority*, p. 71).

56. M. Demai 2.3: R. Judah.

57. Jeremias, *Proclamation*, p. 118.

58. Paul: Gal. 1.14; Phil. 3.6; cf. Acts 23.6; Josephus: *BJ* II.162. (Cohen, however, has doubts about Josephus's Pharisaism; see below at n. 81.)

59. For a brief statement, see Jacob Neusner, *From Politics to Piety*, 1973, esp. pp. 80, 83. He argues that the Pharisees, after Hillel, were essentially *haberim* – a small, pacifist party concerned with purity. He regards this as having been proved by his study of Rabbinic material (*The Rabbinic Traditions about the Pharisees before 70*, 3 vols., 1971). The Pharisaic laws which survive, he argues, primarily have to do with the internal governance of a purity sect. Agricultural laws are a secondary element, but these too affect 'table-fellowship' (vol. III, p. 288). The third group consists of temple rules; but they are not numerous, since the Pharisees did not control the cult (pp. 288, 290). His argument rests, however, on an analysis of traditions assigned to individuals or to houses. Thus the summary does not reflect the numerous anonymous laws which probably represent *common* belief and practice, including large bodies of law on civil matters, worship, feasts, and the temple cult. Neusner is prepared to grant that the Pharisees and others shared a large area of common ground (pp. 287f.), but this is curiously deleted from his definition of Pharisaism as a purity sect. Individual anonymous pericopes dealing with non-purity matters can seldom be shown to be earlier than 70 (or, in fact, be closely dated at all), but one should not convert this difficulty into a denial that the Pharisees before 70 were substantially concerned with these *topics*. If the ground common to all parties – the existence of which Neusner is prepared to grant in general – is added to the definition of Pharisaism, it will be seen that the Mishnah too points towards defining the Pharisees as what Josephus says they were – lay experts in the law – not just as a purity sect.

Neusner notes the problem which Josephus causes for his view in *Rabbinic Traditions* III, pp. 239–44, and he attempted to meet it in 'Josephus's Pharisees. A Complete Repertoire', *Formative Judaism*. Third Series, 1983, pp. 61–82 (first published 1972).

Here he proposes that in Josephus's *War* the Pharisees as a party play no role in politics after about 50 BCE ('with the advent of Herod and Hillel'). His discussion, however, leaves out of account too many passages in the *War*, and it is not persuasive. Thus his statement on p. 269, that the *War* would lead one to think that the Essenes were the most important sect, is contradicted by *BJ* II.162. His view that the Pharisaic party played no role after Herod is contradicted by *BJ* II.411, where it plays a small role at the time of the revolt (ch. 11 below). Throughout Josephus, the Pharisees are a party and they are always interpreters of the law. The only question is their relative influence at any given time (see also below, 2.3.1), not the nature of the party. See now D. R. Schwartz, 'Josephus and Nicolaus on the Pharisees', *JSJ* 14, 1983, pp. 157–71.

In any case the argument which will be presented here and in ch. 10 will stand. If the Pharisees in the time of Jesus were a small sect, dominated by a concern for applying the priestly purity code to the laity, they would not have been able – even if they had wanted – to exclude others from the practice of religion in their own way; and the more exclusivist they were, the fewer would have been their followers. Thus, the closer one puts the Pharisees to the *haberim*, the less significance attaches to any possible conflict between Jesus and the Pharisees.

60. The quotation is from Maccoby, 'Neusner's Mishnah', p. 29. For the Pharisees as exact and accurate interpreters of the law acording to Josephus and other sources, see A. I. Baumgarten, 'The Name of the Pharisees', *JBL* 102/3, 1983, pp. 411–28. Ellis Rivkin has strongly insisted on this definition of the Pharisees and denies their equation with the *haberim*. See 'Defining the Pharisees: The Tannaitic Sources', *HUCA* 40–41, 1969–71, pp. 234–8; *A Hidden Revolution*, 1978.

The new edition of Schürer continues the flat equation of *Pharisees* and *haberim*, quoting the *Rabbinic* passages on the *haberim* and the *'amme ha-arets*. Rivkin's articles appear in the bibliography, but his detailed argument that the Tannaitic sources – much less Josephus – do not equate the Pharisees and the *haberim* is not discussed. See Schürer, ed. Geza Vermes and others, *The History of the Jewish People* II, p. 398.

61. Above, n. 11.

62. Aulén, *Jesus*, p. 59.

63. Ibid., p. 60.

64. Aulén makes it clear that he identifies those offended as the Pharisees: ibid., pp. 61–6.

65. Jeremias, *Proclamation*, p. 112: the ignorance of the *'amme ha-arets* 'stood in the way of their access to salvation.'

66. Nolan, *Jesus before Christianity*, p. 22. Earlier see Rudolf Bultmann, *Primitive Christianity*, ET 1956, p. 66.

67. Baba Metzia 33b (R. Judah b. Ilai).

68. *Paul and Palestinian Judaism*, pp. 110f.

69. On the bleakness of a nineteenth-century Sunday – and consequently its unremunerativeness – , see Dickens, *Little Dorrit*, ch. 3.

70. Baba Metzia 33b; see further *Paul and Palestinian Judaism*, pp. 152–7.

71. Above, n. 63.

72. As by Jeremias, *Proclamation*, p. 117.

73. Above, n. 32.

74. 'Down to the fall of the Temple, the normative Judaism of Palestine is that compromise of which the three principal elements are the pentateuch, the Temple, and the *'amme ha'arez*, the ordinary Jews who were not members of any sect': Morton Smith, 'The Dead Sea Sect in Relation to Ancient Judaism', *NTS* 7, 1960–61, p. 356.

75. Josephus, *Ap.* II.187; see generally 184–98. See further M. Stern, 'Aspects of

Jewish Society: The Priesthood and other Classes', *The Jewish People in the First Century* II (ed. S. Safrai and M. Stern), pp. 561–630, esp. 580–96, 600–12; Schürer/Vermes *The History of the Jewish People* II, pp. 196–236. We return to the relative positions of the priests and the Pharisees in chs. 10 and 11 below.

76. The phrase is Bousset's , *Jesus*, p. 65, but the view is common.

77. Jan Lambrecht, 'Jesus and the Law', *ETL* 53, 1977, p. 79.

78. Jeremias, *Jerusalem in the Time of Jesus*, p. 267. In an extreme extension of Jeremias's view, Farmer writes that the Pharisees 'were recognized by the Romans as legal authorities whose power over the people in the cities and towns of Galilee was their best hope for maintaining social stability in the area' (*Jesus and the Gospel*, 1982, p. 30).

79. The statement on p. 112 of *Proclamation* is clarified on p. 118: the main religious duty of *Judaism* was separation from sinners, naming the Pharisees and the Essenes as representing 'Judaism'. Since the Essenes did not govern Judaism on this point, that leaves only the Pharisees.

80. See Morton Smith, 'Palestinian Judaism'. See also Shaye Cohen, *Josephus in Galilee and Rome*, 1979, pp. 140, 237f., 241.

81. Cohen, ibid., pp. 223f. So also Neusner, 'Josephus's Pharisees', p. 69.

82. Smith, 'Palestinian Judaism', p. 81 (= p. 197).

83. Jeremias, *Jerusalem in the Time of Jesus*, p. 267.

84. Ibid., p. 266.

85. See Michael J. Cook, 'Jesus and the Pharisees', *Journal of Ecumenical Studies* 15, 1978, p. 445.

86. Jeremias, *Jerusalem in the Time of Jesus*, p. 267.

87. See *Paul and Palestinian Judaism*, pp. 157–68.

88. See Schürer/Vermes, *The History of the Jewish People* II, p. 284.

89. See the interesting calculations of numbers in Jeremias, *Jerusalem in the Time of Jesus*, pp. 198–213.

90. Smith ('Palestinian Judaism in the First Century') has proposed that the Galilean synagogues were not dominated by the Pharisees. 'There is strong evidence that there were practically no Pharisees in Galilee during Jesus' lifetime' (*Magician*, p. 157). So also Cohen, *Josephus in Galilee and Rome*, p. 226: 'The Pharisaic movement was centered in Jerusalem and did not become influential in Galilee until after the Bar Kokhba revolt.' Martin Hengel also offers a caution on this point: 'we must avoid overestimating the influence of Pharisaic scholars before 70 A.D. in Galilee' (*Charismatic Leader*, p. 55; cf. p. 45 n. 26). Contrast Farmer, n. 78 above.

91. Lay teachers called 'scribes': e.g. Schürer/Vermes, *The History of the Jewish People* II, pp. 238f. The relationship between 'scribes' and 'Pharisees' is often discussed. See ch. 9 n. 15. My own judgment is that it is more reasonable to equate Pharisees and scribes than Pharisees and *ḥaberim*.

92. Perrin, *Rediscovering*, pp. 91–4.

93. Ibid., p. 91.

94. Ibid., pp. 93f. The equation of 'sinners' and 'Gentiles' is not quite correct, although it may be true that most Gentiles were regarded by most Jews as 'sinners' (see e.g. Gal. 2.15). But an apostate Jew, no matter how heinous his sin and how unrepentant his attitude, was still a Jew. See on this Larry Schiffman, 'At the Crossroads: Tannaitic Perspectives on the Jewish-Christian Schism', *Jewish and Christian Self-Definition II: Aspects of Judaism in the Graeco-Roman Period*, 1981, pp. 115–56.

95. Perrin, p. 94.

96. Jeremias, *Jerusalem in the Time of Jesus*, p. 267.

97. Riches, *Jesus and the Transformation of Judaism*, pp. 99, 108.

98. Käsemann, 'Blind Alleys in the "Jesus of History" Controversy', p. 51.

99. Fuchs, 'The Quest of the Historical Jesus', p. 21.

100. J. Behm, 'μετανοέω, μετάνοια', *TDNT* IV, p. 1002.

101. For these two points, see *Paul and Palestinian Judaism*, pp. 36, 57, 226.

102. See for example W. R. Farmer, 'An Historical Essay on the Humanity of Jesus Christ', *Christian History and Interpretation* (ed. W. R. Farmer and others), 1967, p. 103.

103. Funk, *Language, Hermeneutic, and Word of God*, pp. 17f.

104. E. Schweizer, *Jesus*, p. 29. For this general view see also Schlosser, *Règne*, p. 683.

105. Perrin, *Rediscovering*, p. 97.

106. See also Perrin, *Kingdom*, p. 75. Repentance not exclusive to end-time: ch. 3 at n. 54 above.

107. Perrin's 'evidence' is Tohoroth 7.6, which says that a tax collector defiles a house into which he enters (Perrin, *Rediscovering*, p. 94). I cannot understand why he thought that this meant that the tax collector could not repent.

108. In Rabbinic literature the classic statement on repentance is attributed to R. Simeon (probably b. Yohai): even the completely wicked person who repents at the end will be saved (T. Kiddushin 1.15f.). One passage does not prove a view to be universal, and I cite it to illustrate a view which can be shown to be universal – at least as being virtually universal in all the surviving Jewish literature of the period 200 BCE to 200 CE. There are minor exceptions to the rule in 1QS. One may see the various sections on 'atonement' in each of the first three chapters of *Paul and Palestinian Judaism*.

109. So Perrin, *Rediscovering*, p. 103.

110. Above, p. 109. This point is well made by Aulén, *Jesus*, p. 66.

111. Above, at n. 7. Cf. R. Bultmann, *History*, p. 34: the passage is 'manifestly imaginary, an extended version of Mark 2.14 which, combined with vv. 15–17, gave rise to this story'. Fiedler (*Jesus und die Sünder*, p. 135) argues that the story is so strongly marked by Lucan language and theology that one need not look for a prior story which has been reworked. Jeremias (*Proclamation*, p. 156) treats all the details of the story as factual.

112. Jeremias, *Proclamation*, p. 119. So also Aulén, *Jesus*, pp. 66, 71.

113. Ibid., p. 177. See recently W. R. Farmer, *Jesus and the Gospel*, p. 41; Trautmann, *Zeichenhafte Handlungen*, p. 162; Aulén, *Jesus*, p. 89.

114. Perrin, *Rediscovering*, pp. 90–108.

115. Westerholm, *Jesus and Scribal Authority*, p. 132.

116. For the Rabbinic rule, see Sifra Aḥare Mot pereq 8.1f. Further passages in *Paul and Palestinian Judaism*, p. 179 and notes. Transgression of the Sabbath, for example, ordinarily required a sin-offering (Sanhedrin 7.8; Shabbath 7.1).

117. I am happy to note that this was seen by Aulén, *Jesus*, p. 66: 'One could not find a sign of . . . penance among the sinners with whom Jesus associated.' Basically, however, he accepted the theory that it was the sequence of forgiveness and repentance which was offensive (pp. 66, 71).

118. I agree with Bultmann (*History*, pp. 28, 56f.) that the passages depicting the call of the disciples are 'ideal scenes': they condense 'into one symbolic moment what was in actuality a process' (p. 57). But I still think it likely that at least one tax collector was among Jesus' followers. Pesch has argued that the story of the banquet to which

many tax collectors and sinners came (Mark 2.15–17) is basically authentic ('Das Zöllnergastmahl [Mk 2,15–17]', *Mélanges Bibliques en hommage au R. P. Béda Rigaux* [ed. A. Deschamps and others], 1970, pp. 63–87). The case is admirably argued, but it is a classic example of the careful and meticulous analysis of passages which, I fear, will never tell us much about Jesus. The *general* charge seems reliable, but I remain unpersuaded that several tax collectors gathered in one place in Galilee for a dinner which Jesus attended. Such an event, if it occurred, would tell us more about the density of tax collectors in Galilee than it would about Jesus.

119. This interpretation takes the saying of Mark 2.19 to be an original saying, although the setting for it has been invented. See again Bultmann, *History*, pp. 18f.

120. Moule (*Birth*, p. 24) sees that it is a question whether or not Jesus approved of sacrifice.

121. Jeremias, *Proclamation*, pp. 115f.; Perrin, *Rediscovering*, pp. 107f.; Hengel, *Charismatic Leader*, p. 67; Trautmann, *Zeichenhafte Handlungen*, pp. 161f. From Trautmann's discussion, it would appear that 'eating' always meant 'eschaton'. We must exercise due caution. Table-fellowship, unlike 'the twelve', does not necessarily refer to the kingdom. If we could not correlate the action of eating with sayings which promise 'the lost' inclusion in the coming kingdom, and with the sayings and parables which connect 'banquet' with 'kingdom', we would be on less certain ground. The saying about the fruit of the vine (Mark 14.25 and parallels) alone would establish the eschatological significance of the meal could it be shown unquestionably to be genuine. I take it to be authentic, but cannot show it to be so, beyond appealing to coherence with the depiction of Jesus which is being offered.

122. So Perrin, *Rediscovering*, p. 107.

7. THE GENTILES

1. See ch. 3 section 1, 'From John the Baptist to Paul'.

2. See the brief review in Ferdinand Hahn, *Mission in the New Testament*, ET 1965, pp. 26–41.

3. Jeremias, *Jesus' Promise to the Nations*, ET 1958.

4. Cf. Caird, *Jesus and the Jewish Nation*, p. 14. Jesus thought that the Gentiles would be added in the last days, but not 'by any gradual process of making individual converts to Judaism'.

5. Jeremias, pp. 19–24, 25–39, 51.

6. Ibid., pp. 57–60.

7. Ibid. pp. 40f. See further just below.

8. Ibid., p. 73.

9. John Riches, *Jesus and the Tranformation of Judaism*.

10. See ibid., pp. 69, 76, 95, 99, 107.

11. Ibid., pp. 100f. Riches speaks of Jesus' 'stripping' the word kingdom 'of its existing associations' (*scil.*, those of vengeance) (p. 100) and of his 'deleting' 'conventional associations' (p. 101). Jeremias had claimed that Jesus 'rejects the nationalistic sentiment of hate' (p. 42) and 'detaches the nationalistic idea of revenge from the hope of redemption' (p. 43). How Riches' view differs from that of his unacknowledged predecessor is not clear.

12. Riches, p. 135.

13. Ibid., p. 100.

14. Ibid., pp. 99, 105–8. One would not expect to read in a recent and supposedly scholarly book that the difference between (in effect) Christianity and Judaism is that

one is a religion of love and the other of hate and vengeance. Unfortunately, there is precedent; see above, pp. 200–202. One notes with regret that Jeremias wanted to affirm the same stark dichotomy and that he resorted to an extravagant rewriting of Luke 4.22 in order to accomplish it. The RSV quite reasonably, in view of the context, translates the verse this way: 'And all spoke well of him, and wondered at the gracious words which proceeded out of his mouth. . . .'. This is Jeremias's rendering (*Jesus' Promise to the Nations*, p. 45): ' "They protested with one voice and were furious, because he (only) spoke about (God's year of) mercy (and omitted the words about the Messianic vengeance)." ' In the passage in Luke, anger is not mentioned until v. 28, and then it concerns a different issue.

15. See e.g. the discussions of the Rabbis and Qumran, Riches, pp. 94–7. When he writes of the Rabbis that in their view God 'will not tolerate the presence of that which is ungodly, impure, polluted' (p. 95), one immediately thinks of the saying that 'Beloved is Israel, for even though they are unclean the Shekinah is among them', a statement that occurs in the midst of fairly elaborate prescriptions for purity (Sifre Num. 1). Riches appears to have learned from Neusner that the Rabbis were concerned with purity and to have drawn his own conclusions from that fact, ignoring theirs.

16. Jeremias, *Jesus' Promise to the Nations*, p. 40.

17. Ibid., p. 13.

18. Jeremias's statement that the movement is always 'centripetal' (*Jesus' Promise to the Nations*, p. 60), seems to overlook Isa. 66.19. Hahn (*Mission*, p. 20) correctly points out, however, that here the witnesses are Gentiles themselves.

19. Jeremias, p. 57.

20. Jeremias (ibid., p. 58) read Isa. 60.11 as saying that the Gentiles, *led by* their kings, stream towards Jerusalem. The passage in fact refers to the bringing of foreign tribute (or booty) 'with their kings *led*': that is, in captivity. The entire section Isa. 60.5–16 is about subjugation and tribute – or, failing them, destruction.

21. Jeremias, p. 62, accepted by David Bosch, *Heidenmission*, p. 29.

22. Jeremias, *Jesus' Promise to the Nations*, pp. 61f. On his difficulty about 'late Judaism', given even his own evidence, see above.

23. T. Sanh. 13.2.

24. See B. W.Helfgott, *The Doctrine of Election in Tannaitic Literature* 1954, esp. pp. 140f.; M. Kadushin, *The Rabbinic Mind*, ²1965, esp. p. 28; *Paul and Palestinian Judaism*, pp. 207–11.

25. Above, pp. 96f.

26. The view is still repeated, however, in Ps. Sol. 17.6.

27. Cf. Jeremias, *Jesus' Promise to the Nations*, p. 40.

28. The importance of the question is often overlooked. Hahn (*Mission*), for example, generally sees that eschatological expectation is crucial to the New Testament idea of mission, but his chapter on 'Old Testament and Jewish Presuppositions' deals more with non-eschatological proselytism and general attitude.

29. See Jacob Neusner, *Messiah in Context*, forthcoming.

30. Sanh. 26a–b.

31. The Rabbis appear to have had a well-developed concept of diminished responsibility: the ignorant are also treated more leniently than scholars (Baba Metzia 33b).

32. The most elaborate instance is connected with Caligula's desire to have his statue placed in the temple, *BJ* II.184–203. For Josephus's desire to present a picture of a loyal majority, while narrating uprising after uprising, see e.g. *BJ* II.72f. Cf. also

II.236–40; 244; 294–300. On Josephus's 'axes', see Morton Smith, 'Palestinian Judaism'.

33. See the helpful survey by Barnett, 'The Jewish Sign Prophets'.

34. Thus Riches, *Transformation*, p. 86: 'the relatively impoverished state of the religious traditions which Jesus inherited'.

35. See, for example, Bosch, *Heidenmission*, who competently canvasses opinion on the passages. On the banquet parables and Matt. 8.11f., see pp. 124–31; on Matt. 15.21–28 and 10.5–16, pp. 84–6; on Mark 13.10, pp. 144–71.

36. Jeremias, *Jesus' Promise to the Nations*, p. 29.

37. Bosch, *Heidenmission*, p. 158; G. R. Beasley-Murray, *Jesus and the Future*, 1954, p. 253.

38. Matt. 8.11f.//Luke 13.28f. is generally considered authentic, and Matthew's form the earlier of the two. See, for example, Hahn, *Mission*, pp. 34f. But Matt. 8.12 is more than a little dubious: 'sons of the kingdom' for Jews occurs elsewhere only in Matt. 13.38, and the same use of 'kingdom' appears in 21.43 (the kingdom taken away from you, the Jews), both passages unique to Matthew. 'Outer darkness' occurs in the synoptics elsewhere at Matt. 22.13 and 25.30. 'Wailing and gnashing of teeth', besides appearing in the parallel in Luke 13.28, occurs only in Matt. 13.42, 50; 22.13; 24.51; 25.30. Thus all of Matt. 8.12 is Matthaean, though the verse is partially paralleled in Luke. Schlosser accepts the Lucan form, and thus keeps the entire saying (*Règne*, pp. 607, 614f.). While, on the whole, I want this study to be independent of the synoptic problem, this is one of the numerous points where it is obviously better not to insist on the total independence of Matthew and Luke. Here Luke has a Matthaean phrase. There has been a recent debate between Michael Goulder and Christopher Tuckett as to whether or not Luke shows knowledge of Matthaean phrases and order, but our passage is not discussed. See Goulder, 'On putting Q to the test', *NTS* 24, 1978, pp. 218–34; Tuckett, 'On the Relationship between Matthew and Luke', *NTS* 30, 1984, pp. 130–42. On various grounds I think it better to grant that Luke knew Matthew, though I continue to think that the relationships among the synoptics are complex rather than simple. See 'The Argument from Order and the Relationship between Matthew and Luke', *NTS* 15, 1969, pp. 249–61; 'The Overlaps of Mark and Q and the Synoptic Problem', *NTS* 19, 1972, pp. 453–65.

39. The phrase 'they to the circumcised' in Gal. 2.10 appears to include James as well as Peter and John.

40. Cf. Reumann, *Jesus*, pp. 306f.: 'While the historian today cannot be as sure as he might wish about what Jesus thought [about the future], he can be certain about what his disciples did. They formed a church, a community or fellowship of those who held that God had been at work in Jesus of Nazareth. . . .' More to the point, they carried on his task of preparing Israel for the eschaton.

41. Cf. J. W. Drane, *Paul: Libertine or Legalist*, 1975, p. 74.

42. *Paul, the Law, and the Jewish People*, pp. 18f.

43. See, for example, Pesch, 'Anspruch', pp. 53–6, 68; Hahn, *Mission*, pp. 36–8. There is a thorough discussion in W. D. Davies, *The Gospel and the Land*, n. 46 on pp. 350–52. Davies is dubious about the saying but takes the cleansing of the Gentile court to be significant.

8. THE KINGDOM: CONCLUSION

1. As well as the passages which condemn 'this generation' or which speak of Jewish condemnation and Gentile salvation: Matt. 11.20–4 and par.; Matt. 12.41f. and par. Above, pp. 109f.

2. See the conclusion to ch. 6.

3. Jeremias, *Proclamation*, pp. 116f., 177. Trautmann also notes the existence of the problem. She proposes that it is wrong to think that Jesus would exclude the righteous. Rather he regarded all Jews as sinners and invited tax collectors as an extreme example of all Israel (Trautmann, *Zeichenhafte Handlungen*, pp. 162–4). I cannot discover an adequate foundation for the view that the wicked represent all Israel.

4. E.g. Jeremias and Schlosser, above, ch. 3 nn. 58, 74.

5. Hengel, *Charismatic Leader*, pp. 59–62.

6. Hengel, ibid., pp. 39, 42. The question of whether or not he was misunderstood is taken up below.

7. Above, pp. 200–202.

8. Hengel takes the call to repent for granted as being the heart of Jesus' message.

9. *AJ* XX.203. We return to the persecution of the Christian movement in ch. 10.

10. See above, on Cadbury, pp. 19–21.

11. E.g. Hengel, *Charismatic Leader*, p. 40; Jeremias, *Proclamation*, p. 211.

12. Theissen's appraisal is apt: 'as a renewal movement within Judaism, the Jesus movement was a failure' (Gerd Theissen, *The First Followers of Jesus. A Sociological Analysis of the Earliest Christianity* [= *Sociology of Early Palestinian Christianity*] ET 1978, p. 112.

13. Because of Christian editorial activity, we cannot tell what role, if any, Jesus played in Josephus's description of the period. It is evident, however, that John the Baptist had considerable influence (*AJ* XVIII.118), and this cannot be said of Jesus.

14. See on all this *Paul, the Law and the Jewish People*, pp. 187–90.

15. Hengel, *Charismatic Leader*, pp. 59, 62.

16. Josephus, *AJ* XX.98f.: Roman cavalry killed many of Theudas' followers and decapitated Theudas. *AJ* XX.171f.: 'a large force of cavalry and infantry' attacked the followers of the Egyptian, killed 400 and took 200 prisoners. The Egyptian himself escaped. There is a significantly different account in *BJ* II.261–63. See below at n. 25, and ch. 11.

17. This point, to which we shall return, has recently been emphasized by J. P. M. Sweet, 'The Zealots and Jesus', *Jesus and the Politics of His Day* (ed. E. Bammel and C. F. D. Moule), 1984, pp. 64. See also Bo Reicke, 'Judaeo-Christianity and the Jewish Establishment, A.D. 33–66', ibid., p. 146.

18. See the discussion in Schlosser, *Règne*, pp. 624–41. Schlosser favours the view that Jesus thought of the kingdom as transcendent. See also H. Flender, *Die Botschaft Jesu von der Herrschaft Gottes*, 1968, whose view is closer to the one taken here.

19. Theissen (*First Followers*, p. 9) proposes that they became wandering charismatics. Theissen even extends this to Peter, and proposes that he gave up his family and lived in the wilderness (p. 11). Paul's letters show that Peter was often in Jerusalem, and when he travelled he took his wife, as did others (I Cor. 9.5).

20. See Sweet, 'The Zealots and Jesus', p. 5.

21. E.g. Bornkamm, *Jesus of Nazareth*, p. 159.

22. Above, pp. 98–100 and 149.

23. E.g. Ps. Sol. 17.32; above, ch. 2.

24. Theudas expected to part the Jordan: *AJ* XX.97. For unnamed others, see *BJ* II.258–60; *AJ* XX.167f. Cf. Jonathan in Cyrene, *BJ* VII.437–41.

25. *AJ* XX.170: The Egyptian predicted that the walls of Jerusalem would tumble down. *BJ* II.261–3: he tried to breach them by force.

26. I take the event as historical. See below, ch. 11.

27. For the view that Jesus had no programme in mind, see above, pp. 32, 38.

28. See *Paul and Palestinian Judaism*, pp. 151 n. 19; 294 n. 156; 354 n. 18; 388 n. 4.

29. A discussion of a messianic period which precedes resurrection is a standard part of handbooks on Jewish eschatology. See e.g. Paul Volz, *Die Eschatologie der jüdischen Gemeinde*, 1934, pp. 226f. For the Temple Scroll, see above pp. 84f.

30. Smith, *Magician*, p. 20.

31. Ibid., pp. 142–5.

32. Jesus saw himself as a prophet and as a charismatic, a worker of miracles: Dunn, *Spirit*, pp. 35, 52, 71, 82–4. For emphasis on Jesus as charismatic wonder-worker, see Vermes, *Jesus the Jew*, pp. 58–82. Gerhardsson correctly notes that a prophet has a lot in common with a teacher ('Der Weg der Evangelientradition', p. 92); cf. Riesner, *Jesus als Lehrer*, pp. 276–98. Harvey (*Constraints*, pp. 84–6) is sceptical of the analogy with Theudas and others (and he accepts Josephus's description of their motives, p. 85). Harvey settles for a description of Jesus as one who combined styles (p. 91).

33. Theissen (*First Followers*, pp. 60–2) distinguishes types of 'renewal movements'. Jesus is categorized along with Theudas, the Egyptian, and others, as leader of a 'prophetic movement'. Judas, on the other hand, led a 'resistance movement'. Cf. Barnett's category, 'sign prophet'.

34. Smith, *Magician*, p. 142. The reference is to Mark 15.30 and parr.

35. *AJ* XX.168; cf. *BJ* VII.438. See Theissen, *First Followers*, p. 36.

36. See below, ch. 10 n. 14.

37. Ernst Fuchs ('The Quest of the Historical Jesus', pp. 21f.) proposed that, in accepting sinners, Jesus put himself in God's place. The most that can be said, however, is that he presumed to speak for God.

9. THE LAW

1. Harvey, *Constraints*, p. 36f.

2. Josephus, *AJ* XII.274–76; I Macc. 2.29–41.

3. PSanh. 21b; see G. F. Moore, *Judaism* I, pp. 466f.

4. See the long section *Ap.* II.175–286, especially II.178, 184, 218–21, 232–35, 277f. This of course is idealized and exaggerated. Thus, e.g., the statement that Jews have no desire to emulate the customs of others, II.261. Nevertheless, the argument depends on the fact that the Jews were famous for their loyalty to the law and the tenacity with which it was kept. The idealized picture is based on the reality of general observance. Philo also indicates that Jews were known as distinctive, and that their distinctiveness was keeping the law: e.g. *Legat.* 117. This is, finally, proved by pagan criticism of them for keeping the law. See the brief summary, with bibliography, in *Paul, the Law and the Jewish People*, pp. 102, 117 n. 27. Compare the comments above, ch. 6 at n. 39, on the evidence that the purity laws were generally observed. See further ch. 10 n. 1.

5. Above, pp. 30f., 36f., 51.

6. W. G. Kümmel, 'Äussere und innere Reinheit des Menschen bei Jesus', *Das Wort und die Wörter*, 1973, p. 35.

7. Recently see Jan Lambrecht, 'Jesus and the Law', pp. 76–8.

8. Bultmann, *Jesus and the Word*, p. 63: 'This much is evident, that the idea that Jesus had attacked the authority of the Law was wholly unknown to the Christian community.'

9. Banks, *Jesus and the Law*, p. 242.

10. Ibid., pp. 172, 203, 250.

11. Ibid., p. 242. I agree with many of Banks' strictures on the same page against the extremes of interpreting Jesus as having 'radicalized' or 'abrogated' the law.

12. I use 'midrash' here in its Rabbinic meaning: commentary on Scripture.

13. J. M. Baumgarten, review of Yadin, *The Temple Scroll*, JBL 97, 1978, p. 586. Naturally different groups found different parts of the Scriptures more or less expressive of their self-understanding and consequently quoted them more or less frequently; but there is no exception to the attitude towards the law as unitary and given by God to be found in Jewish literature from around the time of Jesus. This is true even though some may have allegorized its literal meaning away.

14. Westerholm, *Jesus and Scribal Authority*.

15. I do not here take up the question of the adequacy of Westerholm's discussion of the scribes and Pharisees (Westerholm, pp. 26–39). On the difficulty of using New Testament passages to distinguish 'scribe' from 'Pharisee' I am inclined to agree with M. Cook, *Mark's Treatment of the Jewish Leaders*, 1978, pp. 81–97.

16. Westerholm, p. 123.

17. I shall show below that the saying on divorce does not in fact directly challenge the law.

18. See, for example, Dunn, *Spirit*, p. 43, naming 'Sabbath and ceremonial Law'; Braun, *Jesus of Nazareth*, pp. 53–64.

19. Philo, *Migr.* 89.

20. See T. Yom ha-Kippurim 4[5].5; Mek. Bahodesh 7 (Lauterbach II, pp. 249–51), and parallels (*Paul and Palestinian Judaism*, pp. 158–60).

21. Mek. of R. Simeon b. Yohai to Exod. 20.5.

22. See *Paul and Palestinian Judaism*, p. 179 and the literature cited there.

23. Sifra Aḥare Mot pereq 8.1: 'For transgressions which are between man and God the Day of Atonement atones, but for those between man and man the Day of Atonement does not atone until he compensates his fellow.' Cf. Sifre Zuta to Num. 6.26.

24. See e.g. Dunn (*Spirit*, p. 43), who speaks of Jesus' 'sovereign freedom . . . with regard to sabbath and ceremonial law'. For 'sovereign freedom', a cliché of scholarship, see also, for example, Käsemann, 'The Problem of the Historical Jesus', p. 40.

25. An exception is Aulén (*Jesus*, p. 77).

26. Above, pp. 26f. and often. Cf. Jeremias, *Proclamation*, p. 145: three different opponents and three different points of opposition.

27. H. Schürmann, 'Wie hat Jesus seinen tod bestanden und verstanden?', *Orientierung an Jesus* (ed. P. Hoffmann and others), 1973, p. 336.

28. Banks, *Jesus and the Law*, pp. 99f.

29. Ibid., p. 238.

30. I hope that above, in the chapter on the temple, I dealt sufficiently thoroughly with the view that it was only the *abuse* of the temple, by using it to produce private gain, that Jesus protested. For the sake of completeness, I repeat the point here. The den of robbers' saying is probably not original in the pericope. Further, the threat or prediction of the temple's destruction has nothing to do with 'abuse' of it. It is the temple that will be destroyed, not greedy money-changers.

31. A. Schlatter, *Der Evangelist Matthäus*, p. 288.

32. A. Wilder, *Eschatology and Ethics in the Teaching of Jesus*, p. 173. Cf. Perrin, *Rediscovering*, p. 144.

33. Hengel, *Charismatic Leader*, pp. 3–15. Cf. also Harvey, *Constraints*, pp. 59–61. It is a weakness in the theses of Banks and Westerholm not to have seen the significance of the passage, especially after it had been pointed out by Hengel.

34. See Perrin and Hengel, cited in the preceding two notes. Bultmann (*History*, p. 105) regarded at least the saying of Jesus to be authentic. We shall later see that the saying cannot be detached from the question.

35. Cf. T. W. Manson, *The Teaching of Jesus. Studies in its Form and Content*, ²1963, p. 122; Perrin, *Rediscovering*, p. 144; Hengel, *Charismatic Leader*, pp. 3–5, where further literature is cited.

36. Hengel (ibid., p. 4) regards the original introduction as having been, 'Another said, "Let me first go . . .".' The difference is not a substantial one for understanding the passage. O'Neill (*Messiah*, pp. 85f.) argues that characterizing those left behind as (spiritually) dead generalizes the saying to make all those who do not follow Jesus 'dead', while originally the saying applied to only one person. He reconstructs it thus: 'Leave the dead, you must come and proclaim the Kingdom of God.' The point is well made. All we really need is the phrase 'Leave the dead' in order to grasp the offensiveness of the saying.

37. On both points see also Hengel, *Charismatic Leader*, pp. 8–15.

38. Ibid.

39. Hengel, *Charismatic Leader*, p. 12: 'refusal of burial had always been considered among the Greeks and Jews as an unheard of act of impiety and as the severest of punishments for criminals.'

40. Hengel, *Charismatic Leader*, p. 5.

41. Dibelius, *Jesus*, p. 59. Cf. Wilder, above, n. 32.

42. E. Schweizer, *Lordship and Discipleship*, p. 26.

43. Banks, *Jesus and the Law*, p. 97.

44. Banks here (p. 97 n. 3) cites Bultmann (*History*, p. 105) in his support, but Bultmann's position seems to be different. On p. 105 Bultmann includes Luke 9.60a among sayings which 'contain something characteristic, new, reaching out beyond popular wisdom and piety and yet are in no sense scribal or rabbinic nor yet Jewish apocalyptic'. He concludes, 'So here if anywhere we can find what is characteristic of the preaching of Jesus.' It is hard to see how this supports the view that the saying is 'purely proverbial' (Banks, p. 97). On p. 119 of his *History* Bultmann classifies Matt. 8.22 as 'prophetic'.

45. See recently David Dungan, *The Sayings of Jesus in the Churches of Paul*, 1971, part II; Klaus Berger, *Die Gesetzesauslegung Jesu*, 1972, pp. 536–75; Hultgren, *Jesus and his Adversaries*, pp. 120f.

46. Paul carefully distinguishes the woman's act from the man's, showing that he, at least, knew Jewish law. She 'separates from' her husband, he 'sends away' his wife (I Cor. 7.10f.).

47. Schürer, ed. Vermes, *The History of the Jewish People* II, p. 464 n. 1.

48. Westerholm first writes that the Pharisees, who took the biblical commandments to be statutes, 'could not but conclude that the references to divorce in such legal texts as Deut. 24.1 meant that it was a legitimate option' (*Jesus and Scribal Authority*, pp. 122f.). That is, of course, the case. But he later says that in this one case Jesus dealt with a biblical regulation 'which, at least in the Pharisaic view, prescribed (or proscribed) certain actions' (p. 122). But divorce is neither prescribed or proscribed, only remarriage

to one's original wife who had, after divorce, married again. Jesus does not mention this at all, and thus here too he does not deal with a biblical prescription or proscription. For the incorrect view that Jesus abolishes a Mosaic *regulation*, see e.g. Jeremias, *Proclamation*, p. 207.

49. Despite Westerholm, ibid., p. 122.

50. Or Hasmonean: the two are not identical, and the precise identification of the priests who are being criticized depends on the date of CD, which we need not try to determine in detail.

51. Translation by Vermes.

52. For the editions being quoted, see the Bibliography.

53. See Dungan, *Sayings of Jesus*, p. 116.

54. Ibid., p. 117.

55. The antitheses commonly identified as authentic are the first, second and fourth, on murder, adultery and swearing. For the view that these, in effect, deny the law or the authority of Moses, see e.g. Käsemann, 'The Problem of the Historical Jesus', pp. 37f. ('shattering the letter of the law'); Kümmel, *Theology*, p. 52; see the Bibliography in Banks, *Jesus and the Law*, p. 184 n. 1.

56. Especially W. D. Davies, 'Matthew 5:17, 18', *Christian Origins and Judaism*, 1962, p. 44. Davies joins others in denying the authenticity of the other antitheses, and argues that actual denial of the law is limited to the third, fifth and sixth ones (ibid.). See n. 58 below.

57. E.g. Käsemann, n. 55 above.

58. This is true not only of the first, second and fourth antitheses, but also of the third (divorce) and fifth. Thus Davies's view of the inauthentic antitheses – that they oppose the law – needs minor correction (n. 56). The sixth antithesis does not quote a law, and I leave it aside.

59. Strict observance of the two-source hypothesis prevents one from seeing the coherence and significance of this material, since Matt. 5.43–8 is paralleled in Luke (and, by the hypothesis, is therefore from Q); 23.6f. is in both Mark and Luke (and is therefore held to be from Mark), and 23.23–6 is paralleled in Luke (and is therefore also from Q). As I remarked in the Introduction, one needs a complete and convincing solution of the source problem and also a full history of each pericope. It is my own view that we must be prepared to accept a complicated solution of the source problem, one which allows some cross-influence among versions of all three Gospels. Meanwhile, I shall have to rest the case on the internal coherence of this material and also the distinctiveness of its viewpoint. It seems to me to be as clear a 'block' as the controversy stories or the apocalyptic sections. The material is not, however, the composition of the evangelist Matthew, who favoured Gentiles (e.g. 28.19), and who retained the tradition that Jesus associated with tax collectors. For the distinctive position of this block of material on these points, see Matt. 18.15–17; 5.46f.; 6.7.

60. For the interpretation of 5.17 (without 5.48) to mean 'bring to eschatological completion and to transform' (and thus to alter), see Meyer, *Aims*, pp. 147–51. Davies understood 5.17 to mean 'fulfil by radicalizing' ('Matt. 5:17, 18', p. 45).

61. See the discussion in Theissen, *First Followers*, pp. 78f. He is discussing the 'Jesus movement', however, and not necessarily Jesus himself.

62. Cf. Theissen, ibid., p. 79: External relaxation and internal tightening as an interpretation 'fails when the same norms are both intensified and relaxed'.

63. Kümmel, 'Äussere und innere Reinheit'; Käsemann, 'The Problem of the Historical Jesus', p. 40.

64. See 'State of the Question'. See also the summary by Aulén, *Jesus*, p. 49.

65. We may recall that Jewish scholars in particular find no substantial breach of the law by Jesus. See above, p. 55.

66. An exception might be Tiberias, which in Jesus' day was newly founded. We noted before (p. 184) that settlement there was resisted by many, since it involved perpetual corpse-uncleanness. According to Josephus it was settled by 'a promiscuous rabble' (*AJ* XVIII.37), and it may well be that food and Sabbath laws were not regularly observed. But Jesus seems to have had no contact with the city.

67. Bultmann, *History*, p. 39.

68. Harvey, *Constraints*, pp. 38f.

69. Ibid., p. 50.

70. Ibid.

71. For the phrase 'assured result' see Harvey, ibid., p. 49 n. 69. He explains that some aspects of Jesus' behaviour are so 'constantly and consistently attested in the gospel narratives that they can confidently be used as evidence that Jesus, though sharing a number of the beliefs and assumptions of Pharisaism, cannot have been received as a teacher within the Pharisaic tradition' (pp. 49f.). He continues by saying that Jesus was 'frequently accused of not maintaining the standards of religious behaviour' which the Pharisees would have expected (p. 50), citing Mark 2.18 (fasting) and 7.2 (handwashing) as evidence. This line of argument is very weak: (1) No one has proposed that Jesus was a Pharisaic teacher, and Harvey here sets up a proposal which he can easily demolish; (2) 'constantly', 'consistently' and 'frequently' are not accurate descriptions of the evidence. Fasting and handwashing each occurs only once.

72. See e.g. Schürmann, 'Wie hat Jesus seinen Tod bestanden und verstanden?', p. 336.

73. On the passage, see the fine survey by Lambrecht, 'Jesus and the Law'.

74. Lambrecht ('Jesus and the Law', p. 25) points out that 'in the editor's mind the whole of these twenty-two verses form a thematic unity'. I take it that this shows that the evangelist himself did not know the distinction between the handwashing code and the dietary law.

75. Cf. Harvey, *Constraints*, pp. 39f.

76. See e.g. Westerholm, *Jesus and Scribal Authority*, pp. 98–101. Berger (*Die Gesetzesauslegung Jesu*, pp. 476f., 507) argues that even the earliest part of the passage, Mark 7.15, is not authentic. It comes from Hellenistic Judaism and is comprehensible as a debate within Judaism.

77. Mark 7.15 answers the question of Mark 7.5: Lambrecht, 'Jesus and the Law', pp. 56f.; cf. p. 30 n. 13.

78. For the emphasis that Mark 7.15 must refer to food, see Heikki Räisänen, 'Zur Herkunft von Markus 7, 15', *Logia. Les Paroles de Jésus – The Sayings of Jesus* (ed. J. DeLobel), 1982, p. 478; 'Jesus and the Food Laws: Reflections on Mark 7.15', *JSNT* 16, 1982, pp. 81f.; Lambrecht, 'Jesus and the Law', p. 75.

79. This has been often noted. See especially Räisänen's two articles in n. 78. Lambrecht ('Jesus and the Law', pp. 77f.) raises the point, but reaches the conclusion of many: Jesus opposed the law but himself did not know so. This requires, I think, the addition that the disciples were equally dense.

80. Bultmann, *History*, p. 16.

81. So also Hultgren, *Jesus and his Adversaries*, pp. 111–15.

82. So also Harvey, *Constraints*, pp. 37f.

83. Cf. Vermes, *Jesus the Jew*, p. 25. Westerholm (*Jesus and Scribal Authority*, p. 95) comments that 'it seems reasonable to assume that Pharisees would oppose such action [healing] where life was not in danger', and this is possible, even though the kinds of

healing attributed to Jesus in the synoptic Gospels are not forbidden in the Mishnah. Pesch ('Anspruch', p. 68) has also argued that Jesus in Mark 3.1–6 contravenes the Sabbath law either of the Bible or of the Pharisees. But in view of later Rabbinic law it would seem that, even if we take the stories of healing on the Sabbath at face value, no *substantial* transgression was involved.

84. There is an interesting analysis of Mark 3.1–6 in Barrett, *Jesus and the Gospel Tradition*, p. 63. He proposes that the debate 'moves on to different ground' from the 'conventional dispute about what is and what is not permitted on the sabbath': 'there is an egoism that is inconsistent with good Jewish piety'.

85. I leave aside here the question of fasting, which is not even presented as being a matter of law; Jesus is asked why his disciples do not fast when the disciples of John and the Pharisees fast, and he gives an answer which appeals to the presence of the bridegroom (Mark 2.18–22 and parr.). Fasting on the Day of Atonement was prescribed by law (Lev. 16.29), and doubtless other fasts were observed (see Zech 7.3; 8.19: fast days become festivals). The Gospel controversy seems not to be about the Day of Atonement. It may well be an authentic memory that Jesus and his disciples did not fast. Certainly at least one part of the early church did (Matt. 6.16–18), presumably the same part which thought that they should observe the law better than did the Pharisees. That Jesus and his followers did not fast is also indicated in Matt. 11.18f. and par. Still, however, it is not a question of law.

86. So also, for example, Räisänen, 'Zur Herkunft von Markus 7, 15', p. 477.

87. It may be that we should explain this striking saying as an instance in which Jesus claims authority to suspend the law, without implying that a precedent is thereby set or that the law is 'abrogated'. For the category, see B. S. Jackson, 'Jésus et Moïse: le statut du prophète à l'égard de la Loi', *Revue historique de droit français et étranger* 59, 1981, pp. 341–60.

10. OPPOSITION AND OPPONENTS

1. Jews were prepared to fight and die rather than see the temple defiled. The outstanding instance is the threat by Gaius (Caligula) to have his statue set up in the temple. Josephus attributes to 'tens of thousands of Jews' a speech urging their own death rather than the carrying out of Gaius's intention (*AJ* XVIII.262). Philo's evidence is even more dramatic, for he threatens an empire-wide uprising if such an event were to take place. See *Legat.* 159: 'Everyone everywhere, even if he was not naturally well disposed to the Jews, was afraid to engage in destroying any of our institutions'; 192: 'So be it, we will die and be no more, for the truly glorious death, met in defence of laws, might be called life'; 194: the threat by Gaius is against 'the corporate body of the Jews'; 212: all Jews are marked by zeal for the temple; 213–15: Jews are very numerous, too numerous to be contained in a single country, and they pose a danger if outraged; finally Philo piously threatens: 'Heaven forbid indeed that the Jews in every quarter should come by common agreement to the defence. The result would be something too stupendous to be combated.'

Loyalty and devotion to the temple is a special aspect of loyalty and devotion to the law, but the imposing and beautiful temple, to which tens of thousands paid taxes, especially excited loyalty. For the devotion inspired by the temple service, see the *Letter of Aristeas* 92–9: anyone 'will be filled with astonishment . . . at the thought of the sanctity which is attached to each detail of the service'; cf. Josephus's loving and exaggerated description of the first temple, *AJ* VIII.63–129, which surely reflects the grandeur of Herod's temple.

2. 'Abroad' is proved by the payment of the temple tax by Jews 'wherever resident' (*BJ* VII.218); so also Philo, *Legat.* 156.

3. The Qumran sectarians obviously thought that the Jerusalem priesthood was invalid. For other criticism, see e.g. Ps. Sol. 8.13; cf. 1.8; 2.3; T.Mos. 7.

4. Herod locked up and controlled the high priest's robe. Its custody was restored to the priests by Vitellius with the permission of Tiberius himself. After the death of Herod Agrippa I there was a dispute about it. All this shows the immense prestige which the high priest had by virtue of his office, without respect to his character and qualifications. For the robe, see *AJ* XV.403–8; XVIII.90–95.

5. William Horbury, 'New Wine in Old Wine-Skins: IX. The Temple', *ExpT* 86, 1974–75, p. 38.

6. In favour of the theory that prophecy was thought to have ceased, see Jeremias, *Proclamation*, pp. 80–82; Reumann, *Jesus*, p. 220. See the nuanced discussions in Ragnar Leivestad, 'Das Dogma von der prophetenlosen Zeit', *NTS* 19, 1973, pp. 288–99; Peter Schäfer, *Die Vorstellung vom heiligen Geist in der rabbinischen Literatur*, 1972, pp. 89–115; 116–34, 143–6; Dunn, *Spirit*, p. 382 n. 81.

7. John: Matt. 14.3–12 and par.; Theudas: *AJ* XX.97f.

8. Barrett (*Jesus and the Gospel Tradition*, pp. 62–4) correctly speaks of 'an egoism that is inconsistent with good Jewish piety'.

9. Aulén, *Jesus*, p. 55. Cf. the list in Jeremias, *Proclamation*, p. 211.

10. Käsemann, 'The Problem of the Historical Jesus', p. 39.

11. Bornkamm, *Jesus of Nazareth*, p. 97.

12. Ibid., pp. 99–100.   13. It is in John: 8.48.

14. See e.g. Bornkamm, *Jesus of Nazareth*, p. 81; Harvey, *Constraints*, p. 171; cf. Jeremias, *Proclamation*, p. 118 n. 1; Schweizer, *Jesus*, p. 14.

15. Jeremias, *Proclamation*, p. 114.

16. Cf. A. Dupont-Sommer, *The Essene Writings from Qumran*, ET 1961, p. 325, discussing the Prayer of Nabonidus.

17. Cf. 'No one had the right': Dibelius, *Jesus*, p. 126. Against this sort of view Vermes (*Jesus the Jew*, p. 68) correctly comments that there is nothing unique about 'your sins are forgiven'.

18. As does, for example, Harvey, *Constraints*, pp. 170f.

19. Barrett, *Jesus and the Gospel Tradition*, p. 67.

20. Ibid.   21. Reumann, *Jesus*, p. 253.

22. Ibid., p. 152.   23. Ibid., p. 172.

24. Those who regard the passage as authentic will be constrained to defend it against the accusation of being pettifogging, and they may say that its author intended to encourage the right attitude in fasting. Will the same defence be allowed others in Judaism who passed rules?

25. For an explicit example see Jeremias, *Proclamation*, p. 118. Later he states that Jesus opposed the Pharisees for their belief in merit, works of supererogation, casuistry and the like (*Proclamation*, pp. 145–51).

26. *Ap.* II.185–7, 194; cf. 178: difficult to escape punishment. On the other hand Josephus recognizes another point, that the laws are unenforceable and were kept voluntarily: *Ap.* II.218, 220.

27. Above, pp. 183f. and n. 48 (p. 387), p. 251.

28. Josephus consistently says that the Pharisees were 'strict' or 'exact' with regard to the law, even though his description of them in some other respects, especially their relative importance, changed. For their being 'strict', see A. I. Baumgarten, 'The Name of the Pharisees', *JBL* 102, 1983, pp. 413f.

29. That is, the written law: *AJ* XIII.297; XVIII.18.

30. Above, p. 184.

31. Compare my remarks on the false academic security which the use of Billerbeck as 'Rabbinic literature' has long provided: *Paul and Palestinian Judaism*, p. 42.

32. For the last point, see *Paul and Palestinian Judaism*, pp. 551f.; *Paul, the Law and the Jewish People*, pp. 47, 63 n. 142. 154–60.

33. Some of these charges are in parallels in Luke. A charge of ostentation is made against the scribes (not the Pharisees) in Mark 12.38f. See above, pp. 261 and n. 59.

34. David Garland (*The Intention of Matthew* 23, 1979, p. 121) argues that the term 'hypocrites' in Matt. 6.2, 5, 16 does not refer to Pharisees. As the material now stands in Matthew, however, the connection between ch. 6 and ch. 23 can hardly be denied. See W. D. Davies, *The Setting of the Sermon on the Mount*, 1964, pp. 291f.

35. For the admonition to perfection or 'blamelessness', cf. I Thess. 3.13; 5.23.

36. Many regard Matt. 23 as reflecting Matthew's situation, not Jesus'. See, e.g. Cope, *Matthew*, p. 126. Theissen (*First Followers*, pp. 18f.) gives an interesting explanation of the setting of this material: in settled communities rather than in the teaching of wandering charismatics. In general, a lot of Theissen's book on the 'Jesus movement' is based on this and related material, which I have treated as coming from only one segment of the church, not necessarily from the Jesus movement as a whole.

37. Cook ('Jesus and the Pharisees', p. 454) argued against saying that Jesus attacked only some Pharisees ('the hypocritical dregs which even the loftiest of religious movements seems somehow to attract'), pointing out that the Gospels denounce all Pharisees.

38. Jeremias, *Parables*, e.g. pp. 38–40, 132–5. Cf. above, ch. 6, n. 8. The influence of Jeremias's view that the parables attack the Pharisees may be seen, for example, in Robert Funk, *Language, Hermeneutic, and Word of God*, pp. 14–18, 197f.; Aulén, *Jesus*, pp. 66–74; Farmer, 'An Historical Essay on the Humanity of Jesus Christ', p. 116 (accepting Luke 15.1, the Pharisees grumbled); *Jesus and the Gospel*, pp. 36–41. Funk, however, writes that 'the Pharisees' is meant metaphorically (p. 197 n. 13), and he points out that, when the audience changes, Christians can be understood as the targets (pp. 178f.). I gather, however, that he means that Jesus directed the parables against Pharisees and other self-righteous people. On generalizing from 'self-righteous Pharisees' to 'self-righteous Christians', see immediately below.

39. Above, ch. 6, n. 31.

40. See Jeremias, *Parables*, pp. 124f., 135. He claimed that Luke's directing the parables against the Pharisees is authentic, since the tendency (seen in Matthew) was to direct them to disciples (p. 124 n. 41). He apparently did not consider that Luke had a motive too. Eliminating Matthew's setting does not prove Luke's to be authentic. The argument is naive and simplistic.

41. This is seen especially clearly when interpreters slip into the confessional first person while offering supposedly historical and exegetical comments on the text. Such an interpreter has obligated himself to believe what he finds in the text, and consequently he is liable to find in the text what he believes. For an example see Conzelmann, *Theology*, pp. 118f.: 'The demand for penitence [on the part of Jesus] discloses to me that I am not what I should be', etc. With such an attitude, could a truly critical investigation take place? Could the place of repentance in Jesus' message be questioned? For another example, see n. 44 below. In *Paul, the Law and the Jewish People*, pp. 155–7, I quoted an example of the confessional first person from Käsemann and discussed its implications. We take up the implied confessional first person just below.

42. It is a historically defensible statement to say 'Jesus attacked the law' (though I

believe it to be incorrect); but to say that 'Jesus abrogated the law' is a confession of faith, with the confessional 'for us' removed. The same applies to 'shattered', 'destroyed', 'put an end to', and the like. For examples see Leonhard Goppelt, *Jesus, Paul and Judaism*, ET 1964, p. 59 (Jesus was 'the ruination of Pharisaic legalism'), p. 61 (he 'exploded the idea of the Sabbath law'), p. 63 his attitude to the law 'meant the end of Judaism'), p. 69 (Jesus' calling sinners 'was the end of Pharisaism'). Goppelt is an extreme case of a fairly widespread tendency.

43. Luke 15.1f. gives the original setting of the parables which follow: Jeremias, *Parables*, pp. 124, 132. Belief in forgiveness led to Jesus' death; Jeremias, *Jerusalem in the Time of Jesus*, p. 267.

44. For the view that belief in grace led to Jesus' death, see above, ch. 6, pp. 200–202. That Jesus called for the renunciation of achievement, see Bultmann, *Jesus and the Word*, p. 129. See especially Conzelmann, *Theology*, p. 122: 'From this starting point (God and the kingdom of God), it is quite clear that *there can be* no claim on God, that *man* cannot rely on merit. For it is by grace that *I* am what *I* am.' Italics mine. Here we have together the view that Jesus called for true religion (renunciation of one's own claim) and the identification of the author with that position. Conzelmann had previously said that when he ('I') truly realizes the command to turn the other cheek, 'I shall not need any more research work' (p. 121). That is honest, but one notes that critical distance has already been forfeited, and thus the ability to conclude anything about Jesus which does not square with 'my' theology.

45. Scholars sometimes reveal this motive. Note, for example, this explanation by Robert Funk. After writing that 'the Pharisees are incensed because he goes in and eats with sinners', he explains: 'The Pharisees are those who insist on interpreting the word of grace rather than letting themselves be interpreted by it' (*Language, Hermeneutic, and Word of God*, pp. 16f., emphasis removed). See further the application to Christians and others, ibid., pp. 181; Aulén, *Jesus*, p. 72.

46. *Paul, the Law and the Jewish People*, pp. 158f.

47. For the Rabbinic elaboration of 'conditional on intention', see *Paul and Palestinian Judaism*, pp. 92–5, 180, 234.

48. See above, p. 175; ch. 6 n. 24.

49. See the fuller discussion in *Paul, the Law and the Jewish People*, pp. 190–2.

50. On the Jerusalem apostles and Acts, see immediately below.

51. Despite Acts 10.

52. Ch. 3 section 1.

53. See e.g. Arland Hultgren, 'Paul's Pre-Christian Persecutions of the Church: Their Purpose, Locale, and Nature', *JBL* 95, 1976, pp. 97–111, here pp. 97–104.

54. I leave aside here the execution of James the brother of John (Acts 12.1–3), which was apparently connected very loosely, if at all, with the persecution by Jewish authorities.

55. An interesting note in Josephus's account may indicate that the Pharisees also opposed the execution of James. Josephus writes that 'those who were strict (*akribeis*) about the law' were offended (*AJ* XX.201). The term *akribeis* and its cognates, as Baumgarten has pointed out, are regularly used to describe the Pharisees: 'The Name of the Pharisees', pp. 413f., esp. n. 9.

56. Cf. Hengel, review of Brandon, *Jesus and the Zealots, JSS* 14, 1969, p. 237: until Nero Rome left the Christians alone. On the continuing animosity of the chief priests, see also Hengel above, p. 225. One may wonder who were the 'governors and kings' of Mark 13.9 and parr. We know of one king, Agrippa I (Acts 12.1). 'Governors' may have been involved in the punishment of Paul and others (II Cor. 11.25).

57. Morton Smith noted that the real reason for the persecution of Paul was that he transgressed the law, not that he preached a crucified Messiah. He also, however, attributed libertinism to Jesus and the Christian movement generally, and he accounted for the sporadic nature of the persecution of the early church by proposing that they all accepted the principle of I Cor. 9.19f.: occasional conformity to the law when conformity was expedient. I would disagree with Smith about the Jerusalem Christians. James and the 'false brethren' seem to have been conscientious about observing the law. That is, they observed it because they believed in it, not because it was expedient. Their observance had the happy consequence of allowing them to avoid persecution. For Smith's argument, see 'The Reason for the Persecution of Paul and the Obscurity of Acts', *Studies in Mysticism and Religion presented to Gershom G. Scholem* (ed. E. E. Urbach and others), 1967, pp. 261–8.

58. *Paul and Palestinian Judaism*, pp. 551f.

59. On the 'powerful', see ch. 11.

60. So Sweet, 'The Zealots and Jesus', p. 5.

61. Following Hengel: above, pp. 224, 228. This is against the view of T. W. Manson, *The Teaching of Jesus*, pp. 205f.

62. See e.g. Jeremias, *Proclamation*, pp. 145–51; Reumann, *Jesus*, p. 259; Baumbach, *Jesus*, pp. 96f.

63. E.g. Mark 11.8; 15.13; Acts 4.21.

64. Above, p. 226; cf. 239f.

65. *AJ* XVIII.63f.

66. On hostility to Galileans, especially charismatics, see Vermes, *Jesus the Jew*, pp. 80f.

67. For recent discussions of the relationship between scribes and Pharisees, see Westerholm, *Jesus and Scribal Authority*, pp. 26–38; Cook, *Mark's Treatment of the Jewish Leaders*, pp. 81–97. In ch. 6 we discussed the view that the Pharisees were *haberim* and Josephus's view that they were lay teachers of the law. For the present discussion we do not need to reach a decision on precisely how they are to be defined.

68. Jeremias, *Jerusalem at the Time of Jesus*, p. 267. Above, ch. 6 n. 96.

69. Above, n. 62.

70. Reumann, *Jesus*, p. 15, citing Ethelbert Stauffer, *Jesus and the Wilderness Community at Qumran*, ET 1964, p. 21.

71. Above, n. 62.

72. Winter was an early proponent of the view that there was little opposition between Jesus and the Pharisees. See *On the Trial of Jesus*, pp. 174–6, 186.

73. Harvey, *Constraints*, p. 49.

74. Baumbach, *Jesus*, p. 95.

75. Schürmann, 'Wie hat Jesus seinen Tod bestanden und verstanden?', p. 336.

76. Berger, *Das Gesetzesauslegung Jesu*, pp. 576–8. He thinks that the schematization shows that within the Jewish Hellenistic communities there were rigorist groups which either were called Pharisees or which could be identified with the Palestinian Pharisees (p. 578).

77. Michael Cook, 'Jesus and the Pharisees', p. 453; *Mark's Treatment of the Jewish Leaders*, pp. 5, 79f. (with bibliography for and against identifying Jesus' principal opponents as Pharisees). On the evangelists' ignorance of the identity of the opponents, cf. A. F. J. Klijn, 'Scribes, Pharisees, Highpriests and Elders in the New Testament', *NovT* 3, 1959, p. 265.

78. Hultgren, *Jesus and His Adversaries*, p. 159.

79. Ibid., p. 153.

80. Smith, *Magician*, pp. 153–57. The quotation is from p. 157. See above, p. 198 and n. 90.

81. Harvey, *Constraints*, pp. 49f.

82. Ibid., p. 51.

83. On the predominence of the priests in the Sanhedrin and generally in the government of Judaism, see M. Stern, 'Aspects of Jewish Society: The Priesthood and other Classes', esp. pp. 580, 603; Schürer, ed. Vermes, *The History of the Jewish People* II, pp. 199–236, esp. p. 228.

11. THE DEATH OF JESUS

1. A fair part of the Introduction is devoted to scholarly positions on the death of Jesus. There is an admirable summary of views on how to strike the balance between Jewish and Roman involvement in R. E. Brown, *The Gospel According to John XIII–XXI*, 1970, pp. 792f. See also the summary in W. D. Davies and E. P. Sanders, 'Jesus: From the Semitic Point of View', *Cambridge History of Judaism* III, forthcoming. There is also a well-balanced treatment of problems and proposed solutions in G. Sloyan, *Jesus on Trial*, 1973.

2. That Jesus was executed as 'king' is generally accepted, but see especially the detailed argument in Winter, *On the Trial of Jesus*, ch. 12; Nils Dahl, 'The Crucified Messiah', *The Crucified Messiah and other Essays*, pp. 10–36.

3. A. E. Harvey, *Jesus on Trial. A Study in the Fourth Gospel*, 1976, p. 3.

4. Ibid., p. 2.

5. Ibid., p. 3.

6. Above, pp. 232f.

7. Winter, *On the Trial of Jesus*, p. 63.

8. For the distinction, see, for example, W. R. Wilson, *The Execution of Jesus*, 1970, esp. pp. 97, 101–3, 125f.: the temple authorities sought Jesus' life, but for non-religious motives. His action against the temple led to the fear of public disturbance.

9. See, for example, Brown, *John XIII–XXI*, pp. 799f.

10. As Dodd (*Founder*, p. 77) stressed, in Judaism 'national solidarity and religion were inseparable'.

11. Dodd (*Founder*, pp. 149–51) seems to give this parable a role in the fatal conflict.

12. On Luke's deletion of both the word 'blasphemy' and the charge of threatening the temple, see J. M. Creed, *The Gospel According to St Luke*, 1960, p. 276; Hans Conzelmann, *The Theology of St Luke*, ET 1960, pp. 83–7. There has been considerable debate, which cannot be rehearsed here, as to the possibility of Luke's having had an independent source for the Passion Narrative. I take it that Luke's concern to protect the Christian movement from the charge of irreligion is so marked, especially in Acts, that, at least on this point, we do not need to seek a separate source. For Luke's concern to present Christianity as the true and non-threatening form of Judaism, see B. S. Easton, 'The Purpose of Acts', *Early Christianity: The Purpose of Acts and other Papers*, 1954, pp. 42f. In favour of an independent tradition for the Passion Narrative, see J. A. Bailey, *The Traditions Common to Luke and John*, 1963, pp. 32–63; David Catchpole, 'The Problem of the Historicity of the Sanhedrin Trial', *The Trial of Jesus*, (ed. E. Bammel), 1970, pp. 47–65, here p. 54.

13. On a part of Jesus' private teaching which may have been revealed by Judas, see below, p. 309.

14. David Catchpole ('The Answer of Jesus to Caiaphas (Matt. xxvi.64)', *NTS* 17, 1971, pp. 213–26) argues that the phrases in Matthew and Luke are 'affirmative in

content, and reluctant or circumlocutory in formulation' (p. 226). Vincent Taylor (*The Gospel According to St Mark*, p. 569) regarded 'you say that I am', a variant reading in some mss. at Mark 14.62, as original. If this view were accepted, the trial scenes would contain no assertion that Jesus regarded himself as Messiah or Son of God.

15. Harvey (*Jesus on Trial*) proposes that the entire Gospel is constructed as a 'trial', in which the charge of claiming to be equal to God is made and answered.

16. A. Strobel (*Die Stunde der Wahrheit*, 1980, p. 6) states, citing Billerbeck and one additional Rabbinic text, that the basis of the sentence by the Sanhedrin (he assumes there was a sentence) must have been publicly proclaimed and thus that the charge of blasphemy must be authentic. The Rabbinic materials, however, manifestly idealize judicial procedure. If one thinks that Jesus' 'trial' was conducted according to the later Rabbinic rules, then one would have to conclude that it was not conducted at all. The court of the Mishnah is a fantasy one, lacking, among other aspects of reality, a high priest at its head. According to Mishnah Sanhedrin, the court cannot meet at night, witnesses must have cautioned the offender *before* he committed the crime, and a second trial held the next day would be necessary to pass a capital sentence. We shall see below, in considering some passages from Josephus, how trials and executions actually took place.

17. Cf. Brown, *John XIII-XXI*, p. 797.

18. See Bultmann, *History*, pp. 269–71; Martin Dibelius, *From Tradition to Gospel*, ET 1934, p. 182; Boismard, *Synopse des quatre Évangiles* II, p. 409; Creed, *St Luke*, p. 276; Winter, *On the Trial of Jesus*, ch. 3; Sloyan, *Jesus on Trial*, p. 63; Brown, *John XIII-XXI*, p. 796; cf. the summary in J. R. Donohue, *Are You the Christ?*, 1973, pp. 12–30, esp. p. 29 n. 1; pp. 238f.

19. William Horbury ('The Passion Narratives and Historical Criticism', *Theology*, 75, 1972, pp. 58–71) cautions against taking the tendency to incriminate the Jews and exonerate the Romans as having completely controlled the tradition of Jesus' death. Cf. also C. F. D. Moule, 'Some observations on *Tendenzkritik*', *Jesus and the Politics of His Day* (ed. Bammel and Moule), 1984, pp. 91–100.

20. The outstanding example of a thorough-going defence of the historicity of the Marcan account remains the encyclopedic study of Josef Blinzler, *The Trial of Jesus*, ET of 2nd ed., 1959. Cf. now Strobel, *Die Stunde der Wahrheit*. Catchpole defends the basic historicity of the Sanhedrin trial, but follows Luke's order and eliminates the night trial. He also considers the contents of Luke's account to be more primitive than those of Mark's. See 'The Problem of the Historicity of the Sanhedrin Trial'; *The Trial of Jesus*, p. 271.

21. Horbury ('The Passion Narratives and Historical Criticism', p. 69), for example, reasonably suggests that the evangelists possessed 'a common tradition that Jesus was questioned and charged by the Jewish authorities', but arranged it within different frameworks.

22. Reumann, *Jesus*, pp. 64f.

23. Ibid., p. 266.

24. Harvey, *Constraints*, pp. 32, 136, 170f.

25. Ramsay MacMullen, *Roman Government's Response to Crisis* A.D. 235–337, 1976, p. 25. Cf. Elias Bickerman, 'La Chaîne de la tradition pharisienne', *Studies in Jewish and Christian History* II, 1980, pp. 257–69, esp. 257–9.

26. On the census (Luke 2.1), see recently Joseph Fitzmyer, *The Gospel According to Luke I-IX*, 1981, p. 400 ('a vague recollection' of censuses which took place under Augustus Caesar – none corresponding to the sort described in Luke). The reference to Theudas and Judas (Acts 5.36f.) is even 'vaguer': their order is reversed, and

Theudas, who is said to have preceded Jesus, actually lived later. See Josephus, *AJ* XX.97–99.

27. So also Lührmann, 'Markus 14.55–64', pp. 464f.

28. John Bowker, *Jesus and the Pharisees*, pp. 38–52.

29. See recently Strobel, *Stunde der Wahrheit*, pp. 80–92. Harvey (*Constraints*, p. 59) correctly points out that 'deceiver', like 'false prophet', rests on the judgment that one who claims to speak the truth does not. This is a perfectly applicable category, and it is no surprise that it surfaces in later Jewish-Christian debate (see the passages in Strobel). What is lacking is any reason for thinking that it was a formal charge sustained by the Sanhedrin. The Talmudic passages which treat Jesus as a deceiver also say that he was hanged. Is the conviction as deceiver more likely than execution by hanging?

30. Hengel (*Charismatic Leader*, p. 42) proposes that Jesus was executed as a false prophet, and (following Jeremias) he cites evidence outside the trial scene: the scenes of mockery (Mark 14.65 and parr.; 15.29–32 and par.; 15.16–20 and par.; Luke 23.11). These, he says, travesty 'the charge of which he has been accused'. Yet it should be noted that not only is prophesying mocked, but also healing and claiming to be king. This evidence is not adequate to prove that there was a formal charge that Jesus was a false prophet.

31. Above, pp. 200–208.

32. Above, p. 271.

33. Not the prerogative of God: above, pp. 273f.

34. Josephus, *BJ* VI.300–309, quotation from 301 in Thackeray's translation (LCL).

35. Josephus, *AJ* XVIII.116–19.

36. Smith, 'Palestinian Judaism', p. 72 (=188).

37. Smith, *Magician*, pp. 16f., 38–44.

38. Étienne Trocmé, 'L'expulsion des marchands du temple', *NTS* 15, 1968, pp. 1–22, esp. 20–2.

39. Jeremias, *Proclamation*, p. 145. n. 1.

40. Above, ch. 1 n. 1.

41. For the last point, see especially Klausner, *Jesus of Nazareth*, pp. 345–8. For the list of contributing causes, cf. Smith, *Magician*, pp. 38–44.

42. Josephus, *BJ* II.224. He mentions all feasts as times of special preparation by the Romans.

43. Just as this chapter was on its way to the typist, I was able to see an article by David Catchpole arguing that the event is not historical at all. ('The "Triumphal" Entry', *Jesus and the Politics of His Day* [ed. Bammel and Moule], pp. 319–34, esp. 330). I have left the section as it already was, but would now emphasize even more the tentative nature of any conclusions based on the story of the entry.

44. For the difficulty of seeing the passage as showing anything about the public reception of Jesus, see Étienne Trocmé, *Jesus as Seen by His Contemporaries*, pp. 63, 111.

45. Cf. Barrett, *Jesus and the Gospel Tradition*, p. 23.

46. Many scholars have accepted the obvious. See, for example, Dibelius, *Jesus*, pp. 95, 102; Dunn, *Unity and Diversity*, p. 41; W. Beilner, *Christus und die Pharisäer*, 1959, pp. 238–47 (accepting the title 'Messiah'); Smith, *Magician*, pp. 16f., 19. The list could go on and on.

47. Cf. recently Harvey, *Constraints*, p. 136; Barrett, *Jesus and the Gospel Tradition*, p. 23.

48. There is a third reason: Those who do not think that Jesus had in mind an actual

event (thus, for example, Bultmann) naturally are uneasy at the thought that he attributed to himself a role in it!

49. This is a long-standing problem. I repeat here my earlier proposal (p. 234): A teacher who comes into conflict with the Pharisees over the law and who offends the priests by striking at their revenue (the main-line depiction of Jesus), but who appears in visions after his death, does not seem to deserve the title 'Messiah'. But once we grant that the kingdom which Jesus had in mind was actually expected, the problem seems to vanish. For the problem and an interesting answer (that Jesus pointed to Isa. 42.1, where the word occurs), see Harvey, *Constraints*, ch. 6, esp. pp. 137–43.

50. Cf. McKelvey, *The New Temple*, p. 61: 'an acted parable of the coming kingdom of God'.

51. Schweitzer, *Quest*, p. 396.

52. For a summary of protests against seeing the Pharisees as involved in the death of Jesus, see Beilner, *Christus und die Pharisäer*, pp. 235–7. And see especially Winter, *On the Trial of Jesus*, pp. 174–6.

53. Cf. Winter, *On the Trial of Jesus*, p. 147.

54. There are very helpful charts of events, placed in parallel columns, in Reumann, *Jesus*, pp. 59, 68.

55. For the following I draw on Schürer/Vermes, *The History of the Jewish People in the Age of Jesus Christ* II, pp. 199–236; S. Safrai, 'Jewish Self-Government', *The Jewish People in the First Century* I, 1974, pp. 377–99; Ze'ev W. Falk, *Introduction to Jewish Law of the Second Commonwealth* I, 1972, pp. 54–8. All scholars note that the Sanhedrin played varying roles at varying times. See e.g. Safrai, p. 382; Falk, p. 56; Schürer/Vermes, pp. 218–23 (the question of the Sanhedrin's competence under the Romans).

56. Schürer/Vermes, p. 204; cf. Falk, pp. 54f.; Safrai, pp. 384f.

57. Schürer/Vermes, p. 213. Cf. Safrai, p. 384: towards the end of the period of the second temple, 'the pre-eminence of the high priesthood declined, but it was quite considerable even during the last days of the Temple.' Falk (pp. 55f.) depicts the presidency of the Sanhedrin as changing from a member of the priesthood to a Pharisee when a matter of halaka was discussed; cf. Safrai, pp. 388f.

58. Schürer/Vermes, p. 213; Safrai, p. 384.

59. Safrai, p. 386.

60. Schürer/Vermes, p. 213.

61. Of the three treatments being used here, Falk is most dependent on Rabbinic evidence and least discriminating in conflating it with Josephus, Schürer/Vermes the least dependent on the Rabbinic accounts and the most discriminating in use of the sources. As far as I know, despite the large body of literature on the Sanhedrin, there is no work which meticulously distinguishes source from source, including the various works of Josephus from one another. Adolf Büchler, noting the divergence which actually occurs from source to source, and apparently supposing that each source was correct, developed a theory of multiple courts: Büchler, *Das Synedrion in Jerusalem*, 1902. (See Schürer/Vermes, pp. 207f.) While I do not find his argument convincing, his general position has been favoured by others, such as Mantel and Rivkin (for bibliography, see Schürer/Vermes, p. 207 n. 26). In any case, he put his finger on a problem which, I think, has not been satisfactorily resolved. William W. Buehler (*The Pre-Herodian Civil War and Social Debate. Jewish Society in the Period 76–40 B.C. and the Social Factors Contributing to the Rise of the Pharisees and the Sadducees*, 1974) offers an interesting and sometimes revealing study of various terms for the Jewish leaders in

Josephus, but ends by ignoring the *War* in favour of the *Antiquities*. Thus his conclusion about the *dynatoi* (*powerful*) in Josephus (p. 74) ignores his own word study of the *War*, pp. 43–7.

62. Safrai, p. 384; cf. Buehler, *Civil War*, p. 47. Falk (p. 54) is closer to Josephus when he says that the Sadducean priests were excluded from the Sanhedrin.

63. Samaias a Pharisee: *AJ* XV.370. I am indebted to the notes by Ralph Marcus in the LCL edition of Josephus, vol. VII, pp. 504f.

64. Schürer/Vermes, pp. 206f.; Safrai, pp. 381, 389. For the general assumption that *boulē* = Sanhedrin, see Elias Bickerman, 'La Charte séleucide de Jérusalem', *Studies* II, pp. 44–85, esp. pp. 46–9.

65. See above, ch. 6, pp. 193–8; cf. 184, 199.

66. Ralph Marcus, ed., *Josephus* (LCL) VII, p. 373.

67. See Safrai, p. 386 n. 3.

68. Smith, 'Palestinian Judaism', p. 77 = 193.

69. This passage, like all those which bear directly on figures known from the New Testament, is greatly debated. See Strobel, *Stunde der Wahrheit*, pp. 331–6.

70. For a story from an earlier date which makes the same point, see *BJ* I.550: Herod convened a public assembly, charged Tiro and others, and had his opponents beaten to death on the spot.

71. Smith, 'Palestinian Judaism'; cf. above, pp. 188; 195f. Shaye Cohen (*Josephus in Galilee and Rome*) has shown that Josephus's motives were more complicated than this, but I still regard the present point as essentially correct: the Pharisees are elevated in the *Antiquities* in order to support their successors, the Rabbis. Cohen has shown that Josephus was concerned to deny *any* official representative of Judaism (or those whom he depicts as such) – whether Agrippa, the priesthoood, or one of the three 'philosophies' – had any active role in the revolt (pp. 154, 240f.). The present point, however, still stands: with regard to *de facto* control, the chief priests predominated. The motive which Cohen has identified might have inclined Josephus to depict the Pharisees as joining the chief priests in trying to halt the disaffection of the populace, but in fact he assigns them virtually no role at all. The depiction of the Pharisees in the *Antiquities*, on the other hand, as the party which led Judaism on all points, clashes with his own history, as well as with his other summaries assigning governance to the priests.

72. Falk, p. 48, describing 'the political framework'. For the traditional character of government under the leadership of the high priest, see *AJ* XIV.41.

73. Harvey (*Constraints*, p. 42) states that the 'handing over' of Jesus to the Romans must have been the result of a Sanhedrin trial. I see no grounds at all for making that a requirement.

The 'legality' of the trial as depicted in the synoptics, its relationship to Jewish jurisprudence and the competence of the Sanhedrin to deliver a death sentence are matters of vigorous debate. For bibliography and discussion, see Winter, *On the Trial of Jesus*, chs. 3 and 7–9; Catchpole, 'The Problem of the Historicity of the Sanhedrin Trial'. Brown summarizes correctly that 'we simply do not know enough about the customs of the Sanhedrin in Jesus' time' to be certain that what is described in the synoptics could have happened. Brown himself clearly doubts the Matthew/Mark account of two trials (Brown, *John XIII-XXI*, p. 797). I think we can go further: Jesus could have been put forward for execution by the chief priests alone if they could give Pilate adequate cause to have it carried out.

74. On the term 'chief priests', see Schürer/Vermes, pp. 233–36.

75. Harvey, for example, considers 'blasphemy' to be securely attested (*Constraints*,

p. 171), but this contrasts with his own caution elsewhere (see ch. 2 and p. 136). The only 'securely attested' charge is 'king'.

76. See above, n. 52 and ch. 10.

CONCLUSION

1. John Knox, *The Church and the Reality of Christ*, 1962, pp. 53–5.

2. For some uses of 'unique', see above, pp. 137f., 238f. Käsemann, for example, speaks of Jesus' 'unparalleled and sovereign freedom over the law'. ('The Problem of the Historical Jesus', p. 38). It is conceivable that Jesus felt that he could dispose of the law as he wished (sovereign), but unlikely that he was the only person who ever thought so (unparalleled), and in any case not provable historically. James Dunn in more than one case discusses 'uniqueness'. He proposes that Jesus' consciousness of spiritual power was 'unique', but that one cannot with certainty say the same of his 'sense of sonship' (*Jesus and the Spirit*, pp. 37, 47). But in fact, no evidence can be brought to bear which permits discussion of the topic at all.

3. See C. F. D. Moule, *The Phenomenon of the New Testament*, 1967, p. 69.

4. See ch. 3, the subsection on 'judgment'.

5. On parts of the Sermon on the Mount, see above, pp. 260–64, 276f. Goulder's more thoroughgoing proposal of Matthaean authorship (*Midrash and Lection in Matthew*, pp. 250–69) is not entirely convincing (I doubt the lectionary theory), but many of his tests of Matthaean authorship do lead to persuasive results. See, for example, 'the anticipatory epexegetic prohibition[s]' on pp. 79f.

6. Bultmann, *Theology of the New Testament* I, pp. 37–42.

7. Pro: Jeremias; contra: Barrett; see below.

8. I shall still decline to discuss the title 'Son of man', though I incline to the view of Hooker and Moule: there was no set view of the Son of man as a heavenly figure coming on clouds, and there is no reason why Jesus could not have used the phrase for himself in another, or in various meanings. Moule, for example, proposes that he used it, but not as a title; it was a symbol which pointed to suffering and vindication. See C. F. D. Moule, *The Origin of Christology*, 1977, pp. 11–22; Morna Hooker, *The Son of Man in Mark*, 1967, pp. 182–9.

In general, the question of titles should be de-emphasized. None of the terms which we think of as 'titles' had a single meaning in Jesus' day, and in any case he probably did not think 'of himself in terms of titles at all' (Dunn, *Jesus and the Spirit*, p. 15; cf. pp. 39f.; see also Harvey, *Constraints*, pp. 82; 163; 141f.; 145–7).

9. See e.g. Barrett, *Jesus and the Gospel Tradition*, pp. 42–5.

10. Confidence in election 'shaken to pieces', Bornkamm, *Jesus of Nazareth*, p. 78; Jesus shattered 'the letter of the law', Käsemann, 'The Problem of the Historical Jesus', p. 38; he 'shatters' the framework of Jewish piety, ibid.; foundations shaken, above, ch. 8 n. 11; Judaism destroyed, above, p. 278 and n. 42.

11. See Meyer, *Aims*, pp. 242–9.

12. Dodd, *Parables*, pp. 29, 37.

13. Ibid., pp. 83f., 159, 167.

14. Bultmann, *Jesus and the Word*, pp. 51f.

15. Schweitzer, *Quest*, pp. 348, 362f.

16. See 'Introduction: State of the Question', at nn. 4 and 5; ch. 4 at nn. 4–7.

17. At this point one should read Josephus's description of the attack by the Zealots and Idumeans against the high priest and his guards (*BJ* IV.300–18). Josephus says

that it left 8,500 dead. Even allowing for exaggeration, one can see that the temple, even without Roman support, was strongly defended.

18. E.g. Bornkamm, *Jesus of Nazareth*, p. 158.

19. Dodd, *Founder*, pp. 89f.

20. E.g. Nolan, *Jesus Before Christianity*, p. 39; Jeremias, *Proclamation*, p. 119.

21. Conzelmann (*Theology*, p. 118) attributes this view to E. Thurneysen, *Die Bergpredigt*, 1963; but I have been unable to see the work.

22. Bultmann, *Theology of the New Testament* I, pp. 13, 21. Bultmann's view, or so it appears to me, is the modern version of the classical Protestant view that the extreme requirements attributed to Jesus were not actually to be prescribed for society (or for special groups within society), but rather point to justification by faith alone. Bultmann's formulation is that Jesus did not intend these demands to be fulfilled as requirements, but only to bring people face to face with God, who simultaneously saves (apart from works) and demands the whole self. In either case we are asked to believe that Jesus did not concretely mean what he said. See the remarks about his misleading the disciples, p. 129.

23. Above, pp. 200–202; 274–81; 290f.

24. See immediately below.

25. The view that Jesus claimed, either directly or in effect, to be Messiah, is quite common, as is the view that he set himself above Moses. Examples will be seen throughout the section on 'The State of the Question' and in ch. 9. In the view of others he identified himself in some other way, for example as the Son of man (Kümmel, *Theology*, pp. 77–85; cf. n. 8 above). For the view that Jesus died as the Suffering Servant, see Jeremias, *Proclamation*, p. 299. See further just below.

26. Jeremias, *Jerusalem in the Time of Jesus*, p. 267: he was executed for his call to repentance; *Proclamation*, pp. 276–99: as Suffering Servant he died to atone 'for many'.

27. Dodd, *Founder*, p. 109: he died as a self-sacrifice for others; pp. 99–113: he fused the ideas of Messiah and Suffering Servant and applied them to himself, using the phrase 'Son of man'. For the view that Jesus made a skilful combination of scriptural views and titles, see Dodd, *According to the Scriptures*, 1952, pp. 103, 109f.

28. On the non-credal definition of Christianity, and the effect of this on the Christian description of Judaism, see G. F. Moore, 'Christian Writers', pp. 242f.; above, 'State of the Question' at n. 13.

29. Käsemann, 'Blind Alleys in the "Jesus of History" Controversy', p. 51: Jesus was hated because of his belief in grace; 'The Problem of the Historical Jesus', p. 39: he removes the distinction, 'which is fundamental to the whole of ancient thought', between the 'realm of the sacred, and the secular'. . . .

30. Resistance to the view that Jesus was a first-century Jew is common, though it is often accompanied by reassurances that he was one in some respects. Note Käsemann's ambivalence: 'He cannot be integrated into the background of the Jewish piety of his time. Certainly he was a Jew and made the assumptions of Jewish piety, but at the same time he shatters this framework with his claim' ('The Problem of the Historical Jesus', p. 38).

31. C. K. Barrett, 'The Background of Mark 10:45', *New Testament Essays. Studies in Memory of Thomas Walter Manson* (ed. A. J. B. Higgins), 1959, pp. 1–18; *Jesus and the Gospel Tradition*, pp. 35–67. Barrett emphasizes the vicarious nature of the suffering of martyrs, but I would lay equal stress on the view that their cause was vindicated. The Maccabean martyrs were eulogized in works written after the revolt had been *won*.

32. Moule, *The Origin of Christology*, p. 109.

33. Fuchs, 'The Quest of the Historical Jesus', p. 26.

34. Kümmel, *Theology*, pp. 94f.

35. Dodd, *Founder*, p. 109; Jeremias, *Proclamation*, p. 299.

36. Jeremias, *Proclamation*, pp. 276–99.

37. By Barrett: n. 31.

38. Naturally people who make this sort of proposal about Jesus' death do not follow out the logical implication. Dodd, for example, who most explicitly states that Jesus 'voluntarily [took] a course which [led] to his death' (*Founder*, p. 109), also attributed his execution to other causes and argued that Jesus was convicted of blasphemy (p. 158). Similarly Schweitzer argued that Jesus deliberately planned to die, not to atone for others, but to force God to bring in the eschaton (*Quest*, pp. 370f.). Yet he puts the matter in a way that contradicts this: Jesus died because Peter and Judas broke the commandment 'not to tell' (p. 396). What I am indicating here is the logical implication of the view that Jesus intended to die.

39. As does Schweitzer's.

40. 'Self-claim', or something similar, not 'awareness of status', is the appropriate phrase in historical work. 'Awareness of status' implies a theological judgment: God agrees with Jesus' self-claim. For the phrase, see Jeremias, *Proclamation*, p. 250. It is emphasized and made thematic in William Horbury's otherwise useful review of Geza Vermes' *Jesus the Jew: Theology* 77, 1974, pp. 227–32.

41. The observation is not entirely new. Schweitzer long ago said that it is self-evident that 'Mark, Matthew, and Paul are the best sources for the Jewish eschatology of the time of Jesus' (*Quest*, p. 368).

42. *Paul and Palestinian Judaism*, pp. 422f.

43. See below, on motive.

44. Above, pp. 65f.

45. Nolan, *Jesus before Christianity*, p. 28; Taylor, *The Gospel According to St Mark*, pp. 222f. (on Mark 3.5). Taylor grants that the verb 'look around' is Marcan, but sees it as a primitive feature eliminated by the other Gospels.

46. Jeremias, *Parables*, p. 139: the parable was addressed 'to "those who trusted in themselves (instead of in God)" . . . i.e. to the Pharisees'.

47. Jeremias, *Parables*, p. 124. Cf. Farmer's remarks on the 'grumblers' in Matt. 20.11: 'An historical essay on the humanity of Jesus Christ', p. 115.

48. Ch. 1 n. 37; ch. 6 n. 48.

49. Above, p. 270. Besides these examples of devotion to death, we must also remember that the priests had the ability to sway the people (above, pp. 314f.), which shows that they had not lost all moral credibility.

50. I offer a modern analogy. Athletes are said to strive for excellence and scholars for knowledge and insight. In fact, a certain amount of *hubris* accompanies these efforts, as it accompanies all public professions. Further, both groups strive to maximise their earnings and comfort. Some members of each group can even be said to be dominated by pride, arrogance and greed. This mixture of motives, however, does not negate the positive generalizations. We should not start saying that athletes and scholars are hypocrites who profess high ideals but seek only their own gain. We must assume that these observations apply, *mutatis mutandis*, to such groups of ancients as priests and Pharisees.

51. Matt. 23.5; cf. the charge against the hypocrites (doubtless Pharisees in Matthew's redaction) in Matt. 6.

52. Theissen, *The First Followers of Jesus*.

INDEX OF PASSAGES

BIBLE

SYNOPTIC GOSPELS

Passages in the synoptic Gospels which have parallels are indexed under either Matthew or Mark, often under both. Luke has been indexed less completely. In all cases the index to the parallel passage(s) should be checked.

RABBINIC LITERATURE

MISHNAH

TOSEFTA

MEKILTA

SIFRA

SIFRE

BABYLONIAN TALMUD

PALESTINIAN TALMUD

DEAD SEA SCROLLS

APOCRYPHA AND PSEUDEPIGRAPHA

OTHER ANCIENT AUTHORS

INDEX OF NAMES

INDEX OF SUBJECTS

Day of atonement, 200, 207

Death, *see* Jesus' death

Disciples' behaviour and beliefs as pointing to Jesus' own view, 76, 102, 115, 128f., 145, 152, 212, 220f., 231–4, 246–8, 249f., 261, 266, 267–9, 307, 329; *see also* Causes inferred from results; next entry

Disciples, no military or political ambition, 231f., 294f., 318; original expectation, 232f.; not executed, 226, 228, 231, 236, 240, 285, 289, 295, 317f., 329; protected by Rome, 295; ignorant of reasons for Jesus' execution, 299f.

Dispensation (*or* covenant), Mosaic, 252, 255, 260, 269, 271, 293, 301

Dissimilarity, criterion of, 16f., 145, 174, 252f., 307, 332

Divorce, prohibition of, 230, 256–60 & n.48(398f.), 272; points to new order, 233f., 260

Elders, 310f.

End, nearness of, in Paul, 93 & n.10(371f.), 245, 259; common Christian view, 93–5, 102, 145; Jesus' view, 117f. and notes (375), 145, 245, 259; *see also* Eschatology

Entry into Jerusalem, 31, 306–9, 317

Ephthasen, meaning of, 134 & nn.47, 52, 53(377f.), 136, 140

Eschatology, Jewish, 23, 77–90, 95–8, 106–8, 113f.; widespread, 124f.; influenced view of Gentiles, 216 & n.28(393)

Eschatology, as context for Jesus, 8, 21, 90, 91–5 & n.2(371), 152, 169, 212, 264; context of early Christian movement, 94f., 118, 129, 264; predates Jesus' death, 95, 129, 230–2, 320, 324

Eschatology, Jesus', in Christian scholarship, 23, 27; Jesus' own, 75 & n.71(369), 77, 125, 152–5, 232 (including disciples), 235, 306, 320, 329, 334; determined view of law, 267–9; of other prophets, 234f.; *see also* End; Jewish restoration theology; Israel, restoration of

Essenes (Dead Sea sect), 20, 45f., 193, 256

Evangelists, embarrassed by temple scene and saying, 75, 301; embarrassed by betrayal, 99f., 102; added sayings about repentance, 109, 113; cf. 223; reluctant to have Jesus claim Messiahship (except Mark), 297; desired to incriminate Jews and exculpate Romans, 298 & n.19(407); favoured Gentile mission, 219; lacked knowledge of Jesus' motives and aspects of career, 159f.; of cause and effect, 299f., 301, 302; of motives of Jewish leaders, 299f., 339; of 'who did what' and 'who was who', 300, 311; of Jesus' opponents, 405 n.77; wrote according to conventions of day, 304; *see also* Church, tendencies of; individual listings.

Execution, cause of, 177, 195, 293, 294f., 296–306; specific cause of, 301f., 304f., 309; not accounted for by teaching, 223f., 225; reason proposed here, 232f.; general grounds ascertainable, 301; agents of, 196f., 199, 293; whether explained by issue of law, 245; carried out by Rome, 294, 317; evangelists' ignorance of reasons for, 299f.; events leading up to (evangelists' views), 296–309

Exegesis of sayings, difficulty of, 129, 131–3, 148f.; *see also* Sayings

Exorcisms, whether or not proof of presence of kingdom, 134f. & nn.54, 56(378), 137f. & n.67(379), 140, 153, 157f., 160, 161f., 163, 166; as giving rise to claim of divinity, 165 & n.39(383), 168; use of imitation in, 166; possible cause of conflict, 271f.; *see also* Miracles

External acts, required in Judaism, 275